HANDBOOK OF ADOLESCENT DEVELOPMENT

What specifically characterises adolescents? What does it mean to be young at the beginning of the twenty-first century?

Handbook of Adolescent Development tries to fill a gap in the literature on adolescent development and behavior. All the authors of the various chapters have been invited to include as many findings on European adolescents as possible. Through this specific emphasis, the handbook provides a complement to other reviews of the literature that are mostly based on North American samples.

The contributors are all eminent researchers in the field and the individual chapters cover their specific areas of expertise. Theories of adolescence, along with emotional, physical and cognitive issues are explored. Topics covered include: families, peer relations, school and leisure time as well as problem areas such as depression, drug consumption and delinquency. *Handbook of Adolescent Development* also incorporates a comprehensive review of the literature in the area and considers avenues for future research.

This multidisciplinary text will be of interest to those studying and researching in the fields of developmental psychology, sociology, demography, epidemiology and criminology.

Sandy Jackson was a Senior Lecturer in Developmental Psychology at the University of Groningen (the Netherlands). He founded the European Association for Research on Adolescence (EARA) and served as its President for many years (1991–2000). He was one of the co-founders of the European Society for Developmental Psychology (ESDP) and served as its Secretary for an extensive period of time.

Luc Goossens is Professor in Developmental Psychology at the Catholic University of Leuven (Belgium). He served as President (2004–2006) of the European Association for Research on Adolescence (EARA). His research interests focus on the study of identity formation, parent–adolescent relationships, and adolescent loneliness.

Handbook of Adolescent Development

Sandy Jackson and Luc Goossens

Psychology Press
Taylor & Francis Group

HOVE AND NEW YORK

First published 2006 by Psychology Press
27 Church Road, Hove, East Sussex BN3 2FA

Simultaneously published in the USA and Canada
by Psychology Press
270 Madison Avenue, New York NY 10016

Psychology Press is an imprint of the Taylor & Francis Group, an Informa business

Reprinted 2008

Typeset in Times by RefineCatch Limited, Bungay, Suffolk
Printed and bound in Great Britain by
TJ International Ltd, Padstow, Cornwall
Cover design by Jim Wilkie

This publication has been produced with paper manufactured to strict
environmental standards and with pulp derived from sustainable
forests.

British Library Cataloguing in Publication Data
A catalogue record for this book is available from the British Library

Library of Congress Cataloging in Publication Data
Handbook of adolescent development / edited by Sandy Jackson and Luc Goossens.
    p.   cm.
Includes bibliographical references and index.
ISBN 1–84169–200–X
1. Adolescence.   2. Teenagers.   I. Jackson, Sandy, 1937–   .   II. Goossens, Luc.
HQ796.H2558   2006
305.235'5—dc22   2006002769

ISBN13: 978–1–84169–200–5
ISBN10: 1–84169–200–X

Contents

List of Figures

List of Tables

List of contributors

Professor Françoise D. Alsaker
Universität Bern
Psychologisches Institut
Muesmattstrasse 45
3000 Bern 9
Switzerland

Dr. Sofia Buelga
Universidad de Valencia (Estudio General)
Area de Psicologia Social
Avda. Blasco Ibañez 21
46010 Valencia
Spain

Isabelle Chossis
Centre Hospitalier Universitaire Vaudois
(CHUV) – Lausanne
Unité Multidisciplinaire de Santé des
Adolescents (UMSA)
Rue du Bugnon 21
CH-1005 Lausanne
Switzerland

Dr. Elvira Cicognani
Università degli Studi di Bologna
Departimento di Scienze dell'Educazione
Via Zamboni 34
40126 Bologna
Italy

Dr. Andreas Dick-Niederhauser
Universität Bern
Psychologisches Institut
Muesmattstrasse 45
3000 Bern 9
Switzerland

Professor August Flammer
Universität Bern
Psychologisches Institut
Muesmattstrasse 45
3000 Bern 9
Switzerland

Luc Goossens
Catholic University of Leuven
Department of Psychology
Tiensestraat 102
B-3000 Leuven
Belgium

Professor Leo B. Hendry
University of Glamorgan
School of Humanities and Social Sciences
Department of Psychology
Pontypridd CF3 1DL
Wales, UK

Professor Marion Kloep
University of Glamorgan
School of Humanities and Social Sciences
Department of Psychology
Pontypridd CF3 1DL
Wales, UK

Professor Willem Koops
University of Utrecht
Faculty of Social Sciences
Department of Developmental Psychology
Heidelberglaan 1
Postbox 80140
3508 TC Utrecht
The Netherlands

Professor Jane Kroger
University of Tromsö
Department of Psychology
N-9037 Tromsö
Norway

Professor Henri Lehalle
Université Paul Valéry
(Montpellier III)
Département de Psychologie
Route de Mende
34199 Montpellier Cedex 5
France

Dr. Marisol Lila
Universidad de Valencia (Estudio General)
Area de Psicologia Social
Avda. Blasco Ibañez 21
46010 Valencia
Spain

Professor Pierre-André Michaud MD
Head, Unité multidisciplinaire de santé des
adolescents
Centre hospitalier universitaire vaudois
Beaumont 48
1011 Lausanne
Switzerland

Professor Gonzalo Musitu
Universidad de Valencia (Estudio General)
Area de Psicologia Social
Avda. Blasco Ibañez 21
46010 Valencia
Spain

Dr. Bram Orobio de Castro
University of Utrecht
Faculty of Social Sciences
Department of Developmental Psychology
Heidelberglaan 1
Postbox 80140

3508 TC Utrecht
The Netherlands

Professor Augusto Palmonari
Università degli Studi di Bologna
Departimento di Scienze dell'Educazione
Via Zamboni 34
40126 Bologna
Italy

Dr. Marcella Ravenna
Università di Ferrara
Facoltà di Lettere e Filosofia
Dipartimento di Scienze Umane
Via Savonarola 27
44100 Ferrara
Italy

Dr. Monica Rubini
Università degli Studi di Bologna
Departimento di Scienze
dell'Educazione
Via Zamboni 34
40126 Bologna
Italy

Dr. Ron H. J. Scholte
Catholic University of Nijmegen
Faculty of Social Sciences
Department of Special Education: Family and
Behavior
Montessorilaan 3
Post box 9104
6500 HE Nijmegen
The Netherlands

Joan-Carles Suris
Institut Universitaire de Médecine Sociale et
Préventive (UMSP)
Groupe de Recherche sur les Adolescents
(GRSA)
Rue du Bugnon 17
CH-1005 Lausanne
Switzerland

Marcel van Aken
Utrecht University
Heidelberglaan 1
Postbox 80140
35608 TC Utrecht
The Netherlands

Professor Bruna Zani
Università degli Studi di Bologna
Departimento di Scienze dell'Educazione
Via Zamboni 34
40126 Bologna
Italy

Preface

This book has a long and complicated history. Work on it got underway in June 1997 when the European Commission, through its SOCRATES-ERASMUS programme, awarded money for a so-called European module (EM) on adolescent development to a consortium of European universities. The latter comprised eight universities: the Catholic University of Leuven (Belgium), which acted as the coordinating institution, the University of Bergen (Norway), the University of Berne (Switzerland), the University of Bologna (Italy), the University of Groningen (the Netherlands), the University of Montpellier III (France), the Catholic University of Nijmegen (currently the Radboud University, the Netherlands), and the University of Valencia (Spain). The European Module (Reference 27945-IC-1.96.1.BE), entitled 'Youth and Adolescence: The European Dimension' was intended to introduce students to the diversity of adolescent development in the different regions of Europe. The course materials on this general theme, which were jointly developed by all the consortium partners, were to be taught at all the universities involved in the project. In brief, joint curriculum development was to lead to a European course on adolescent development that could be inserted, so to speak, into the existing curricula at the various universities that took part in the project (hence the name 'European module').

Representatives from all universities first met in Leuven in November 1997 and over the next few years in Montpellier (March 1998), Groningen (November 1998), Bologna (June 1999), Nijmegen (November 1999), and, finally, Valencia (March 2000). Few chapters, however, were ready when the contract with the European Commission expired in June 2000. The original plans for jointly developed teaching materials were then transformed into the somewhat more ambitious project of a European handbook of adolescent development. Thanks to Sandy Jackson's personal links with the world of publishing, a contract for such a handbook was signed with Psychology Press in July 1999. The team of authors, all of whom hailed from the eight universities involved, was expanded with colleagues from Italy, Norway, the Netherlands, Switzerland, and the United Kingdom, who could provide additional know-how on areas of expertise that were not well represented in that original group.

Work on this unwieldy project progressed slowly. On Tuesday, September 11, 2001, when Sandy travelled by train from Groningen (in the Netherlands) to Leuven (in Belgium) for what he saw as the final editorial meeting, he had no access to modern means of communication on that journey. On his arrival in my home town, I told him to turn on the TV set in his hotel room so that he could see the tragic events of that fateful day unravel before his very eyes. Sandy's protracted illness and untimely demise in July 2003 caused further delays in the production schedule of the book. The book manuscript was finally ready by the summer of 2004. Each chapter was reviewed by an expert on the topic over the following months and the authors were invited to incorporate reviewers' comments in their final revision and to completely update their chapter by November 2005.

Now that the volume is finally completed, I would like to thank a number of people who, over the years, have contributed to the project in various ways. I want to extend my gratitude to Piet Henderickx and Leen Wyndaele, both at the International Relations Office of my home university, who guided me through the application process with the European Commission and helped me to comply with all the renewal and reporting requirements. Special thanks go to all the colleagues from our seven collaborating universities. I have fond memories of the biannual meetings with this core group of authors: Françoise Alsaker (then in Bergen and now in Berne), August Flammer (Berne), Augusto Palmonari and Giusy Speltini (Bologna), Sandy Jackson (Groningen), Henri Lehalle (Montpellier), Marcel van Aken (then at the Catholic University of Nijmegen and now at the University of Utrecht), and Gonzalo Musitu, Marisol Lila, and Sofia Buelga (Valencia).

I also express my gratitude to the authors who joined the group at a later stage, that is, Bruna Zani, Elvira Cicognani, Monica Rubini, and Marcella Ravenna (Italy), Jane Kroger (Norway), Ron Scholte, Willem Koops, and Bram Orobio de Castro (the Netherlands), Pierre-André Michaud, Isabelle Sossis, and Joan-Carles Suris (Switzerland), and Leo Hendry and Marion Kloep (United Kingdom). Special thanks go to Pierre-André Michaud and Willem Koops, who kept urging me to publish the book. I would also like to thank, in alphabetical order, the reviewers of the 18 chapters in this handbook, that is, Trevor G. Bond (Australia), Harke Bosma (the Netherlands), B. Bradford Brown (USA), John Coleman (United Kingdom), Maia Dekovic (the Netherlands), Eirini Flouri (United Kingdom), Beth D. Kivel (USA), Reed Larson (USA), Bonnie Leadbetter (Canada), Judith Smetana (USA), and all the colleagues who chose to send in their review anonymously. Thank you for your generous and constructive comments and your support.

On behalf of the chapter authors, I extend my deepest gratitude to all the people at Psychology Press who have encouraged and supported us over the last few years. Special thanks go to Michael Forster, founder of Psychology Press, who never lost faith in the project, and to Lucy Kennedy, Senior Commissioning Editor, who kept urging us to get the book ready for publication. I also want to thank editorial assistants Claire Lipscombe and Lizzie Catford, and Tara Stebnicky, Senior Editorial Assistant, who skilfully guided us through the final round of reviews and ensuing updates, and the manuscript preparation process, respectively. I am most grateful to my co-workers and former co-workers Wim Bevers (now at the University of Ghent), Koen Luyckx, Eline Sierens, and Bart Soenens, who carefully prepared extensive comments on earlier drafts of the chapters and urged the authors to adhere to APA-style as strictly as possible. Koen also acted as a skilful data manager who stored extra electronic copies of all chapters on his computer and saved the entire project from complete disaster when my hard disk crashed. Helen Baxter (of Helen Baxter Editorial Services) did a wonderful job when copy editing the final version of the chapters.

I also want to express my gratitude to the European Commission who provided funding during the initial phase of the project and to all my colleagues, both at the Center for Developmental Psychology in Leuven and within the European Association for Research on Adolescence (EARA), who kept asking me for an update on the status of this handbook.

Finally, I want to dedicate this handbook to my parents, Louis Goossens and Suzanne Persijn, who provided me with expert guidance and unconditional support throughout adolescence and all the other hazardous periods of development.

Luc Goossens
March 2006

Adolescent development: Putting Europe on the map

Luc Goossens

This handbook tries to fill a gap in the literature on adolescent development and behavior. All the authors of the various chapters have been invited to include as many findings on European adolescents as possible. Through this specific emphasis, the present handbook is meant to provide a complement to other reviews of the literature that are mostly based on empirical studies conducted on North American samples. This project seems to come at an appropriate time, because there is an increasing contribution from developmentalists based outside the United States to the available knowledge base on child development. The children whose development is reported are also inceasingly more likely to be living outside the United States (Super, 2005). Exact figures on international representation in research on adolescence are currently lacking, but there is a growing realization that some aspects of development may proceed with different trajectories in different environments.

In this introductory chapter, we will define what we mean by the terms 'adolescence' and 'Europe' and we will indicate how cross-cultural comparisons of adolescent development can be made. Comparative work within Europe and between European cultures and the United States, however, should never represent the end point of cross-cultural research on adolescence. Rather, such comparisons should provide a stepping stone toward a global science of adolescent development, a science that no longer restricts the study of young people to selected regions of the world.

1. Boundaries of adolescence

Adolescence is the transitional period between childhood and adulthood. Its onset, therefore, is marked by the biological changes of puberty, whereas its upper boundary is defined by the transition to the adult status. In terms of age, these boundaries are somewhat flexible. For many years, the Society for Research on Adolescence (SRA) has announced on the cover of its flagship journal, *The Journal of Research on Adolescence*, that it devoted itself to research on the second decade of life. Aspiring members of that society are still asked to indicate on the application form whether they are mainly interested in research on early adolescence (10 to 15 years of age), mid-adolescence (15 to 18 years), or late adolescence (18 to 22 years). Adolescence, therefore, effectively spans the age period of 10 to 22.

There are clear indications that the adolescent period tends to increase in length, at least in the Western world. One reason for this extension is that the first phases of pubertal development tend to take place at an earlier age (Herman-Giddens et al., 1997; Herman-Giddens, Wang, & Koch, 2001). Another important reason is that many individuals remain financially dependent on their parents well into their twenties and seem to postpone the transition to adulthood for many years. This socio-cultural trend has prompted certain authors to refer to the late teens and early twenties as a separate stage of development that is labeled 'emerging adulthood' (Arnett, 2000, 2004b). This new stage of life refers to the age period of 18 to 30, with a focus on ages 18 to 25. Alternative terms for this period have been suggested. Keniston (1971) referred to this period as 'youth', but this particular use of the term is problematic, because the word has long been used and continues to be used as a term for the combined periods of childhood and adolescence. 'Emerging adulthood', therefore, seems a more suitable term to refer to this transitional period, which is a distinct phase demographically, subjectively, and in terms of identity exploration.

An important demographic feature of emerging adulthood is that there is a great deal of variability and instability, for instance, in terms of residential status and relationship formation. From ages 18 to 25, some adolescents continue to live with their parents, whereas others enjoy a status of semi-autonomy during the college years, with some of them returning home after graduation (Arnett, 2000). During that same period some young people experience a period of cohabitation with a romantic partner, whereas

others live on their own or are married. There are marked differences between European countries in this regard. Young people in Southern European countries tend to live with their parents much longer than do their agemates in Northern European countries (Cherlin, Scabini, & Rossi, 1997). Recent European data also indicate that the traditional sequence of events in which different markers of the transition to adulthood followed one another in orderly fashion, with completion of one's formal education followed by entrance into occupational life and entrance into marriage and parenthood, has been replaced with multiple transition patterns (Chisholm & Hurrelmann, 1995).

At the subjective level, adulthood is no longer defined in terms of marriage, which used to be an important marker in earlier times. Questionnaire studies in the United States (Arnett & Taber, 1994) revealed that individualistic qualities rank among the top criteria used by young people in their late teens and early twenties to define adulthood. These characteristics are: accepting responsibility for oneself, making independent decisions, and becoming financially independent. Subsequent research on young people in other Western countries revealed that these individualistic criteria for adulthood are widely endorsed across the cultures examined, with some interesting cultural variations (Arnett & Galambos, 2003).

In terms of identity formation, emerging adulthood marks the transition from the tentative explorations of adolescence to more serious and focused attempts at self-definition. Such a transition can be observed in the areas of love, work, and worldviews. Adolescent dating, which is primarily recreational in nature, gives way to more intimate and serious explorations in which young people ask themselves what kind of person they wish to have as a long-term partner. Adolescent jobs, mainly in the service sector (e.g., fast food restaurants), do not provide young people with knowledge and experience that is related to their future occupations. During the years of emerging adulthood, however, young people ask themselves what kind of job they would be good at and what type of work would suit them as a long-term profession. Finally, adolescent worldviews, which are still strongly influenced by parental views, are re-examined during emerging adulthood and re-shaped into a set of beliefs that young people have arrived at through their own reflection (Arnett, 2000).

In terms of demographics, subjective characteristics, and identity, therefore, significant advances are made toward full attainment of adult maturity during emerging adulthood. Yet the volatility of this age period implies that these temporary solutions are primarily meant to broaden the range of experiences before taking on enduring adult responsibilities. Much remains open during this stage of life. For these reasons, emerging adulthood refers to a distinct period that cannot be captured adequately by traditional terms such as 'adolescence' or 'young adulthood'. This observation further helps to explain why emerging adulthood only exists in Western countries. These cultures allow young people a prolonged period of exploration during the late teens and early twenties (Arnett, 2000).

This optimistic portrayal describes ages 18 to 25 as the most volitional years of life, when many things are left to young people's independent decision. The extension of adolescence, however, can be described in more pessimistic terms as well. The 'maturity gap', that is, the age period between biological and social adulthood, is viewed as an important contributing factor to adolescent delinquency. Many young people engage in delinquent acts during that period because these activities provide access to adult status or adult privileges (Moffitt, 1993). As the maturity gap widens, the delinquency rate may continue to be high during emerging adulthood, when many issues regarding adult roles are not yet settled in a definitive way. Recent longitudinal research does in fact indicate that delinquent careers that are taken up in adolescence are extended into emerging adulthood (i.e., until age 26; Moffitt, Caspi, Harrington, & Milne, 2002).

Another problem is that young people who continue to be dependent on their parents into their late twenties are increasingly targeted as consumers by a recreation industry that is entirely geared toward mass culture (e.g., music and fash-

ion) and by that very fact bars access to true adulthood (Côté & Alahar, 1996). One may legitimately ask, therefore, whether many emergent adults will ever reach adulthood in the psychological sense of the term (Côté, 2000). At any rate, young people will be forced to make a number of important decisions for themselves, as traditional value systems have lost much of their influence. The latter phenomenon, which sociologists call 'individualization', can have both positive and negative consequences for the young (Neubauer & Hurrelmann, 1995).

Whatever value one may attach to the extended transitional period between adolescence and adulthood, it is clear that a reconceptualization of the traditional boundaries of adolescence is in order. Researchers seem to be well-advised to focus on two adjacent periods of development that may be collectively referred to as 'adolescence and emerging adulthood'. It is to those two periods that this handbook is devoted, with a somewhat stronger emphasis on the traditional period of adolescence, now redefined as ages 10 to 18, than on emerging adulthood (ages 18 to 25). Viewed in a somewhat broader perspective, this latest shift in the conceptualization of life stages constitutes yet another phase in the long and dynamic history of the scientific use of terms such as 'adolescence', 'youth', and 'young adulthood' (Klein, 1990).

2. Europe: An old continent and an emergent reality

Europe is known as the 'Old Continent' and terms such as 'European' have been used for centuries. During the last decades, however, the continent has gone through a remarkable process of political change that has profoundly altered our understanding of age-old terms and divisions. It seems appropriate, therefore, to define the current boundaries of Europe in terms of the new entities that have come into existence as a result of that recent process of cooperation and integration.

Europe as conceived in this handbook is not restricted to the 12 countries of the Eurozone (or 'Euroland'), where a common currency was introduced on 1 January 2002, or to the countries that made up the European Union (EU) up to 30 April 2004. Attention will be directed to a somewhat larger economic entity, that is, to the countries that made up the European Economic Area (EEA) up to that same date (March 2004). This area comprises the 15 member states of the EU at that particular moment in time (Austria, Belgium, Denmark, Finland, France, Germany, Greece, Ireland, Italy, Luxemburg, the Netherlands, Portugal, Spain, Sweden, and the United Kingdom) and three additional countries (Iceland, Liechtenstein, and Norway). A final, strategic extension adds Switzerland to the countries of interest in this handbook. As a result, the area covered effectively coincides with what is commonly known as Western Europe. Throughout this handbook, the main focus will be on that geographical area.

Occasionally, the focus will be extended to the 10 countries that joined the European Union on 1 May 2004. These countries are the three Baltic states (Estonia, Latvia, and Lithuania), several countries in Eastern and Central Europe (the Czech Republic, Hungary, Poland, Slovakia, and Slovenia) and some states in Southern Europe (Cyprus and Malta). Other aspiring member states in Eastern and Southern Europe (such as Bulgaria, Romania, and Turkey), which have also entered into enlargement negotiations with the European Union, will receive less systematic attention in this handbook.

While these political changes were taking place, important developments also occurred on the European continent with regard to the formal organization of scholarly activity related to adolescence. A new scholarly society, the European Association for Research on Adolescence (EARA), was established by its first, inspirational leader, Alexander ('Sandy') Jackson. A native from Scotland, Sandy had moved to the Netherlands where he worked for many years (Bosma & Koops, 2004). The first meeting of EARA was held in 1988 in Paris. In the two decades that followed, with biennial conferences in Groningen, the Netherlands (1990), Bologna, Italy (1992), Stockholm, Sweden (1994), Liège, Belgium (1996), Budapest, Hungary (1998), Jena, Germany (2000), Oxford, United Kingdom (2002) and

Porto, Portugal (2004) and through the leadership of the EARA presidents who succeeded Jackson – Monique Bolognini (Switzerland), Hakan Stattin (Sweden), and Luc Goossens (Belgium) – the organization flourished and provided a platform for continuous exchange of new ideas, new methodological tools, and new findings. Within this particular context, researchers increasingly began to struggle with the question of whether North American findings on adolescence could be generalized easily to European adolescents and whether adolescent development takes on a different form in each of the European countries represented within the association. These concerns, in turn, prompted greater interest in cross-cultural comparisons regarding psychological development in the phase of adolescence.

3. Cross-cultural comparisons of adolescent development

At first sight, there seems to be little reason to assume that adolescent behavior and development will be different in the United States than in Europe or will take on a different form in a particular European country than in another one. After all, all adolescents who are embedded in a predominantly European context (i.e., Europe, North America, and Australia) have many things in common, including a common set of basic values as handed on to them by the older generation and in fact, a long European–American cultural tradition. However, important differences do seem to exist, at least among European countries, in the objective social condition of late adolescents and emerging adults. The European Community Household Panel Survey, for instance, revealed large differences across European countries in young people's transition to adulthood. Their level of educational attainment, early experiences on the labor market, the age at which they leave the parental home, and their living standards all show important differences (Iacovou & Berthoud, 2001). From a sociological point of view (Hendry & Kloep, 1999) these differences are understandable, because each country or society handles the transition from the childhood to the adult status in a different way.

Whether adolescents in different European countries also show differences in psychological characteristics (such as self-esteem) is less clear as of yet. Comparative research on those characteristics looks like a difficult undertaking, because representative samples of adolescents have to be drawn from each country involved in the comparative effort. Finding two comparable samples of adolescents across different cultures always represents a difficult challenge.

These difficulties may be avoided, and the 'next-best-solution' to doing comparative research be adopted, by focusing on cultures rather than nations and by adopting an anthropological approach to defining cultures. The term culture is defined by cross-cultural psychologists and anthropologists as 'the total way of life of a people' (Schlegel, 2000, p. 71). The latter comprises language, political systems, and historical background, among other things. People coming from two different countries that differ on all these dimensions may therefore be considered as coming from two different cultures (Alsaker & Flammer, 1999). If we want to estimate how many cultures there are in Europe, we first have to define our working unit, so to speak.

3.1 Basic cultural units

Anthropologists have proposed the culture-bearing unit (or 'cultunit' for short) as the basic cultural unit. A cultunit is defined as a group of 'people who are domestic speakers of a common distinct language and who belong either to the same state or to the same contact group' (Naroll, 1973, p. 731). The latter implies that the members of the cultunit meet and interact with one another on a regular basis. To identify the various cultunits in a given geographical area, one can proceed in two steps. First, the language boundaries are drawn on the map of that region in a distinctive manner (e.g., by red lines). Second, the state boundaries are indicated in another, equally distinctive way (e.g., by blue lines). The various cultunits are then defined by the intersections of the two types of lines.

Such an approach will identify a substantial number of cultunits in contemporary Europe. In most countries, a single cultunit will suffice. Some countries will comprise two or more cultunits. In Switzerland, for instance, one can find two cultunits: a larger German-speaking one and a smaller French-speaking one. All cultunits may be further divided into subunits in terms of the dialect or regional variety of the common (or 'standard') language that is used in the home. Similarities across cultunits may be represented in a hierarchical system (or 'culture tree') with common groupings such as Western Europe and Eastern Europe (as defined in the previous section) as superordinate categories.

Moving to the level of cultunits rather than nations or countries has important strategic advantages. When comparing adolescents in different countries, the different samples have to be truly representative of their respective countries. When the samples are considered to represent culture-bearing units, the situation is different. Each sample is then thought of as a group of people who are under the influence of a particular set of cultural variables. A sample of adolescents from a particular city or region in Italy, for instance, is not completely representative of all young Italians aged 12 to 22. Yet, because these young people speak Italian and their life is governed by the Italian political system, which in turn is shaped by that country's particular history, the Italian culture is manifest in that sample. Such a sample, therefore, can be compared to a sample of German adolescents as long as the German culture (i.e., language, political institutions, and history) is clearly manifest in that sample. Whether differences that obtain between the two samples truly reflect cultural differences or additional differences between the two cultures is an empirical matter. Including other Italian and German samples (e.g., from different regions in their respective countries) can help to clarify the nature of these differences.

Studies that are directly comparative in their design, and therefore uniquely powerful in their conclusions, are scarce. An important study that illustrates the benefits of a comparative approach to adolescent development is the EURONET study (Alsaker & Flammer, 1999). Thirteen samples of adolescents (aged 14 to 16) were included in this study. There were six Western European samples (France, Finland, Germany, Norway, and the German-speaking and French-speaking parts of Switzerland) and six samples from East and Central Europe (Bulgaria, the former Czechoslovak Federal Republic, Hungary, Poland, Romania, and Russia). All 12 samples were compared to a sample of adolescents from the United States. An additional sample of ethnic Hungarians living in Romania was added at a later stage.

A basic question of the study was whether and how age and gender interact with culture. In essence, these interactions were limited. The findings revealed that age and gender differences that have emerged from research on United States samples were replicated on the EURONET samples. In all countries, for instance, older adolescents spent more time dating and hanging around with peers. Boys and girls behaved in accordance with traditional gender stereotypes in all samples. In addition to these results, the EURONET study yielded two types of finding that are likely to emerge from any cross-cultural study of adolescence. These findings pertain to (a) differences across cultures in mean levels for certain variables and (b) different correlates of a given phenomenon in different cultures.

3.2 *Differences in mean values across cultures*

The EURONET study revealed both similarities and differences among the various cultunits, but there were no distinct national profiles. The final conclusion of the study, therefore, was that European adolescents are 'basically alike and excitingly different' (Alsaker & Flammer, 1999, p. 165). Some of the traditional distinctions among European cultures seemed to be confirmed by the results. The four Eastern European samples (Bulgaria, Poland, Romania, and Russia) were completely different from all other countries in terms of their daily life and basic values. These adolescents more often reported the presence of grandparents or other relatives in the household. They also rated social responsibility (which included taking care of one's parents) as more important than did Western adolescents. The United States sample was comparable to the Western European samples in many respects.

Occasionally, however, Eastern European adolescents more closely resembled the United States sample than the Western European samples did. Visible success (e.g., 'earning much money' and 'becoming famous') were rated as more important by both Eastern European and United States adolescents. This finding may reflect the fact that the data were collected in 1992, that is, soon after the Eastern part of Europe opened up to the Western world and the new opportunities offered to the young seemed without limit.

Through a strategic choice of cultunits, the EURONET study allowed for a comparative study of the effects of national boundaries as opposed to language boundaries. The results were mixed. In some cases, national boundaries turned out to be more important than linguistic ones. Adolescents from the French-speaking part of Switzerland, for instance, closely resembled their agemates from the German-speaking part of Switzerland in terms of their time use (e.g., time spent on school and on meals). In other cases, linguistic boundaries seemed more important than national borders. Adolescents from the Hungarian minority living in Romania more closely resembled other Hungarian adolescents than their Romanian agemates.

3.3 *Different correlates in different cultures*

This topic was not a major concern in the EURONET study, which mainly concentrated on comparisons of mean levels across cultures. When the topic was addressed – for instance, when examining the correlates of adolescent well-being – few cross-cultural differences emerged. The associations between subjective well-being, on the one hand, and strain, control expectancy and problem-oriented coping, on the other, were very similar across countries or cultunits. In all 13 samples, high levels of strain were associated with lower levels of well-being, whereas higher levels of control expectancy and problem-oriented coping were associated with greater well-being (Alsaker & Flammer, 1999).

Other studies have effectively found different correlates of a given phenomenon in a sample of European adolescents as compared to a sample of United States adolescents. Different aspects of parenting style, for instance, were associated with adolescent self-esteem in Germany and the United States (Barber, Chadwick, & Oerter, 1992). Support and control, two classical dimensions of parenting style, were found to be associated significantly with adolescent self-esteem in the United States sample, but were unrelated to that same variable in the German sample. A more general indicator of the overall quality of the relationship between parents and adolescents, which tapped feelings of security and availability in that relationship, was associated with higher self-esteem in both samples.

Such patterns of findings suggest that there may be important cultural differences in the link between the adolescent–parent relationship and adolescent development. Specifically, German adolescents must feel valued in their relationship with their parents through other processes than the ones examined in the North American literature (such as support and control). These other factors could include communication and decision-making processes through which German parents induce feelings of self-worth in their adolescent children.

This comparative study on correlates of adolescent self-esteem merely serves to illustrate the strategic value of cross-cultural comparisons. In addition to their evident descriptive function, such comparative studies can serve an explanatory function as well, by pointing to potential processes through which development arises or by providing clues about the relevant mechanisms involved (Tudge, Shanahan, & Valsiner, 1997). Again, this is not to say that numerous or large differences between European and United States adolescents are to be expected. More recent research, for instance, has revealed far greater similarity in the effects of traditional dimensions of parenting style on adolescent development and behavior across cultures (Steinberg, 2001). However, cross-national research is particularly needed to distinguish generality from specificity in particular results (Petersen, Silbereisen, & Sörensen, 1996). To reach that objective, the available database on adolescent behavior and development has to be expanded still further and researchers have to move beyond the boundaries

of the Western world. Put differently, cross-cultural comparisons should not be limited to United States–European contrasts.

4. Globalization of adolescent research

Research that moves beyond the boundaries of the European–American part of the world, and the implicit conception of the stages of life shared by all its inhabitants, is bound to reveal the influence of the cultural life course (Caspi, 1987; Levine, 1982). Ethnographic analyses have shown that, in all cultures, shared expectancies about how lives should be lived play a central role in crucial phases of life. The prescribed behaviors regulated by these expectancies can be very different from Western conventions. The transition rites in early adolescence that marked the transition to the adult status in many non-Western, pre-industrialized cultures and that have no counterpart in contemporary Western cultures (Herdt & Leavitt, 1998) are a case in point here.

Of course, pre-industrialized societies no longer exist in their original form, as their members have come to adopt many aspects of Western lifestyle, through a process alternatively known as globalization or modernization. Across the world, however, one can find many instances of local cultural constructions of development and the various stages of life. These constructions are examined by the scientific discipline of psychological anthropology (Casey & Edgerton, 2005). Analyses as conducted by experts in this field of inquiry have revealed that the concepts of 'childhood' and 'adolescence' carry a different meaning for members of different sociocultural communities across the globe. Hence the experience of these stages of life takes on a different form across cultures as well (Weisner & Lowe, 2005).

North American scholars of adolescence have increasingly come to adopt the view long embraced by psychological anthropologists, that is, that the experience of adolescence can differ markedly as a function of time and place (Larson & Wilson, 2004). Some years ago, a joint taskforce, funded by the Society for Research on Adolescence (SRA) and the International Society for the Study of Behavioral Development (ISSBD) tried to project some trends for the future that directly touch on adolescents' lives (Larson & Mortimer, 2000). One of the trends identified by this taskforce – the 'Adolescence in the 21st century' group – was the ever increasing level of contact between adolescents from different parts of the world. A direct result of this trend, typically referred to as globalization, is that adolescent scholars in the future will need to be more international in their expertise. The taskforce decided to publish an edited book on the adolescent experience in eight regions of the world (Brown, Larson, & Saraswathi, 2002). In addition to North America and Europe, these regions comprised Sub-Saharan Africa, India, the Middle East, Southeast Asia, China and Japan, Russia, and Latin America. This is not an isolated effort. A recent textbook on adolescence and emerging adulthood (Arnett, 2004a) adopts an explicitly cross-cultural approach in that adolescent development in North America is systematically compared to young people's experiences in other cultures. One of the important messages to emerge from these books is that researchers should not routinely assume that North American findings will be confirmed by adolescents from other cultures.

The increased contact between adolescents from different continents may have both advantages and drawbacks. There is indeed growing concern that this new trend will lead to globalization. This latter term needs to be carefully defined. A process of globalization is effectively taking place in the sense that the experience of adolescence around the world has increasingly become more homogeneous as a result of widespread schooling. The latter trend, in turn, is a by-product of the increasing spread of industrialization and urbanization. While they are in school, adolescents have limited contact with adults and primarily turn to one another for social contacts. During their spare time, they all listen to the same type of popular music and are wearing the same type of Western casual clothing all over the world. Some authors fear that this emergence of a global youth culture (Banks, 1997; Mody, 2001), or the homogenization of daily adolescent experience, will ultimately lead to a homogenization of cultural forms. Put rather

more mildly, other authors expect that identity problems will become much more common in non-Western cultures as adolescents in these cultures are increasingly confronted with two sets of cultural values, the one offered by their own traditional culture and the one implied in Western media messages (Arnett, 2001). In short, the globalization of adolescent culture appears as a real threat or a true challenge to contemporary youth in non-Western cultures.

Fortunately, anthropologists (Schlegel, 2000) and cross-cultural psychologists (Dasen, 2000) are convinced that these dangers do not loom large. Traditional cultures have proved to be remarkably impervious to Western influences, as far as their basic value systems are concerned. Cultural transmission, apart from the adoption of consumer goods, is by no means an automatic process. New ideas are typically transformed and incorporated into the existing culture. This means that each culture reacts in its own way to Western products and customs.

Adolescent culture has two general features that make it readily transportable from one culture to another: it makes few demands on the listener or consumer and it is typically grounded in universal values (e.g., love and friendship) rather than local ones. These same qualities, however, also make it rather ephemeral. One could argue that as the Western type of adolescent culture becomes more widespread, adults all over the world will be able to draw on a common source of memories and that cultural differences will gradually be blurred by this new trend. This is not a real danger, however. It is well-known that, as adolescents develop into adults, key factors that shape the world of adults, such as income or class, increase in importance at the expense of universal values (Schlegel, 2000). Adolescents, moreover, are not inevitably socially isolated from adults because some Western cultures (e.g., Germany and Northern Italy) have developed ways to keep young people involved in the adult worlds of work and community life and this may well happen in non-Western cultures as well (Schlegel, 2003).

In a related argument, cross-cultural psychologists (e.g., Dasen, 2000) argue that increased contact with Western ideas need not lead to increased conflict between parents and adolescents in traditional societies, as long as there is some basic form of continuity with the past and cultural identity and basic values such as family solidarity are preserved during the acculturation process.

5. Conclusion

This introductory chapter has illustrated that scholars of adolescence currently witness exciting new developments. Recent societal and psychological trends extend adolescence, alter the classical markers of the transition to adulthood, and – through increased contact between cultures – may well change the traditional meaning of adolescence across the globe (Larson, Brown, & Mortimer, 2002). In a literature that has long been dominated by North American research, it seems appropriate therefore to pay greater attention to adolescent development in other parts of the world, such as Europe, and to compare these European findings to what is known from earlier research on adolescents in the United States.

These comparative efforts are but a first step toward a global science of adolescent development that deliberately relies on comparisons of both European and North American adolescents with their agemates from Asia, Africa, Australasia, and Latin America when sketching a comprehensive picture of adolescence. The hope is expressed that this handbook, which systematically tries to include relevant findings on European adolescents whenever possible, can contribute to this emergence of a new, more global, and pluralistic view of adolescence (Larson, 2002).

Acknowledgement

The author is greatly indebted to Marcel van Aken for his insightful comments on an earlier draft of this chapter.

References

Alsaker, F.D., & Flammer, A. (Eds.). (1999). *The adolescent experience: European and American adolescents in the 1990s.* Mahwah, NJ: Lawrence Erlbaum Associates, Inc.

Arnett, J.J. (2000). Emerging adulthood: A theory of development from the late teens through the twenties. *American Psychologist, 55,* 469–480.

Arnett, J.J. (2001, Fall). Globalization and adolescent development. *Society for Research on Adolescence Newsletter,* pp. 1–2,8.

Arnett, J.J. (2004a). *Adolescence and emerging adulthood: A cultural approach* (2nd ed.). Upper Saddle River, NJ: Prentice Hall.

Arnett, J.J. (2004b). *Emerging adulthood: The winding road from the late teens through the twenties.* New York: Oxford University Press.

Arnett, J.J., & Galambos, N. (Eds.). (2003). *Exploring cultural conceptions of the transition to adulthood* (New Directions for Child and Adolescent Development, Nr. 100). San Francisco: Jossey-Bass.

Arnett, J.J., & Taber, S. (1994). Adolescence terminable and interminable: When does adolescence end? *Journal of Youth and Adolescence, 23,* 517–537.

Banks, J. (1997). MTV and the globalization of popular culture. *Gazette: International Journal for Communication Studies, 59,* 43–60.

Barber, B.K., Chadwick, B.A., & Oerter, R. (1992). Parental behaviors and adolescent self-esteem in the United States and Germany. *Journal of Marriage and the Family, 54,* 128–141.

Bosma, H.A., & Koops, W. (2004). Social cognition in adolescence: A tribute to Sandy (A. E.) Jackson (1937–2003). *European Journal of Developmental Psychology, 1,* 281–288.

Brown, B.B., Larson, R., & Saraswathi, T.S. (Eds.). (2002). *The world's youth: Adolescence in eight regions of the globe.* New York: Cambridge University Press.

Casey, C., & Edgerton, R.B. (Eds.). (2005). *A companion to psychological anthropology: Modernity and psychocultural change.* Malden, MA: Blackwell.

Caspi, A. (1987). Personality in the life course. *Journal of Personality and Social Psychology, 53,* 1203–1213.

Cherlin, A.J., Scabini, E., & Rossi, G. (Eds.). (1997). Delayed home leaving in Europe and the United States [Special issue]. *Journal of Family Issues, 18*(6).

Chisholm, L., & Hurrelmann, K. (1995). Adolescence in modern Europe: Pluralized transition patterns and their implications for personal and social risk. *Journal of Adolescence, 18,* 129–158.

Côté, J.E. (2000). *Arrested adulthood: The changing nature of maturity and identity.* New York: New York University Press.

Côté, J.E., & Allahar, A.L. (1996). *Generation on hold: Coming of age in the late twentieth century.* New York: New York University Press.

Dasen, P.R. (2000). Rapid social change and the

turmoil of adolescence: A cross-cultural perspective. *International Journal of Group Tensions, 29*, 17–49.

Hendry, L.B., & Kloep, M. (1999). Adolescence in Europe: An important life phase? In D. Messer, & S. Millar (Eds.), *Exploring developmental psychology: From infancy to adolescence* (pp. 383–399). London: Arnold.

Herdt, G., & Leavitt, S.C. (Eds.). (1998). *Adolescence in Pacific island societies.* Pittsburgh, PA: University of Pittsburgh Press.

Herman-Giddens, M.E., Slora, E.J., Wasserman, R.C., Bourdony, C.J., Bhapkar, M.V., Koch, G.G. et al. (1997). Secondary sexual characteristics and menses in young girls seen in office practice: A study from the Pediatric Research in Office Settings Network. *Pediatrics, 99*, 505–512.

Herman-Giddens, M.E., Wang, L., & Koch, G. (2001). Secondary sexual characteristics in boys: Estimates from the National Health and Nutrition Examination Survey III, 1988–1994. *Archives of Pediatrics and Adolescent Medicine, 155*, 1022–1028.

Iacovou, M., & Berthoud, R. (2001). *Young people's lives: A map of Europe.* Colchester, England: University of Essex, Institute for Social and Economic Research.

Keniston, K. (1971). *Youth and dissent: The rise of a new opposition.* New York: Harcourt Brace Jovanovich.

Klein, H. (1990). Adolescence, youth, and young adulthood: Rethinking current conceptualizations of life stage. *Youth and Society, 21*, 446–471.

Larson, R.W. (2002). Globalization, societal change, and new technologies: What they mean for the future of adolescence. *Journal of Research on Adolescence, 12*, 1–30.

Larson, R.W., Brown, B.B., & Mortimer, J.T. (Eds.). (2002). Adolescents' preparation for the future: Perils and promise [Special issue]. *Journal of Research on Adolescence, 12*(1).

Larson, R., & Mortimer, J.T. (2000, July). *Adolescence in the 21st century: A worldwide perspective.* Symposium conducted at the Sixteenth Biennial Meetings of the International Society for the Study of Behavioral Development (ISSBD), Beijing, People's Republic of China.

Larson, R., & Wilson, S. (2004). Adolescence across time and place: Globalization and the changing pathways to adulthood. In R. M. Lerner, & L. Steinberg (Eds.), *Handbook of adolescent development* (2nd ed., pp. 299–330). Hoboken, NJ: John Wiley & Sons.

Levine, R.A. (1982). *Culture, behavior, and personality: An introduction to the comparative study of psychosocial adaptation* (2nd ed.). New York: Aldine.

Mody, B. (Ed.). (2001). Mediated adolescence around the world [Special issue]. *Gazette: The International Journal of Communication Studies, 65*(1).

Moffitt, T.E. (1993). Adolescence-limited and life-course persistent antisocial behavior: A developmental taxonomy. *Psychological Review, 100*, 674–701.

Moffitt, T.E., Caspi, A., Harrington, H., & Milne, B.J. (2002). Males on the life-course persistent and adolescence-limited antisocial pathways: Follow-up at age 26 years. *Development and Psychopathology, 14*, 179–207.

Naroll, R. (1973). The culture bearing unit in cross-cultural surveys. In R. Naroll, & R. Cohen (Eds.), *Handbook of method in cultural anthropology* (pp. 721–765). New York: Columbia University Press.

Neubauer, G., & Hurrelmann, K. (Eds.). (1995). *Individualization in childhood and adolescence.* Berlin: de Gruyter.

Petersen, A.C., Silbereisen, R.K., & Sörensen, S. (1996). Adolescent development: A global perspective. In K. Hurrelmann, & S. T. Hamilton (Eds.), *Social problems and social contexts in adolescence: Perspectives across boundaries* (pp. 3–37). New York: Aldine de Gruyter.

Schlegel, A. (2000). The global spread of adolescent culture. In L. J. Crockett, & R. K. Silbereisen (Eds.), *Negotiating adolescence in times of social change* (pp. 71–88). New York: Cambridge University Press.

Schlegel, A. (2003). Modernization and changes in adolescent social life. In T. S. Saraswathi (Ed.), *Cross-cultural perspectives on human development: Theory, research, and applications* (pp. 236–257). New Delhi: Sage.

Steinberg, L. (2001). We know some things: Parent–adolescent relationships in retrospect and prospect. *Journal of Research of Adolescence, 11*, 1–19.

Super, C.M. (2005). The globalization of developmental psychology. In D. B. Pillemer, & S. B. White (Eds.), *Developmental psychology and social change: Research, history, and policy* (pp. 11–33). New York: Cambridge University Press.

Tudge, J., Shanahan, M.J., & Valsiner, J. (Eds.). (1997). *Comparisons in human development: Understanding time and context.* New York: Cambridge University Press.

Weisner, T.S., & Lowe, E.D. (2005). Globalization, childhood, and psychological anthropology. In C. Casey, & R. B. Edgerton (Eds.), *A companion to psychological anthropology: Modernity and psychocultural change* (pp. 315–336). Malden, MA: Blackwell.

2

Theories of adolescence

Luc Goossens

Following a brief introduction on the role of developmental theories in the history of the scientific study of adolescence, a series of classical theories of adolescence is presented. Several attempts at conceptual integration of these theories are also reviewed. The latest generation of developmental theories, collectively referred to as contextualist theories, will also be discussed in some detail, with particular emphasis on applications of these theories to the study of adolescent development. Throughout the chapter, special attention will be devoted to the numerous contributions of European authors to classical theories of adolescence. Finally, the implications of recent, contextualist theories for European research on adolescence will be outlined.

1. Developmental theories: Their role in the history of adolescent psychology

Generally speaking, theories of development (Lerner, 2002; Miller, 2002) are concerned with or focus on systematic changes in behavior over time (see Flammer, 1996). This focus presents developmental psychologists with three tasks: (a) to

describe changes in one particular domain of behavior (e.g., cognition or emotion), (b) to describe changes in associations among different domains of behavior, and (c) to explain the course of development that has been described in those domains. Developmental theories that address these three tasks offer two contributions to empirical researchers: (a) they organize and give meaning and coherence to what would otherwise remain isolated facts, and (b) they guide further empirical work by allowing researchers to deduce testable assumptions from the general statements of the theory and to effectively put these hypotheses to the test (Miller, 2002).

All theories of development address at least four basic issues, be it explicitly or implicitly. Phrased as questions, these issues read as follows:

1. What is the underlying conception of development and of human nature in general?
2. Is development basically quantitative or qualitative in nature?
3. How do the individual ('nature') and the

environment ('nurture') contribute to development?

4. What is it that develops? (Miller, 2002).

The answers that developmentalists provide to these questions, and that ultimately reflect their philosophical outlook on life itself, will have a strong impact on the topic or the subject matter they want to study and the methods they are inclined to use (Lerner, 2002).

By way of illustration, the variety of answers provided by different theories will be reviewed briefly for two of the four questions. With regard to the first question, essentially two types of developmental theory can be distinguished: the organismic and the contextual. Adherents of these views think of the developing person, and, in fact, of the world as a whole, in terms of a living organism and a historical event, respectively. With regard to the fourth question, many theorists tend to concentrate on a specific aspect of the developing person, such as feelings, cognition, or personality. For each of them, this particular aspect represents the 'essence' or core domain of development, which leads to additional differences in emphasis in the various theories developed over time.

By and large, two distinct phases may be distinguished in the history of the scientific study of adolescence. These phases were characterized by a predominance of organismic and contextualist theories, respectively. It is important to realize, however, that each of these types of theory predominated during one of two overlapping phases in that history, each of which was characterized by a different relationship between theory and empirical research on adolescence. The first, organismic phase, which began in the early years of the 20th century and lasted until the 1970s, was characterized by grand theoretical models, whereas empirical research during that phase was largely atheoretical and descriptive in nature.

The second, contextualist phase, which began in the 1970s and continues to this day, is characterized by somewhat less ambitious theoretical models and an intimate link between theory and empirical research. During this phase, researchers with an active interest in developmental processes

as influenced by the broader context began to study adolescence to test their theoretical notion that development may be decribed as the set of a person's changing relationships to his or her environment (Lerner & Steinberg, 2004; Steinberg & Lerner, 2004). The research prompted by these concerns (see reviews by Lerner & Galambos, 1998; Petersen, 1988; Steinberg & Morris, 2001) also led to an increased interest in applied issues and to the promotion of positive youth development in particular (Benson, Mannes, Pittman, & Ferber, 2004; Larson, 2000). One could even claim that a third phase is currently emerging in the history of the scientific study of adolescence. In this emergent phase, the findings from research on adolescence and associated theorizing are increasingly used to advance civil society and to forge strong collaborative links between researchers, policy makers, and practitioners (Lerner, Fischer, & Weinberg, 2000). This chapter will focus on the theories developed during the first two phases of this history, which will be referred to as the classical and the contextualist theories, respectively.

2. Four classical types of theory on adolescence

All theories of adolescence, being theories of development, will by necessity adopt a specific position regarding the four basic questions addressed in developmental theories, as described in the previous section. For historical reasons, however, the important themes that differentiate among the various theories of adolescent development are organized in a slightly different way. They revolve around two questions:

1. Is adolescence a distinct phase in development?
2. Is the period of adolescence characterized by increased levels of emotional turmoil, that is, by 'storm and stress'?

This particular way of rephrasing the important theoretical issues does of course give a certain degree of specificity to theories of adolescence (Miller, 1989).

The various psychological theories that address these two questions are typically organized into four broad categories. These categories refer to (a) biological, (b) psychoanalytic, (c) social–cultural, and (d) cognitive theories of adolescence, respectively (Berzonsky, 2000; Miller, 1989; Muuss, 1996). (See Flammer & Alsaker, 2002, for an overview of sociological theories of adolescence or youth.) Each of these four types of theory is presented in this section.

Most of the classical theories of adolescence, Freud's psychoanalytic theory and Piaget's cognitive theory in particular, are organismic theories. In the organismic model, in which the world is conceptualized as a living organism, the individual is conceived of as active and the emphasis is on the impact of the individual ('nature') on development. Living organisms, such as plants or animals, are to be considered in dynamic fashion in this model. This means that an organism is not just a static collection of cells or organs. Rather it is defined in terms of distinct steps in an organic process (e.g., egg, caterpillar, cocoon, and butterfly), with particular emphasis on the principal features of the organic system that will ultimately be achieved (i.e, the butterfly stage). Development, therefore, is the result of inherent properties and goals of the developing individual (Lerner, 2002).

The fact that the end state or goal of development (i.e., 'genital sexuality' in Freud's theory or 'formal operations' in Piaget's, respectively) is postulated in advance in these theories has other consequences as well. Adherents of organismic theories are also more inclined to posit qualitative changes, which leads them to phrase stage theories of development. Piaget's classical theory of cognitive development, which posits a universal sequence of transitions to ever more sophisticated forms of thought (e.g., from concrete to more abstract forms of thinking), based on an internal dynamic (i.e., increasingly higher levels in the way thinking is organized), is an example of this approach.

2.1 Biological theories of adolescence

The first scientific account of adolescence and, in fact, the first biological theory of psychological development in that period, was proposed by Granville Stanley Hall in his two-volume book *Adolescence* (Hall, 1904). Hall truly was a founding father of psychology in the United States. He received the first Ph.D. in psychology in that country, founded its first psychological journal, and served important functions in professional associations of psychologists such as the American Psychological Association (APA) (White, 1992). In his thinking about development, however, he was strongly influenced by European thinkers. Many of these European ideas Hall seems to have picked up in the course of two extensive study visits to Germany and extensive reading afterwards (Ross, 1972). In the second half of the nineteenth century, European thinking was dominated, in large part, by the theory of evolution.

Inspired by this biological theory, Hall (1904) applied the so-called law of recapitulation to psychological development. In essence, this view implies that the development of the species (or phylogenesis) is recapitulated in the development of the individual (or ontogenesis). In his own account of human development, which he consistently referred to as 'genetic psychology', Hall therefore distinguished four periods of individual development that corresponded to four long periods in our development as a species (Dacey & Kenny, 1997).

In the first phase, infancy (0 to 4 years), children recapitulate the animal stage of our development as a species. Mental development is still quite primitive and motor and sensory development are very important during that period. In the second phase, childhood (4 to 8 years), children recapitulate the anthropoid phase of our development as a species (in which humans closely resembled the primates or human-like apes). Hunting and fishing were important means of subsistence during that nomadic stage. This explains, according to Hall, why children in the corresponding phase of individual development have such a strong interest in those activities and in playing with toy weapons and hiding in caves (which our ancestors were supposed to have done in the corresponding 'anthropoid' stage). In the third phase, preadolescence (or the juvenile stage; 8 to 12 years), young people recapitulate the half-barbarian phase of our development as a species.

In the latter phase, humans first began to settle and work the land permanently (which explains why preadolescents are so fond of building camps) and routine training and drills (which still work well with preadolescents) began to be used in agrarian societies. The fourth and final phase, adolescence, began with puberty, which according to Hall took place around 13 or even 14 years of age, and continued well into the twenties (roughly up to 25 years of age). This phase corresponds with the civilized phase in our development as a species. During adolescence the so-called higher emotions, that set us apart as humans and were slow to develop in our own history as a species, were thought to emerge. Due to inherent properties of these emotions, periods of strong emotional upheaval, or 'storm and stress' are to be expected during adolescence.

Two aspects of Hall's theory of adolescence stand out as unusual:

- Hall's notion of adolescence was different from our current definition of that period. His operational definition of adolescence was 'the years from 14 to 24' (Hall, 1904, Vol. 1, p. xix).
- He thought that 'storm and stress' was bound to emerge during adolescence for structural reasons. Because the higher emotions (i.e., reason, true morality, religion, sympathy, love, and esthetic enjoyment) are a recent and somewhat tenuous acquisition in the development of the human species, they stand in continuous opposition to their counterparts and have to be continually re-asserted against them, so to speak. (In other words: these higher emotions are not permanently inherited yet.)

This particular feature of emotional life in adolescence explains the frequent oscillations between emotional extremes that are so characteristic of adolescents. The 12 oppositions that Hall describes are the following:

1. inertness and excitement
2. pleasure and pain
3. self-confidence and humility
4. selfishness and altruism
5. good and bad conduct
6. solitude and society
7. sensitiveness and dullness
8. curiosity and apathy
9. knowing and doing
10. conservatism and iconoclasm
11. sense and intellect
12. wisdom and folly.

With real sensitivity to the adolescent experience, Hall (1904, Vol. 2, pp. 71–94) describes all these oppositions in detail. He sketches, for instance, how adolescents can be truly elated at times and feel deeply depressed on other occasions (Opposition 2), how they tend to love being alone and to enjoy looking at the stars at one point in time and to be completely immersed in social activities and all sorts of social clubs at other moments (Opposition 6), and how they are oversensitive to other people's critique on their own behavior, while being utterly insensitive to others' feelings and sufferings (Opposition 7). Because of the high potential represented by the positive poles of these dualities, adolescence represented for Hall a second birth (i.e., into our own uniquely human form) and the 'best decade of life' (Hall, 1904, Vol. 1, p. xviii).

Hall's theory, of course, implies some sort of inheritance of acquired characteristics in subsequent generations, an idea that is now completely discredited. He did not refer to genes (which were not generally known in his days), but in the neo-Lamarckian era that he lived in, Hall assumed that memories (or 'traces') of earlier experiences were transmitted to later generations in the 'echo chamber' of our individual souls (Arnett, 1999). Similar ideas had found rather widespread acceptance in the second half of the 19th century and Hall's theory seems to have undergone numerous neo-Lamarckian influences. An intellectual biography of Hall's ideas (Grinder, 1967) traced their origins back to European authors like Lamarck, Darwin, Haeckel, and Spencer and to American authors like John Fiske, a leading proponent of Spencer's ideas in the United States.

Hall's genetic psychology also led him to offer some suggestions for educational reform. In the early phases of individual development, when the evolutionary momentum is still strong, educators should try not to intervene in development. Catharsis was assumed to be at work in development, which meant that every stage of development should be allowed free expression if development were to proceed smoothly. By allowing children to express their 'natural cruelty' in milder forms (e.g., by twisting a friend's arm), they would be rendered immune from expression of cruelty at later stages in development (Grinder, 1969). This 'Nature-is-right' idea was easily accepted by many educators in Hall's time, because another European author, Jean-Jacques Rousseau, had expounded similar ideas some time earlier.

Educating adolescents, however, is a different affair altogether. Because the higher emotions were late to emerge in the development of the species, their evolutionary momentum is weak. The full expression of these emotions should therefore be actively encouraged and nurtured by parents and other educators. If and when adults do so in continuous fashion, the whole of humankind could be brought to a higher level of functioning still, which would naturally be transmitted to the following generations. In doing so, adolescence can be prolonged (indefinitely, at least in principle) and a new generation of human beings ('superanthropoids' as Hall called them) would come into existence in whose minds the higher emotions are engrained more deeply than in the generation of adolescents that Hall described in his work.

The whole of Hall's 'genetic psychology' was aimed at determining so-called 'sensitive periods' or 'critical periods' for different psychological functions or emotions (Hall referred to them as 'nascent periods') in which educators could assist young people, either at a distance (in the phases before adolescence) or in much more active fashion (in adolescence). To this aim, he pioneered the use of open-ended questionnaires on a given topic (or topical 'syllabi' in Hall's terminology). Teachers were asked to carefully observe the children or adolescents entrusted to them and to detail in brief written reports, for instance, the age of occurrence and precise form of instances of altruistic behavior. This part of Hall's work should have yielded valuable information on developmental norms. Few such norms, however, can be found in his books, because it proved to be extremely difficult to process the rich data for the syllabi (several hundreds of even thousands of reports per study) that were sent to Hall and his team by diligent teachers all over the United States.

This brief description of Hall's theoretical views of adolescence and the limited achievements of his empirical work on psychological development serves to make an important point. Hall was not a maturationist, as he is occasionally described to be. He did not think of development as an unfolding of physical structures and behaviors according to a biological blueprint (Crain, 2000), or to be more precise: he accepted such a notion for the phases that preceded adolescence only. In all probability, Hall is associated with the maturationist viewpoint, because one of his students, Arnold Gesell, came to embrace such an extreme view. In Gesell's work, we find a detailed normative description of development up to and including the phase of adolescence (ages 10 to 16 for Gesell), complete with vivid descriptions of the '12-year-old', the '14-year-old' and the '16-year-old' (Gesell, Ilg, & Ames, 1956).

An evaluation of Hall's complex theory must, by necessity, be a balanced one. In fact, contemporary authors tend to value the three key aspects of his work in radically different ways:

- His general developmental principle (recapitulation) has long been refuted by additional findings in comparative biology and evolutionary theory.
- His sharp insight into the psychology of adolescence (i.e., the 12 oppositions pertaining to the higher emotions) continues to be valuable until the present day.
- His belief in the plasticity (or malleability) of adolescent development makes him a precursor of contemporary contextualist theories of adolescence (as described later in this chapter) and was truly innovative and provocative in his own time (Cairns, 1998).

Psychoanalytic theories of adolescence

In sharp contrast to Hall's theory, psychoanalysis does not assign a decisive role to the phase of adolescence. Earlier phases, labelled the oral, anal, and oedipal (or phallic) stages, occupy a much more central role in the theory advanced by Sigmund Freud. During these phases of early childhood, children experience various types of sexual and aggressive impulses (or drives). Following a brief interlude in middle childhood (labelled the 'latency' phase), these drives are re-awakened by the biological changes of puberty. Freud addressed the issue in one of his essays ('The Transformations of Puberty') in general terms (Freud, 1953). He mainly asserted that puberty is marked by the emergence of the mature or genital form of sexuality which implies that all of the earlier sexual impulses (i.e., oral and anal drives) have to be subsumed under the primacy of genital or adult sexuality. This view does, of course, imply another version of the recapitulation theory advanced by Hall (1904). Psychological development in adolescence recapitulates earlier phases in the development of the individual rather than phases from the development of the human species (as was the case in Hall's theory).

Incidentally, this is more than a superficial analogy. There are direct links between Hall and Freud. Hall was the first (in 1909) to invite Freud and some of his co-workers, including Carl Gustav Jung, to the United States for a series of lectures. This event represented the first form of academic recognition of psychoanalysis anywhere in the world (Rosenzweig, 1992). What seems to have attracted Hall in Freud was his historical or archeological approach, in which the different layers of personality each referred to a different period of development and each layer only made sense in relation to these different periods of development considered as a whole. Hall was even more interested, it seems, when he heard late in his life of Jung's notion of the collective unconsciousness as a reservoir of psychical experiences and religious images of the human race (Ross, 1972).

Sigmund Freud left it to his youngest daughter Anna, who, like him, lived in Vienna first and in London afterwards, to fully develop the psychoanalytic version of the recapitulation theory (Gallatin, 1975). She saw puberty as a period of increased activity of the drives ('storm and stress'). This increase is first quantitative in nature (i.e., higher level of general arousal) and qualitative later on. Oedipal feelings, that is, sexual impulses directed at the parent of the opposite sex and aggressive impulses directed toward the same-sex parent, are re-awakened and are all the more dangerous because the adolescent has reached full sexual maturity and bodily strength. Strong mechanisms of defense, therefore, have to be put into place to curb these impulses.

In addition to well-known Freudian mechanisms of defense, Anna Freud described two special mechanisms, which she labeled ascetism and intellectualization, respectively. Ascetism means that adolescents deny themselves any type of pleasure, for fear of losing control over their sexual impulses. Adolescents who commit themselves to highly demanding schedules of studying or sports can provide an example of this particular mechanism of defense. Intellectualization implies that personal conflicts of a highly emotional nature are transformed into abstract philosophical arguments, stripped of emotion (Miller, 1989). As an illustration, one can refer to young adolescent males who calmly assert that all tyrants all over the world have to be deposed immediately. On closer inspection, such adolescents typically have a somewhat strained relationship with their father whom they find too strict as a parent (Freud, 1966).

In her later work on adolescence, Anna Freud came to regard the 'storm and stress' of adolescence as normal. If it failed to manifest itself in some adolescents, this should not be seen as a sign of adaptive functioning. Rather, one should routinely assume that the mechanisms of defense used by these young people are too strong, because the re-emergence of oedipal longings was believed to be inevitable (Freud, 1969, 1971). This drive/defense view became the cornerstone of the classical psychoanalytic theory of adolescence (Blos, 1962).

A new perspective on the psychoanalysis of adolescence was introduced by Peter Blos (1979), who had first worked with Anna Freud in Vienna and had later moved to the United States. These new ideas were phrased within the framework of object relations theory. Object relations or object representations are (mostly unconscious) inner representations of one's relationships with important people in one's life, such as one's parents. (These important people are labeled 'objects' in psychoanalytic parlance.) Blos (1979) states that adolescence is a second separation–individuation phase in life, which in important ways parallels the first such phase, which occurs in the first two to three years of life. In that phase, described by Margaret Mahler and her co-workers (Mahler, Pine, & Bergman, 1975), young children distance themselves physically from their mother. In the course of this process, they are first absorbed into their own autonomous functioning ('practicing phase'), seek close proximity to the mother figure again ('rapprochement'), and finally develop a primitive sense of self. According to Blos (1979), adolescents go through similar phases as they strive to distance themselves psychologically from their parents. His new psychoanalytic view, therefore, is once again a recapitulation theory.

Both Anna Freud and Peter Blos, however, did recognize that adolescence represents a distinct phase in psychological development. This is evident from the developmental objectives they set out for adolescents. For Anna Freud, the ultimate goal for adolescents was the integration of adult sexuality into their developing personality. Peter Blos likewise suggested the shedding of outdated forms of dependency on parents and the achievement of age-appropriate forms of autonomy as major objectives for adolescents. For all psychoanalysts, therefore, adolescence represents both a recapitulation and a complete reworking of older impulses, representations, and conflicts. A final note on the psychoanalytic position regarding adolescence is that one ultimately has to come to an integration or synthesis of the classical drive/defense view (Adelson & Doehrman, 1980) and the more recent object relational view. Both perspectives refer to parallel tasks that the developing adolescent has to deal with simultaneously (Lerner, 1987).

2.3 Social–cultural theories of adolescence

Many theories about adolescence, including social-learning theory, hold that adolescent behavior is shaped to a certain extent by the reactions from their immediate social environment, that is, by reactions from their parents and peers. Other views within the broader class of social theories of adolescence focus on the role of the broader social environment, that is, the cultural context in which adolescents live. The period of adolescence has managed to capture the attention of social and cultural anthropologists from the first quarter of the 20th century onwards. In her book, *Coming of age in Samoa*, Margaret Mead (1928) set out to examine whether the 'storm and stress' of adolescence was universal. It is clear from the date of publication of her work, that she must have been referring to Hall's work, because the psychoanalytic version of the 'storm and stress' theory was yet to be fully developed at that time. In fact by the 1920s, 'storm and stress' had developed into a popular stereotype of adolescence that comprised three components. Adolescents were thought:

1. to evidence frequent mood swings
2. to have strained relationships with their parents
3. to be prone to risk taking which leads to higher levels of delinquency among adolescents (Arnett, 1999).

Mead (1928) herself referred to 'storm and stress' as a broad category of adolescent behaviors that included idealism and rebellion against parental authority.

In her study, Mead (1928) conducted individual interviews with 50 girls from a remote island in American Samoa, in the eastern part of the Samoan archipelago (Polynesia). These girls were distributed about evenly across three phases of pubertal development: pre-pubertal, pubertal, and post-pubertal. In these interviews, Mead could find no signs of 'storm and stress' among these girls. Because the biological changes of puberty were considered to be universal, and American adolescents were all supposed to suffer from emotional turmoil, this finding led Mead to presume that there were differences between the two cultures (Samoa and the United States) that accounted for this difference in experienced 'storm and stress'.

In her speculative account of these differences, Mead (1928) came up with two explanations. First, she pointed out that life on Samoa was simpler because adolescents were not confronted with difficult decisions that had a strong impact on their lives (as was the case in the United States). Second, she referred to the general casual nature of the Samoan lifestyle, which extended toward a more casual attitude toward premarital sex. Mead's work on Samoa, therefore, had a message for Western civilization, which is typical for many of her books (McDermott, 2001). The implication was that adolescence would be less troublesome for young people in America if they were less pressured into taking important decisions and if the general nature of the American culture were to be more casual. At any rate, Mead's (1928) work led to the conclusion that the degree of 'storm and stress' experienced by adolescents also depends, to a certain degree at least, on the broader cultural milieu.

A few years after Mead's death, her ideas from her Samoan work were seriously challenged by one of her colleagues in social and cultural anthropology. Derek Freeman had spent some time on another island in the western part of the Samoan archipelago and had come to conclusions that were radically different from Mead's. He maintained that Mead had failed to understand the Samoan culture as a whole and adolescence on Samoa in particular. His analyses of juvenile court cases, for instance, indicated that there was considerable 'storm and stress' on Samoa as well (Freeman, 1983). Mead would further have been duped by her native informants into believing that Samoan youths in the 1920s could indulge in premarital sex with few restrictions (Freeman, 1999). These allegations led to the most hotly debated issue in social and cultural anthropology in recent years and arguably one of the 10 liveliest debates in science ever (Hellman, 1998), the so-called Mead–Freeman controversy. Careful re-analyses of Mead's original work (Côté, 1992) and of the entire Mead–Freeman controversy (Côté, 1994, 2000) indicate that

Mead's main finding *can* be upheld. She could have phrased her conclusions somewhat more conservatively (e.g., by pointing out that they applied only to the island that she had visited and not to the whole of Samoa, as she occasionally implied). Her explanations of the observed difference between the Samoan and American cultures continue to be speculative. There seems to be no reason, however, to doubt that adolescence was indeed a somewhat easier phase of life on that particular island in American Samoa in 1925–1926 when Mead did her fieldwork there than it was in the United States at that time. The fact that the island concerned is strongly Americanized now and that other islands in the same archipelago in Polynesia may have presented a different state of affairs is not all that important. To make her point, Mead needed just a single example of a non-Western culture (which had had relatively limited contact with the Western world) where the experience of adolescence was conspicuously different from its experience in the American culture at that time, and she seems to have found just that on a remote island in the Central Pacific in the 1920s. Her main conclusion, therefore – that adolescent 'storm and stress' is not universal and is co-determined by the cultural milieu, among other factors – continues to stand the test of time (Côté, 1992).

Mead did not care to interview a control group of American adolescents, simply because she assumed 'storm and stress' to be universal in the United States. Subsequent research (e.g., Offer & Sabshin, 1974) has revealed, however, that marked difficulties as implied in the popular stereotype of adolescence are not widespread in that culture either. Disturbances in the self-image were only found in about 20% of American adolescents. In addition, most adolescents turned out to have positive relationships with their parents (Arnett, 1999).

2.4 Cognitive theories of adolescence

Cognitive theories of adolescence state, in essence, that adolescent behaviors that are of some concern to adults have their origins in the cognitive changes that take place at the onset of adolescence. In his classical work on adolescent thinking (Inhelder & Piaget, 1958), Swiss psychologist Jean Piaget made exactly that point. Two different types of thinking, concrete operations vs. formal operations, were shown to underlie children's and adolescents' reasoning about simple scientific experiments, respectively. In the final chapter of the book Inhelder and Piaget (1958) considered the broader implications of the transition to formal thinking. Adolescents can think about their own thinking and reality becomes secondary to possibility, in the sense that the world that we live in is just one of the many possible worlds that one can envisage.

This new type of insight lies at the core of adolescent idealism, which was described by Margaret Mead (1928) as an intrinsic element of the 'storm and stress' of adolescence. Adolescents, Inhelder and Piaget (1958) state, are strongly inclined to develop philosophical, ethical, and political systems in an attempt to change the world for the better. These solutions are inherently naïve, because the possibilities of solving important social problems through logical reasoning are limited. When adolescents come to realize this, they take an important step toward adulthood, that is (a) their insertion into society and (b) the formation of their socially corrected and socially sanctioned personality.

Reasoning along similar lines, David Elkind (1967) claimed that the advent of formal thought would lead adolescents to develop certain misconceptions about the self and others that he referred to as 'adolescent egocentrism'. This type of egocentrism would lead to two mental constructions. Because adolescents are preoccupied with themselves, they tend to think that others are paying just as much attention to them as they are doing themselves. This leads to the construction of an imaginary audience. Adolescents believe they are constantly being watched, hence the term 'audience', but this is seldom effectively the case (and that is why the audience only exists in their own minds). As a complement to this lack of differentiation between self and others, adolescents tend to overdifferentiate their feelings from the feelings of others. This gives rise to a second mental construction that Elkind (1967) called the personal fable. Adolescents tell themselves a story about themselves that is not true to reality. The personal fable leads to adolescent feelings of uniqueness, omnipotence, and invulnerability.

Adolescents' belief in the imaginary audience helps explain many of their typical behaviors. When they feel critical about themselves, they are convinced that others feel equally critical. That is why adolescents tend to be self-conscious and why shame is such an important emotion for them. When they admire themselves, adolescents project these positive feelings unto their imaginary audience. That explains why adolescents who have just bought a new outfit they find 'cool' cannot understand that others do not think much of their new clothes. The personal fable helps to account for the oft heard cry from adolescents that no one can understand their feelings. It also accounts for the risks that adolescents take while driving recklessly or while having unprotected sex. They simply do not believe that harm can come their way. Many of the phenomena that can be explained in terms of the twin cognitive constructions of the imaginary audience and the personal fable are often explained in psychoanalytic terms.

3. Integrative approaches

As the classical theories describe a whole range of changes during adolescence and empirical research on adolescence was largely unrelated to these theoretical frameworks in the first phase of the development of the discipline, several attempts have been made to integrate the various theoretical viewpoints and to integrate the growing body of research with those theories. In this section, two such approaches will be described that focus on complementarity among the classical theories and on the effect of cumulative changes, respectively.

3.1 Complementarity

It is clear from the foregoing description that each type of theory tends to emphasize a different aspect of the developing person, such as feelings, cognitions, or involvement in social interaction. Many authors have therefore suggested that no single type of theory can provide a complete picture of adolescent development. Researchers, therefore, are strongly encouraged to combine different theoretical perspectives to arrive at a composite picture of the developing adolescent (Berzonsky, 2000; Miller, 1989).

There is a second reason why researchers are well advised to 'think together' different theories of adolescence. All the available types of theories are formulated at a level that is far too general. As soon as one enters into greater detail, one is naturally led to include elements from other theoretical frameworks in the explanation of typical adolescent behaviors. Psychoanalytic explanations naturally lead into a discussion of social factors. Incorporating adult sexuality into one's personality will inevitably be done in interaction with others. Cognitive explanations of adolescent idealism lead to social factors that explain its demise, as we have seen in the previous section. The twin constructions of the imaginary audience and the personal fable will also disappear gradually through social interaction. In intimate conversations, for instance, adolescents come to realize that most other people have feelings similar to their own. Conversely, changes in social interaction presuppose cognitive changes as well, which allow the adolescent to think of social interaction in new and more complex ways (Lehalle, 1996).

Some authors have even suggested that the same adolescent phenomena can be explained from different theoretical perspectives. The imaginary audience and the personal fable, for instance, have been explained in terms of developments in adolescent object relations. This explanation, which is thought to complement the original cognitive account, assigns a different role to each of these mental constructions. As adolescents try to distance themselves from their parents, they still want to be connected to others and that is why they construct an imaginary audience. At the same time, their belief in the personal fable gives them the strength to go their own way (Goossens, Beyers, Emmen, & van Aken, 2002; Lapsley, 1993).

Such attempts at integration have led some authors to conclude that a comprehensive theory of adolescence can be developed as some sort of

'conceptual umbrella'. Gallatin (1975) maintained that such a theory was developed by Erik Erikson (1968), who also studied with Anna Freud in Vienna and later moved to the United States (Friedman, 1999). Erikson assigned equal importance to the individual and his or her social environment in adolescent identity formation. At the individual level, adolescents have to define their own personal life style. This personal approach to life has to be recognized by the social environment. On closer inspection, three dimensions can be distinguished in Erikson's theory, which sum up most of the theories discussed in the previous section. These are (a) the biological dimension (as in the drives that occupy a central place in psychoanalytic theory), (b) the social dimension (as in the cultural influences emphasized in social-cultural theories), and (c) the individual dimension (because no two people can have the same identity). One may object that cognitive elements are not included in Erikson's theory of identity. It can be shown, however, that Erikson assigned an important role to the cognitive changes of adolescence that give rise to adolescents' time perspective which is important in making plans for the future (Gallatin, 1975). In summary, Erikson's theory of adolescent identity formation can effectively be claimed to incorporate elements from all the main theories of adolescence.

3.2 Cumulative changes

An alternative approach to the many changes of adolescence is to consider the developmental sequencing of these changes and its impact on adolescents. British psychologist John Coleman (1974) asked himself why so many adolescents managed to cope well with the many changes of adolescence. A small minority (about 20%) seems to experience serious problems with these changes, which, of course, implies that 80% of all adolescents do comparatively well. To answer this question, the author developed the focal model of adolescent development (Coleman, 1974; Coleman & Hendry, 1999). The model states that, for most adolescents the different changes (which were all social relationship issues for Coleman) successively come into focus, in the sense of being most prominent. Put differently: most adolescents deal with one issue at the time when working through their relationships with their parents, same-sex friends, opposite-sex friends, groups of agemates, and authority figures. Only a small group (about 20% of all adolescents) are forced by the circumstances to deal with several or all issues at the same time and evidence the signs of adolescent 'storm and stress' (because they are overwhelmed by their problems).

Empirical support for Coleman's (1974) focal model was provided in North American research on the effects of cumulative change on early adolescents. Five types of important life events were distinguished in this study: school change, pubertal change, early dating, geographical mobility (e.g., moving to a new neighborhood), and major family disruption (e.g., parental divorce). The greater the number of important life events the adolescents were confronted with, the more negative effects they experienced. They felt worse (i.e., lower self-esteem) and did worse in school (i.e., poorer school results; Simmons & Blyth, 1987; Simmons, Burgeson, Carlton-Ford, & Blyth, 1987).

In an interpretation that went somewhat beyond the data, the authors surmised that adolescents need at least one 'arena of comfort', that is, one domain of their lives (e.g., family life) that is undisturbed and to which they can withdraw and become reinvigorated. Under these conditions, adolescents can deal successfully with problems that present themselves in other domains of their lives. However, if adolescents experience disruptions in all important domains of their lives, they are bound to experience substantial problems (Simmons & Blyth, 1987; Simmons et al., 1987).

Subsequent research (Call & Mortimer, 2001) has found empirical support for this notion. An arena of comfort was defined as an interpersonal context in which adolescents experienced support from others and four such potential arenas were distinguished: the family, the peer group, school, and (part-time) work. The findings supported earlier results in that adolescents who reported more arenas in which they were provided with social support exhibited a stronger sense of well-being. Only a small group (about 10%) did not have any arena of comfort and they reported the lowest level of well-being. Finally, moderating (or compensating) effects were obtained. Stressors that related to family change (e.g., changes in father's employment status) had a smaller negative impact on adolescent self-esteem and well-being among those young people who experienced support from both friends and supervisors at work. Supportive relationships in school, and with teachers in particular, had similar buffering effects on adolescent well-being when the family moved geographically.

The fact that empirical findings are in line with the predictions made by the focal model does not solve all the questions one can address to that model. An important issue that needs to be dealt with is the role of the person in the focal model. An implication of the model seems to be that some adolescents at least may actively choose to deal with one important issue at the time and try to organize their lives in such a way that they can effectively do so (Goossens & Marcoen, 1999; Jackson & Bosma, 1992). Empirical support for this important assumption, however, has not been forthcoming. Despite this important gap in current knowledge, research on cumulative changes in adolescence and the theoretical models that can account for such effects provides a potential avenue to conceptual integration of the various changes that different theories of adolescence tend to concentrate on.

4. Contextualist theories

The prime metaphor for development in the contextual model is that of an historical event or a tapestry, which are both situated in time and space (Lerner, 2002). Each behavior has meaning only in its socio-historical context (and therefore represents a historical event or historical act). Alternatively, the horizontal threads of time and the vertical threads of space can be thought to produce the pattern of human life. Viewed within this metaphor, each part of the tapestry makes sense in the context of the whole texture. Both metaphors used (i.e., the historical event and the tapestry) imply that the emphasis in development is neither on the individual ('nature') nor on the environment ('nurture') but rather on their interaction.

A 'pure' contextual model of development, however, is difficult to conceive of because that would treat each event as a purely historical accident. Researchers have therefore tried to combine the best of both world views by incorporating elements of the contextual model into the organismic models that had served developmentalists so well for such a long time. The new elements in this combined organismic–contextual model try to account adequately for the role of time and place in development (Lerner, 2002). Three instantiations of this combined model are discussed in some detail in this section. These three theories are (a) ecological theory, (b) life course theory, and (c) developmental contextualism.

4.1 Ecological theory

Ecological theory was developed by Urie Bronfenbrenner (1979, 2005), an American author who migrated from Russia to the United States with his entire family when he was about 5 years of age. The theory essentially provides a detailed description of the environment in which psychological development takes place. The theory is often called the 'bio-ecological' theory, to make clear that it wants to address all levels in the interaction between individuals and their environment, from the lowest (i.e., biological) to the highest (i.e., cultural) level. True to this ambition, Bronfenbrenner (1979) describes different types of system within the environment that fit into one another, like a series of nesting Russian dolls (Muuss, 1996). Bronfenbrenner identified four of these behavioral systems, which he defined in terms of how directly they impinge on an adolescent's development (Thomas, 2001).

The setting that affects the adolescent most directly is called the microsystem. A microsystem is a pattern of activities and relationships within a particular face-to-face setting in the immediate environment. Typical microsystems for adolescents are the family, the peer group, and the school context. At the next higher level, Bronfenbrenner defines the meso-system as the system that encompasses the linkages and processes that operate between two or more of the developing adolescent's microsystems. Parental attempts to co-structure the adolescent's relationships with her friends would be an example of such a linkage between two microsystems, that is, between the family and the peer group.

Behavioral systems beyond the meso-system are referred to as exo-systems. Such a system represents a context that, although not directly influencing the developing adolescent (e.g., the workplace of the father), nevertheless has an influence on the adolescent's behavior and development. Such a linkage within that particular meso-system can occur, for instance, when father returns home from a stressful day at the office and is less effective that evening in his role as parental caregiver (Lerner, 2002). The macrosystem, finally, is the highest level in Bronfenbrenner's hierarchy of levels, that is, the level most remote from the adolescent's immediate experience. This system is the cultural milieu which may comprise macro-institutions such as the nation's government and public policy. This macrosystem encompasses all the other systems (i.e., the micro-, meso-, and exo-systems).

In more recent years, Bronfenbrenner has come to realize that he had only developed a comprehensive theory of the environment in which psychological development takes place. He then set out to devise an equally well-developed theory of the developing person. While doing so, he came to grasp that he also had to devise a more fully developed vision of the process that operates between person and environment and of the role of historical time in this entire process. In short, he designed a Person-Process-Context-Time theory (or PPCT theory, for short). Some elements of this ambitious undertaking have already been worked out in some detail.

With regard to process, Bronfenbrenner (1995; Bronfenbrenner & Morris, 1998) broadened his conception of the microsystems. He did so by advancing two basic propositions. First, he states that so-called proximal processes are operating within these systems and that those processes are the primary mechanisms that initiate and sustain human development. Second, he maintains that the power and direction of these proximal processes depend on the characteristics of the developing person, the characteristics of all systems within the environment, the nature of the developmental outcomes under consideration, and the social continuities and changes occurring over time (both in the life course of the individual and in the historical period in which the person lives).

Bronfenbrenner (1995) stipulates that proximal processes, in order to be effective, must be reciprocal interactions that occur on a regular basis over extended periods of time. Classical aspects of parenting style, or periods in which parenting style is translated into concrete parenting activities, are primary examples of proximal processes that operate in the microsystem of the family. Parental support of the adolescent's learning activities (alternatively referred to as responsiveness to the adolescent's needs) or active parental monitoring of the adolescent's activities and whereabouts (when conceived of as ongoing reciprocal activities) are useful illustrations here.

With regard to the developing person, Bronfenbrenner now distinguishes three types of characteristic that influence development or, to be more precise, that have an impact on the proximal processes (Bronfenbrenner & Morris, 1998). 'Force characteristics' are dispositions (e.g., control of emotions, activity level, creativity, and ego control) that can set proximal processes in motion and continue to sustain their operation. 'Resource characteristics' (e.g., experience, knowledge, and skills) are required for the effective functioning of proximal processes or can hamper their functioning (e.g., in the case of chronic illness). 'Demand characteristics', finally, invite or discourage reactions from the social environment in such a way that the operation of proximal processes is fostered or disrupted. Factors that act in the spontaneous process of attraction and rejection, such as physical attractiveness or unattractiveness, are a case in point here.

The whole array of new concepts, such as proximal processes, and the forces, resources, and demands within the developing person that set and keep them in motion, represents an important first step toward the full articulation of Bronfenbrenner's (1995) all-encompassing Person-Process-Context-Time (PPCT) model.

Some elements of that comprehensive model, and the role of historical time in individual development in particular, have already been clarified in other conceptual frameworks such as life course theory, which is described in the next section.

4.2 *Life course theory*

The sociological concept of the life course refers to the succession of life stages (i.e., childhood, youth, adulthood, mid-life, and old age) as it is influenced by social and cultural factors (Hunt, 2005). Life course theory integrates several theoretical orientations and therefore, emphasizes both the role of social structure and individual agency (Mortimer & Shanahan, 2003). As a result, the theory takes into account the social surroundings of the individual and traces the stories of people's lives over time in an ever-changing society. Through this integrative approach, life course theory in the particular form developed by Glen Elder Jr. represents an effort to include historical influences in developmental research, which has rarely been attempted. (See Elder, Modell, & Parke, 1993, for exceptions to this general rule.)

The empirical basis for the theory was provided by the author's longitudinal analyses on two samples that were first studied in the 1920s when they were children or adolescents and followed ever since at regular intervals. One of these samples (born in 1920), the Oakland sample, was followed from their entry into adolescence (Grade 7) until they were in mid-life. In later work, a sample from a somewhat younger cohort (born in 1929), the Berkeley sample, was also followed for an extensive period. Although publications on these samples have appeared in print since the 1970s (Elder, 1999), the basic principles of life course theory were only derived from that work in the 1990s (Elder, 1998a, 1998b).

A first central concept in the new theory are life paths or social trajectories, such as education, work, and family. A succession of transitions occurs within each of these trajectories (e.g., getting one's first job, the birth of a first child) and there are age-graded normative expectations associated with these transitions (i.e., optimal ages at which one is expected to make each of these transitions). The whole of these life paths, which typically are not neatly synchronized among them, is referred to as the life course. A second concept are the influences of the historical context, which offers opportunities and imposes certain restrictions. A third concept, finally, is the developmental trajectory of the individual who makes certain choices regarding the different transitions in his or her life.

Life course theory, therefore, provides a framework for studies that attempt to relate social pathways to history and to developmental trajectories. A whole series of age-related expectations structure the social pathways in our life, but historical conditions bring new opportunities or new restrictions to these pathways, and individuals create their own developmental trajectories through life by the choices they make regarding these social pathways. The core of the theory can be summarized in four basic principles.

The first principle ('historical time and place') states that: 'The life course of individuals is embedded in and shaped by the historical times and places they experience over their life-time' (Elder, 1998a, p. 3). In his own work, Elder (1999) has been able to detail how the historical circumstances of the Great Depression in the 1930s and World War II had a profound impact on the psychological development of the young people in both the Berkeley and the Oakland cohorts.

The second principle ('timing in lives') states that: 'The developmental impact of a succession of life transitions or events is contingent on when they occur in a person's life' (Elder, 1998a, p. 3). In his historical analyses, Elder was able to contrast the effect of the Great Depression on young people of different ages. The participants in the Oakland cohort (born in 1920) experienced this series of historical events when they were adolescents, after they had had a prosperous childhood. The participants in the Berkeley cohort (born in 1929), by contrast, experienced the Great Depression when they were children and spent their adolescence in the years of World War II. This difference in timing led to a different experience of the adolescent period in the two cohorts.

There were few signs that the Oakland cohort experienced a stressful period of adolescence. Adolescents in the Berkeley cohort, however,

had low aspirations as adolescents and developed a 'dependency' syndrome in adolescence (e.g., they tended to feel victimized, to withdraw from adversity, and to exhibit self-defeating behavior). These feelings of personal and social inadequacy, in all probability, reflected the joint influence of economic deprivation early in their lives (in the 1930s) and the peculiar circumstances that applied during the war years. A positive finding was that the participants in the Berkeley cohort did substantially better when they had developed into mature adults (Elder, 1980).

The third principle ('linked lives'), states that: 'Lives are lived interdependently, and social and historical influences are expressed through this network of shared relationships' (Elder, 1998a, p. 4). Elder's work shows many cases in which children and adolescents experience the effect of the historical conditions through the older generation, that is, their parents. In all families that experienced economic hardships, regardless of the age of the children, three types of changes could be observed. These comprised changes in the household economy (e.g., because father was unemployed, mother and the older adolescents in the family had to find a job), changes in family relationships (e.g., mother's relative power was increased), and social strains in the family (e.g., increased conflict and emotional distress; Elder, 1980).

A family stress model of economic deprivation was developed in which loss of income and indebtedness led to increases in depressive feelings and marital negativity among parents. These processes in turn undermined effective parenting, which increased the likelihood of behavioral problems in the younger generation (Elder, 1998a, 1998b). Subsequent longitudinal research on the aftermath of the Great Farm Crisis in the United States in the 1980s, suggested some important qualifications to that model. The initial findings on young adolescents (Grade 7) in the early 1990s, who had experienced the Great Farm Crisis as children, effectively revealed increased problem behaviors. A few years later, by Grade 10, however, there no longer were such negative effects. These findings were attributed to particular characteristics that are commonly found among people in rural areas, who tend to have strong ties to the land. These characteristics include an extensive social network of relatives and active involvement of the younger generation in meaningful activities on the farm and in the broader community. Historical conditions, therefore, interact with characteristics of the developing person and his social environment to produce the eventual developmental outcome (Elder & Conger, 2000).

The fourth principle ('human agency'), finally, states that: 'Individuals construct their own life course through the choices and actions they take within the opportunities and constraints of history and social circumstances' (Elder, 1998a, p. 4). An illustration of this principle is provided when older adolescents find themselves a job and decide to leave the family and to make the transition to adulthood at an early age, and in so doing construct their own life course.

In all their generality, the four principles of life course theory, when taken together, provide a useful framework for researchers who want to include the role of historical conditions into their explanatory framework. This theoretical framework will undoubtedly be expanded as other historical eras and different geographical regions are examined in future longitudinal work on adolescents.

4.3 Developmental contextualism

Developmental contextualism (Lerner, 2002; Muuss, 1996) provides a basic theoretical framework that could support and theoretically enlarge the findings revealed in all other contextual approaches. Summarizing the contributions of these theories, one can state that there are many (bi-directional) relationships between the developing individual and aspects of his or her environment (e.g., family members, peers, teachers, the neighborhood, the cultural milieu, and the historical context). Developmental contextualism simply suggests to regard the whole pattern of these dynamic person–context interactions as the key phenomenon of psychological development.

This view has important implications:

• The developing person changes continually, because his or her relationships with the environment are in constant flux. At least one of these many relationships is bound to change at any point in time.

• Human development is characterized by a great potential for systematic change, that is, by plasticity, at any point in the life span. This plasticity is not absolute, however, as certain biological restrictions apply.

• Applied research and intervention research in particular should be relatively easy, because it merely involves that the relationship with one aspect of the environment is changed. As a consequence, developmental contextualism transcends the traditional distinctions between person and context, individual and environment, nature and nurture, and fundamental and applied research.

Bronfenbrenner's (1995) ecological theory and Elder's (1998a) life course theory are all members of the family of contextualist theories, of which developmental contextualism is the prime representative.

For all of its merits, developmental contextualism faces the real danger that it may remain an abstract formalism, that is, some sort of philosophical 'relationalism'. There is a continuing need, therefore, for concrete applications of the theory that attest to its usefulness and viability. Two such applications can be found with regard to adolescence. The first application deals with the effect that different types of relationships with the context can have on adolescents. Optimal conditions apply when there is a 'goodness-of-fit' (or 'match') between person and context. Individuals are strongly motivated and tend to do well in social environments that fit well with their social needs. Conversely, when the social environment does not match the needs of the individual, a decrease will be observed in motivation, interest, and achievement.

Examples of lack of fit have been found in early adolescence. In that phase of development, young people strive to have greater autonomy in their lives. In the first years of secondary school, however, they tend to have less control over their learning activities in school than they used to have in the upper grades of elementary school. Secondary schools tend to be bigger and more impersonal and teachers in these schools prefer working with the entire class as a whole rather than in small groups, which are all features of the environment that contribute to a decrease in autonomy in early adolescence (i.e., the early years of secondary school). Empirical research has shown that this mismatch between individual and school context effectively has deleterious effects on early adolescents' school performance. The most compelling evidence in support of this view were longitudinal findings showing that as the degree of incongruence increased, school achievements decreased (Eccles, Lord, & Buchanan, 1996).

A second application deals with active regulation of person–context relationships. Borrowing from life-span developmental psychology, Lerner has recently applied a general model of developmental regulation to adolescents' search for identity (Lerner, Freund, De Stefanis, & Habermas, 2001). This 'Selection-Optimization-Compensation' (or SOC) model suggests that adolescent identity formation includes an initial phase of goal selection (e.g., the decision to start focusing one's attention in the initial search for possible options regarding one's vocational identity). In a second phase of goal pursuit, adolescents will have to learn the necessary skills to achieve their self-selected objectives (e.g., testtaking skills for academic goals). Finally, they will have to engage in goal maintenance or alteration in the face of difficulties. The latter implies that they have to learn from their mistakes and redefine their objectives when necessary (Lerner et al., 2001). Both of these applications (the SOC model and the goodness-of-fit concept) provide a first glimpse of the potential advantages offered by developmental contextualism in the study of adolescence.

5. Conclusion

At the end of this chapter, it seems appropriate to return to the two classical questions that help researchers to differentiate among the many theories of adolescence. To the first question, which asks whether adolescence is a distinct phase in development, all theories provide an affirmative answer (including psychoanalytic theories, as we have seen). Contemporary, contextualist theories will emphasize, for instance, that adolescence is characterized by a unique meso-system (ecological theory) or by a specific succession of important transitions and age-related expectations in the various life paths that constitute that specific part of the life course (life course theory).

To the second question which asks whether adolescence is characterized by increased emotional turmoil ('storm and stress'), as the popular stereotype of that period would have it, the various theories provide different answers. The degree to which adolescence is experienced as a difficult period depends on the cultural milieu (social–cultural theories), the concurrent experience of important life events or transitions (focal model and accumulation theories), or the historical era (life course theory). To sum up: whether 'storm and stress' emerges or not and how strongly it is experienced depends on the entire pattern of relationships that adolescents have with their environment (developmental contextualism).

Contextualist theories of adolescence may be usefully applied in adolescent research in Europe. The concept of development that emerged from these theories and associated research was summarized by Lerner (1998) in terms of four principles. These entail that development is best viewed (a) as a combination of both systematic changes and plasticity, and as characterized by (b) dynamic interaction with the environment, (c) historical embeddedness and temporality, and (d) limited generalizability. This means that, because these contemporary theories of adolescence assign an important role to historical and local conditions, and because historical time and local influences will inevitably be different in Europe as compared to the United States, research on European samples provides additional tests of contextualist theories and its results will help to place the findings obtained on American samples in a broader perspective. Recent historical events in Europe, such as the collapse of the former Eastern bloc, and the process of German unification that got underway in the aftermath of those changes and is continuously being monitored ever since (Juang, Silbereisen, & Wiesner, 1999) have provided unique opportunities to study the way in which adolescents are influenced by and react to social change (Crockett & Silbereisen, 2000; Noack, Hofer, & Youniss, 1994; Nurmi, 1998).

Looking back on the entire chapter, one may also conclude that European authors have contributed substantially to the development of the classical theories of adolescence. This tradition seems to have got lost in the latest generation of theories of adolescence and should be revived, because all of these contextualist theories are largely based on North American findings and have been devised by authors residing in the United States. International collaboration between European and North American scholars in particular should be encouraged. Referring to the history of developmental psychology as a whole, Cairns (1998, p. 92) noted that: 'Over the past 100 years, the insights and emphases of developmental investigators in Europe have often been on a different frequency than those in North America, and the reverse held as well. When exceptions occurred . . . the whole discpline was revitalized.' Similar revitalizing effects on adolescent psychology are bound to emerge as the discipline grows more international.

References

Adelson, J., & Doehrman, M.J. (1980). The psychodynamic approach to adolescence. In J. Adelson (Ed.), *Handbook of adolescent psychology* (pp. 99–116). New York: John Wiley & Sons.

Arnett, J.J. (1999). Adolescent storm and stress, reconsidered. *American Psychologist, 54*, 317–326.

Benson, P.L., Mannes, M., Pittman, K., & Ferber, T. (2004). Youth development, developmental assets, and public policy. In R. M. Lerner, & L. Steinberg (Eds.), *Handbook of adolescent development* (2nd ed., pp. 781–814). Hoboken, NJ: John Wiley & Sons.

Berzonsky, M.D. (2000). Theories of adolescence. In G. Adams (Ed.), *Adolescent development: The essential readings* (pp. 11–27). Oxford: Blackwell.

Blos, P. (1962). *On adolescence: A psychoanalytic interpretation*. New York: Free Press.

Blos, J. (1979). *The adolescent passage*. New York: International Universities Press.

Bronfenbrenner, U. (1979). *The ecology of human development: Experiments by nature and design*. Cambridge, MA: Harvard University Press.

Bronfenbrenner, U. (1995). Developmental ecology through space and time: A future perspective. In P. Moen, G. H. Elder Jr., & K. Lüscher (Eds.), *Examining lives in context: Perspectives on the ecology of human development* (pp. 619–647). Washington, DC: American Psychological Association.

Bronfenbrenner, U. (Ed.). (2005). *Making human beings human: Bio-ecological perspectives on human development*. Thousand Oaks, CA: Sage.

Bronfenbrenner, U., & Morris, P.A. (1998). The ecology of developmental processes. In W. Damon, & R. M. Lerner (Eds.), *Handbook of child psychology: Vol. 1. Theoretical models of human development* (5th ed., pp. 993–1028). New York: John Wiley & Sons.

Cairns, R.B. (1998). The making of developmental psychology. In W. Damon, & R. M. Lerner (Eds.), *Handbook of child psychology: Vol. 1. Theoretical models of human development* (5th ed., pp. 25–105). New York: John Wiley & Sons.

Call, C.T., & Mortimer, J.T. (2001). *Arenas of comfort in adolescence: A study of adjustment in context*. Mahwah, NJ: Lawrence Erlbaum Associates, Inc.

Coleman, J.C. (1974). *Relationships in adolescence*. London: Routledge.

Coleman, J.C., & Hendry, L. (1999). *The nature of adolescence* (3th ed.). London: Routledge.

Côté, J.E. (1992). Was Mead wrong about coming of age in Samoa? An analysis of the Mead/Freeman controversy for scholars of adolescence and human development. *Journal of Youth and Adolescence, 21*, 499–527.

Côté, J.E. (1994). *Adolescent storm and stress: An evaluation of the Mead/Freeman controversy*. Hillsdale, NJ: Lawrence Erlbaum Associates, Inc.

Côté, J. (Ed.). (2000). The Mead–Freeman controversy in review [Special issue]. *Journal of Youth and Adolescence, 29*(5).

Crain, W. (2000). *Theories of development: Concepts and applications* (4th ed.). Upper Saddle River, NJ: Prentice Hall.

Crockett, L.J., & Silbereisen, R.K. (Eds.). (2000). *Negotiating adolescence in times of social change*. New York: Cambridge University Press.

Dacey, J., & Kenny, M. (1997). *Adolescent development* (2nd ed.). Madison, WI: Brown & Benchmark.

Eccles, J.S., Lord, S., & Buchanan, C.M. (1996). School transitions in early adolescence: What are we doing to our young people? In J. A. Graber, J. Brooks-Gunn, & A. C. Petersen (Eds.), *Transitions through adolescence: Interpersonal domains and context* (pp.

251–284). Mahwah, NJ: Lawrence Erlbaum Associates, Inc.

Elder, G.H. Jr. (1980). Adolescence in historical perspective. In J. Adelson (Ed.), *Handbook of adolescent psychology* (pp. 3–46). New York: John Wiley & Sons.

Elder, G.H. Jr. (1998a). The life course as developmental theory. *Child Development, 69*, 1–12.

Elder, G.H. Jr. (1998b). The life course and human development. In W. Damon, & R. M. Lerner (Eds.), *Handbook of child psychology: Vol. 1. Theoretical models of human development* (5th ed., pp. 939–991). New York: John Wiley & Sons.

Elder, G.H. Jr. (1999). *Children of the great depression: Social change in life experience* (25th anniversary edition). Boulder, CO: Westview Press. (Original work published 1974)

Elder, G.H. Jr., & Conger, R.D. (2000). *Children of the land: Adversity and success in rural America.* Chicago: University of Chicago Press.

Elder, G.H. Jr., Modell, J., & Parke, R.D. (Eds.). (1993). *Children in time and place: Developmental and historical insights.* New York: Cambridge University Press.

Elkind, D. (1967). Egocentrism in adolescence. *Child Development, 38*, 1025–1034.

Erikson, E.H. (1968). *Identity: Youth and crisis.* New York: Norton.

Flammer, A. (1996). *Entwicklungstheorien. Psychologische Theorien der menschlichen Entwicklung* (2. Aufl.) [Theories of development: Psychological theories of human development (2nd ed.)]. Bern, Switzerland: Huber.

Flammer, A., & Alsaker, F.D. (2002). *Entwicklungspsychologie der Adoleszenz: Die Erschliessung innerer und äusserer Welten im Jugendalter* [Developmental psychology of adolescence: Unlocking the inner and outer worlds of youth]. Bern, Switzerland: Huber.

Freeman, D. (1983). *Margaret Mead and Samoa: The making and unmaking of an anthropological myth.* Cambridge, MA: Harvard University Press.

Freeman, D. (1999). *The fateful hoaxing of Margaret Mead: A historical analysis of her Samoan research.* Boulder, CO: Westview Press.

Freud, A. (1966). The ego and the mechanisms of defense. In *The writings of Anna Freud* (Vol. 2). New York: International Universities Press. (Original work published 1936)

Freud, A. (1969). Adolescence. In *The writings of Anna Freud* (Vol. 5, pp. 136–166). New York: International Universities Press. (Original work published 1958)

Freud, A. (1971). Adolescence as a developmental disturbance. In *The writings of Anna Freud* (Vol. 7, pp. 39–47). New York: International Universities Press. (Original work published 1969)

Freud, S. (1953). Three essays on the theory of sexuality. In J. Strachey (Ed. and Trans.), *The standard edition of the complete psychological works of Sigmund Freud* (Vol. 7, pp. 135–243). London: Hogarth Press. (Original work published 1905)

Friedman, L.J. (1999). *Identity's architect: A biography of Erik H. Erikson.* London: Free Association Books.

Gallatin, J.E. (1975). *Adolescence and individuality: A conceptual approach to adolescent psychology.* New York: Harper & Row.

Gesell, A., Ilg, F.L., & Ames, L.B. (1956). *Youth: The years from ten to sixteen.* New York: Harper & Row.

Goossens, L., Beyers, W., Emmen, M., & van Aken, M.A.G. (2002). The imaginary audience and personal fable: Factor analyses and concurrent validity of the 'New Look' measures. *Journal of Research on Adolescence, 12*, 193–215.

Goossens, L., & Marcoen, A. (1999). Relationships during adolescence: Constructive vs. negative themes and relational dissatisfaction. *Journal of Adolescence, 22*, 65–79.

Grinder, R.E. (1967). *A history of genetic psychology: The first science of human development.* New York: John Wiley & Sons.

Grinder, R.E. (1969). The concept of adolescence in the genetic psychology of G. Stanley Hall. *Child Development, 40*, 355–369.

Hall, G.S. (1904). *Adolescence: Its psychology and its relation to physiology, anthropology, sociology, sex, crime, religion, and education* (2 vols). New York: Appleton.

Hellman, H. (1998). *Great feuds in science: Ten of the liveliest debates ever.* New York: John Wiley & Sons.

Hunt, S. (2005). *The life course: A sociological introduction.* Houndmills: Palgrave Macmillan.

Inhelder, B., & Piaget, J. (1958). *The growth of logical thinking from childhood to adolescence: An essay on the construction of formal operational structures* (A. Parsons, & S. Milgram, Trans.). London: Routledge & Kegan Paul. (Original work published 1955)

Jackson, S., & Bosma, H.A. (1992). Developmental research on adolescence: European perspectives for the 1990s and beyond. *British Journal of Developmental Psychology, 10*, 319–337.

Juang, L.P., Silbereisen, R.K., & Wiesner, M. (1999). Predictors of leaving home in young adults raised in Germany: A replication of a 1991 study. *Journal of Marriage and the Family, 61*, 505–515.

Lapsley, D.K. (1993). Toward an integrated theory of adolescent ego development: The 'New Look' at adolescent egocentrism. *American Journal of Orthopsychiatry*, *63*, 562–571.

Larson, R.W. (2000). Toward a psychology of positive youth development. *American Psychologist*, *55*, 170–183.

Lehalle, H. (1996). *Psychologie des adolescents* [Psychology of adolescents] (4th ed.). Paris: Presses Universitaires de France.

Lerner, H. (1987). Psychodynamic models. In V. B. Van Hasselt, & M. Hersen (Eds.), *Handbook of adolescent psychology* (pp. 53–76). New York: Pergamon.

Lerner, R.M. (1998). Theories of human development: Contemporary perspectives. In W. Damon, & R. M. Lerner (Eds.), *Handbook of child psychology: Vol. 1. Theoretical models of human development* (5th ed., pp. 1–24). New York: John Wiley & Sons.

Lerner, R.M. (2002). *Concepts and theories of human development* (3rd ed.). Mahwah, NJ: Lawrence Erlbaum Associates, Inc.

Lerner, R.M., Fischer, C.B., & Weinberg, R.A. (2000). Toward a science for and of the people: Promoting civil society through the application of developmental science. *Child Development*, *71*, 11–20.

Lerner, R.M., Freund, A.M., De Stefanis, I., & Habermas, T. (2001). Understanding developmental regulation in adolescence: The use of the selection, optimization and compensation model. *Human Development*, *44*, 29–50.

Lerner, R.M., & Galambos, N. (1998). Adolescent development: Challenges and opportunities for research, programs, and policies. *Annual Review of Psychology*, *49*, 413–446.

Lerner, R.M., & Steinberg, L. (2004). The scientific study of adolescent development: Past, present, and future. In R. M. Lerner, & L. Steinberg (Eds.), *Handbook of adolescent development* (2nd ed., pp. 1–12). Hoboken, NJ: John Wiley & Sons.

Mahler, M., Pine, F., & Bergman, A. (1975). *The psychological birth of the human infant.* New York: International Universities Press.

McDermott, R. (2001). A century of Margaret Mead. *Teachers College Record*, *103*, 843–867.

Mead, M. (1928). *Coming of age in Samoa: A psychological study of primitive youth for Western civilization.* New York: Norton.

Miller, P.H. (1989). Theories of adolescent development. In J. Worell, & F. Danner (Eds.), *The adolescent as decision-maker: Applications to development and education* (pp. 13–46). San Diego, CA: Academic Press.

Miller, P.H. (2002). *Theories of developmental psychology* (4th ed.). New York: Worth.

Mortimer, J.T., & Shanahan, M. (Eds.) (2003). *Handbook of the life course.* New York: Springer-Verlag.

Muuss, R.E. (1996). *Theories of adolescence* (6th ed.). New York: McGraw-Hill.

Noack, P., Hofer, M., & Youniss, J. (Eds.). (1994). *Psychological responses to social change: Human development in changing environments.* Berlin: de Gruyter.

Nurmi, J.-E. (1998). Growing up in contemporary Europe: An overview. In J.-E. Nurmi (Ed.), *Adolescents, cultures, and conflicts: Growing up in contemporary Europe* (pp. 3–17). New York: Garland.

Offer, D., & Sabshin, M. (1974). *Normality: Theoretical and clinical concepts of mental health* (rev. ed.). New York: Basic Books.

Petersen, A.C. (1988). Adolescent development. *Annual Review of Psychology*, *39*, 583–607.

Rosenzweig, S. (1992). *Freud, Jung, and Hall the kingmaker: The historic expedition to America (1909) with G. Stanley Hall as host and William James as guest.* Lewiston, NY: Hogrefe and Huber.

Ross, D. (1972). *G. Stanley Hall: The psychologist as prophet.* Chicago: University of Chicago Press.

Simmons, R.G., & Blyth, D.A. (1987). *Moving into adolescence: The impact of pubertal change and school context.* New York: Aldine de Gruyter.

Simmons, R.G., Burgeson, R., Carlton-Ford, S., & Blyth, D.A. (1987). The impact of cumulative change in early adolescence. *Child Development*, *58*, 1220–1234.

Steinberg, L., & Lerner, R.M. (2004). The scientific study of adolescence: A brief history. *Journal of Early Adolescence*, *24*, 45–54.

Steinberg, L., & Morris, A.S. (2001). Adolescent development. *Annual Review of Psychology*, *52*, 83–110.

Thomas, R.M. (2001). *Recent theories of human development.* Thousand Oaks, CA: Sage.

White, S.H. (1992). G. Stanley Hall: From philosophy to developmental psychology. *Developmental Psychology*, *28*, 25–34.

3

Pubertal maturation

Françoise D. Alsaker and August Flammer

LEARNING OBJECTIVES

This chapter aims to help you to understand puberty as a biological, psychological, and social event. It does so by considering:

1. basic aspects of pubertal maturation in terms of hormonal, biological, and bodily changes
2. importance of the timing of the onset of puberty
3. the differential meaning of puberty for girls and boys
4. the complexity of the relations and interactions between the biological, psychological, and social facets of puberty.

Basically, puberty refers to physical and reproductive maturation. This will be covered in the first section of this chapter. However, physiological changes do not occur in a vacuum. Young people are aware of the changes and so are their parents, teachers and peers. This means that the experience of puberty is also linked to societal norms. The second section will be about adolescents' psychological experience of and their reactions to the bodily changes that arise during puberty.

1. Somatic changes

Most species survive through reproduction of individual living organisms. These living organisms first go through a phase of growing up in order to be able to survive more or less independently. The next phase sees the development of the capacity to reproduce and this is followed by a phase of reproduction and the nurturing of offspring. The second of these phases is called pubertal maturation. Pubertal maturation is the result of physiological developments in the individual reproductive system. It includes a whole

set of hormonal, physiological, and morpho-
logical changes that are also subject to interpretation and evaluation in a given socio-cultural and
historical context.

Changes referring to the core reproduction system are called *primary* sexual characteristics
whereas the visible changes in the sexual organs
as well as accompanying features such as breast
development are called *secondary* sexual characteristics. In this chapter, we first present the most
important pubertal changes that are easily visible
(secondary sexual characteristics), and turn then
to the hormonal background.

1.1 Bodily changes and bodily appearance

Externally, pubertal maturation manifests itself
mainly through drastic alterations in body shape
(morphology) and appearance. These alterations
are primarily produced by changes in the hormonal system, but they vary to a large extent
between individuals, for example, in terms of
onset and duration.

While growth is a rather stable process in childhood (Rogol, Roemmich, & Clark, 2002) and
while young boys' and girls' bodies do not look or
develop very differently, the onset of puberty
brings dramatic changes in these domains. Common to both genders is a marked increase in body
growth (so-called *growth spurt* or *peak height
velocity*). Prior to puberty, girls and boys grow
approximately 5 or 6 cm a year. During the
growth spurt, girls grow on average 9 cm a year
and boys reach an average peak height velocity of
10.3 cm a year (Rogol et al., 2002). The growth
spurt spreads somehow asynchronically over the
whole body, typically starting with the extreme
parts of the limbs (hand, feet, arms and legs) and
finally reaching the trunk. The attendant changes
in body proportions lead to alterations in many
bodily movements. This is why some youngsters
sometimes make a surprisingly uncoordinated or
awkward impression.

The timing and sequence of bodily changes are
somewhat different between boys and girls. In boys
they appear in a rather arranged order, namely:

1. growth of testicles and scrotum, appearance
   of the first pubic hair

2. increased penis growth, first facial hair,
   increased muscularity
3. first spontaneous ejaculation
4. growth spurt, appearance of axillary hair,
   and deepening of the voice.

Further modifications are observed in the skin,
which becomes rougher and produces more tallow,
whereby acne and a strong body smell can develop.
During this time, the male breast may 'over-
develop' and for some, this may produce fears
of becoming 'feminine'. Such overdevelopments
typically level out somewhat later, but they often
represent a source of worry in adolescent boys.

In girls, the developmental sequence of the visible sex characteristics is somewhat less strict. It
usually begins with elevation of the breasts
(breast budding) followed by the appearance of
pubic hair. This order may also be reversed. For
example, Brooks-Gunn and Reiter (1990)
reported that pubic hair developed prior to breast
budding in approximately 20% of girls. A main
change at this early stage consists in the redistribution of body fat, whereby the girl's body
gradually takes a woman's shape. After this,
modifications in the genital organs take place
(enlargement of the uterus, the vagina, the clitoris
and the labia). At about the same time the growth
spurt comes to an end; a clear difference from
boys whose growth spurt occurs later in the
developmental process. Menarche (first menstru-
ation) takes place relatively late and fertility is
reached even later. Interestingly, girls seldom
grow more than 4% after menarche. This means
that in extreme cases where intervention is needed
to stop growth, it has to be done before menarche.

A frequently mentioned feature of pubertal
maturation is that boys develop one and a half to
two years later than girls. However, the first
changes in the male body (genitals) appear only a
few months after the first female body changes
(breast budding) (Finkelstein, 1980). By contrast,
the growth spurt occurs much earlier in the
female pubertal process than in the male and the
further easily perceptible indicators in boys
(beard, voice) appear very late. This makes the
biological difference seem larger than it is.

Also, while lean body mass (also called fat-free

mass), bone mass, and body fat are approximately equivalent in boys and girls prior to puberty (although girls have slightly more body fat at an age of 10), and they both experience changes in body composition, these changes are very different for the two genders (Rogol et al., 2002). In addition to the redistribution of fat in girls, their body also develops more fat and girls have twice as much body fat than boys at the end of puberty (Archibald, Graber, & Brooks-Gunn, 2003). The relative increase in muscle mass (lean body mass) is larger in boys than in girls (Garn & Clark, 1976; Rogol et al., 2002). Following growth spurt, boys experience a spurt in the growth of bone and muscles and a loss of fat in the limbs (Rogol et al., 2002), i.e., they experience a remarkable growth in strength. Girls, in contrast, experience a drop in sports performances. At the conclusion of puberty, the muscle–fat ratio is about 3:1 in young men and 5:4 in young women (Steinberg, 1989). These sex differences are primarily biologically determined and justify, for example, separate sports competitions for women and men. By the same token, intensive sports training strongly influences these ratios and leads to greater similarity between men and women in this respect (Brooks-Gunn & Warren, 1985; Schölmerich, 1996).

1.2 *Role of the hormones*

The function of the hormonal system is to coordinate the activities of the various body systems. A multiplicity of hormones is involved in the regulation of the internal environment, however, full details are beyond the scope of this chapter.

Hormones are produced in ductless glands and transported in the blood. They work as messengers from one organ (the endocrine gland) to another (the target organ). The target organs contain receptors for specific hormones. The hormones regulate the function of the target organ (slow down or speed up) by inducing cellular processes. The basis of the interplay between the endocrine gland and the target organ is called the *negative feedback system*, i.e., a substance that increases in concentration induces its own regulation downwards. For example, LH (see later) stimulates the production of the male sex hormone testosterone. When a certain level of concentration is reached, testosterone inhibits the further production of LH, thereby inducing a decrease in its own level. In similar fashion, the target organ also produces a set of different chemical messengers that work on the endocrine gland to modify its hormonal production.

Sex hormones are the specific hormones produced by the internal sex organs (the gonads, i.e., the ovaries and testicles) in both sexes. They are the main contributors to the characteristic appearance of the adult male/female.

The body produces sex hormones at all stages of life, although only in very small amounts before puberty. There are male and female sex hormones and the body produces both kinds from infancy and in about the same proportion in both sexes before puberty. At puberty, the amount and proportion change. For instance, the male testosterone concentration in the bloodstream (an androgen) is about 18 times higher in male puberty than in childhood; estradiol, one of the female sex hormones, increases its concentration by a factor eight from childhood to female puberty (Nottelmann et al., 1987). However, there are large individual variations (Susman, Dorn, & Chrousos, 1991). Also, estrogens in females are partly gained peripherally from the conversion of androgens in subcutaneous fat tissues (so called aromatase).

Some years before the maturation of the internal sex organs (gonads), the adrenal gland increases its secretion of androgens (the so-called adrenarche). Before puberty, through mechanisms that are not yet fully understood, the secretion of GnRH (gonadotrophic-releasing hormone) from the hypothalamus is inhibited. Somehow, the maturation of the central nervous system leads to the removal of this inhibition and the hypothalamus starts to activate the pituitary gland by sending out pulses of GnRH, before the actual beginning of puberty (Figure 3.1).

The pituitary gland then starts to produce sex-specific proportions of luteinizing hormones (LH) and follicle-stimulating hormones (FSH), which trigger increased growth of the ovaries in the female and the testes in the male. These then produce the actual sex hormones, i.e., the family

FIGURE 3.1

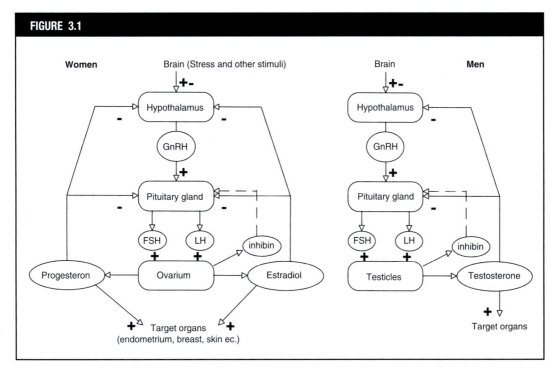

Hormonal processes involved in pubertal development.

of estrogens and the family of androgens. Estrogens and androgens in combination with LH and FSH trigger the production and maturation of the female eggs and the male semen as well as the growth and the maintenance of the visible sex characteristics. For a long time, researchers thought it was easy to define the onset of puberty, simply by using endocrinological indicators. However, more recent research has shown that, relative to body weight, peak sex hormone production takes place shortly before birth and that after a standstill, with the next peak around the seventh year of life (Grumbach, Grave, & Mayer, 1974; Susman, Inoff-Germain, Nottelmann, Loriaux, Cutler, & Chrousos, 1987), whereas gonadarche and the anatomical development of sexual characteristics starts only two to five years later.

Pubertal processes and individual differences in the onset of puberty seem to be partly genetically determined (Marshall, 1978). For example, Graber, Brooks-Gunn, and Warren (1995) found

a correlation of .23 between mothers' age at menarche and that of their daughters at menarche (see also Campbell & Udry, 1992) and Surbey (1990) was able to explain genetically some 10 to 15% of the variance in menarche age. A study by Meyer, Eaves, Heath, and Martin (1991), including 1888 pairs of monozygotic and dizygotic twins, also demonstrated clear genetic effects on the timing of menarche. Interpreting exact percentages of the genetic determination of age at menarche should, however, be considered with caution. Percentages vary tremendously between studies and methods used to establish heritability. Given relatively stable environments across generations, as is the case in most middle-class Western environments, associations between mothers' and daughters' age at menarche will be inflated (see Ellis, 2004, for a detailed discussion).

Rich and manifold nutrition as well as psychological and somatic well-being seem to promote an early onset of puberty (Graber et al., 1995), while chronic diseases, stress, and extensive sportive activity seem to delay it (Ellis, 2004). However, the data are not fully conclusive. In a study by Moffitt, Caspi, Belsky, and Silva (1992), for example, family conflict and father absence predicted an earlier age of menarche; others, however, have demonstrated that aversive family environments have dramatic retarding effects on growth and pubertal maturation (Money & Wolff, 1974). For a more extensive review see Alsaker (1995b) and Ellis (2004).

1.3   Timing of physiological changes

Psychological as well as biological processes vary. They vary within the individual over time (intra-individual differences) and between the individuals (inter-individual differences, or simply individual differences).

1.3.1   Individual differences

As pointed out earlier, there are large and predictable differences between the sexes. We have also indicated that the onset and the duration of the individual pubertal processes vary considerably within and among individuals of the same sex. According to Tanner (1972) the onset of visible pubertal changes has a range of four to five years, i.e., it can start between 8 and 13 years in girls and between 9½ and 13½ years in boys. Contrariwise, an early onset of the pre-pubertal peak of sex hormone production does not necessarily predict an early onset of anatomical sexual development. Some young people are early and rapid initially and slower later, while others are late at the beginning and fast later. Still others are extremely early or extremely late.

Some parents worry about their child's extremely short body length (mainly boys) or extremely high growth (especially in girls). There are hormone treatments to prevent such extreme growth patterns, but the pros and contras of such interventions are not yet clearly established (Degenhardt, 1996). Most doctors today are hesitant about using such treatments, except for children who have been diagnosed as having hormonal deficiencies.

1.3.2   Secular trends

Over the past one and a half centuries or so,

European adolescent girls seem to have entered puberty earlier and earlier. This is referred to as secular acceleration (*saeculum* = century). Within 110 years (between 1860 and 1970) the onset of menarche in European countries has come down from around 16 to about 13 years of age (Tanner, 1989). This means that over this interval of time, the acceleration was about nine months per generation. To be fair, such data tap only menarche. Since menarche occurs at the end of the pubertal process, it is an open question whether this acceleration also included the onset of the various pubertal processes. This secular trend seems to be due to nutritional progress (variety, abundance, food science) and healthier lifestyle and it has generally been held that there remains no further potential for further acceleration to take place. Average menarcheal age reported in recent studies is around 13. However, data from the United States reporting a mean age of 12 years at menarche in some ethnic groups have led to increased preoccupations and some hypotheses have been put forward regarding a possible further acceleration (for details see Archibald et al., 2003). First, the role of environmental toxins (pesticides) that would work during pregnancy has been suggested. These toxins might have some similar influence on the body as estrogens. Second, the dramatic increase in obesity has been suggested to lead to earlier maturation, due to increases in the production of the hormone leptin. And third, some data may indicate a relationship between family stress and earlier maturation. This, however, cannot serve as an explanation for a general trend towards earlier maturation without suggesting that families were far more harmonious in the past (see also Ellis, 2004, for a thorough discussion of the relationship between stress and hormones).

The secular acceleration has – almost unnoticed – dramatically changed living and socialization conditions of young people. Their childhood has been reduced by one-fourth! This means that at the present time even primary school children may be confronted with the inner and outer changes of puberty, at a time when they have to decide about their future schooling and to show high scholastic achievement in order to be able to enter higher levels of secondary education (see Flammer & Alsaker, this volume). In addition, individual differences in puberty onset may represent unfair learning and achievement conditions for some adolescents (Simmons, Blyth, van Cleave, & Bush, 1979). Petersen, Sarigiani, and Kennedy (1991) took the body growth spurt as an indicator of possibly the greatest inner and outer pubertal changes and found that 12% of American boys experienced this event within plus or minus six months of the transition to high school. For girls, the proportion was 43%! Regression analyses showed that this coincidence was statistically related to depressive mood experience in girls.

One might wonder whether the secular acceleration of pubertal maturation is accompanied by an accelerated mental and social development. This question is not easy to answer empirically. Some relation between physical and mental precocity has been reported (see Kohen-Raz, 1974) and there is some evidence of a small IQ advantage for early maturers (see Tanner, 1972). As for intelligence test scores, adolescents in the Western part of the world (like school children and adults) show far better results today than decades or a century ago (Flammer, App & de Pretto, 1977; Flynn, 1987, 1999).

1.3.3 Socio-cultural differences

In many countries differences between girls living in the countryside and those in cities have been found, the former maturing later than the others. This, however could not be replicated in a recent study conducted in Switzerland (Deppen, Jeannin, Michaud, Suris, & Alsaker, submitted). However, those Swiss girls from rural areas often perceived themselves erroneously as early maturers.

According to Eveleth and Tanner (1976) large differences have also been reported between girls in different economic conditions. In India, for example, the average menarcheal age of the rich was 12.8 years and that of the poor 14.5 years. The corresponding figures for Melanesian girls on Guinea were 15.5 and 18.4 (Eveleth & Tanner, 1976). In Europe the difference was estimated at around five to six months (Eveleth & Tanner, 1976; see also Brundtland & Walloe, 1976, for Norwegian data from the 19th century).

Differences have also been observed between countries. These can be partly attributed to genetic (racial) differences and partly to variations in the economies of the countries concerned. Several studies in the United States have yielded somewhat different results as regards onset of puberty in white and black girls. Herman-Giddens et al. (1997) reported that black American girls show the first changes in apparent sexual characteristics (breast budding) approximately one year before white American girls do. In their overview, Archibald et al. (2003) additionally referred to studies focusing on menarche and showing no or rather small (around four months) differences between ethnic groups in the United States. In Europe, south–north differences have been found: southern girls have been reported to mature earlier (12.5) than northern girls (13.4). Interestingly, these differences between Europeans of different origin can also be found in Australian immigrants (Eveleth & Tanner, 1976). In addition, American girls of European origin mature slightly earlier than European girls in Europe. The Chinese and the Japanese are, on average, as early as European girls (around 13.0), but the Melanese in New Guinea are substantially later (between 15.5 and 18.4, depending on their living conditions).

1.3.4 Measurement issues

We have talked about changes accompanying pubertal maturation on several levels. We started by pointing out that the overall appearance of adolescents changes and referred this back to hormonal level. How are these changes measured? While some indicators are easy to identify, but possibly not very telling, more valid indicators are of a very private character and often raise ethical concerns. Some authors have used parents' or researchers' observations of adolescents to determine their pubertal status. Others have used medical examinations or hormonal assays.

1.3.4.1 Pubertal status

Pubertal status refers to the level of development reached by an individual in terms of physical changes at a given time. The following list provides examples of measures that have been used by researchers. For a thorough and critical review of methods used to measure puberty, the reader is referred to Coleman and Coleman (2002):

1. Global visual inspection of clothed adolescents by researchers, using facial hair/breast development, body proportion, and general coordination to determine the global status on a five-point Likert scale (e.g., Steinberg, 1981).

2. Global self-ratings or parents' ratings following a description of the kind of changes that happen around puberty. Answers indicate whether these changes have occurred and if so when (two years ago, one year ago, etc.; e.g., Alsaker, 1992).

3. Age at peak height velocity calculated on the basis of longitudinal objective measures (e.g., Simmons & Blyth, 1987).

4. Examination of the naked body (usually done by doctors or nurses) using Tanner's criteria of stages of breast, genital, and pubic hair development (e.g., Dorn et al., 2003). Drawings accompanied by a description of each stage are usually used and raters are trained.

5. Self-reports or parents' reports using the drawings just discussed. This method has yielded the best validity among the different self-report and parent report instruments (Coleman & Coleman, 2002).

6. Specific self-ratings following written descriptions of the different bodily changes (e.g., breast development, pubic hair, facial hair etc.) occurring at puberty (e.g., Pubertal Development Scale, PDS, by Petersen, Crockett, Richards, & Boxer, 1988). The adolescents are asked whether respective growth has 'not begun', 'barely begun', etc.

7. Self-report of menarche, whether it has occurred and if so, when. Menarche being a salient event in pubertal development, the recall of age at menarche has proved to be fairly accurate (Coleman & Coleman, 2002).

8. Since pubertal maturation has been found to be highly related to ossification (e.g., Behrman, Kliegman, Nelson, & Vaughan, 1992), X-rays of the wrist have sometimes been employed to determine the young adolescents' level of maturation.

9. Finally, hormone levels have been used (e.g., Susman et al., 1985). Since hormonal changes occur before bodily changes are visible, this method may detect pubertal maturation at very early stages. However, hormone concentrations cannot be used instead of measures of body changes. For example, Dorn et al. (2003) have shown that pubic hair stages were uncorrelated with a wide range of pubertal hormones.

In conclusion, given the private nature of some pubertal changes and the possible reticence of adolescents to answer these kinds of question, and also to participate in studies including medical examination or blood sampling, the 'exact' pubertal status is mostly very difficult to specify. For example, even though reports on maturational status obtained from young adolescents, their mothers and physicians are highly intercorrelated, they are far from being fully concordant (around .65 in 13-year-old girls; Brooks-Gunn, Warren, Rosso, & Gargiulo, 1987). Also, even trained raters of Tanner's stages (physicians and nurses) do not deliver totally overlapping scores. Interrater agreement of around 90% is considered good (Dorn et al., 2003). Nevertheless, depending on the aims of studies, exact measures of pubertal status are not always necessary. Visible and global signs of puberty, such as body shape, may actually be of greater importance for adolescents' psychosocial adjustment than changes that are less directly evident. And in some cases, the subjective perception of timing may be the method of choice. Still, given the wide variation in the sequence of pubertal changes, and the possible independence of some of the changes, measures considering only one single aspect of pubertal maturation should be avoided.

1.3.4.2 Pubertal timing
Research distinguishes between (absolute) pubertal status and (relative) pubertal timing. Pubertal timing is relative to expected pubertal maturation

at a given age or within specific reference groups such as school class (Brooks-Gunn, Petersen, & Eichorn, 1985), i.e., it refers to inter-individual differences in the onset of pubertal changes. Whether timing should be calculated on the basis of age norms or comparisons within a specific sample, depends on the research issue being investigated.

The most commonly used method is to calculate standardized scores within reference groups for each gender. Very often adolescents whose scores are more than one standard deviation above the mean are considered to be early maturers and those who are one standard deviation below are considered late maturers relative to their reference group. Those in between are considered to be 'on time'.

1.3.4.3 Perceived pubertal timing

Pubertal timing is especially important as far as it is perceived by the adolescents themselves. In the literature, adolescents' own perception of their pubertal maturation as compared to peers is called perceived pubertal timing or subjective pubertal timing. This aspect of timing is commonly operationalized by asking adolescents to globally describe their physical maturity relative to their peers (Alsaker, 1992). In some studies perceived/subjective pubertal timing has been used as an approximation of actual timing (e.g., Graber, Lewinsohn, Seeley, & Brooks-Gunn, 1997; Graber, Seeley, Brooks-Gunn, & Lewinsohn, 2004; Siegel, Yancey, Aneshensel, & Schuler, 1999). Whereas some authors have argued for the use of perceived timing as an equivalent measure of actual timing because it was found to be correlated with height and weight (Graber et al., 1997), and with self-reported or clinical evaluation of pubertal development (Berg-Kelly & Erdes, 1997; Siegel et al., 1999) other authors have pointed to the fact that actual and perceived timing are only moderately related (around 60% of off-time maturers judging themselves as being on time as compared to their peers; Alsaker, 1992; Stattin & Magnusson, 1990).

Also, perceived timing has been proved to affect different aspects of psychosocial adjustment (e.g., Buchanan, 1991; Wichstrøm, 2001)

and to be a significant predictor of sexual activities when actual timing was controlled (Deppen et al., submitted).

2. Psychosocial aspects of pubertal maturation

One may consider the effects of pubertal changes on psychosocial adjustment from a *biological perspective* (e.g., effects of endocrinological changes), from an *individual* point of view (e.g., in terms of coping with normative and non-normative developmental tasks; Alsaker, 1996), and from the perspective of the *social* context (e.g., in terms of social roles or cultural influences). Our presentation is organized along these three approaches, although most researchers today would agree in considering that individual and social factors interact and mediate between the biological maturational process and psychosocial outcomes.

2.1 A biological perspective: Role of hormones in mood and behavior

The mechanisms linking hormones to mood and to behavior are not yet well-established. However, it seems likely that the considerable increase in hormones that occurs during puberty has at least some activating effects on, for example, excitability and arousability (see Brooks-Gunn & Warren, 1989). These may bring the adolescent's physiology into a state of disequilibrium that may have emotional and behavioral effects. In addition, given that the prevalence of some clinical disorders such as depression has been shown to increase in early adolescence, it has been postulated that hormonal factors account for some part of this effect (Brooks-Gunn & Warren, 1989; Buchanan, Eccles, & Becker, 1992).

In general, results from studies on the effect of hormones on behavior are disappointing. They have shown that the levels of hormones known to increase during pubertal maturation are only inconsistently associated with behavior and mood. This means that associations are found in some studies between specific hormones and outcomes but that the associations differ in terms of hormones and outcome variables (for more details see Alsaker, 1995b; Archibald et al., 2003; Buchanan et al., 1992). When effects are found, during adolescence or later, they relate predominantly to *testosterone* and its correlation with mild expressions of aggressiveness (Inoff-Germain, Arnold, Nottelmann, Susman, Cutler, & Chrousos, 1988), reports of proneness to react aggressively when provoked (Olweus, Mattson, Schalling, & Low, 1980) and dominance (Udry & Talbert, 1988) in boys (see also Susman, Dorn, & Schiefelbein, 2003). Udry, Billy, Morris, Groff, and Raj (1985) also found individual testosterone level to be a strong predictor of sexual motivation and behavior in boys (inter-individual perspective). However, intra-individual changes in hormone levels over a three-year period in pubertal adolescents were not accompanied by changes in sexual behavior (Halpern, Udry, Campbell, & Suchindran, 1992). Effects in girls are even weaker and less consistent. The weakness of the empirical evidence may be due to the low reliabilities of the measures (Halpern & Udry, 1992). However, *estrogen* has been shown to be associated with higher levels of activity and more positive moods, whereas lack of estrogen may be associated with depression and negative moods (see Buchanan et al., 1992).

Even within this biological frame of reference, most effects include mediational variables. The most important ones are probably subjective expectations and interpretations. For example, an internally aroused girl certainly feels very different when she is being tested while standing in front of the blackboard in school than when she is going to a movie with friends. In addition, these interpretations are by themselves moderated by social expectations and norms. Many parents, for example, expect their pubertal youngsters to be emotional, eruptive, and unpredictable.

2.2 Models of influence

As we have seen, other factors that may influence adolescents' reactions to pubertal maturation are individual characteristics and the social context. Individuals differ in the extent to which they *perceive* their bodily changes. They also have different expectations and attitudes towards pubertal changes and show different habitual reactions to challenges and stress. Both awareness of bodily changes and interpretations may depend on self-

reflection and cognitive differentiation as well as personality orientation, including attributional style and defensiveness (Alsaker, 1995b). They also depend on the availability of information and social feedback. The adolescent's changing appearance acts as a signal to and triggers reactions from others that are independent of his or her own wishes (see Brooks-Gunn & Warren, 1989, for a short review of reactions from parents and peers).

Furthermore, adolescents compare themselves with their own reference groups. That is, two young people who, objectively speaking, are equally mature may perceive themselves as on time, early, or late, depending on the level of maturation of their peers (see perceived/subjective timing earlier in this chapter).

Because adolescents' position between childhood and adulthood is in a state of constant change and because of the lack of clearly defined roles or behavior norms for this age period (Flammer & Alsaker, 2002), adult reactions towards adolescents vary considerably. In pluralistic societies such as Western ones, norms typically vary greatly between social groups or what we may call subcultures. Such subcultures may be conceived of in terms of social class, educational level, ethnicity, religion, rural or urban areas and even of communities (see Richards & Petersen, 1987, for an example of the latter, and Alsaker, 1995a, for a discussion of socialization at puberty).

However, one area of great importance to maturing girls is regulated by astonishingly homogeneous norms within Western societies, i.e., attractiveness. Agreement as to what constitutes attractiveness is as high among 8 year olds as among 11 and 17 year olds (Cavior & Lombardi, 1973). The problem is that the Western body ideal for girls is far from reality. It clearly emphasizes prepubertal leanness and body proportions that are closer to men's bodies than to girls' (e.g., in terms of size of legs). This means that if pubertal development occurs normally, the girl's body moves far from the feminine ideal.

Several models of the influence of pubertal changes on psychosocial adjustment have been proposed. Most of these address the issue of the timing of the onset of bodily changes. The specific models usually discussed in the literature are (1) the stage termination model, (2) the deviance model, and (3) the goodness of fit model.

The *stage termination model* (also called the developmental readiness model) suggests that the particular developmental tasks pertaining to a particular developmental stage require a certain amount of time to be resolved adequately, before the next developmental tasks can be worked on. For example, early maturation is claimed to interrupt the task of ego development prior to the pubertal stage (Petersen & Taylor, 1980). Another related hypothesis considers early maturation as a non-normative developmental task (Alsaker, 1996) and poses that early maturers' task differs from the task confronting their peers, as they are less prepared to cope with pubertal and emotional changes (Ge, Conger, & Elder, 2001a). This model is also currently referred to as the early maturation or *early timing hypothesis*.

The *deviance* model (also called the social clock model or the *off-time hypothesis*) states that off-time maturation (i.e., early and late maturation) places young adolescents in a socially 'deviant' category and thus leads to negative effects (Petersen & Taylor, 1980). According to this model, an interaction between timing, grade, and gender should be expected. Negative effects should be stronger for early-maturing girls in lower grades. For boys, negative effects of timing should be stronger in higher grades, when late-maturing boys would be the very last to enter puberty.

The *goodness of fit* model is based on the assumption that persons and contexts are distinct entities with their specific characteristics (Lerner, 1985). Consequently, a good fit between characteristics of the adolescent and requirements inherent to the context, are considered a prerequisite for psychological adjustment. Whereas on-time maturers may be generally satisfied with the rate and timing of their pubertal changes, they may be at risk in a context that emphasizes the values of a prepubertal body. The value of this model has been demonstrated for young female dancers (Brooks-Gunn & Warren, 1985).

The deviance and the goodness of fit models are highly related to one another and it is sometimes difficult to say whether empirical results give support to the one or the other.

In contrast to these three models of pubertal timing, three further models are related to pubertal maturation itself. The first is called the *simultaneous change* model (Simmons & Blyth, 1987). It states that pubertal development interacts with other changes and that negative effects partly depend on the number of changes occurring simultaneously with pubertal maturation. The second is called the *ideal of thinness* model (Blyth, Simmons, & Zakin, 1985) and it posits that, given the widespread ideals of thinness for girls in the Western cultures, pubertal maturation will have a negative effect on girls' body image, but not on that of boys. The third model has only been considered in two studies (Caspi & Moffitt, 1991; Ge et al., 2003) and is called the *stressful change* hypothesis. It posits that adolescents in the midst of pubertal maturation experience most stress and are expected to show most problems.

In conclusion, the developing young adolescent stimulates reactions from others, but is also an active processor of information and thus an actor in her/his own psychosocial development (Lerner, 1985). Reactions to pubertal changes may well be influenced by hormonal factors, earlier personality and social development and the social context, but they are not determined by these factors. As a result, even in equivalent contexts of development, adolescents will still be expected to show a high diversity of reactions. The adolescent's development during pubertal maturation is not merely one of adaptation to new characteristics arising primarily from physiological changes, but also one of adjustment to a changing social environment (Alsaker, 1996; Petersen & Taylor, 1980) and of integration of discrepant reactions, expectations and unrealistic norms.

2.3 *Correlates of maturation and timing*

The influence of pubertal development on sexual ideation and behavior as well as the relationship between pubertal timing and adolescents' sexuality will not be treated in the present chapter. Instead, the reader is referred to the chapter in this volume concerning adolescent sexuality (Zani & Cicognani).

2.3.1   Social relationships – peers

If we consider the central role that peers play in early adolescence and the importance of the wider social context, we should expect peer relations to be affected by pubertal maturation or its timing. Two of the models presented earlier may be helpful in formulating at least general expectations. These are the deviance model and the goodness of fit model. Following these models, one should expect early maturation to have a positive effect on peer relationships in contexts where a higher level of maturation is highly valued, and vice versa. In view of the importance of social comparison in adolescence, off-time maturing might also have some negative effects on peer relationships and one might ask whether off-time maturers seek alliance with adolescents who are on the same maturational level.

Studies in which these issues have been addressed have generally shown no or inconsistent effects of pubertal development on number of friends (Stattin & Magnusson, 1990; Susman et al., 1985), perceived popularity (Simmons & Blyth, 1987; Zakin, Blyth, & Simmons, 1984), or rejection by peers (Silbereisen, Petersen, Albrecht, & Kracke, 1989), both in girls and in boys.

One result is worth mentioning. In a large Swedish longitudinal study, Stattin and Magnusson (1990) have shown that early-maturing girls had older friends than other girls and twice as many who were already in employment. It seemed that off-time maturers tried to find matching friends and in doing so, redefined their peer network. This has certainly positive sides (e.g. as to one's body image), but it may also lead to more risk behavior. The latter was actually reported in the study by Stattin and Magnusson (see later).

2.3.2   Family relationships

Why should we expect pubertal maturation to alter parent–adolescent relationships? Paikoff and Brooks-Gunn (1991) have proposed three models; two of them will be presented here. The first implies a direct and/or indirect effect (through emotional and behavioral changes) of hormonal changes on parent–adolescent interaction. Only one study could be found that has addressed the possible influence of pubertal hormones on parent–adolescent relationships. The researchers (Inoff-Germain et al., 1988), observed adolescents in interaction with their parents and focused primarily on aggressive behavior. In boys, some association was shown between testosterone index and an adrenal androgen and moderate signs of anger. In girls, estradiol and androstenedione levels were related to defiance, dominance and anger toward parents.

The second model suggests that changes in secondary sex characteristics and also the rate and timing of change have a signal effect that brings about changes in the parents' and adolescents' expectations towards one another.

Where *pubertal maturation* is concerned, two studies indicate general changes (Greif & Ulman, 1982), as well as some perturbation in mother–daughter relationships on menarche (Hill, Holmbeck, Marlow, Green, & Lynch, 1985a, 1985b), i.e. when pubertal maturation is almost achieved. Other authors have also reported increased conflicts and diminished closeness in parent–adolescent relationship at later stages of maturation in girls (Crockett & Petersen, 1987; Steinberg, 1987, 1988), but not in boys.

In boys, the same perturbation in relation to parents seems to occur at around the middle of pubertal development, i.e., at an earlier maturational stage than in girls. Observational studies also reveal less affective and more assertive interactions in families with adolescents who are in the middle of the maturational process (Papini, Datan, & McCluskey-Fawcett, 1988). These adolescents also reported more intense conflicts than other adolescents with their parents with respect to personal habits (Papini & Clark, 1989).

The general conclusion is that pubertal maturation is related to greater emotional autonomy and less closeness to parents (see further Alsaker, 1995b; Paikoff & Brooks-Gunn, 1991).

Studies focusing on *pubertal timing* have also led to inconsistent conclusions ranging from less conflict (Paikoff, Brooks-Gunn, & Warren, 1991) to more conflict or dissatisfaction with the parental relationships in early-maturing girls (Hill et al., 1985a; Petersen, 1985; Savin-Williams & Small, 1986; Stattin & Magnusson, 1990). In boys, the general conclusion is that early maturing is accompanied by positive parent–adolescent interactions (Savin-Williams & Small, 1986; Simmons & Blyth, 1987), whereas late maturing sometimes shows the opposite effect (Clausen, 1975; Jones & Mussen, 1958).

2.3.3 Body image and body-related problems

Dissatisfaction with one's own body during the period of pubertal maturation seems to be strongly related to height in boys and weight in girls. Early-maturing boys are usually most satisfied with their height (Simmons & Blyth, 1987), whereas early-maturing girls generally complain about their weight (Duke-Duncan, Ritter, Dornbusch, Gross, & Carlsmith, 1985; Stattin & Magnusson, 1990).

We have already noted that pubertal maturation in girls is accompanied by increases in body fat and weight (Garn & Clark, 1976). In line with this finding, girls' dissatisfaction with weight correlates with pubertal development and particularly affects early-maturing girls (Duke-Duncan et al., 1985; Stattin & Magnusson, 1990). Tanner (1962) noted that girls who matured very early tended to be both shorter and heavier than on-time girls of the same maturational level. Cairns and Cairns (1994) even reported an association between early maturing and a less attractive appearance. Early-maturing girls not only rated themselves as less attractive than their peers, they were also rated as less attractive by their peers. It is no wonder then that early maturing has proved to be a more powerful predictor of body dissatisfaction than pubertal maturation itself.

However, the effect of timing on body image depends to a large extent on social context (see e.g., Brooks-Gunn, Attie, Burrow, Rosso, & Warren, 1989). Whereas early maturing is generally reported as having a negative effect on body image, Brooks-Gunn and colleagues (Brooks-Gunn et al., 1989) demonstrated that among dancers even being on time was associated with significantly less satisfaction than being late. A recent study (Ge, Elder, Renerus, & Cox, 2001c) demonstrated the impact of girls' perceptions of their weight on self-esteem, depression and somatic symptoms, when pubertal development and actual BMI were controlled. Here again, the influence of the social context was clearly shown: the effect was found for Anglo-American and Hispanic-American girls, but not for African–American girls.

An interesting cultural difference should also be noted here. While some authors have shown greater dissatisfaction in early maturers with increasing grade in North America (6th to 8th grade, Petersen & Crockett, 1985; 6th to 10th grade, Simmons & Blyth, 1987), the strongest effects of early timing have been found in the *youngest* girls in two large Norwegian samples and a Swiss sample (including 4th to 9th graders, Alsaker, 1992, 1997). The reason for this difference is unclear.

The next question is, whether these early-maturing girls have developed concerns about their weight and eating habits. Data from a North American sample (Brooks-Gunn et al., 1989) and a Norwegian sample (Alsaker, 1997) show that early maturing is related to concerns about eating and – in the Norwegian sample – even to actual dieting.

Early-maturing boys typically feel more attractive (Tobin-Richards, Boxer, & Petersen, 1983) and are more satisfied with their bodies, looks, and muscle development than other boys (Blyth, Simmons, Bulcroft, Felt, VanCleave, & Bush, 1981; Çok, 1990; Simmons & Blyth, 1987). Correspondingly, late developers, who are shorter and usually weaker than their peers, are more dissatisfied with their bodies (Alsaker, 1992). Some recent results, however, point to a new trend (Künzli-Hämmerli, 1995; Speltini, 1996). This relates to the appearance of pubic hair and body hair in pubertal boys which does not square with the image of the hairless man as presented by modern advertisements.

Psychosomatic symptoms are reported to a greater extent by early-maturing girls than by others (Alsaker, 1997; Aro & Taipale, 1987; Stattin & Magnusson, 1990). Aro and Taipale demonstrated an effect of both maturation and timing.

The more developed and the earlier development occurs, the more symptoms were reported. The recent Swiss–Norwegian study showed the same effect in early-maturing girls and boys in both Norway and Switzerland (Alsaker, 1997). Early maturers reported around twice as many symptoms as their peers (Figure 3.2).

2.3.4 Internalizing problems
The prevalence of *depression* is higher in adolescents than in children. This could be due to many factors and one might question whether pubertal processes per se play some role in the onset or intensification of such problems. Some studies have indicated that, especially in girls, a proneness to depression may be related to pubertal maturation (Rutter, 1986).

Pubertal status, measured in terms of bodily changes, has been found to correlate with negative moods and their intensity (Buchanan, 1991). Most results, however, are associated with pubertal timing. Although Dorn et al. (2003) have underlined inconsistencies in results between different studies, most authors put emphasis on the

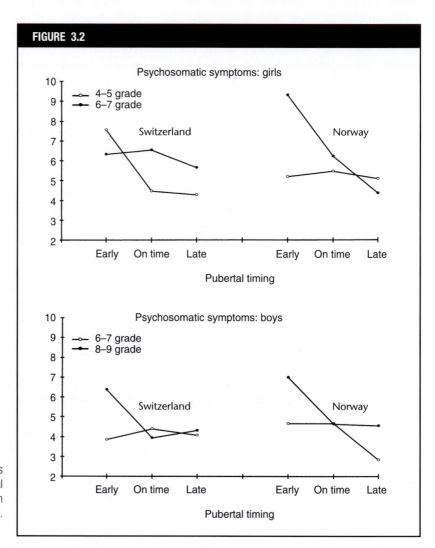

FIGURE 3.2

Psychosomatic symptoms in different maturational groups of adolescents in Norway and Switzerland.

overall trend in the results and maintain that there is substantial evidence today that early-maturing girls go through diverse internalizing psychological problems (Alsaker, 1995b; Archibald et al., 2003; Ge et al., 2003; Hayward, 2003). For example, early-maturing girls have been found to score higher on Offer's psycho-pathology scale (including a wide range of symptoms; Brooks-Gunn & Warren, 1985; Petersen & Crockett, 1985), on depressive symptoms or indicators of major depression (e.g., Alsaker, 1992, 1997; Ge, Conger, & Elder, 2001a; Graber et al., 1997; Hayward et al., 1997; Stattin & Magnusson, 1990) and on sadness (Brooks-Gunn & Warren, 1985). Also, two recent studies demonstrated similar results in a population of African–American (Ge et al., 2003) and Finnish girls (Kaltiala-Heino, Kosunen, & Rimpelä, 2003). In the same vein, using hormonal assets, Susman et al. (1985) have shown that girls with higher levels of FSH than their same-age peers (i.e., who were presumably early maturers) also scored higher on Offer's emotional tone and psy-chopathology sub-scales. The emotional tone scale is reported to tap essentially sadness (Sus-man et al., 1985). Using *perceived* pubertal tim-ing, Graber et al. (2004) found young adults (age 24) who had reported themselves as being early maturers during adolescence, to show higher life-time prevalence rates of major depression dis-orders (MDD) than the former on-time and late maturers. Further analyses revealed that they experienced onset of MDD throughout ado-lescence. At age 24, however, no differences existed between the timing groups. Nevertheless, the subjectively early maturing young women were less satisfied with their life, family and friends. In sum, given the diversity of methods used to assess timing of onset of puberty, results are very consistent, and clearly indicate that early-maturing girls are at risk for internalizing problems.

Results on emotional problems and pubertal status or timing in boys have been less clear. Some researchers have found that *early-maturers* report less sadness (Crockett & Petersen, 1987; Susman et al., 1985). Others report no association with sadness, but more with psychopathology in general (Petersen & Crockett, 1985). Still others have found that early-developing boys report more depressive symptoms in Norway and Switzerland (Alsaker, 1992, 1997) and recently in Finland (Kaltiala-Heino et al., 2003). And in the United States early-maturing boys have recently been shown to score higher on internalizing dis-tress including depression, anxiety, and somatic symptoms one and three years after their timing status had been defined (Ge et al., 2001b). This was true also after controlling for the level of internalized distress at the first time of measurement.

The results just presented corroborate earlier results from the Berkeley Guidance Study (the Peskin study as cited in Petersen & Taylor, 1980) showing that early maturers were more sombre and anxious than others. Also a higher level of pubertal maturation in itself has been reported to correlate positively with depressive symptoms and anxiety (Susman et al., 1991). Finally, late maturers have also been found to report more sadness (e.g., Nottelmann et al., 1987; Siegel et al., 1999 – in terms of perceived timing in the latter study) and in at least three studies (Alsaker, 1992; Graber et al., 1997; Kaltiala-Heino et al., 2003) both early and late maturers were found to be more depressed than their on-time peers.

In sum, as contained by Alsaker (1996) and Ge et al. (2001b), the undifferentiated view of early maturation as a positive event for boys needs to be modified. The results are less clear than in girls (Ge et al., 2001a), but they definitely demonstrate that early maturation is a burden at least to some adolescent boys.

2.3.5 Externalizing problems

Simmons and Blyth (1987) found that younger post-menarcheal girls (i.e., early maturers in their study) scored higher on school-related behavior problems than other girls. This result is in line with findings reported by Stattin and Magnusson (1990) for early-maturing girls and findings indi-cating that girls with precocious puberty showed more behavior problems during IQ testing and their parents also reported more behavior prob-lems (Ehrhardt et al., 1984). One might argue that pronounced early maturing may produce a large gap between actual maturity and the expectations of others. School might lead to boredom, impatience and, consequently to more conflicts (Moffitt, 1993). It should be noted, however, that neither Duke-Duncan et al. (1985) nor Alsaker (1997) found effects of timing on school adjustment or on attitudes towards school.

An association between alcohol consumption and early maturing has been reported by several authors. Four studies deserve some specific attention, as they all included longitudinal data. Magnusson and colleagues (Magnusson, Stattin, & Allen, 1986; Stattin & Magnusson, 1990) have reported clear effects of early maturing on what they have called 'norm-violative activity' in general in Swedish girls. Early-maturing girls had more pronounced drinking habits at the age of 14; 63% of these girls reported having been drunk on at least one occasion. Among late maturers of the same age, only 29% had had such an experience. The effect disappeared at age 16. No systematic pattern was found when the girls' drinking habits were re-assessed 10 years later. Aro and Taipale (1987) also reported a similar effect of early maturing on girls' alcohol consumption around age 15 and found that it vanished at around age 16. They also found grade effects to be more important than pubertal timing in predicting drinking behavior. Wichstrøm (2001) has also reported somewhat similar findings in a large Norwegian sample. He found early-maturing girls to report a higher number of intoxications and of alcohol units consumed on each occasion. The association between early timing at the first time of measurement (age 13 to 16 years) and alcohol consumption two years later was still significant but clearly lower, when alcohol consumption at Time 1 was controlled. Finally, Wiesner and Ittel (2002) reported that early timing predicted alcohol use and cigarette smoking one year after measurement of pubertal timing and also after controlling for substance use at Time 1 in a German sample. Both in Wichstrøm's and in Wiesner and Ittel's studies the major predictor of substance use at Time 2 was substance use at Time 1. However, early timing was able to predict an increase in substance use. That means that early maturation may affect

young girls' alcohol use at an early stage and that these behaviors are consolidated during adolescence.

Other types of norm breaking were also more frequent in early-maturing girls than in others (Magnusson et al., 1986). Their norm-breaking activities ranged from use of hashish and hard drugs, to provocations, stealing and the like. However, the same early-maturing girls were only slightly more represented in criminal records at age 26. In contrast, Duke-Duncan et al. (1985) using self-report of deviant behavior – contact with police or smoking – found no effect of pubertal timing in girls.

A very interesting feature of the Magnusson study is that norm-breaking activities in early-maturing girls could be attributed to their peer network. Early-maturing girls had older friends than on-time and late maturers. These older peers were also tolerant toward norm-breaking behaviour (Stattin & Magnusson, 1990). In the Silbereisen et al. (1989) study, early-maturing girls also had more contact with 'deviant' peers. The conclusion might therefore be that early-maturing girls are at risk from developing norm-breaking behavior habits, but that the effect is mediated by their social network. Results from two catholic girls' schools also give support to the mediating role of the social context. Early-maturing girls in these schools showed no tendencies to norm-breaking behavior (Henneberger & Deister, 1996).

Results for boys show that being off time (both early and late) can be a disadvantage. In the Duke-Duncan et al. (1985) study, early-maturing boys reported higher occurrences of contact with police and smoking than their peers. Ge et al. (2001b) found early maturers to be more hostile than their peers and to become slightly (but significantly) more hostile within the three years following their categorization as early maturers. Wichstrøm (2001) found early-maturing boys to report a higher number of intoxications and of alcohol units consumed on each occasion. The results were similar to the results presented earlier as regards girls, but they were much stronger. Also Wiesner and Ittel (2002) reported similar findings among boys as they did among girls in their German sample: early maturers used more alcohol and smoked more than the on-time and late maturers.

As to late maturers, they have also been reported to be at risk regarding later alcohol problems in Sweden (Anderson & Magnusson, 1990), to drink more often than their on-time peers, provided that they were with peers in Germany (Kracke, 1993) but to drink significantly less than their peers in Norway (Wichstrøm, 2001). This last author points out that these boys may often be excluded from typical drinking parties, because they look immature. So possibly the Norwegian results corroborate the German ones.

Early maturation has been demonstrated to be a risk factor as regards a variety of problems in adolescence. However, it should be emphasized that it does not mean that early timing necessarily leads to problem behavior. There are convincing indications that early maturation being a stressful task tends to *accentuate* already existing tendencies towards problem behavior (Caspi & Moffitt, 1991).

3. Conclusion

This chapter leads to three fundamental messages that point well beyond the specific content of the chapter.

First, pubertal changes are indeed at the core of development in adolescence. However, they are not the only ones and they nearly always affect the adolescent's behavior in interaction with other factors. None of these factors can be dismissed but none, by the same token, can predict behavior by and of itself.

Second, these other factors are related to psychological and social processes. Social processes are always culturally and historically determined. A fortiori, even puberty is a cultural and historical phenomenon. Like developmental psychology in general, the psychology of puberty has to be rewritten for every culture in every epoch (Flammer, 1996). Needless to say within each culture and epoch there still are huge individual differences. There is no such thing as 'the' early maturers, or 'the' late maturer, or 'the' on-time maturer.

Third, the reader may be disappointed by the many inconsistent findings. Part of the inconsistency may, of course, be due to unreliable measurement or to biased sampling methods, or possibly to different research interests. However, it is also rooted in the topic. These studies were conducted in different cultures and subcultures and no study can include all factors that are of possible importance.

References

Alsaker, F.D. (1992). Pubertal timing, overweight, and psychological adjustment. *Journal of Early Adolescence, 12,* 396–419.

Alsaker, F.D. (1995a). Is puberty a critical period for socialization? *Journal of Adolescence, 18,* 1–18.

Alsaker, F.D. (1995b). Timing of puberty and reactions to pubertal changes. In M. Rutter (Ed.), *Psychosocial disturbances in young people: Challenges for prevention* (pp. 39–82). New York: Cambridge University Press.

Alsaker, F.D. (1996). The impact of puberty. *Journal of Child Psychology and Psychiatry, 37,* 249–258.

Alsaker, F.D. (1997). Pubertät als Belastung [Puberty as burden]. In A. Grob (Ed.), *Kinder und Jugendliche heute: belastet – überbelastet?* (pp. 129–148). Zurich, Switzerland: Ruegger.

Anderson, T., & Magnusson, D. (1990). Biological maturation and the development of drinking habits and alcohol abuse among young males: A prospective longitudinal study. *Journal of Youth and Adolescence, 19,* 33–41.

Archibald, A.B., Graber, J.A., & Brooks-Gunn, J. (2003). Pubertal processes and physiological growth in adolescence. In G. R. Adams, & M. Berzonsky (Eds.), *Blackwell handbook of adolescence* (pp. 24–47). Malden, MA: Blackwell.

Aro, H., & Taipale, V. (1987). The impact of timing of puberty on psychosomatic symptoms among fourteen- to sixteen-year old Finnish girls. *Child Development, 58,* 261–268.

Behrman, R.E., Kliegman, R.M., Nelson, W.E., & Vaughan, V.C. (1992). *Nelson textbook of pediatrics.* Philadelphia, PA: W. B. Saunders.

Berg-Kelly, K., & Erdes, L. (1997). Self-assessment of sexual maturity by mid-adolescents based on a global question. *Acta Paediatrica, 86,* 10–17.

Blyth, D.A., Simmons, R.G., Bulcroft, R., Felt, D., VanCleave, E.F., & Bush, D.M. (1981). The effects of physical development on self-image and satisfaction with body-image for early adolescent males. *Research in Community and Mental Health, 2,* 43–73.

Blyth, D.A., Simmons, R.G., & Zakin, D.F. (1985). Satisfaction with body image for early adolescent females: The impact of pubertal timing within different school environments. *Journal of Youth and Adolescence*, *14*, 207–225.

Brooks-Gunn, J., Attie, H., Burrow, C., Rosso, J., & Warren, M.P. (1989). The impact of puberty on body and eating concerns in athletic and non-athletic contexts. *Journal of Early Adolescence*, *9*, 269–290.

Brooks-Gunn, J., Petersen, A.C., & Eichorn, D. (1985). The study of maturational timing effects in adolescence. *Journal of Youth and Adolescence*, *14*, 149–161.

Brooks-Gunn, J., & Reiter, E.O. (1990). The role of pubertal processes. In S. S. Feldman, & G. R. Elliott (Eds.), *At the threshold: The developing adolescent* (pp. 16–53). Cambridge, MA: Harvard University Press.

Brooks-Gunn, J., & Warren, M.P. (1985). The effects of delayed menarche in different contexts: Dance and non-dance students. *Journal of Youth and Adolescence*, *14*, 285–300.

Brooks-Gunn, J., & Warren, M.P. (1989). Biological and social contributions to negative affect in young adolescent girls. *Child Development*, *60*, 40–55.

Brooks-Gunn, J., Warren, M.P., Rosso, J., & Gargiulo, J. (1987). Validity of self-report measures of girls' pubertal status. *Child Development*, *58*, 829–841.

Brundtland, G.H., & Walloe, L. (1976). Menarcheal age in Norway in the 19th century: A re-evaluation of the historical sources. *Annals of Human Biology*, *3*, 363–374.

Buchanan, C.M. (1991). Pubertal development, assessment of. In R. M. Lerner, A. C. Petersen, & J. Brooks-Gunn (Eds.), *Encyclopedia of adolescence* (pp. 875–883). New York: Garland.

Buchanan, C.M., Eccles, J.S., & Becker, J.B. (1992). Are adolescents the victims of raging hormones? Evidence for activational effects of hormones on moods and behavior at adolescence. *Psychological Bulletin*, *111*, 62–107.

Cairns, R.B., & Cairns, B.D. (1994). *Lifelines and risks: Pathways of youth in our time*. New York: Cambridge University Press.

Campbell, B.C., & Udry, J.R. (1992). *Mother's age at menarche, not stress, accounts for daughter's age at menarche*. Paper presented at the Biennial Meeting of the Society for Research on Adolescence, Washington, DC.

Caspi, A., & Moffitt, T.E. (1991). Individual differences are accentuated during periods of social change: The sample case of girls at puberty. *Journal of Personality and Social Psychology*, *61*, 157–168.

Cavior, N., & Lombardi, D.A. (1973). Developmental aspects of judgment of physical attractiveness in children. *Developmental Psychology*, *8*, 67–71.

Clausen, J.A. (1975). The social meaning of differential physical and sexual maturation. In S. E. Dragastin, & G. H. Elder (Eds.), *Adolescence in the life cycle: Psychological change and social context* (pp. 25–47). Washington, DC: Hemisphere.

Çok, F. (1990). Body image satisfaction in Turkish adolescents. *Adolescence*, *25*, 409–413.

Coleman, L., & Coleman, J. (2002). The measurement of puberty: A review. *Journal of Adolescence*, *25*, 535–550.

Crockett, L.J., & Petersen, A.C. (1987). Pubertal status and psychosocial development: Findings from the early adolescence study. In R. M. Lerner, & T. T. Foch (Eds.), *Biological and psychosocial interactions in early adolescence* (pp. 173–188). Hillsdale, NJ: Lawrence Erlbaum Associates, Inc.

Degenhardt, A. (1996). Der Einfluss von Körpergrösse, Reifestatus und sozialer Belastung auf Selbstbildaspekte hochwüchsiger Madchen [The influence of body height, maturational status and social stress on aspects of the self-image of tall girls]. In R. Schumann-Hengsteler, & H.M. Trautner (Eds.), *Entwicklung im Jugendalter* (pp. 57–76). Göttingen, Germany: Hogrefe.

Deppen, A., Jeannin, A., Michaud, P-A., Suris, J-C., & Alsaker, F.D. (submitted). Subjectively off-time but objectively on-time: Genesis and impact of subjective pubertal timing on health and behaviours of adolescent girls. *Social Science and Medicine*.

Dorn, L.D., Dahl, R.E., Williamson, D.E., Birmaher, B., Axelson, D., Perel, J. et al. (2003). Developmental markers in adolescence: Implications for studies of pubertal processes. *Journal of Youth and Adolescence*, *32*, 315–324.

Duke-Duncan, P., Ritter, P.L., Dornbusch, S.M., Gross, R.T., & Carlsmith, J.M. (1985). The effects of pubertal timing on body image, school behavior, and deviance. *Journal of Youth and Adolescence*, *14*, 227–235.

Ehrhardt, A.A., Meyer-Bahlburg, H.F.L., Bell, J.J., Cohen, S.F., Healey, J.M., Stiel, R. et al. (1984). Idiopathic precocious puberty in girls: Psychiatric follow-up in adolescence. *Journal of the American Academy of Child Psychiatry*, *23*, 23–33.

Ellis, B.J. (2004). Timing of pubertal maturation in girls: An integrated life history approach. *Psychological Bulletin*, *130*, 920–958.

Eveleth, P., & Tanner, J. (1976). *Worldwide variation in human growth*. New York: Cambridge University Press.

Finkelstein, J.W. (1980). The endocrinology of adolescence. *Pediatric Clinics of North America, 27*, 53–69.

Flammer, A. (1996). *Entwicklungstheorien* [Developmental theories]. Bern, Switzerland: Huber.

Flammer, A., & Alsaker, F.D. (2002). *Entwicklungspsychologie der Adoleszenz. Die Erschliessung innerer und äusserer Welten im Jugendalter* [Development in adolescence. The opening of inner and outer worlds]. Bern, Switzerland: Huber.

Flammer, A., App, U., & de Pretto, J. (1977). Zur Aequivalenz von Intelligenztests bei zwölfjährigen Schweizer Kindern [On the equivalence of IQ tests in 12-year-old Swiss children]. *Vierteljahresschrift für Heilpädagogik und ihre Nachbargebiete, 46*, 29–36.

Flynn, J.R. (1987). Massive gains in 14 nations: What IQ tests really measure. *Psychological Bulletin, 101*, 171–191.

Flynn, J.R. (1999). Searching for justice: The discovery of IQ gains over time. *American Psychologist, 54*, 5–20.

Garn, S.M., & Clark, D.C. (1976). Trends in fatness and the origins of obesity. *Pediatrics, 57*, 443–456.

Ge, X., Conger, R.D., & Elder, G.H. Jr. (2001a). Pubertal transition, stressful life events and the emergence of gender differences in adolescent depressive symptoms. *Developmental Psychology, 37*, 404–417.

Ge, X., Conger, R.D., & Elder, G.H. Jr. (2001b). The relation between puberty and psychological distress in adolescent boys. *Journal of Research on Adolescence, 11*, 49–70.

Ge, X., Elder, G.H. Jr., Regnerus, M., & Cox, C. (2001c). Pubertal transitions, perceptions of being overweight, and adolescents' psychological maladjustment: Gender and ethnic differences. *Social Psychology Quarterly, 64*, 363–375.

Ge, X., Kim, I.J., Brody, G., H, Conger, R.D., Simons, R.L., Gibbons, F.X. et al. (2003). It's about timing and change: Pubertal transition effects on symptoms of major depression among African American youths. *Developmental Psychology, 39*, 430–439.

Graber, J.A., Brooks-Gunn, J., & Warren, M.P. (1995). The antecedents of menarcheal age: Heredity, family environment and stressful life events. *Child Development, 66*, 346–359.

Graber, J.A., Lewinsohn, P.M., Seeley, J.R., & Brooks-Gunn, J. (1997). Is psychopathology associated with the timing of pubertal development? *Journal of the American Academy of Adolescent and Child Psychiatry, 36*, 1768–1776.

Graber, J.A., Seeley, J.R., Brooks-Gunn, J., & Lewinsohn, P.M. (2004). Is pubertal timing associated with psychopathology in young adulthood? *Journal of the American Academy of Child and Adolescent Psychiatry, 43*, 718–726.

Greif, E.B., & Ulman, K.J. (1982). The psychological impact of menarche on early adolescent females: A review of the literature. *Child Development, 53*, 1413–1430.

Grumbach, M.M., Grave, G.D., & Mayer, F.E. (Eds.). (1974). *Control of the onset of puberty*. New York: John Wiley & Sons.

Halpern, C.T., & Udry, J.R. (1992). Variations in adolescent hormone measures and implications for behavioral research. *Journal of Research on Adolescence, 2*, 103–122.

Halpern, C.T., Udry, J.R., Campbell, B., & Suchindran, C. (1992). *Hormonal influences on adolescent male sexual activity*. Paper presented at the Biennial Meeting of the Society for Research on Adolescence, Washington, DC.

Hayward, C. (Ed.). (2003). *Gender differences at puberty*. New York: Cambridge University Press.

Hayward, C., Killen, J.D., Wilson, D.M., Hammer, L.D., Litt, I.F., Kraemer, H.C. et al. (1997). Psychiatric risk associated with early puberty in adolescent girls. *Journal of the American Academy of Adolescent and Child Psychiatry, 36*, 255–262.

Henneberger, A., & Deister, B. (1996). Jugendliche wählen ihre Umwelt. Die Bedeutung von Entwicklungsaufgaben im Lebenskontext. [Adolescents choose their environment: The meaning of developmental tasks in life context]. In R. Schumann-Hengsteler, & H. M. Trautner (Eds.), *Entwicklung im Jugendalter* (pp. 119–140). Göttingen, Germany: Hogrefe.

Herman-Giddens, M.E., Slora, E.J., Wassermann, R.C., Bourdony, C.J., Bhapkar, M.V., Koch, G.G. et al. (1997). Secondary sexual characteristics and menses in young girls seen in office practice: A study from the pediatric research in office settings network. *Pediatrics, 99*, 505–511.

Hill, J.P., Holmbeck, G.N., Marlow, L., Green, T.M., & Lynch, M.E. (1985a). Menarcheal status and parent–child relations in families of seventh-grade girls. *Journal of Youth and Adolescence, 14*, 301–316.

Hill, J.P., Holmbeck, G.N., Marlow, L., Green, T.M., & Lynch, M.E. (1985b). Pubertal status and parent–child relations in families of seventh-grade boys. *Journal of Early Adolescence, 5*, 31–44.

Inoff-Germain, G., Arnold, G.S., Nottelmann, E.D., Susman, E.J., Cutler, G.B., Jr., & Chrousos, G.P. (1988). Relations between hormonal levels and observational measures of aggressive behavior of young adolescents in family interactions. *Developmental Psychology*, *24*, 129–139.

Jones, M.C., & Mussen, P.H. (1958). Self-conceptions, motivations, and interpersonal attitudes of early- and late-maturing girls. *Child Development*, *29*, 491–501.

Kaltiala-Heino, R., Kosunen, E., & Rimpelä, M. (2003). Pubertal timing, sexual behaviour and self-reported depression in middle adolescence. *Journal of Adolescence*, *26*, 431–545.

Kohen-Raz, R. (1974). Physiological maturation and mental growth at pre-adolescence and puberty. *Journal of Child Psychology and Psychiatry and Allied Disciplines*, *15*, 199–213.

Kracke, B. (1993). *Pubertät und Problemverhalten bei Jungen* [Puberty and problem behavior in boys]. Weinheim, Germany: Beltz.

Künzli-Hämmerli, S. (1995). *Körperbezogene Kognitionen und Handlungen in der Pubertät* [Body-related cognitions and behavior at puberty]. Unpublished master's thesis, University of Berne, Switzerland.

Lerner, R.M. (1985). Adolescent maturational changes and psychosocial development: A dynamic interactional perspective. *Journal of Youth and Adolescence*, *14*, 355–372.

Magnusson, D., Stattin, H., & Allen, V.L. (1986). Differential maturation among girls and its relevance to social adjustment: A longitudinal perspective. In D. L. Featherman, & R. M. Lerner (Eds.), *Life-span development and behavior* (Vol. 7, pp. 135–172). New York: Academic Press.

Marshall, W. (1978). Puberty. In F. Falkner, & J. Tanner (Eds.), *Human growth* (Vol. 2, pp. 141–181). New York: Plenum.

Meyer, J.M., Eaves, L.J., Heath, A.C., & Martin, N.G. (1991). Estimating genetic influence on the age-at-menarche: A survival analysis approach. *American Journal of Medical Genetics*, *39*, 148–154.

Moffitt, T.E. (1993). Adolescence-limited and life-course-persistent antisocial behavior: A developmental taxonomy. *Psychological Review*, *100*, 674–701.

Moffitt, T.E., Caspi, A., Belsky, J., & Silva, P.A. (1992). Childhood experience and the onset of menarche: A test of a sociobiological model. *Child Development*, *63*, 47–58.

Money, J., & Wolff, G. (1974). Late puberty, retarded growth and reversible hyposomatotropinism (psychological dwarfism). *Adolescence*, *9*, 121–134.

Nottelmann, E.D., Susman, E.J., Dorn, L.D., Inoff-Germain, G., Loriaux, D.L., Cutler, G.B. et al. (1987). Developmental processes in early adolescence. *Journal of Adolescent Health Care*, *8*, 246–260.

Olweus, D., Mattson, A., Schalling, D., & Low, H. (1980). Testosterone, aggression, physical, and personality dimensions in normal adolescent males. *Psychosomatic Medicine*, *42*, 253–269.

Paikoff, R.L., & Brooks-Gunn, J. (1991). Do parent–child relationships change during puberty? *Psychological Bulletin*, *110*, 47–66.

Paikoff, R.L., Brooks-Gunn, J., & Warren, M.P. (1991). Effects of girls' hormonal status on depressive and aggressive symptoms over the course of one year. *Journal of Youth and Adolescence*, *20*, 191–215.

Papini, D.R., & Clark, S. (1989). Grade, pubertal status, and gender-related variations in conflictual issues among adolescents. *Adolescence*, *24*, 977–987.

Papini, D.R., Datan, N., & McCluskey-Fawcett, K.A. (1988). An observational study of affective and assertive family interactions during adolescence. *Journal of Youth and Adolescence*, *17*, 477–492.

Petersen, A.C. (1985). Pubertal development as a cause of disturbance: Myths, realities, and unanswered questions. *Genetic, Social, and General Psychology Monographs*, *111*, 205–232.

Petersen, A.C., & Crockett, L. (1985). Pubertal timing and grade effects on adjustment. *Journal of Youth and Adolescence*, *14*, 191–206.

Petersen, A.C., Crockett, L., Richards, M.H., & Boxer, A.M. (1988). A self-report measure of pubertal status: Reliability, validity, and initial norms. *Journal of Youth and Adolescence*, *17*, 117–133.

Petersen, A.C., Sarigiani, P.A., & Kennedy, R.E. (1991). Adolescent depression: Why more girls? *Journal of Youth and Adolescence*, *20*, 247–271.

Petersen, A.C., & Taylor, B. (1980). The biological approach to adolescence: Biological change and psychological adaptation. In J. Adelson (Ed.), *Handbook of adolescent psychology* (pp. 117–155). New York: John Wiley & Sons.

Richards, M., & Petersen, A.C. (1987). Biological theoretical models of adolescent development. In V. B. Van Hasselt, & M. Hersen (Eds.), *Handbook of adolescent psychology* (pp. 34–52). New York: Pergamon.

Rogol, A.D., Roemmich, J.N., & Clark, P.A. (2002). Growth at puberty. *Journal of Adolescent Health*, *31*, 192–200.

Rutter, M. (1986). The developmental psychopathology of depression: Issues and perspectives. In M. Rutter, C. E. Izard, & P. B. Read (Eds.), *Depression in young people: Developmental and clinical perspectives* (pp. 3–30). New York: Guilford.

Savin-Williams, R.C., & Small, S.A. (1986). The timing of puberty and its relationship to adolescent and parent perceptions of family interactions. *Developmental Psychology, 22*, 342–347.

Schölmerich, A. (1996). Frühe Kindheitserfahrungen und Eintritt in die Reifezeit [Early childhood experiences and entry into the age of maturation]. In R. Schumann-Hengsteler, & H. M. Trautner (Eds.), *Entwicklung im Jugendalter* (pp. 41–56). Göttingen, Germany: Hogrefe.

Siegel, J.M., Yancey, A.K., Aneshensel, C.S., & Schuler, R. (1999). Body image, perceived pubertal timing, and adolescent mental health. *Journal of Adolescent Health, 25*(2), 155–165.

Silbereisen, R.K., Petersen, A.C., Albrecht, H.T., & Kracke, B. (1989). Maturational timing and the development of problem behavior: Longitudinal studies in adolescence. *Journal of Early Adolescence, 9*, 247–268.

Simmons, R.G., & Blyth, D.A. (1987). *Moving into adolescence: The impact of pubertal change and school context.* New York: Aldine de Gruyter.

Simmons, R.G., Blyth, D.A., Van Cleave, E.F., & Bush, D.M. (1979). Entry into early adolescence: The impact of school structure, puberty and early dating on self-esteem. *American Sociological Review, 44*, 948–967.

Speltini, G. (1996, August). *Boys and girls at puberty: Their representation of physical and psychosocial development.* Paper presented at the XIVth Biennial Meetings of the International Society for the Study of Behavioural Development, Quebec City, Canada.

Stattin, H., & Magnusson, D. (1990). *Pubertal maturation in female development.* Hillsdale, NJ: Lawrence Erlbaum Associates, Inc.

Steinberg, L. (1981). Transformations in family relations at puberty. *Developmental Psychology, 17*, 833–840.

Steinberg, L. (1987). Impact of puberty on family relations: Effects of pubertal status and pubertal timing. *Developmental Psychology, 23*, 451–460.

Steinberg, L. (1988). Reciprocal relation between parent–child distance and pubertal maturation. *Developmental Psychology, 24*, 122–128.

Steinberg, L. (1989). *Adolescence* (2nd ed.). New York: McGraw-Hill.

Surbey, M.K. (1990). Family composition, stress, and the timing of human menarche. In T. E. Zeigler, & F. B. Bercovitch (Eds.), *Socioendocrinology of primate reproduction* (pp. 11–32). New York: John Wiley & Sons.

Susman, E.J., Dorn, L.D., & Chrousos, G.P. (1991). Negative affect and hormone levels in young adolescents: Concurrent and predictive perspectives. *Journal of Youth and Adolescence, 20*, 167–190.

Susman, E.J., Dorn, L.D., & Schiefelbein, V.L. (2003). Puberty, sexuality and health. In I.B. Weiner, R. M. Lerner, M. A. Easterbrooks, & J. Mistry (Eds.), *Handbook of psychology: Vol 6. Developmental psychology* (pp. 295–324). Hoboken, NJ: John Wiley & Sons.

Susman, E.J., Inoff-Germain, G., Nottelmann, E.D., Loriaux, D.L., Cutler, G.B., Jr., & Chrousos, G.P. (1987). Hormones, emotional dispositions, and aggressive attributes in young adolescents. *Child Development, 58*, 1114–1134.

Susman, E.J., Nottelmann, E.D., Inoff-Germain, G.E., Dorn, L.D., Cutler, G.B., Jr., Loriaux, D.L. et al. (1985). The relation of relative hormonal levels and physical development and social–emotional behavior in young adolescents. *Journal of Youth and Adolescence, 14*, 245–264.

Tanner, J.M. (1962). *Growth at adolescence.* Oxford: Blackwell.

Tanner, J.M. (1972). Sequence, tempo, and individual variation in growth and development of boys and girls aged twelve to sixteen. In J. Kagan, & R. Coles (Eds.), *Twelve to sixteen: Early adolescence* (pp. 1–24). New York: Norton.

Tanner, J.M. (1989). *Foetus into man: Physical growth from conception to maturity* (2nd ed.). Cambridge, MA: Harvard University Press.

Tobin-Richards, M.H., Boxer, A.M., & Petersen, A.C. (1983). The psychological significance of pubertal change: Sex differences in perceptions of self during early adolescence. In J. Brooks-Gunn, & A. C. Petersen (Eds.), *Girls at puberty: Biological and psychological perspectives* (pp. 127–154). New York: Plenum.

Udry, J.R., Billy, J.O.G., Morris, N.M., Groff, T.R., & Raj, M.H. (1985). Serum androgenic hormones motivate sexual behavior in adolescent boys. *Fertility and Sterility, 43*, 90–94.

Udry, J.R., & Talbert, L.M. (1988). Sex hormone effects on personality at puberty. *Journal of Personality and Social Psychology, 54*, 291–295.

Wichstrøm, L. (2001). The impact of pubertal timing on adolescents' alcohol use. *Journal of Research on Adolescence, 11*, 131–150.

Wiesner, M., & Ittel, A. (2002). Relations of pubertal timing and depressive symptoms to substance use in early adolescence. *Journal of Early Adolescence, 22,* 5–23.

Zakin, D.F., Blyth, D.A., & Simmons, R.G. (1984). Physical attractiveness as a mediator of the impact of early pubertal changes for girls. *Journal of Youth and Adolescence, 13,* 439–450.

4

Affect, emotion, and loneliness in adolescence

Luc Goossens

This chapter concentrates on emotions in adolescence and will devote special attention to loneliness, an emotion often associated with that stage of life. Adolescents' lonely plight cannot be discussed without reference to solitude, a notion that is related to yet distinct from loneliness. Throughout this chapter, considerable attention will be given to the interactive and socio-cultural context of emotions. It will be emphasized that emotions are typically experienced within relationships and that feelings of loneliness, for instance, can take on a different form in different types of relationship. Results of European studies on adolescent emotions and loneliness will be referred to, whenever available, and cross-cultural differences in loneliness will be discussed.

1. Adolescent emotions

Research over the past two decades, conducted exclusively with American samples, has provided

unique insights into the emotional world of adolescence. Using a non-intrusive method, researchers have empirically tested a classical theory of adolescent emotionality and have examined the determinants and adjustment consequences of adolescent emotions.

1.1 The "storm and stress" theory of adolescent emotionality

Increased emotionality is part and parcel of the "storm and stress" theory that the general public holds about adolescence. The essence of this theory is the idea that adolescence is a difficult period of life. The notion of "storm and stress" was introduced into scientific psychology by G. Stanley Hall (1904), who maintained that adolescents oscillate continually between emotional extremes. Psychoanalytic theorists concurred with this view and even described increased emotionality in adolescents as a normal and adaptive state of affairs. (See Chapter 2, Theories of adolescence, in this volume.)

The general public typically endorses a somewhat broader version of the "storm and stress" theory, which includes three key elements. In essence, this version of the theory states that adolescents (a) tend to experience mood disruptions, (b) have frequent conflicts with their parents, and (c) have higher rates of risk behaviors, including acts of delinquency, than children. Empirical research has long shown that several key elements of this stereotypical view of adolescence do not apply to all adolescents or even to the majority of them. Most adolescents, for instance, have a positive relationship with their parents. The original core of Hall's (1904) "storm and stress" theory, however – increased emotionality – had received less systematic attention in empirical research, until recently (Arnett, 1999).

In common parlance, adolescents are said to suffer from increased emotionality or to be more moody than children and adults. On closer inspection, the term "moodiness" can have two different meanings. The term can imply that the frequency of negative emotions (e.g., feeling sad or angry) increases during adolescence (Larson, 1991). A second possible meaning of the term is that adolescents experience greater emotional variability than do other age groups. This means that they experience greater mood swings or tend to experience both emotional highs and emotional lows more frequently than do children and adults. A central feature of lay conceptions of adolescent "storm and stress", finally, is that adolescent moodiness, whichever way defined, has a biological origin in the hormonal changes of puberty.

1.2 Measuring adolescent affect
In recent years, adolescents' emotions or immediate affects have been studied using the experience sampling method (ESM; Csikszentmihalyi & Larson, 1987; Larson, 1989). The participants in ESM studies are asked to carry an electronic pager (or "beeper") and a booklet of self-reports for a week. At random points in time during that week, they are sent an electronic signal (typically one "beep" per 2-hour block). At the signal, they

are to describe on the self-report form (a) their objective situation (e.g., where they are, what they are doing, and whom they are with), and (b) their subjective states (e.g., their emotions and motivation). Because the typical participant completes about 40 self-reports over the course of a week, the experience sampling method presents researchers with a representative sample of the daily life of that individual, a sample that is obtained with minimal intrusion in his or her daily activities.

1.3 Research on adolescent emotions
When ESM is used with rather large groups of adolescents, reliable estimates of their average emotional state and accompanying variability can be obtained and compared to the emotional states experienced by children and adults. Participants use six seven-point scales (ranging from −3 to +3) when describing their affective states. These scales are: happy–sad, irritable–cheerful, friendly–angry, alert–drowsy, strong–weak, and excited–bored. Participants' scores are recoded in such a way that higher scores reflect more positive affect.

1.3.1 Frequency of negative emotions
Research (Larson & Lampman-Petraitis, 1989) indicates that early adolescents have a lower average value on the six affect scales than do children at the end of elementary school. Young people, therefore, increasingly experience negative emotions across the transition from childhood to adolescence, as predicted by the "storm and stress" theory of adolescent emotionality. Inspection of the frequency with which children and adolescents use each of the seven points on these scales gives a somewhat more detailed view of these age-related changes. The greatest age differences occurred for the extremely positive scale points (+2 and +3), which were used much less frequently by adolescents as compared to children (Larson & Lampman-Petraitis, 1989). This shift was part of a broader "fall from grace", or a "general deflation of childhood happiness" (Larson & Richards, 1994a, p. 85) in which adolescents also felt "great" and "proud" much less often. An additional finding was that the mildly

negative scale points (−2 and −1) were used slightly more frequently by adolescents than by children. The findings, therefore, provide support for a modified "storm and stress" theory. Adolescents' average affect is slightly more negative than children's average score, as expected. This result, however, is caused by a reduction of positive feelings and a slight increase of mildly rather than strong negative feelings.

Additional research on older adolescents (Larson, Moneta, Richards, & Wilson, 2002a) revealed that late adolescence is associated with a slowing of the emotional changes of early adolescence. The characteristic downward shift in emotions in early adolescence, in the direction of more negative and fewer extreme positive states, does not continue into late adolescence.

1.3.2 Variability
Emotional variability can be captured by individuals' standard deviation on each of the six affect scales (computed across all self-reports obtained from a given individual). A comparison of adolescents and adults indicated that the former group had significantly higher standard deviations, on average, than the latter (Larson, Csikszentmihalyi, & Graef, 1980). However, a comparison between children in the upper grades in elementary school and adolescents in the first three grades in secondary school failed to yield significant differences in standard deviations on any of the six scales (Larson & Lampman-Petraitis, 1989). These findings suggest that the emotional variability of early adolescence is largely a continuation of a childhood condition, not a new phenomenon associated with this age period (Larson, 1991). Additional longitudinal research on older adolescents (Larson et al., 2002) suggested that this variability may not continue into late adolescence. Emotional variability at one point in time showed only a modest correlation with emotional variability four years later. With increasing age, there was also greater stability among youth in their relative levels of emotionality.

One may well wonder, then, why increased emotionality, defined as greater mood swings, has been included in the popular notion of adolescent

"storm and stress". A possible explanation, of course, is that mood swings are simply tolerated or endured more easily when parents and other adults are dealing with children. Put differently, adults expect greater emotional maturity or equanimity when interacting with early adolescents and get annoyed when these expectations are not being met, hence the stereotype of greater emotional variability in adolescence.

1.3.3 Associations with psychological adjustment
Correlations between emotional intensity (or average affect) and emotional variability (or standard deviation) and psychological adjustment were examined using established self-report measures of both internalizing problems (such as the children's depression inventory, CDI; Kovacs, 1992) and externalizing problems (such as the externalizing subscale of the youth self-report form, YSR; Achenbach, 1991). Both the frequency of negative emotions and emotional variability were associated with either type of problem behaviors. Adolescents who reported more negative emotions and more labile emotions reported more depressive symptoms (Larson, Raffaelli, Richards, Ham, & Jewell, 1990; Silk, Steinberg, & Morris, 2003) and more externalizing problem behaviors (such as anti-social behavior; Silk et al., 2003). Less effective regulation of these emotions (as assessed through an adaptation of the ESM procedure) were also related to adolescent adjustment. Adolescents who more frequently used disengagement (such as denial) and involuntary engagement strategies (such as rumination or acting impulsively) reported more depressive symptoms and externalizing problem behaviors (Silk et al., 2003). In sum, it appears that increased moodiness and failure to regulate these emotions in appropriate ways represents a non-specific risk factor for the development of psychopathology in adolescence (Steinberg & Avenevoli, 2000).

1.4 Possible explanations
In addition to pubertal development, as emphasized in the "storm and stress" theory, a whole series of potential determinants of the early

adolescent shift toward more negative emotions has been examined. These determinants refer to both individual characteristics and contextual influences.

1.4.1 Pubertal development

Contrary to popular belief, few associations were obtained between pubertal status or pubertal timing, on the one hand, and early adolescents' average emotional state and emotional variability, on the other. No significant effects were found for girls (Richards & Larson, 1993). These findings are in line with earlier research using classical, "one-time" assessments of adolescent affect (Brooks-Gunn & Warren, 1989; Buchanan, Eccles, & Becker, 1992; Inoff-Germain, Arnold, Susman, Nottelmann, Cutler, & Chrousos, 1988). Some positive effects emerged for boys. Boys who were more advanced in pubertal maturation or went through the changes of puberty earlier than their agemates did, experienced more positive affect and reported more frequently that they felt strong. These findings may reflect the benefits that a more athletic body has for adolescent boys (Richards & Larson, 1993). Taken together, the results for girls and boys are in line with a well-established fact on the effects of puberty, that is, that the effects of hormonal changes tend to be small and exist only in interaction with other, socio-cultural factors (Brooks-Gunn, Graber, & Paikoff, 1994; Susman, 1997). (See Chapter 3, Pubertal maturation, in this volume.)

1.4.2 Cognitive processing

The cognitive changes of adolescence can also offer a partial explanation for the age changes in negative emotionality. As adolescents reach the stage of formal operations, they can think about their own experiences in novel and more abstract ways. This is illustrated in an ESM study in which participants were invited to describe the reasons for strong emotional states in somewhat greater detail. Careful content coding of these descriptions revealed that the events described frequently dealt with mildly negative emotions (such as feeling hurt, disappointed, or mad). A common feature of these emotions is that expectations are not being met (Larson & Asmussen, 1991).

Children tend to explain such events by referring to the concrete, immediate situation (e.g., they simply put the blame on the other partner in the interaction). Adolescents give more complex explanations that pertain to relationships and to other people's feelings. Adolescents can also acknowledge multiple levels of meaning and ambiguities, which make their problems seem worse than the interpersonal frictions reported by children. Adolescents are also confronted with novel sets of expectations and with the emergence of romantic attachments in particular. Typical descriptions of these affectively charged events by young adolescent females, therefore, read something like: "I am mad at Melissa because she seemed so close with Kevin (whom I greatly fancy myself)."

The idea that greater cognitive sophistication can lead to increased levels of negative emotions was confirmed in studies using other methodologies than ESM. Hauser and Safyer (1994) examined associations between emotions revealed during a semi-structured interview and ego development. Adolescents who were functioning at a higher level of ego development, which entailed that they were more aware of the complexities of personal relationships, exhibited more diverse emotions and more anxiety.

The results of these studies can be interpreted using differential emotions theory (DIT; Abe & Izard, 1999). This theory holds that each emotion has distinct motivational properties and serves different adaptive functions. A developmental extension of the theory posits that certain emotions become more prominent in particular periods of life such as adolescence. It is as if the complexity of certain emotional reactions is truly understood for the first time because of the cognitive abilities that emerge in that period.

1.4.3 Important life events

Increased negative emotionality in adolescents seems to be due, at least in part, to environmental causes. Analyses of major life events in young people's life, as reported by the child and a parent, revealed that young adolescents encountered more negative life events than did children. These negative events occurred in the domains of family (e.g., get along worse with a parent), friends (e.g., broke up with a boyfriend/girlfriend), and school (e.g., changed schools). Young people who experienced more negative events experienced a greater frequency of negative states. Additional analyses indicated that accumulation of negative life events had a stronger association with daily negative affect among adolescents than among children (Larson & Ham, 1993). The association between the number of negative life events encountered and average affect also held for older adolescents (Larson et al., 2002). Because the average number of negative life events experienced increases from late childhood to adolescence and tends to level off or even decreases in late adolescence, this factor may explain, at least in part, the age trends observed in adolescent emotionality (i.e., the downward shift in early adolescence, followed by a leveling off from mid-adolescence onwards).

1.4.4 Interactive contexts

A final explanation of negative emotions in adolescence, which is not incompatible with earlier explanations, is that emotions are experienced within the context of social relationships. More specifically, processes of emotional transmission may occur within the family. This explanation was examined in an ESM study in which the target adolescent and both their mother and father were asked to carry electronic pagers for a week and were beeped all three at the same points in time (Larson & Richards, 1994a, 1994b).

The analyses, of course, have to be restricted to those cases in which (a) both parties (i.e., adolescent–mother or adolescent–father) completed an ESM form twice within a brief period of time (in two consecutive time blocks) and (b) one or both of the parties reported being with the other for at least one of these reports. In time-series analyses, correlations or regression equations can be computed between affect at Time 1 and Time 2, as experienced by the two parties involved (Larson & Almeida, 1999). Cases in which one party's emotion at one report in time predicts the other party's emotion at the next report (e.g., father's affect at Time 1 predicts adolescent's affect at Time 2 or adolescent's affect at

Time 1 predicts mother's affect at Time 2) point to processes of emotional transmission in the family.

Analyses in two-parent families revealed that father's affect at Time 1 significantly predicted son's and mother's affect at Time 2. This effect also held when the analyses were restricted to those cases in which father was at work at Time 1 (Larson & Richards, 1994a). This finding indicates that fathers' emotions at work influence the emotions experienced by other family members at subsequent times (which is not the case for working mothers; Larson & Richards, 1994a). Emotional transmission also took place from the younger generation to the older one. Daughters' affect at Time 1 predicted both mothers' and fathers' affect at Time 2 (Larson & Richards, 1994b).

In one-parent, mother-headed families, there was a significant path from mothers' anxiety and anger at Time 1 to adolescents' anxiety and anger at Time 2. This effect only held for sequences of events within the family. Several factors moderated the emotional transmission of negative emotions in one-parent families. Emotional transmission was less pronounced when mother had more time to herself and more pronounced when mother experienced greater stress (because of her busy schedule) and when she used certain coercive parenting techniques (Larson & Gillman, 1999).

1.5 Conclusion: "Storm and stress" revisited

Experience sampling or "beeper" studies have failed to confirm the "storm and stress" theory of adolescent emotionality as originally developed by Hall (1904) and endorsed by the general public. Increased emotionality was only found in mild forms among adolescents and proved to be unrelated to the biological changes of puberty. However, a series of other contributing factors was identified, such as encountering more negative life events, interpreting interpersonal frictions in more negative terms, and being exposed more frequently to transmission of negative affect within the family. Particularly when adolescents cannot find adequate ways in which to regulate the emotions associated with those factors (Silk et al., 2003), they are at risk for depressed moods and various types of problem behaviors. This configuration of factors may explain, at least in part, why an estimated one-third of adolescents experience depressed moods at any given time. Depressed moods, in turn, are important precursors of clinical depression (Petersen, Compas, Brooks-Gunn, Stemmler, Ey, & Grant, 1993).

Researchers, therefore, can support a modified version of the "storm and stress" theory of adolescent emotionality. It is certainly not the case that all adolescents suffer from increased emotionality. However, emotional problems such as increased frequency of negative emotions can lead to depressed moods in adolescence, if and when certain conditions apply (Arnett, 1999).

2. Adolescent loneliness and solitude

In this part of the chapter, the concepts of loneliness and solitude (or aloneness), which are often confused with one another in the literature, are carefully distinguished. The measures used to assess each construct are briefly described, the most important age trends in adolescence are summarized for both constructs, and their respective sets of correlates are reviewed.

2.1 Conceptual distinctions

At the purely conceptual level, loneliness and solitude can be readily distinguished. Loneliness is a subjective feeling. It is typically defined as "the upleasant experience that occurs when a person's network of social relationships is deficient in some important way, either qualitatively or quantitatively" (Perlman & Peplau, 1981, p. 31). Loneliness, therefore, results from a discrepancy between the desired level of quality of one's relationships and the level that is actually experienced. When a person's relationships do not live up to his or her expectations, that person will feel lonely. Solitude (or aloneness), by contrast, refers to an objective situation, that is, the mere fact of having no one else around. In technical terms, it is typically defined in terms of communicative isolation from others (Larson, 1990). People are alone when they cannot exchange information or affect with other people. Viewed in this way, an

adolescent would not be alone in a solitary house when conversing with another adolescent on the phone, because there is exchange of information.

In many studies, however, the distinction between the subjective feeling of loneliness and the objective state of being alone is somewhat blurred. The main reason for this confusion is that people often feel lonely when they are alone, even though they can feel lonely in a crowd just as well. Many people will also state that they feel alone and researchers often examine subjective attitudes toward time spent alone, rather than the mere incidence of solitude or the average experience of time spent on one's own. These qualifications notwithstanding, it is important to keep in mind the conceptual distinction between loneliness and solitude throughout the remainder of this chapter.

2.2 Loneliness: Assessment, age trends, and correlates

2.2.1 Assessment

In studies on North American adolescents, loneliness is typically measured by means of the UCLA loneliness scale (Russell, Peplau, & Cutrona, 1980). (The acronym "UCLA" stands for the University of California at Los Angeles, where the instrument was developed originally.) In this unidimensional measure, loneliness is conceived of as a unitary phenomenon that takes on essentially the same form across relationships or social contexts and varies only in intensity. All items of this scale, therefore, refer to the generalized other (using terms such as "people" or "others"). In line with the conceptual definition of loneliness, some items contain (mostly implicit) evaluations of one's relationships (e.g., "I feel in tune with the people around me"; reverse scored), whereas others directly tap the negative feelings of abandonment associated with negative evaluations of one's relationships (e.g., "I feel isolated from others"; Shaver & Brennan, 1991).

2.2.2 Age trends

Classical theories of loneliness have assigned special importance to adolescence, or the age period immediately preceding it. According to Sullivan (1953), the full scope of loneliness can only be experienced from pre-adolescence onwards. Based on his own experience of that age period (Evans, 1996), Sullivan maintained that the emergent capacity for intimacy can be fulfilled in a deeply rewarding relationship with a same-sex peer or "chum". However, if no such relationship can be established during that same period, a deep-felt sense of loneliness can ensue. Sullivan's view has long been abandoned, because subsequent research (Asher, Hymel, & Renshaw, 1984; Rotenberg & Hymel, 1999) has revealed that children can and do feel lonely at times and can accurately describe what loneliness is (Galanaki, 2004). However, adolescence continues to be regarded as a period of life when loneliness is particularly prevalent.

Adequate comparisons of the incidence of loneliness across broad age categories (e.g., children, adolescents, adults, and the elderly) are rare. But several surveys reveal that high percentages of adolescents (ages 12 to 18) report feeling lonely (Brennan, 1982). Several reasons are invoked to explain this high level of loneliness during adolescence (the meaning and relevance of which is unclear in the absence of good comparative data across age categories). These factors include a reorganization of the attachment system (with the main emphasis shifting from parents to peers and ultimately to an opposite-sex partner; Weiss, 1982), active exploration regarding identity issues (Brennan, 1982; Perlman, 1988), and sheer accumulation of developmental changes (e.g., pubertal changes, novel social expectations, and cognitive changes; Ostrov & Offer, 1980). Because issues of attachment and identity are gradually resolved throughout adolescence and age-normative changes tend to accumulate at the onset of adolescence, loneliness can be expected to peak in early adolescence and to gradually decrease thereafter.

Using the UCLA scale, several authors have managed to confirm the expected decreasing age trend in adolescent loneliness. Mahon (1983) found that early adolescents (13 years of age) scored significantly higher than did mid- and late adolescents (15 and 20 years of age, respectively).

In another study, middle adolescents (17 years of age) were found to score higher than did college students (19 years; Schultz & Moore, 1988).

2.2.3 Correlates

Research on the correlates of adolescent loneliness has concentrated on college students and typically lacks a strong developmental orientation. Three theoretical frameworks have guided the search for empirical correlates of loneliness (see Marangoni & Ickes, 1989, and Goossens & Marcoen, 1994, for a review). Two of these approaches can directly be related to the conceptual definition of loneliness. Some authors claim that loneliness ensues when important social needs are not being met ("social needs" approach). Numerous studies concur that qualitative aspects of one's relational network (e.g., satisfaction or felt support) are far more important as predictors of loneliness than are purely quantitative aspects (e.g., frequency of contact). Other authors state that cognitive processes (e.g., comparison with internal standards of relational quality) generate feelings of loneliness and determine their full impact ("cognitive processes" approach). Adherents of this perspective have typically concentrated on lonely people's attribution style, that is, their characteristic way of explaining personally relevant events. Feelings of loneliness are more intense and last longer when their causes are perceived as uncontrollable by the individual.

The "social behavior and personality" approach is less intimately related to the conceptual definition of loneliness, but has strong intuitive appeal. It basically states that lonely individuals behave in ways that inadvertently make them into less interesting partners in social interaction (e.g., inappropriate approaches to self-disclosure). Characteristic aspects of their personality (such as low self-esteem or social anxiety) are thought to underly these reticent or clumsy behaviors (Jones & Carver, 1991; Jones, Rose, & Russell, 1990). In all probability, the three types of determinant, as identified in the social needs, cognitive processes, and social behavior and personality approaches, tend to go hand in hand and should be integrated into a comprehensive model of adolescent loneliness. In one study, for instance, college students felt less lonely if they were more satisfied with their relationships with their friends (social needs approach) and if they thought that they were capable of intimate relationships (social behavior and personality approach; Boldero & Moore, 1990).

2.3 Solitude: Assessment, age trends, and correlates

Unwanted solitude, as experienced during solitary confinement or extended periods of sensory deprivation is singularly unpleasant. Yet, solitude that is actively strived for can have a constructive role in psychological adjustment. Time spent on one's own can lead to greater insight, emotional self-renewal, and increased creativity in some people (Long & Averill, 2003; Storr, 1997; Suedfeld, 1982). For some people then, time spent on their own, provided that it is a voluntary and rewarding experience, can have positive effects on psychological adjustment. Developmental psychologists have asked themselves at which point in development individuals come to grasp those advantages of time alone and to use solitude as a constructive domain of experience. To investigate this issue, they (a) devised measures to capture people's experience of being alone, (b) charted the developmental course of these phenomena, and (c) examined the associations between time spent alone and its key correlate, that is, psychological adjustment. Adolescents' psychological well-being was assessed in those studies by means of parents' reports of problem behaviors, teachers' reports of classroom adjustment, objective measures such as school results (grade point average), and self-reported depression.

2.3.1 Assessment

How adolescents experience time on their own and how they feel about that particular "experiential niche" in their lives can be examined in at least three different ways. First, the percentage of time spent alone can be determined by means of the experience sampling method (ESM). Second, the average affect when alone can be estimated using the same method.

Finally, a person's attitude toward being alone can be determined by means of questionnaire measures, such as the preference for solitude scale (PSS; Burger, 1995) or sentence completion tests, such as the London sentence completion test (LSCT; Coleman, 1974). In the PSS, participants are asked to select the sentence that describes them best, either "I enjoy being with other people" or "I enjoy being by myself" (with the latter option reflecting greater preference for solitude). In sentence completion tests, participants have to complete sentence stems such as "When there is no one else around I . . ." and "If a person is alone . . .". The positive or negative nature of the endings they provide to these incomplete sentences give indications about their general attitude to being alone.

2.3.2 Age trends

Some authors claim that children are born with the need to be alone from time to time (Bucholz, 1997), learn to endure being alone while knowing that their mother is nearby (Winnicott, 1958), or gradually come to distinguish between feeling lonely and being alone (Galanaki, 2004). Other authors (Larson, 1997; Long & Averill, 2003; Marcoen & Goossens, 1993) have emphasized that important changes take place in experience of and attitude toward being alone during adolescence. Larson (1990) developed a lifespan theory of solitude in which he sketched the experience of being alone in childhood, adolescence, adulthood, and old age. Children rarely strive to be on their own and when they find themselves without company, they cannot seem to make constructive use of time spent alone. For adolescents, solitude begins to have conscious and deliberate functions (e.g., as an opportunity for privacy). Time alone probably increases greatly for emerging adults who are not married and live alone, but is greatly reduced for those who are married and have young children. Similarly, in middle adulthood, one has to adjust to the portion of solitude that is associated with one's roles and life situation. Academics, for instance, have to get used to long hours of solitary writing or studying. The old, finally, spend more time alone and feel more comfortable when alone than do younger age groups. From this theory, one may deduce that, as people grow older, they (a) spend a greater amount of time alone, (b) feel better when they effectively are on their own, and (c) adopt a more positive attitude toward being on their own.

Research using the ESM procedure indicates that the percentage of time alone does increase from childhood to adolescence. European–American adolescents spend about one-quarter of their waking hours physically alone. When time alone is expressed as a percentage of the participants' non-school time, fifth graders spent 24% of the time on their own, whereas seventh graders did so for 37% of the time (Larson & Richards, 1991). This trend is part of a broader set of changes in which overall time with parents decreases (Larson, Richards, Moneta, Holmbeck, & Duckett, 1996) and suggests that early adolescents who are not yet allowed to spent large amounts of time outside the parental home spent more time in the privacy of their own room. In other cultural groups, where the decrease in time spent with the family does not take place in early adolescence, such as African–American adolescents (Larson, Richards, Sims, & Dworkin, 2001) and adolescents in India (Larson, Verma, & Dworkin, 2002b), the increase in time spent alone is much smaller.

The average affect when alone, however, does not improve from Grade 5 through Grade 9 (Larson, 1997) in European–American adolescents. An additional finding in this regard is that, throughout adolescence, young people's affect is lower alone than when they are with others (Csikszentmihalyi & Larson, 1984; Larson & Richards, 1991). Additional research on adolescents from other cultural groups is in order here.

Adolescents' attitude toward being alone grows more positive with advancing age. Research on English (Coleman, 1974), New Zealand (Kroger, 1982), United States (Kroger, 1985), and Belgian adolescents (Goossens & Marcoen, 1999a) using sentence completion tasks have revealed that positive reactions to the sentence stems tend to increase as adolescents grow older, whereas negative reactions tend to decrease.

2.3.3 Correlates

The associations that the three types of measure have with psychological adjustment are somewhat variable. For the percentage of time spent alone, a curvilinear rather than the expected linear association with well-being was obtained. European–American adolescents who spent an intermediate amount of time on their own (e.g., between 25% and 45% of their non-class time) scored better on all measures of psychological well-being than the other two groups (who spent lower and higher amounts of time alone, respectively; Larson, 1997; Larson & Csikszentmihalyi, 1978). Additional analyses revealed that this curvilinear effect does not hold among children (Grades 5 to 6), but emerges in early adolescence (Grades 7 to 9). Finally, the curvilinear effect also failed to emerge among early adolescents in India (Larson et al., 2002b) and may, therefore, reflect a culturally specific finding.

Results regarding the affective experience of time spent alone depend on the type of analysis performed. When the absolute quality of experience of time spent alone is examined, (i.e., only time alone is attended to), the results are encouraging. The adolescents who reported more favorable affect when alone were better adjusted on all measures of psychological adjustment. However, a correction for the overall level of affective experience seems to impose itself, because some adolescents report low levels of positive affect across all relational contexts (i.e., both when they are with others *and* when they are alone), whereas other adolescents always report higher levels of positive affect, regardless of relational context.

When overall mean affect is included in the analysis, the significant relations with well-being disappear or negative associations are obtained (with depression, e.g.). Positive scores when correcting for the overall quality of experience across relational contexts indicate that adolescents feel better when alone than when they are in the company of others. The more they are inclined to feel that way, the more depressed they are. The statistical background for the reversal of effects when correcting for overall quality of affective experience is the strong positive correlation between overall affect and well-being (or put differently: between more negative average affect and problem behaviors, as decribed earlier in this chapter). The more positive the overall level of affect (across relational contexts), the higher the scores on well-being. These positive and negative effects (for absolute and relative experience of being alone, respectively) hold for children and adolescents (Larson, 1997).

Associations between attitude to being alone and adjustment have not been examined in adolescents. However, some questionnaire studies on adults have yielded interesting results. A measure of solitary comfort (which included items such as "I enjoy being by myself") was negatively related to depression and physical symptoms and positively to satisfaction with life (Larson & Lee, 1996). However, higher preference for being alone (assessed by means of the PSS) was associated with greater maladjustment (i.e., higher scores on social anxiety and alienation; Waskovic & Cramer, 1999). In line with the findings obtained for average affect when being alone, these results may reflect a difference between absolute attitudinal measures (which tap someone's positive attitude toward being alone) and relative attitudinal measures (which measure whether people's attitude to being alone is more positive than their attitude to being accompanied by others). Higher scores on absolute attitudinal measures may be beneficial, whereas higher scores on relative attitudinal measures (such as the PSS) are associated with lower levels of adjustment. Additional research on the link between solitude and adjustment among adolescents is certainly in order (Buchholz & Catton, 1999).

Data obtained with the experience sampling method (ESM) further indicate that time spent alone can have short-term positive effects, in addition to its immediate effects, on adolescent experience. In a time-series analysis of hour-to-hour changes in affective states, adolescents reported feeling better after being alone. When analyzing average affect in two consecutive time blocks, one can compare two particular sequences of relational contexts. In one of these sequences, adolescents are alone at Time 1 and in the company of others at Time 2, whereas in the other sequence, they are in the company of others at both time points. When comparing average affect at Time 2 in those two sequences, adolescents feel somewhat better after being alone (Sequence 1) than at other comparable times (Sequence 2; Larson, 1997; Larson, Csikszentmihalyi, & Graef, 1982). This positive aftereffect of solitude does not hold for children, but emerges in early adolescence (Larson, 1997).

Summing up the results on adjustment effects of solitude, it seems that adolescents are well-advised to strike some sort of happy balance between two extreme options. Adolescents should be able to spend some time on their own, but excessive periods of time alone have deleterious effects on psychological adjustment. Feeling well when alone has positive effects on adjustment, but feeling comparatively better when alone has negative consequences. Research on adults suggests that a positive attitude toward being alone has positive consequences, but a preference for time spent alone over time spent in the company of others may have negative effects on adjustment as well. The findings on positive aftereffects of time spent alone on subsequent mood presents some sort of a paradox (Larson, 1999). The immediate experience of solitude is tinged with negative emotions among adolescents and does not improve as adolescents grow older. Yet, like a bitter-tasting but salutary medicine, solitude seems to have a positive aftereffect on adolescents' emotional state.

By way of a general conclusion, one may state that adolescence is the phase of life when some young people begin to use time alone constructively. Several factors may account for the observed age differences in adolescent solitude. First, advanced reasoning skills (formal operations) may allow adolescents to think about and use solitude in ways that had been unavailable to them in the past. Solitude may be used for self-reflection, coping, and emotional self-regulation. Second, developmental changes in adolescents' social relationships may make solitude more useful to adolescents. Relationships with parents are being re-evaluated and relationships with peers take on new and initially tentative forms. In this context of shifting allegiances, solitude may provide a much-needed opportunity to relax and step back from social life. Third, solitude may be instrumental in the ongoing adolescent process of identity formation, as different identity options may be actively considered and worked through during periods of solitude. In all three ways, adolescents' solitude is a valuable resource because it represents a strategic retreat from an active social life that complements healthy adjustment in other social domains of daily life (Larson, 1997). This conclusion should not obscure the fact that solitude during adolescence can have both positive and negative implications for psychological adjustment. Future research may re-address this seemingly dual nature of time spent alone in adolescence by differentiating healthy forms of solitude from unhealthy forms (Larson, 1997).

3. Integrating research on adolescent loneliness and solitude: A European research program

As a complement to North American research on loneliness and solitude (as described in previous sections of this chapter), a research program was initiated in Europe, in the Dutch-speaking part of Belgium (Marcoen & Goossens, 1993). Key features of the program are its more complex approach to measuring loneliness and related phenomena and its strong developmental orientation. The latter is exemplified in the strong emphasis on normative age trends in loneliness and on associations that loneliness holds with core developmental phenomena in adolescence.

3.1 A multidimensional measure

The development of the loneliness measure used in the research program was inspired by two basic ideas. First, it was hypothesized that different levels of loneliness can be experienced in different relationships. Children and adolescents, for instance, may feel very satisfied with their relationships with their parents, but may feel lonely in their relationships with their peers. Separate subscales were therefore developed in which each item explicitly referred to either parents or peers (rather than to the generalized other, as is done in the unidimensional UCLA loneliness scale). Second, it was thought vital to measure both

loneliness and attitude toward solitude. Based on earlier work using sentence completion tests, an attempt was made to tap both positive and negative attitudes to being alone.

Information on adolescent attitude toward being alone was considered crucial because it could help to place adolescents' scores on the loneliness subscales in a somewhat broader perspective. Specifically, adolescents' attitude toward being alone were thought to moderate the relation between solitude and the experience of loneliness. An adolescent's affinity for aloneness could act as a buffer against feeling lonely when alone. Conversely, adolescents' aversion to aloneness might increase their vulnerability to feeling lonely when alone (Goossens & Beyers, 2002).

The measure designed in accordance with the program's conceptual framework, the Louvain loneliness scale for children and adolescents (LLCA; Marcoen, Goossens, & Caes, 1987), contains four subscales. These scales measure (a) loneliness in the relationships with parents (e.g., "I feel left out by my parents"), (b) loneliness in the relationships with peers (e.g., "I feel sad because I have no friends"), (c) aversion to aloneness (e.g., "When I am alone, I feel bad"), and (d) affinity for aloneness (e.g., "I want to be alone"), respectively.

Several studies have concentrated on the distinctiveness of these four subscales. Low intercorrelations have been obtained among all four of them. This finding implies that parent- and peer-related loneliness do represent two distinct forms of loneliness and that, in the absence of a strong negative correlation between aversion to and affinity for aloneness, the latter constructs are not to be considered as opposites (Marcoen et al., 1987). Each of these scales probes largely independent aspects of adolescents' attitude toward being alone. Construct validity of the four scales was established in that each subscale was associated with theoretically relevant criterion measures in its own specific way (Marcoen & Goossens, 1993). Confirmatory factor analysis (CFA) using a broad set of alternative measures of the constructs also indicated that each subscale does indeed tap a separate construct, as hypothesized (Goossens & Beyers, 2002).

3.2 Normative developmental trends

Each of the subscales was found to exhibit a specific developmental trend (Marcoen & Goossens, 1993). Across a broad age range (Grades 5 through 11), parent-related loneliness showed a curvilinear trend. Average scores on this subscale decreased from Grade 5 to Grade 7 and then gradually increased again, most markedly between 15 and 18 years of age. Scores on the peer-related loneliness subscale decreased during adolescence, and particularly so in early adolescence. Adolescents' scores on the aversion to aloneness subscale exhibited a similar age trend (i.e., a gradual decline, which was most pronounced in early adolescence – Grades 5 through 7). The average age trend for the affinity for aloneness subscale was somewhat more complex. Earlier studies (e.g., Marcoen et al., 1987) across the entire age range (Grades 5 through 11) failed to yield significant age effects. Subsequent studies that covered a more limited age range found significant increases in affinity for aloneness, particularly between ages 15 and 18 (Marcoen & Goossens, 1993). With some caution, therefore, it may be inferred that peer-related loneliness and aversion to being alone decrease with advancing age, whereas parent-related loneliness and affinity for aloneness tend to increase throughout adolescence.

These average age trends confirm earlier findings with the unidimensional UCLA loneliness scale and with sentence completion tests on adolescent attitudes toward solitude (as described in earlier sections of this chapter). An important addition to the existing body of knowledge on adolescent loneliness, however, is the increasing trend in parent-related loneliness. As adolescents grow older, they are less satisfied with their relationships with their parents. Whether these age trends also hold in other European cultures is unclear at present. A recent study on Irish adolescents across a more restricted age range confirmed most of the age trends found in the Dutch-speaking part of Belgium, except for parent-related loneliness. In this group of younger adolescents a decrease in parent-related loneliness was found, which may represent the initial phase of a broader, curvilinear pattern of development

(de Roiste, 2000). Additional cross-cultural research is needed on this particular point.

3.3 Associations with developmental tasks in adolescence

Several suggestions in the literature about the developmental origins of adolescent loneliness and solitude were put to an empirical test within the multidimensional framework embodied in the LLCA. In these studies, differential patterns of association with key developmental variables have been obtained for most, if not all of the four subscales.

Because some authors (e.g., Weiss, 1982) maintain that loneliness emerges in adolescence because of a gradual transformation of the attachment system, adolescents' attachment style was related to their experience of loneliness and their attitude to being alone. Adolescents who were securely attached scored significantly lower on both parent- and peer-related loneliness than did their agemates with different, insecure attachment styles. Adolescents who were strongly dependent on their parents felt more negative about being on their own. Insecurely attached adolescents (who exhibited either avoidant or anxious–ambivalent attachment) felt more positive about being alone (Goossens, Marcoen, Van Hees, & Van De Woestijne, 1998).

Loneliness and solitude were also related to categorical and continuous measures of adolescent identity. Several authors (Larson, 1997; Perlman, 1988) hold that greater loneliness and a more positive attitude toward being alone will ensue, at least temporarily, as identity issues are increasingly being considered by the adolescent. When concentrating on interpersonal aspects of identity, theoretically meaningful differences emerged between four categorical types of identity or identity statuses (Marcia, 1980). Adolescents in the foreclosure status, who hold strong identity commitments which they failed to explore in depth because they typically adopted these viewpoints from their parents, obtained the lowest scores of all four types on parent-related loneliness. Adolescents in the diffusion status, who have weak identity commitments and do not actively explore different identity options, scored higher on the parent-related loneliness subscale than did the foreclosures. Diffusions also scored higher than the moratorium and achievement groups on peer-related loneliness. All three non-diffused groups may be considered to represent "stronger" types of identity because they exhibit strong commitments (foreclosures), active exploration (moratorium), or both (achievement; Marcoen & Goossens, 1993).

No significant associations were found with either aversion to or affinity for aloneness when categorical measures of identity were used (Marcoen & Goossens, 1993). However, when using continuous measures of identity commitment and exploration, a significant association was obtained between college students' affinity for aloneness and the degree to which they explored different identity options (Goossens & Marcoen, 1999b).

As a global evaluation of the ongoing European research program (described in this section), one may state that it effectively complements North American research on the topic through (a) its more complex view on measuring loneliness, aloneness, and their interrelations (and the multidimensional measure to match that conception), (b) its more inclusive picture of normative age trends in both loneliness and solitude, and (c) its empirical tests of associations that loneliness and solitude are presumed to hold with important developmental tasks of adolescence (such as continuing to be attached to parents and developing one's own identity).

However, the European program has failed to live up to its full promise, because the added value of the multidimensional approach to measuring loneliness and solitude has not been demonstrated convincingly. To do so, one would have to compare groups of adolescents with different patterns of scores on the four subscales and to show that they score differently in terms of general well-being, for instance. If adolescents' attitude toward being alone truly affects their experience of loneliness, one should find differences between, say adolescents who feel lonely but do not have an aversion to being alone and their agemates who feel lonely and simply cannot stand being on their own. Such a "person-oriented" or

clustering approach should inspire future steps in the research program.

4. Socio-cultural differences in loneliness

Studies on cross-cultural differences in loneliness have typically contrasted two types of culture. Various dichotomies are being used to capture the basic distinction between those two classes of culture. They are referred to as individualistic vs. collectivistic cultures (Triandis, 1995), as cultures having an independent vs. an interdependent orientation (Markus & Kitayama, 1991), or as atomistic societies vs. organic communities (Mijuskovic, 1992). In individualistic cultures, an independent construal of self is dominant. There is a stronger emphasis on an autonomous self that is relatively distinct from others in the environment. In collectivistic cultures, by contrast, an interdependent construal of self is dominant. There is much greater emphasis on the interrelatedness of the individual to others in the environment. Individualistic cultures are found in the United States, Canada, and Western Europe. Collectivistic cultures are found in Asia, Latin America, and Southern Europe. Most cross-cultural studies of loneliness in adolescence, therefore, have compared one culture from the first category to a culture from the second. These comparisons have concentrated on (a) the experience of loneliness, (b) its perceived causes, and (c) the way in which young people cope with loneliness.

4.1 Experience of loneliness

A general conception that inspired several studies on cross-cultural differences in loneliness is that cultures may differ in the average level of loneliness experienced, but that the correlates of loneliness in the different cultures are essentially the same (Jones, Carpenter, & Quintana, 1985). The second part of this assertion was confirmed in a study that found essentially the same set of variables to predict loneliness in the United States and in Puerto Rico. In both cultures, personality and interpersonal constructs (e.g., perceived lack of social skills and feelings of alienation) accounted for a substantial part of the variance in UCLA loneliness scores (Jones et al., 1985).

Cross-cultural differences in average level of loneliness, however, present greater problems to scholars of adolescence. At the conceptual level, it is hard to predict whether loneliness will be higher in one type of culture or another. In collectivistic cultures there is, generally speaking, a trend toward lesser loneliness, because a spirit of unity, interdependence, and reciprocal support is encouraged. However, when loneliness is experienced in that type of culture, it could take on a more extreme form (Mijuskovic, 1992). Based on the conceptual definition of loneliness, one would also expect higher levels of loneliness in collectivistic cultures, because the expectations or standards for relational quality will be higher in that type of culture, which implies that loneliness is more likely to emerge. Finally, cultural differences in linguistic tools to describe loneliness may also contribute to differences in average level of loneliness as experienced in different cultures (Jones et al., 1985).

At the empirical level, the results seem to depend on the type of loneliness measure used. In two studies that used the UCLA loneliness scale to compare college students from the United States to students from Puerto Rico (Jones et al., 1985) and from the People's Republic of China (Anderson, 1999), respectively, the students from the two collectivistic (i.e., non-North American) cultures scored significantly higher. The reverse held when an alternative, multidimensional measure of the experience of loneliness was used. Canadian high school students (aged 12 to 18) scored higher than their Portuguese agemates on emotional distress (e.g., feeling hurt), social inadequacy and alienation (e.g., feeling like a boring and uninteresting person) and interpersonal alienation (e.g., feeling unloved). These last results were believed to reflect a stronger tendency toward self-reflection regarding one's inner turmoil and to self-blaming when confronted with failure. Such a tendency, it was claimed, is more likely to emerge in individualistic cultures (Rokach & Neto, 2001).

4.2 Causes of loneliness

Research on the perceived causes of loneliness essentially takes two forms. A first approach is to relate people's general attributional style to the level of loneliness they experience. Adherents of this approach present adolescents with a narrative account of an interpersonal failure. Such a story reads as follows: "You have just attended a party for new students and failed to make any new friends." The participant is asked to select a reason from a list of potential causes for this interpersonal failure, ranging from lack of ability (e.g., "I am not good at meeting people at parties") to external circumstances (e.g., "Other circumstances (e.g., people, situations, etc.) produced the outcome"; Anderson, Jennings, & Arnoult, 1988). Participants' scores on the attribution measure, which reflect their general attributional style, are then related to their scores on standard measures of loneliness such as the UCLA loneliness scale. A second approach is to specifically ask the participants for the causes they believe to be at the origin of their feelings of loneliness, using an instrument specifically designed for that purpose.

Rather clear-cut differences across cultures can be expected when adopting the first approach (i.e., when examining general attributional style). In individualistic cultures, people tend to blame external circumstances for their occasional interpersonal failures. In this way, they can ward off feelings of loneliness. People in collective cultures, however, may be less inclined to attribute interpersonal failures to external circumstances, because that would threaten their perceptions of and ties to groups that are highly relevant to them. Instead, they would be more inclined to atttribute interpersonal failures to internal, stable, and uncontrollable causes (e.g., lack of ability). A style that is considered to be dysfunctional in Western cultures, therefore, seems to be more in keeping with the interdependent orientation in collectivistic cultures, where it may even represent the dominant pattern (Anderson, 1999).

A comparison of college students from the United States and from the People's Republic of China (Anderson, 1999) revealed that the latter group of students effectively referred to lack of ability more often than did the former one when explaining interpersonal failures. This difference in explanatory style largely explained the observed cross-cultural difference on the UCLA loneliness scale, with Chinese students scoring higher. That is, the difference between the two cultural groups was substantially reduced if differences in general attributional style across cultures were statistically controlled.

Additional analyses revealed that the correlations among the attribution variables and the loneliness scale were essentially the same in the two cultures. These findings indicate, therefore, that the dysfunctional attributional style, originally identified in individualistic cultures, has equally deleterious effects on feelings of loneliness in collectivistic cultures, where it is more prevalent (Anderson, 1999). This result is of course in keeping with the general notion that cultures differ in the average level of loneliness experienced, but that the correlates of loneliness in the different cultures are comparable.

Few theoretical predictions regarding cross-cultural differences can be advanced when using the second approach (i.e., when asking directly about the perceived causes of loneliness). Personal, relational, and situational causes of loneliness (Rokach, 1989) were distinguished in an exploratory study on Canadian and Portuguese high school students. Within this framework, Canadian adolescents were more inclined to point out personal inadequacies (e.g., lack of courage in social contacts) and deficient relationships from the past (e.g., having emotionally distant parents) as causes of their current loneliness than were their Portuguese counterparts. These findings were thought to reveal a stronger awareness of one's own contribution to loneliness and a lower level of cohesion within the family that characterizes individualistic cultures (Rokach & Neto, 2000a).

4.3 Coping with loneliness
In research on adults, four ways of coping with loneliness are typically distinguished. These coping strategies are referred to as:

- social contact (e.g., visiting someone or calling a friend)
- active solitude (e.g., engage in one's favorite hobby, such as reading or listening to music)
- distraction (e.g., spend money, go shopping)

- sad passivity (e.g., sit and think, watch TV).

Among these strategies, seeking social contact and active solitude were orginally considered the more active and therefore the more functional types of coping (Rubenstein & Shaver, 1982). Subsequent research, however, has suggested that passive coping styles (such as sad passivity) can also hold some adaptive potential, as a preparation for subsequent, more active forms of coping. These studies have led to a more process-oriented view on coping with loneliness.

In one three-stage model of coping (Rokach, 1990), for instance, passive coping strategies occupy a central place in the initial phases of coming to terms with loneliness. In the first phase (acceptance), lonely people adjust to their newly discovered plight and engage in various forms of solitary involvement (e.g., hobbies) and in reflexive solitude (e.g., sit and think in an effort to restructure the situation). In a second phase (transition), lonely people take stock and restructure their resources. They do so by either seeking professional help or by thinking about their relationships in a different way (e.g., coming to realize the importance of social relationships in life). In the third and final phase (reaching out), lonely people start building a new network of social relationships, which can involve both a rekindling of extant relationships (e.g., with family members) or the development of new relationships (e.g., romantic attachments). In addition to the strategies structured in the three phases of the coping process, a whole series of inadequate strategies can be distinguished (such as avoidance and social isolation).

Research on high school students in the United States has confirmed the potential value of sad passivity as a way of coping with loneliness, at least in the initial stages of the coping process. The proportion of sad passive activities (e.g., watching TV) seemed more important than the number of sad passive activities utilized. Sad passivity was used by both lonely and non-lonely adolescents, but the non-lonely adolescents resorted to this method only temporarily and as a preparation for a more active coping style (Van Buskirk & Duke, 1991).

Cross-cultural research on adolescent coping with loneliness is rare. The exploratory study of high school students from Canada and Portugal, which also used a measure of adolescents' coping styles, yielded findings that can be related to the three-phase model of coping with loneliness, and to the second, transitional phase in particular. Compared to the Portuguese sample, Canadian adolescents were more inclined to seek professional help, to pray more often, and to increase their attendance at religious services. In addition, they resorted to inadequate strategies (such as distancing and denial of the problem) more often than did their Portuguese agemates. The greater tendency to seek help from a professional or to seek answers to one's problems in prayer was seen as a typical aspect of North American cultures, such as the Canadian culture (Rokach & Neto, 2000b).

When considering the whole of the available research on cross-cultural differences in adolescent loneliness, it is clear that many issues remain unresolved. The empirical findings seem to depend on the type of loneliness measure used and on the way in which subjectively defined causes of loneliness are approached. In addition, one cannot escape the impression that it seems somewhat simplistic to describe cultures in terms of a single underlying dichotomy such as individualistic vs. collectivistic. In some studies, on cultural differences in coping with loneliness in particular, additional contrasts between the two cultures compared have already been invoked to explain the differences observed (e.g., differences in attitudes toward religion). This seems to suggest that the theoretical framework that opposes cultures with an independent and an interdependent construal of self, or atomistic societies and organic communities, can offer interesting suggestions at best. Additional research on cross-cultural differences in adolescent loneliness is definitely called for.

5. Conclusion

Through a set of complementary techniques (i.e., experience sampling method and traditional questionnaires), the available knowledge base on adolescents' emotional life has been expanded significantly during the last two decades. During that same period, psychologists have acquired a deeper insight into adolescent loneliness and solitude. As a result of these new insights, classical theories, such as the "storm and stress" theory of adolescent emotionality, have been revised substantially.

Increasing attention is being devoted to the relational context of adolescent emotions in general and adolescent loneliness in particular. Recent research on emotional transmission in the family and efforts to distinguish relationship-specific types of loneliness are cases in point here. The cultural context of adolescent loneliness and solitude has also been examined in some detail. In future research, greater attention could be paid to the fact that the meaning and significance attributed to time spent alone also differs substantially across cultures (Larson, 1999).

Comparable attention, however, should be devoted to cross-cultural differences in adolescent emotions. It seems unfortunate in this regard that most of the "beeper" research, which provides unique insights into adolescent emotions, has been conducted in the United States. Regarding emotions, it is well-known, for instance, that some cultures are characterized by greater emotional expressiveness, as compared to others. Different cultures may also organize their young people's lives in radically different ways. As all cultures make the transition from a pre-industrial to an industrial or post-industrial society, their youth is gradually freed from household and paid labor. However, there seems to be two patterns of reaction to this historical evolution. The typical Western reaction, as exemplified in the United States and Europe, has been to turn substantial amounts of this time over to young people themselves, which resulted in an increase in free time. The typical Eastern reaction, as exemplified in countries such as South Korea, has been to entrain much of this time in extra schoolwork (Larson & Verma, 1999). Differences in time use, average affect, and consequences for adolescent adjustment are bound to be associated with these two reactions. ESM research in countries such as South Korea (Lee & Larson, 2000) and India (Verma, Sharma, & Larson, 2002) has shown that adolescents in those cultures spend more time on their schoolwork and experienced more negative emotions, particularly while doing their homework. Spending more time on schoolwork was also related to more internalizing problems.

Finally, more research on European adolescents' time use and associated emotions is needed. Some studies using the experience sampling method (ESM; Della Fave & Bassi, 2000) or diary methods (Alsaker & Flammer, 1999) have provided information on European adolescents' time use and motivational states. But detailed analyses of changes in average affect or emotional lability across the transition to adolescence are currently still lacking. Even within the Western hemisphere, interesting differences in adolescent emotionality may obtain between cultures, and between North American and European cultures in particular.

References

Abe, J.A.A., & Izard, C.E. (1999). The developmental functions of emotions: An analysis in terms of differential emotions theory. *Cognition and Emotion*, *13*, 523–549.

Achenbach, T.M. (1991). *Manual for the Youth Self-Report and 1991 Profile*. Burlington: University of Vermont, Department of Psychiatry.

Alsaker, F.D., & Flammer, A. (Eds.) (1999). *The adolescent experience: European and American adolescents in the 1990s*. Mahwah, NJ: Lawrence Erlbaum Associates, Inc.

Anderson, C.A. (1999). Attributional style, depression, and loneliness: A cross-cultural comparison of American and Chinese students. *Personality and Social Psychology Bulletin*, *25*, 482–499.

Anderson, C.A., Jennings, D.L., & Arnoult, L.H. (1988). Validity and utility of the attributional style construct at a moderate level of specificity. *Journal of Personality and Social Psychology*, *55*, 979–990.

Arnett, J.J. (1999). Adolescent storm and stress, reconsidered. *American Psychologist*, *54*, 317–326.

Asher, S.R., Hymel, S., & Renshaw, P. (1984). Loneliness in children. *Child Development*, *55*, 1456–1464.

Boldero, J., & Moore, S. (1990). An evaluation of de Jong-Gierveld's loneliness model with Australian adolescents. *Journal of Youth and Adolescence*, *19*, 133–147.

Brennan, T. (1982). Loneliness at adolescence. In L. A. Peplau, & D. Perlman (Eds.), *Loneliness: A sourcebook of current theory, research and therapy* (pp. 269–290). New York: John Wiley & Sons.

Brooks-Gunn, K., Graber, J.A., & Paikoff, R.L. (1994). Studying links between hormones and negative affect: Models and measures. *Journal of Research on Adolescence*, *4*, 469–486.

Brooks-Gunn, J., & Warren, M.P. (1989). Biological and social contributions to negative affect in young adolescent girls. *Child Development*, *60*, 40–55.

Buchanan, C.M., Eccles, J.S., & Becker, J.B. (1992). Are adolescents the victims of raging hormones? Evidence for activational effects of hormones on mood and behavior at adolescence. *Psychological Bulletin*, *111*, 62–107.

Buchholz, E.S. (1997). *The call of solitude: Alonetime in a world of attachment*. New York: Simon & Schuster.

Buchholz, E.S., & Catton, R. (1999). Adolescents' perception of aloneness and loneliness. *Adolescence*, *34*, 203–213.

Burger, J.M. (1995). Individual differences in preference for solitude. *Journal of Research in Personality*, *29*, 85–108.

Coleman, J.C. (1974). *Relationships during adolescence*. London: Routledge.

Csikszentmihalyi, M., & Larson, R. (1984). *Being adolescent: Conflict and growth in the teenage years*. New York: Basic Books.

Csikszentmihalyi, M., & Larson, R. (1987). Validity and reliability of the experience sampling method. *Journal of Nervous and Mental Disease*, *175*, 526–536.

Delle Fave, A., & Bassi, M. (2000). The quality of experience in adolescents' daily lives: Developmental perspectives. *Genetic, Social, and General Psychology Monographs*, *126*, 347–367.

de Roiste, A. (2000). Peer- and parent-related loneliness in Irish adolescents. *Irish Journal of Psychology*, *21*, 237–246.

Evans, F.B. III (1996). *Harry Stack Sullivan: Interpersonal theory and psychotherapy*. London: Routledge.

Galanaki, E. (2004). Are children able to distinguish among the concepts of aloneness, loneliness, and solitude? *International Journal of Behavioral Development*, *28*, 435–443.

Goossens, L., & Beyers, W. (2002). Comparing measures of childhood loneliness: Internal consistency and confirmatory factor analysis. *Journal of Clinical Child and Adolescent Psychology*, *31*, 252–262.

Goossens, L., & Marcoen, A. (1994). Eenzaamheid in de adolescentie [Loneliness in adolescence]. In

J. D. Bosch, H. A. Bosma, D.N. Oudshoorn, J. Rispens, & A. Vyt (Eds.), *Jaarboek ontwikkelingspsychologie, orthopedagogiek en kinderpsychiatrie 1, 1994–1995* (pp. 190–210). Houten, The Netherlands: Bohn Stafleu Van Loghum.

Goossens, L., & Marcoen, A. (1999a). Relationships during adolescence: Constructive vs. negative themes and relational dissatisfaction. *Journal of Adolescence, 22*, 65–79.

Goossens, L., & Marcoen, A. (1999b). Adolescent loneliness, self-reflection, and identity: From individual differences to developmental processes. In K. J. Rotenberg, & S. Hymel (Eds.), *Loneliness in childhood and adolescence* (pp. 225–243). New York: Cambridge University Press.

Goossens, L., Marcoen, A., Van Hees, S., & Van De Woestijne, O. (1998). Attachment style and loneliness in adolescence. *European Journal of Psychology of Education, 13*, 529–542.

Hall, G.S. (1904). *Adolescence: Its psychology and its relation to physiology, anthropology, sociology, sex, crime, religion, and education*. New York: Appleton.

Hauser, S.T., & Safyer, A.W. (1994). Ego development and adolescent emotions. *Journal of Research on Adolescence, 4*, 487–502.

Inoff-Germain, G., Arnold, G.S., Susman, E.J., Nottelmann, E.D., Cutler, G.B. Jr., & Chrousos, G.P. (1988). Relations between hormone levels and observational measures of aggressive behavior of young adolescents in family interactions. *Developmental Psychology, 24*, 129–139.

Jones, W.H., Carpenter, B.N., & Quintana, D. (1985). Personality and interpersonal predictors of loneliness in two cultures. *Journal of Personality and Social Psychology, 48*, 1503–1511.

Jones, W.H., & Carver, M.D. (1991). Adjustment and coping implications of loneliness. In C. R. Snyder, & D. R. Forsyth (Eds.), *Handbook of social and clinical psychology: The health perspective* (pp. 395–415). New York: Pergamon.

Jones, W.H., Rose, J., & Russell, D. (1990). Loneliness and social anxiety. In H. Leitenberg (Ed.), *Handbook of social and evaluation anxiety* (pp. 247–266). New York: Plenum.

Kovacs, M. (1992). *Children's Depression Inventory: Manual.* North Tonawanda, NY: Multi-Health Systems.

Kroger, J. (1982). Relationships during adolescence: A developmental study of New Zealand youths. *New Zealand Journal of Educational Studies, 17*, 119–127.

Kroger, J. (1985). Relationships during adolescence: A cross-national comparison of New Zealand and United States teenagers. *Journal of Adolescence, 8*, 47–56.

Larson, R. (1989). Beeping children and adolescents: A method for studying time use and daily experience. *Journal of Youth and Adolescence, 18*, 511–530.

Larson, R.W. (1990). The solitary side of life: An examination of the time people spend alone from childhood to old age. *Developmental Review, 10*, 150–183.

Larson, R. (1991). Adolescent moodiness. In R. M. Lerner, A. C. Petersen, & J. Brooks-Gunn (Eds.), *Encyclopedia of adolescence* (pp. 658–662). New York: Garland.

Larson, R.W. (1997). The emergence of solitude as a constructive domain of experience in early adolescence. *Child Development, 68*, 80–93.

Larson, R.W. (1999). The uses of loneliness in adolescence. In K. J. Rotenberg, & S. Hymel (Eds.), *Loneliness in childhood and adolescence* (pp. 244–262). New York: Cambridge University Press.

Larson, R.W., & Almeida, D.M. (1999). Emotional transmission in the daily lives of families: A new paradigm for studying family process. *Journal of Marriage and the Family, 61*, 5–20.

Larson, R., & Asmussen, L. (1991). Anger, worry, and hurt in early adolescence: An enlarging world of negative emotions. In M. E. Colten & S. Gore (Eds.), *Adolescent stress: Causes and consequences* (pp. 21–41). New York: Aldine de Gruyter.

Larson, R., & Csikszentmihalyi, M. (1978). Experiential correlates of time alone in adolescence. *Journal of Personality, 46*, 677–693.

Larson, R., Csikszentmihalyi, M., & Graef, R. (1980). Mood variability and the psychosocial adjustment of adolescents. *Journal of Youth and Adolescence, 9*, 469–490.

Larson, R., Csikszentmihalyi, M., & Graef, R. (1982). Time alone in daily experience: Loneliness or renewal? In L.A. Peplau, & D. Perlman (Eds.), *Loneliness: A sourcebook of current theory, research and therapy* (pp. 40–53). New York: John Wiley & Sons.

Larson, R.W., & Gillman, S. (1999). Transmission of emotions in the daily interactions of single-mother families. *Journal of Marriage and the Family, 61*, 21–37.

Larson, R., & Ham, M. (1993). Stress and storm and stress in early adolescence: The relationship of negative events with dysphoric affect. *Developmental Psychology, 29*, 130–140.

Larson, R., & Lampman-Petraitis, C. (1989). Daily emotional states as reported by children and adolescents. *Child Development, 60*, 1250–1260.

Larson, R., & Lee, M. (1996). The capacity to be alone as a stress buffer. *Journal of Social Psychology, 136*, 5–16.

Larson, R.W., Moneta, G., Richards, M.H., & Wilson, S. (2002a). Continuity, stability, and change in daily emotional experience across adolescence. *Child Development, 73*, 1151–1165.

Larson, R., Raffaelli, M., Richards, M.H., Ham, M., & Jewell, L. (1990). Ecology of depression in late childhood and early adolescence: A profile of daily states and activities. *Journal of Abnormal Psychology, 99*, 92–102.

Larson, R., & Richards, M.H. (1991). Daily companionship in late childhood and early adolescence: Changing developmental contexts. *Child Development, 62*, 284–300.

Larson, R., & Richards, M.H. (1994a). *Divergent realities: The emotional lives of mothers, fathers, and adolescents*. New York: Basic Books.

Larson, R., & Richards, M.H. (1994b). Family emotions: Do young adolescents and their parents experience the same states? *Journal of Research on Adolescence, 4*, 567–583.

Larson, R.W., Richards, M.H., Moneta, G.B., Holmbeck, G., & Duckett, E. (1996). Changes in adolescents' daily interactions with their families from ages 10 to 18: Disengagement versus transformation. *Developmental Psychology, 32*, 744–754.

Larson, R.W., Richards, M.H., Sims, B., & Dworkin, J. (2001). How urban African–American adolescents spend their time: Time budgets for locations, activities, and companionship. *American Journal of Community Psychology, 29*, 565–597.

Larson, R.W., & Verma, S. (1999). How children and adolescents spend time across the world: Work, play and developmental opportunities. *Psychological Bulletin, 125*, 701–736.

Larson, R., Verma, S., & Dworkin, J. (2002b). Adolescents' family relationships in India: The daily family lives of Indian middle-class teenagers. In J. J. Arnett (Ed.), *Readings on adolescence and emerging adulthood* (pp. 133–141). Upper Saddle River, NJ: Prentice Hall.

Lee, M., & Larson, R. (2000). The Korean "examination hell": Long hours of studying, distress, and depression. *Journal of Youth and Adolescence, 29*, 249–271.

Long, C.R., & Averill, J.R. (2003). Solitude: An exploration of benefits of being alone. *Journal for the Theory of Social Behaviour, 33*, 21–44.

Mahon, N.E. (1983). Developmental changes and loneliness during adolescence. *Topics in Clinical Nursing, 5*, 66–76.

Marangoni, C., & Ickes, W. (1989). Loneliness: A theoretical review with implications for measurement. *Journal of Social and Personal Relationships, 6*, 93–128.

Marcia, J. (1980). Identity in adolescence. In J. Adelson (Ed.), *Handbook of adolescent psychology* (pp. 159–187). New York: John Wiley & Sons.

Marcoen, A., & Goossens, L. (1993). Loneliness, attitude towards aloneness, and solitude: Age differences and developmental significance during adolescence. In S. Jackson, & H. Rodriguez-Tomé (Eds.), *Adolescence and its social worlds* (pp. 197–227). Hove, UK: Lawrence Erlbaum Associates Ltd.

Marcoen, A., Goossens, L., & Caes, P. (1987). Loneliness in pre- through late adolescence: Exploring the contributions of a multidimensional approach. *Journal of Youth and Adolescence, 16*, 561–577.

Markus, H.R., & Kitayama, S. (1991). Culture and the self: Implications for cognition, emotion, and motivation. *Psychological Review, 98*, 224–253.

Mijuskovic, B. (1992). Organic communities, atomistic societies, and loneliness. *Journal of Sociology and Social Welfare, 19*, 147–164.

Ostrov, E., & Offer, D. (1980). Loneliness and the adolescent. In J. Hartog, J. R. Audy, & Y. A. Cohen (Eds.), *The anatomy of loneliness* (pp. 170–185). New York: International Universities Press.

Perlman, D. (1988). Loneliness: A life-span, family perspective. In R. Milardo (Ed.), *Families and social networks* (pp. 190–220). Newbury Park, CA: Sage.

Perlman, D., & Peplau, L.A. (1981). Toward a social psychology of loneliness. In R. Gilmour, & S. Duck, (Eds.), *Personal relationships: 3. Relationships in disorder* (pp. 31–56). London: Academic Press.

Petersen, A.C., Compas, B.E., Brooks-Gunn, J., Stemmler, M., Ey, S., & Grant, K.E. (1993). Depression in adolescence. *American Psychologist, 48*, 155–168.

Richards, M.H., & Larson, R. (1993). Pubertal development and the daily subjective states of adolescents. *Journal of Research on Adolescence, 3*, 145–169.

Rokach, A. (1989). Antecedents of loneliness: A factorial analysis. *Journal of Psychology, 123*, 369–384.

Rokach, A. (1990). Surviving and coping with loneliness. *Journal of Psychology, 124*, 39–54.

Rokach, A., & Neto, F. (2000a). Causes of loneliness in

adolescence: A cross-cultural study. *International Journal of Adolescence and Youth, 8,* 65–80.

Rokach, A., & Neto, F. (2000b). Coping with loneliness in adolescence: A cross-cultural study. *Social Behavior and Personality, 28,* 329–342.

Rokach, A., & Neto, F. (2001). The experience of loneliness in adolescence: A cross-cultural comparison. *International Journal of Adolescence and Youth, 9,* 159–173.

Rotenberg, K.J., & Hymel, S. (Eds.). (1999). *Loneliness in childhood and adolescence.* New York: Cambridge University Press.

Rubenstein, C., & Shaver, P. (1982). *In search of intimacy.* New York: Delacorte Press.

Russell, D., Peplau, L.A., & Cutrona, C.E. (1980). The revised UCLA loneliness scale: Concurrent and discriminant validity evidence. *Journal of Personality and Social Psychology, 39,* 472–480.

Schultz, N.R. Jr., & Moore, D. (1988). Loneliness: Differences across three age levels. *Journal of Social and Personal Relationships, 5,* 275–284.

Shaver, P.R., & Brennan, K.A. (1991). Measures of depression and loneliness. In J. P. Robinson, P. R. Shaver, & L. S. Wrightsman (Eds.), *Measures of personality and social psychological attitudes* (pp. 195–289). San Diego, CA: Academic Press.

Silk, J.S., Steinberg, L., & Morris, A.S. (2003). Adolescents' emotion regulation in daily life: Links to depressive symptoms and problem behavior. *Child Development, 74,* 1869–1880.

Steinberg, L., & Avenevoli, S. (2000). The role of context in the development of psychopathology: A conceptual framework and some speculative propositions. *Child Development, 77,* 66–74.

Storr, A. (1997). *Solitude.* London: HarperCollins. (Original work published 1989)

Suedfeld, P. (1982). Aloneness as a healing experience. In L. A. Peplau, & D. Perlman (Eds.), *Loneliness: A sourcebook of current theory, research, and therapy* (pp. 40–53). New York: John Wiley & Sons.

Sullivan, H.S. (1953). *The interpersonal theory of psychiatry.* New York: Norton.

Susman, E.J. (1997). Modeling developmental complexity in adolescence: Hormones and behavior in context. *Journal of Research on Adolescence, 7,* 283–306.

Triandis, H.C. (1995). *Individualism and collectivism.* Boulder, CO: Westview Press.

Van Buskirk, A.M., & Duke, M.P. (1991). The relationships between coping style and loneliness in adolescents: Can "sad passivity" be adaptive? *Journal of Genetic Psychology, 152,* 145–157.

Verma, S., Sharma, D., & Larson, R.W. (2002). School stress in India: Effects on time and daily emotions. *International Journal of Behavioral Development, 26,* 500–508.

Waskovic, T., & Cramer, K.M. (1999). Relation between preference for solitude scale and social functioning. *Psychological Reports, 85,* 1045–1050.

Weiss, R.S. (1982). Attachment in adult life. In C. M. Parkes, & J. Stevenson-Hinde (Eds.), *The place of attachment in human behavior* (pp. 171–184). London: Tavistock.

Winnicott, D. (1958). The capacity to be alone. *International Journal of Psychoanalysis, 39,* 416–420.

5

Cognitive development in adolescence: Thinking freed from concrete constraints

Henri Lehalle

Cognitive development refers to the successive levels of intellectual adaptation, from birth to adulthood. It consists of the general and slowly constructed competencies along with the various procedures and intellectual processing one individual might use in specific situations where a logical problem must be solved, whether at school or in everyday life. The analysis of cognitive development during adolescence remains strongly influenced by the seminal work of Inhelder and Piaget (Inhelder, 2001; Inhelder & Piaget, 1955).

According to the classic version of Piaget's theory (Piaget, 1956) cognitive development progresses through three successive periods. The first period, from birth to about 24 months, incorporates a progressive coordination of actions with the physical world. The second period starts with the development of the ability to represent objects and actions by means of symbols. Note that, for Piaget (1945), symbolic representations emerge from the previous period of sensori-motor development. Language is just one example of the symbolic function: others include drawings, symbolic games, etc. Logical coordination of these representations does not occur until a later period of development. This new coordination occurs between about 6 or 7 and 11 or 12 years of age and takes the form of concrete operations which are gradually elaborated across the various domains of intellectual functioning. The third and final period, called stage of formal operational thinking, can be viewed as a third level of coordination which permits the construction of an abstract frame of reference for the earlier concrete operations. It corresponds to the period of adolescence.

Almost all the experimental tasks used to characterize formal stage and formal operations were originally developed by Inhelder (1954; see Bond, 2001) in order to study the functional, rather than the structural, aspects of cognition. Functioning concerns behaviors in specific situations whereas structures refer to general competencies. So, when Inhelder proposed her formal stage situations, she was already thinking about the transition from general competencies to specific reasonings in particular contexts. But, at the same time, Piaget was still working on logico-mathematical structures and modeling (Piaget, 1952, 1954). Then, the seminal book on adolescent cognition (Inhelder & Piaget, 1955) was a puzzling blend of new empirical findings, from Inhelder, and sophisticated logical interpretations from Piaget.

Of course, fifty years later, this chapter will not be limited to the Piagetian classic analysis. After Neimark (1975), there were numerous reviews either focusing on formal operations (Bond, 1998, 2001; Demetriou & Efklides, 1981; Gray, 1990; Lehalle, 1985, 2001) or taking the Piagetian view as a starting point for further improvements (Graber & Petersen, 1991; Keating, 2004; Moshman, 1998a; Smith, 1993). Indeed, new findings and theories were proposed, especially from Pascual-Leone (de Ripaupierre & Pascual-Leone, 1979) and Fischer (1980). Some of them constitute the "neo-Piagetian group" (Demetriou, 1988) and were motivated mainly by the desire to explain the contextual and individual variabilities that Piaget's theory did not even attempt take into account (de Ribaupierre, 1997).

At the present time, research into cognitive development appears to be a divergent and not really integrated field, in spite of what Demetriou (1988) wished for. Except for some attempts (Bideaud, 1999; de Ribaupierre, 1997; Sternberg, 1988), there are not many deep confrontations between the various new proposals that exist more in juxtaposition than truly discussed beyond the terminology used and with respect to empirical validations.

In this chapter, we start with the concrete purpose of selecting and defining the main new cognitive skills in the transition from childhood to adolescence. Because of what studies after Piaget have shown, this part will have to be precise how adolescent cognition really differs from child cognition. Second, developmental changes in societal conceptualization, scientific knowledge, and identity construction will be considered from a cognitive perspective. Finally, possible explanations of cognitive evolution will be suggested.

1. New cognitive skills in the transition from childhood to adolescence

From the large corpus of experimental tasks (starting with Inhelder, 1954) commonly used to assess the cognitive change in adolescence, five main properties can be selected to characterize the new cognitive skills that are elaborated during this period. The choice of the word "skill" comes from Fischer (1980) and stresses the fact that every new cognitive process is constructed in context, that is, in the various situations at stake. There is no general processing that could be applied *without effort* in a situation, although common cognitive aspects may be observed in numerous functional domains. This is what Fischer, Kenny, and Pipp (1990) humorously called the "Calvinist principle", i.e.: "The person must actively construct every new skill" (p.166).

1.1 Coordination of several measurable dimensions

Measuring skill on one dimension (such as length, weight, etc.) belongs typically to the concrete level and implies an understanding of the logical properties of numbers. But, the multiplicative coordination of two or more dimensions is acquired afterwards. Let us examine the difficult construction of the proportionality laws.

Proportionality reasoning consists of an integration or reunion of at least two additive reasonings, already effective in every quantitative dimension at stake. For instance (Noelting, 1982), a given quantity of orange juice is mixed with a given quantity of water and this concentration has to be compared with another one which does not have the same quantity of orange juice or of water. Here, there are at least two dimensions to be compared: orange juice and water, each of them being evaluated on an additive scale (for example: the number of glasses of each poured into the mixture).

The additive measurement is already mastered and experienced in childhood and the underlying logic matches the logic embedded in a true concept of number and counting. Moreover, some very simple proportions (e.g., half a glass with one sugar compared to the entire glass with two sugars) can be understood at around 9 years of age (Lehalle & Savois, 1985; Stavy, 1981). Furthermore, ratios such as "1/2 and 2/4" or "1/3 and 2/6" can be successfully compared, even at the preformal stage (Longeot, 1969), when the configurations "2/4" or "2/6" are rearranged to show that they are made of twice the previous ones ("1/2" or "1/3"). We can note also, that for Piaget (Piaget & Szeminska, 1941) multiplicative operations are an extension of additive operations and can be easily understood from multiple correspondences (e.g., two flowers in each vase) according to the same general concrete logic.

Nevertheless, complex proportionality problems (i.e., when numbers prevent any immediate figurative representation) are only very gradually solved in the adolescent period. Indeed, since the problem is not obviously represented, it becomes necessary, first, to consider and to organize the complete system of transformations at stake (that is with an integration of the possible transformations in each of the quantitative dimensions), second, to understand that *multiplicative* operations (not additive ones, as younger folk already do) must be processed.

Proportionality reasoning has been documented in numerous contexts: probability (Piaget & Inhelder, 1951), concentrations (e.g., orange juice and water; Noelting, 1982; Noelting, Rousseau, Bond, & Brunel, 2000), physical systems (balance beam equilibrium, weight traction on a sloping plane; Inhelder & Piaget, 1955), both physical and geometric system (projection of shadows; Inhelder & Piaget, 1955). However, the balance beam task was probably the most frequently used for new experiments and theorizations (see Box 5.1 on the balance beam problem).

1.2 A combinatorial approach

According to Piaget (Inhelder & Piaget, 1955) adolescents may show a combinatory scheme. When facing a problem with several independent finite factors or elements, adolescents are supposed to use a systematic procedure to list all the possibilities that may appear.

In the Piaget and Inhelder's work on chance and probability (1951), there were many examples of that skill. For instance, children were presented to a bag containing, for example, 40 marbles: 20 red marbles (R) and 20 blue ones (B). They had to anticipate the colors of the pairs if they drew lots two at a time. There were three boxes in which to place the successive pairs: one for the RR pairs, one for the BB pairs, one for the mixed pairs. From about 12 to 13 years of age, adolescents used a combinatory skill. They could indicate the most probable distribution: 10 BB, 10 RR; 20 mixed. However, even at around 9 years, children already knew there would be more mixed pairs. Moreover, if fewer marbles of more than two colors were placed into the bag, adolescents could adjust their successive anticipations to the events previously noted.

Another example was the chemical combination of colorless liquids (Inhelder & Piaget, 1955). In this task, children were presented to four similar flasks with colorless and odorless liquids inside 1: diluted sulphuric acid; 2: water; 3: oxygenated water; 4: thiosulphate. Moreover, a smaller flask (labeled g) contained potassium iodide. Then, two more glasses were displayed: in one glass there was a mix of liquids "1" and "3", the other glass contained the liquid "2" (water), but children were not aware of which liquids were in these glasses. While participants watched, the experimenter added several drops of g to each of these two glasses. Thus, the liquid in the glass containing "1 + 3" (not in the "2" glass), turned yellow (as a chemistry reader could anticipate!). Participants had to reproduce the color, using whichever liquids they chose from the five flasks.

The developmental trends in this task are very informative. Young children pick liquids at random and observe the result. Children at 7 to 9 years of age take one term in correspondence with each other, or one term with all the others

---

Box 5.1.   Balance beam problem

The balance beam problem was originally presented by Inhelder (1954), then by Inhelder and Piaget (1955) and many others. Apparatus and procedure may vary among authors, but the general experimental principles are always the same. Children are presented with quite a long beam that can "balance" on a fulcrum. Some weights may be placed on either side of the beam, at different lengths, and it is possible to quantify (or count) both weight and distance from the fulcrum. With young children, Inhelder used several dolls (as weight) that could be hung on the beam and "balance". Siegler (1978) used a well-known apparatus: pegs were equally spaced on each side of the beam and metal disks of the same weight could be placed on them, letting the child "count" on both dimensions: distance and weight.

The problem is to discover the proportional law between weights and distances, when equilibrium is preserved. Questions may be of different sorts: find the right weight at a given distance to "balance" weights already placed on the other side (or find the right distance, etc.), anticipate what will happen (bending right, or left, or "balance") with a given configuration on each side, etc.

The proportionality law is only used from about 12/13 years of age and remains difficult for many adolescents. Inhelder and Piaget (1955) thought that the difficulty was a matter of coordination between all the transformations at stake. They expressed this coordination in terms of reversibility and propositional logic (see Box 5.2).

After Piaget, the balance beam problem continued to be a sort of fetish task: every serious new theorization took on the challenge to try to explain the developmental trends in this task!

For instance, Pascual-Leone (de Ribaupierre & Pascual-Leone, 1979) described 24 steps for the functional construction of the balance's proportionality rule. In each step the formula used the codes and concepts from the Pascual-Leone's *Theory of Constructive Operators*. Moreover, Case (1985) was able to present and to validate successive cognitive stages "from birth to adulthood" through adapted forms of the balance problem (in particular Siegler's form). Later, connectionist models were developed on the balance beam situation (McClelland, 1989; Shultz, 1996, 2003).

(in that case there is no more a yellow color . . . because liquid "4" fades the mix, as a very good chemistry reader could anticipate!); then quantitative hypothesis (i.e., more or less "water") or sequential hypothesis (procedure) may be invoked by children, according to the current logic at this stage. But, around 9 to 11 years, children can think about other possible combinations (2 by 2, or 3 by 3). However, Inhelder and Piaget's observations suggest that a systematic method for listing all possible combinations constitutes a formal stage skill (starting from 12 or 13 years of age), which is more and more easily activated and performed with age.

The main point here is that adolescents consider a given event as one event among many others, with the possibility of organizing in a systematic way all the events they think about. In sum, Piaget viewed the formal stage as a change in the relation between what is "real" and what is "possible". At the concrete stage, logical structuration concerns the direct representation of experience, and the possible events can be considered only from this direct representation. For instance, the child may think of a given combination of marbles (or liquids), then of another one starting from the first, etc. without any system for listing all the combinations. With the formal stage, a given representation (i.e. what is "actual"

for the child) is immediately considered as a particular case among others.

However, this combinatorial skill may be considered more as an attitude than as a new competence which could be performed without effort in any case. In fact, even before adolescence, children can solve simple combinatory problems, as we saw earlier. See Longeot (1969) who placed at the concrete stage the fact that children can find, without systematic method, the six permutations of three colored tokens. Conversely, too complex combinatorial problems may overload the processing capacity of a truly normal formal stage person (Gréco, 1988).

As a consequence, a complete combinatorial scheme does not constitute an adolescent cognitive competence per se. However, it indicates a new attitude. When adolescents are facing a new situation, they attempt to organize the possibilities in a systematic way, whereas children simply follow what is successively activated.

1.3 Scientific reasoning: Isolation of variables and proof logic

How can we be sure that a given factor does influence a phenomenon? Conversely, how can we be sure that it does not? Such questions arise in a scientific context, of course, but they also occur in daily life, when we have to find why something does not work or when we want to ascertain what factors contribute to success (for instance, when making a delicious dish).

If the problem is to prove that a factor is effective, one must exclude other possible factors, and the best way to do that is to construct an experiment following the famous tenet that "all things are equal, except for the variable or factor to be tested". Moreover, a factor can be viewed as not effective if, in controlled conditions, there is no systematic link between the factor and the phenomenon.

When we are processing in this way, we implicitly use a logic of true proof that Inhelder and Piaget (1955) have analyzed in terms of the propositional logic. It follows that experimental reasoning is considered as one of the formal stage skills constructed during adolescence. This skill supposes a successive focusing on possible hypothesis and explicit control of the identified factors.

Control aspects are close to combinatorial skill (see earlier). Facing experimental results, younger children may fail to differentiate and organize the factors at stake. When two factors are both modified, with the consequence of an attested effect, children may falsely conclude that *both* factors have an influence. For instance, in the classic case of searching what factors influence pendulum oscillations, children may conclude there is an effect of both string length *and* weight, if oscillations are compared in the two following cases: "short length and high weight", then "long length and low weight". In fact, string length is the unique effective factor.

Further researches have partly confirmed earlier Inhelder and Piaget's findings (1955). For instance, Danner and Day (1977) have shown that adolescents (from two age groups: 13 years and 17 years) can quite easily learn to systematically control factors in experiments (according to the formal stage criterion used in this study). But it is not the case for the younger group (10 years).

Nevertheless, a primitive form of factor control may be observed in children (Lawson & Wollman, 1976; Lehalle, 1994). As Lehalle (1994) pointed out, this primitive control is not supported by propositional logic but by what Piaget called

multiplication co-univoque. It refers to the possibility of conceiving that one effect may be due to several factors. For instance (this task was originally used by Lawson and Wollmann, 1976), suppose we have to find which of two tennis balls bounces higher, but we try one ball on the ground and the other on a piece of cardboard. Most children will say "Oh, that's not fair!" and suggest using the same condition for testing the balls. They know that bouncing depends on the surface properties of the ground, not only on the properties of the ball.

So, what is really new in adolescent experimental skills can be set out in two central features: (a) the possibility of differentiating, combining, and controlling many factors (a combinatorial skill); (b) the generalization of experimental control to *any potential factors*, not only to those factors known to be effective in a particular situation. It follows the "all things equal . . ." rule.

The same kind of cognitive evolution can be stressed about hypothesis formulation. Following what Piaget already suggested in 1924, a truly hypothetico-deductive reasoning implies: (a) to consider a possible explanation even though we do not agree with it; it may be a peer opinion and, because of that, this skill can be viewed as a social skill (Piaget, 1924); (b) to delay any judgment about the truthfulness of this explanation; (c) to logically deduce consequences from the hypothetical explanation up to some factual falsifiable predictions which lead to an experiment.

Obviously, this kind of competence constitutes a major progression in adolescent cognition, noticeably experienced in adolescent discussions and debates. However, children can already indicate some suppositions about the possible causes of a phenomenon. Can their suppositions be regarded as true "hypotheses"? Sodian, Zaitchik, and Carey (1991) have shown, among first and second grade children, a kind of differentiation between hypothetical beliefs and factual evidence. But the authors acknowledge they have greatly simplified the task, leaving out important aspects of the classic scientific reasoning. The kind of "hypothesis" they consider simply consists of a supposed property of an "object" (for instance: "Can this unknown animal smell well?").

Obviously, this is a supposed feature, not a supposed relation between a possible cause, among other possible causes, and an effect. Moreover there is not a long or sophisticated deductive process between "hypothesis" and "prediction". It is a very short inference to understand that: "If this animal can smell well, it can smell this bland food." There is no more a necessity for controlling factors, since alternatives are clearly predefined by the experimenters and the children have just to reach a conclusion, using a simple serial correspondence between smelling aptitude and strong or bland food. Note that serial correspondence belongs to concrete logic, according to the Piagetian view.

Then, the adolescent competence about hypotheses may be restricted to the hypotheses they can formulate and manage from their own (i.e., not predefined), especially in the case of searching effective factors (i.e., not knowing them before the experiment), among possible numerous factors to be controlled, and with a real deductive processing from hypotheses up to predictions.

In sum, a complete form of scientific reasoning is elaborated during adolescence, but some partial primitive aspects were effective earlier. These primitive aspects are supported by a concrete logic: co-univocal multiplication or serial correspondence.

1.4 Distinction between theoretical laws and empirical reports

There are few studies on the distinction between theoretical laws and empirical evidence, yet this is a very good indicator of the cognitive change from children to adolescent thinking. Children can appreciate the world on a concrete and empirical level: measuring, classifying, ordering, comparing, etc. This is already a rational approach. But adolescents are supposed to gradually develop the possibility of considering a pure theoretical construction as a pertinent and valid representation of reality, even if this representation does not exactly fit reality because of some disrupting constraints.

Again, an Inhelder task (Inhelder & Piaget, 1955), the conservation of motion on a horizontal plane, is a good illustration. In this task,

children or adolescents are presented to some balls differing in matter, weight and volume. Balls can be thrown out with a spring on a horizontal plane (the apparatus is actually not very different from a pinball). The question is to think about the reasons why balls are falling nearer or further away, why they slow down and, finally, stop. Children are able to refer to some movement explanations and to possible causes for slowing down and stopping. But adolescents (from 14 or 15 years of age) can understand that if the parasite factors (air resistance, friction forces) were absent, the balls *should not* slow down or stop. It is a sort of distinction between *de jure* aspects (what it should be on a theoretical level) and *de dicto* (what is observed, in fact, because of some factors we have to consider). As usual (see Box 5.2), Piaget attributed this skill to propositional logic: the previously quoted understanding "if parasite factors were absent, then no stopping" was interpreted as an example of contraposition or *modus tollens* in propositional logic (from "stopping implies given factors" – that is "p implies q" – it is followed by contraposition "no given factors implies no stopping" – that is "not-q implies not-p", then the theoretical conservation of motion becomes a necessary conclusion).

Even if we don't agree with the Piagetian logical interpretation of the distinction between theoretical laws and empirical evidence, one may consider the obvious generality of this new skill. On an academic level, the Euclidian geometry cannot be understood without a distinction between a pure theorical construction and imperfect realizations in the real world. In daily life as well, one may use the same distinction. For instance, if we have to carpet a room, a not very sophisticated way to start consists of proceeding according on a concrete level, taking tiles one by one and placing them one after the other, doing the best each successive time the carpet one is placed down. Another, more sophisticated and formal way, is to use, *as a guide*, a theoretical and complete representation of the hoped results, with parallel lines, etc. Obviously, this theoretical frame cannot exactly fit the realization, because of some practical difficulties, imperfect tiles, no strictly parallel walls, etc.

Box 5.2.   Piaget's use of propositional logic

Piaget used propositional logic as a model of the new *underlying* cognitive competencies in adolescence (formal operational stage). The balance beam problem and proportionality scheme will serve as an example.

Let us call p = to increase weight (and not-p = to decrease weight), q = to increase distance (and not-q = to decrease distance). It is thus easy to see that any weight increasing may be compensated (reversibility) either by weight decreasing (reverse N) or by distance increasing (converse R). Moreover, each of the four possible transformations (p, not-p, q, not-q) has a reverse N and a converse R, which are one of the three other transformations.

But we can go further, with Piaget, and consider transformations that take into account *both* weight and distance for *one* transformation. Indeed, Piaget noted that the starting point, at the formal stage in the balance beam situation, is to consider that "weight increasing *and* distance decreasing" on one side of the beam *is the same as* "weight decreasing *and* distance increasing" on the other side. This new consideration may be translated into our codes, that is (p and not-q) = R (not-p and q). Now, we are in the binary propositional logic system: a combinatory of true values for two propositions with R and N defined in the system. Indeed, each of the present four transformations: (p and not-q), (not-p and q), (not-p or q), (p or not-q), has a reverse N and a converse R, which are one of the three other transformations. For instance, as we have just seen, starting with (p and not-q), which means "increasing weight and decreasing distance", we may define *in the model* the converse R which is (not-p and q) and also the reverse (not-p or q), that is "decreasing weight or increasing distance". At the same time, these four transformations are four operations among the 16 binary operations of the propositional logic, when we make judgments about the truth value of the combination of two propositions (p and q) and their negations (not-p and not-q).

In Inhelder and Piaget (1955), we find numerous analyses like just these. Piaget's use of propositional logic can be understood with the following riders.

It is a model of underlying, not explicit, structuration. Children or adolescents think about weight, distance, equilibrium, not deductive reasoning in itself. In the case of the proportionality scheme, the logical model is supposed to characterize the prerequisite qualitative transformations (N and R) that are necessary for applying an explicit quantitative processing (i.e. the multiplicative arithmetic operation to find the right weight or the right distance).

As a consequence, the propositional logic, in Piaget's formal operational stage analysis, does not concern verbal reasoning. In Inhelder and Piaget (1955) there is no situation where adolescents should operate on verbal materials, such as syllogisms or conditional reasoning, which are supposed to correspond to propositional logic.

In fact, Piaget started from actual spontaneous reasonings, in such and such situations, and *translated* these reasonings in propositional logic terms, to consider that propositional logic, as a whole, could be a good model of the new underlying cognitive competencies in adolescence.

1.5 "Abstract" thinking

Adolescent thinking, compared to the child one, is generally simply considered as "abstract" thinking. Indeed, most of the previous considerations belong to some kind of abstractness. However, although everybody in common talk about adolescents seems to easily understand what abstract thinking is (and does not show any need of further explanation), there are, in fact, many difficulties in precisely defining what this abstract property is.

On the one hand, abstractness may be viewed as a gradual growing process, from birth to adulthood. Then, there are no abstractions per se, but many *levels* of abstractness, the next level being more abstract than preceding ones. Indeed, if "more abstract" means that one can select common properties of elements previously considered and think about those properties as a unique element, then such developmental trends can be described at every developmental level (for instance, using a single word to indicate a category of distinct but similar objects). According to this view, adolescent thinking, compared to

child thinking, is not "abstract", it is actually "more abstract".

Nevertheless, it is equally lawful, on the other hand, to reserve the term "abstraction" to indicate not the developmental process at stake, but a given level in the process, the one which is gradually observed from adolescence. That was the choice made by Fischer (Fischer, 1980; Fischer et al., 1990). See Box 5.3 for a presentation of the development of abstractions, according to Fischer's skill theory.

The main point from skill theory is to consider that abstractions are first isolated structurations of previously constructed representations. Afterwards, abstractions may gradually be organized, through mapping and correspondences between previously isolated abstractions, up to more general systems made of several abstractions that are linked together.

2. Cognitive analysis of developmental domains in adolescence

The various functional domains are often supposed to partly depend on a general cognitive

Box 5.3.   Fischer's skill theory and the development of abstractions

Fischer's skill theory (1980; Fischer, Yan, & Stewart, 2003) describes cognitive development in four periods or four main "tiers": reflexes, actions (from about 3–4 months, up to 20–24 months), representations (from about 20–24 months, up to 10–12 years), and abstractions (from about 10–12 years, up to 24–26 years). In each tier, there are the same successive levels (or "sub-stages", according to a more common terminology not used by Fischer) and the final level of one tier is the first level of the next one (i.e., a given new tier comes from coordinations in the previous one).

Let us be precise about what Fischer calls "abstractions", with examples taken from Fischer et al. (1990). As for the other tiers, the abstract tier consists of a succession of four levels, which correspond to successively more complex links between abstractions. Ages in brackets are an approximation of the earliest evidence of the skill when children are given some kind of support ("optimal level"); the "functional levels" (i.e., no support: children or adolescents behave on their own) are delayed.

The first level (from 10–12 years of age) allows only *single abstractions*, that is, people are able to consider common aspects of several concrete instances. "Intangible categories" may illustrate what single abstractions are. Each category is defined from concrete instances and there are no relations between categories that are considered singly, for example, law, justice, society. In arithmetics, people at this level can abstractly define a single operation, for instance "addition", from various examples.

The second level, *abstract mapping* (from 14–16 years), maps two single abstractions. It means that some relations are stressed between the two given abstractions. For instance, in arithmetics, it becomes possible to indicate how closely two operations are related. "Close" means that only one dimension is considered for comparing the arithmetic operations. Here true comparisons are only possible for the following pairs: addition and subtraction, multiplication and division, multiplication and addition, division and subtraction.

The third level (from 19–21 years) consists of *abstract systems*. Relations between two abstractions are now deeply analyzed, with a correspondence between varieties in one abstraction and varieties in the second one. In other words, at this level, there is a differentiation in each abstraction and a correspondence between the differentiated aspects from the two abstractions. For instance, in arithmetics, "addition and division" can be analyzed according to two aspects: the direction of change (addition increases whereas division decreases) and the type of units (one number at a time for addition and group of numbers for division). The same goes, but separately, for "subtraction and multiplication". In sum, with abstract systems, two or more dimensions or criteria are used to compare two abstractions. It implies a sort of differentiation into each abstraction.

Finally (from 24–26 years) the fourth abstract level, *general principle*, "involves the integration of two or more [. . .] abstracts systems in terms of some general theory, ideology, or framework" (Fischer et al., 1990, p. 171). For instance, a "theory" of the four operations can be formulated, using the two dimensions (increase/decrease and single number/group of numbers) for classifying those operations on a 2×2 table. However, we can note that this "theory" of the four arithmetical operations is not complete: if we try to multiply 6 by 0.5, the result is not "increasing". Yet both addition and multiplication are considered as "increasing" in our example of "general principle" proposed by the authors. This is probably due to the fact that, as also indicated by the authors, the categorizing tasks used to assess the levels comprised only simple operations with positive whole numbers.

Others examples of "abstractions" are presented by Fischer et al. (2003) mainly from social and interpersonal domains.

developmental factor. For instance, the formal stage competencies have been considered as a necessary but not sufficient condition for achieving Kohlberg's sequence in moral judgments (Bideaud, 1980; Tomlinson-Keasey & Keasey, 1974), as if late moral stages were grounded on formal operational thought. But, if we consider that cognition is always contextualized, it is logically impossible to assess a cognitive level without context. As a consequence, there is no "pure cognitive tasks", even the Piagetian ones, which could indicate a competence per se.

However, this statement does not imply that there are no general competencies. But, if general competencies can be defined, they are simply the common cognitive aspects that an observer detects through the various domains. It does not mean that competencies would be independent of any content in the individual minds. It does not mean, either, that cognitive progress should be synchronous across domains, or that Piagetian tasks should be mastered immediately (as for the hypothetical relation between moral stages and formal operational thinking).

That is the reason why, after the specification of five cognitive skills in adolescence taking examples mainly from scientific concerns, we have now to show how cognitive development may be inherent in several other domains of adolescent development. Of course, these following statements have strong connections with other chapters in this handbook: moral and socio-cognitive chapters for social aspects, the school chapter for scientific knowledge, and the identity chapter for personal concerns. Here, however, the focus will be on the general cognitive aspects embedded in various functional domains.

2.1 *Thinking about society and social regulation*

Developmental change in adolescents' thinking on society and social rules can be interpreted according to the general cognitive evolution during this period.

From a very broad view, as it was originally proposed by Inhelder and Piaget (1955), cognitive transformations in adolescence induce a modification in the relation between what is "real" and what is "possible" (see earlier, on combinatorial skills). Of course children, before adolescence, can extend their view beyond immediate events, but these extensions to some kind of potentialities are drawn from concrete or actual situations which are just transformed with no general system that could encompass both actual and potential aspects. Then the "possible" depends on the "real". But in adolescence, immediate events and present situations are considered through some kind of general systems. Then the "real" depends on the "possible" because the real is only one possibility among many others and all possibilities tend to be organized in a systematic way through general principles.

It is not surprising, therefore that adolescence is clearly a period during which present social organisations are questioned. Indeed, society and current values are considered as one possibility among many potential other systems. This is a great source of improvement for the social group because social functioning is not accepted without discussion any more. Instead, it is evaluated in comparison with ideals and with other social systems that exist elsewhere.

Some years ago, Adelson (1975) was able to point out how cognitive development appears in adolescent thinking about political ideology. In this article, Adelson presented a synthesis of several studies, in particular one extensive survey involving about 1000 adolescents, aged 11 to 18, from various countries (United States, Great Britain, West Germany). The survey used interviews in which youngsters had to imagine that

1000 people leave their country to form a new society; discussion was conducted concerning problems that would inevitably arise about social and political order in this situation; the discussion permitted various questions on crime and justice, interactions of state and citizens, utopian possibilities of government, etc.

From the results, Adelson stressed the main cognitive transitions that take place in adolescent years. The first one is labelled "abstractness", since middle and late adolescents are gradually able to manage abstract concepts, whereas it remains difficult for young adolescents to think in abstract categories. As Adelson wrote: "The young adolescent can imagine a church, but not the church, the teacher and the school but not education, the policeman and the judge and the jail but not the law, the public official but not the government" (1975, p. 68).

Moreover, other cognitive transformations, indicated by Adelson (1975), belong as well to the new possibilities of generalization and to the skill of thinking freely from concrete instances (even if the gains during adolescence are sometimes judged "modest"). Thus, we can observe:

- progress in historical perspective, with an understanding of the determination of the future by present and past events, and by the successive historical decisions
- progress from a static to a dynamic view of the political universe, for instance about the laws which were previously considered as permanent and unalterable but are now viewed as a potentially changing collective decision, involving the possibility of abolition and amendments
- progress in the analysis of social situations, with an awareness of competing interests inducing the necessity of compromises because the problem is no more to find who is right and who is wrong but to search the best formula for each party in the frame of general principles
- indeed, there are also progress in grasping general principles (such as "democracy") which are now increasingly related and

understood beyond the mere knowledge of the words used to indicate these principles.

More recently, new descriptions of cognitive development offer the opportunity to more precisely analyze how social concepts imply complex cognitive organizations. For instance, Lamborn, Fischer, and Pipps (1994) have used skills theory (Fischer, 1980, see Box 5.3) to distinguish successive steps in understanding honesty and kindness in social interactions. These steps match the levels of abstractness in Fischer's theory.

At the level of "single abstractions", honesty and kindness are isolated terms which allow to identify a common theme in at least two concrete situations. Single abstractions overtake the possibility to recognize honesty or kindness in *successive* concrete situations (that was already the case for the previous level labelled "concrete concepts"). Abstractions grasp *common aspects* of several examples. For instance, if "Tom helps Beth with English *and* shares his lunch with Mark", then both Beth and Mark obviously need help, but they cannot help Tom in return because he does not need any help; in sum, Tom is kind and "kindness" is caring by helping someone in need, even if he/she cannot help in return. Single abstractions allow people to understand such general statement about several concrete situations (Tom with Beth *and* Tom with Mark).

The next level consists of "abstract mappings" which indicate some kind of relation between two abstractions. Abstract concepts are defined, as in the previous level, but it is further possible to characterize how abstractions are related in more complex social concepts. For instance, in social lies, honesty is opposed to kindness, and this opposition constitutes the relation between the two abstractions. For example, somebody *lies* by telling a friend that his/her painting is good (while this is not really the case!), but at the same time this person is also *kind* facing his/her friend.

Finally, "abstract systems" relate previously differentiated abstractions. As an example, let us consider what is a complete understanding of "constructive criticism", for instance in the context of evaluating a friend's painting. First, we have to differentiate two kinds of honesty because sometimes we have to praise and sometimes we have to criticize (both are honesty but in opposite directions, in which case, this is an abstract mapping). Second, we have to differentiate two kinds of kindness, because sometimes we have to build confidence and sometimes we have to help to improve (again this is abstract mapping with an opposition between two abstractions). Third, we have to relate the two mappings, building the concept of "constructive criticism" which integrates the two previously differentiated abstractions: indeed, you are both kind and honest in "constructive criticism" when praising is used to build confidence and criticizing is used to induce improvement.

Stories like these were constructed, by Lamborn et al., according to successive cognitive levels. Participants, aged from 9 to 20 years, were presented with each story; they had to indicate the main points of the story. Since one story corresponds to one level, the step is "pass or fail" according to what the participant can indicate about the story. A scalogram analysis displays a quite perfect hierarchy according to the theoretical sequence. It is difficult to be precise at what age the successive levels are passed, because, according to skill theory, it depends on experimental condition and support. Roughly speaking, it is important to know that progress along the sequence appears during adolescence: in the case of honesty and kindnesss, mean ages for single abstractions are around 11 to 13 years, for abstract mappings around 13 to 17 years and for abstract systems around 17 to 20 years.

While the previous research was grounded on Fischer's theory, Marini and Case (1994) have presented a similar study but starting from Case's theory. This study does not really concern social concepts but rather social interactions. The point is to anticipate the behavior of a character. This anticipation stems from what the character has done previously. As in Fischer's framework, stories were constructed according to a theoretical developmental sequence (Case's theory), with more and more complex features letting participants predict further behaviors of the character. Again a scalogram analysis displays an acceptable hierarchy in accordance with Case's proposals. Moreover, this hierarchy is similar to what is observed in a scientific domain (it was, of course, the balance beam task). So, Case's theory appears to be supported on a general level. In sum, this theory allows people to order items according to the number of informations we have to take into account for solving the item.

In conclusion, social knowledge in adolescents can be analyzed as an example of the various cognitive improvements that appear during this period. This was done both from general views (Adelson, 1975; Inhelder & Piaget, 1955), and from more precise predictions grounded on more recent cognitive models (Lamborn et al., 1994; Marini & Case, 1994).

2.2 Increasing scientific knowledge

Scientific knowledge was the main source of examples in the first part of this chapter, when the new cognitive skills in adolescence were described. Then, it is easy for the reader to realize how cognitive development is implicated in the acquisition of scientific knowledge. It is a matter of conceptualization, as we have seen about the social domain. Indeed, various forms of abstraction and generalization could be stressed about scientific concepts, for instance about numbers, since number development is far from achieved at 7 years (Lehalle, 1998; Rittle-Johnson & Siegler, 1998; Box 5.4 on Gréco, 1963).

It is also a matter of method and logic because combinatorial skill and experimental reasoning are used to get information and to sort out pertinent cues and evidence.

General models of cognitive development have been elaborated in particular about scientific domains. We earlier took Fischer's theory as an example of the neo-Piagetian approaches to new general descriptions (see Box 5.3). But the pertinence of general models does not mean that scientific knowledge constitutes an homogeneous domain. Some years ago, Martorano (1977) showed that formal tasks are far from belonging to the same level of difficulty. In this study, tasks that imply a combination of elements (permutations, factors control) seem to be easier than tasks that imply a coordination of dimensions (for

instance, the proportionality tasks). Thus Piagetian tasks were paradoxically used to recognize sub-domains among the too large scientific domain. As another example, extensive studies have been conducted by Demetriou (Demetriou & Efklides, 1988). In these studies, numerous participants (usually 300 or more in one study) from a broad age range (4 to 50 years) were interviewed on a large number of tasks. Factor analysis of the results led to consider six groups of tasks, that is, six sub-domains or "capacities" as labeled by the authors:

- *quantitative-relational*: aspects of quantification and quantificative concepts (for instance: measurement, number, conservation, proportionality tasks)
- *qualitative-analytic*: identification of objects properties and comparison between them (for instance: classification, seriation, analogical reasoning tasks)
- *imaginal-spatial*: representational aspects (for instance: Piagetian tasks on mental imagery, coordination of perspective, spatial reasoning tasks)
- *causal-experimental*: how objects interact and how we know how they interact (for instance: combinatory, permutations, isolation of variables in experiments, experimental designs, theory formation tasks)
- *verbal-propositional*: verbal reasoning (for instance: syllogistic and propositional reasoning tasks)
- *metacognitive-reflecting*: "how I work?" (for instance: tasks requiring reflection on one's own cognitive performance).

In Demetriou's theorization, these capacities constitute only one aspect of cognition. Further analyses (Demetriou, Efklides, Papadaki, Papantoniou, & Economou, 1993) have postulated that cognition develops across three fronts: (a) progress in the various specific domains (the five first capacities just indicated, with metacognition excluded); (b) progress in cognitive control (here is the metacognitive aspect which was the previously sixth "capacity"); (c) progress in functional

> **Box 5.4.   Number development in adolescence (from Gréco, 1963)**
>
> Piagetian contribution to the understanding of number concept is not limited to the seminal book by Piaget and Szeminska (1941) where the natural numbers come from a new synthesis (at 6 or 7 years) made up of classification and seriation, with the necessity of the conservation of quantity.
>
> At the beginning of the 1960s, in Geneva, Piaget's collaborators conducted important new studies on number. Among them, Gréco (in particular, Gréco, 1963) aimed at a better understanding of number structuration that leads to necessary inferences based on the iterative property of the successive whole numbers. Thus, number development was considered in depth after seven years, up to the adolescent period.
>
> Gréco's experimental paradigm consisted of the construction, with participants, of successive piles, which represent successive numbers. For instance: one token in the first pile, then two tokens in the next pile, then three tokens, etc. (up to 25). In a different condition, another material may be set up with boxes of matches (one match in the first box, two in the next one, etc.). This experimental paradigm had two important features. First, participants must be absolutely sure that there is always a difference of one unit between two adjacent piles or boxes (this is "iteration"). Second, when a number is increasing, it is impossible to directly evaluate the cardinal quantity in a given set. With tokens, piles are irregularly displayed and two adjacent large piles look very similar. With boxes of matches it is easy to close the boxes in order to focus on a pure deductive skill from the iterative properties of the successive numbers.
>
> There were many tasks adapted from this paradigm. One of them used colored tokens in ordered piles. The first questions concerned the possibility (or not) of splitting a given pile into two piles of exactly the same quantity. Of course, the immediate reaction of anybody is to search for the cardinal quantity of the whole pile. But if you are informed that a previous pile cannot be split, you are sure that the target pile may be, but not the next, etc. without knowing the exact number of each pile. In other words, you have grasped the alternation between even and uneven numbers.
>
> After that, in Gréco's study, participants were questioned about dividing into three equal parts. Again, if a given pile can be divided into three parts, can the next pile be divided into three parts as well or not? And what about the one after that? etc. The same for dividing into five parts, then into four. Finally, the problem was to understand a very abstract and general numerical law, which stipulates that the periodicity of the multiples of a number n is n.
>
> From 9 or 10 years children become progressively aware of this numerical law. At 9 or 10 years, children can find all the piles that could be exactly divided by a given divisor. This is called "horizontal generalization". But, when children had found all the successive correct piles that can be divided, for instance, into two parts, they cannot immediately find the correct piles in the case of another divisor. For instance, some children predicted, for a divisor of 3, exactly the same piles as for a divisor of 2! The generalization from one divisor to another one is called "vertical generalization". It is instructive to observe, in Gréco's results, that when the vertical generalization had begun, it followed successive divisors and could not jump directly, for instance, from 3 to 5. Success in vertical generalization is observed around 10–12 years. But, taking other situations into account, not reported here, it appears that a complete abstraction from cardinal values, which implies the processing on pure iteration, was observed at about 12–14 years. Younger children need to imagine hypothetical quantities (even if they know they are probably not the right ones) to process on these examples and come to a conclusion.
>
> Finally, from Gréco's studies and those from other researchers in the Piagetian group, we can conclude that number development follows two general levels of abstraction. The first level (in childhood) concerns the qualitative differences between objects, and allows counting and natural numbers (for counting we have to neglect the specific properties that differentiate the counted objects; this is the Piagetian abstraction principle). The second level (in adolescence) starts from numbers, but allows people to understand general numerical laws whatever the numbers may be. For abstracting general laws we have to go beyond the specific cardinal values of the numbers.

processing (including working memory, speed of processing, etc.).

As a whole, it is obvious that cognitive development is implicated in scientific knowledge acquisitions. But, even if general models can be drawn, the scientific domain is quite heterogeneous, leading to intra- and interindividual differences.

2.3 Thinking about oneself

Moshman (1998b) has recalled that "Erikson himself proposed that formal operations may be a necessary, though not sufficient, condition for the construction of identity" (1998b, p. 4). Further, he quoted a very explicit passage from Erikson (1968):

The cognitive gifts developing during the first half of the second decade add a powerfull tool to the task of youth. Piaget calls the gains in cognition made toward the middle teens the achievement of "formal operations". This means that the youth can now operate on hypothetical propositions and can think of possible variables and potential relations [. . .]. Such cognitive orientation forms not a contrast but a complement to the need of the young person to develop a sense of identity, for, from among all possible and imaginable relations, he must make a series of ever-narrowing selections of personal, occupational, sexual, and ideological commitment. (1968, p. 245)

How can we understand these proposals? The first way is to consider cognitive development and identity construction separately, with an implicit assumption that cognitive development corresponds to the competencies assessed by Piagetian tasks. Again, we are in the previously criticized paradigm where cognitive development is evaluated through one domain, scientific knowledge. This way is partially illustrated by Boyes and Chandler (1992, quoted by Moshman, 1998b) who did not find a significant relation between formal stage and identity status, but, instead, found a strong association between formal operational thinking and higher epistemic levels (i.e., at these epistemic levels, one considers knowledge as an active or subjective construction), and there is also a strong association between higher epistemic levels and the more advanced identity status.

The second way is to think about the cognitive transformations at stake *in* the construction of identity. Thus, cognitive development is not really an external tool for identity, or a prerequisite condition. But, when adolescents consider their own situation and perspectives, they may proccess according to the general new trends that could be observed in other domains. Indeed, as Erikson suggested (in the earlier quotation from Moshman), the construction of identity during adolescence can be viewed as illustrating some of the new cognitive skills presented in this chapter. For instance, the present personal situation is no more considered as an inevitability; instead the present personal situation is evaluated as one possibility among many others. In some cases (for instance, about professional choices), possibilities may be systematically explored (which corresponds to a combinatorial skill). Moreover, if the adolescent can think about his/her own previous child personality, this implies a new representative level in the personality domain, where the child personality constitutes the target of the new representative level. Furthermore, if identity construction comprises some kind of pressure to avoid contradictions and to integrate various aspects in a coherent system, logical skills are unavoidably involved. And finally, as a whole, progress in abstraction are

necessarily linked to the core meaning of the concept of identity, according to Moshman's definition: "An identity is an explicit theory of oneself as a person" (1998b, p. 1).

Of course, cognitive aspects are not the only ones in the construction of identity. That is the reason why they may constitute a necessary but not a sufficient condition of identity achievement. But this statement does not imply that success in formal stage tasks (i.e., in the scientific domain) should be a prerequisite for achieving identity.

3. In search of explanations and theoretical frameworks

Most researchers on cognitive development are greatly occupied with the descriptive characterization of stages, sequences, and architectures of the growing cognition. But developmentalists are also concerned by the more problematic and far from achieved attempt towards explanations, mechanism and developmental factors.

It would appear, especially from the previously quoted synthesis on the post-Piagetian field (Bideaud, 1999; de Ribaupierre, 1997), that some common concerns and debatable preoccupations can be drawn from present theorizations, event if these theorizations are still mostly divergent.

If there were a race, twelve years or so ago, between theorists (as Sternberg, 1988, humorously suggested) the constructivist approach would probably be the winner. This approach constitues the general framework for understanding cognitive development (Bideaud, 1999). Indeed, cognitive progress does not come solely from maturation or social and environmental pressure, but it is the result of the *reactions* from individuals to the successive *external incitements*.

From the starting point of constructivism, three main questions will be considered. Can cognitive development be explained by progress in attentional resources? What are the contributions of recent new kinds of model? How can the obvious cognitive variability be coordinated with general cognitive statements? Finally, a distinction between developmental processes, developmental mechanism, and developmental factors will be emphasized.

3.1 Cognitive and memory developments

In the neo-Piagetian group, a common explanation of cognitive growth was to consider progress in attentional resources (Case, 1985; de Ribaupierre & Pascual-Leone, 1979; Halford, 1993). Beyond the great diversity of authors' proposals, the general idea is based on four statements: (a) cognitive tasks, especially the Piagetian ones, can be divided into cognitive elements which have to be processed at the same time; (b) with cognitive stages, the number of these elements increases; (c) in addition, attentional resources in children progress with age; (d) it follows that when the tasks need more and more attentional resources, they will be progressively solved with age, in relation with the improvement of attentional resources. As an example, consider the successive 24 steps for solving the balance beam problem in Pascual-Leone's theory (de Ribaupierre & Pascual-Leone, 1979): in each step various schemes are described and the number of schemes which have to be simultaneously boosted in the mental space are computed.

From this perspective, cognitive development must be considered in the framework of functional constraints, especially the working memory load (de Ribaupierre & Hitch, 1994; Roulin & Monnier, 1996). But the question is to know if the attentional capacities really do increase with age, or if some kind of chunking makes free some part of the total fixed processing space (several possibilities are suggested by Case, 1985).

In fact, according to Ericsson and Kintsch (1995), capacities in short-term memory depend on long-term memory and it seems difficult to postulate a general attentional capacity free from contexts. For instance, chess players do not necessarily show superior performances on memory tasks in other contexts than the chess context. The same for the mental calculators; they exhibit exceptional memory for digits, but they show capacities within the normal range for other types of materials. It follows that there is no one general memory capacity, which could be free from contexts and experience. Consequently, the increase in memory capacities with age can be understood as the *consequence* of practice and development, not as the *cause* which could explain cognitive development.

3.2 Contribution of new models

Present theoretical evolution in the field of cognitive development leads to mathematical models of developmental changes.

Thus, dynamic systems models (van Geert, 1997) aim at more realistic descriptions of developmental processes, since actual growth curves are rarely linear. In these models, mathematical equations, for transitions between successive times, aim to take into account sudden jumps, slowing down, regressions, etc. According to this approach, development is considered as a complex system in evolution, as for other complex systems, for instance, the weather system or the population densities. Many factors interact. There are long-term determinations, and small differences at the start may produce great differences later on. Moreover, dynamic equations clearly show how weak modifications in developmental parameters lead to very different growth curves: in some cases, predictible progressions tend towards a given point; in other cases, evolutions are chaotic and not really predictable. But a striking question remains to appreciate the pertinent cues leading to a description of the cognitive system complexity at a given point in time.

Besides, connectionist models (Elman, Bates, Johnson, Karmiloff-Smith, Parisi, & Plunkett, 1996) exam the possibilities of formal networks to learn adapted responses in cognitive tasks. These networks are made of units which behave according to what the real neurons are supposed to, and they can solve Piagetian tasks, even at the formal stage level (see Shultz, 1996, for the balance beam problem). Of course, these models are just simulations of development. Although they model the neuronal activity, they do not indicate the actual developmental process (Lehalle, 1998). No child can learn to solve the balance beam problem through the repetition of 100 presentations. Nevertheless, connectionist models have a great interest in showing that learning is possible without the necessity to postulate previous innate knowledge or explicit cognitive control. It is just a matter of architecture and developmental mechanism, that is, developmental laws operating between input and output.

Nevertheless, these new approaches do not lead to a rejection of traditional structural models (Lehalle, 1998). Structural models can be used in two very different ways. First, if cognitive organisations are similar in various domains, the similarities may be defined in general or "structural" forms: see the new descriptions of cognitive stages in the neo-Piagetian field (for instance, Fischer, 1980). Second, structural models, especially the logical ones, may describe not the "structures as a whole", but the structural and implicit necessities which implicitly control the cognitive activity in a given context. For instance, it is convenient to differentiate "categories" (in particular, perceptual categories) from "logical class", because the former is supported by a relation of similarity that is not transitive (if A looks like B, and B like C, it does not necessarily follow that A looks like C; think, for instance, of three birds), whereas the latter is supported by common properties (what is a bird?, what is a duck?) and class inclusion (ducks are included in the category of birds) which correspond, in particular, to the transitive operational rule.

3.3 Variabilities
When a person grows up, he or she goes through general developmental stages, but at the same time, he or she becomes an individual different from others. Thus, cognitive development is intrinsically linked to differentiation.

First, intra-individual variabilities indicate, as we have seen already, that every cognitive domain and every skill in a situation must be actively constructed (Fischer et al., 1990). Consequently, when a high level of performance is observed in a situation, the same level is not automatically observed in a new situation. This is due to the fact that structurations are first *implicit* structurations of *explicit* contents. In fact, structurations appear twice: at first, they correspond to implicit constraints in specific situations (in this case, they are weakly generalizable), later on, they may be abstracted from the various situations and considered on an explicit level, which induces

generalization and lessens intra-individual variability.

There is also an inter-individual variability, especially on Piagetian tasks. Indeed, few adolescents can reach the formal stage level in the standardized classic tasks coming from Inhelder and Piaget (1955). (See, for example, Longeot, 1969; Martorano, 1977; Neimark, 1975.) These results may be interpreted as if the formal stage were not a general cognitive stage but rather a personal characteristic observed in some people.

But, following Piaget (1972), two considerations have to be underlined. First, it is conceivable that individuals can reach the formal stage but only in specific contexts or situations, for instance, about professional concerns. In fact, Piagetian tasks belong to the scientific domain which is a specific context. When people fail in this context, it does not mean that he or she will fail to present formal schemes in all other contexts. Moreover (Danner & Day, 1977), prompts can elicit formal operations in adolescents (13 and 17 years) but not in 10-year-old children. It means that an underlying competence does exist in adolescents, but not yet in late childhood.

Second, even if a final stage were not so frequent, it does not mean that this stage is not a good candidate for being a milestone in cognitive development. On the contrary, it could be that both individual and historical progress will conduct up to this stage. Thus, a study conducted in France (Flieller, 1999) shows that today's adolescents exhibited a higher level of cognitive development in Piagetian standardised tasks than similar samples of adolescents 20 or 30 years ago.

3.4 A distinction between developmental processes, developmental mechanisms and developmental factors
The previous discussion leads us to consider that cognitive development must be approached through the distinction between developmental processes, developmental mechanisms and developmental factors.

The developmental processes refer to successive progresses with age that are captured through the description of developmental sequences or stages.

But processes are supported by biologically innate mechanisms which produce transformations at every period of age. In the Piagetian view, these mechanisms correspond to equilibration. But connectionist models, as well, have tried to identify the basic developmental laws or learning rules. On the neuronal level, mechanisms correspond to the innate properties of neuronal activity, considered at various timescales (see Hebb's law). On the psychological level, the same mechanisms may be approached in more descriptive terms through developmental transformations such as integration, differentiation, generalization, or abstraction. But there is a bi-univoque mapping between these two levels of empirical investigation (neural and psychological). Moreover, if developmental mechanisms are identified, they have to be effective and recognized at every level of development, even though they concern different levels of skill.

Developmental factors stress what may release the mechanisms that in turn produce developmental processes. Factors comprise common incitements from social and physical worlds but also specific influences and experiences which induce inter-individual variability. However, this inter-individual variability must be understood more as an orientation towards activities in specific domains than as true differences in cognitive capacity.

4. Conclusion

As a whole, it is convenient to conclude that most adolescents acquire abstract cognitive skills in the contexts they experience, with no immediate generalization through other contexts. As a consequence, cognitive assessment of gereral stages is intrinsically doubtful (Lehalle & Mellier, 1984). One can be sure of the competence if an individual presents some evidence of a given cognitive level in a specific situation. But we cannot decide the absence of competence if an individual fails to present the appropriate level in a specific situation because it remains always possible that he/she could present this level in a more familiar context or situation.

In sum, the previously quoted "Calvinist principle" (Fischer et al., 1990) allows an optimist view on cognitive construction and competence among adolescents: when an adolescent fails a cognitive task, it does not mean that he/she should fail all the tasks from the same cognitive level.

References

Adelson, J. (1975). The development of ideology in adolescence. In S. E. Dragastin, & G. H. Elder (Eds.), *Adolescence in the life cycle* (pp. 63–78). Washington, DC: Hemisphere Publishing Corporation.

Bideaud, J. (1980). Développement moral et développement cognitif [Moral development and cognitive development]. *Bulletin de Psychologie, 33*(345), 589–601.

Bideaud, J. (1999). Psychologie du développement: Les avatars du constructivisme [Developmental psychology: The misadventures of constructivism]. *Psychologie Française, 44–3*, 205–220.

Bond, T.G. (1998). Fifty years of formal operational research: The empirical evidence. *Archives de Psychologie, 66*, 221–238.

Bond, T.G. (2001) Building a theory of formal operational thinking: Inhelder's psychology meets Piaget's epistemology. In A. Tryphon, & J. Vonèche (Eds), *Working with Piaget: Essays in honour of Bärbel Inhelder* (pp. 65–83). London: Psychology Press.

Case, R (1985). *Intellectual development: Birth to adulthood*. Orlando, FL: Academic Press.

Danner, F.W., & Day, M.G. (1977). Eliciting formal operations. *Child Development, 48*, 1600–1606.

Demetriou, A. (Ed.). (1988). *The neo-Piagetian theories of cognitive development: Toward an integration*. Amsterdam: Elsevier.

Demetriou, A., & Efklides, A. (1981). The structure of formal operations: The ideal of the whole and the reality of the parts. In J. A. Meacham, & N. R. Santilli (Eds.), *Social development in youth: Structure and content* (pp. 20–46). Basel, Switzerland: Karger.

Demetriou, A., & Efklides, A. (1988). Experiential structuralism and neo-Piagetian theories: Toward an integrated model. In A. Demetriou (Ed.), *The neo-Piagetian theories of cognitive development: Toward an integration* (pp. 173–223). Amsterdam: Elsevier.

Demetriou, A., Efklides, A., Papadaki, M., Papantoniou, G., & Economou, A. (1993). Structure and development of causal-experimental thought: From early adolescence to youth. *Developmental Psychology, 29*(3), 480–497.

Elman, J.L., Bates, E.A., Johnson, M.H., Karmiloff-Smith, A., Parisi, D., & Plunkett, K. (1996). *Rethinking innateness*. Cambridge, MA: MIT Press.

Erikson, E.H. (1968). *Identity: Youth and crisis*. New York: Norton.

Ericsson, K.A., & Kintsch, W. (1995). Long-term working memory. *Psychological Review, 102*(2), 211–245.

Fischer, K.W. (1980). A theory of cognitive development: The control and construction of hierarchies of skills. *Psychological Review, 87*(6), 477–531.

Fischer, K., Kenny, S.L., & Pipp, S.L. (1990). How cognitive processes and environmental conditions organize discontinuities in the development of abstractions. In C. L. Alexander, & E. J. Langer (Eds.), *Higher stages of human development* (pp. 162–187). New York: Oxford University Press.

Fischer, K.W., Yan, Z., & Stewart, J. (2003). Adult cognitive development: Dynamics in the developmental web. In J. Valsiner, & K. Connolly (Eds.), *Handbook of developmental psychology* (pp. 491–516). Thousand Oaks, CA: Sage.

Flieller, A. (1999). Comparison of the development of formal thought in adolescent cohorts aged 10 to 15 years (1967–1996 and 1972–1993). *Developmental Psychology, 35*(4), 1048–1058.

Graber, J.A., & Petersen, A.C. (1991). Cognitive changes at adolescence: Biological perspectives. In K. R. Gibson, & A. C. Petersen (Eds.), *Brain maturation and cognitive development* (pp. 253–279). New York: Aldine de Gruyter.

Gray, W.M. (1990). Formal operational thought. In W. F. Overton (Ed.), *Reasoning, necessity, and logic: Developmental perspectives* (pp. 227–253). Hillsdale, NJ: Lawrence Erlbaum Associates, Inc.

Gréco, P. (1963). Le progrès des inférences itératives et des notions arithmétiques chez l'enfant et l'adolescent [The progress of iterative inferences and arithmetical concepts in childhood and adolescence]. In P. Gréco, B. Inhelder, B. Matalon, & J. Piaget, *La formation des raisonnements récurrentiels* (pp. 143–281). Paris: Presses Universitaires de France.

Gréco, P. (1988) Préface [Preface]. In J. Bideaud, *Logique et bricolage chez l'enfant*, Lille: Presses Universitaires de Lille.

Halford, G.S. (1993). *Children's understanding: The development of mental models*. Hove, UK: Lawrence Erlbaum Associates Ltd.

Inhelder, B. (1954/2001) Les attitudes expérimentales de l'enfant et de l'adolescent, *Bulletin de Psychologie, 7*, 272–282. (Translated T. Bond, The experimental approaches of children and adolescents.)

In A. Tryphon, & J. Vonèche (Eds), *Working with Piaget: Essays in honour of Bärbel Inhelder* (pp.193–209). London: Psychology Press.

Inhelder, B., & Piaget, J. (1955). *De la logique de l'enfant à la logique de l'adolescent* [The growth of logical thinking from childhood to adolescence]. Paris: Presses Universitaires de France.

Keating, D.P. (2004). Cognitive and brain development. In R. M. Lerner, & L. Steinberg (Eds.), *Handbook of adolescent psychology* (2nd ed.) (pp. 45–84). Hoboken, NJ: John Wiley & Sons.

Lamborn, S.D., Fischer, K., & Pipp, S. (1994). Constructive criticism and social lies: A developmental sequence for understanding honesty and kindness in social interactions. *Developmental Psychology, 30*, 495–508.

Lawson, A.E., & Wollman, W.T. (1976). Encouraging the transition from concrete to formal cognitive functioning. *Journal of Research in Science Teaching, 13*(5), 413–430.

Lehalle, H. (1995). *Psychologie des adolescents* [Psychology of adolescents] (4th ed.). Paris: Presses Universitaires de France (Original work published 1985).

Lehalle, H. (1994). Aspects logiques et génétique du raisonnement expérimental [Logical and developmental aspects of experimental reasoning]. In M. Blancheteau, & A. Magnan (Eds.), *Psychologie expérimentale et psychologie du développement* (pp. 271–290). Paris: L'Harmattan.

Lehalle, H. (1998). Sagesse et illusions de la modélisation [Wisdom and illusions of models], *Bulletin de Psychologie, 51*(435). Special issue in honor of Jean Piaget, 249–263.

Lehalle, H. (2001). Le développement cognitif des adolescents. Caractéristiques générales et variabilités [Cognitive development in adolescents. General aspects and variability]. In C. Golder, & D. Gaonac'h (Eds.), *Enseigner à des adolescents. Manuel de psychologie* (pp. 58–75). Paris: Hachette.

Lehalle, H., & Mellier, D. (1984). L'évaluation des opérations intellectuelles: La question du langage . . . et quelques autres [Assessment of intellectual operations: Language matters . . . and some other questions]. *Rééducation Orthophonique, 22*(137), 213–232.

Lehalle, H., & Savois, C. (1985). Signification et ancrage significatif dans une situation dite de "proportionnalité" [Meaning and meaningful anchoring in a so-called "proportionality" situation]. *Archives de Psychologie, 53*, 345–364.

Longeot, F. (1969). *Psychologie différentielle et théorie*

opératoire de l'intelligence [Differential psychology and operative theory of intelligence]. Paris: Dunod.

Marini, Z., & Case, R. (1994). The development of abstract reasoning about physical and social world. *Child Development, 65*, 147–159.

Martorano, S.C. (1977). A developmental analysis of performance on Piaget's formal operation tasks. *Developmental Psychology, 13*(6), 666–672.

McClelland, J.L. (1989). Parallel distributed processing: Implications for cognition and development. In R. G. M. Morris (Ed.), *Parallel distributed processing: Implications for psychology and neurobiology* (pp. 9–45). Oxford: Clarendon Press.

Moshman, D. (1998a). Cognitive development beyond childhood. In W. Damon (Ed.), *Handbook of child psychology. Volume II: Cognition, perception and language* (5th ed.) (pp. 947–978). New York: John Wiley & Sons.

Moshman, D. (1998b). Identity as a theory of oneself. *The Genetic Epistemologist, 26*(3), 1–9.

Neimark, E.D. (1975). Intellectual development during adolescence. In F. D. Horowitz, E. M. Hetherington, S. Scarr-Salapatek, & G. M. Siegel (Eds.) *Review of child development research, Volume 4* (pp. 541–594). Chicago: University of Chicago Press.

Noelting, G. (1982). *Le développement cognitif et le mécanisme de l'équilibration* [Cognitive development and the mechanism of equilibration]. Chicoutimi, Québec: Gaëtan Morin.

Noelting, G., Rousseau, J-P., Bond, T., & Brunel, M-L. (2000). Can qualitative stage characteristics be revealed quantitatively? *Archives de Psychologie, 68*, 259–275.

Piaget, J. (1924). *Le jugement et le raisonnement chez l'enfant* [Judgment and reasoning in the child]. Neuchâtel and Paris: Delachaux et Niestlé.

Piaget, J. (1945). *La formation du symbole chez l'enfant* [Play, dreams and imitation in childhood]. Neuchâtel and Paris: Delachaux et Niestlé.

Piaget, J. (1952). Equilibre et structures d'ensemble [Equilibrium and structures of the whole]. *Bulletin de Psychologie, 6*, 4–10.

Piaget, J. (1954). La période des opérations formelles et le passage de la logique de l'enfant à celle de l'adolescent [The period of formal operations and the transition from the child logic to the adolescent one]. *Bulletin de Psychologie, 7*, 247–253.

Piaget, J. (1956). Les stades du développement intellectuel de l'enfant et de l'adolescent [The stages of intellectual development in children and adolescents]. In P. Osterrieth, J. Piaget, R. de Saussure, J.

M. Tanner, H. Wallon, R. Zazzo et al., *Le problème des stades en psychologie de l'enfant* (pp. 33–42). Paris: Presses Universitaires de France.

Piaget, J. (1972). Intellectual evolution from adolescence to adulthood. *Human Development, 15*, 1–12.

Piaget, J., & Inhelder, B. (1951). *La genèse de l'idée de hasard chez l'enfant* [The origins of the idea of chance in children]. Paris: Presses Universitaires de France.

Piaget, J., & Szeminska, A. (1941). *La genèse du nombre chez l'enfant* [The child's conception of number]. Neuchâtel and Paris: Delachaux et Niestlé.

Ribaupierre, A. de (1997). Les modèles néo-piagétiens: Quoi de nouveau? [The neo-Piagetian models: What's new?]. *Psychologie Française, 42*(1), 9–21.

Ribaupierre, A. de, & Hitch, G.J. (Eds.). (1994). *The development of working memory*. Hove, UK: Lawrence Erlbaum Associates Ltd.

Ribaupierre, A. de, & Pascual-Leone, J. (1979). Formal operation and M power: A neo-Piagetian investigation. *New Directions for Child Development, 5*, 1–43.

Rittle-Johnson, B., & Siegler, R.S. (1998). The relation between conceptual and procedural knowledge in learning mathematics: A review. In C. Donlan (Ed.), *The development of mathematical skills* (pp. 75–110). Hove, UK: Psychology Press.

Roulin, J.L., & Monnier, C. (1996). La mémoire de travail [The working memory]. In F. Eustache, B. Lechevalier, & F. Viader (Eds.), *La mémoire. Neuropsychologie clinique et modèles cognitifs* (pp. 237–278). Bruxelles: De Boeck University.

Shultz, T.R. (1996). Models of cognitive development. In V. Rialle, D. Fisette, & D. Payette (Eds.), *Penser l'esprit. Des sciences de la cognition à une philosophie cognitive* (pp. 393–450). Grenoble: Presses Universitaires de Grenoble.

Shultz, T.R. (2003). *Computational developmental psychology*. Cambridge, MA: MIT Press.

Siegler, R.S. (1978). The origins of scientific reasoning. In R. S. Siegler (Ed.), *Children's thinking: What develops?* (pp. 109–149). Hillsdale, NJ: Lawrence Erlbaum Associates, Inc.

Smith, L. (1993). *Necessary knowledge: Piagetian perspectives on constructivism*. Hove, UK: Lawrence Erlbaum Associates Ltd.

Sodian, B., Zaitchik, D., & Carey, S. (1991). Young children's differentiation of hypothetical beliefs from evidence. *Child Development, 62*, 753–766.

Stavy, R. (1981). Teaching inverse function via the concentration of salt water solution. *Archives de Psychologie, 49*, 267–287.

Sternberg, R.J. (1988). A day at developmental downs: Sportscast for race #2 – Neo-Piagetian theories of cognitive development. In A. Demetriou (Ed.), *The neo-Piagetian theories of cognitive development: Toward an integration* (pp. 1–23). Amsterdam: Elsevier.

Tomlinson-Keasey, C., & Keasey, C.B. (1974). The mediating role of cognitive development in moral judgment. *Child Development, 45,* 291–298.

van Geert, P. (1997). Variability and fluctuation: A dynamic view. In E. Amsel, & K. A. Renninger (Eds.), *Change and development: Issues of theory, method, and application* (pp. 193–212). Mahwah, NJ: Lawrence Erlbaum Associates, Inc.

6

Self-concept, self-esteem, and identity

Françoise D. Alsaker and Jane Kroger

LEARNING OBJECTIVES

The first aim of this chapter is to provide basic knowledge on central concepts within the literature on the self, self-concept, self-esteem, and identity. The second aim is to give an understanding of the importance of the adolescent period for the development of self-concept and identity. Finally, we will present an overview of the empirical research done in these areas.

Theories and researches on self-concept, self-esteem, and identity will be presented separately. In the first section of the chapter, we will present models of self-concept and self-esteem and research on gender differences, on change and stability, and on selected areas of influence. In the second section, we turn to identity. After presenting models of identity formation, methods of assessment, empirical findings, and critical comments on the identity status paradigm, current issues in the identity status literature are discussed.

Introduction

Defining the "self", either for research purposes or for personal matters, is an intricate task. As to research purposes, several authors (e.g., Green-wald, 1982; Harter, 1983) have already pointed to the fact that the self-literature is overflowing with concepts and that the definitions offered are very often ambiguous, incomplete and overlapping. Wylie's (1974) primary criticism of this field of research was that the constructs frequently seemed to point to no clear empirical referents. Wylie suggested that research in this field would benefit from moving from molar (e.g., the self) to molecular concepts (such as specific self-representations). This distinction is one of the reasons why we chose to focus on more specific concepts in this chapter and to address self-concept and identity in two definite and separate sections.

The terms, self-concept, self-esteem, and identity have become increasingly important topics of both theory and research in psychology over the past 40 years. Furthermore, each of these topics has come to hold special meanings in the psychological literature. Self-concept generally refers to an individual's characteristic features, beliefs, attitudes, and feelings of and about the self. Self-concept generally holds a descriptive element of some important attributes of oneself. So, for example, an adolescent's self-concept might include such thoughts as "I am tall for my age, but popular and a lover of nature." Self-esteem, by contrast, refers to how one evaluates one's own personal attributes. It may also denote the degree of self-worth one feels. An adolescent with low self-esteem might say, "I expect that others won't like me because I am such a boring person." Identity refers to how one uses knowledge about oneself to find vocational, ideological, and sexual roles within a society that best express "who one is". Identity has a contextual element a feeling of "being at home" within particular social roles that "fit". An adolescent might say the following about his or her identity: "Now I can see who I am and want to be – a person with a strong sense of justice that must work to help the powerless in society". As shown in these examples, self-concept/self-esteem and identity are closely related to one another. However, the two fields of research have developed in different conceptual traditions that seldom refer to one another. The latter has definitely contributed to the feeling of confusion we have already mentioned. Before we turn to the specifics of self-concept, self-esteem, and identity, we want to shed some light on the particular position of the adolescent period for the development of these personality characteristics.

The various chapters in this book point to a major characteristic of the adolescent period that is crucial to our discussion: adolescence is a time of change and transition. Transitions generally mean new orientations, which also imply the danger of disorientation. As discussed by Alsaker and Flammer (this volume), the physiological changes of puberty challenge the child's view of her/himself. The pubertal changes are challenging because they really bring totally new physical and emotional experiences. Younger children may have observed that they grow, and they are usually proud of it, but the growth of body hair or of the breasts, for example, is something totally new. Several of these changes also bring new sensations, and they are associated with representations of being an adult. Also, bodily changes work as signals to others and trigger new reactions. Such reactions may, for example, consist of higher demands put on the young adolescent, who does not look like a child, and should not behave like a child anymore. The challenges of puberty may more generally be associated with discrepancies between the young adolescent's perception of himself in terms of maturation and the reactions from adults.

Positive reactions to the new body appearance may also represent a challenge. For example, when older boys start showing a special interest in pubertal girls, the adolescent girl is confronted with an unknown type of attention. The attention of these boys is actually directed toward new facets of her appearance. It is not directed toward the girl she was, but toward the young woman she is becoming and may challenge her sense of identity.

Early adolescence is also a period when relations to others (peers as well as parents) are in transition and a time when many adolescents also experience changes in their school environment, such as moving from elementary school to junior high school. In many countries, adolescents have to make decisions that will have a great impact on their further academic and working career and thus play a crucial role for their self-definition.

All these changes happen at a time when formal operational thought emerges, i.e., a time when a shift from a concrete to a more abstract mode of thinking is taking place. This cognitive stage brings with it an ability to think about the self in an abstract way, to go beyond the self and to consider others' thoughts as well as one's own (Ellis & Davis, 1982). As a consequence, adolescence is also characterized by an increase in self-awareness (Rosenberg, 1979) and a greater capacity and inclination for introspection (Hansell, Mechanic, & Brondolo, 1986; Rosenberg, 1986). Earlier research on the content of children's and adolescents' self-concept has shown that there is a shift from the concrete to the abstract, from referring to external characteristics, to referring to activities and then to internal or psychological dimensions (see Fishbein, 1984; Harter, 1983). Also, interpersonal attributes and social competence seem to become salient in young adolescents' self-descriptions (Damon & Hart, 1988). Some authors (e.g., Ewert, 1984) have pointed to the rapidity of the progresses adolescents make in acquiring a psychological vocabulary and in becoming sensitive to their own and others' feelings. However, these rapidly growing cognitive abilities may also result in overgeneralizations about others and the self, because the ability to use abstract reasoning is not yet fully developed (Harter, 1983).

The many challenges encountered by adolescents have been recognized long ago, and this circumstance has led some authors to describe the adolescent years as a time of great inner turmoil (e.g., Hall, 1904) having implications for conceptions of self and identity. This "storm and stress" view of adolescence has been strongly criticized (e.g., Offer, Ostrov, & Howard, 1984; Rutter, Graham, Chadwick, & Yule, 1976). Studies focusing on normal adolescent populations (e.g., Offer, 1969; Rutter et al., 1976) have generally yielded little support for a turmoil hypothesis. The prevailing standpoint with respect to the issue of possible turmoil seems to be that (early) adolescence is a difficult time of adjustment even though the development of most adolescents is not characterized by extreme inner turmoil or affective crises. Rather, the numerous adolescent challenges may make great demands on the young person's ability to adjust her/his self-evaluations to incoming new information about her/himself. As a consequence, it is natural to assume, as does Rosenberg (1986), that adolescence may generally be considered as a time of self-concept difficulties.

Assuming that a person's self-concept changes with self-relevant experiences, we should expect self-representation of adolescents to undergo great changes. However, it is important to remember that the same events may be experienced very differently by different people. It would therefore be naive to expect some given event to have the same impact on all adolescents' self-concept or identity.

1. Self-concept and self-esteem

1.1 Historical frame of reference
Research on self-concept has its roots in writings from the end of the 19th and beginning of the 20th centuries. As noted by Harter (1998), there has been a resurgence of interest for these early writings during the last decade. Therefore, a short summary of this early literature is given in this section.

There is still considerable consensus in the literature about a basic dichotomy of self as a subject (knower, agent, or "I") and self as an object (also percept or "me"). The distinction was introduced in 1890 by James (James, 1950), who stated that the "I" was the active component of the self, the one that perceived the "Me". For James, there was no substantial "I" component that could be assessed separately from experiences, and he advanced the notion that the self as an object was more promising for purposes of research. The self-concept, thus, refers to James' Me-self.

Baldwin then introduced the idea of the complementarity of "ego" and "alter" (the other): "My sense of myself grows by imitation of you, and my sense of yourself grows in terms of my sense of myself" (Baldwin, 1897, p. 7). Accordingly, the symbolic interactionists conceived of the self primarily in terms of social processes. For Cooley (1902), the perception of what we believe others think about us was a central process in the construction of the self-concept. Cooley therefore introduced the term of "looking-glass-self". Mead (1934) elaborated some of Cooley's ideas, emphasizing the importance of the interpersonal interaction. In Mead's view, the child constructs a representation of some generalized other, whose perspective s/he uses to evaluate her/himself.

1.2 Different approaches to self-concept and self-esteem

Whereas self-concept has often been considered to be a descriptive component of self (Beane & Lipka, 1980), most authors agree on defining self-esteem in terms of an evaluative component. This distinction was already present in James' writings and elaborated by several authors many decades ago. Some authors, then, proposed a definition of self-esteem in terms of self-evaluation and self-worth (Brisset, 1972), while others defined it as an attitude toward the self (Burns, 1979; Rosenberg, 1965, 1979). Despite this apparently clear distinction between self-concept and self-esteem, the concepts are often used interchangeably.

There is a basic question as to whether or not it is possible to consider self-concept (i.e., self-perception and self-description) without including an evaluative component; this conceptualization involves adding an emotional aspect to the cognitive one. Actually, Rosenberg (1979) pointed out that humans do not seem to be able to perceive anything without passing judgment, and that it is difficult to establish the accuracy of an individual's self-concept because it is "largely couched in the terms of natural language". And "natural language" is "completely shot through with evaluative overtones" (p. 29). This implies that all self-perceptions are essentially *self-evaluations*. The inclusion of an affective component represents a shift in the conceptualization of the self-concept over the last decades, acknowledged in a recent review (van der Meulen, 2001).

Rosenberg (1979), who has provided the most detailed conceptualization of self-concept until now, defined self-concept as "the totality of the individual's thoughts and feelings having reference to himself as an object" (p. 7). Rosenberg proposed that self-concept be considered in terms of content (social identity, dispositions, and physical characteristics), structure (relationships between components of the self-concept), and what he termed dimensions of self-attitudes (intensity, stability, etc.). Self-concept refers here to what Rosenberg called the extant self-concept. His conceptualization also included the desired self (ideal self) and the presenting self, which refers to how one presents oneself to others (these last two aspects are not considered in this chapter). Rosenberg (1979) does not provide an exhaustive list of self-concept elements. However, when exemplifying his theoretical assumptions, he refers to specific elements in terms of evaluations of one's intelligence, attractiveness, and morality, or attitudes towards one's social class, ethnic heritage, etc. With regard to structure, Rosenberg called our attention to the concept of centrality (i.e., importance) of the various components of self-concept and their hierarchical organization.

There is now general agreement among researchers about considering self-concept as a *multidimensional* (or multifaceted) construct. This perspective on the self-concept was introduced by Shavelson (Shavelson, Hubner, & Stanton, 1976; Shavelson & Marsh, 1986) and further elaborated by Harter (1983). The term multidimensional refers to the different facets of an individual's behavior and experiences that may be the target of self-evaluations. Such facets include academic competence, social competence, appearance (looks), athletic competence, and also the individual as a whole. The latter dimension is usually referred to as global self-esteem or global self-evaluation and is used as a synonym to the concept of self-esteem (or self-worth). The concept of global self-evaluation, as used here, is not an overall concept, but in fact a specific one, referring to a specific process. Whereas specific self-evaluations are targeted towards specific and relatively concrete domains of competence, the process of global self-evaluation is directed towards the person as a whole. The concept of global self-evaluation has implications for how we should measure self-esteem. Rosenberg (1979) pointed out that simply to add up different components in order to assess the whole (i.e., the global facet of self-evaluation) is to ignore the fact that the global component is the product of a complex synthesis of elements. An individual's global self-esteem may be positive even if the same individual evaluates himself negatively in different specific domains. Consequently, Rosenberg's (1979) approach to the study of self-esteem has been to focus directly on individuals' global self-evaluations, employing items that were not related to any particular situations or areas of competence, but rather to the person's general feelings of worth and competence – or to their negative counterparts. Rosenberg actually introduced this notion of a separate "global self-esteem" very early in his writings (Rosenberg, 1965) and Harter included a general/global self-worth subscale in her self-concept instruments (1982; Harter, Waters, & Whitesell, 1998).

Shavelson et al. (1976) have proposed that the various components of self-concept are organized hierarchically, with general/global self-concept at the apex. Interestingly, in Shavelson's work, self-concept is explicitly defined as being evaluative. Thus, even if the author uses the term, self-concept, in his description of the hierarchical model, self-concept may be replaced by the term self-evaluation or self-esteem. Shavelson's model is based on the assumption that experiences of competence in a specific field lead to the formation of specific self-evaluations related to this field. Self-evaluations in related fields are then aggregated to form broader categories. Finally, the "general self-concept" is assumed to be formed on the basis of these "lower level" evaluations. Proponents of this hierarchical model usually also take into account the *relative importance* of specific components for an individual. The relative importance is called centrality in Rosenberg's model (1979).

The 1976 hierarchical model of Shavelson et al. assumes causal relationships between the different facets of self-evaluation. In this model, the global component may be built up on the basis of lower level components. However, we should keep in mind that the general component may also influence the perception of competence in specific areas and/or the direction and formation of other self-evaluative components. Therefore, the complexity of the multifaceted self-concept is probably better represented in a model that allows paths between the different domains of self-evaluation – in other words, from the global facets to the specific ones.

The focus on distinct dimensions of the self-concept has led to differentiated but sometimes seemingly contradictory findings. One example is that school achievement is only moderately associated with adolescents' global self-esteem, but that it correlates highly with the academic facet of self-esteem (Alsaker, 1989; Harter, 1982).

Another important move in the conceptualization of the self was made by Harter (1999; Harter et al., 1998), who introduced the notion of *relational self-worth*. This concept takes into consideration the fact that individuals evaluate themselves differently in various relationships. In fact, three-fourths of adolescents seem to experience significant variations in their self-worth according to the relational context in which they evaluate themselves. As an example, a young girl might report a high level of self-worth when she is together with her best friend and a moderate or even low level of self-worth when she is with her parents.

The concept of multiple selves is also used frequently today in the self-concept literature (Harter, 1999). Multiple selves builds on the fact that individuals adopt different roles in various contexts. Harter uses a six-sided polygon, on which each side represents a specific situation (i.e., in the classroom, with a group of friends, with my best friend, with my father, with my mother, with a romantic interest), to ask participants to generate six attributes or characteristics of themselves in these different situations. Next to that, adolescents are invited to identify contradictory characteristics of themselves. An important developmental task in adolescence is to find some way to deal with these sometimes contradictory elements of one's self-concept. Harter's (1999) findings seem to indicate that the number of opposing attributes increases between early and middle adolescence (see also section 1.4).

1.3 Gender differences

Gender differences in self-concept are usually not large, but they are consistent. Girls seem more vulnerable than boys to self-representations. Girls have more negative global self-evaluations than boys (e.g., Alsaker & Olweus, 1993; Simmons & Blyth, 1987). Interestingly, the significant but modest mean-score differences reported by Alsaker and Olweus (1993) reflect a large difference in the distribution of girls and boys at the extreme poles of the scale. There were approximately 25% more girls than boys with extremely negative self-evaluations and approximately 50% more boys than girls at the other pole of the scale, with extremely positive self-evaluations. It is well known that negative self-evaluation forms part of a depression syndrome (e.g., Battle, 1980; Foulds & Bedford, 1977). Since there do not seem to be any clear sex differences in perceived general self-worth in the two or three years preceding early adolescence (e.g., Harter, 1982), it may be tentatively assumed that these findings are associated with the gender difference in depression-related symptomatology that begins to emerge in early adolescence (see Chapter 16, this volume).

Data also consistently indicate that girls perceive themselves as less stable than boys with regard to their self-concept, a difference that increased with age in the two studies addressing this issue (Alsaker & Olweus, 1993; Rosenberg, 1986).

Several authors (e.g., Maccoby & Jacklin, 1974; Rosenberg & Simmons, 1975) have found some evidence for sex differences in variables related to the academic area. Boys have tended to have greater academic self-confidence or to place more importance on achievement than girls. Girls also report somewhat lower perceived academic competence in spite of slightly better school achievement (e.g., Alsaker, 1989).

1.4 Developmental patterns

1.4.1 Age-related changes
Different studies have come to somewhat conflicting conclusions as to whether or not there are age-related changes in self-esteem during early adolescence. Some authors have concluded that there is no clear evidence of an association between chronological age and self-esteem (Harter, 1982; Wylie, 1979), or for a view of adolescence as a period of discontinuity in self-representations or evaluations (Dusek & Flaherty, 1981). By the same token, O'Malley and Bachman (1983) reviewed five studies and concluded that there was reasonably solid evidence of age-related differences in self-esteem

between 13 and 23 years, and that the direction of change was one of improvement with age. Some other studies (Rosenberg, 1979; Simmons & Blyth, 1987; Simmons, Rosenberg, & Rosenberg, 1973) have indicated that self-concept disturbances are more likely to be associated with particular life changes that occur at certain ages (e.g., school transition) than with age per se.

Alsaker and Olweus (1993) used a cohort-longitudinal design with four adjacent cohorts of students ($N = 1689$) followed over two years to study the development of self-attitude (global negative self-evaluations and perceived instability of self) in early adolescence (age range 11–16 years). They found no clear relationship between age/grade and self-evaluations, although there was a weak trend towards improved self-esteem in boys and increased self-instability in the higher age range for both girls and boys. They found no support for a "stressful periods" hypothesis or discontinuity view with respect to self-evaluations. Possible changes in self-evaluations were very gradual and quite small. However, Alsaker and Olweus (1993) also reported a consistent "relative age" effect, implying that younger students within a grade had more negative self-attitudes. This result indicates the operation of social comparison processes that deserve more attention.

Another approach to the study of age-related changes in self-concept is the study of the contents of self-representations. The transition from childhood into adolescence brings changes from concrete and straightforward descriptions of oneself to more differentiated and complex evaluations. In her overview on the development of self-representations, Harter (1998) emphasized early adolescents' ability to think abstractly, and to coordinate concepts. The early adolescent may integrate trait labels in abstractions. For example, s/he may integrate attributes such as being a smart and creative person into the more abstract self-construct of being intelligent. As noted in an earlier section, at this age, social skills and attributes that influence social interaction seem to be salient (Damon & Hart, 1988). However, the early adolescent seems to lack the cognitive control that is necessary to integrate all – sometimes contradictory – facets of self-concept into a consistent theory. Therefore, the self-representations remain segregated (Fischer, 1980; Harter, 1998). In middle adolescence, the interconnection of concepts and abstractions develops further. Thus, the adolescent becomes able to recognize that s/he, for example, may be both cheerful and depressed. This period also brings increases in introspection and awareness of the inconsistency in behavior or self-representations across situations and roles. However, the adolescent cannot integrate the (seeming) contradictions of the self-facets yet. During early adolescence, inconsistency is generally upsetting to the individual, who tends to demonstrate all or-none-thinking, and to oscillate between the inconsistent aspects of his/her self-perception. In late adolescence, the drive towards a unified or consistent self-concept can be satisfied through higher abilities to coordinate concepts. The adolescent gradually becomes able to integrate contradicting self-facets in constructing higher order abstractions (e.g., being a flexible or an inconsistent person; Harter, 1998).

1.4.2 Stability

Some authors, such as Morse and Gergen (1970) have argued that the self-concept is highly mutable and dependent on the situational context (see earlier discussion on multiple selves). Contrariwise, proponents of consistency or self-maintenance theories (e.g., Lecky, 1945) assume a motive to act or to interpret events in accordance with one's self-concept, in order to maintain it unchanged. As part of a "construction system", global self-evaluations are expected to have a certain degree of stability helping us to organize our experiences in a meaningful way.

At this point, it is important to point to the distinction between cross-situational and longitudinal consistency (e.g., Epstein, 1977; Mischel, 1969). Mischel (1969), who was a proponent of the need to consider the role of the situation in personality features, argued at the same time that self-perceptions show considerable stability over time. There is, in fact, evidence for short-term changes in self-esteem, depending on situational factors (Harter, 1998). The position of Markus and Kunda (1986) is of particular interest on this point. Markus and Kunda use the

term working self-concept to refer to a rather malleable subset of a relatively stable system of self-representations. Other authors have used concepts such as baseline vs. barometric self-concept (Rosenberg, 1986; see later), or trait vs. state self-esteem (see Harter, 1998, for a review of these positions) to refer to the fact that self-representations may be both malleable and stable.

Under normal circumstances, self-representations will have a certain degree of stability and yet will develop and change with new experiences across the lifespan (Alsaker & Olweus, 2002; Epstein, 1973). However, change becomes somewhat less likely with increasing age. Thus, the highest degree of stability in self-representation should be expected in periods with little environmental or maturational change, whereas less stability would be anticipated in periods where events challenge individuals' views of themselves, as it is the case in adolescence.

There have been relatively few studies on the longitudinal stability of self-esteem. However, Alsaker and Olweus (1992) have reanalyzed previous developmental studies of self-esteem and compared earlier results with their own data. As could be expected, stability coefficients (autocorrelations) decreased as the interval between measurement points increased. For example, over a period of six months, the average correlation was .70, and it decreased smoothly (around .60 for one year and one and a half years) until it reached its lowest level for intervals of two years or more (around .40). The analyses also indicated a somewhat stronger decrease of the stability coefficients with time interval for girls than for boys; this result was especially true for longer time intervals.

Interestingly, boys' stability coefficients generally increased with age. Boys who were older at the first time of measurement yielded higher stability coefficients than younger boys, independent of the time interval between the measurements. Girls showed a slightly different pattern. Even though the same general trend was found, girls who were in the sixth grade at Time 1 showed less stability in self-evaluations than others. These girls were typically experiencing a shift from elementary to junior high school between the measurement points. The authors explained the lower stability coefficients as a likely consequence of changes in these young adolescents' social and academic environments (see Simmons & Blyth, 1987). Results support a "gradual consolidation hypothesis" stating that global negative self-evaluations are likely to become relatively more crystallized with increasing age. The results also indicate a decreasing impact of later experiences under ordinary conditions (Alsaker & Olweus, 2002).

These findings have clear implications. As self-evaluations tend to become more and more stable with age, awaiting a spontaneous "recovery" for highly negative self-representations would be naive. As a result, early adolescents showing strong tendencies towards self-deprecation, or other self-related problems, should be taken seriously and offered suitable treatment. Rosenberg (1965, 1979) has called our attention also to the individual's perception of the stability of his/her self-concept. Rosenberg refers to the degree to which a person "experiences rapid shifts and fluctuations of self-attitudes from moment to moment" (Rosenberg, 1986, p.126). This aspect of the process of self-evaluation is sometimes also referred to as the barometric self and contrasted with the average level of self-evaluation in an individual over time or across situations. Thus, a person may experience situational or longitudinal instability but still maintain a generally positive or negative attitude to him/herself. Nonetheless, empirical studies have often shown that adolescents who report a high degree of perceived instability generally also report more negative self-evaluations. This dimension of self-evaluation has received considerably less research attention than self-esteem. The data from the Rosenberg cross-sectional study (Rosenberg, 1979) pointed to a marked increase in perceived instability from ages 8 through 13. Additionally, Alsaker and Olweus (1993) found some evidence of increased instability in the period from grade 8 to grade 9. This finding fits well with earlier work, suggesting increased awareness of inconsistency among self-facets during middle adolescence and also supports the assumption that adolescence is a highly challenging time for individuals' working models of self.

1.5 Sources and correlates of self-esteem

Harter (1999) has come to the conclusion that perceptions of competence, on the one hand, and approval from significant others, on the other, provide a powerful explanation for individual differences in self-esteem. These two sources of self-esteem are additive, but they also work together to improve or impair adolescents' self-esteem. Among all possible factors that may have an impact on self-esteem or be associated with it, we chose three areas that are central in adolescents' lives: school, pubertal development, and negative experiences with peers. Other factors are treated more or less explicitly in other chapters (e.g., chapters on school, peer relations, and family).

1.5.1 School

As noted previously, Simmons and Blyth (1987) have considered the transition from elementary to junior high school as a particular stressor on adolescents' self-esteem. Alsaker and Olweus (1993), however, were unable to document any negative effects of the transition from elementary to junior high school in Norway. This difference may reflect differences in the character of the school transition in the United States and Norway. The gap between the elementary and junior high school environments in the United States seems to be much more important than it is in European countries. Unfortunately, results from other countries on this issue are not available.

School achievement is only weakly related to global self-evaluation (Alsaker, 1989; Wylie, 1979). However, correlations between perceived competence (academic self-concept) and achievement are usually higher. Harter (1982) reported correlations between "perceived cognitive competence" and test scores to range from .27 to .54. in samples of students in the third through the ninth grade. The latter correlations tend to be somewhat higher in higher grades (Alsaker, 1989). Also global self-concept and academic self-concept usually correlate moderately (r around .40). However, we should keep in mind that school may provide strong experiences of competence or incompetence that can be crucial to the individual's self-worth. These experiences of one's own competence are not necessarily linearly associated with academic results; they may depend on the personality of the student as well as on personality characteristics and communication styles of the teachers.

1.5.2 Pubertal maturation

Different aspects of pubertal timing and of weight have been examined in relation to global negative self-evaluations, body image, and perceived instability of self-concept. (Results on body image are discussed in Chapter 3, this volume, and not reiterated here. Suffice it to say that the general concern with appearance in the adolescent period seems to make body image an important factor with respect to global self-esteem (e.g., Levine & Smolak, 2002; Tobin-Richards, Boxer, & Petersen, 1983).)

With some exceptions, most studies have reported pubertal status and pubertal timing to be unrelated to self-esteem in *girls* (e.g., Brack, Orr, & Ingersoll, 1988; Brooks-Gunn & Ruble, 1983; Simmons & Blyth, 1987). However, Jaquish and Savin-Williams (1981) reported that girls who were more mature, independent of the timing of this maturation process, had a higher self-esteem than their less mature peers.

Considering how girls perceive themselves in terms of maturation as compared to their same-age peers, a German and a Norwegian study have yielded rather different results. German girls who perceived themselves as early maturers were found to have more positive self-attitudes (Silbereisen, Petersen, Albrecht, & Kracke, 1989). The Norwegian study, based on highly similar instruments, demonstrated the opposite effect (Alsaker, 1992). Furthermore, Norwegian girls who perceived themselves as early maturers were found to score higher on perceived instability of self (Alsaker, 1992) and to show more variability in self-esteem (measured three times a week, over a period of four weeks; Buchanan, 1991).

These somewhat dissimilar results possibly reflect the influence of social and cultural contexts. In fact, Simmons and colleagues have shown that pubertal status may interact with the social context in terms of school transition. Whereas menstrual status was unrelated to self-evaluation before school transition, they found that the girls who had lowest self-esteem were those who experienced menarche and school transition at the same time (Blyth, Simmons, & Zakin, 1985).

Most studies reviewed here have yielded no effects of pubertal status on self-esteem in *boys* (Blyth, Simmons, Bulcroft, Felt, VanCleave, & Bush 1981; Brack et al., 1988; Simmons & Blyth, 1987). When a relation has been reported (Alsaker, 1992), it was to the detriment of late maturers.

Menarche, considered a special event in the pubertal development of girls, has received much attention. Even if menarche has repeatedly been shown to be accompanied by negative feelings, some studies have also shown that menarche may have positive effects in terms of self-definition (Garwood & Allen, 1979; Greif & Ulman, 1982).

In sum, even if pubertal development is a great challenge to self-representation, it is not associated with a general impairment of self-esteem or body image. However, the association between increased weight and off-time maturation with body dissatisfaction and self-esteem clearly indicates that some adolescents are negatively affected by this challenge.

1.5.3 Negative experiences with peers: Victimization

Relationships between peers and with parents are generally sources of positive self-experiences that are treated in greater detail elsewhere in this volume. However, negative experiences with peers, such as rejection and victimization, are generally expected to lead to the formation of negative self-perceptions. Studies based on sociometric measures of rejection (i.e., unpopularity) have reported no association between rejected status and self-esteem among schoolchildren (Patterson, Kupersmidt, & Griesler, 1990). This paradoxical result partly reflects the fact that unpopularity in one's class does not tell the whole truth about individuals' actual experiences of rejection. First, so-called rejected children are not rejected by all peers; they may be part of a small group of friends, and their general unpopularity does not necessarily affect their self-esteem. Second, being unpopular does not mean that one necessarily experiences negative behaviors from peers.

In his first studies on victimization by peers, Olweus (1978) found that victimization was strongly related to poor self-esteem. This effect has been replicated in various studies (e.g., Boulton & Smith, 1994; Slee & Rigby, 1993). The general amount of victimization in the class (as perceived by the subject him/herself) has also predicted level of self-esteem beyond what was predicted by individual experiences of victimization alone (see Alsaker & Olweus, 2002). These findings are in line with Harter's (1998) proposal that appraisal from peers in more public domains (such as school setting) is "far more predictive of self-esteem than is approval from one's close friends" (p. 584).

Alsaker and Olweus (2002) have also shown that changes in victimization experiences over time co-varied clearly with changes in self-evaluation for girls as well as for boys. That is, subjects who were exposed to an increase in victimization over time increased their negative self-evaluations over time. Conversely, subjects who experienced a decrease in victimization tended to improve in self-esteem. And the greater the changes in victimization, the larger the changes in self-esteem.

At the same time, it should be emphasized that an individual's self-esteem is multiple determined and that a considerable proportion of individuals in a school are only minimally or not at all involved in victimization problems. Accordingly, changes in self-esteem, in both positive and negative directions, will occur for other reasons than changes in victimization by peers, and this is particularly true of individuals who are not seriously involved in bully/victim problems.

The results presented in this chapter show clearly that a (pre)adolescent's self-image, though relatively (interindividually) stable over shorter periods of time, may at the same time undergo fairly marked (intraindividual) changes. Such intraindividual changes may depend on the kind of experiences and events the preadolescent experiences. Assuming that an individual's self-representations are reasonably flexible and open to new information, one should expect self-evaluations to change with changes in relationships (e.g., the first romantic relationships).

However, due to the general consolidation process of self-perceptions on the basis of repeated experiences, new experiences should be less likely to influence self-representations over time.

Based on the writings of Stern (1985), who proposed a detailed conceptualization of representations of the self and others in interactions, we want to argue that extensive exposure to a certain type of experience may cause an overconsolidation of self-perceptions, even in the presence of clear changes in the social environment. This overconsolidation of self-perceptions may be particularly true when repeated interactions with others trigger intense emotional self-experiences, such as feelings of helplessness, worthlessness, mental pain or shame. This phenomenon would be typical of the self-experiences of maltreated, abused, and most probably also of victimized children.

1.6 Role of the self-concept for adolescent development

Self-concept and self-esteem are quite interesting from a developmental perspective because of their likely centrality to an individual's general adjustment, quality of life, and planning for the future. Given that all self-evaluations may be active in forming our perceptions and decisions (Markus & Wurf, 1987), self-evaluations are assumed to play a crucial role in the extent to which adolescents will engage in different activities, relationships etc., and thus shape their future development.

For example, an adolescent who has a positive attitude toward her/himself is more apt to give a positive impression of her/himself. This positive self-presentation is likely to trigger positive reactions from others, which in turn facilitates first contacts. In addition, adolescents who are convinced of their self-worth will be more likely to engage in new contacts than adolescents who think they are "nothing" (Goetz & Dweck, 1980). The latter group of people are usually convinced that nobody could be interested in being friends with them. In conclusion, adolescents with a higher self-esteem are more likely to make friends in new contexts. This process, in turn, can work as a protective factor against rejection, bullying etc.

The active role of self-representations in the individual's development may be positive in the case of positive self-evaluations but also detrimental to development in the case of self-derogation. Thus negative self-representations lead very often to vicious circles that are difficult to stop. Large-scale school programs for the enhancement of self-esteem have become rather popular in the United States in the last decades. However, self-esteem is influenced by so many sources, that it seems rather naive to hope to enhance self-esteem in all children and adolescents using the same intervention. Also, it is questionable whether all adolescents need self-esteem enhancement training. In fact the study by Alsaker and Olweus (1992, 1993) has shown that approximately 7% of adolescents are affected by highly negative self-evaluations and that most students had a healthy self-esteem. It would definitely be more appropriate to work intensively with these smaller groups of adolescents who are in great need for intervention and who do not necessarily gain from global interventions. Also, as repeatedly pointed out by Seligman (1995, 1998), one cannot produce a sense of self-esteem without first giving individuals an opportunity to enhance their competence and thus their sense of being competent. This argument leads us to the next debate in the self-literature.

A rather tenacious assumption has been that a certain proportion of subjects reporting high self-esteem may in fact report a spurious high self-esteem, mostly based on defensiveness. Arguments in favor of a distinction between genuinely positive self-evaluations and inflated self-esteem are based on the assumption that humans have a need for positive self-regard (see Epstein, 1973). Therefore, defense mechanisms are supposed to be activated when self-esteem is threatened. A competing hypothesis contends that the self-evaluative process is motivated mainly by a need to maintain one's self-concept as it is (self-consistency motive; e.g., Blyth & Traeger, 1983; Lecky, 1945). According to this hypothesis, events that do not fit with previous conceptions of oneself would be likely to be ignored or distorted. Following the latter arguments we may understand how false negative

as well as false positive self-evaluations may be maintained. Despite the apparent conflict between the arguments presented in defense of the two perspectives, and the diverging empirical findings, both motives are usually assumed to be important.

Returning to the issue of genuine versus spurious high self-esteem, we may note that the self-esteem motive as well as the self-consistency motive imply the use of some defense mechanisms (Rosenberg, 1979). The question thus arises as to what should be considered functional and dysfunctional self-evaluations.

We may draw a parallel to findings in the field of depression. Several studies have shown that non-depressed subjects usually have positively biased perception, while subjects showing depressive tendencies are more likely to be realistic in their self-evaluation (e.g., Alloy & Abramson, 1979; Brewin, 1988). Other results (Harter, 1986) have shown that students reporting high self-esteem seemed to have an inflated judgment of their competence in comparison to their teachers' reports. Also Colvin, Block, and Funder (1995) have reported negative short- and long-term consequences of self-enhancement. Too "realistic" perceptions may be related to self-derogation and positively biased perceptions may be considered fairly adaptive ways to protect self-esteem (Rosenberg, 1979). Contrariwise, too "unrealistic" self-appraisals would provide a rather unreliable basis for predictions.

In summary, there is little evidence that slightly inflated self-esteem is maladaptive. By the same token, there is considerable evidence showing that negative self-evaluations are associated with psychological maladjustment (e.g., Battle, 1980; Harter, 1998; Wilson & Krane, 1980). An important task for future research, as regards the issue of realistic versus biased perceptions, would therefore be to investigate the processes leading to biased negative self-perception.

2. Identity

Self-concept and identity are closely related areas. Both constructs can provide answers to the question, "Who am I?" But these two concepts do differ in important ways. Baumeister (1986) has defined the difference between the two as a difference in the level of reply. He notes that self-concept is one's *description* of who one is, while identity is one's *definition* of who one is. It may be possible for an attribute to be a part of one's self-concept, but not a part of one's identity. For example, "I sometimes procrastinate", may be part of one's self-concept, but not a part of one's identity ("I am generally a person who makes a commitment and follows it through"). Furthermore, self-concept is most frequently used to describe an individual's own attributes, while identity is generally defined in terms of one's biological and psychological characteristics in relation to a social context.

Erik Erikson (1963), the first psychologist seriously to write about issues of identity, stressed that identity is a three-part product of psyche, soma, and society. By this statement, Erikson meant that identity is the unique combination of our psychological interests, drives, needs, and defenses with our biological gender, attributes, strengths, and limitations, in interaction with opportunities offered by a social and cultural milieu. A feeling that "This is me and a place where I belong" occurs when there is an optimal sense of identity. In Erikson's words: "[Optimal identity's] most obvious concomitants are a feeling of being at home in one's body, a sense of 'knowing where one is going' and an inner assuredness of anticipated recognition from those who count" (Erikson, 1968, p.165). Thus, identity involves a feeling of self-sameness and continuity over time, as one comes to recognize and be recognized by others we choose to help us define our life directions.

How does a sense of identity develop? In Erikson's (1968) view it is the work of adolescents to undertake identity-defining commitments that will lead them into adult life. These commitments generally involve finding some vocational direction, a meaningful set of philosophical values by which to live one's life, and satisfying forms of sexual and sex role expression. How does this process unfold? Indeed, Erikson has characterized "*Identity vs. role confusion*" as the fifth task of healthy personality development; this task normally comes to the fore during adolescence and involves finding some optimal balance between identity and role confusion. In Erikson's view, one must experiment, explore, examine different possibilities for oneself, undergo some *role confusion*, in order to make later, more meaningful identity commitments.

A sense of identity emerges through the *identity formation process*, according to Erikson (1968). This identity formation process involves trying on potential adult roles and values "for fit", and discarding what does not work well. It involves blending earlier childhood identifications into a new product, which is greater than the sum of its individual parts. Identity formation occurs as one sifts through identifications with the people important to one during childhood and decides which attributes and values to retain as "one's own" and which to discard. "The final identity, then, as fixed at the end of adolescence, is superordinated to any single identification with individuals of the past: it includes all significant identifications, but it also alters them in order to make a unique and reasonably coherent whole of them" (Erikson, 1968, p.161). In Erikson's view, it is important that societies offer a psychosocial *moratorium* period to adolescents, a time of delay and permissiveness granted to youths before expecting commitments to adult roles sanctioned by the society itself. During this time, it is critical, in Erikson's (1968) view, that societies tolerate role experimentation among adolescents and not label these explorations as deviant behavior. Negative labeling by society may offer the adolescent an identity such as "delinquent" or "promiscuous", which may only too readily be accepted by youths in search of a niche in the wider social milieu. Through such labeling, youths may be only too happy to live up to society's negative labels. Optimal identity formation occurs through a psychosocial moratorium phase, in which there is active exploration by youths followed by meaningful commitments to adult vocational, ideological, and sexual values.

2.1 Ways of assessing identity

More recently, social scientists have attempted, empirically, to study identity and the identity formation process of adolescence. Some approaches have focused on the relationship of Erikson's "Identity vs. role confusion" task to other psychosocial tasks in the eight stage lifespan sequence (e.g., Constantinople, 1967, 1969; Rosenthal, Gurney, & Moore, 1981). Those adopting this approach have developed self-report inventories to examine and clarify the place of identity in relation to other Eriksonian stages. These writers argue that one cannot do justice to Erikson's model by focusing on only one psychosocial stage of development; rather, identity vs. role confusion must be understood in relation to all seven other psychosocial stages.

A second approach has focused on the "Identity vs. role confusion" task alone, conceptualizing its resolution as lying somewhere on a continuum between high and low points (e.g. Simmons, 1970). With this approach, researchers have examined identity achievement in quantitative terms as an entity one "has" to greater or lesser degree. Thus, scales of identity achievement vs. role confusion have been developed that provide a score regarding how identity achieved one is. Scales of this type have been used to examine identity achievement in relation to other personality variables such as locus of control, dogmatism, interpersonal trust, and self-concept (LaVoie, 1976; Tan, Kendis, Fine, & Porac, 1977).

A third general approach to studying identity has been through specific dimensions of identity described by Erikson. Thus, Blasi and Glodis (1995) focus on one's phenomenological experience of identity, while van Hoof (1999) focuses on spatial and temporal dimensions of identity. The identity status model developed by James Marcia (1966, 1967) has been the most popular dimensional approach to date, focusing on the identity dimensions of exploration and commitment processes. Marcia has identified four different styles (or *identity statuses*) by which adolescents make identity-defining decisions; these identity statuses are defined on the basis of exploration and commitment variables. Marcia and others have found associations between the identity statuses and various personality features, family antecedents, developmental patterns, as well as styles of resolving later Eriksonian tasks

(Kroger, 2004; Marcia, Waterman, Matteson, Archer, & Orlofsky, 1993).

2.2 Marcia's identity statuses

Elaborating Erikson's task of "Identity vs. role confusion", Marcia (1966) identified and empirically validated four different ways in which late adolescents may approach (or not) the task of forming identity commitments within any given social context; these four styles, or identity statuses are termed identity achievement, moratorium, foreclosure, and diffusion. Identity achieved individuals have formed their commitments based on their own terms, following an active period of exploration and search. During this exploration, they have sought ways in which they might best express their own values, preferences, and beliefs within the possible options presented by society, and the commitments they have eventually made reflect their own strivings for meaningful forms of self-expression. Foreclosed individuals, by contrast, have formed their identity-defining commitments without prior exploration; their commitments are thus attained by identification with significant others, primarily their parents. A reflective attempt to match individual talents, interests, and values with the offerings of a social context is lacking in adopting a foreclosed identity position. Moratorium and diffuse individuals have not formed identity-defining commitments; however, the moratorium adolescent is very much in the process of trying to find personally meaningful ways of expressing vocational, ideological, and sexual preferences while the diffuse adolescent is not. Those in the diffuse identity status may or may not have attempted previous identity explorations, but they have been unable to form commitments.

Marcia developed the identity status interview to assess ego identity status (Marcia, 1966). While this interview has undergone revision in areas of content for particular samples and modification for use with different age groups (see Marcia et al., 1993), it has remained a popular instrument for the assessment of ego identity status. Its form for late adolescents generally probes the domains of vocational, political, religious, and sexual values in an attempt to determine the extent of an individual's commitments within each of these identity-defining domains as well as the process by which any commitments were or are being formed. More recently, domains of ethnicity and family/career priorities have also been used in some identity status research (Marcia et al., 1993). Marcia (2000, personal communication) stresses that domains should be areas of salience for the particular individuals in question; thus attitudes toward one's ethnicity or sexual orientation may be used in identity status assessments of particular samples where these issues are of special relevance. The interview generally takes approximately 30 minutes to administer and is taperecorded for later assessment and reliability checks. Reliabilities for two independent raters for each domain generally has been about 80% agreement. Generally an individual is given an identity status rating within each identity domain, as well as an overall rating reflecting his or her primary mode of dealing with salient identity domains.

Several efforts have also been made to develop paper-and-pencil measures of ego identity status. Adams, Bennion, and Huh (1989) and Adams (1999) have developed the extended objective measure of ego identity status (EIS-EOM-2), a 64-item instrument that assesses an individual's identity status in both ideological and interpersonal areas. More specifically, the measure uses a Likert-scale format to assess the presence or absence of exploration and commitment within the following identity-defining domains: vocational, political, religious, philosophy of life values (all comprising the ideological domain), and friendship, dating, sex role, and recreational values (comprising the interpersonal domain). Individuals receive domain and overall identity status ratings with this measure, which has shown adequate levels of validity and reliability (Adams et al., 1989).

Within Europe, Bosma's (1992) Groningen identity development scale has also been developed as a measure of ego identity status for use with Dutch adolescents, and Meeus, Iedema, Helsen, and Vollebergh (1999) have developed a scale measure of identity exploration and commitment variables.

2.3 *Personality correlates*

Over the past 40 years of identity status research, particular personality variables have consistently been associated with each of the four identity positions. Early attempts to validate the identity statuses found identity achieved individuals to be high and diffuse individuals to be low on a continuous measure of ego identity (ego identity-incomplete sentences blank; Marcia, 1967), as one would predict.

Additionally, identity achieved individuals have consistently scored well under conditions of stress and have been found to use more rational and planful decision-making strategies than individuals of other identity statuses (e.g., Blustein & Philips, 1990; Klaczynski, Fauth, & Swanger, 1998; Marcia, 1966, 1967). The identity achieved have also been low in self-monitoring behaviors, meaning that they do not regulate their expressive self-presentation to maintain desirable public appearances (Kumru & Thompson, 2003). They also have been found to use the more adaptive defense mechanisms (adaptive narcissism, internal locus of control) and to have high levels of ego development, self-esteem, and openness to new experiences (Berzonsky & Adams, 1999; Cramer, 1995; Tesch & Cameron, 1987). Berzonsky and Kuk (2000) found that the more self-exploration that students had engaged in (those in both identity achieved and moratorium identity statuses), the more willing they were to undertake tasks in a self-directed manner without needing to look to others for reassurance and emotional support. The identity achieved also most frequently use the highest post-conventional level of reasoning on tasks requiring moral decision making (Skoe & Marcia, 1991). They also have scored as more intrapsychically differentiated from others and more secure in their attachment patterns compared with individuals of other identity statuses (Kroger, 1995). In a longitudinal study of attachment and identity status from age 16 to age 18 years, Zimmermann and Becker-Stoll (2002) found that secure attachment profiles were associated with identity achievement, whereas dismissive attachment profiles were associated with identity diffusion. Longitudinally, identity diffusion age 16 predicted attachment profile two years later (dismissive). Perhaps as a result of their higher intrapsychic differentiation from others, identity achievement individuals also have more intimate forms of relationships (Dyk & Adams, 1990).

Late adolescent moratoriums have consistently scored high on measures of anxiety (Marcia, 1967; Sterling & Van Horn, 1989) as well as greater openness to experience and use of an experiential orientation (Boyes & Chandler, 1992; Stephen, Fraser, & Marcia, 1992). They have also scored highest of all identity statuses on a measure of identity distress (Berman, Montgomery, & Kurtines, 2004). Moratoriums, like the identity achieved, have scored significantly lower on self-monitoring than the identity diffuse in the domain of ideological identity (Kumru & Thompson, 2003). They have also shown higher use of the defense mechanisms of denial, projection, and identification to keep their anxieties at bay, compared with those of other identity statuses (Cramer, 1995). Moratorium adolescents also have appeared more volatile in their interpersonal relationships, particularly with authority figures, and have had more mixed attachment profiles (Donovan, 1975; Kroger, 1995). While they have been able to describe what they desire in an intimate relationship, they generally have not formed such a relationship with a partner (Josselson, 1987, 1996). However, in many other ways, late adolescents in the moratorium status resemble identity achieved youths. Moratoriums have shown similarly high levels of cognitive complexity, moral reasoning, and failure to rely on others' judgments in making decisions (Skoe & Marcia, 1991; Slugoski, Marcia, & Koopman, 1984).

Adolescents who have a foreclosed identity status have consistently scored higher on measures of authoritarianism compared with those in all other identity statuses (e.g., Cote & Levine, 1983; Marcia, 1966, 1967). In addition, foreclosures have also scored lowest on measures of anxiety and openness to new experience, in contrast to all other identity status groups (Stephen et al., 1992; Tesch & Cameron, 1987). It is likely that the rigid adherence of adolescent foreclosures to the directives of authority figures does not allow room for anxiety; similarly, lack of openness to new experiences keeps any anxiety that might result from alternative identity considerations at bay. Foreclosures have also made use of defensive narcissism to bolster their self-esteem (Cramer, 1995, 1997). In terms of cognitive processes, foreclosed adolescents have primarily scored at pre-conventional or conventional levels of moral reasoning and have used less integratively complex cognitive styles compared with adolescents of other identity statuses (Skoe & Marcia, 1991; Slugoski et al., 1984). In relationships with others, foreclosed individuals have engaged in stereotypic or merger styles of interaction (Dyk & Adams, 1990; Josselson, 1987, 1996). These youths have appeared less intrapsychically differentiated from parental figures, more non-secure (anxious or detached) in attachment profiles compared with those of other identity statuses (Kroger, 1985, 1995; Kroger & Haslett, 1988; Papini, Micka, & Barnett, 1989).

Adolescents who have been rated as identity diffuse have shown low levels of self-esteem and autonomy (Marcia, 1966, 1967). They have scored highest of all identity groups on measures of hopelessness (Selles, Markstrom-Adams, & Adams, 1994). Interpersonally, adolescent diffusions have scored as isolated or stereotypic on measures of intimacy and have been characterized as distant and withdrawn (Donovan, 1975; Orlofsky, Marcia, & Lesser, 1973). They have also demonstrated high self-monitoring behaviors in the ideological domain of identity, regulating their expressive self-presentations according the social signals given by others (Kumru & Thompson, 2003). Parents of adolescent diffusions have been reported as distant and rejecting, thus making it difficult for their offspring to internalize a strong parental figure during earlier years (Josselson, 1987, 1996).

2.4 Antecedents and consequences

Family antecedents associated with the various identity statuses have been undertaken through studies that are correlational in design. Thus it is possible only to speculate on early family conditions which may be associated with the various identity positions at the time of adolescence. Indeed, an adolescent's identity status may determine various forms of parental behaviors. With this limitation in mind, researchers have found various styles of family communication to be associated with the identity statuses or exploration and commitment processes. Bosma and Gerrits (1985), Campbell, Adams, and Dobson (1984), Grotevant and Cooper (1985), and Willemsen and Waterman (1991) have all found that families who stress both individuality and connectedness have adolescent sons and daughters who explore various identity alternatives prior to making identity-defining commitments. In addition, families emphasizing strong emotional attachment coupled with little support for expressions of adolescent individuality was characteristic of the adolescent foreclosed. Diffuse adolescents generally reported little emotional attachment to families, who, in turn, communicated a laissez-faire attitude to their offspring.

Attachment patterns have also been studied in relation to the identity statuses. For both male and female university students, strong identification with father predicted identity foreclosure over the course of their university studies (Cram, 1998). For both genders, weak identification with mother predicted the diffusion status; additionally for men, weak identification with father also predicted identity diffusion (Cram, 1998). Strong identification with the mother predicted identity achievement among women, while strong identification with mother predicted both identity achievement and foreclosure among men from this same longitudinal investigation. Parent identification was unrelated to the moratorium status, most likely reflecting the changeability of this non-committed status. Identity achieved and moratorium individuals have also perceived parental values more accurately than those in other identity statuses (Knafo & Schwartz, 2004).

Studies have also found particular behaviors associated with the various identity statuses. One investigation, longitudinal in design, compared a subsample of 300 gifted children rated as most and least likely to be successful from Terman's entire sample of gifted individuals. During young adulthood, these individuals were examined in terms of occupational identity status; significant

relationships were found between occupational identity status and occupational success (Zuo & Cramond, 2001). Gifted children who were rated as likely to be successful were found to be primarily occupational identity achievers during young adulthood, while those rated unsuccessful as children were most likely to be diffuse in their occupational identity status by young adulthood. Most investigations into the relationship between identity status and behaviors, however, have been correlational in design as well as few in number. Thus, little is known about behaviors resulting from an adolescent's particular style of identity resolution (identity status). The diffusion identity status has been associated with particular problem behaviors. Jones (1992) found identity diffuse high school students to report more frequent substance abuse than peers in the other three identity statuses. Josselson (1996) also reported adolescent women in the diffusion status to live "more ragged" lives than those in other identity groups. In terms of motivation for substance abuse, identity achieved and moratorium adolescents were more likely to list curiosity as their reason for using drugs than foreclosure and diffuse youths (Christopherson, Jones, & Sales, 1988). Diffusion adolescents, by contrast, listed boredom and peer influence as the primary reason for their use of drugs.

Behavioral interactions with peers have also been observed for individuals of various identity groups. Slugoski et al. (1984) observed late adolescent males, who had been identified according to identity status, interact on a group decision-making task. Identity achieved and moratorium participants asked for others' opinions more frequently than those of other identity statuses, while foreclosures showed higher frequencies of antagonism compared with those in other identity statuses.

2.5 Developmental patterns

Over the past 30 years, much has been learned about the stability of the various identity statuses and most likely patterns of change when movement does occur. Some research has also been undertaken on conditions associated with different types of identity status movement. Over the years of late adolescence and young adulthood, longitudinal research has consistently shown that among samples of students attending university, at least 50% of adolescents studied remained foreclosed or diffuse across all identity domains (e.g., Adams & Fitch, 1983; Cramer, 1998; Kroger, 1988, 1995; Pulkkinen & Kokko, 2000; Marcia, 1976; Waterman, Geary, & Waterman, 1974; Waterman & Goldman, 1976). Despite the challenges and opportunities for meeting new people and subject matter, large percentages of individuals are seemingly entering adult life without exploration of and commitment to identity-defining roles and values on their own terms. These researches, however, have been primarily undertaken in North America, and developmental studies of identity status changes in other contexts are beginning.

Longitudinal and retrospective research which has examined intraindividual patterns of change has also consistently indicated the moratorium position to be the least stable of the identity statuses (Adams & Fitch, 1983; Cramer, 1998; Kroger, 1988; Kroger & Haslett, 1987; Marcia, 1976). It is likely that the moratorium position generates such uncomfortable levels of anxiety that one is unlikely able to sustain identity-related indecisions over long time intervals. In longitudinal and retrospective research examining interindividual patterns of development, there is furthermore evidence that areas of vocational decision making may have less protracted decision-making time intervals than relational and sexual domains (Kroger & Haslett, 1987).

Longitudinal studies addressing identity status changes from late adolescence through adulthood have found considerable instability to the identity achievement status (e.g. Fadjukoff, Pulkkinen, & Kokko, 2005; Hart, 1989; Josselson, 1996; Mallory, 1984; Pulkinnen & Kokko, 2000). Stephen et al. (1992) have suggested that for those who have achieved a sense of identity by early adulthood, continuing cycles of moratorium–achievement–moratorium–achievement (*mama cycles*) may characterize further adult identity development, and these patterns have been apparent in studies by Josselson (1996) and Kroger and Haslett (1987, 1991). In Finland, Pulkinnen and Kokko

(2000) suggest achievement-foreclosure cycles to be more characteristic of their random sample of men and women assessed at ages 27 and 36 years. Results of this pattern may be attributed to both macro and micro factors. The collapse of the Soviet Union, which borders Finland, occurred between data collection points and brought serious political uncertainly and recession to Finland. The collapse may have impacted on identity-defining commitments of many formerly achieved individuals to seek greater security amidst social disorganization experienced very close at hand.

Where identity status movement occurs, the most common pattern of development over late adolescence and young adulthood has been from the foreclosed to the moratorium to the achievement identity status according to the few studies assessing identity status over more than two data collection points (e.g. Adams, Montemayor, & Brown, 1992; Goossens, Marcoen, & Janssen, 1999; Kroger & Haslett, 1987, 1991). Conditions primarily associated with such changes in these age groups have been exposure to new events or circumstances and new internal awarenesses (Josselson, 1996; Kroger & Green, 1996). Certain university climates within departments have been examined in relation to identity status; those environments de-emphasizing social awareness issues were less attractive to committed identity statuses (Adams & Fitch, 1983). Meeus (1996) offers a comprehensive review of some of these developmental findings.

Longitudinal studies of identity development in both Belgium and the Netherlands have been assessing variables related to identity status development. Luyckx, Goossens, & Soenens (in press) have data on 402 university students assessed four times over two years. Their data measures four dimensions of identity commitment and exploration factors. Among their many findings were the following: adolescents who broadly explore various alternatives do not feel confident and certain about current commitments with increasing age; exploration of possible identity commitments in depth increased over time, although identification with commitments significantly decreased with time. In general, commitment making and exploration in breadth were closely related to exploration and identification with commitment over time. Meeus et al. (1999) have used a measure of identity status somewhat different to that of Marcia's identity statuses to examine the relationship between relational and societal identity status and well-being among approximately 1500 Dutch adolescents. Both domains decreased in diffusion over time, but the relational domain increased in the "achieving identity status" while the societal domain increased in the "closure" identity status.

2.6 Criticism of the identity status paradigm

Over the past two decades, several critical commentaries of the identity status approach have appeared (e.g. Blasi & Glodis, 1995; Côté & Levine, 1988; Meeus et al., 1999; van Hoof, 1999). One focus of criticism has been on whether or not Marcia's identity status approach captures Erikson's theoretical conception of identity (Blasi & Glodis, 1995; van Hoof, 1999). A second focus has been on whether or not adequate validity has been established for the identity statuses (van Hoof, 1999). Another line of criticism has addressed whether or not identity status change follows a developmental continuum or a random sequence of movement (e.g. Côté & Levine, 1988; Meeus et al., 1999); one further critique questions whether the identity statuses capture identity development at all (van Hoof, 1999).

How does one measure Erikson's concept of ego identity? Blasi and Glodis (1995, p. 410) have criticized the identity status construct for failing to address phenomenological dimensions of identity: "[Measures assessing ego identity status] neglect to address the experience of one's fundamental nature and unity, which, in Erikson's descriptions, constitutes the subjective side of the phenomenon." From a somewhat different perspective, Côté and Levine (1988) point to a theoretical hiatus between Marcia's formulations of identity and Erikson's theory. Côté and Levine note that while the identity status paradigm has focused on at least one essential element expressed in Erikson's writings on identity (the formation of commitments during the identity

formation process), the identity status construct has largely ignored not only the role of developmental contexts but also the interaction between person and environment. A further charge comes from van Hoof (1999), who argues that Marcia's identity statuses ignore what she believes to be the core of identity – spatial–temporal continuity. She also points to construct under-representation of Erikson's theory in the identity status approach and questions what construct actually underlies the ego identity statuses.

In response to these measurement criticisms, Marcia has at no time claimed that his attempt to operationalize identity via the identity statuses captures all dimensions that Erikson included in his concept of ego identity. Any attempt to do so would be simply unwieldy, if not impossible. Exploration and commitment variables used by Marcia to define the identity statuses were taken directly from part of Erikson's discussions of the identity formation process, so that the identity statuses do reflect an operationalization of at least some of Erikson's dimensions of ego identity. Similarly, the identity-defining roles and values of vocation, ideology, and sexuality, deemed by Erikson to be so critical for adolescents in the identity formation process, are those same values which are examined in commonly used measures of Marcia's ego identity status. Clearly, Marcia's identity status approach has been based on some of Erikson's key ideas regarding ego identity. However, to try to capture the complexity of Erikson's ego identity concept with a single measure would simply not be possible.

Berzonsky and Adams (1999) have succinctly addressed the question of whether or not the identity status construct is a valid measure of Eriksonian identity. They point out that in the need to be precise and specific, operationally defining a construct involves a trade-off, often in the loss of theoretical richness and scope. Multiple measurements are also necessary to establish construct validity. The identity statuses are an operational attempt to define and expand some, but not all, of Erikson's rich, clinically based observations included in his identity construct. Certainly, it is important and necessary to operationalize and research other dimensions of Erikson's identity construct. The identity status construct has given rise to well over 600 empirical studies of various personality variables, family antecedents, and developmental consequences associated with the various identity (Kroger, Martinussen, Marcia, & Green, unpublished raw data). As van Hoof (1999) has pointed out, however, a number of these studies have failed to hypothesize relationships that are directly grounded in Eriksonian theory. Future identity status research should take heed of this criticism as well as focus on additional identity dimensions that Erikson has described.

A second issue under discussion has been the construct validation of the identity statuses themselves. Van Hoof (1999) has adopted the rather conservative position that each of the four identity statuses must respond statistically differently to variables used to help establish their construct validity. She points out that, most commonly, only one or two identity statuses differ significantly from remaining identity statuses on measures of constructs used for validation purposes. She concludes, therefore, that construct validity of the four different identity positions has not been established. Waterman (1999) has addressed this issue by noting that any typological or complex stage system in psychology that would be unlikely to satisfy this stringent criterion for construct validation. Validation of a construct, Waterman and others have argued, should require that a distinctive pattern of responses be demonstrated. Thus, construct validation of the identity statuses should require not that each identity status be related significantly different from every other identity status on dependent variables used to help establish construct validation. Rather, only a distinctive and hypothesized pattern of responses should be associated with the four identity status positions.

Furthermore, one would not expect individuals in each identity status to score significantly differently from those in every other identity status on some variables used to help establish construct validity (although some data do discriminate among the four identity positions; see Adams & Berzonsky, 1999). Thus, for example, moratoriums would be theoretically expected to score higher than the other identity statuses on a measure of anxiety because of the uncertainty and indecision likely to be associated with the identity formation process. However, they may not score *significantly* higher than every other identity status, and no theoretical expectations would be held for the inter-relationships among remaining identity statuses. According to more commonly used criteria for the establishment of construct validity in psychology, considerable evidence has accrued for expected patterns of responses for each of the four ego identity statuses. However, a useful direction for future research would be a meta-analysis of variables commonly researched in relation to the identity statuses. This procedure would provide a mean estimate of effect size and make it possible to study variation among studies in actual effect sizes, ultimately enabling one to determine whether or not the mean effect could be generalized across settings (Hunter & Schmidt, 1990).

Are the identity statuses capable of capturing identity development? A common finding among longitudinal and cross-sectional studies of identity development over late adolescence is that approximately 50% of participants sampled as they are about to enter young adulthood remain foreclosed or diffuse in identity status (see Kroger, in press, for a review of these investigations). Such findings have led van Hoof (1999) to question whether or not the identity statuses are even capable of capturing the identity formation process of late adolescence. However, the fact that such large percentages of adolescents do not progress to more complex forms of identity development does not invalidate the model's sensitivity to change; it simply means that large numbers of adolescents do not attain more complex levels of identity development. And such findings are completely consistent with findings from the related literatures of ego development (Loevinger, 1976), moral reasoning (Kohlberg, 1984), and self-other differentiation (Kegan, 1982, 1994); all of these developmental schemes have been linked with the identity statuses, and all have shown similar failures among large percentages of young adults to reach the highest levels of developmental complexity described by the respective models (see Kroger, in press, for a review of these studies). Failure of large numbers of late adolescents in a variety of western contexts to reach moratorium and achieve identity statuses positions is likely to reflect a reality of life – that while many young adults will have made identity commitments (i.e. be achieved or foreclosed in identity status), the developmental complexity of identity achievement is an elusive phenomenon.

What are common identity status movement trajectories? Where identity status movement occurs, longitudinal studies have most commonly found movement from less mature (foreclosure and diffusion) to more mature (moratorium and achievement) positions. This pattern of development is common for studies focusing on both adolescence and adulthood (Kroger, in press). Van Hoof (1999) has argued that patterns of stability or decrease in the moratorium status in longitudinal identity status studies speak against the notion of a developmental continuum. However, it is difficult to interpret what change or stability in the moratorium status may actually mean. Kroger and Haslett (1991) found that time estimates for the probability of movement from the moratorium status over a one-year interval during late adolescence/young adulthood to be very high (ranging from 50–100% across various subgroups of the larger sample), and Waterman (1999) notes that it is unlikely a late adolescent will remain in the moratorium status for very long. However, there are frequently long intervals between data collection points in longitudinal identity status studies (sometimes, one year but frequently three to 10 years). Thus it is likely that considerable movement in and out of the moratorium position will take place during this time interval.

A further research issue that has made developmental understanding of the moratorium status difficult to interpret is the fact that longitudinal studies of late adolescents have typically assessed identity status at the entry and exit point of university attendance (e.g. Cramer, 1998; Kroger, 1988, 1995; Waterman & Goldman, 1976). Yet these measurement times are very unlikely to

capture the moratorium identity status position for those late adolescents who will undergo change. It is only after youths have had time for exposure to the diversity of new ideas and people in the university environment that one would expect to see individuals enter a moratorium position as well as some considerable time before graduation, when identity-defining decisions about the future need to be made. Indeed studies by Fitch and Adams (1983) and Waterman and Waterman (1971) that focused on late adolescents in a 9–12 month period after university entrance, found considerable increases in the numbers of moratorium students in this time interval. While investigations do indicate that where identity status movement occurs it most commonly is from a less to more mature identity status, longitudinal investigations tracing identity status movements over shorter time intervals are essential in future identity status research. It is only through such studies that we will be able to evaluate any continuum of identity statuses and come to understand both the common and the unique patterns of identity development in which adolescents engage on the road to adult life.

2.7 Current issues in identity research

There exists today in the field of identity status research a number of issues still in need of research attention. While various personality correlates of the identity statuses have now been consistently articulated, many process issues remain to be examined. To date, most published identity status research has been conducted within North America, and much remains to be learned about the process of identity development in other socio-cultural contexts. For example, use of the EOM-EIS-2 (Adams et al., 1989) in the north Norwegian context has consistently found lower levels of both exploration and commitment among Norwegian late adolescent university students compared with five samples of students from different geographic regions of the United States (Jensen, Kristiansen, Sandbekk, & Kroger, 1998; Stegarud, Solheim, Karlsen, & Kroger, 1999). It may be that the Norwegian mixed liberal welfare state, which stresses equality among all individuals, may de-emphasize strong individual exploration and commitment processes among its youth, compared to North American contexts, which place higher emphases on individualistic values. Late adolescent patterns of identity exploration and commitment may be strongly related to opportunities and constraints presented by various social, political, and economic forces; future identity research might well examine patterns of identity development across countries holding similar political and economic values for some clarification of the relationship between identity development and socio/political/economic forces.

Additionally, domains of issues salient to identity development may vary greatly across contexts. Within North America itself, identity domains regarded as most important to late adolescents have undergone some change over time (see Marcia et al., 1993 for a review); identity researchers in other contexts might well find important differences in the salience of issues around which young people develop a sense of meaningful identity-defining values. For example, in both New Zealand and Norway, the domain of religion has not been one of great importance in identity definition (Jensen et al., 1998; Kroger, 1988). Furthermore in Norway, a good translation for the domain of dating could not even be identified, for the formal concept of "dating" was not a part of the adolescent Norwegian experience (see also Alsaker & Flammer, 1999, for a discussion of the uniqueness of the concept of dating in North America).

The process of identity development needs to be examined in greater detail. Measurement of identity statuses needs to be made over longer periods of time and at more frequent intervals than is currently characteristic of longitudinal identity research. Furthermore, presentation of such data needs to be given in such a way that it is possible to examine intraindividual patterns of change. At present, there are very few longitudinal studies of identity status where it has been possible to assess individual identity status changes over more than two data collection points. (Some noteworthy exceptions have been researched by Adams et al., 1992; Fadjukoff et al., 2005; Goossens et al., 1999; Hart, 1989;

Josselson, 1996; Mallory, 1984.) These studies provide interesting possibilities for insight into conditions associated with identity progression, stability, and regression over time. Future longitudinal studies that enable a description of the frequencies of various identity status trajectories and conditions associated with these various movement patterns will offer an important contribution to identity research. One's tolerance of experienced conflict and/or the ability to imagine alternative future selves examined in work by Kalakoski and Nurmi (1998) may be important factors associated with identity progression trajectories in future research. The role of emotions in the strength and content of commitments (Vleioras & Bosma, 2005) is also an important new consideration in examining change processes; emotions may have important links in identity status trajectories of progression, stability, and regression. And new methodologies need to be developed to study the change process. Recent efforts in the Netherlands by Kunnen and Klein-Wassink (2003) to distinguish different steps in the identity accommodation process via case analysis presents a novel way of understanding development more systematically. These are some of the many identity process issues that await future investigation in this exciting area of adolescent identity development.

3. Conclusion

This chapter has discussed the concepts of self-concept, self-esteem, and identity. The term, self-concept, generally refers to one's characteristic features, basic beliefs, attitudes and feelings of and about the self. Self-concept usually holds a descriptive element. By contrast, self-esteem generally refers to how one evaluates oneself, including the degree of self-worth one holds. Identity generally refers to a person's feeling of "fit" between a social context and his or her own psychological and physiological characteristics. Adolescence is generally a time of transition, as physiological maturation, newly developing psychological needs and interests, and differing social expectations often represent great challenges to one's self-concept, self-esteem, and sense of identity.

The fields of self-concept, self-esteem, and identity have rather different historical origins and differing research traditions. Recent models of self-concept have generally recognized the multidimensional nature of this construct. Current research on self-concept thus often addresses such issues as how a person describes his or her academic, athletic, and social competence, physical appearance, and the self as a whole. Self-esteem research has focused on such issues as the relationship between one's global evaluations and particular areas of competence or specific kinds of situations. Gender differences have consistently appeared in self-concept and self-esteem research among adolescents, with girls more prone to global negative self-evaluations than boys. Girls have also presented themselves as less stable in their self-concepts than boys. In spite of somewhat conflicting results for age-related developmental changes in self-concept and self-esteem over the years of adolescence, the main conclusion seems to be that the self-concept becomes more differentiated, but that there are no clear normative changes in terms of self-esteem.

The field of adolescent identity research has been greatly influenced by Erikson's initial usage of the identity concept and later writings on identity. Research on identity has been occupied with such questions as the relationship between Erikson's fifth psychosocial task of "Identity vs. role confusion" and other Eriksonian psychosocial stages of development. A popular framework for studying adolescent identity today has been via Marcia's identity status paradigm, an expansion of Erikson's original ideas. Marcia's identity statuses (achievement, moratorium, foreclosure, and diffusion) represent qualitatively different types of resolutions to identity questions. Researches involving the identity statuses have focused on family antecedents, developmental consequences, and personality and behavioral correlates associated with these four identity resolutions. Current research issues in the identity literature include the need to examine intraindividual identity trajectories over more than two points in time throughout adolescence and young adulthood and more in-depth studies of the adolescent identity formation process itself. Self-concept, self-esteem, and identity research all hold rich opportunities for future explorations of development during the transitional years of adolescent life.

References

Adams, G.R. (1999). *The objective measure of ego identity status: A manual on theory and test construction.* Unpublished manuscript, University of Guelph, Canada.

Adams, G.R., Bennion, L., & Huh, K. (1989). *Objective measure of ego identity status: A reference manual.* Unpublished manuscript, University of Guelph, Canada.

Adams, G.R., & Fitch, S.A. (1983). Psychological environments of university departments: Effects on college students identity status and ego development stage. *Journal of Personality and Social Psychology, 44*, 1266–1275.

Adams, G.R., Montemayor, R., & Brown, B.B. (1992). *Adolescent ego-identity development: An analysis of patterns of development and the contributions of the family to identity formation during middle and late adolescence.* Unpublished manuscript, University of Guelph, Canada.

Alloy, L., & Abramson, L. (1979). Judgment of contingency in depressed and non-depressed students: Sadder but wiser? *Journal of Experimental Psychology, 108*, 441–485.

Alsaker, F.D. (1989). School achievement, perceived competence and global self-esteem. *School Psychology International, 10*, 147–158.

Alsaker, F.D. (1992). Pubertal timing, overweight, and psychological adjustment. *Journal of Early Adolescence, 12*, 396–419.

Alsaker, F.D., & Flammer, A. (1999). *The adolescent experience: European and American adolescents in the 1990s.* Hillsdale, NJ: Lawrence Erlbaum Associates, Inc.

Alsaker, F.D., & Olweus, D. (1992). Stability of self-evaluations in early adolescence: A cohort-longitudinal study. *Journal of Research on Adolescence, 2*, 123–145.

Alsaker, F.D., & Olweus, D. (1993). Global self-evaluations and perceived instability of self in early adolescence: A cohort longitudinal study. *Scandinavian Journal of Psychology, 34*, 47–63.

Alsaker, F.D., & Olweus, D. (2002). Stability and change in global self-esteem and self-related affect. In T. M. Brinthaupt, & R. P. Lipka, *Understanding the self of the early adolescent* (pp. 193–223). New York: State University of New York Press.

Baldwin, J.M. (1897). *Social and ethical interpretations in mental development: A case study in psychology.* New York: Macmillan.

Battle, J. (1980). Relationship between self-esteem and depression among high school students. *Perceptual and Motor Skills, 51,* 157–158.

Baumeister, R.F. (1986). *Identity: Cultural change and the struggle for self.* New York: Oxford University Press.

Beane, J.A., & Lipka, R.P. (1980). Self-concept and self-esteem: A construct differentiation. *Child Study Journal, 10,* 1–6.

Berman, S.L., Montgomery, M.J., & Kurtines, W.M. (2004). The development and validation of a measure of identity distress. *Identity: An International Journal of Theory and Research, 4,* 1–8.

Berzonsky, M.D., & Adams, G.R. (1999). Re-evaluating the identity status paradigm: Still useful after 35 years. *Developmental Review, 19,* 104–124.

Berzonsky, M.D., & Kuk, L.S. (2000). Identity status, identity processing style, and the transition to university. *Journal of Adolescent Research, 15,* 81–98.

Blasi, A., & Glodis, K. (1995). The development of identity: A critical analysis from the perspective of self as subject. *Developmental Review, 15,* 404–433.

Blustein, D.L., & Phillips, S.D. (1990). Relation between ego identity statuses and decision-making styles. *Journal of Counseling Psychology, 37,* 160–168.

Blyth, D.A., Simmons, R.G., Bulcroft, R., Felt, D., VanCleave, E.F., & Bush, D.M. (1981). The effects of physical development on self-image and satisfaction with body-image for early adolescent males. *Research in Community and Mental Health, 2,* 43–73.

Blyth, D.A., Simmons, R.G., & Zakin, D.F. (1985). Satisfaction with body image for early adolescent females: The impact of pubertal timing within different school environments. *Journal of Youth and Adolescence, 14,* 207–225.

Blyth, D.A., & Traeger, C.M. (1983). The self-concept and self-esteem of early adolescents. *Theory into Practice, 22,* 91–97.

Bosma, H.A. (1992). Identity in adolescence: Managing commitments. In G. R. Adams, T. P. Gullotta, & R. Montemayor (Eds.), *Adolescent identity formation* (pp. 91–121). Newbury Park, CA: Sage.

Bosma, H.A., & Gerrits, R.S. (1985). Family functioning and identity status in adolescence. *Journal of Early Adolescence, 5,* 69–80.

Boulton, M.J., & Smith, P.K. (1994). Bully/victim problems in middle-school children: Stability, self-perceived competence, peer perceptions and peer acceptance. *British Journal of Developmental Psychology, 12,* 315–329.

Boyes, M.C., & Chandler, M. (1992). Cognitive development, epistemic doubt, and identity formation in adolescence. *Journal of Youth and Adolescence, 21,* 277–304.

Brack, C.J., Orr, D.P., & Ingersoll, G. (1988). Pubertal maturation and adolescent self-esteem. *Journal of Adolescent Health Care, 9,* 280–285.

Brewin, C.R. (1988). *Cognitive foundations of clinical psychology.* Hillsdale, NJ: Lawrence Erlbaum Associates, Inc.

Brisset, D. (1972). Toward a classification of self-esteem. *Psychiatry, 35,* 255–263.

Brooks-Gunn, J., & Ruble, D.N. (1983). The experience of menarche from a developmental perspective. In J. Brooks-Gunn, & A. C. Petersen (Eds.), *Girls at puberty: Biological and psychosocial perspectives* (pp. 155–177). New York: Plenum.

Buchanan, C.M. (1991). Pubertal development, assessment of. In R. M. Lerner, A. C. Petersen, & J. Brooks-Gunn (Eds.), *Encyclopedia of adolescence* (pp. 875–883). New York: Garland.

Burns, R.B. (1979). *The self-concept: Theory, measurement, development and behaviour.* London: Longman.

Campbell, E., Adams, G.R., & Dobson, W.R. (1984). Familial correlates of identity formation in late adolescence: A study of the predictive utility of connectedness and individuality in family relations. *Journal of Youth and Adolescence, 13,* 509–525.

Christopherson, B.B., Jones, R.M., & Sales, A.P. (1988). Diversity in reported motivations for substance use as a function of ego-identity development. *Journal of Adolescent Research, 3,* 141–152.

Colvin, C.R., Block, J., & Funder, D.C. (1995). Overly positive self-evaluations and personality: Negative implications for mental health. *Journal of Personality and Social Psychology, 68,* 1152–1162.

Cooley, C.H. (1902). *Human nature and the social order.* New York: Charles Scribner's Sons.

Constantinople, A. (1967). Perceived instrumentality of the college as a measure of attitudes toward college. *Journal of Personality and Social Psychology, 5,* 196–201.

Constantinople, A. (1969). An Eriksonian measure of personality development in college students. *Developmental Psychology, 1,* 357–372.

Côté, J.E., & Levine, C. (1983). Marcia and Erikson: The relationship among ego identity status, neuroticism, dogmatism, and purpose in life. *Journal of Youth and Adolescence, 12,* 43–53.

Cramer, P. (1995). Identity, narcissism, and defense mechanisms in late adolescence. *Journal of Research in Personality, 29*, 341–361.

Cramer, P. (1997). Identity, personality, and defense mechanisms: An observer-based study. *Journal of Research in Personality, 31*, 58–77.

Cramer, P. (1998). Freshman to senior year: A follow-up study of identity, narcissism and defense mechanisms. *Journal of Research in Personality, 32*, 156–172.

Damon, W., & Hart, D. (1988). *Self-understanding in childhood and adolescence.* New York: Cambridge University Press.

Donovan, J.M. (1975). Identity status and interpersonal style. *Journal of Youth and Adolescence, 4*, 37–55.

Dusek, J.B., & Flaherty, J.F. (1981). The development of the self-concept during the adolescent years. *Monographs of the Society for Research in Child Development, 46* (4, Serial No. 191).

Dyk, P.H., & Adams, G.R. (1990). Identity and intimacy: An initial investigation of three theoretical models using cross-lag panel correlations. *Journal of Youth and Adolescence, 19*, 91–109.

Ellis, D.W., & Davis, L.T. (1982). The development of self-concept boundaries across the adolescent years. *Adolescence, 17*, 695–710.

Epstein, S. (1973). The self-concept revisited, or a theory of a theory. *American Psychologist, 28*, 404–416.

Epstein, S. (1977). Traits are alive and well. In D. Magnusson, & N. S. Endler (Eds.), *Personality at the cross-roads: Current issues in interactional psychology* (pp. 83–98). Hillsdale, NJ: Lawrence Erlbaum Associates, Inc.

Erikson, E.H. (1963). *Childhood and society* (2nd ed.). New York: Norton.

Erikson, E.H. (1968). *Identity: Youth, and crisis.* New York: Norton.

Ewert, O.M. (1984). Psychische Begleiterscheinungen des pubertalen Wachstumsspurts bei männlichen Jugendlichen – eine retrospektive Untersuchung [Psychological conditions accompanying pubertal growth spurts in male adolescents: A retrospective study]. *Zeitschrift für Entwicklungspsychologie und Pädagogische Psychologie, 16*, 1–11.

Fadjukoff, P., Pulkkinen, L., & Kokko, K. (2005). Identity processes in adulthood: Diverging domains. *Identity: An International Journal of Theory and Research, 5*, 1–20.

Fischer, K.W. (1980). A theory of cognitive development: The control and construction of hierarchies of skills. *Psychological Review, 87*, 477–531.

Fishbein, H.D. (1984). *The psychology of infancy and childhood: Evolutionary and cross-cultural perspectives.* Hillsdale, NJ: Lawrence Erlbaum Associates, Inc.

Fitch, S.A., & Adams, G.R. (1983). Ego identity and intimacy status: Replication and extension. *Developmental Psychology, 19*, 839–845.

Foulds, G.A., & Bedford, A. (1977). Self-esteem and psychiatric syndromes. *British Journal of Medical Psychology, 50*, 237–242.

Garwood, S.G., & Allen, L. (1979). Self-concept and identified problem differences between pre- and postmenarcheal adolescents. *Journal of Clinical Psychology, 35*, 528–537.

Goetz, T.E., & Dweck, C.S. (1980). Learned helplessness in social situations. *Journal of Personality and Social Psychology, 39*, 246–255.

Goossens, L., Marcoen, A., & Janssen, P. (1999). *Identity status development and students' perception of the university environment: From identity transitions to identity trajectories.* Unpublished manuscript, Catholic University of Leuven, Belgium.

Greenwald, A.G. (1982). Is anyone in charge? Personalysis versus the principle of personality unity. In J. Suls (Ed.), *Psychological perspectives on the self* (Vol. 1, pp.151–181). Hillsdale, NJ: Lawrence Erlbaum Associates, Inc.

Greif, E.B., & Ulman, K.J. (1982). The psychological impact of menarche on early adolescent females: A review of the literature. *Child Development, 53*, 1413–1430.

Grotevant, H.D., & Cooper, C.R. (1985). Patterns of interaction in family relationships and the development of identity exploration in adolescence. *Child Development, 56*, 415–428.

Hall, G.S. (1904). *Adolescence.* New York: Appleton.

Hansell, S., Mechanic, D., & Brondolo, E. (1986). Introspectiveness and adolescent development. *Journal of Youth and Adolescence, 15*, 115–132.

Hart, B. (1989). *Longitudinal study of women's identity status.* Unpublished doctoral dissertation. University of California, Berkeley.

Harter, S. (1982). The perceived competence scale for children. *Child Development, 53*, 87–97.

Harter, S. (1983). Developmental perspectives on the self-system. In P. H. Mussen, & E. M. Hetherington (Eds.), *Handbook of child psychology: Vol. 4. Socialization, personality and social development* (4th ed., pp. 275–385). New York: John Wiley & Sons.

Harter, S. (1986). Processes underlying the construction, maintenance and enhancement of the self-concept in children. In J. Suls, & A. G. Greenwald

(Eds.), *Psychological perspectives on the self* (Vol. 3, pp. 137–181). Hillsdale, NJ: Lawrence Erlbaum Associates, Inc.

Harter, S. (1998). The development of self-representations. In W. Damon, & N. Eisenberg (Eds.), *Handbook of child psychology: Vol. 3. Social, emotional, and personality development* (5th ed., pp. 553–617). New York: John Wiley & Sons.

Harter, S. (1999). *The construction of the self: A developmental perspective*. New York: Guilford.

Harter, S., Waters, P., & Whitesell, N.R. (1998). Relational self-worth: Differences in perceived worth as a person across interpersonal contexts among adolescents. *Child Development*, *69*, 756–766.

Hunter, J.E., & Schmidt, F.L. (1990). *Methods of meta-analysis: Correcting error and bias in research findings*. Newbury Park, CA: Sage.

James, W. (1950). *Principles of psychology*. Chicago: Encyclopaedia Britannica. (Original work published 1890)

Jaquish, G.A., & Savin-Williams, R.C. (1981). Biological and ecological factors in the expression of adolescent self-esteem. *Journal of Youth and Adolescence*, *10*, 473–486.

Jensen, M., Kristiansen, L., Sandbekk, M., & Kroger, J. (1998). Ego identity status in cross-cultural context: A comparison of Norwegian and United States university students. *Psychological Reports*, *83*, 455–460.

Jones, R.M. (1992). Ego identity and adolescent problem behavior. In G. R. Adams, T. P. Gullotta, & R. Montemayor (Eds.), *Adolescent identity formation* (pp. 216–233). Newbury Park, CA: Sage.

Josselson, R. (1987). *Finding herself: Pathways to identity development in women*. San Francisco: Jossey-Bass.

Josselson, R. (1996). *Revising herself: The story of women's identity from college to midlife*. New York: Oxford University Press.

Kalakoski, V., & Nurmi, J.E. (1998). Identity and educational transitions: Age differences in adolescent exploration and commitment related to education, occupation, and family. *Journal of Research on Adolescence*, *8*, 29–47.

Kegan, R. (1982). *The evolving self: Problem and process in human development*. Cambridge, MA: Harvard University Press.

Kegan, R. (1994). *In over our heads: The mental demands of modern life*. Cambridge, MA: Harvard University Press.

Klaczynski, P.A., Fauth, J.M., & Swanger, A. (1998). Adolescent identity: Rational vs. experiential pro-cessing, formal operations, and critical thinking beliefs. *Journal of Youth and Adolescence*, *27*, 185–207.

Knafo, A., & Schwartz, S.H. (2002). Identity formation and parent–child value congruence in adolescence. *British Journal of Developmental Psychology*, *22*, 439–458.

Kohlberg, L. (1984). *Essays in moral development, Vol. 2. The psychology of moral development*. San Francisco: Harper & Row.

Kroger, J. (1985). Separation-individuation and ego identity status in New Zealand university students. *Journal of Youth and Adolescence*, *13*, 65–77.

Kroger, J. (1988). A longitudinal study of ego identity status interview domains. *Journal of Adolescence*, *11*, 49–64.

Kroger, J. (1995). The differentiation of "firm" and "developmental" foreclosure identity statuses: A longitudinal study. *Journal of Adolescent Research*, *10*, 317–337.

Kroger, J. (2004). *Identity in adolescence: The balance between self and other* (3rd ed.) London: Routledge.

Kroger, J. (in press). Why is identity achievement so elusive? *Identity: An International Journal of Theory and Research*.

Kroger, J., & Green, K. (1996). Events associated with identity status change. *Journal of Adolescence*, *19*, 477–490.

Kroger, J., & Haslett, S.J. (1987). An analysis of ego identity status changes from adolescence through middle adulthood. *Social and Behavioral Sciences Documents*, *17*, (Ms. 2792).

Kroger, J., & Haslett, S.J. (1988). Separation-individuation and ego identity status: A two-year longitudinal study. *Journal of Youth and Adolescence*, *17*, 59–81.

Kroger, J., & Haslett, S.J. (1991). A comparison of ego identity status transition pathways and change rates across five identity domains. *International Journal of Aging and Human Development*, *32*, 303–330.

Kumru, A., & Thompson, R.A. (2003). Ego identity status and self-monitoring behavior in adolescents. *Journal of Adolescent Research*, *18*, 481–495.

Kunnen, E.S., & Klein-Wassink, M.E. (2003). An analysis of identity change in adulthood. *Identity: An International Journal of Theory and Research*, *3*, 347–366.

LaVoie, J.C. (1976). Ego identity formation in middle adolescence. *Journal of Youth and Adolescence*, *5*, 371–385.

Lecky, P. (1945). *Self-consistency: A theory of personality*. New York: Island Press.

Levine, M.P., & Smolak, L. (2002). Body image development in adolescence. In T. F. Cash, & T. Pruzinsky (Eds.), *Body image: A handbook of theory, research, and clinical practice* (pp.13–21). New York: Guilford.

Loevinger, J. (1976). *Ego development: Conceptions and theories.* San Francisco: Jossey-Bass.

Luyckx, K., Goossens, L., & Soenens, B. (in press). A developmental contextual perspective on identity construction in emerging adulthood: Change dynamics in commitment formation and commitment evaluation. *Developmental Psychology.*

Maccoby, E.E., & Jacklin, C.N. (1974). *The psychology of sex differences.* Stanford, CA: Stanford University Press.

Mallory, M. (1984). *Longitudinal analysis of ego identity status.* Unpublished doctoral dissertation, University of California, Davis.

Marcia, J.E. (1966). Development and validation of ego identity status. *Journal of Personality and Social Psychology, 3,* 551–558.

Marcia, J.E. (1967). Ego identity status: Relationship to change in self-esteem, "general maladjustment", and authoritarianism. *Journal of Personality, 35,* 118–133.

Marcia, J.E. (1976). Identity six years after: A follow-up study. *Journal of Youth and Adolescence, 5,* 145–150.

Marcia, J.E., Waterman, A.S., Matteson, D.R., Archer, S.L., & Orlofsky, J.L. (1993). *Ego identity: A handbook for psychosocial research.* New York: Springer-Verlag.

Markus, H.R., & Kunda, Z. (1986). Stability and malleability of the self-concept. *Journal of Personality and Social Psychology, 51,* 858–866.

Markus, H.R., & Wurf, E. (1987). The dynamic self-concept: A social psychological perspective. *Annual Review of Psychology, 38,* 299–337.

Mead, G.H. (1934). *Mind, self, and society from the standpoint of a social behaviorist.* Chicago, IL: University of Chicago Press.

Meeus, W. (1996). Studies on identity development in adolescence: An overview of research and some new data. *Journal of Youth and Adolescence, 25,* 569–598.

Meeus, W., Iedema, J., Helsen, M., & Vollebergh, W. (1999). Patterns of adolescent identity development: Review of literature and longitudinal analysis. *Developmental Review, 19,* 419–461.

Mischel, W. (1969). Continuity and change in personality. *American Psychologist, 24,* 1012–1018.

Morse, S.R., & Gergen, K. (1970). Social comparison, self-consistency, and the presentation of self. *Journal of Personality and Social Psychology, 16,* 148–156.

Offer, D. (1969). *The psychological world of the teen-ager.* New York: Basic Books.

Offer, D., Ostrov, E., & Howard, K.I. (1984). The self-image of normal adolescents. *New Directions for Mental Health Services, 22,* 5–17.

Olweus, D. (1978). *Aggression in the schools: Bullies and whipping boys.* Washington, DC: Hemisphere.

O'Malley, P., & Bachman, J. (1979). Self-esteem and education. *Journal of Personality and Social Psychology, 37,* 1153–1159.

O'Malley, P.M., & Bachman, J.G. (1983). Self-esteem: Change and stability between ages 13 and 23. *Developmental Psychology, 19,* 257–268.

Orlofsky, J.L., Marcia, J.E., & Lesser, I.M. (1973). Ego identity status and the intimacy versus isolation crisis of young adulthood. *Journal of Personality and Social Psychology, 27,* 211–219.

Papini, D.R., Micka, J.C., & Barnett, J.K. (1989). Perceptions of intrapsychic and extrapsychic functioning as bases of adolescent ego identity status. *Journal of Adolescent Research, 4,* 462–482.

Patterson, C.J., Kupersmidt, J.B., & Griesler, P.C. (1990). Children's perceptions of self and of relationships with others as a function of sociometric status. *Child Development, 61,* 1335–1349.

Pulkkinen, L., & Kokko, K. (2000). Identity development in adulthood: A longitudinal study. *Journal of Research in Personality, 34,* 445–470.

Rosenberg, F., & Simmons, R.G. (1975). Sex differences in the self-concept in adolescence. *Sex Roles, 1,* 147–159.

Rosenberg, M. (1965). *Society and the adolescent self-image.* Princeton, NJ: Princeton University Press.

Rosenberg, M. (1979). *Conceiving the self.* New York: Basic Books.

Rosenberg, M. (1986). Self-concept from middle childhood through adolescence. In J. Suls, & A. G. Greenwald (Eds.), *Psychological perspectives on the self* (Vol. 3, pp. 107–136). Hillsdale, NJ: Lawrence Erlbaum Associates, Inc.

Rosenthal, D. A, Gurney, R.M., & Moore, S.M. (1981). From trust to intimacy: A new inventory for examining Erikson's stages of psychosocial development. *Journal of Youth and Adolescence, 10,* 526–537.

Rutter, M., Graham, P., Chadwick, O.F.D., & Yule, W. (1976). Adolescent turmoil: Fact or fiction? *Journal of Child Psychology and Psychiatry, 17,* 35–56.

Seligman, M.E.P. (1995). *The optimistic child.* Boston, MA: Houghton-Mifflin.

Seligman, M.E.P. (1998). What is the "good life"? *Monitor*, *2*.

Selles, T., Markstrom-Adams, C., & Adams, G.R. (1994, February). *Identity formation and risk for suicide among older adolescents*. Paper presented at the Biennial Meetings of the Society for Research on Adolescence, San Diego, CA.

Shavelson, R.J., Hubner, J.J., & Stanton, G.C. (1976). Self-concept: Validation of construct interpretation. *Review of Educational Psychology*, *46*, 407–441.

Shavelson, R.J., & Marsh, H.W. (1986). On the structure of self-concept. In R. Schwarzer (Ed.), *Anxiety and cognition* (pp. 305–330). Hillsdale, NJ: Lawrence Erlbaum Associates, Inc.

Silbereisen, R.K., Petersen, A.C., Albrecht, H.T., & Kracke, B. (1989). Maturational timing and the development of problem behavior: Longitudinal studies in adolescence. *Journal of Early Adolescence*, *9*, 247–268.

Simmons, D.D. (1970). Development of an objective measure of identity achievement status. *Journal of Projective Techniques and Personality Assessment*, *34*, 241–244.

Simmons, R.G., & Blyth, D.A. (1987). *Moving into adolescence: The impact of pubertal change and school context*. New York: Aldine de Gruyter.

Simmons, R.G., Rosenberg, F., & Rosenberg, M. (1973). Disturbances in the self-image at adolescence. *American Sociological Review*, *38*, 553–568.

Skoe, E.E., & Marcia, J.E. (1991). A measure of care-based morality and its relation to ego identity. *Merrill-Palmer Quarterly*, *37*, 289–304.

Slee, P.T., & Rigby, K. (1993). Australian school children's self appraisal of interpersonal relations: The bullying experience. *Child Psychiatry and Human Development*, *23*(4), 273–282.

Slugoski, B.R., Marcia, J.E., & Koopman, R.F. (1984). Cognitive and social interactional characteristics of ego identity statuses in college males. *Journal of Personality and Social Psychology*, *47*, 646–661.

Stegarud, L., Solheim, B., Karlsen, M., & Kroger, J. (1999). Ego identity in cross-cultural context: A replication study. *Psychological Reports*, *85*, 457–461.

Stephen, J., Fraser, E., & Marcia, J.E. (1992). Moratorium–achievement (mama) cycles in lifespan identity development: Value orientations and reasoning system correlates. *Journal of Adolescence*, *15*, 283–300.

Sterling, C.M., & Van Horn, K.R. (1989). Identity and death anxiety. *Adolescence*, *23*, 321–326.

Stern, D.N. (1985). *The interpersonal world of the infant: A view from psychoanalysis and developmental psychology*. New York: Basic Books.

Tan, A.L., Kendis, R.J., Fine, J.T., & Porac, J. (1977). A short measure of Eriksonian ego identity. *Journal of Personality Assessment*, *41*, 279–284.

Tesch, S.A., & Cameron, K.A., (1987). Openness to experience and development of adult identity. *Journal of Personality*, *5*, 615–630.

Tobin-Richards, M.H., Boxer, A.M., & Petersen, A.C. (1983). The psychological significance of pubertal change: Sex differences in perceptions of self during early adolescence. In J. Brooks-Grunn, & A. C. Petersen (Eds.), *Girls at puberty: Biological and psychological perspectives* (pp. 127–154). New York: Plenum.

van der Meulen, J.J. (2001). Developments in self-concept theory and research: Affect, context, and variability. In H. A. Bosma, & E. S. Kunnen (Eds.), *Identity and emotions: Development through self-organization* (pp. 10–32). Cambridge: Cambridge University Press.

van Hoof, A. (1999). The identity status approach: In need of fundamental revision and qualitative change. *Developmental Review*, *19*, 497–556.

Vleioras, G., & Bosma, H.A. (2005). Predicting change in relational identity commitments: Exploration and emotions. *Identity: An International Journal of Theory and Research*, *5*, 35–56.

Waterman, A.S. (1999). Identity, the identity statuses, and identity status development: A contemporary statement. *Developmental Review*, *19*, 591–621.

Waterman, A.S., Geary, P.S., & Waterman, C.K. (1974). Longitudinal study of changes in ego identity status from the freshman to the senior year at college. *Developmental Psychology*, *10*, 387–392.

Waterman, A.S., & Goldman, J.A. (1976). A longitudinal study of ego identity status development at a liberal arts college. *Journal of Youth and Adolescence*, *5*, 361–369.

Willemsen, E.W., & Waterman, K.K. (1991). Ego identity status and family environment: A correlational study. *Psychological Reports*, *69*, 1203–1212.

Wilson, A.R., & Krane, R.V. (1980). Change in self-esteem and its effects on symptoms of depression. *Cognitive Therapy and Research*, *4*, 419–421.

Wylie, R.C. (1974). *The self concept: Vol. 1. A review of methodological considerations and measuring instruments*. Lincoln, NE: University of Nebraska Press.

Wylie, R.C. (1979). *The self concept: Vol. 2. Theory and research on selected topics*. Lincoln, NE: University of Nebraska Press.

Zimmermann, P., & Becker-Stoll, F. (2002). Stability of attachment representations during adolescence: The influence of ego-identity status. *Journal of Adolescence, 25*, 107–124.

Zuo, L., & Cramond, B. (2001). An examination of Terman's gifted children from the theory of identity. *Gifted Child Quarterly, 45*, 251–259.

7

Moral development in adolescence: How to integrate personal and social values?

Henri Lehalle

Moral development consists of progressive individual concern about social norms and social values. It comprises two aspects: a conceptual level including moral judgments and norms representation, and a pragmatic level regarding moral actions and commitment.

Adolescence is a critical period of: (a) increasing social experience; (b) claiming personal thought; (c) elaborating identity choices especially about ideology (Alsaker & Kroger, this volume); and (d) constructing abstract cognitive skills (Lehalle, this volume). It follows that deep transformations and inter-individual differentiations should be commonly observed in moral domains.

Following Piaget (1932), the cognitive–developmental approach to moral development was predominant in the 1960s and 1970s, especially from Kohlberg's proposals (Kohlberg, 1969). This approach leads to several procedures aiming to evaluate moral judgments in the frame of some general developmental stages (first part of the chapter). However, the studies on moral development were increasingly concerned with the contextual intra-individual variability of judgments and with the effective differentiation that individuals may operate among social norms (second part). Furthermore, especially during adolescence, it is important, first, to consider individual differences in moral development, particularly with respect to issues such as sex differences and delinquency, and, second, to approach causal factors of personal differentiation and change (third part of the chapter). Finally, several open questions will be considered in the conclusion of this chapter.

1. Assessment methods and general stages

The cognitive–developmental perspective on morality states that people progress along several successive stages, depending on more accurate cognitive competencies constructed through social experiences and individual adaptation. Piaget (1932) initiated the description of moral stages based on individual judgments about socio-cognitive dilemmas. However, in this seminal book, Piaget was mainly concerned with moral development in childhood, not so much in adolescence. Therefore the Piagetian moral dilemmas used plausible events appearing in the daily experience of children during the 1930s. Nevertheless, Piaget was able to stress the main trend of moral development: from *heteronomy* (i.e., individuals conform to the norms that authority figures present) to *autonomy* (i.e., when the moral pressure is grounded in personal considerations).

Kohlberg (1969) extended Piaget's procedure and cognitive approach to adolescents' concerns, keeping the same idea of successive stages related to cognitive development. Later, more developed procedures were proposed for either practical purposes or theoretical reasons.

1.2 Kohlberg's stage system and dilemmas procedure

A dilemma is an hypothetical story (see examples in Box 7.1) where a protagonist has to decide how he/she should behave in a given social situation when several conflictual reasons may be put forward for choosing the better way of acting. A dilemma always induces one to make a decision among some other possibilities. However, it is, rather, the justifications – that is, the reasons why a participant decides something – that lead to a moral categorization according to successive stages.

When analyzing the justifications collected mainly from interviews with adolescents, Kohlberg (1969) was able to describe six general stages

of moral judgment. The stage characteristics are summarized in Box 7.2. These stages are grouped, in twos, forming three more general levels. The first level is "preconventional". People in this level base their decision on the possible consequences of behaviors, in terms of risk and benefit for the protagonists. The second level, "conventional", takes into account the collective norms and obligations underlying the choice. The third level, "postconventional", consists of a progressive appeal to the moral principles a person has to conform to, even against the collective norms and current laws.

Developmental trends along these six stages are particularly noticeable during adolescence. Kohlberg (1969) presented statistics on moral judgments belonging to the various stages. These statistics were gathered from several countries. Main results showed, from ages 10 to 16: (a) a decreasing of stages 1 and 2; (b) an increasing of stage 3 between 10 and 13, and of stage 4 between 10 and 16; (c) stage 5 appeared quite frequently at age 16 in the US sample; (d) stage 6 was rare in every sample. However (Rest, Davison, & Robbins, 1978; Teo, Becker, & Edelstein, 1995), further researches indicated low frequencies of the postconventional thinking, even in adulthood, and a strong effect due to number of years of formal education. In sum, we can admit that stages 3 and 4 become the most frequent stages during adolescence, with a correlative decline in stages 1 and 2. Only some late adolescents reach postconventional thinking, provided that environmental, cultural and educational influences make it possible. But moral judgments continue to improve after the adolescent period, probably as a series of spurts and plateaux (Dawson-Tunik, Commons, Wilson, & Fischer, 2005).

Kohlberg's proposals have been constantly adapted, following the first presentations in the 1960s, both on methodological aspects and theoretical stage analysis. First, the scoring procedure was clarified and took the form of *moral judgment interview* (MJI) (Colby and Kohlberg, 1987; Colby et al., 1987). On the theoretical side, the six stages system was revised and modified, in particular by Kohlberg himself.

For instance, a "transitional" stage was

Box 7.1.   Two out of the six dilemmas used by Rest (1979) in the *Defining Issues Test*

Heinz and the drug (DIT version, Rest 1979)
Somewhere in Europe a woman was near death from a particular cancer. There was one drug that the doctors thought might save her. It was a form of radium that a druggist in the same town had recently discovered. The drug was expensive to make, but the druggist was charging 10 times what the drug cost to make. He paid $200 for the radium and charged $2000 for a small dose of the drug. The sick woman's husband, Heinz, went to everyone he knew to borrow the money, but he could only get together about $1000, which is half the cost. He told the druggist that his wife was dying, and asked him to sell it cheaper or let him pay later. But the druggist said: "No, I discovered the drug and I'm going to make money from it." Heinz got desperate and began to think about breaking into the man's store to steal the drug for his wife.
   Should Heinz steal the drug?

Escaped prisoner (DIT version, Rest 1979)
A man has been sentenced to prison for 10 years. After one year, however, he escaped from prison, moved to a different part of the country, and took on the name of Thompson. For 8 years he worked hard, and gradually he saved enough money to buy his own business. He was fair to his customers, gave his employees top wages, and gave most of his own profits to charity. Then one day, Mrs. Jones, an old neighbor, recognized him as the man who had escaped from prison 8 years before, whom the police had been looking for.
   Should Mrs. Jones report Mr. Thompson to the police and have him sent back to prison?

Box 7.2.   Kohlberg's stages (Kohlberg & Ryncarz, 1990)

Preconventional level
● Stage 1: "Punishment and obedience"
The avoidance of punishment and the obedience to powerful authorities lead to not doing physical damage to people and property. At this stage, there is no social decentration, no consideration for the interests of others or no attempt to relate conflicting points of view.
● Stage 2: "Individual instrumental purpose and exchange"
The main objective is to meet one's own interests and needs. Everybody is supposed to search for his/her own purposes. Then it is suitable to make fair deals in terms of concrete exchange. It implies that the personal point of view is now separated from those of authorities and others.
Conventional level
● Stage 3: "Mutual interpersonal expectations, relationships and conformity content"
It is important to play a good role according to close group expectations. Sharing feelings and agreements take primacy over individual interests. Then, people are concerned with others and what they feel. They keep mutual relationships, maintaining trust, loyalty, respect, and gratitude.
● Stage 4: "Social system and conscience maintenance"
The criteria shift from close people to social system and society: doing one's duty, upholding social order, and maintaining the welfare of society and groups. The viewpoint of the system is emphasized. Laws have to be respected. Then, individual concerns and obligations are considered with respect to the whole society or institution.

Postconventional and principled level
● Stage 5: "Prior rights and social contract or utility"
In this stage, people acknowledge that values and rules are relative to one's group. Moreover, it is suitable to preserve this variability and to elaborate social contracts in order to safeguard individual values and rights. Contracts must be respected and laws are a kind of contract. Thus, people begin to be aware of some absolute values and rights (such as life, liberty, etc.), which have to be upheld in any society, regardless of what the majority of people may think. However, when the moral and legal points of view are conflicting, it remains difficult, at this stage, to integrate these opposed aspects.
● Stage 6: "Universal ethical principles"
Moral judgments are now guided by universal ethical principles that all humanity should follow (justice, equality of human rights, respect for the dignity of human beings as individuals). One acts in accordance with these principles even though they do not fit the present laws. This real "moral" point of view can be recognized by any rational individual. It comes from the feeling that the respect for other persons defines ends not means.

---

inserted between the conventional and postconventional levels. This transitional stage (labeled stage 4½) looks closed to some current stereotypes on adolescence. It consists of doubtful feelings about "duty" and "moral rights". Individuals seem to stand outside their own society with no real commitment. At the same time there are not, or at least not yet, clear personal principles. Since the appeal for collective norms decreases, the choices sound personal and subjective, but these personal accounts are different from those expressed in the preconventional level.

Furthermore, in a late presentation of the moral stage system, Kohlberg and Ryncarz (1990) have included a seventh stage, which lies beyond the sixth stage of moral principles. Indeed, one may think of some motives for elaborating the moral principles. After all, if principles are personal, and if there is the potential for their being preferred over laws, how can we ensure that these principles are really "moral"? This is why, relying on moral exemplars, from Socrates to Martin Luther King Jr, Kohlberg and Ryncarz proposed a seventh stage where moral principles – already invoked in stage 6 – are explicitly grounded in a more general philosophical thought emphasizing natural laws from a cosmic perspective.

These two precisions about the 4½ and seventh stages lead to consider Kohlberg's system as an evolving perspective, far from a rigid and definitive conceptualization. In fact, beyond the suggestive clarity of the constructive links joining the successive six stages, many problems arise, first, about the stage conceptualization itself.

Indeed, the commonly accepted "structural properties" of Kohlberg's stages are not really valid: they are not true structures, with formal description and logical rules of composition, as in Piaget's structuralism. Kohlberg's stages are just general statements that are supposed to summarize a coherent position about social norms. These statements are not a direct transcription of what a person acts or decides when facing dilemmas. They convey, rather, the underlying justifications or motives for action and decision making.

As a consequence, a given decision may belong in more than one stage. For instance, calling on the majority opinion in a group may be relevant to stage 2 (if this is a means of making practical arrangements between people, or a manner to escape from personal involvement), stage 3 (if the purpose is to appreciate what the close group would desire), stage 4 (if it corresponds to a strict application of the majority law, with legal concerns), stage 5 (if it expresses the necessity of knowing what the concerned group thinks, since opinions and rules are relative), or stage 6 (if the majority law reaches the status of a democratic and universal principle).

Moreover, a given stage is not characterized by one single aspect. It is, rather, a matter of multidimensional construct, and several properties may be alternately emphasized. For instance, consider stage 3: we may focus on a conformist aspect (to be a "good" boy or girl), on a new level of decentration (to consider close group values), or on social objectives (to search positive and smooth individual interactions; Edwards, 1982).

1.3 Defining issues test (DIT) and Rest's collective procedure

Rest (1979, for the revised manual) has proposed a collective procedure to assess moral judgment. This procedure, in comparison with the previous individual interviews (especially the MJI method) presents the great advantage of being strictly objective, but at the cost of an act of faith about participants' understanding of the successive items. Indeed, the main characteristic of this instrument consists of the presentation of successive hypothetical issues that participants have to consider. Moral assessment depends on the importance individuals assign to the issues because every significant issue corresponds to one of the various stages of moral judgment. Other issues allow to control the reliability of participants' responses.

Finally, a given participant is characterized by an individual profile, made of the proportion of the choices belonging to the various stages. Sometimes, researchers simply use the proportion of postconventional judgments (" principled" or "P score": that is "stage 5" plus "stage 6") as a dependent variable.

The DIT have induced numerous studies among adolescents, youth and adults. Rest et al. (1978) have already conducted a review of cross-sectional, longitudinal and sequential studies. This instrument seems to be valid and findings suggest a positive evolution in moral judgment during adolescence and youth, followed by a plateau in development in early adulthood when formal education stops. This long-term development based on the DIT does not fit the long-term shape of development (alternation of spurts and plateaux) suggested by Dawson-Tunik et al. (2005) from studies using the MJI procedure

Besides, the DIT assessments depend on the accuracy of the a priori correspondence between issues and moral stages. The recognition method used by Rest has two main difficulties. We cannot be sure that the various issues really belong to the various stages, and we cannot be sure that a given issue is truly understood according to the authors' intent. Moreover, participants have to maintain a high level of attention during the test and it seems difficult simultaneously to manage the 12 issues that follow a given dilemma. Finally, it is likely that performance in the DIT could be due, at least for some part, to verbal abilities, as suggested by Sanders, Lubinsky, and Benbow (1995) comparing gifted adolescents with their average-ability peers.

1.4 Direct assessment of moral maturity: The sociomoral reflection measure – short form

Gibbs, Basinger, and Fuller (1992) have proposed an instrument (SRM-SF) which is very different from Kohlberg's original method. This instrument was elaborated to develop simpler measures than MJI and DIT. The first main difference concerns the dilemmas method. Although the authors recognize some advantages to the dilemmas method, which provides concrete situational details and allows participants to react "in fresh and spontaneous ways" (p. 37), they also report current critics about Kohlberg's dilemmas which are sometimes considered as artificial and irrelevant. Moreover, they estimate that moral judgment and thought can be truly evaluated through easier procedures.

The second main difference between SRM-SF and MJI (or DIT), lies in a deep modification of the stages system. From a superficial view, one may think that stages 5 and 6 are simply discarded, since there are now only four stages, which look somewhat like Kohlberg's stages 1 to 4. In fact, some of the stage 5 and 6 properties are now considered as a differentiation of stage 3 and 4. Let us explain this point.

In SRM-SF, two global levels of moral development are considered. The first level is labeled "*immature*". It comprises two stages. In stage 1, decisions are grounded on physical power,

authority status, absolute judgments, undifferentiated moral labels and unilateral social perspective. Stage 2 is reached when moral thinkers are aware of the reciprocity of social interactions; they can then understand the necessity of pragmatic deals and exchanges: if one helps a friend, it is because he or she may return the favor.

The second moral level comprises two stages of *mature sociomoral reflection*. The important point is that people from this mature level are able to consider the fundamental bases of moral behaviors. Stage 3 remains in the interpersonal sphere but it stresses some interpersonal expectations of prosocial feeling, caring and conduct; normative expectations and values are now considered in the frame of interpersonal interactions. The transition between stages 3 and 4 may be characterized by an appraisal of the relativism of personal values. Finally, in stage 4, society as a whole is considered as a complex system: moral values and obligations are now evaluated from this new global perspective.

Moreover, both stage 3 and stage 4 are differentiated in type A and type B, following what Kohlberg has suggested in 1984 (quoted by Gibbs et al., 1992). In type A, moral aspects are considered, basically, in specific contexts or situations (either for stage 3 interpersonal or stage 4 societal concerns), whereas in type B moral reflection is generalized to ideals and universal considerations (again about either interpersonal or societal concerns). Therefore, some aspects of the traditional stage 5 and stage 6 remain through these principled and universal aspects of type B thought.

In sum, Gibbs et al. (1992) proposed two general levels of moral development: first "immature" then "mature". The mature level comprises two stages (interpersonal then societal) and two types in each stage, depending on the degree of abstraction and generalization of moral judgments.

The SRM-SF procedure (Gibbs et al., 1992) takes the form of a brief questionnaire about topics such as: keeping promises, telling the truth, saving a life, not taking things that belong to others, obeying the law, etc. In each of the 11 questions, participants have, first, to indicate, on a three-point scale, how important it is to act according to the suggested way, when dealing with, for example, a friend or parents, and, second, to indicate why is it more or less important to behave in this way.

Therefore, moral concerns are directly set out, that is, not through a dilemma. Nevertheless, moral reflection appears to be activated by the contextual support of thinking about a friend or parents, and by the open question aiming at explaining or justifying the preceding rating.

Results suggest that the mature level is constructed during adolescence. A shift in the mean global stage (from stage 2 to stage 3), appears between 12 and 14 years old. But stage 4 is not the mean global stage until adulthood. Moreover, there is a highly significant correlation between SRM-SF and MJI ($r(43) = .69$, $p < .0001$).

SRM-SF, then, constitutes a very useful instrument, for practical reasons, although it is not frequently used as a mainstream instrument. Indeed, the mature stages and types are probably more realistic than the infrequent traditional stages 5, 6, or 7. But one may think that this moral maturity level looks a little too conformist. In fact, it was "morally" satisfying, with Kohlberg's stage 6, to conceive that moral development may progress up to a level where people are ready to fight against more unfair social order. Furthermore, a true developmental perspective does not imply that final stages are necessarily the most frequent stages in adolescence or adulthood.

1.5 Back to the dilemmas, but real-life dilemmas

If moral development concerns not only judgments about hypothetical cases, but also and perhaps mainly, decisions and reflections about personal conflicts, it is appropriate to explore procedures based on real-life dilemmas. There is not a lot of research using this method, but we can anticipate a growing interest for it in the future.

For instance, Wark and Krebs (1996) compared moral maturity of undergraduate students (average age 20) in the MJI and in a situation adapted from Walker et al. (quoted by Wark & Krebs, 1996) where participants had to recall and discuss two significant real-life moral conflicts: one personal, that is with a personal involvement in the event, and one impersonal, implying that the person reporting the dilemma is not directly involved in it. Results indicate a higher score of moral maturity through MJI. Indeed, 88% of the participants scored higher on Kohlberg's dilemmas than on the impersonal real-life dilemmas, and 95% scored higher on Kohlberg's dilemmas than on the personal real-life dilemmas. Thus, personal dilemmas appear to induce the lowest moral maturity score.

Moreover, Wark and Krebs (1996) were able to categorize real-life dilemmas into the four following types: *philosophical dilemmas*, such as abortion, euthanasia, capital punishment (participants are not directly involved but had to think about them), *antisocial dilemmas* (about rules transgressions or reacting to temptation, such as having unprotected sex, cheating in an exam or at poker with friends), *social pressure* to violate one's value or identity (for instance, pressure by father to accept religion or pressure by family on lifestyle and career), *prosocial dilemmas* (for example, when participants experienced conflicting demands, as from divorced parents, or when they had to react to others' needs: help a criminal friend, take car key from a drunk friend, stop mother from taking drugs).

From these categories, it appears that real-life dilemmas may be used to make clear what people consider as moral concerns and conflicts. That was the main objective of the research conducted by Walker, Pitts, Hennig, and Matsuba (1995). In this research, participants from four age groups – adolescence (16–19 years), early adulthood (18–25 years), middle adulthood (35–48 years) and late adulthood (65–84 years) – were mainly interviewed about real-life dilemmas and also about their conception of morality and moral people. The authors stress the fact that, despite the variability of the dilemmas recalled, most of the reasonings were readily scorable in Kohlberg's system. Adolescents and young adults did not differ in their moral levels, same thing when middle and older adult groups are compared, but the two older groups reasoned at a more mature level than did the two younger groups (note that middle-aged adults were partly university students, and older adults were participants in programs for retired people).

It follows that real-life dilemmas can be very useful for moral assessment. Remember that Piaget (1932) had carefully created dilemmas and situations according to the daily life of children in the 1930s. The use of real-life dilemmas with 1990s adolescents has the same objective. However, it is also convenient to question adolescents about situations they have never met. Indeed, every citizen may have his/her own opinion about social problems such as euthanasia or capital punishment that they have not personally experienced and it is significant to note that participants in Wark and Krebs' research often chose this kind of philosophical dilemma as a "real-life" dilemma.

2. Sequential aspects of the general stages

The first question about every stage system is to appreciate the ordered properties of the sequence: is it necessary to follow the growing process step by step? In the case of Kohlberg's stages, there is a lot of evidence in favor of sequentiality. First, longitudinal data (Rest et al., 1978) showed a decrease in lower stages and an increase in higher stages, especially during the adolescent period. For instance, a specific study (quoted by Rest et al., 1978) on adolescents from 14 years to 18 years of age at the first testing, observed an average percentage of 53% adolescents moving up and 15% moving down two years later, followed by 66% of moving up and 7% of moving down four years later. Clearly, an upward trend is predominant in the individual change patterns.

Moreover, Walker (1982) tried to influence the initial dominant stage of 10- to 13-year-old girls and boys. There were five experimental conditions: (a) participants were presented to a conflicting reasoning scorable at the stage just lower (−1 stage) than the stage they have shown; (b) presentation of a +1 stage reasoning; (c) presentation of a +2 stage reasoning; (d) presentation of a reasoning from the same stage; (e) control condition with no treatment. At one week and seven weeks later, there was no regression in the dominant stage, even in the −1 stage condition. Changes in the upward direction are particularly noticeable in +1 and +2 conditions. These changes are always +1 stage changes, even in the +2 stage condition.

Another study by Walker, de Vries, and Bichard

(1984) showed that, whatever the participants' stage, understanding of statements belonging to higher stages depends on the proximity between the current participant's stage and the stage of the given statement. Understanding is evaluated by the correctness of paraphrases. There were 96.6% of correct paraphrases when statements came from the same stage, but 67.2% when it came from a +1 stage, 20.8% from a +2 stage, and 00% from a +3 stage.

However, it is well known that individuals are not characterized by one single stage. On the contrary, any individual may present responses belonging to several stages. If a single stage is retained, according to some kind of procedure, it is only a "dominant" or a "modal" stage, as we saw earlier. Developmental evolution, then, can be analyzed by considering the range of effective stages. In this case, the sequential properties of moral development are attested by the shape of the transitional processes from one stage to the next (Thoma & Rest, 1999; Walker & Taylor, 1991). Figure 7.1 (from Walker & Taylor, 1991) shows the theoretical successive stages distributions in accordance with a sequential evolution: it corresponds to a progressive shift along the sequence. In their results, gathered from children, adolescents, and adults in a two-year follow-up study, Walker and Taylor (1991) observed 158 (69.6%) patterns of change, consistent with the theoretical patterns presented in Figure 7.1.

From these studies, we can conclude that: (a) Kohlberg's sequence of general stages is an acceptable approach to the developmental process at stake; (b) the intra-individual variability is consistent with the stage sequence; (c) however, it would be inappropriate, in most cases, to characterize adolescents by one single stage; (d) conversely, moral assessment should take into account the range of the various stages any one adolescent may present.

3. Context variabilities and differentiation between several rule systems

The previous paragraphs have stressed that moral development can be analyzed in terms of general successive stages. But the intra-individual variability we have discussed earlier indicates that, at

FIGURE 7.1

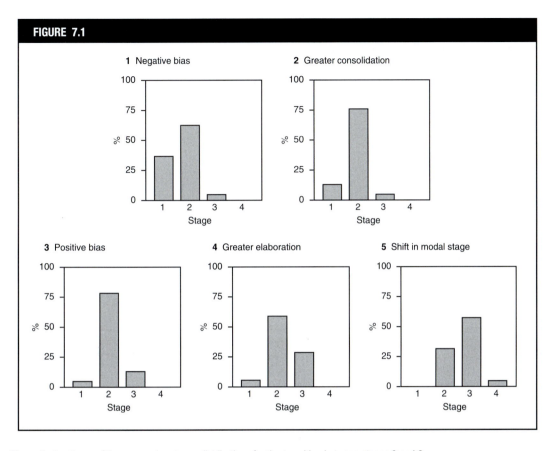

Theoretical patterns of the successive stages distributions for the transition between stages 2 and 3.

the same time, we have to consider possible sources of variation (Lehalle, Buelga, Aris, Chapelle, & Levy, 2000). Indeed, intra-individual variability is not a mere fluctuation around a modal stage. It may be due to identifiable differences between situations. This possibility does not disagree with stage analysis, since it is likely that a more elaborated reasoning appears first in specific situations (as Piaget pointed out, in some of the first research, in referring to "horizontal *décalages*"). In the following paragraphs, we will examine situational variations and two further extensions of intra-individual possible variations: the debate about moral action *vs* moral judgment, and the differentiation between several categories of social norms.

3.1 Moral levels and dilemmas characteristics

The question is to consider modifications in participants' decisions following a change in moral dilemmas. Sobesky (1983) initiated into this field by proposing four versions of the Heinz dilemma to each participant from two age groups: high school students (mean age 16.1 years) and college students (mean age 19.6 years). It appears that students were less certain to steal when the negative consequences were greater for Heinz (i.e., Heinz is sent to prison). Conversely, students were more certain about stealing when the wife could be saved. Moreover, when the consequences for Heinz were low, the average P score (stages 5 plus 6) was higher, as if participants needed to strongly justify an unpunished illegal act. But, when the consequences for the wife were greater, *P* score was lower, as if there were no necessity so strongly to justify a successful illegal act.

Teo et al. (1995) did not construct variations on a single dilemma (as Sobesky did), but they examined the various dilemmas used by Colby et al. (quoted by Teo et al., 1995). Thus, if authoritative issues (i.e., when the matter concerns prescriptions from authorities and institutions) are opposed to non-authoritative issues (i.e., aspects of fairness, needs, and people's rights), higher stages were observed with the non-authoritative issues, in younger groups (10 and 13–14), and there was no difference in older groups. Moreover, if personal dilemmas (which deal with conflicts in the frame of personal interactions) are opposed to transpersonal dilemmas (where topics stress formal roles, social functions, institutions), these transpersonal dilemmas pulled for higher stages, at least for the four "middle" age groups (16–30 years of age). This is not really surprising if we remember that stage 4, not stage 3, goes beyond personal matters up to societal concerns.

Another example comes from a study by Aris (1999), who considers how participants may experience feelings of a hypothetical nature. Aris started from the unavoidable Heinz dilemma, by considering the personal interest of protagonists. If somebody can steal a drug to save his wife (with moral considerations), will the same decision and considerations occur if the question is to save a neighbor? Adolescents from two age groups (12 and 14 years of age) appear very sensitive to this induced variable. They decide more often to act against norms in case of personal interest, but they produce more principled justifications in dilemmas without personal interest, as if it would be necessary to strongly justify a gratuitous act.

It would be of interest to promote this topic of research in order to sort out the more important characteristics of dilemmas. A property such as "personal interest" may be common in numerous possible situations, and linked to predictable variations in participants' judgments. Eventually, any dilemma could be thought of as a specific cluster of properties that interact until a "decision" emerges from this interaction.

3.2   *Moral action and moral judgment*

Intra-individual variability leads to the more general question of the relationship between moral judgments and moral behavior. Of course, morality is always embedded in concrete concerns, but the problem is to know if moral actions can be linked to moral assessment in hypothetical judgments, like judgments in Kohlberg's paradigm. In other words, are people who are "moral" when they have to judge behaviors still moral when they have to behave? A priori, one may think that people should act in accordance with what they think and what they do. As a consequence, moral action and moral judgment should be correlated. But this very evident and simple question has no definitive answer.

In a review by Blasi (1980), the link between moral reasoning and moral action appears generally positive but the relations are often weak and may vary from one domain to another. In fact, the judgment/action debate constitutes an open and budding field (Killen & Hart, 1995). Two opposite theoretical conceptions are obvious. On one hand, moral actions would be strongly context dependent, which leads to predict a large range of variability across circumstances and no strong relations between reasoning and actions. On the other hand, individual conceptions and personal principles should impose consistence and coherence in various situations, which lead to observation of positive relationships between judgments and actions. The truth probably lies somewhere between these two poles. Following Hart and Killen (1995), it is appropriate to consider that moral actions are not entirely contextualized, and it is suitable to conceive moral development as a constructivist process with an active control and structuration from individuals. Furthermore, consistence and coherence may be viewed as a cognitive–developmental outcome, after a long run where variability is the rule and decisions depend on circumstances and contexts.

Moreover, it would be of interest to distinguish several steps between "judgments" and "actions", by considering the experimental procedures. There are two extremes: on one side, the Kohlbergian hypothetical stories are pure judgments; on the other side, effective individual behaviors in

> **Box 7.3. Examples of social events from the five-rule system (McConville & Furth, 1981)**
>
> **Legal rules**
> - A girl frequently goes into department stores and takes clothes and records without paying for them
> - Tom likes to drive fast and frequently goes above the speed limit
>
> **Ascriptive rules**
> - Jim is a college student. He wants to get an A in his history course. On the day of the exam, he sits next to the smartest guy in the class and copies from him
> - Bill often stays out later than his parents permit
>
> **Conventional rules**
> - The Smith family members don't exchange Christmas presents
> - A couple's wedding is arranged by their parents. They do not meet until the day of the wedding
>
> **Interpersonal rules**
> - Mary is eating lunch with a group of girls. Another girl, who is a friend of Mary's, asks if she could sit with them. Mary says she can't
> - Jack lets Fred use his bicycle on the condition that he can use Fred's skateboard the next day. Fred, however, refuses to let Jack use his skateboard when he asks for it.
>
> **Moral rules**
> - Mr. Brown is accused of robbing a bank. His neighbor, Mr. Smith, knows that Mr. Brown was at home at the time the robbery was committed and therefore could not have done it. Mr. Smith, however, doesn't bother to tell anyone that Mr. Brown is innocent, because he doesn't like him
> - Carol knows that Mary would be upset if people found out that her father had been in jail but Carol tells people anyway.

context are pure actions (e.g., resistance to temptation in the laboratory setting or moral evaluation through naturalistic observations). But there are, at least, two intermediate steps: (a) when the hypothetical stories are chosen in relation to participant's concerns (e.g., Scharf, quoted by Jurkovic, 1980); (b) when data come from participants' reports about real-life moral dilemmas (Walker et al. 1995). Further research will probably take these distinctions into account.

3.3 Categories of social norms

If moral judgments vary according to different contexts, it is appropriate to understand how social norms are actually categorized by adolescents. Turiel (quoted by McConville & Furth, 1981) was the first to suggest a distinction between social *conventions*, which are arbitrary but not intrinsically wrong, and *moral* obligations, which must be respected, even though there are no explicit rules or law for them.

McConville and Furth (1981) have extended Turiel's distinction between conventions and morality and drawn up a five-rule system. In addition to morality and conventions, they consider the *legal domain* (when transgressions are forbidden by law), *ascriptive rules* (which are explicit rules in a specific social context, for instance, at school or in the family), and *interpersonal rules* (which concern fairness between peers). See Box 7.3 where the social events used by McConville and Furth (1981) are reported and classified according to the five-rule system.

In this research, events such as those given in Box 7.3 were presented to 80 adolescents from four age groups (13 to 19). The presentation was in threes, with two events from the same category and one from another one. The adolescents had to indicate which of the two situations were alike and, together, differed from the third. Thus, it was a forced-choice task. Moreover, adolescents were asked to explain their choice. Results indicated that legal and moral rules situations are most frequently recognized whereas interpersonal situations are the least paired; pairing of ascriptive or conventional situations depends on the rule in contrast. Interestingly, there is no age trend in the pairing, but explanations of the choices are more "systemic", that is more explicit, with age. When explanations are taken into account, the legal system appears as the best recognized, and the interpersonal domain as the most poorly. The ascriptive rules were processed almost like the legal ones, but the moral and conventional rules were less explicit.

Lehalle, Chapelle, Decaluwé, and Aris (1998) used the same situations (adapted from McConville and Furth, 1981), but with a free classification task mostly analyzed through cluster analysis (here, the cluster analysis indicated how often different stories were classified together). In this case, legal system was again the most differentiated, but moral obligations appeared to be very close to interpersonal rules. When taking into account more recent results grounded on the same method (Lévy & Lehalle, 2002), adolescents' moral landscape appears to be made of three main regions: (a) the *conventional* land where social rules are usually respected but transgressions are not forbidden, (b) the country of *constraints*, which comprises the land of *laws* and the land of *ascriptive rules* (both lands concern what is explicitly forbidden, nevertheless the two categories are quite well-differentiated), (c) the country of *care*, which groups together *morality* and *interpersonal* relationships (these categories are not well-differentiated and concern *what we have to respect as regards others*, although there is no real sanction to be anticipated). Moreover, in agreement with McConville and Furth (1981), results suggest that, during adolescence, the criteria for categorizing social norms become more abstract. In early adolescence, there are more categorizations from superficial features such as "it's to do with school". But, in late adolescence, there are more categorizations according to explicit social norms.

4. Inter-individual differences

Following common sense, and probably daily experience also, it is evident that morality and moral commitment are not exactly equally distributed among individuals. But developmental analysis in adolescence has first to clarify and sometimes to moderate the range of inter-individual differences; second, differences may be conceived in terms of differentiation and not only in terms of maturity or competencies; finally, possible sources of influences may be viewed as developmental factors.

4.1 Delinquency or moral commitment

Delinquency is an example of the necessity to examine carefully individual differences, beyond common sense. Of course, one may expect that young delinquents would be scored at a lower moral stage than other adolescents. This was the main conclusion of Blasi (1980) reviewing 15 studies mostly grounded on Kohlberg's interviews. However, Blasi already argues that a range of moral reasoning stages can be present among delinquents.

Thus, Jurkovic (1980) suggested a more differentiated picture of moral reasonings in adolescent delinquents. If we compare results of heterogeneous groups of delinquents with matched non-delinquent groups, most researches display low levels of moral reasoning in delinquent groups, as Blasi stressed. But it appears that some delinquents can show high levels of moral reasoning, and several authors failed to find differences in moral maturity between the two groups they interviewed. This leads Jurkovic to conclude, first, that delinquency as a legal classification does not strictly imply *less mature* moral reasoning (conversely, conventional level of morality does not prevent from delinquency); second, that other variables have to be taken into account, since there is a variability into the "delinquent *vs* non-delinquent" variability. In particular, Jurkovic refers to research that has shown that psychopathic or sociopathic delinquents present many more preconventional levels than other delinquents. In other words (Jurkovic, 1980), there are variabilities in adolescent delinquent groups and: "Just as these youngsters differ in their personality and behavioral style, so do they differ in their level of moral judgment" (p. 716).

Thus, it is advisable to go beyond mere dichotomies such as delinquent/non-delinquent or moral/amoral and to consider variability in delinquent groups and the links between this variability and the socio-personal maturity from a developmental perspective (Van Poppel & Born, 1994).

Moreover, variability in social groups leads us to consider, in parallel with delinquent adolescents, the cases of exceptional altruistic adolescents. Following Hart, Yates, Fegley, and Wilson

---

Box 7.4.   Moral commitment in inner-city adolescents (Hart et al., 1995)

Let us abandon stereotypes about "inner-city adolescents" living in a "poor urban area". Among these marginalized and deprived populations, there are also admirable figures with a great sense of moral commitment and care for others. Hart et al. (1995) have proposed a theoretical analysis of what could differentiate these exceptional adolescents (called "care exemplars"). Data came from two studies by the authors, and also from some cases analysis. The first study was done in Camden (New Jersey) and consisted mainly of comparing, on several variables, 15 exemplary youths (African–American and Latino adolescents) with a matched sample of adolescents. The second source of data stemmed from participants in a school-based community service program (150 African–American adolescents in Washington, DC).

In order to reach a better understanding of moral commitment and action, Hart et al. (1995) focussed on people's conceptions of themselves and others, that is, how people conceive self and identity with respect to others' needs and socio-economic situations.

Care exemplars adolescents appeared to be different on the following aspects. First, they were more likely to describe themselves in terms of moral personality traits and moral goals. Second, they presented more integration of ideal self and parental representations into their self-concept; for instance, a subset of the terms they used for describing themselves was also used to describe the ideal self. Third, they have constructed a kind of theory of themselves which consists of using principles to organize and make sense of the self's characteristics. Fourth, they showed a stronger representation of their self-evolution, that is, a greater continuity and connection between past and future selves.

All these personality characteristics support a constructivist view of moral development.

(1995), the question is to delineate what the specificities of these exceptional youths are, with respect to their individual history and personal adjustment (see Box 7.4).

4.2 Gender differentiation

Gilligan (1977) is well known for her claim that Kohlberg's theory is male oriented because of a focus on justice and law, whereas females would be oriented toward an ethic of care. If this gender difference were valid, then females would be put at a disadvantage in Kohlbergian assessments because legal and justice concerns are scored at stage 4, while interpersonal interests and care aspects are supposed mainly to belong to stage 3. This ultra-traditional view of Gilligan has been strongly criticized, in particular on methodological aspects (Brabeck, 1983; Wark & Krebs, 1996).

In fact, there is no evidence that gender induces any difference in moral maturity. For instance, Walker (quoted by Brabeck, 1983) first examined research on 29 samples of children and early adolescents: only four of them reported significant sex differences, and, indeed, showed more mature development for females. Second, among 32 samples of late adolescents, Walker found only eight studies indicating significant sex differences, in this case, however, more mature development for males.

Similarly, Rest (1979) reviewed 22 samples of DIT research including gender variable, and only two of them reported a significant difference in P score (stage 5 plus stage 6) between males and females, with about 6% of the variance accounted for the sex variable, leading Rest (1979) to conclude: "Whenever sex differences do occur, it would probably be a good idea to check for the influence of other variables, such as IQ, education or SES" (p. 75).

In fact, the controversy over Gilligan's approach could be solved by taking into account the distinction between "moral maturity" and "moral orientation" (Wark & Krebs, 1996). The former implies a position on a developmental ordered sequence, such as Kohlberg's. The latter stresses people's major preoccupations: mainly justice and legal system or mainly care aspects and interpersonal relations. Wark and Krebs' findings (from 19- to 20-year-old students) indicated a significant main effect for gender in moral orientation (more care orientations in females) but there was no significant effect for gender in moral maturity.

This result suggests that one may have a personal orientation for care concerns, but the same person can also take into account justice and legal aspects when facing Kohlberg's dilemmas. Moreover, in Wark and Krebs' study (1996), moral orientation is not split into either justice mode or care mode: numerous people, instead, present both orientations, with (or without) a predominance of one of them.

4.3 Possible sources of moral differentiation

When we compare delinquents and non-delinquents, or boys and girls, nothing reveals itself about the possible causes for the differences. Furthermore, differences in social environment may produce developmental differences. This is the case for peers (Scholte & van Aken, this volume), family (Lila, van Aken, Musitu, & Buelga, this volume) and culture (Hendry & Kloep, this volume). But the point is also to use factual evidence in order to approach plausible explanations of moral differentiation.

Regarding peers, it is evident that moral thinking and moral commitment are oriented through discussion and affiliation in peer group. There is a special case of peer influence in adolescence (Scholte & van Aken, this volume). Moreover, following Piaget (1932), it is likely that decentration and care concerns are more easily performed when dealing with a peer than with adults or anybody else. Then, peer experience and conflicts in peer relations may promote moral development. But there is another way to consider the peer factor. Indeed, some studies have attempted to clarify how various modalities of the individual integration in peer groups may differentiate moral development. But, in Schonert-Reichl's study (1999) among early adolescents around 12 years of age, significant correlations between several dimensions of group integration and moral scores (MJI) are not regular or very strong. However we can note that: (a) in girls, moral reasoning is positively correlated with leadership status and prosocial behavior; (b) in boys, moral reasoning is positively correlated with leadership status, as for girls, but also with antisocial behavior, and (negatively) with withdrawn behavior; (c) moral reasoning is clearly related, both for girls and boys, to the number of close friends but not to the number of friends; (d) about the quality of friendship for boys, moral reasoning is *lower* when conflicts are reported to be resolved quickly and easily; (e) finally, indicators of the degree of friendship activities are positively related to moral reasoning for girls, but not for boys. These results suggest that peer influence on moral reasoning is due to the specific social experiences that peer group induces: conflict resolutions, discussions in close relationships, positive insertion in peer groups (which implies the resolution of conflicts).

Family influences on adolescent moral maturity are not as easily validated as one may think. If we consider one possible direct influence from parents, Speicher (1994) found significant but moderate correlations between parents' and offsprings' moral reasoning. Moreover, when background variables are controlled (for instance age, IQ, education, etc.) the parents' moral level may predict the moral judgment of the *daughter* but not of the son. Furthermore, as Speicher (1994) noted and probably because of formal education, numerous adults reach a higher moral score than their parents, which excludes the idea that there is a direct influence from parents. Finally, if we think about an indirect effect of education style, Pratt, Arnold, Pratt, and Diessner (1999) observed no significant correlation between parents' authoritativeness and moral level of 14- to 16-year-old adolescents. These surprising results lead, first, to view moral development as a product of numerous interactive factors, and, second, to consider the proposition, yet again, that moral development is a constructive process, implying that the effect of any environmental impulse depends on adolescent reaction. Adolescents do not always develop in ways adults or parents want them to.

Cultural influences on adolescent moral thinking were already considered by Kohlberg (1969). However, Kohlberg claimed the universality of his stage sequence, despite slight differences between developmental curves from different cultural groups. Some years later, Snarey (1985) reviewed cross-cultural research. His conclusion supports a Kohlbergian view. Indeed, Kohlberg's dilemmas appear to be relevant in various cultures, provided that some superficial adjustments are made to fit the specificity of cultural environments. Moreover, the sequential stages constitute a fair approximation of developmental trends. But the question is to what extent different cultures work in promoting moral development? This is not a matter of a cultural hierarchy on a common moral dimension. Indeed, there are, in every culture, philosophical traditions and thought about moral topics, such as the meaning of life, social control, care for others, etc., which lead to cultural settings for socio-moral development. Second, on moral concerns, the intra-cultural variability among individuals appears to be more important than inter-cultural variability (Wainryb & Turiel, 1995).

In fact, because of the specificities of cultural contexts, cross-cultural research is useful for studying specific variables, but not for comparing cultures per se. For example, Edwards (1982), studying moral development among youth in Kenya, stressed the importance of such variables as family modernization, number of years lived away from home (which increases social experience and autonomy, therefore moral level), cultural diversity at school (which seems to impulse moral maturity because the diversity allows experiencing other modes of thinking and living). Furthermore, if people appear to stay at stage 3 in a given culture (see Edwards, 1982, about traditional community leaders in Kenya), one must consider that this stage is perhaps the best adapted in that context, that is when there is no utility to take into account social system beyond the close group and when there is not much information available about it. In other words, as we formulated earlier (Bril & Lehalle, 1988/1998) moral development in a culture is necessary . . . *when it is possible*.

In sum, when peers, family or cultural setting are supposed to influence moral development in adolescents, it is convenient to think about the causal underlying process of moral change. Taking into account lessons from research such as that quoted earlier, Lehalle, Aris, Buelga, and Musitu (2004) have suggested a socio-cognitive approach that proposes five determining factors of moral improvement in adolescence: (a) a strictly cognitive factor inducing to go beyond specific contexts to process on general features or common principles (i.e., then we have to save the neighbor as well!); (b) a role of the effective participation in decision and social functioning, in the frame of the groups adolescents belong to (school, family, sport team, etc.); (c) a better understanding of how the whole society works (i.e. information about institutions, justice, law, social support and solidarity, etc.); (d) a *personal* experience of other modes of thinking and behavior (to meet people from other cultures as people from other social settings and social groups); (e) an improvement in self-reflection in relation to the past (parent and familial history) and the future (what can I do with my life?).

5. Conclusion

Throughout this chapter, we have attempted some answers to three main questions: (a) how to define, delimit and assess moral development?; (b) how to take into account intra- and inter-individual variability?; (c) how to approach possible sources of moral development?

Clearly, the study of moral development leads to a better understanding of individual attempts to coordinate personal and social values. This is one of the main developmental tasks in adolescence. However, although moral development during adolescence has been studied and documented during the last three decades, there still remain disturbing questions and unresolved problems.

One problem concerns the search for valid explanations of these developmental trends. If general stages, despite the variability, appear to be a fair enough descriptive approximation of long-term evolution, what are the mechanisms and determinants for this evolution? Kohlberg always claimed that cognitive factors are of major importance. But it is not an obvious way of clarifying links between cognitive development and the various domains where cognitive development may be involved (Lehalle, this volume). Of course, progress in abstraction leads to more general concepts about society, justice, etc. Furthermore, the traditional formal stage implies an ability to consider present society and current social rules as one possibility among many others. It follows a reflection on desirable changes in order to improve the present rules. Cognitive processes, thus, are truly implicated.

But moral development depends on affective incentives as well. Adolescents are influenced by the figures they meet, especially if they go through a period of reflection about what could be possible in society or what is really important in life, both for them and for others.

Social factors must also be considered (Edwards, 1982). Indeed, the increasing social experience during adolescence implies the necessity to solve social conflicts and induces the experience of social regulation and social diversity, which, in turn, may induce, according to Kohlberg, more relative judgments and a better coordination between individual needs and social demands.

But is it really advisable to maintain a conceptualization of development, always ending, as in Kohlberg's system, with an idyllic stage of perfect achievement? Of course, according to Piaget, the process of equilibration is always "*majorant*". The implication of this, then, is that developmental changes should always be upwards. Nevertheless, positive evolutions depend on contexts and circumstances. As a consequence, a complete developmental view must explain not only moving up but also moving down (as observed in some cases by Rest et al., 1978), in addition to stagnation. It is obvious that moving down in longitudinal studies not only comes from measurement errors. Were we to have a better understanding of the developmental mechanisms and factors in the long run, we could approach why individual changes may follow different paths, depending on what happens in individual lives.

This chapter, as a whole, therefore, supports a constructivist view on moral development. Moral judgments and moral commitments are built through individual reactions to circumstances and environmental impulses. Thus, although there is a sort of stagnation after adolescence or after formal education, it is advisable to emphasize, according to this constructivist view, that positive changes are always potential, not only in the adolescent period but also in adulthood (Dawson-Tunik et al., 2005).

References

Aris, C. (1999, September). *Intra-individual variations in adolescents' moral judgments related to "personal interest" enclosed in moral dilemmas*. IXth European Conference on Developmental Psychology, Spetses, Greece.

Blasi, A. (1980). Bridging moral cognition and moral action: A critical review of the literature. *Psychological Bulletin, 88*(1), 1–45.

Brabeck, M. (1983). Moral judgment: Theory and research on differences between males and females. *Developmental Review, 3*, 274–291.

Bril, B., & Lehalle, H. (1988/1998). *Le développement psychologique est-il universel? Approches interculturelles* [Is psychological development universal? Cross-cultural approaches] (3rd ed.). Paris: Presses Universitaires de France.

Colby, A., & Kohlberg, L. (1987). *The measurement of moral judgment Vol. 1*. Cambridge: Cambridge University Press.

Colby, A., Kohlberg, L., Speicher, B., Hewer, A., Candee, D., Gibbs, J.C. et al. (1987). *The measurement of moral judgment Vol. 2*. Cambridge: Cambridge University Press.

Dawson-Tunik, T.L., Commons, M., Wilson, M., & Fischer, K. (2005). The shape of development. *European Journal of Developmental Psychology, 2*, 163–195.

Edwards, C.P. (1982). Moral development in comparative perspective. In D. A. Wagner, & H. W. Stevenson (Eds.), *Cultural perspectives on child development* (pp. 248–279). San Francisco: W. H. Freeman & Co.

Gibbs, J.C., Basinger, K.S., & Fuller, D. (1992). *Moral maturity: Measuring the development of sociomoral reflection*. Hillsdale, NJ: Lawrence Erlbaum Associates, Inc.

Gilligan, C. (1977). In a different voice: Women's conceptions of self and of morality. *Harvard Educational Review, 47*, 481–517.

Hart, D., & Killen, M. (1995). Introduction: Perspectives on morality in everyday life. In M. Killen, & D. Hart (Eds.), *Morality in everyday life: Developmental perspectives* (pp. 1–20). Cambridge: Cambridge University Press.

Hart, D., Yates, M., Fegley, S., & Wilson, G. (1995). Moral commitment in inner-city adolescents. In M. Killen, & D. Hart (Eds.), *Morality in everyday life: Developmental perspectives* (pp. 317–341). Cambridge: Cambridge University Press.

Jurkovic, G.J. (1980). The juvenile delinquent as a moral philosopher: A structural-developmental perspective. *Psychological Bulletin, 88*(3), 709–727.

Killen, M., & Hart, D. (Eds.). (1995). *Morality in everyday life: Developmental perspectives*. Cambridge: Cambridge University Press.

Kohlberg, L. (1969). Stage and sequence: The cognitive-developmental approach to socialization. In D. A. Goslin (Ed.), *Handbook of socialization theory and research*. Chicago, IL: Rand McNally College Publishing Company.

Kohlberg, L., & Ryncarz, R.A. (1990). Beyond justice reasoning: Moral development and consideration of a seventh stage. In C. N. Alexander, & E. J. Langer (Eds.), *Higher stages of human development* (pp. 191–207). New York: Oxford University Press.

Lehalle, H., Aris, C., Buelga, S., & Musitu, G. (2004). Développement cognitif et jugement moral: De Kohlberg à la recherche des déterminants de la différenciation du développement moral [Socio-cognitive development and moral judgment: From Kohlberg to the search of differentiating factors of moral development]. *L'Orientation Scolaire et Professionnelle, 33*(2), 289–314.

Lehalle, H., Buelga, S., Aris, C., Chapelle, D., & Levy, E. (2000). Variabilities in moral development during adolescence: Is it still possible to support a developmental view on social norms acquisition? *European Review of Applied Psychology, 50*(2), 283–292.

Lehalle, H., Chapelle, D., Decaluwé, L., & Aris, C. (1998, June). *A free classification of some socially negative behaviors by French and Norwegian adolescents.* The 6th Biennial Conference of the European Association for Research on Adolescence, Budapest, Hungary.

Lévy, E., & Lehalle, H. (2002). La catégorisation des infractions aux règles sociales chez les adolescents: Au-delà des circonstances, les progrès de l'abstraction [Evolution of social norms categorization in adolescents: Contexts power and abstraction growth]. *Enfance, 54*(2), 187–206.

McConville, K., & Furth, H.G. (1981). Understanding of social rule systems in adolescence. In J. A. Meacham, & N. R. Santilli (Eds.), *Social development in youth: Structure and content* (pp. 145–159). Basel, Germany: Karger.

Piaget, J. (1932). *Le jugement moral chez l'enfant* [The moral judgment of the child]. Paris: Presses Universitaires de France.

Pratt, M.W., Arnold, M.L., Pratt, A.T., & Diessner, R. (1999). Predicting adolescent moral reasoning from family climate: A longitudinal study. *Journal of Early Adolescence, 19*(2), 148–175.

Rest, J.R. (1979). *Revised manual for the defining issues test: An objective test of moral judgment development.* Minneapolis, MN: Minnesota Moral Research Projects.

Rest, J.R., Davison, M.L., & Robbins, S. (1978). Age trends in judging moral issues: A review of cross-sectional, longitudinal, and sequential studies of the defining issues test. *Child Development, 49,* 263–279.

Sanders, C.E., Lubinsky, D., & Benbow, C.P. (1995). Does the defining issues test measure psychological phenomena distinct from verbal ability?: An examination of Lykken's query. *Journal of Personality and Social Psychology, 69*(3), 498–504.

Schonert-Reichl, K.A. (1999). Relations of peer-acceptance, friendship adjustment, and social behavior to moral reasoning during early adolescence. *Journal of Early Adolescence, 19*(2), 249–279.

Snarey, J.R. (1985). Cross-cultural universality of social-moral development: A critical review of Kohlbergian research. *Psychological Bulletin, 97*(2), 202–232.

Sobesky, W.E. (1983). The effect of situational factors on moral judgments. *Child Development, 54,* 575–584.

Speicher, B. (1994). Family patterns of moral judgment during adolescence and early adulthood. *Developmental Psychology, 30*(5), 624–632.

Teo, T., Becker, G., & Edelstein, W. (1995). Variability in structured wholeness: Context factors in L. Kohlberg's data on the development of moral judgment. *Merrill-Palmer Quarterly, 41*(3), 381–393.

Thoma, S.J., & Rest, J.R. (1999). The relationship between moral decision making and patterns of consolidation and transition in moral judgment development. *Developmental Psychology, 35*(2), 323–334.

Van Poppel, E., & Born, M. (1994). Identification and interpersonal maturity: Contribution to a developmental approach of juvenile delinquency. In E. G. M. Weitekamp, & H. J. Kerner (Eds.), *Cross-national longitudinal research on human development and criminal behavior* (pp. 353–370). Dordrecht, Amsterdam: Kluwer.

Wainryb, C., & Turiel, E. (1995). Diversity in social development: Between or within cultures? In M. Killen, & D. Hart (Eds.), *Morality in everyday life: Developmental perspectives* (pp. 283–313). Cambridge: Cambridge University Press.

Walker, L.J. (1982). The sequentiality of Kohlberg's stages of moral development. *Child Development, 53,* 1330–1336.

Walker, L.J., Pitts, R.C., Hennig, K.H., & Matsuba, M.K. (1995). Reasoning about morality and real-life moral problems. In M. Killen, & D. Hart (Eds.), *Morality in everyday life: Developmental perspectives* (pp. 371–407). Cambridge: Cambridge University Press.

Walker, L.J., & Taylor, J.H. (1991). Stage transitions in moral reasoning: A longitudinal study of developmental processes. *Developmental Psychology*, *27*(2), 330–337.

Walker, L.J., Vries, B. de, & Bichard, S.L. (1984). The hierarchical nature of stages of moral development.

Developmental Psychology, *20*(5), 960–966.

Wark, G.R., & Krebs, D.L. (1996). Gender and dilemma differences in real-life moral judgment. *Developmental Psychology*, *32*(2), 220–230.

The many faces of adolescent autonomy: Parent–adolescent conflict, behavioral decision-making, and emotional distancing

Luc Goossens

Autonomy in adolescence is not a unitary construct and may take on a different form in different relationships, such as the relationships with parents, peers, and romantic partners (Spear & Kulbok, 2004). Even within a single relationship, adolescents may display signs of responsible independence in different ways. This chapter focuses on adolescents' relationships with their parents and describes the different types of

autonomous functioning within that particular context, their ramifications for adolescent adjustment, and their intercorrelations.

1. Three types of autonomy

Most scholars of adolescence agree that adolescents can display up to three different types of autonomy in their relationships with their parents. Opinions diverge, however, on the exact nature of those types. Many authors adhere to the classical distinction between behavioral, emotional, and value autonomy (Douvan & Adelson, 1966; Noom, Dekovic, & Meeus, 2001). *Behavioral autonomy* refers to "active, overt manifestations of independent functioning, including the regulation of one's own behavior and decision-making" (Sessa & Steinberg, 1991, p. 42). Emotional autonomy, as described in the psychoanalytic or neo-analytic literature (Blos, 1979), takes on a specific meaning in adolescence. In their emotional world, children think of their parents as omnipotent figures, to whom they turn for help and advice in many situations. Developing *emotional autonomy* implies that adolescents, prompted by the biological changes of puberty, cast off these childish representations of their parents and relinquish their dependencies on them. This deidealization of the parental figures leads to a more mature conception of parents as individuals who also have a life of their own, beyond their role as parents. As a result of these representational advances, adolescents are no longer at the behest of unconscious feelings, often of an ambivalent nature, toward their parents, as children tend to be. This emotional advance, in turn, allows adolescents to acquire greater control of their emotional life. *Value autonomy*, finally, refers to the development of one's own system of values and morals.

Other authors suggest an alternative distinction between behavioral, emotional, and cognitive autonomy (Collins, Gleason, & Sesma, 1997a; Zimmer-Gembeck & Collins, 2003). The first two have similar meanings as in the earlier typology. Cognitive autonomy involves a subjective sense of control over one's life. One key criterion is that judgments and choices are derived from one's own individually held principles, rather than from the expectations of others (Collins et al., 1997a). Thus defined, cognitive autonomy appears to be strongly related to value autonomy, as defined in the earlier typology.

By combining the two typologies, researchers can examine how adolescents come to exercise increasing control over their behavior, their emotional life, and their emerging system of values, and gradually develop a concomitant sense of

self-control. Limited research, however, has been conducted on the last two aspects, that is, value autonomy and cognitive autonomy. The available body of evidence on adolescent autonomy, therefore, deals mostly with the first two aspects, that is, behavioral autonomy, and emotional autonomy.

Both types of autonomy are thought to have adaptive value for adolescents. This is almost self-evident for the overt form of self-determination that behavioral autonomy represents. But emotional autonomy, as a more covert form of autonomous functioning, is equally adaptive for adolescents. It is through the process of gaining emotional autonomy that adolescents come to rely on their own internal resources and take responsibility for their own actions. In sum, by gaining both behavorial and emotional autonomy vis-à-vis their parents, adolescents come to be mature, competent young people (Silverberg & Gondoli, 1996). This idea is often expressed in negative terms. Scholars of adolescence and laypeople alike state that if adolescents never distance themselves from their parents, both in their behavior and in their emotional world, they will never be able to function truly as adults.

2. Behavioral autonomy

Research on behavioral autonomy deals with two interrelated concepts, that is, parent–adolescent conflict and behavioral decision making. The link between the two concepts is intuitively clear, because conflicts frequently emerge when adolescents want to make independent decisions over certain issues and parents are not prepared or willing to let them do so. In addition, both concepts are examined using highly similar instruments, because adolescents are typically presented with a list of issues that may give rise to conflict or over which they may or may not exert full decisional autonomy.

2.1 *Parent–adolescent conflict*

In instruments like the issues checklist (Prinz, Foster, Kent, & O'Leary, 1979; Robin & Foster, 1984), adolescents are asked to indicate for each issue how frequently conflict has emerged with their parents over the last two weeks and to rate the intensity of those conflicts. The scores may be summed across items to yield composite scores for conflict frequency and intensity or the results may be analyzed issue by issue. In variations of these standard instruments, adolescents are asked to indicate what type of solution they and their parents have managed to find for the conflicts that have recently emerged.

Using these straightforward measures of the construct, many of the long-held views on parent–adolescent conflict, as derived from classical theories of adolescent development, have been put to an empirical test. The psychoanalytic approach to adolescence, for instance, saw parent–adolescent conflict as an essential force in driving young people out of their family of origin and into the outside world. This notion suggests that this type of conflict shows a typical age trend, with increasing conflict in early adolescence and a significant decrease thereafter, when adolescents have found their place outside the parental home. Despite its positive consequences for adolescents' orientation to the outside world, parent–adolescent conflict was thought to have dysfunctional effects on the family. Finally, because of its functional role in development, parent–adolescent conflict was thought to be ubiquitous and unavoidable (Hill & Holmbeck, 1986). Each of these facets of that traditional view was refuted in more recent theorizing and empirical research.

Conflicts with parents per se do not seem to drive adolescents out of their families of origin. Important changes within families, such as the marked decrease in the time that adolescents spend with their parents, proved unrelated to the amount of conflict. So, young people who experience more conflict with their parents do *not* spend less time with their families. Rather, opportunities and pulls to be away from home (such as having a driver's license or a job) were associated with the decreasing trend in time spent with the family from mid-adolescence onwards (Larson, Richards, Moneta, Holmbeck, & Duckett, 1996).

Meta-analysis revealed that the presumed inverted U-curve did not adequately describe age-related changes in parent–adolescent conflict. The combined evidence from multiple studies

actually reveals linear declines in the frequency of conflicts with parents from early to late adolescence. However, the intensity of these disagreements increases from early adolescence to mid-adolescence (with limited change from mid-adolescence to late adolescence; Laursen, Coy, & Collins, 1998).

Conflicts with parents do not have exclusively dysfunctional effects on family relationships either. Depending on the way it is expressed and its resolution, conflict may have positive effects on adolescents' relationships with their parents, because it provides an important learning experience for them (Cooper, 1988). Well-resolved conflicts in particular can greatly enhance one's understanding of the other party's feelings and motives. Research, however, reveals that most disagreements between parents and adolescents are resolved through submission or disengagement of one of the parties involved. Compromise, which would constitute a true learning experience, is relatively rare (Collins & Laursen, 2004a).

Parent–adolescent conflict is not as widespread and inevitable as was once believed. This type of conflict is endemic in a limited number of families, most of which have a long history of internal disputes from childhood onwards. The most accurate description of the situation, therefore, seems to be that conflict between parents and adolescents is found in "all families some of the time and in some families most of the time" (Montemayor, 1983).

Finally, researchers have found that parents and adolescents have conflicts about a limited number of issues. These issues, moreover, have hardly changed in recent history. Most disagreements involve mundane topics such as "not doing one's duties at home (such as cleaning one's room)", "physical appearance", "time to come in at night (or curfew)", "type of friends one hangs out with", and "drinking or smoking" (Montemayor, 1983). Different theoretical explanations have been advanced to clarify why conflicts between adolescents and their parents center around such seemingly unimportant issues. (See Holmbeck, 1996, for a review of those explanations.)

Socio-cognitive theories, which focus on

parents' beliefs and expectations regarding their children's development (Goodnow & Collins, 1990), figure prominently among such accounts. One of those theories, the expectancy-violation model (Collins, Laursen, Mortensen, Luebker, & Ferreira, 1997b), holds that parents know fairly well what to expect from their offspring during childhood, based on their long history of daily interaction with their children. During adolescence, however, divergences between parents' expectations regarding appropriate behavior and adolescents' actual behavior are much more likely to occur. Parents hope to transfer certain responsibilities to their children (e.g., choice of appropriate clothes) and jurisdiction over certain activitities (e.g., whether to spend time with friends or with family) will inevitably shift from parents to adolescents at some point during that period of development. Discrepancies among parents' and adolescents' views on those issues may be detected by asking adolescents of different ages how important it is that they are able to engage in those adolescent activities and by asking parents how important it is that their child wants to do so. Empirical research (Collins & Luebker, 1994; Collins et al., 1997b) has revealed little concordance between the views of both parties involved. This lack of concordance, in turn, is bound to lead to increased conflict between parents and adolescents.

Another theory, the social-domain theory of parental authority (Smetana, 2002), states that parents and adolescents hold different opinions on who has the final say regarding certain aspects of their lives. Rather than asking parents and adolescents about their respective expectations regarding adolescent behavior, adherents of this theory ask both parties involved whether parental authority can be rightfully exerted in various areas of life. Discrepancies are again found to emerge, because parents and adolescents hold different views about parental authority. These discrepancies, in turn, will lead to increased conflict between parents and adolescents. The fact that adolescents who are less likely to endorse parental authority across a range of issues report more conflict with their parents provides basic support for the theory (Fuligni, 1998).

Both theories are highly similar in many respects, because the types of issue in adolescents' life that lead to divergent expectations regarding appropriate behavior are also the ones over which disputes regarding parental authority are most likely to arise. Subtle differences, however, do exist between the two theories. The expectancy-violation model states that discrepancies between parents' and adolescents' expectations regarding appropriate behavior are most likely to emerge in early adolescence. Those expectations are continually revised and updated, which results in a gradual convergence of the views of both parties involved and a concomitant decrease in parent–adolescent conflict. The model is therefore described more accurately as the expectancy-violation-realignment model (Collins et al., 1997b). The social domain theory of parental authority, by contrast, allows for the possibility that divergences between parents' and adolescents' views, at least about some issues of central concern to parents, continue to exist or even increase over time. Both approaches, however, suggest that conflict is the primary vehicle through which adolescents try to renegotiate their place within the family (Collins & Laursen, 2004a). Research on adolescent decision making provides additional information on this gradual process of change in several ways.

2.2 Behavioral decision making

In instruments very similar to the issues checklist, adolescents are asked to indicate whether they can decide all for themselves about a number of issues. Across all Western countries, the number of issues on which adolescents do so increases as a function of age in both cross-sectional (Cicognani et al., 1996) and longitudinal research (Zani, Bosma, Zijsling, & Honess, 2001). For issues over which adolescents do not exert full control, researchers can ask to what degree they are involved in the decision-making process, when they expect to be granted autonomy over the issues at hand, and whether they think their parents' claim to authority over those issues is legitimate. These additional questions yield information regarding family decision making, timetables for expectations regarding autonomy, and conceptions about parental authority, respectively.

2.2.1 Family decision-making style

In the family decision-making scale (Lamborn, Dornbusch, & Steinberg, 1996), adolescents are again presented with a list of issues and asked who decides about these things at their homes. They can select one of three options: unilateral parental decision, joint decision, and unilateral adolescent decision making. A proportion score is then calculated separately for each of the three styles of decision making within the family.

Alternatively, adolescents can rate their degree of decisional autonomy for each issue on a five-point scale ranging from "My parents decide without discussing with me" (coded as 1) to "My parents leave it entirely up to me" (coded as 5; Smetana, Campione-Barr, & Daddis, 2004). Adolescents' scores on those measures show a clear association with age. Unilateral parental decision making decreases with age, whereas unilateral adolescent decision making increases over time (Lamborn et al., 1996).

Associations with adolescent adjustment were straightforward for two of the family decision-making styles. Both cross-sectional (Dornbusch et al., 1985; Dornbusch, Ritter, Leiderman, Roberts, & Fraleigh, 1987; Dornbusch, Ritter, Mont-Reynaud, & Chen, 1990) and longitudinal analyses showed that unilateral adolescent decision making is associated with poorer adjustment and with greater involvement in deviant activities in particular. Joint decision making, by contrast, is related to more positive adjustment and to lower rates of deviance in particular. The findings were less clear for unilateral parental decision making, which can be expected to have somewhat different yet equally deleterious effects on adolescent adjustment. The pattern of associations obtained differed as a function of ethnic group. Among European–American adolescents, unilateral parental decision making was associated with poorer psychosocial development, as expected. Among African–American adolescents, however, that same style of family decision making was correlated with less involvement in deviance and higher academic competence (Lamborn et al., 1996).

2.2.2 Timetables for decisional autonomy

In instruments such as the teen timetable questionnaire (Feldman & Quatman, 1988) both parents and adolescents are asked about the average age at which adolescents should be able to decide about a list of issues. Averaged across a number of respondents, these expected ages for the various issues yield a developmental timetable for the acquisition of behavioral or decisional autonomy. Parents and adolescents typically hold onto different timetables. The average order of the items in terms of the age at which autonomy is to be granted, as derived from parents' responses, closely mirrors the order derived from their children's responses. On average, however, adolescents feel they should be granted decisional autonomy earlier than their parents are willing to grant it to them. Averaged across all issues, this time difference was estimated to range between six months in a sample of 13 to 15 year olds in the Netherlands (Jackson, Bosma, & Zijsling, 1997) and a year in a sample of 10 year olds in the United States (Feldman & Quatman, 1988). This characteristic difference in timing may in and by itself lead to conflicts between the two parties involved.

Associations between parents' age expectations and adolescent adjustment have rarely been examined, but the available evidence suggests longitudinal associations between fathers' expectations for early autonomy and less optimal academic and social outcomes in their adolescent sons. Specifically, fathers' early autonomy expectations at preadolescence (age 10) were related to lower school grades, lower school effort, greater misconduct, and a greater number of sexual partners in mid-adolescence (age 14; Feldman & Wood, 1994). These findings seem to point out the importance of optimal pacing of autonomy expectations and the dangers of precocious autonomy in particular. Cross-cultural research, finally, has revealed clear differences that set the Chinese culture apart from other cultures. Adolescents in Hong Kong (Feldman & Rosenthal, 1991) and adolescents of Chinese descent in the United States (Feldman & Rosenthal, 1990; Fuligni, 1998) and Australia (Feldman & Rosenthal, 1990) believed that they would be allowed to decide for themselves at a later age than did adolescents of European descent in both the United States and Australia. A comparison of first- and second-generation Chinese adolescents in the United States and Australia revealed that their autonomy expectations gradually become more like those of their counterparts of European descent, but this acculturation process was relatively slow (Feldman & Rosenthal, 1990).

2.2.3 Adolescents' conception of parental authority

In interviews (Smetana, 1988) and, increasingly, in self-report questionnaires (Smetana & Daddis, 2002), adolescents and parents are again presented with a list of issues and asked about parents' right to make rules (i.e., parental legitimacy) or their duty to make rules (i.e., parental obligations). In addition, both parties involved are asked for the reasons that most closely fit their thinking about the issues at hand (i.e., the justifications for the respective stances adopted on those issues). The finding from studies using this methodology show that adolescents do not challenge their parents' authority in every domain of life. Rather, they continue to accept their parents' authority as legitimate in some domains and assert their rights to personal jurisdiction in other domains (Smetana, 1995a).

2.2.3.1 Social domain theory

The different domains are distinguished in accordance with a much broader theoretical framework that has come to be known as the domain-specific approach to moral and social development (see Smetana & Turiel, 2003, for a review). According to this view, three domains may be distinguished in the social world that are referred to as morality, social conventions, and personal issues, respectively. Morality deals with individuals' prescriptive understanding of how people ought to behave toward each other. These prescriptive moral judgements are based on concepts of welfare, justice, and rights. Moral rules cannot be changed because the moral transgressions that the rules try to prevent inevitably have negative consequences for others and are, therefore, intrinsically wrong. Social conventions are arbitrary, agreed-on, and shared regularities that

coordinate the interactions of individuals within social groups. Because they apply to a particular social context only, conventional rules can be changed by common consent and alternative rules can be devised that promote the smooth and efficient functioning of the group equally well. Personal issues pertain only to the individual and are therefore considered to be outside the realm of moral concern and conventional regulation. In every culture, individuals assert claims to an arena of personal discretion and personal freedom, although this area varies as a function of one's standing in the social hierarchy (Turiel, 2002).

In the social world of families with adolescents, those three domains are easily recognized. Moral rules pertain to family members' welfare and rights (e.g., not hitting siblings, not stealing money from parents). Conventional rules assure effective functioning of the family unit as a whole through rules that are consensually agreed on (e.g., doing assigned chores or cleaning up after a party). Personal issues, by contrast, pertain to the actor only and are viewed as beyond moral concern and conventional regulation. Sleeping late on a weekend or watching music videos are examples of such issues (Smetana, 1988).

2.2.3.2 Adolescents' views on parental authority

Adolescents accept parental authority as legitimate in both the moral and conventional domains and parent–adolescent conflicts rarely emerge over issues that pertain to those domains. These findings may reflect the hierarchical organization within the family. Personal issues are mostly described by both parties involved as "something that is up to the individual" (and the individual alone) and as having nothing to do with right or wrong, although parents tend to do so somewhat less frequently than do their adolescent children. As a consequence, conflict over those issues is also relatively rare. Important divergences in opinion, however, do emerge for issues that can be viewed as containing elements of more than one domain and parent–adolescent conflict emerges mostly around those issues (see Smetana, 2002, for a review).

The most striking examples of such contentious

topics are multifaceted issues, in which parents are inclined to emphasize the conventional elements, whereas adolescents see the same issue as falling under their personal jurisdiction. When adolescents do not clean up their room, for instance, parents will emphasize conventional rules of cleanliness or acceptable standards of maintenance, whereas adolescents tend to see their room as their personal territory over which they exercise full personal control. Wearing "street wear" (such as skateboarder clothes) may likewise be construed as a violation of the family's conventional dress code or as an aspect of behavior over which adolescents can exercise full personal freedom (Smetana, 1988). Friendship issues, such as hanging out with unconventional friends, are another case in point, although parents also state psychological or interpersonal reasons for trying to interfere with such friendships. In that case, they tend to worry about negative effects on their children's behavior and development. Finally, health or safety-related issues, such as using alcohol, can also lead to divergences in opinion. However, conflicts are less likely to occur for those issues, because adolescents tend to accept their parents' obligation to state rules for those behaviors (Smetana & Asquith, 1994).

Demands for personal autonomy increase gradually in childhood and adolescence. There are indications that a personal domain is already established, in a somewhat restricted form, in early childhood. Mothers typically allow young children to decide for themselves on minor issues, such as which types of fruit or vegetable to eat or which color clothes to wear. During adolescence, however, young people's appeal to personal autonomy increases clearly with advancing age, as they try to include more acts into the personal domain and to bring those acts under personal jurisdiction (Smetana, 2002).

2.2.3.3 Cultural differences
The three domains (moral, conventional, and personal) are all clearly distinguished from one another by adolescents from different cultures, although the precise content of the personal domain may vary from one culture to another. These differences may help explain the cultural differences in the links between unilateral parental decision making and adjustment and in autonomy timetables noted earlier in this chapter. Faced with pervasive racism and prejudice in the environment, parents of African–American adolescents may rightly view certain activities, such as wearing a particular style of clothes or going to the mall with a group of young people, as fraught with risks, whereas the same activities do not represent major risks to adolescents from other ethnic groups. Enforcing unilateral parental decision making regarding those activities may therefore have uniquely positive effects for this particular ethnic group (Smetana & Chuang, 2001; Smetana, Crean, & Campione-Barr, 2005). Similarly, Chinese adolescents in Hong Kong may be confronted with less lenient timetables for behavioral autonomy because their parents are concerned with their welfare and safety in the dense urban environment of Hong Kong (Yau & Smetana, 1996).

2.2.3.4 Recent extensions
The distinction between social domains or types of topic, which proved so useful in research on adolescents' conceptions of parental authority, may also apply to other aspects of adolescent decision making. In recent years, the domain distinction has also been introduced into research on (a) family decision-making style and (b) teen timetables. For both research topics, personal issues should yield somewhat different results than do other types of issues. A subset of personal issues was therefore identified through factor analysis on the lists of issues used and contrasted with other empirically identified clusters of issues, such as conventional, multifaceted, or prudential issues (e.g., issues that have negative health or safety consequences for the adolescent; Daddis & Smetana, 2005). Regarding family decision making, adolescents rated themselves as more autonomous over personal than all other issues (Smetana et al., 2004). Regarding teen timetables, age expectations for decisional autonomy were earlier for personal issues than for prudential issues (Daddis & Smetana, 2005).

Greater parental control over the personal domain also proved to have negative associations with adolescent adjustment across different cultures. Specifically, higher such control correlated with more depressive symptoms among Japanese adolescents (Hasabe, Nucci, & Nucci, 2004), lower self-esteem in African–American adolescents (Smetana et al., 2004) and lower school grades among adolescents in Brazil (Nucci, Hasabe, Lins-Dyer, 2005). Finally, mothers' earlier timetables for decisional autonomy in the personal domain in mid-adolescence predicted increased autonomous decision making in that same domain three years later (Daddis & Smetana, 2005). These findings suggest that mothers' ideas about the desired pacing of adolescent autonomy in mid-adolescence influence their autonomy granting. Such results indicate that it is not only through adolescents' consistent claims for greater personal jurisdiction that the boundaries of parental authority change during adolescence, but also through gradual changes in parenting behaviors as displayed by both mothers and fathers presumably. The transformation of the parent–child relationship that takes place during adolescence therefore seems to be a transactional process (Smetana, 2005). Correlations across various aspects of adolescents' decisional autonomy, such as age expectations for autonomy and the actual degree of decision making obtained, also suggests the usefulness of integrated approaches to measuring the construct.

2.2.4 Integrated approaches

More sophisticated approaches to measuring decisional autonomy in adolescence entail that several questions are asked about each issue and that patterns of responses across those questions are identified and analyzed. Such an approach has been adopted in several cross-cultural studies on adolescent autonomy, most of which have been conducted outside the United States.

The perspectives on adolescent decision-making (PADM) scale (Bosma et al., 1996), for instance, is a list of 21 behavioral issues in which four questions are asked about each of these. All questions can be answered by "yes" or "no". Specifically, these questions were (a) whether the adolescent decides for him or herself about the issue at hand (*adolescent choice*), (b) whether

the parents feel that the adolescent should not perform that behavior (and therefore are likely to impose restrictions on that behavior; *parental feelings*), (c) whether there are often arguments between the adolescent and his or her parents about that issue (*arguments*), and (d) whether the adolescent thinks it is normal for young people of his or her age to decide for themselves about the issue (*normality*). For smoking, for instance, the four statements were as follows:

> "I decide myself whether I smoke or not."
> "My parents feel I should not smoke."
> "I often have arguments with my parents about smoking."
> "I think it is normal for someone of my age to decide for himself or herself about smoking."

The pattern of responses across the four statements can be determined for each item separately and then summed across the items. Among the 16 potential patterns of responses to each item, four constellations (which make up more than 50% of all the patterns used) were examined in some detail. In the description of those patterns, Y stands for "yes" and N for "no" answers to the four questions in the order listed earlier. *Accepted parental authority* (or NYNN) means that adolescents do not decide for themselves, that parents take a restrictive position on the issue, that there are no arguments, and that adolescents do not think it is normal to decide for themselves. *Norm-supported conflict* (or YYYY) implies that adolescents decide for themselves, that parents take a restrictive position on the issue, that arguments occur, and that adolescents think it is normal to decide for themselves. *Norm-supported compromise* (YYNY) means that adolescents decide for themselves, that parents take a restrictive position on the issue, that there are no arguments, and that adolescents think it is normal to decide for themselves. *Norm-supported autonomy*, finally (or YNNY) implies that adolescents decide for themselves, that parents do not have strong feelings about the issue, that no arguments occur, and that adolescents think it is normal to decide for themselves.

Detailed analyses of adolescents' decisional autonomy using these constellations were performed in a European cross-cultural study in which adolescents from three countries took part. Teens from the cities of Groningen (the Netherlands), Bologna (Italy), and Cardiff (Great Britain) were thought to represent the Dutch, Italian, and British culture-bearing units, respectively, as found in Europe. (See Goossens, Chapter 1, this volume.) Large numbers of 13 and 15 year olds and their parents completed the PADM scale and a second wave of data was collected two years later, when the adolescents were 15 and 17 years of age, respectively (Jackson, Bosma, & Zijsling, 1998). Additional information on parent–adolescent relationships was obtained by means of a conflict management scale (Honess et al., 1997; Jackson, Cicognani, & Charman, 1996) and individual interviews on decisional autonomy with parents of young adolescents (Cicognani & Zani, 1998). Construct validity of the PADM was established through correlations in the expected direction with the parent–adolescent communication scale (PACS) and the family satisfaction scale (Olson, MacCubbin, Barnes, & Hill, 1983) on British (Honess et al., 1997), Dutch (Jackson, Bijstra, Oostra, & Bosma, 1998), and Italian (Bosma et al., 1996) adolescents. Specifically, a higher incidence of arguments was associated with less positive communication and with lower satisfaction.

The general picture of results indicated that most adolescents managed to achieve a fair degree of decisional autonomy in a non-conflictual manner. Summed across the items, the constellations of norm-supported autonomy and norm-supported compromise were used most often, followed by accepted parental authority and norm-supported conflict (which was rare). With advancing age, there was a decrease in unquestioning obedience to parents (i.e., decreasing use of the constellation labeled accepted parental authority), in favor of complete endorsement of adolescent autonomy (i.e., increasing use of norm-supported autonomy), a more conflictual style of interaction (i.e., increasing use of norm-supported conflict), or a newly found equilibrium (i.e., increasing use of norm-supported compromise; Cicognani et al., 1996). Gender differences in decisional autonomy were rare. Girls used the constellation

norm-supported compromise (YYNY) more often than did their male counterparts.

Statistically significant but subtle differences emerged between the adolescents from the three European cultures. Dutch adolescents used the constellation accepted parental authority more frequently, whereas British adolescents used both norm-supported conflict and norm-supported autonomy more often. However, because these differences were minimal (about three points on a 21-point scale), the researchers concluded that the development of autonomy followed similar scripts in the different countries, with differences mostly in terms of timing.

These differences in cultural scripts became more apparent when adolescents' responses concerning specific issues were analyzed. Some differences reflected broad cultural differences in the general emphasis of socialization. Dutch adolescents had few degrees of freedom about issues related to behaviors inside the parental home (such as chores, time to go to bed, manners, and language). For Dutch parents, it seemed to be of the utmost importance that their children kept things at home clean, tidy, and organized. Italian adolescents, by contrast, had less freedom to decide on behaviors outside the home (such as going out and which friends to hang out with). Their parents seeemed more concerned about what others might think of their children outside the parental home. Other differences seemed more limited in scope. The lower degree of autonomy reported by Italian adolescents regarding visits to relatives, for instance, can be explained by the importance of the extended family in the Italian culture where visits to grandparents and other relatives are made frequently (Cicognani et al., 1996).

Another integrated approach to measuring decisional autonomy was adopted in a comparative study of adolescents from Chile, the Philippines, and the United States (Darling, Cumsille, & Pena-Alampay, 2005). For each issue, three questions were asked (again answered with "yes" or "no"). These questions were "Do your parents have clear rules or expectations about this issue?" (*rules*), "Is it OK for your parents to set rules?" (*legitimacy of parental authority*), and "If you and your parents disagree, do you have to obey?" (*obligation to obey*). Conflicts between parents and adolescents were most likely to emerge when particular constellations of responses across the three questions were obtained. Specifically, conflict did emerge when (a) adolescents did not endorse their parents' right to set rules and the latter did set rules, (b) when adolescents questioned the legitimacy of their parents' authority but felt at the same time obliged to obey them, or (c) when adolescents did not endorse their parents' right to set rules, but believed they had to obey them, and parents did set out rules to regulate their children's behavior. Put differently, no conflict will occur when parents do not set rules to regulate their children's behavior or when the latter do not feel obliged to obey them if they do. This observation helps explain the differences in the frequency of conflict across the cultures examined. Chilean adolescents were less likely to acknowledge the legitimacy of their parents' authority than Filipinos did, but they reported fewer conflicts with their parents. The explanation for this apparent contradiction is that Filipino parents set more rules and that Filipino adolescents felt more obliged to obey them.

Finally, the pattern approach as exemplified in this cross-cultural study has also revealed differences in adolescents' reactions to different types of issue (again identified empirically using factor analysis). Across cultures, adolescents were least inclined to endorse their parents' right to set rules or their obligation to obey them for multifaceted issues (in which they tend to emphasize the personal elements). Parents, however, are very likely to set rules for these issues (in which they tend to emphasize the conventional elements; Darling et al., 2005). In short, integrated approaches to measuring decisional autonomy in adolescence yield findings that are broadly in line with expectations derived from the social domain theory of parental authority, but also suggest additional dimensions worthy of consideration.

3. Emotional autonomy: The "detachment debate"

Researchers with an active interest in emotional autonomy have all used the same operational measure of the construct. Careful examination of its correlations with various measures of adjustment and competence suggests that emotional autonomy, as measured by that scale, is a maladaptive form of autonomy. Several lines of research have been initiated to account for this unexpected finding. Theoretical frameworks have been developed and advanced statistical analyses have been conducted to explain under which circumstances emotional autonomy from one's parents can be more or less adaptive for adolescents.

3.1 Measuring the construct

For a long time, no measure of the psychoanalytic concept of emotional autonomy was available. Empirical research on the construct got underway in the mid-1980s, when the emotional autonomy scale (EAS; Steinberg & Silverberg, 1986) was constructed, based on the theoretical notions developed by Blos (1979). The 20-item scale comprises four subscales. *Deidealization* refers to the perception of one's parents as fallible human beings (e.g., "My parents never make mistakes"; reverse scored). *Non-dependency* taps the absence of childish dependencies on one's parents (e.g., "When I've done something wrong, I depend on my parents to straighten things out for me"; reverse scored). *Individuation* stands for perceived lack of parental knowledge and understanding (e.g., "My parents know everything there is to know about me"; reverse scored). *Parents as people*, finally, refers to the perception of one's parents as individuals who can move beyond their role as parents (e.g., "I might be surprised to see how my parents act at a party").

Over the years, different versions of the scale have been developed, ranging from a 14-item version (Lamborn & Steinberg, 1993), over a 12-item (Beyers & Goossens, 1999, 2001; Beyers, Goossens, Van Calster, & Duriez, 2005; Beyers, Goossens, Vansant, & Moors, 2003), to a nine-item version (Bray, Getz, & Baer, 2000; Schmitz & Baer, 2001). Using these shorter forms, which are typically said to tap adolescents' emotional separation from their parents (rather than the broader construct of emotional autonomy), a clear developmental trend has been uncovered.

Emotional separation shows a clear increase from late childhood to early adolescence, that is, until Grade 8 (Chang, McBride-Chang, Stewart, & Au, 2003; Steinberg & Silverberg, 1986), followed by a smaller increase until Grade 12 (Beyers & Goossens, 1999; Steinberg & Silverberg, 1986). This particular age trend suggests a link with the pubertal processes of early adolescence. Research did, in fact, reveal that emotional separation increases as a function of physical maturation (but is unrelated to pubertal timing; Steinberg, 1987). This pattern of results supports the notion that biological maturation accelerates the process through which adolescents become more autonomous from their parents (Steinberg, 1988, 1989) and attests to the validity of the EAS.

3.2 A maladaptive form of autonomy?

Contrary to expectations, high scores on the various forms of the EAS are associated with less positive outcomes for adolescents. This is particularly evident for the overall quality of the relationships with parents, as reported by adolescents. Adolescents who score high on the EAS are less attached to their parents and experience greater parental rejection (Ryan & Lynch, 1989), report lower degrees of authoritative parenting (McBride-Chang & Chang, 1998; Smetana, 1995b), are subjected to higher degrees of psychological control by their parents (Steinberg, 1987), and report higher degrees of conflict in the family (Goossens, 1997).

Adolescents with higher scores for emotional separation from parents are more involved in all sorts of problem behavior. This association is particularly clear for internalizing problems. Emotional separation from parents is associated with greater frequency of both depression (Beyers & Goossens, 1999; Chou, 2000; Lamborn & Steinberg, 1993) and anxiety (Papini & Roggman, 1992), using symptom-based measures designed for use with the general population. The association is well-established for externalizing problems as well. Adolescents with higher scores for emotional separation from parents show greater substance use (Turner, Irwin, & Millstein, 1991; Turner, Irwin, Tschann, & Millstein, 1993) and increased alcohol use (Bray et al., 2000), are more

frequently involved in physical fights (Turner et al., 1993), and score higher on summary indices of problem behaviors (Beyers & Goossens, 1999; Chen & Dornbusch, 1998; Chou, 2003; Lamborn & Steinberg, 1993).

The findings are less clear for adolescents' self-image. Some studies found positive associations between the EAS and measures of self-esteem and psychosocial maturity (Beyers & Goossens, 1999), whereas other studies found negative correlations with those measures (Chen, 1999; Lamborn & Steinberg, 1993; Steinberg & Silverberg, 1986). Results on adolescents' academic competence are equally confused. Depending on the study, adolescents' emotional separation from their parents is associated with lower school grades (Beyers & Goossens, 1999; Chen & Dornbusch, 1998; McBride-Chang & Chang, 1998) or shows inconsistent relations with academic results (e.g., a positive correlation for boys and a negative one for girls; Lamborn & Steinberg, 1993).

These well-documented findings on the negative correlates of the EAS have led some authors (Ryan & Lynch, 1989) to conclude that the scale is not measuring a healthy, age-appropriate form of separation from the parents but rather an unhealthy form of detachment. The latter term refers to a severing of developmentally appropriate ties with the parents, which deprives the adolescent of an important source of guidance, affection, and nurturance. Because of this theoretical opposition between supposedly adaptive separation and supposedly non-adaptive detachment, the debate on the adaptive or maladaptive nature of emotional separation in adolescence was labeled the "detachment debate" (Silverberg & Gondoli, 1996).

A number of existing theoretical perspectives readily provide explanations for the negative correlates of the EAS. Giving up long-held idealized representations of one's parents is distressing for the adolescent and may lead to increases in depressive mood in what psychoanalytic or neo-analytic authors describe as a mourning process (Blos, 1979). Increased distancing from parents may cause some adolescents to become strongly oriented toward peers and to become engaged in deviant peer groups and youth delinquency (Fuligni & Eccles, 1993). However, several authors felt compelled to develop new explanatory frameworks. In these explanations, they claim essentially that the negative consequences of emotional separation for adolescent adjustment occur mainly for particular subgroups of adolescents or when the timing of this separation is suboptimal.

3.3 Relational context

Research on the associations between emotional separation from parents and adolescent adjustment, as summarized in the previous section, is highly decontextualized. Such an approach overlooks the possibility that these associations take on a different form depending on the relational climate within the family (Lamborn & Steinberg, 1993). Alternative approaches that take this possibility seriously have shed new light on the separation–adjustment link.

Adherents of these approaches emphasize that emotional separation from parents is, in essence, a relational construct. The positive or negative consequences of emotional distancing for adolescent adjustment, therefore, are hard to determine without making reference to the object from whom the adolescent is becoming autonomous. The overall quality of the parent–adolescent relationship, operationally defined as relational support from or attachment to parents, becomes a key variable in this approach. The working hypothesis in all empirical studies is that young people who distance themselves emotionally from parents they feel attached to show much healthier profiles of adjustment than their agemates who have achieved emotional separation from parents whom they see as unsupportive (Lamborn & Steinberg, 1993).

The working hypothesis actually comes in two versions. The weaker version posits that the negative consequences of emotional separation for adjustment are less pronounced in adolescents who are strongly attached to their parents. The stronger version states that emotional separation, when it occurs in the context of a supportive parent–adolescent relationship, carries some advantages. The latter form of the hypothesis is consistent with classical models of adolescent individuation, which hold that young people should actively strive for a balance between individuality and connectedness (Grotevant & Cooper, 1986; Steinberg, 1990) and is supported by observational studies of actual family interactions (Allen, Hauser, Bell, & O'Connor, 1994; Grotevant & Cooper, 1985; Hauser, Powers, Noam, Jacobson, Weiss, & Follansbee, 1984). The hypothesis, in both forms, can be tested empirically in two different ways.

3.3.1 Attachment–separation configurations

Using this statistical method, researchers conceptually define four groups of adolescents (e.g., through a median split on each variable) that represent the different combinations of the two variables at hand. To test the weaker version of the hypothesis, they compare adolescents who score high on both variables (labeled *individuated youths*) to the adolescents who score high on emotional separation but low on attachment (so-called *detached adolescents*). More positive profiles of adjustment for the former group support the hypothesis. A test of the stronger version of the hypothesis involves a comparison of adolescents who score high on both variables (*individuated youths*) to those who score low on emotional separation but high on attachment (so-called *connected youths*). Again, more positive profiles of adjustment for the former group support the hypothesis. This method also yields a fourth group of adolescents who score low on both variables (so-called *ambivalent youths*) and for which no specific expectations can be advanced regarding their comparative profile of adjustment.

Results of empirical comparisons among those groups were mixed. Individuated adolescents had a more positive self-image and better results in school than did both detached adolescents (supporting the weaker version of the hypothesis) and connected adolescents (supporting the stronger version of the hypothesis). However, combining high levels of emotional separation from and attachment to parents also had its drawbacks. Individuated adolescents scored higher than did connected adolescents on both internalizing and externalizing problems (Lamborn & Steinberg, 1993).

Subsequent research, however, failed to replicate those findings. In some studies, no significant differences emerged among the four groups of adolescents (Beyers & Goossens, 1999). Other studies have tried to replicate the findings using attachment–separation groups that were derived empirically, by means of cluster analysis, for instance, rather than being defined conceptually. Such an approach, however, failed to corroborate the existence of the ambivalent group (Delaney, 1996) or even the crucial individuated group (Lee & Bell, 2003). The most reliable finding that emerges from the comparisons among empirically derived groups is that connected adolescents are more competent and show superior adjustment than do detached adolescents, a finding that has no bearing on the working hypothesis in either form.

3.3.2 Attachment × separation interactions

Using this statistical method, researchers extend classical regression analyses by adding an interaction term (defined as the product of the variables attachment and separation) to the regression equation when trying to predict adolescent adjustment (Holmbeck, 1997). If this interaction term turns out to be significant, follow-up tests are conducted to determine whether the interaction has a general shape consistent with the basic working hypothesis (Holmbeck, 2002).

Applications of this method yielded significant interaction effects, but the joint effect of attachment and separation on adjustment took an unexpected form. Higher scores of emotional separation predicted more positive adjustment among adolescents who lived in less favorable family environments (e.g., they experienced lower parental support or had depressed mothers who could not provide them that support; Fuhrman & Holmbeck, 1995; Garber & Little, 2001). These findings make sense intuitively, because adolescents will have a natural tendency to distance themselves emotionally from less supportive homes or less available parents and will feel more competent and well-adjusted when these distancing efforts are successful. But the working hypothesis would, of course, predict such positive associations between emotional separation and adjustment among adolescents living in more supportive family environments.

So, depending on the statistical method used, empirical results provide mixed support for the relational context approach (i.e., when focusing on attachment–separation configurations) or directly go against the expectations derived from this explanatory framework (i.e., when examining attachment × separation interactions). (See Silverberg & Gondoli, 1996, for additional comments on this controversy.)

3.4 Optimal timing

An emergent theoretical framework to explain the effects of emotional separation on adolescent adjustment has been derived from longitudinal analyses using latent growth curve (LGC) modeling based on structural equation modeling (SEM; Beyers, 2001; Bray, Adams, Getz, & McQueen, 2003). (See Bray, Adams, Getz, & Baer, 2001, for an alternative approach based on hierarchical linear modeling or HLM.)

Two types of finding from these longitudinal analyses are worth noting. First, adolescents who have high initial scores on emotional separation show a greater increase in alcohol use in subsequent years (Bray et al., 2003). Second, two different trajectories of development have been identified for emotional separation. Consistent with earlier speculations (Silverberg & Gondoli, 1996), adolescents who started at a high initial level of separation (and show limited increase later on) had a more problematic profile of adjustment than did their agemates who had a lower initial level of separation but increased slowly thereafter (Beyers, 2001). The longitudinal studies, then, converge on the conclusion that accelerated growth of emotional separation bodes more poorly for adolescent subsequent adjustment than does a more gradual increase in emotional distancing from parents, which may represent the developmental norm (as suggested by the cross-sectional age trends described earlier in this chapter).

Similar findings have been found in a longitudinal study on behavioral autonomy and even suggest correlated changes in autonomy and adjustment. Two groups of male adolescents were identified. One group, the antisocial group, had embarked on an antisocial career at an early age (i.e., was arrested by the police at least once by the age of 14) and persisted along this antisocial path later on (which resulted in further arrests). The other group, the well-adjusted boys, initially scored below the mean for the full sample on a measure of antisocial behavior and continued to do so throughout the study. A process of degradation of family management was observed, which basically entailed that adolescents acquired behavioral autonomy at too early an age, and this process was much more pronounced in the group of antisocial boys. This pattern of results suggests that as parents reduce their involvement in their sons' decision making and/or adolescents claim decisional autonomy at an early age they show increasing or continually high levels of antisocial behavior (possibly through their increasing involvement in deviant peer groups; Dishion, Nelson, & Bullock, 2004). This analysis of the longitudinal consequences of premature adolescent autonomy, combined with the longitudinal analyses on emotional separation, support the notion that the negative consequences of emotional separation from parents may apply, for the most part, to those youngsters who distance themselves too early or too rapidly from their parents.

4. Linking behavioral and emotional autonomy

Although conceptual distinctions can be made between behavioral and emotional autonomy, the two concepts are related to one another. Behavioral decision making (as measured by means of the PADM) and emotional separation from parents (as measured by means of the EAS) show a modest positive intercorrelation (Beyers & Goossens, 1999). This correlation suggests that developments in one domain of autonomy can foster healthy growth in another. Adolescents who accept their parents as fallible and give up their idealized representations of their parents are more likely to take a greater number of decisions by themselves. Put simply: *gains in emotional autonomy lead to gains in behavioral autonomy*. Conversely, gains in behavioral decision making (as an indicator of behavioral autonomy) may allow adolescents to take important steps toward greater emotional separation from their parents (as an indicator of emotional autonomy). Specifically, they may create a greater emotional distance from their parents and seek out their advice and assistance less often (Steinberg, 1985).

But because the correlation between the two constructs is far from being perfect, one can also assume that behavioral and emotional autonomy develop independently of one another, rather than in tandem (Sessa & Steinberg, 1991). Family structure can have an impact on the development of both types of autonomy and may lead to developmental incongruence among the two of them. A combination of high behavioral autonomy and low emotional autonomy, for instance, is more likely to be found among adolescent girls who are raised in mother-headed single-parent families. In that particular family structure, many young girls develop a close and dependent relationship with their mother following divorce, and have high levels of responsibility and power in decision making. This combination of behavioral autonomy in the context of a close and interdependent relationship with the mother may create problems for young girls in the development of emotional autonomy. They may not deidealize their mother to the same extent as their agemates in intact families do and they may continue to be dependent on her for guidance and assistance for a longer time.

This hypothesis suggests that parents should actively strive to avoid a situation in which there are conflicting demands across different domains of autonomous functioning. Adolescents, for their part, should avoid developmental incongruences between different types of autonomy or even actively strive for balanced development of all types of autonomy in the relationships with their parents. Such incongruities may take on a number of different forms. When emotional autonomy exceeds the level of behavioral autonomy granted to an adolescent, unhealthy rebellion from already deidealized parents may be provoked (Sessa & Steinberg, 1991). These hypotheses and speculations, however, have not been yet been examined in empirical research.

5. Conclusion

This chapter has provided an overview of the main findings in the two areas subsumed under the generic term "adolescent autonomy". Many commonalities exist across the two research traditions. For both types of autonomy, increasing attention is being paid to their associations with adolescent adjustment and the picture is far from being clear at the moment. Behavioral autonomy and emotional separation from parents may carry both positive and negative implications for adolescent behavior and development that have to be elucidated further in future research. There is also growing interest for issues of timing in both areas, as reflected in research on the effects of desired pacing of autonomy expectations on subsequent development of behavioral autonomy and on the optimal timing and preferred pace of development in emotional separation.

At the same time, however, important differences continue to exist between the two research traditions. Research on behavioral autonomy has come to focus much more explicitly on cultural differences in average level of autonomy and on differential patterns of associations with adjustment across different cultural groups. Emotional separation from parents is equally bound to have a different meaning and, potentially, differential associations with adolescent adjustment in different cultures (Silverberg & Gondoli, 1996). Future research will have to concentrate more systematically on those cross-cultural differences.

Finally, the reader should keep in mind that all the findings reviewed in this chapter refer to a particular interpersonal context, that is, the parent–adolescent relationship. The defining features of this relationship, in which parents initially exert a strong influence on their children's behavior and are idolized by them, undoubtedly has an impact on the type and degree of autonomy that adolescents can hope to establish within that context. Research has shown that adolescents readily distinguish among their relationships with parents, peers, and romantic partners and that each of these relational contexts offers different opportunities for personal and social development (Collins & Laursen, 2004b). Future studies on adolescents' behavioral and emotional autonomy, therefore, should encompass both parent–adolescent and peer relationships.

References

Allen, J.P., Hauser, S.T., Bell, K.T., & O'Connor, T.G. (1994). Longitudinal assessment of autonomy and relatedness in adolescent–family interactions as predictors of adolescent ego-development and self-esteem. *Child Development, 65*, 179–194.

Beyers, W. (2001). *The detachment debate: The autonomy-adjustment link in adolescence.* Unpublished PhD thesis, Catholic University of Leuven, Belgium.

Beyers, W., & Goossens, L. (1999). Emotional autonomy, psychosocial adjustment and parenting: Interactions, moderating and mediating effects. *Journal of Adolescence, 22*, 753–769.

Beyers, W., & Goossens, L. (2001). Psychological separation and adjustment to university: Moderating effects of gender, age, and perceived parenting style. *Journal of Adolescent Research, 18*, 363–382.

Beyers, W., Goossens, L., Van Calster, B., & Duriez, B. (2005). An alternative substantive factor structure for the emotional autonomy scale. *European Journal of Psychological Assessment, 21*, 147–155.

Beyers, W., Goossens, L., Van Sant, I., & Moors, E. (2003). A structural model of autonomy in middle and late adolescence: Connectedness, separation, detachment, and agency. *Journal of Youth and Adolescence, 32*, 351–365.

Blos, P. (1979). *The adolescent passage.* New York: International Universities Press.

Bosma, H.A., Jackson, A.E., Zijsling, D.H., Zani, B., Cicognani, E., Xerri, M.L. et al. (1996). Who has the final say? Decisions on adolescent behaviour within the family. *Journal of Adolescence, 19*, 277–291.

Bray, J.H., Adams, G.J., Getz, J.G., & Baer, P.E. (2001). Developmental, family, and ethnic influences on adolescent alcohol usage: A growth curve approach. *Journal of Family Psychology, 15*, 301–314.

Bray, J.H., Adams, G.J., Getz, J.G., & McQueen, A. (2003). Individuation, peers, and adolescent alcohol use: A latent growth analysis. *Journal of Consulting and Clinical Psychology, 71*, 553–564.

Bray, J.H., Getz, J.G., & Baer, P.E. (2000). Adolescent individuation and alcohol use in multi-ethnic youth. *Journal of Studies on Alcohol, 61*, 588–597.

Chang, L., McBride-Chang, C., Stewart, S.M., & Au, E. (2003). Life-satisfaction, self-concept, and family relations in Chinese adolescents and children. *International Journal of Behavioral Development*, *27*, 182–189.

Chen, Z.Y. (1999). Ethnic similarities and differences in the association of emotional autonomy and adolescent outcomes: Comparing European–American and Asian–American adolescents. *Psychological Reports*, *84*, 501–516.

Chen, Z.Y., & Dornbusch, S.M. (1998). Relating aspects of adolescent emotional autonomy to academic achievement and deviant behavior. *Journal of Adolescent Research*, *13*, 293–319.

Chou, K.L. (2000). Emotional autonomy and depression among Chinese adolescents. *Journal of Genetic Psychology*, *161*, 161–168.

Chou, K.L. (2003). Emotional autonomy and problem behavior among Chinese adolescents. *Journal of Genetic Psychology*, *164*, 473–480.

Cicognani, E., & Zani, B. (1998). Parents' educational styles and adolescents' autonomy. *European Journal of Psychology of Education*, *13*, 485–502.

Cicognani, E., Zani, B., Xerri, M.L., Jackson, S., Bosma, H., Zijsling, D. et al. (1996). *The development of decisional autonomy within the family: A cross-national study*. Unpublished manuscript, University of Bologna, Italy.

Collins, W.A., Gleason, T., & Sesma, A., Jr. (1997a). Internalization, autonomy, and relationships: Development during adolescence. In J. E. Grusec, & L. Kuczynski (Eds.), *Parenting and children's internalization of values: A handbook of contemporary theory* (pp. 78–99). New York: John Wiley & Sons.

Collins, W.A., & Laursen, B. (2004a). Parent–adolescent relationships and influences. In R. M. Lerner, & L. Steinberg (Eds.), *Handbook of adolescent psychology* (2nd ed., pp. 331–361). Hoboken, NJ: John Wiley & Sons.

Collins, W.A., & Laursen, B. (2004b). Changing relationships, changing youth: Interpersonal contexts of adolescent development. *Journal of Early Adolescence*, *24*, 55–62.

Collins, W.A., Laursen, B., Mortensen, N., Luebker, C. & Ferreira, M. (1997). Conflict processes and transitions in parent and peer relationships: Implications for autonomy and regulation. *Journal of Adolescent Research*, *12*, 178–198.

Collins, W.A., & Luebker, C. (1994). Parent and adolescent expectancies: Individual and relational significance. In J. G. Smetana (Ed.), *Social-cognitive models of parenting* (pp. 65–80). San Francisco: Jossey-Bass.

Cooper, C.R. (1988). Commentary: The role of conflict in adolescent–parent relationships. In M. R.

Gunnar, & W. A. Collins (Eds.), *21st Minnesota symposium on development: Development during the transition to adolescence* (pp. 181–187). Hillsdale, NJ: Lawrence Erlbaum Associates, Inc.

Daddis, C., & Smetana, J.G. (2005). Middle-class African American families' expectations for adolescents' behavioral autonomy. *International Journal of Behavioral Development*, *29*, 371–381.

Darling, N., Cumsille, P., & Pena-Alampay, L. (2005). Rules, legitimacy of parental authority, and obligation to obey in Chile, the Philippines, and the United States. In J. G. Smetana (Ed.), *Changing boundaries of parental authority during adolescence* (pp. 47–60). San Francisco: Jossey-Bass.

Delaney, M.E. (1996). Across the transition to adolescence: Qualities of parent/adolescent relationships and adjustment. *Journal of Adolescence*, *16*, 274–300.

Dishion, T.J., Nelson, S.E., & Bullock, B.M. (2004). Premature adolescent autonomy: Parent disengagement and deviant peer process in the amplification of problem behavior. *Journal of Adolescence*, *27*, 515–530.

Dornbusch, S.M., Carlsmith, J.M., Bushwall, P.L., Ritter, P.L., Leiderman, P.H., Hastorf, A.H. et al. (1985). Single parents, extended households, and the control of adolescents. *Child Development*, *56*, 326–341.

Dornbusch, S.M., Ritter, P.L., Leiderman, P., Roberts, D., & Fraleigh, M. (1987). The relation of parenting style to adolescent school performance. *Child Development*, *58*, 1244–1257.

Dornbusch, S.M., Ritter, P.L., Mont-Reynaud, R., & Chen, Z. (1990). Family decision making and academic performance in a diverse high school population. *Journal of Adolescent Research*, *5*, 143–160.

Douvan, E., & Adelson, J. (1966). *The adolescent experience*. New York: John Wiley & Sons.

Feldman, S.S., & Quatman, T. (1988). Factors influencing age expectations for adolescent autonomy: A study of early adolescents and parents. *Journal of Early Adolescence*, *8*, 325–343.

Feldman, S.S., & Rosenthal, D.A. (1990). The acculturation of autonomy expectations in Chinese high schoolers residing in two Western nations. *International Journal of Psychology*, *25*, 259–281.

Feldman, S.S., & Rosenthal, D.A. (1991). Age expectations of behavioral autonomy in Hong Kong, Australian, and American youth: The influence of family variables and adolescents' values. *International Journal of Psychology*, *26*, 1–23.

Feldman, S.S., & Wood, D.N. (1994). Parents' expectations for preadolescent sons' behavioral autonomy: A longitudinal study of correlates and outcomes. *Journal of Research on Adolescence, 4*, 45–70.

Fuhrman, T., & Holmbeck, G.N. (1995). A contextual-moderator analysis of emotional autonomy and adjustment in adolescence. *Child Development, 66*, 793–811.

Fuligni, A.J. (1998). Authority, autonomy, and parent–adolescent conflict and cohesion: A study of adolescents from Mexican, Chinese, Filipino, and European background. *Developmental Psychology, 34*, 782–792.

Fuligni, A., & Eccles, J. (1993). Perceived parent-adolescent relationships and early adolescents' orientation toward peers. *Developmental Psychology, 29*, 622–632.

Garber, J., & Little, S.A. (2001). Emotional autonomy and adolescent adjustment. *Journal of Adolescent Research, 16*, 355–371.

Goodnow, J.J., & Collins, W.A. (1990). *Development according to parents: The nature, sources, and consequences of parents' ideas.* Hillsdale, NJ: Lawrence Erlbaum Associates, Inc.

Goossens, L. (1997). Emotionele autonomie, relationele steun en de perceptie van de gezinssituatie door adolescenten [Emotional autonomy, relational support, and adolescents' perception of the family situation]. In J. R. M. Gerris (Ed.), *Jongerenproblematiek: Hulpverlening en gezinsonderzoek* (pp. 92–103). Assen, The Netherlands: van Gorcum.

Grotevant, H.D., & Cooper, C.R. (1985). Patterns of interaction in family relationships and the development of identity exploration in adolescence. *Child Development, 56*, 415–428.

Grotevant, H.D., & Cooper, C.R. (1986). Individuation in family relationships: A perspective on individual differences in the development of identity and role-taking skills in adolescence. *Human Development, 29*, 82–100.

Hasabe, Y., Nucci, L., & Nucci, M.S. (2004). Parental control of the personal domain and adolescent symptoms of psychopathology: A cross-national study in the United States and Japan. *Child Development, 75*, 815–828.

Hauser, S.T., Powers, S.I., Noam, G.G., Jacobson, A.M., Weiss, B., & Follansbee, D.J. (1984). Family contexts of adolescent ego development. *Child Development, 55*, 195–213.

Hill, J.P., & Holmbeck, G.N. (1986). Attachment and autonomy during adolescence. In G. Whitehurst (Ed.), *Annals of child development* (Vol. 3, pp. 145–189). Greenwich, CT: JAI Press.

Holmbeck, G.N. (1996). A model of family relational transformations during the transition to adolescence: Parent–adolescent conflict and adaptation. In J. A. Graber, J. Brooks-Gunn, & A. C. Petersen (Eds.), *Transitions through adolescence: Interpersonal domains and context* (pp. 167–199). Mahwah, NJ: Lawrence Erlbaum Associates, Inc.

Holmbeck, G.N. (1997). Toward terminological, conceptual, and statistical clarity in the study of mediators and moderators: Examples from the child-clinical and pediatric psychology literatures. *Journal of Consulting and Clinical Psychology, 65*, 599–610.

Holmbeck, G.N. (2002). Post-hoc probing of significant moderational and mediational effects in studies of pediatric populations. *Journal of Pediatric Psychology, 27*, 87–96.

Honess, T.M., Charman, E.A., Zani, B., Cicognani, E., Xerri, M.L., Jackson, A.E. et al. (1997). Conflict between parents and adolescents: Variation by family constitution. *British Journal of Developmental Psychology, 15*, 367–385.

Jackson, A.E., Cicognani, E., & Charman, L. (1996). The meaning of conflict in parent–adolescent relationships. In L. Verhofstadt-Denève, I. Kienhorst, & C. Braet (Eds.), *Conflict and development in adolescence* (pp. 75–91). Leiden, The Netherlands: DSWO Press.

Jackson, S., Bijstra, J., Oostra, L., & Bosma, H. (1998). Adolescents' perceptions of communication with parents relative to specific aspects of relationships with parents and personal development. *Journal of Adolescence, 21*, 305–322.

Jackson, S., Bosma, H., & Zijsling, D. (1997). Beslissen jongeren zelf over alles? Grenzen voor ouders en opvoeders [Do adolescents make their own decisions? Boundaries for parents]. In J. R. M. Gerris (Ed.), *Jongerenproblematiek: Hulpverlening en gezinsonderzoek* (pp. 77–91). Assen, The Netherlands: van Gorcum.

Jackson, S., Bosma, H., & Zijsling, D. (1998, February). *Progress to personal decision-making in adolescent development: Studies in three European countries.* In J.-E. Nurmi (Chair), *Strategies, decision-making, and relationships in adolescence: The role of the cultural context.* Symposium conducted at the 7th biennial meeting of the Society for Research on Adolescence (SRA), San Diego, CA.

Lamborn, S.D., Dornbusch, S.M., & Steinberg, L. (1996). Ethnicity and community context as moderators of the relations between family decision-making and adolescents' adjustment. *Child Development, 67*, 283–301.

Lamborn, S.D., & Steinberg, L. (1993). Emotional autonomy redux: Revisiting Ryan and Lynch. *Child Development, 64*, 483–499.

Larson, R.W., Richards, M.H., Moneta, G., Holmbeck, G.N., & Duckett, E. (1996). Changes in adolescents' daily interactions with their families from ages 10 to 18: Disengagement and transformation. *Developmental Psychology, 32*, 744–754.

Laursen, B., Coy, K.C., & Collins, W.A. (1998). Reconsidering changes in parent–adolescent conflict across adolescence: A meta-analysis. *Child Development, 69*, 817–832.

Lee, J.M., & Bell, N.J. (2003). Individual differences in attachment–autonomy configurations: Linkages with substance use and youth competencies. *Journal of Adolescence, 26*, 347–361.

McBride-Chang, C., & Chang, L. (1998). Adolescent-parent relations in Hong Kong: Parenting styles, emotional autonomy, and school achievement. *Journal of Genetic Psychology, 159*, 421–436.

Montemayor, R. (1983). Parents and adolescents in conflict: All families some of the time and some families most of the time. *Journal of Early Adolescence, 3*, 83–103.

Noom, M.J., Dekovic, M., & Meeus, W. (2001). Conceptual analysis and measurement of adolescent autonomy. *Journal of Youth and Adolescence, 30*, 577–595.

Nucci, L., Hasabe, Y., & Lins-Dyer, M.T. (2005). Adolescent psychological well-being and parental control of the personal. In J. G. Smetana (Ed.), *Changing boundaries of parental authority during adolescence* (pp. 17–30). San Francisco: Jossey-Bass.

Olson, D.H., MacCubbin, H.I., Barnes, H., & Hill, R. (1983). *Families: What makes them work?* Beverly Hills, CA: Sage.

Papini, D.R., & Roggman, L.A. (1992). Adolescent perceived attachment to parents in relation to competence, depression, and anxiety: A longitudinal study. *Journal of Early Adolescence, 12*, 420–440.

Prinz, R.J., Foster, S.L., Kent, R.N., & O'Leary, K.D. (1979). Multivariate assessment of conflict in distressed and non-distressed mother–adolescent dyads. *Journal of Applied Behavioral Analysis, 12*, 691–700.

Robin, A.L., & Foster, S.L. (1984). Problem-solving communication training: A behavioral family-systems approach to parent–adolescent conflict.

Advances in Child Behavior Analysis and Therapy, 3, 195–240.

Ryan, R.M., & Lynch, J.H. (1989). Emotional autonomy versus detachment: Revisiting the vicissitudes of adolescence and young adulthood. *Child Development, 60*, 340–356.

Schmitz, M.G., & Baer, J.C. (2001). The vicissitudes of measurement: A confirmatory factor analysis of the emotional autonomy scale. *Child Development, 72*, 207–219.

Sessa, F.M., & Steinberg, L. (1991). Family structure and the development of autonomy during adolescence. *Journal of Early Adolescence, 11*, 38–55.

Silverberg, S.B., & Gondoli, D.M. (1996). Autonomy in adolescence: A contextualized perspective. In G. R. Adams, R. Montemayor, & T. P. Gullotta (Eds.), *Psychosocial development during adolescence* (pp. 12–61). Thousand Oaks, CA: Sage.

Smetana, J.G. (1988). Adolescents' and parents' conceptions of parental authority. *Child Development, 59*, 321–335.

Smetana, J.G. (1995a). Context, conflict, and constraint in adolescent–parent authority relationships. In M. Killen & D. Hart (Eds.), *Morality in everyday life: Developmental perspectives* (pp. 225–255). New York: Cambridge University Press.

Smetana, J.G. (1995b). Parenting styles and conceptions of parental authority during adolescence. *Child Development, 66*, 299–316.

Smetana, J.G. (2002). Culture, autonomy, and personal jurisdiction in parent–adolescent relationships. *Advances in Child Development and Behavior, 29*, 51–87.

Smetana, J.G. (Ed.) (2005). *Changing boundaries of parental authority during adolescence* (New directions for child and adolescent development, Nr. 108). San Francisco: Jossey-Bass.

Smetana, J.G., & Asquith, P. (1994). Adolescents' and parents' conceptions of parental authority and personal autonomy. *Child Development, 65*, 1147–1162.

Smetana, J., Campione-Barr, N., & Daddis, C. (2004). Longitudinal development of family decision making: Defining healthy behavioral autonomy for middle-class African–American adolescents. *Child Development, 75*, 1418–1434.

Smetana, J.G., & Chuang, S. (2001). Middle-class African–American parents' conceptions of parenting in the transition to adolescence. *Journal of Research on Adolescence, 11*, 177–198.

Smetana, J.G., Crean, H.F., & Campione-Barr, N.

(2005). Adolescents' and parents' changing conceptions of parental authority. In J. G. Smetana (Ed.), *Changing boundaries of parental authority during adolescence* (pp. 31–46). San Francisco: Jossey-Bass.

Smetana, J.G., & Daddis, C. (2002). Domain-specific antecedents of parental psychological control and parenting: The role of parenting beliefs and practices. *Child Development, 73,* 563–580.

Smetana, J., & Turiel, J. (2003). Moral development during adolescence. In G. R. Adams, & M. D. Berzonsky (Eds.), *Blackwell handbook of adolescence* (pp. 247–268). Malden, MA: Blackwell.

Spear, H.J., & Kulbok, P. (2004). Autonomy and adolescence: A concept analysis. *Public Health Nursing, 21,* 144–152.

Steinberg, L. (1985). *Adolescence.* New York: Knopf.

Steinberg, L. (1987). Impact of puberty on family relations: Effects of pubertal status and pubertal timing. *Developmental Psychology, 23,* 451–460.

Steinberg, L. (1988). Reciprocal relation between parent–child distance and pubertal maturation. *Developmental Psychology, 24,* 122–128.

Steinberg, L. (1989). Pubertal maturation and parent–adolescent distance: An evolutionary perspective. In G. R. Adams, R. Montemayor, & T. P. Gullotta (Eds.), *Biology of adolescent behavior and development* (pp. 71–97). Newbury Park, CA: Sage.

Steinberg, L. (1990). Autonomy, conflict, and harmony in the family relationship. In S. S. Feldman & G. Elliot (Eds.), *At the threshold: The developing adolescent* (pp. 255–276). Cambridge, MA: Harvard University Press.

Steinberg, L., & Silverberg, S.B. (1986). The vicissitudes of autonomy in adolescence. *Child Development, 57,* 841–851.

Turiel, E. (2002). *The culture of morality: Social development, context, and conflict.* New York: Cambridge University Press.

Turner, R.A., Irwin, C.E., Jr., & Millstein, S.G. (1991). Family structure, family processes, and experimenting with substances during adolescence. *Journal of Research on Adolescence, 1,* 93–106.

Turner, R.A., Irwin, C.E., Jr., Tschann, J.M., & Millstein, S.G. (1993). Autonomy, relatedness and the initiation of health risk behaviors in early adolescence. *Health Psychology, 12,* 200–208.

Yau, J., & Smetana, J.G. (1996). Adolescent–parent conflict among Chinese adolescents in Hong Kong. *Child Development, 67,* 1262–1275.

Zani, B., Bosma, H.A., Zijsling, D.H., & Honess, T.M. (2001). Family context and the development of adolescent decision-making. In J. E. Nurmi (Ed.), *Navigating through adolescence: European perspectives* (pp. 199–225). New York: Routledge Falmer.

Zimmer-Gembeck, M.J., & Collins, W.A. (2003). Autonomy development during adolescence. In G. R. Adams, & M. D. Berzonsky (Eds.), *Blackwell handbook of adolescence* (pp. 175–204). Malden, MA: Blackwell.

9

Families and adolescents

Marisol Lila, Marcel van Aken, Gonzalo Musitu, and Sofia Buelga

LEARNING OBJECTIVES

The general aim of this chapter is to contribute to a better understanding of the role of families on adolescence. More specifically, we want to focus on the specifics of families in Europe, and the diversity of these. Second, we will focus on the family relationships as a context of adolescent functioning. After this, we will focus on a systemic view on adolescents' families, and the transitions that occur within these families during this period of the lifespan. Throughout the chapter, we will describe the level of the individual (i.e., adolescent development, but also parental beliefs, styles, and practices), the level of dyadic relationships (parent–child relationship and sibling relationships), and the level of the family as a system. At the end of this chapter, we will draw some conclusions and focus again on a European perspective.

1. Introduction

In the last 20 years research related to adolescence has undergone a change of paradigm by shifting from the analysis of individual (physical, cognitive and emotional) development in isolation, to the analysis of development within social contexts (Frydenberg, 1997; Gecas & Seff, 1990). In particular, special attention has been given to adolescent development within the family context. This should come as no surprise, if we consider the major importance of the family in human societies, despite differences among its many particular manifestations. Every individual, throughout his/her entire life, is embedded in a network of relationships and activities somehow connected by family ties (Musitu & Allatt, 1994). As such, families fulfill an important role in the economic, affective and sexual life of individuals.

Indeed, families are considered to be among the most important aspects in most people's lives, even more important than other elements, such as work, money or friends (Commission of the European Communities, 1993). When a human being reaches adolescence, the importance of the family does not diminish. On the contrary, during this stage family plays a major role in important aspects of adolescent development, such as identity formation (Harter, 1990), autonomy acquisition (Noack, Kerr, & Olah, 1999; Steinberg, 1998) and, in general terms, the psychosocial adjustment of the adolescent.

In this chapter, we will be dealing with several issues related to adolescents and their family contexts. First, we will analyze some changes and transformations undergone by European families. As will be observed, our conclusions stress the importance of increasing tolerance and acceptance among Europeans for family diversity, rather than of actual changes in family structure, its formation or dissolution (Peterson & Steinmetz, 1999). Nevertheless, one conclusion also is that the nuclear family is still the prevailing family type in most European countries. After this, a section is dedicated to the effects on adolescents of having divorced parents and of living in single-parent or reconstructed families.

This chapter also briefly deals with some of the adolescents' developmental tasks in which family plays an important role. We close the chapter with a general view of the socialization processes, beliefs and parenting styles, the effects of these on adolescents' adjustment and, with regards to the interdependence of the members of a family system, the bi-directional nature of family socialization (or parenting).

Finally, changes undergone by families as a result of development, or after dissolution or during the transition to a reconstructed family must be analyzed from a global or systemic perspective (Cox & Paley, 1997). Therefore, in the last section of this chapter, the family is defined and viewed as a system. Some of the key issues that are pointed out in this section are the stages in the family life course, family stress, family communication and functioning, and interdependence among the members of the system.

2. Families in Europe

Although agreement on the importance of the family is practically unanimous, it is difficult to reach a shared definition of family, partly because of the wide variety of family types. In this section, we will briefly deal with the definition of a family, the main changes that have taken place in this respect during the last decades and some of the consequences of these changes for adolescents.

2.1 Definition and transformations in European families

The notion of 'family' may seem obvious at first. In our society, company, sexual activity, mutual care and support, education and child rearing are considered to be an essential part of the nuclear family, being the most prevalent family type in the western world. The concept of a nuclear family refers to the family as a small unit formed in the event of a man and a woman legally bound through marriage. The nuclear family is then formed when a child is born. The members of this type of family share a common household and its structure is determined by affective ties, a common identity and mutual support. This approach to the family, which could be considered by some to arise from 'common sense', somehow reflects traditional beliefs about sex, emotions and parenting relationships.

However, this 'common sense' belief of a family may not be a correct and exhaustive representation of how people organize their lives (Bernardes, 1997; Jones, Tepperman, & Wilson, 1995). Indeed, the multiplicity of family structures over time and cultures is so vast that it becomes extraordinarily difficult – if not impossible – to give a definition of family that could include all of them. There does not seem to be a particular family standard or a prototypical contemporary family (Smith, 1995). Many authors claim that there are many possible definitions of a family, arising from different theoretical perspectives, rather than a single and comprehensive definition (e.g., Bernardes, 1997; Doherty, Boss, LaRossa, & Schumm, 1993). These definitions become determined by the theoretical framework and epistemological standpoints assumed by the

Box 9.1.   Some elements of the transformation of European families

Decrease of the birth rate indices
With regards to the birth rate per 1000 inhabitants a decrease in most EEC countries is observed (Eurostat, 1996). In addition, from 1970 until 1995 the average age of women giving birth for the first time increased with 2 or 3 years. In 1970 the maximum age was 28.3 in Italy and the minimal 26.7 in Denmark, whereas in 1995 the average age of first child birth ranged between a maximum of 30.2 years in Ireland and a minimum of 27.7 in Austria (Observatoire Européen des Politiques Familiales Nationales, 1998).

Population aging
Either due to the later age of women when giving birth for the first time, or due to additional causes, such as the longer life expectancy of the elderly, it is certain that Europe is facing an aging problem of its population. The later age of first child birth seems to hinder the reproduction of the population in all the European countries, since a required minimum of 2.1 children per woman is not achieved. Far from these minimum levels, in all the European countries the fecundity index ranges between 1.4 and 1.87 (Kiely, 1998; Observatoire Européen des Politiques Familiales Nationales, 1998).

Changes in family formation
Besides the trend to bear the first child at a later age than in previous decades, there is also a European trend to marry or live with a partner at a later age. Thus, the average age of the first marriage, in comparison to the 1970s, shows an average increase of 3–4 years in all the European countries. Denmark and Sweden are the countries where this trend seems to be the largest. Even though the decrease in the number of marriages observed in all the European countries could be explained, in part, by this delay in the age of marriage, it is also certain that in many countries cohabitation is more and more regarded as an alternative household style (Hammer, 1998; McGlone & Millar, 1998). Also, there is an increase in the number of births outside the marriage and in the context of cohabitation. Regardless of the differences between the European countries in number of births frequency in this context, it has doubled in all these countries since 1970 (Observatoire Européen des Politiques Familiales Nationales, 1998).

Changes in the process of dissolution of families
Since the 1970s many European countries show a significant increase of separations and divorces, which stabilized in some countries during the 1980s. The divorce rate is not uniform among the European countries. It varies from one country to another depending in many cases on inherent difficulties in the process of the dissolution of marriage. In 1995 Belgium and Sweden were the European countries with the highest divorce rate, while Greece, Portugal, Spain and Italy showed the lowest rates in Europe (Observatoire Européen des Politiques Familiales Nationales, 1998).

researcher, as well as the family socio-cultural context that the researcher chooses to analyze.

For example, a decrease has been observed of households in Europe representative of the model of a traditional nuclear family, with a father, a mother and at least one child. Rather, much more diverse modes of the family have become prevalent. Among some of the events which have contributed to the changing definitions of the family in most European countries, we find the decrease of birth rate indices and the consequent aging of the population, the rapid transformation in the formation and dissolution of families, and the subsequent diversification of the family types and households (Observatoire Européen des Politiques Familiales Nationales, 1998). (See Box 9.1.)

The phenomena described in Box 9.1 caused several changes at the end of the 20th century and beginning of the 21st century. In spite of the fact that the prevailing family type in all European countries is still, as in previous decades, the nuclear family formed by children and their bio-logical parents, in all European countries there is a general decrease in the number of households that represent this traditional model of nuclear family. Currently, the family of the European adolescent is not as permanent as in previous decades. On the contrary, in many cases adolescents are acquainted with or live in alternative family households, which can be just as enriching as the others (see Box 9.2).

Certain demographic factors such as the decrease of the birth rate index, the growth of life expectancy and a progressive aging process of the population explain the fact that adolescents now live in 'longer and narrower' families than before (Alberdi, 1999). This description refers, on the one hand, to the decrease of traditional marriage, and, on the other hand, to the increase of cohabitation experienced by current family systems. Adolescents co-exist with their grandparents and great-grandparents, but they live in separate households most of their life, if the elders are self-sufficient and autonomous.

Box 9.2.   Diversity of family types

Despite the fact that most children live with their married biological parents, a growing minority of other family types – single-parent families, families with cohabitating parents, reconstructed families – have emerged during these decades.

Cohabitation
The presence of this family unit differs substantially from one country to another. Kiernan and Estaugh (1993) identify three groups of countries: those where cohabitation is firmly established, like Sweden and Denmark. Second, those countries where cohabitation represents a previous transitional stage to marriage, like Austria, Finland, France, Germany, Benelux and United Kingdom. Finally, the third group of countries are those where cohabitation is not well established and not very frequent, like Ireland and southern Europe.

Single-person households
There are a growing number of single-person households in Europe. In fact, in Germany and in Denmark the number of this type of households is higher than other types of family unit. For example, 33.9% of German households and 44.8% of Danish households are single person. It is important to note that the occurrence of living alone varies according to age (young, adult, elder person) and sex (man or woman). To live alone at different ages is also related to different marital status; young persons living alone are mostly single, adults are mostly separated or divorced and elderly widowed (Zanatta, 1997).

Single-parent families
A single-parent family can be considered to consist of a father or a mother who is not living with a partner, either married or in cohabitation. Parents or responsible tutors may or may not cohabit with other people – friends or their own parents – and live at least with one child under 18. In 1995 the percentage of this type of families was 19.6% in the UK, 18.8% in Denmark and 13.8% in Belgium. Percentages are much lower (less than 10%) in southern European countries (Eurostat, 1996).

Stepfamilies
Even though reconstructed families are the third most frequent family type in almost all European countries, its frequency is significantly lower than that of complete families and single-parent families. Sweden and Denmark show the highest percentages of this type of families. This type refers to a family that, after separation or divorce, is later reconstituted by the father or the mother with custody of the children and a new partner. Under this label some authors also include those couples that reconstruct their lives without children (Zanatta, 1997).

Living in with parents
Another trend observed in the nuclear family in certain European countries, mainly in southern countries – Spain, Italy and Greece – is the increase of the cohabitation of the offspring in the paternal household. In Italy, for example, 90.1% of children aged under 24 still live with their parents and the percentage of subjects between 25 and 34 years of age continues to be high. According to Sgritta (1998) and Zanatta (1998), students and unemployed children are those who live with their parents until a later age. However, even 31.8% of employed children remain at the parents' home. These authors also point out that the late departure from the paternal house is not only due to economical and material reasons, but also to the values, traditions and cultural customs of this country. Italian families and families from the south of Europe present a more protective attitude towards their children than families from other central and northern countries (Sgritta, 1998; Zanatta, 1998).

Moreover, adolescents cohabit now with fewer brothers and sisters than before. Approximately 25% of European children who live with their biological parents do not have siblings (Bahle & Rothenbacher, 1998).

In addition to the basic demographic patterns of family households, there is also a wider range of structures that are reflected in the roles adopted by the different family members. For example, if we look at labor participation, we observe a growing trend in the last few years of the percentage of married women who work in Europe in a wider range of occupations and at a wider range of ages than in any other historical period since the Industrial Revolution. This has also affected the family structure, since it fosters a type of household with two economic providers – dual-career families – rather than the more traditional model of one provider (Hammer, 1998).

Some of the most interesting issues from a psychosocial perspective are the consequences of divorce on children and adolescents, and how living in a single-parent or reconstructed household affects them (see Box 9.2). In the following section we will focus on some studies related to these questions.

2.2 Adolescents and family diversity: Divorce, single-parent families and stepfamilies

Due to the increase of divorces and their growing impact on family life and structure, there has been during the last decades a significant increase of the number of studies that analyze the effects on the various family members of family dissolution and transformation – for instance, into a single-parent or stepfamily. Even though divorce was formerly regarded as a deviant state (Raschke, 1987), and considered to be the reason for the problems experienced by family members, nowadays most scholars consider that divorce is not, in itself, a triggering event for problematic situations. The situation of adolescents in a divorce can deteriorate or improve depending on some other factors or family functioning variables, such as parental conflict (Bigner, 1998; Nicholson, 1996), or economic problems and lack of resources, which in many cases are the main reasons for separation (Entwisle & Alexander, 1995). In this same research line, Ellwood and Stolberg (1993) found that family composition significantly fosters or hinders the stressing events, and it also affects family economics. However, it does not influence children's levels of *adjustment* (Steinmetz, 1999). Indeed, some studies show that children present a high social and emotional adjustment after their parents' divorce, in comparison to other children and adolescents who remain in family systems where conflict between parents is acute and frequent (Bigner, 1998).

Even though the short-term consequences of divorce for young children have been thoroughly studied, this is not the case for the consequences of divorce on adolescents. Some of the most frequent reactions found in adolescents in response to their parents' divorce include (Bigner, 1998): fear of being abandoned, rejected or unloved by the parent who does not hold the child's custody; interference with identity development and formation; fear of failure of his/her future marital relationship; criminal or problematic behavior; high levels of conflicts with parents and academic difficulties – academic performance – (Bisnaire, Firestone, & Rynard., 1990; Brody & Forehand,

1990; Hetherington et al., 1992; Smetana, Yau, Restrepo, & Braeges., 1991). By the same token, some of the most powerful predictors for children's positive adjustment are parental consistency, appropriate discipline, low levels of parental hostility and acceptance behaviors (Ellwood & Stolberg, 1993).

With regards to long-term consequences, a classic study by Hetherington, Cox and Cox (1976), showed that a large part of the sample had reached full normality or balance in the second year after divorce. In a later research carried out by Wallerstein and Kelly (1980), a significant minority of the survey sample presented some type of disorder five years after a divorce. Nevertheless, it must be said that this discrepancy in the results could be explained by the different criteria employed at the initiation of the study. The first study established legal divorce as the time of initiation, whereas the second one considered the initiating point the physical separation of parents. In a more recent longitudinal study carried out by Dunlop and Burns (1995) with a sample of youngsters who had experienced their parents' divorce during adolescence, no evidence was found for a long-term maladjustment. Ten years after their parents' divorces these youngsters were no different from other peers with non-divorced parents in terms of anxiety levels, depression and self-esteem.

Studies about parent–child relationships in single-parent families also show inconsistent results: in some studies, it is found that these relationships are normally tense, specially after divorce or remarriage (Wallerstein & Kelly, 1980), whereas in other studies it is found that many (especially adolescent) children develop very close relationships with the single parent, acting in many occasions as their confidant (Amato 2000; Lewin, 1993). In accordance with these outcomes related to children living in single-parent families, Buchanan, Maccoby and Dornbusch (1996) did not find any differences between levels of depression or academic achievement between adolescents who live with their mothers or those living with their fathers; however, the adolescent tends to show more behavioral problems (such as substance use) when they live with their fathers.

It has been thoroughly documented that, after divorce, children generally assume more roles and responsibilities within the household. If a remarriage takes place further changes may occur, with the stepfather or stepmother and stepsiblings likely to change or transform some of the roles previously held by a son or daughter. Consequently, these may experience a certain loss of family status (Hetherington, 1989). Furthermore, transitions frequently result in families moving from one house to another, and this may have subsequent effects on academic, social or recreational activities of children. Empirical evidence relates the negative changes caused by divorce and a break from the household routines, to the child's poor adjustment (Amato, 1993).

One of the issues that has consistently been underlined in this field of research is the fact that the impact on children of divorce and cohabitation in single-parent or stepfamilies varies according to their gender and age. Also, the way problems are shown changes with age. For instance, children are more prone to experience separation anxiety, whereas adolescents are more likely to get involved in risk behaviors (Doherty & Needle, 1991). Adjustment problems after parental divorce seem to be worse in the youngest children, probably due to the skill limitations still experienced by these in order to understand the changes which take place in the family environment. Older children have more skills to help them adjust to changes and stress, and they also have their own network of friends (Bigner, 1998; Steinmetz, 1999). In contrast, after remarriage or parent's cohabitation with a second or third partner, adjustment problems seem to increase for older children and adolescents. The addition of a new authority source, i.e., a stepfather or a stepmother, can be a difficult process for older children who are in a developmental stage characterized by their struggle to gain more autonomy and independence from the family (Hetherington, 1989).

As for the differences by gender, it has been found that boys and girls react similarly to high levels of inter-parental conflict, with an increasing risk of externalizing and internalizing problems. However, when sons/daughters are faced with marital disharmony but without a high level of inter-parental conflict, boys and girls may differ in their reactions. For the boys, a moderate level of parental disharmony is related to higher levels of externalizing problems; for girls, by way of contrast, this same family situation is associated to higher levels of internalizing problems (Grych & Fincham, 1990).

Another important question is the apparent interaction between children's gender and the gender of parents with custody. Some studies have reported more behavior problems for children living with a parent of opposite gender, fewer displays of pro-social behavior and poorer self-esteem, whereas children living with a parent of the same gender seems to experience problems in interactions with peers of opposite gender (Camara & Resnick, 1989). Moreover, Buchanan et al. (1996) found that, even though most adolescents feel close to the parent they live with, no matter the parent's gender, both sons and daughters feel closer to mothers than to fathers (Amato, 2000).

Research indicates that boys tend to benefit to a larger extent from a new marriage and a new type of family than girls, whereas girls, on the contrary, experience more suffering. Boys may show short-term behavior problems, but in the long run, boys living in stable stepfamilies show fewer behavior problems than boys in unstable single-parent or nuclear families. Girls living in stepfamilies have a higher levels of behavior problems than girls living in nuclear or single-parent families, no matter the duration of the new marriage or coupling (Bray, 1988). The reasons for these differences by gender of adjustment to family transitions experienced by sons and daughters may be explained by the changes that take place in parental and family relationships. The first years of adolescence seem to be a critical life time to adjust to parents' remarriage and new couplings. This is probably due to the fact that, along with the typical tensions experienced at these ages, such as the ones arising from the increment of autonomy demands, new ones arise from the family transitional situation and the acceptance of a new adult figure in their lives (Hetherington & Jodl, 1994).

3. Family relationships and adolescence

Family relationships undoubtedly play an important role for an adequate development in adolescence. These relationships affect the way the young negotiate the main tasks in adolescence, their implication in behavioral problems generally associated to this period of people's lives and their ability to establish long, close relationships. Some of these elements regarded as particularly important in families with adolescent children are the promotion of children's autonomy and independence, the degree of monitoring fostered by parents and the quantity and type of conflict between family members. Every process is dealt with thoroughly in other chapters in this handbook, and therefore we will just make a short recollection of them. After that, we will be focusing in more detail on the specific relationships within a family: the parent–child relationship, and we will shortly address the emerging literature on sibling relationships.

3.1 Effects of changes in the adolescent

In Alsaker and Flammer (this volume), we have seen that rapid and drastic somatic changes occur during puberty. The biological/hormonal changes during this period, but also the changes in physical appearance that follow, have important consequences for the relationships within families with adolescent children. The models proposed by Paikoff and Brooks-Gunn (1991) postulate effects of hormonal changes on parent–child interaction, either direct (hormonal) effects, or indirect effects, through emotional or behavioral changes in the adolescent or through the signal value of changes in secondary sex characteristics. The conclusion that these models reach is that pubertal maturation is related to greater emotional autonomy and to less closeness to parents. In addition, Alsaker and Flammer clearly show how not only pubertal maturation by itself, but also pubertal *timing*, has consequences for adolescent families: especially early maturing girls show more conflict and dissatisfaction in relationships with their parents (Buchanan et al., 1992).

Equally drastic changes take place during adolescence in the domain of social cognition. Selman (1980) described how these social–cognitive changes reflect themselves in changing conception of the parent–child relationships. In research on emotional autonomy (e.g., Lamborn & Steinberg, 1993, see also Goossens, this volume), parental de-idealization, the realization that parents are independent persons, with their own ideas, responsibilities, and, also, their own flaws, can be seen as a consequence of this social–cognitive development. This realization, in its turn, has consequences for the parent–adolescent relationship: Steinberg (1990) found that conflicts between parents and children might result from these changes in the adolescent. In addition, in a discussion between Ryan and Lynch (1989) and Lamborn and Steinberg (1993), it becomes clear that adolescents' perception of support in the relationships with their parents may be a powerful mediator in the relation between autonomy (as a result of social–cognitive change) and conflictive relationships: in the context of supportive adolescent–parent relationships, emotional autonomy may have developmental advantages, whereas in the context of relationships characterized by low support, it may have some deleterious effects.

One of the most relevant developmental tasks in adolescence of the process of achieving a positive, stable adult identity is the *autonomy acquisition* (Steinberg, 1998; see also Goossens, this volume). The main element of this task is the adolescents' gradual separation or detachment in the relations with their parents; this implies to give up parental dependence, which is unavoidable in childhood. And even though this detachment was originally viewed as a harmful process in family relationships, studies developed by Youniss and Smollar (1985) and Grotevant and Cooper (1986) reveal that, on the contrary, solid family relationships are indispensable for a successful development of autonomy (Noack et al., 1999).

A typical element of family relationships in adolescence related to adolescents' autonomy acquisition is the increase of *family conflict* (Arnett, 1999; Jackson, Cicognani, & Charman, 1996). Despite the fact that this occurs in most families, it is also true that there are individual and cultural differences, which increase or decrease the probability of family conflict. In relation to cultural variables, it has been found that conflict is more likely to occur in individualistic cultures (Dasen, 2000). Some of the individual variables associated to a higher probability of parent–child conflict are the depressive mood of an adolescent (Cole & McPherson, 1993), substance consumption (Petersen, 1988) and early maturity of girls (Buchanan et al., 1992).

One of the conflictive elements at these ages is related to the different views adopted by parents and children about the quantity and *degree of parental control* over different aspects of adolescents' lives. These claim for themselves a growing number of areas previously considered being under parental control. For instance, adolescents are less willing to accept parental influence on the election of friends or clothes. Research data collected by Zani, Bosma, Zijsling, and Honess (2001) and obtained from a sample of adolescents aged 13 and 15 and their respective parents clearly show that, as adolescents grow older, there is an increase of the areas of disagreement with their parents and they regard as normal for someone of their age to take their own decisions, thus demanding a higher level of autonomy in those areas (see also Bosma et al., 1996). Another element associated with the degree of monitoring or monitoring, which has recently been considered also to be a modulating variable in parent–child relationships, is *confidence*. This variable also depends on the level of knowledge that parents have about their children's lives. A study by Kerr, Stattin, and Trost (1999), which was carried out with over 1000 Swedish adolescents, revealed that the aspect most closely associated with parental confidence towards their children is the level of knowledge about the daily activities that are described by adolescents to their parents in a spontaneous way. Likewise, these studies revealed that the relation between children's delinquency and dysfunctional family relations were affected by parental confidence.

3.2 Parent–child relationship as a socialization context

The socialization process has certainly been one of the family roles most widely acknowledged. In particular, family socialization refers to the set of interactive processes that take place in the family environment aimed to instill a certain system of values, norms and beliefs into children (Maccoby, 1980). The socialization process does not end with childhood; it is a process that continues during adolescence, even though important transformations are required because the child and family system change during this transition. Both developmental changes – biological, psychological and emotional – as well as contextual changes experienced by adolescents call for a change of approach to socialization strategies and forms of relation between parents and children (Holmbeck, Paikoff, & Brooks-Gunn, 1995), that is, a major change in the family system.

One of these contextual changes during adolescence is the process by which other contexts different from the family become new important socialization environments: peer groups, school environment, the mass media etc., gradually become a referent and, on occasion, these come into conflict with the family. However, according to Kuczynski and Grusec (1997), parents are potentially placed in the best position to provide their children with an adequate and pro-social socialization. In first place, although there are many chances of varying and reducing parenting monitoring, there are biological reasons for the contextual influence that parents have over their children; the parent–child dyad presents a biological bias that facilitate parental influence. Second, there are also cultural reasons; in spite of serious opponents in their socializing role, our society grant parents the main authority over their children's care. Parents have a series of legal rights and responsibilities in the field of child care that allows them to control their children. Third, parents have more occasions than anybody else to establish meaningful relationships with their children. Since the very first moment after the child's birth, and throughout many years, parents feed, look after, protect, care and play with them, all these being activities that promote a strong link between parents and child. Finally, parents play a major role in socialization processes because they have more opportunities than anyone else to control and understand their children's behavior.

Every reason that is proposed by these authors concerning the importance of parenting continues to be present to a greater or lesser extent when children become adolescent.

The parenting process has obviously been studied from multiple theoretical perspectives, and various socialization elements have been underlined. In this section, we are going to deal briefly with some issues studied in depth by scholars. First, we will focus on parental beliefs. Second, some of the socialization mechanisms, that is to say, parenting styles and practices, will be analyzed. Third, we will focus on the relation between these mechanisms and the outcomes in adolescents. Finally, we will put forward an issue that has recently stirred much discussion in this field: the directionality of socialization.

The beliefs about parenting held by parents are considered to be important precursors of parenting styles and practices (McGillycuddy-De Lisi & Sigel, 1995). These beliefs (both implicit and explicit) are assumed to guide the parental behavior towards their adolescents. For instance, one of the relevant sets of parental beliefs is about when and at what age the different developmental tasks of the adolescent should take place (i.e., the age at which developmental tasks or tasklets are supposed to be normative). These parental beliefs can be seen as sources of influence on adolescents, on parents themselves, and on the parent–adolescent relationship. The study of parental beliefs is particularly important for the European perspective of this handbook, because cultural differences in parental beliefs have been found (Goodnow, 1997). These differences may have implications regarding the diversity of parenting in various European countries.

In order to fully understand parenting processes, Darling and Steinberg (1993) suggest that it is essential to establish a clear difference between socialization goals, parenting practices – used by parents to assist their children in achieving these goals – and the parenting style or emotional environment in which socialization occurs, that is, between content aspects – parenting practices and goals – and contextual aspects – parenting styles. According to these authors, a parenting style is a set of parents' attitudes towards their children that create an 'emotional climate' in which parents' behaviors are expressed. These behaviors consist of those aimed to achieve a socialization goal – that is, parenting practices – as well as those not aimed to achieve this goal, such as gestures, changes of voice tone, body language or the spontaneous expression of emotions. Moreover, the set of values or socialization goals deals with the child's achievement of skills and specific behaviors (social skills, academic skills, etc.), and his/her development of more general characteristics (curiosity, independence, critical thinking).

Indeed, all these aspects of family socialization are closely related to the cultural context of individuals. According to Bronfenbrenner and Crouter (1983), the processes that link parents' and children's behaviors are not universal; they differ in accordance with the characteristics of the participants or the contexts in which these processes occur. Values and cultural patterns determine the real behavior of parents and the manner in which children interpret their parents' goals and behaviors, as well as the way in which adolescents organize their own behavior.

Most classic research on parenting styles underlines two basic dimensions or factors that explain most variance in parenting behaviors and, even though different terms were used, there is a great similarity between the dimensions previously proposed. Thus, all these could be grouped under the dimensions of parental support and parental monitoring. Based on these two factors, many authors have attempted to describe a parenting-style typology in order to analyze the precedents and consequences of the various forms of socialization.

One classic piece of research and undoubtedly one of the most quoted in relation to parental monitoring and child autonomy is that of Diana Baumrind (1978). According to this author, the key element of the parental role for the development of their children's socialization is their ability to get them to accept other people's demands, while, at the same time, retaining their sense of personal integrity. She also distinguishes three types of parenting style with regards to the monitoring dimension: (a) the authoritarian style, in which parents value obedience and impose a restriction on their child's autonomy; (b) the permissive style, in which parents provide all the possible autonomy, as long as the child's physical safety is not jeopardized; and, (c) the authoritative style, in which parents attempt to channel their children's activities in a rational and problem-directed manner.

In later years, Maccoby and Martin (1983) have established a categorization of the parenting styles in accordance with the two orthogonal dimensions of responsiveness – parental reinforcement contingency – and demandingness – number and type of parents' demands. This categorization includes four parenting styles: *authoritative* (responsive and controlling parents) – parents present a responsive style to their children's demands but, similarly, they expect their children to respond to their demands; *authoritarian* (controlling but not responsive parents) – children experience a parenting style characterized by power assertion, and they are expected to obey rules without placing demands on their parents, physical punishment being more likely to occur in these households; *permissive* (responsive but not controlling parents) – parents are reasonably responsive but avoid regulating their children's behavior, impose few rules and place few demands for a mature behavior on their children, avoid the use of punishment and tend to be tolerant to a wider range of behaviors; *rejecting–neglecting* (not responsive and not controlling parents) – parents tend to limit the time employed in parenting tasks, also reducing their time to deal with the drawbacks associated to these tasks.

3.3 Parenting styles and adolescent adjustment

Not only has there been a general agreement among scholars in relation to the main dimensions underlying parenting styles, but there has also been a rapid and common agreement about the association between children outcomes and parenting styles. 'Model children' or, according to Baumrind (1978), 'instrumentally competent' children, were an outcome of households where parents presented a certain type of behavior. These parents were affectionate, they established

rational, straightforward norms, allowed their children certain level of autonomy and were able to clearly communicate their expectations and reasons for them (Darling & Steinberg, 1993).

Generally speaking, research on outcomes of different parenting styles on adolescents indicates that the authoritative style – at least in western cultures – is more related than the other parenting styles to high adjustment levels (Steinberg, Mounts, Lamborn, & Dornbusch, 1991), psycho-social maturity (Steinberg, Elmen, & Mounts, 1989), psychosocial competence (Lamborn, Mounts, Steinberg, & Dornbusch, 1991), self-esteem (Noller & Callan, 1991) and academic achievement (Dornbusch, Ritter, Leiderman, Roberts, & Fraleigh, 1987). By the same token, adolescents with authoritarian and coercive parents: (a) are less prone to get involved in exploring identity alternatives; (b) are more likely to adopt external moral standards instead of internalizing norms; (c) have lower levels of self-confidence and self-esteem; and (d) are more prone to experience problems when using their own judgment as behavioral guidance. Moreover, these adolescents are more likely to have problems in relation to many aspects of their autonomy, since their own identity sense is underdeveloped, they are less reliant on their competence and more sensitive to parental pressure because they have learned to depend on external sources of approval and guidance (Noller & Callan, 1991). Adolescents whose parents adopt inductive and democratic styles, on the contrary, are able to make their own decisions and formulate adequate plans. Surprisingly, these adolescents make decisions and plans that are more satisfactory to their parents. The paradox lies in the fact that authoritative homes tend to produce adolescents strongly identified with their parents and who have internalized their parents' rules and values.

In particular, Steinberg (1990) found that when one or more components of the authoritative style are absent, some adverse outcomes become evident. Adolescents from authoritarian households present high levels of obedience but low levels of competence. Adolescents from permissive households rely more on themselves, but show high levels of substance consumption and academic difficulties. Finally, adolescents from negligent households show an important decrease of competence levels and the highest levels of behavioral problems, in comparison to other parenting styles. After analyzing these outcomes, it seems obvious that responsiveness as well as demandingness is related to different sets of outcomes in the development of adolescents. While responsiveness seems to be related to self-esteem and social abilities, demandingness seems to increase self-control and social responsibility (Holmbeck et al., 1995).

In general terms, current research on parenting styles and their relation with the various indicators of adolescent adjustment confirm the need to make more detailed distinctions between the dimensions of parenting styles. Indeed, even though the distinction between psychological control and behavioral control was made over 30 years ago (Barber, Olsen, & Shagle, 1994), there is too little research on differential effects of these two types of control. Barber et al. found that psychological control was a better predictor for adolescents' internalized problems, such as feelings of loneliness and depression, whereas behavioral control was a better predictor for externalized problems, such as alcohol consumption or truancy. Research by Gray and Steinberg (1999) obtained similar results. These authors distinguished three core dimensions of authoritative parenting (acceptance–involvement, strictness–supervision and psychological autonomy granting), and presented differential associations of these dimensions with various aspects of adolescent functioning.

For instance, these authors found that adolescents who perceived in their parents high levels of involvement, autonomy concession and structuring, evaluated more positively their own behavior, psychosocial development and mental health. However, adolescents achieve better academic results when they perceive high levels of involvement and autonomy concession, but also low levels of supervision and monitoring.

Other elements normally not associated with an authoritative style, such as sensibility, predictability and parental involvement also play an important role in the future adjustment of adolescents. Indeed, there is evidence that parental sensibility is negatively related to behavioral problems in children (Rothbaum & Weisz, 1994), unpredictable and contradictory parenting styles are positively related to behavioral problems (Patterson & Dishion, 1985) and parental involvement is positively related to the adolescents' academic performance and psychological well-being (Schwarz & Silbereisen, 1996). A study by Juang and Silbereisen (1999) which grouped these three dimensions under the label of 'supportive parenting', revealed that adolescents with parents who regularly apply this type of parenting present lower levels of depression and delinquent behavior, higher levels of self-efficiency and a better academic performance.

3.4 Directionality

A key issue in the parenting field is the directionality associated to this process. Even though 30 years have passed since Bell (1968) introduced the idea of the children's influence on parents' behavior, most of the subsequent definitions of parenting have continued to be, implicitly, unidirectional (Kerr et al., 1999; Kuczynski & Lollis, in press). These assume children are placed in a world with pre-existing meanings, rules and expectations that are maintained by their parents and the significant others in their cultural context and, through interaction with their social environment, they gradually internalize these ideas (Kuczynski, Marshall, & Schell, 1997). However, mainly during the stage of adolescence, the important socializing role of children cannot be ignored. Nevertheless, Baumrind had already suggested that children contributed to their own development through the influence on their parents. This author viewed the socialization process as a dynamic one: the parenting style used alters the children's openness to their parents' actions to socialize them. In particular, the authoritative style increases the paternal effectiveness by producing changes in children's characteristics that, at the same time, reinforce parents' skills to act as socialization agents. According to Grotevant and Cooper (1998), the directionality of socialization in Baumrind's model could be explained in terms of the different directions that take place in the various parenting styles. Thus, in the authoritarian and permissive style, control in the relationships mainly occurs in a one-way direction. In the case of the authoritarian style, this moves from parents to child; in the case of the permissive style, this moves from child to parents. Both styles differ from the authoritative one, since this implies a bi-directional socialization between parents and children.

Some of the most recent models in connection with parenting have been focused on the need of establishing a change in some basic premises, such as *process directionality* – from uni-directional to bi-directional, that is to say, children also play an active role in the process of socialization by influencing their parents. This new approach implies a change in the interpretation of *agency* or *causality*, power and parenting outcomes. Indeed, in relation to causality or agency, parents are no longer considered as the only socialization agents. Children are not mere passive subjects and become active agents in the process by assessing and interpreting their parents' ideas and selecting those regarded as appropriate by them. The *relational power* is no longer exclusively associated to parents; on the contrary, parents and children interact in close and interdependent relationships where each one is vulnerable and, at the same time, has power over the other. Furthermore, children enjoy more power in their relationships with their parents than with any other adult people. Finally, the *socialization outcomes* do not necessarily need to be assessed according to the similarity between parents and children; the discrepancies between them do not necessarily mean failure in socialization, rather they can become desirable outcomes in development (Lollis & Kuczynski, 1997).

3.5 Sibling relationships

Most of the research on adolescents and their families has focused on the relationship between adolescents and their parents. The relationships between adolescents and their siblings have been studied less frequently. Furman and Buhrmester (1985) were among the first to notice that siblings can be important members of an adolescent's social network. Since then, some research on

conflict in sibling relationships, or sibling rivalry, has been developed. Basically, studies find that the level of conflict in sibling relationships is higher than in any other relationship adolescents are involved with (including the parents).

The scant literature on sibling relationships has so far focused almost exclusively on conflict, but recently some studies have looked at positive contributions of siblings to adolescent development. Positive effects of sibling support on adolescents' self-esteem and lack of loneliness were found, and some studies even found compensatory effects of sibling support for adolescents with a lack of peer support (East & Rook, 1992; Stocker, 1994), although these latter effects were not always replicated (Seginer, 1998; van Aken & Asendorpf, 1997). In addition, older siblings were recently found to be important sources for advice about life plans and personal problems (Tucker, Barber, & Eccles, 1997), but also for the timing of the first sexual encounter (Widmer, 1997). In a study on the influence of sibling support and sibling problem behavior on psychosocial adjustment in adolescence, Branje, van Lieshout, van Aken, and Haselager (2004) found that support from an older sibling increased strongly from age 11 to age 13, with a smaller increase later on. Also, sibling support was found to have additional effects on adolescents' adjustment, even after controlling for parental and friend support. However, sometimes sibling support was related to more problem behavior, indicating that a good relationship with a sibling may encourage the modeling of 'bad' sibling behavior.

In sum, the results of studies on sibling relationships thus far suggest that these relationships can perform important roles in the families of adolescents, although certainly more work needs to be done before we can understand the specific positive or negative aspects of these relationships.

4. Family systems and adolescence

One of the theories most widely accepted in the study of family is the system theory. In this approach, the family is defined as an organized, interdependent group of units linked by behavior rules and dynamic functions in permanent interaction and exchange with the exterior. In particular, a family as a system is characterized by the following features (Lewis & Feiring, 1998):

- There may be more than two elements or family members. The term 'element' refers not only to each individual member, but also to dyads (e.g., mother–child) and, even to triads if there is more than one child in the family.

- Elements are interdependent – a change in one of the elements affects the whole system. The effects of some elements over the rest can be direct (e.g., father on the child) or indirect (e.g., the effects of parents' relation on the child). Moreover, systems can consist of subsystems (e.g., mother–father dyad) and, at the same time, they can be embedded in wider systems (e.g., the community). That is, systems are found organized hierarchically.

- Elements are non-additive, and thus the sum of individual elements does not equal the total family system. Individual behaviors cannot explain the global functioning of the family.

- The elements in the system change and yet maintain the system. This double process of continuity and growth takes place through a dynamic balance between two apparently contradictory functions: the homeostatic tendency and the transformation capacity. Flexibility is necessary in order to secure change and development, whereas stability is essential in order to achieve an internal family space well-defined.

- Both systems and families are goal oriented. Some of these goals or functions assumed by the family system are protection, care giving, nurturance, play, learning and social control.

4.1 Stages in a family lifespan

From a systemic perspective, it is considered that families move through a series of stages or nodal points of development (Carter & McGoldrick, 1989). In each stage of its lifespan, a family reorganizes itself in order to enter successfully the next stage. The crisis generated at each transitional point may foster a new movement that favors family development or, on the contrary, it may cause a stagnation of family development. In

this sense, Olson and collaborators (1983) have proposed seven different stages: (1) young couple without children; (2) family with children at pre-school ages (older child aged 0–5); (3) family with schoolchildren (older child aged 6–12); (4) families with adolescent children (older child aged 13–18); (5) disintegrated families (older child aged over 19); (6) 'empty-nest' family (all children have left the parental household) and (7) family with retired members (husband aged over 65). The stage with adolescent older children is defined as a stage of preparation, in which adolescents prepare to leave the parental household, and in which important restatements in relation to family style take place, which show the differences in expectations and world conceptions between adolescents and their parents.

In another description of the family life span, Minuchin and Fishman (1981) propose four stages: (1) couple formation, (2) family with babies, (3) family with schoolchildren or adolescent children and (4) family with adult children. These authors underline the fact that during adolescence the group of peers becomes a referential element for children. The importance of this group for the adolescents frequently disarranges the rules or patterns established by the family. At this moment families start to interact with a powerful system that often becomes a competitor. Moreover, adolescents' growing capacity enables them to demand changes from their parents. Issues such as autonomy and monitoring are renegotiated at all levels. Developmental changes and necessities experienced by adolescents are perceived by families as disruptors of their functioning, thus requiring a rearrangement of their norms of interaction. It is at this stage that the separation process of children from their families takes place and this change affects the family as a whole. Having said that, children are not the only family members who grow and change. Another source of pressure and demands may influence families at this stage: the parents' parents. At the same time that middle-aged parents experience autonomy and support problems with their children, a renegotiation of the entrance of grandparents inside the family household may also take place, due to health problems or after the death of one of the grandparents. Furthermore, at this stage of children's development two emotional problems difficult to resolve may appear: the need of parents to focus their attention again on the relationship with their partners due to the decrease of parental functions, and the need to develop a professional activity that is often intense at this time.

4.2 Family stress, functioning and communication

There is a long tradition in developing models of family stress and its measurement. Among these models, one should definitely describe the pioneering work of Reuben Hill in the late 1940s and the reformulations of this model developed by the McCubbin group (McCubbin, Patterson, & Lavee, 1983) and Boss (1987).

Along with normative resources of family stress associated to each stage of their life span, families may additionally undergo unexpected or non-normative stressing events, such as economic crisis, a sudden death or a chronic illness of one of their members. These non-normative sources of family stress, in opposition to the normative stressing events associated with the lifespan, are not foreseeable in the sense that they are not considered to be part of a family development. On the contrary, these are unexpected events with repercussions that result in important changes of the family system. A key issue is how families perceive and handle the stressing events. If the resources are already saturated or wasted due to the co-occurrence of other vital changes, members of a family may not be able to carry out further adjustments when faced with new stressing social events (McCubbin, Thompson, & McCubbin, 1996). Therefore, due to its active and open nature, a family system, and its functioning become affected by any type of tensions or changes. These changes call for an adjusting process, that is, a permanent transformation of family interactions and norms, which will allow, on the one hand, family continuity and, on the other hand, the development of the individual family members (Pardeck, 1989).

Some authors such as Olson or McCubbin have pointed out that *family functioning*, that is,

the set of attributes of a family system which show the regularities shared by families in their modes of actions, evaluations or behaviors (McCubbin & Thompson, 1987), allows to distinguish some families from others and also to predict the future developmental course of events and the strategies employed to face the co-occurrence of various stressing events. In the forerunner study carried out by Olson, McCubbin, Barnes, Larsen, Muxen, and Wilson (1983), the authors identify two family functioning dimensions in the circumplex model: family connectedness and family adaptability. *Family connectedness* is the emotional link between family members, and *family adaptability* is related to the system's ability to change its power structure and the relationships between roles and norms in stressing situations and developmental stages. From these dimensions, different family typologies can be obtained in order to distinguish families with a potentially vulnerable development from those stronger families with more resources available in difficult situations.

In Olson's model, communication is a facilitating variable of family functioning. Positive, effective communication between family members facilitates the resolution of family transitional periods in an adaptive way, whereas negative communication hinders family development. In many occasions, family communication becomes both the origin and the result of the family system incapability to evolve in a harmonious mode. Thus, the presence of problems of family communication becomes a very reliable indicator of the inadequacy of the family functioning for their members' well-being.

Grotevant and Cooper (1986) have identified the different aspects involved in family communication that reinforce psychosocial competence in adolescence. These authors have developed a model of an individuating process; this process is characteristic of intra-family relationships and accounts for the interdependence between individuals and connectedness among family members. The concept of individuation is regarded consistent with the notion of family connectedness. Both concepts represent the two extremes of a dimension: on the one hand, clustering – which is related to a high level of connectedness and where family members behave and think in a similar fashion – and, on the other, detachment – which implies low levels of connectedness and family members appear quite independent and do not exert much influence on the other members. Individuated relationships present a balance between individuality and connectedness. This model consists of four factors. The first two reflect individuality features: self-assertion, which is defined as the capability to hold a particular point of view and to communicate this in a clear way, and separation, that is, the capacity to express the difference between oneself and the others. The remaining two factors deal with differentiated aspects of support and involvement in the family: these are permeability – to show responsiveness and openness to other people's ideas – and mutuality – to show sensibility and respect in one's relations with the others. From Grotevant and Cooper's research (1986), it can be concluded that the co-occurrence of these factors in intra-family relationships determines the developmental context in adolescence, thus contributing to the adolescents' development of their identity and self-esteem. It also promotes the acquisition of interpersonal capabilities, such as role taking and skills for negotiation (Zani, 1993).

It should be noted that in the literature the differences by gender of adolescents or parents become clearly apparent. Adolescents make a clear distinction between their mothers and their fathers in relation to the issues they talk about, the period of time they spend together and the tone adopted in discussions or quarrels (Noller & Callan, 1991). Generally speaking, adolescents perceive their mothers as more receptive to listen to their problems and to help them in sentimental issues than their fathers. This perception is even more acute in girls: mother–daughter communication is generally more likely and open to discussing than father–daughter communication. Boys, on the contrary, talk about themselves less openly than girls and do not draw such a clear distinction between what issues they comment on with their mothers or with their fathers (Youniss & Ketterlinus, 1987).

4.3　Interdependence between members of a system

As we have mentioned already, one of the basic assumptions in the conceptualization of family as a system is the notion of interrelation or interdependence. Thus, changes in one of the elements affect the whole system. Indeed, as described earlier (in 3.1), adolescence is a time of rapid transitions in the biological, cognitive and emotional domains, and even though the adolescents mainly experience these changes, these also affect the adolescents' contexts in which they are integrated, such as the family context.

A source often ignored of the changes in the parent–adolescent relationship is the development of parents. Silverberg (1996, see also Silverberg & Steinberg, 1990) describes how adolescents' parents are also undergoing changes in their lives and ways of thinking, often triggered by the changes experienced by their adolescent children. She states that personal change and new developmental tasks occur not only for the adolescents, but also for their parents. Although she also shows how this is somehow troublesome for all parents, but appears to be biased by factors such as parental gender, investment in paid work, and socio-economic status; from a transactional view it should surely be expected that these changes for parents affect the quality of family relationships.

In addition to analyzing how the changes of one element affect the whole system, some recent studies have also provided evidence for the usefulness of a general systemic framework for the analysis of families with adolescent children. Some aspects of such a systemic framework is described in section 3.5, where sibling relationships and parental differential treatment were discussed. One other fascinating outcome is reported in Reiss et al. (1995). These authors found that parental hostility towards a sibling is associated with lower levels of problematic behavior in adolescents, even after controlling for parental hostility towards both the adolescents. In a similar fashion, O'Connor, Hetherington, and Reiss (1998) reported that the regression coefficients obtained from the quality of family relationships, which predict adolescents' antisocial behavior and depression, varied from one family type to another. For example, in families with high levels of marital conflict, the quality of sibling relationships was closely related to the adolescents' psychopathology and competence, thus suggesting the protecting effect of sibling relationships within these families. Schauerte, Branje, and van Aken (2003) found that in families in which some members reported a low level of support but others did not, no clear relations with problem behavior and well-being were found. In families where all members reported a low level of support these relations were clearly present.

Another recent development in the study of the system of family relationships concerns the work on parental differential treatment. There is growing evidence that parent–child relationships differ not only between families, but also *within* families. Differential parental treatment, i.e., the part of the parent–child relationship that is unique for a child, and not shared with other siblings, is associated with a variety of child outcomes. That is, adolescents who are treated less favorably by their parent, as compared to a sibling, are reported to have higher levels of problematic behavior (see, e.g., Tamrouti, Dubas, Gerris, & van Aken, 2004).

In sum, although studies based on this system paradigm model are still relatively rare, these first results seem to provide evidence for systemic processes within these families. As O'Connor et al. (1998) formulated: 'Different constellations of family relationships give rise to qualitatively different family processes that, in turn, modify the relative salience of relationships on individual adjustment' (p. 371). Although results have not as yet depicted a clear idea of these family processes, at least they confirm the fact that one needs to understand not only the elements of adolescent families (e.g., all the persons, all the dyadic subsystems), but also their interrelations.

5. Conclusion

In this chapter, we have presented some of the features of the family context of European adolescents, as well as the relations and processes that take place within this context. Three important conclusions can be drawn from this chapter.

First, even though the nuclear family is still the prevailing type in all European countries, diversity and change are a common element in this social unit. Indeed, according to the authors of the last *Handbook of marriage and the family*, family diversity is no longer an exception and it is gradually becoming the standard (Peterson & Steinmetz, 1999).

Second, we have found that in parent–child relationships during adolescence, an authoritative style of parenting, characterized by parents' efforts to channel their children's activities in a flexible and responsive manner, is associated with high levels of psychosocial functioning of adolescents. However, we have also observed that a bi-directional notion of the parent–adolescent relationship (in which not only do parents influence their children, but also that children play an active role in socialization by influencing their parents) seems to be important for a better understanding of adolescents and their families.

Third, we have seen that the study of families with adolescents is becoming increasingly complex. Traditionally, research focused on parent–child relationships, but more recent studies have focused on other relationships within the family context (e.g., relationships between siblings), and there is an increasing number of studies with a systemic approach, in which not only the relationships are studied, but also the interrelations between those relationships.

References

Alberdi, I. (1999). *La nueva familia española* [The new Spanish family]. Madrid: Taurus.

Amato, P.R. (1993). Children's adjustment to divorce: Theories, hypotheses, and empirical support. *Journal of Marriage and the Family, 55*, 23–38.

Amato, P.R. (2000). Diversity within single-parent families. In D. H. Demo, K. R. Allen, & M. A. Fine (Eds.), *Handbook of family diversity*. Oxford: Oxford University Press.

Arnett, J.J. (1999). Adolescent storm and stress, reconsidered. *American Psychologist, 54*, 317–326.

Bahle, T., & Rothenbacher, F. (1998). La politique familiale en Allemagne: Après la réunification, le choc de la mondialisation [Family policy in Germany: After reunification, the shock of globalization]. In B. Ditch, H. Barnes, & J. Bradshaw

(Eds.), *Evolution des politiques familiales nationales en 1996*. York: Commission Européenne.

Barber, B.K., Olsen, J.E., & Shagle, S.C. (1994). Associations between parental psychological and behavioural control and youth internal and externalised behaviours. *Child Development, 65*, 1120–1136.

Baumrind, D. (1978). Parental disciplinary patterns and social competence in children. *Youth and Society, 9*, 239–276.

Baumrind, D. (1980). New directions in socialisation research. *American Psychologist, 35*, 639–652.

Baumrind, D. (1991). Effective parenting during the early adolescent transition. In P. A. Cowan, & E. M. Hetherington (Eds.), *Advances in family research: Vol. 2* (pp. 111–163). Hillsdale, NJ: Lawrence Erlbaum Associates, Inc.

Bell, R.Q. (1968). A reinterpretation of the direction of effects in studies of socialisation. *Psychological Review, 75*, 81–95.

Bernardes, J. (1997). *Family studies: An introduction*. London: Routledge.

Bigner, J.J. (1998). *Parent–child relations: An introduction to parenting*. Englewood Cliffs, NJ: Prentice Hall.

Bisnaire, L.M., Firestone, P., & Rynard, D. (1990). Factors associated with academic achievement in children following parental separation. *American Journal of Orthopsychiatry, 60*, 67–76.

Bosma, H.A., Jackson, A.E., Zijsling, D.H., Zani, B., Cicognani, E., Xerri, M.L. et al. (1996). Who has the final say? Decisions on adolescent behavior within the family. *Journal of Adolescence, 19*, 277–291.

Boss, E.G. (1987). Family stress. In M. B. Sussman, & S. K. Steinmetz (Eds.), *Handbook of marriage and the family*. New York: Plenum.

Branje, S.J.T., van Lieshout, C.F.M., van Aken, M.A.G., & Haselager, G.J.T. (2004). Perceived support in sibling relationships and adolescent adjustment. *Journal of Child Psychology and Psychiatry, 45*, 1385–1396.

Bray, J.H. (1988). Children's development during early remarriage. In E. M. Hetherington, & J. D. Arasteh (Eds.), *Impact of divorce, single parenting and step parenting on children* (pp. 279–298). Hillsdale, NJ: Lawrence Erlbaum Associates, Inc.

Brody, G., & Forehand, R. (1990). Interparental conflict, relationship with the noncustodial father, and adolescent post-divorce adjustment. *Journal of Applied Developmental Psychology, 11*, 139–147.

Bronfenbrenner, U., & Crouter, A.C. (1983). The evolution of environmental models in developmental research. In P. Mussen (Ed.), *Handbook of child development: Vol. 1* (4th ed., pp. 357–414). New York: John Wiley & Sons.

Buchanan, C.M., Eccles, J., & Becker, J. (1992). Are adolescents the victims of raging hormones? Evidence for activational effects of hormones on moods and behavior at adolescence. *Psychological Bulletin, 111*, 62–107.

Buchanan, C.M., Maccoby, E.E., & Dornbusch, S.M. (1996). *Adolescents after divorce*. Cambridge, MA: Harvard University Press.

Camara, K.A., & Resnick, G. (1989). Styles of conflict resolution and cooperation between divorced parents: Effects on child behaviour and adjustment. *Journal of Orthopsychiatry, 59*, 560–575.

Carter, E.A., & McGoldrick, M. (1989). *The changing family life cycle*. Boston, MA: Allyn & Bacon.

Cole, D.A., & McPherson, A.E. (1993). Relation of family subsystems to adolescent depression: Implementing a new assessment strategy. *Journal of Family Psychology, 7*, 119–133.

Commission of the European Communities (1993). *Europeans and the family. Results of an opinion survey. Eurobarometer 39.0*. Brussels: Commission of the European Communities.

Cox, M.J., & Paley, B. (1997). Families as systems. *Annual Review of Psychology, 48*, 243–267.

Darling, N., & Steinberg, L. (1993). Parenting style as context: An integrative model. *Psychological Bulletin, 113*, 487–496.

Dasen, P.R. (2000). Rapid social change and the turmoil of adolescence: A cross-cultural perspective. *International Journal of Group Tensions, 29*, 17–49.

Doherty, W.J, Boss, P.G., LaRossa, R., & Schumm, W.R. (1993). Family theories and methods: A contextual approach. In P. G. Boss, W. J. Doherty, R. LaRossa, W. R. Schumm, & S. K. Steinmetz (Eds.), *Sourcebook of family theories and methods: A contextual approach* (pp. 3–30). New York: Plenum.

Doherty, W.J., & Needle, R.H. (1991). Psychological adjustment and substance use among adolescents before and after a parental divorce. *Child Development, 62*, 328–337.

Dornbusch, S.M., Ritter, P.L., Leiderman, P.H., Roberts, D.F., & Fraleigh, M.J. (1987). The relation of parenting style to adolescent school performance. *Child Development, 58*, 1244–1257.

Dunlop, R., & Burns, A. (1995). The sleeper effect: Myth or reality? *Journal of Marriage and the Family, 57*, 375–386.

East, P., & Rook, K. (1992). Compensatory patterns of support among children's peer relationships: A test using school friends, non-school friends, and siblings. *Developmental Psychology*, *28*, 163–172.

Ellwood, M.S., & Stolberg, A.L. (1993). The effects of family composition, family health, parenting behavior and environmental stress on children's divorce adjustment. *Journal of Child and Family Studies*, *2*, 23–36.

Entwisle, D.R., & Alexander, K.L. (1995). A parent's economic shadow: Family structure versus family resources as influences on early school achievement. *Journal of Marriage and the Family*, *57*, 399–409.

Eurostat (1996). *The European Community Household Panel: Volume 1 – Survey methodology and implementation*. Luxemburg: Eurostat.

Frydenberg, E. (1997). *Adolescent coping*. London: Routledge.

Furman, W., & Buhrmester, D. (1985). Children's perceptions of the personal relationships in their social networks. *Developmental Psychology*, *21*, 1016–1024.

Gecas, V., & Seff, M.A. (1990). Families and adolescents: A review of the 1980s. *Journal of Marriage and the Family*, *52*, 941–958.

Gelles, R.J. (1995). *Contemporary families: A sociological view*. Newbury Park, CA: Sage.

Goodnow, J.J. (1997). Parenting and the transmission and internalization of values: From social-cultural perspectives to within-family analyses. In J. E. Grusec, & L. Kuczynski (Eds.), *Parenting and children's internalisation of values: A handbook of contemporary theory* (pp. 333–361). New York: John Wiley & Sons.

Gray, M.R., & Steinberg, L. (1999). Unpacking authoritative parenting: Reassessing a multidimensional construct. *Journal of Marriage and the Family*, *61*, 574–587.

Grotevant, H.D., & Cooper, C.R. (1986). Individuation in family relationships: A perspective on individual differences in the development of identity and role-taking skill in adolescence. *Human Development*, *29*, 82–100.

Grotevant, H.D., & Cooper, C.R. (1998). Individuality and connectedness in adolescent development. Review and prospects for research on identity, relationships, and context. In E. Skoe, & A. von der Lippe (Eds.), *Personality development in adolescence*. London: Routledge.

Grych, J.H., & Fincham, F.D. (1990). Marital conflict and children's adjustment: A cognitive-contextual framework. *Psychological Bulletin*, *108*, 267–290.

Hammer, T. (1998). Social parameters in adolescent development. In E. Skoe, & A. von der Lippe (Eds.), *Personality development in adolescence*. London: Routledge.

Harter, S. (1990). Self and identity development. In S. S. Feldman, & G. R. Elliot (Eds.), *At the threshold: The developing adolescent* (pp. 352–387). Cambridge, MA: Harvard University Press.

Hauser, S.T., Powers, S.L, & Noam, G.G. (1991). *Adolescents and their families: Paths of ego development*. New York: Free Press.

Hetherington, E.M. (1989). Coping with family transitions: Winners, losers, and survivors. *Child Development*, *60*, 1–14.

Hetherington, E.M., Clingempeel, W.G., Anderson, E.R., Deal, J.E., Hagan, M.S., Hollier, E.A. et al. (1992). Coping with marital transitions. *Monographs of the Society for Research in Child Development*, *57*, 2–3.

Hetherington, E.M., Cox, M., & Cox, R. (1976). Divorced fathers. *Family Coordinator*, *25*, 417–428.

Hetherington, E.M., & Jodl, K.M. (1994). Stepfamilies as settings for child development. In A. Booth, & J. Dunn (Eds.), *Stepfamilies: Who benefits? Who does not?* (pp. 55–79). Hillsdale, NJ: Lawrence Erlbaum Associates, Inc.

Holmbeck, G.N., Paikoff, R.L., & Brooks-Gunn, J. (1995). Parenting adolescents. In M. H. Bornstein (Ed.), *Handbook of parenting. Vol. 1. Children and parenting* (pp. 91–118). Hillsdale, NJ: Lawrence Erlbaum Associates, Inc.

Jackson, A.E., Cicognani, E., & Charman, L. (1996). The measurement of conflict in parent–adolescent relationships. In L. Verhofstadt-Denève, I. Kienhorst, & C. Braet (Eds.), *Conflict and development in adolescence* (pp. 75–91). Leiden, The Netherlands: DSWO Press.

Jones, L., Tepperman, L., & Wilson, S. (1995). *The futures of the family*. Englewood Cliffs, NJ: Prentice Hall.

Juang, L.P., & Silbereisen, R.K. (1999). Supportive parenting and adolescent adjustment across time in former East and West Germany. *Journal of Adolescence*, *22*, 719–736.

Kerr, M., Stattin, H., & Trost, K. (1999). To know you is to trust you: Parents' trust is rooted in child disclosure of information. *Journal of Adolescence*, *22*, 737–752.

Kiernan, K., & Estaugh, V. (1993). *Cohabitation: Extra-marital childbearing and social policy*. London: Family Policy Studies Centre.

Kuczynski, L., & Grusec, J.E. (1997). Future directions for a theory of parental socialisation. In J. E. Grusec, & L. Kuczynski (Eds.), *Parenting and* children's internalization of values (pp. 399–414). New York: John Wiley & Sons.

Kuczynski, L., & Lollis, S. (in press). Four foundations for a dynamic model of parenting. In J. R. M. Gerris (Ed.), *Dynamics of parenting*. Hillsdale, NJ: Lawrence Erlbaum Associates, Inc.

Kuczynski, L., Marshall, S., & Schell, K. (1997). Value socialisation in a bidirectional context. In J. E. Grusec, & L. Kuczynski (Eds.), *Parenting and children's internalization of values* (pp. 23–50). New York: John Wiley & Sons.

Kiely, G. (1998). Rapport sur l'Irlande pour l'année 1996 [Report on Ireland for the year 1996] In B. Ditch, H. Barnes, & J. Bradshaw (Eds.), *Evolution des politiques familiales nationales en 1996*. York: Commission Européenne.

Lamborn, S.D., Mounts, N.S., Steinberg, L., & Dornbusch, S.M. (1991). Patterns of competence and adjustment among adolescents from authoritative, authoritarian, indulgent, and neglectful families. *Child Development, 62*, 1049–1065.

Lamborn, S., & Steinberg, L. (1993). Emotional autonomy redux: Ryan and Lynch revisited. *Child Development, 64*, 483–499.

Lewin, E. (1993). *Lesbian mothers: Accounts of gender in American culture*. Ithaca, NY: Cornell University Press.

Lewis, M., & Feiring, C. (1998). *Families, risk, and competence*. Mahwah, NJ: Lawrence Erlbaum & Sons.

Lollis, S., & Kuczynski, L. (1997). Beyond one-hand clapping: Seeing bidirectionality in parent–child relations. *Journal of Social and Personal Relationships, 14*, 441–461.

Maccoby, E.E. (1980). *Social development: Psychological growth and parent–child relationships*. New York: Harcourt Brace Jovanovich.

Maccoby, E., & Martin, J. (1983). Socialisation in the context of the family: Parent–child interaction. In E. M. Hetherington, & P. H. Mussen (Eds.), *Handbook of child psychology: Vol. 4. Socialisation, personality, and social development* (4th ed., pp. 1–101). New York: John Wiley & Sons.

McCubbin, H., Patterson, J., & Lavee, Y. (1983). *One thousand army families: Strengths, coping and supports*. St Paul, MN: University of Minnesota, Family Social Science.

McCubbin, H., & Thompson, A. (Eds.). (1987). *Family assessment: Resiliency, coping and adaptation. Inventories for research and practice*. Madison, WI: University of Wisconsin Publishers.

McCubbin, H.L, Thompson, A.L, & McCubbin, M.A. (1996). *Family assessment: Resiliency, coping and adaptation. Inventories for research and practice*. Madison, WI: University of Winsconsin Publishers.

McGillicuddy-De Lisi, A.V., & Sigel, I.E. (1995). Parental beliefs. In M. Bornstein (Ed.), *Handbook of parenting: Vol. 3. Status and social conditions of parenting* (pp. 333–358). Hillsdale, NJ: Lawrence Erlbaum & Sons.

McGlone, F., & Millar, J. (1998). Rapport sur les tendances et les développements au Royaume-Uni en 1996 [Report on trends and developments in the United Kingdom in 1996]. In B. Ditch, H. Barnes, & J. Bradshaw (Eds.), *Evolution des politiques familiales nationales en 1996*. York: Commission Européenne.

Minuchin, S., & Fishman, H. (1981). *Family therapy techniques*. Cambridge, MA: Harvard University Press.

Musitu, G., & Allatt, P. (1994). *Psicosociologia de la familia* [Psycho-sociology of the family]. Valencia, Spain: Albatros.

Nicholson, J.M. (1996). *Child behaviour problems in stepfamilies: Assessment and intervention*. PhD thesis, University of Queensland, Brisbane, Australia.

Noack, P., Kerr, M., & Olah, A. (1999). Family relations in adolescence. *Journal of Adolescence, 22*, 713–717.

Noller, P., & Callan, V. (1991). *The adolescent in the family*. London: Routledge.

Observatoire Européen des Politiques Familiales Nationales (1998). Synthèse des politiques familiales nationales en 1996 [A synthesis of national family policies in 1996]. In B. Ditch, H. Barnes, & J. Bradshaw (Eds.), *Evolution des politiques familiales nationales en 1996*. York: Commission Européenne.

O'Connor, T.G., Hetherington, E.M., & Reiss, D. (1998). Family systems and adolescent development: Shared and non-shared risk and protective factors in non-divorced and remarried families. *Development and Psychopathology, 10*, 353–375.

Olson, D.H., McCubbin, H.I., Barnes, H., Larsen, A., Muxen, M., & Wilson, M. (1983). *Families: What makes them work?* London: Sage.

Paikoff, R.L., & Brooks-Gunn, J. (1991). Do parent–child relationships change during puberty? *Psychological Bulletin, 110*, 47–66.

Pardeck, J.T. (1989). The Minuchin family stress model: A guide for assessing and treating the impact of marital disruption on children and families. *International Journal of Adolescence and Youth, 4*, 367–377.

Patterson, G.R., & Dishion, T.J. (1985). Contributions of families and peers to delinquency. *Criminology, 23*, 63–79.

Petersen, A.C. (1988). Adolescent development. *Annual Review of Psychology, 39*, 583–607.

Peterson, G.W., & Steinmetz, S.K. (1999). Introduction: Perspectives on families as we approach the twenty-first century – Challenges for future handbook authors. In M. B. Sussman, S. K. Steinmetz, & G. W. Peterson (Eds.), *Handbook of marriage and the family* (pp. 1–12). New York: Plenum.

Raschke, H.J. (1987). Divorce. In M. B. Sussman, & S. K. Steinmetz (Eds.), *Handbook of marriage and the family* (pp. 597–624). New York: Plenum.

Reiss, D., Hetherington, E.M., Plomin, R., Howe, G.W., Simmens, S.J., Henderson, S.H. et al. (1995). Genetic questions for environmental studies: Differential parenting and psychopathology in adolescence. *Archives of General Psychiatry, 52*, 925–936.

Rothbaum, F., & Weisz, J.R. (1994). Parental caregiving and child externalizing behavior in non-clinical samples: A meta-analysis. *Psychological Bulletin, 116*, 55–74.

Schauerte, C., Branje, S.J.T., & van Aken, M.A.G. (2003). Familiäre Unterstützungsbeziehungen: Familientypen und ihre Bedeutung für die einzelnen Familienmitglieder. *Psychologie in Erziehung und Unterricht, 50*, 129–142.

Schwarz, B., & Silbereisen, R.K. (1996). Anteil und Bedeutung autoritativer Erziehung in verschiedene Lebenslagen [Contribution and meaning of authoritative parenting in various conditions of life]. In J. Zinnecker, & R. K. Silbereisen (Eds.), *Kindheit in Deutschland: Aktueller Survey über Kinder und ihre Eltern* (pp. 229–242). Weinheim: Juventa.

Seginer, R. (1998). Adolescents' perceptions of relationships with older siblings in the context of other close relationships. *Journal of Research on Adolescence, 8*, 287–308.

Selman, R. (1980). *The growth of interpersonal understanding: Developmental and clinical analyses.* New York: Academic Press.

Sgritta, B.G. (1998). L'Italie en 1996 [Italy in 1996]. In B. Ditch, H. Barnes, & J. Bradshaw (Eds.), *Evolution des politiques familiales nationales en 1996.* York: Commission Européenne.

Silverberg, S.B. (1996). Parents' well-being and their children's transition to adolescence. In C. D. Ryff, & M. M. Seltzer (Eds.), *The parental experience in midlife* (pp. 215–254). Chicago, IL: University of Chicago Press.

Silverberg, S., & Steinberg, L. (1990). Psychological well-being of parents at midlife: The impact of early adolescent children. *Developmental Psychology, 26*, 658–666.

Smetana, J.G., Yau, J., Restrepo, A., & Braeges, J.L. (1991). Adolescent–parent conflict in married and divorced families. *Developmental Psychology, 27*, 1000–1010.

Smith, S. (1995). Family theory and multicultural family studies. In B. B. Ingoldsby, & S. Smith (Eds.), *Families in multicultural perspective.* New York: Guilford.

Steinberg, L. (1990). Interdependence in the family: Autonomy, conflict, and harmony in the parent–adolescent relationship. In S. S. Feldman, & G. L. Elliott (Eds.), *At the threshold: The developing adolescent* (pp. 255–276). Cambridge, MA: Harvard University Press.

Steinberg, L. (1998). *Adolescence* (4th ed.). New York: McGraw-Hill.

Steinberg, L.D., Elmen, J.D., & Mounts, N. (1989). Authoritative parenting, psychosocial maturity, and academic success among adolescents. *Child Development, 60*, 1424–1436.

Steinberg, L., Mounts, N., Lamborn, S.D., & Dornbusch, S.M. (1991). Authoritative parenting and adolescent adjustment across varied ecological niches. *Journal of Research on Adolescence, 1*, 19–36.

Steinmetz, S.K. (1999). Adolescence in contemporary families. In M. B. Sussman, S. K. Steinmetz, & G. W. Peterson (Eds.), *Handbook of marriage and the family* (pp. 371–423). London: Plenum.

Stocker, C.M. (1994). Children's perceptions of relationships with siblings, friends, and mothers: Compensatory processes and links with adjustment. *Journal of Child Psychology and Psychiatry, 35*, 1447–1459.

Tamrouti, I., Dubas, J.S., Gerris, J.R.M., & van Aken, M.A.G. (2004). The relation between the absolute level of parenting and differential parental treatment with adolescent siblings' adjustment. *Journal of Child Psychology and Psychiatry, 45*, 1397–1406.

Tucker, C., Barber, B., & Eccles, J. (1997). Advice about life plans and personal problems in late adolescent sibling relationships. *Journal of Youth and Adolescence, 26*, 63–76.

van Aken, M.A.G., & Asendorpf, J.B. (1997). Support by parents, classmates, friends and siblings: Covariation and compensation across relationships. *Journal of Social and Personal Relationships, 14*, 79–93.

Wallerstein, J., & Kelly, J. (1980). *Surviving the breakup:*

How children and parents cope with divorce. New York: Basic Books.

Widmer, E. (1997). Influence of older siblings on initiation of sexual intercourse. *Journal of Marriage and the Family, 59,* 928–938.

Youniss, J., & Ketterlinus, R.D. (1987). Communication and connectedness in mother– and father–adolescent relationships. *Journal of Youth and Adolescence, 16,* 265–280.

Youniss, J., & Smollar, J. (1985). *Adolescent relations with mothers, fathers, and friends*. Chicago, IL: University of Chicago Press.

Zanatta, A.L. (1997). *Le nuove famiglie* [The new families]. Bologna, Italy: Il Mulino.

Zanata, A.L. (1998). L'Italie en 1996: Rapport spécial sur les enfants en Italie [Italy in 1996: Special report on children in Italy]. In B. Ditch, H. Barnes, & J. Bradshaw (Eds.), *Evolution des politiques familiales nationales en 1996*. York: Commission Européenne.

Zani, B. (1993). Dating and interpersonal relationships in adolescence. In S. Jackson, & H. Rodriguez-Tomé (Eds.), *Adolescence and its social worlds* (pp. 95–119). Hove, UK: Lawrence Erlbaum associates, Inc.

Zani, B., Bosma, H.A., Zijsling, D.H., & Honess, T.M. (2001). Family context and the development of adolescent decision-making. In J. E. Nurmi (Ed.), *Navigating through adolescence: European perspectives* (pp. 199–225). New York: Routledge Falmer.

10

Peer relations in adolescence

Ron H. J. Scholte and Marcel A. G. Van Aken

1. Introduction

Adolescents are embedded in myriad relationships, most significantly peer relationships and relationships with parents. Relationships involve a sequence of interactions between two individuals who know one another. The interactions are influenced by preceding interactions and, in turn, will influence future interactions (Hinde, 1997). Especially during adolescence peer relationships increase in importance. Peers are not necessarily of the same age, but the key characteristics of peers is that they are of the same level of social, emotional, and cognitive development. Peer relationships are usually based on equality in terms of knowledge and social rank (Hartup, 1983) and are more horizontal than parent–adolescent relationships, which tend to be more vertical. Peer relationships are important because of their significance for normal personal growth and development. They are not only advantageous, however, but can also have negative or detrimental effects for adolescent adjustment and development.

In this chapter, we will first focus on the characteristics, dynamics, and effects of adolescent friendships. Second, we will examine the peer groups that adolescents can be part of. Third, the peer relations in terms of the social status will be highlighted. Fourth, bullying and victimization, as a specific kind of negative peer relations will be described. Fifth, it will be described that although peer relationships become increasingly important in adolescence, the parent–adolescent relationships are still significant for adolescents' lives. The relative importance of peers compared to parents will be examined, thereby focusing on perceived support as an important aspect of parent–adolescent and friend relationships. During adolescence, romantic and sexual relationships also emerge. These will not be described in the present chapter but can be found in **Chapter 11**.

The American or European culture, and the cultures of the separate countries within Europe, is the larger social context in which all groups are embedded and refers to the socio-cultural environment. This environment can influence relationships resulting in similarities or cultural differences in relationships. Because most of the research on adolescent relationships comes from the USA, European studies will be described and compared with the American literature.

2. Friendships: Characteristics, dynamics, and effects

2.1 Friendship characteristics

Friendships are special kinds of peer relationship because they include two persons who like each other. Friendships are characterised by reciprocity and commitment (Hartup, 1993) between two individuals who see themselves similar in feelings and orientations. In contrast to family relationships, friendships are more fluid and are initiated, transformed and dissolved more frequently. Peer relationships and friendships have significance for the learning of attitudes and values (Hartup, 1989), the development of perspective taking and the self-system (Mead, 1934), and the formation of identity (Erikson, 1968). In addition, in the social interactions with peers the adolescents acquire social skills such as conflict management and aggression regulation. Thus, having high-quality friendships are important for children and adolescents' success in the peer social world (Berndt, 2004).

Friendships can only be formed and maintained when common ground and affirmation are present between the friends. Friendships differ from other peer relationships in that they have more affective ties. In describing friendships, one can distinguish between 'best friends', good friends and close friends (Hartup, 1993). Best friends are two individuals who mutually nominate each other as best friend: reciprocity is the central feature in identifying best friends. During adolescence, the number of self-reported best friends decreases from four or five in early adolescence to one or two in late adolescence. It should be noted that reciprocated best friendships are rarer than is indicated by adolescents' self-reports, since more adolescents claim to have a reciprocated best friend than there actually are (Epstein, 1983). Because in many studies no differentiation is made between friends and reciprocal best friends, these two

terms will be used as synonyms throughout this chapter.

Over the past 20 years there has been a growing empirical interest in the characteristics and the functions of friendship and in its developmental significance. Despite this growing interest only very few theoretical explanations of friendship and its contribution to development exist. One of the most useful theories is Sullivan's (1953) interpersonal theory of development. Sullivan proposed that different social needs emerge at different periods in life and at different stages of development. At every developmental stage a new social need emerges that is added to the already existing needs. In (pre)adolescence, the need for interpersonal intimacy emerges, and friendship is especially suited to fulfill this need. In Sullivan's view, intimacy, together with collaboration between friends aimed at satisfying the others' needs, is a critical aspect of true friendship in adolescence. Even more, social interactions between friends are necessary for an individual to overcome loneliness and to remain happy and psychologically healthy (Buhrmester, 1990). Sullivan (1953) argued that friendship offers the opportunity to fulfill specific social needs. According to Sullivan, there are five basic social needs: (1) tenderness, (2) companionship, (3) acceptance, (4) intimacy, and (5) sexuality, the first four of which can be fulfilled in adolescents' friendships. Social needs, however, are not the only needs that play a role in friendships. Needs such as gaining agency, power, and excitement can also be distinguished (Buhrmester, 1996). These needs are more individualistic or agentic in nature, whereas the needs proposed by Sullivan are more social and communal. Empirical evidence for these two broad categories of needs was found in a study by Buhrmester (1996) in which factor analysis of 20 interpersonal needs that were used by major personality, social psychology, and developmental theorists supported the dualistic perspective.

A second theory that is of specific relevance for understanding adolescent friendships is Selman's (1980) theory of interpersonal perspective taking. Whereas Sullivan focused on the emergence of specific social needs in adolescence, Selman's theory describes the social cognitive skills that develop during adolescence and that are important for establishing healthy interpersonal relationships. Adolescents, in contrast to children at a younger age, are capable of establishing and maintaining intimate relationships because they can think in more complex ways about themselves and other adolescents, and about the relationships that exist between them. According to Selman's theory, adolescents are able to mutually recognize their personal views and influence and also take the perspective of the other person involved in the relationship.

2.2 Dynamics of friendships: Formation, stability and dissolution

Friendships vary considerably in duration, some only last for some weeks while others will last a lifetime. In adolescence, many friendships are relatively stable across time and in this respect differ from friendships in childhood. More than 70% of the adolescents have friendships that will at least last one year (Hartup, 1993). Nevertheless, friendship dissolution often occurs. Dissolution is a multi-determined phenomenon and can be caused by various reasons. Whereas adolescents may choose one another on the basis of similarities to become friends, similarity becomes less important once the friendship is established. Instead, friends search for social and emotional resources such as intimacy and support. High-quality friendships, which offer these resources are likely to last over a longer period while friendships low in quality are likely to lead to dissolution. Low quality is usually associated with low levels of intimacy, support or closeness, and higher levels of disagreement, competition, and conflict.

As the work by Laursen (1993, 1995) shows, however, conflicts not necessarily contribute negatively to a friendship, but may have positive effects as well. Conflicts can even be seen as a potential developmental force (Shantz & Hartup, 1992). Conflicts are ubiquitous in adolescents' close relationships, including close relationships with parents and friends. Conflicts between friends, defined as interpersonal disagreement are as frequent as one every six hours of interaction

(Laursen, 1995). Friends, in contrast to non-friends, may be more concerned about resolving the conflict. Adolescents recognize that conflicts can irreparably damage their friendships. They also recognize, however, that conflicts can have positive effects in that conflicts provide opportunities for friendship growth and improvement of the relationship. It is hypothesised (e.g., Laursen, 1993) that the effects of conflicts differ according to the relationship and the closeness of the participants in the relationship. Closer relationships like friendships (and adolescent–parent relationships) will more often face conflicts than less close relationships. At the same time, the feelings associated with conflicts are less negative and the social interaction will almost always continue after a conflict, with the relationship often being perceived as being improved (Laursen, 1993). In addition, Krappmann (1991) states that moderate levels of conflict between peers foster healthy individual development. The reason is that friendships are interdependent and rewarding relationships and adolescents therefore have a lot to lose when these relationships terminate.

Thus adolescents have a higher commitment to their friends and are more willing to invest in their relationship. By conflict resolution, distress and inequity can be reduced, thereby maintaining the relationship. Compared to conflict resolution with parents, adolescents use more negotiation and less power assertion and disengagement, thus confirming the horizontal relationship that exists between friends. In friendships there is usually no intense competition and striving for dominance, which allows the adolescent and his or her friends to solve disagreement satisfactorily, fostering friendship growth.

2.3 Effects of friendships

In an influential review of more than 80 articles in which friends were compared to non-friends, Newcomb and Bagwell (1995) examined the effects of positive and negative friendship features on a wide range of behaviors. They found that friends, compared to non-friends showed more closeness, faithfulness and amity. Friendships, more than other peer relations served as a context for social, emotional and cognitive development such as the validation of self-worth, and fulfill specific social needs such as security and emotional support. In order to adequately describe the effects of friendships, however, one has to distinguish between three aspects (Hartup, 1996). These aspects concern (a) whether or not one has friends, (b) who the friends are, and (c) what the quality of the friendship is. In the next section we will describe each of these aspects in more detail.

2.3.1 Significance of having friends

To examine the significance of having friends, a number of researchers have compared children and adolescents who have friends with those who do not (Hartup, 1993; Newcomb & Bagwell, 1995). In general, these cross-sectional studies show that children and adolescents who have friends are socially more competent and psychologically more healthy than friendless children and adolescents. They are more sociable, cooperate more, have fewer difficulties with others, and have a higher self-esteem. All these conclusions, however, should be interpreted with caution. First, almost all of the studies on having friends versus not having friends are correlational and causality can thus not be inferred. Having friends may increase self-esteem and sociability but it may also be that adolescents who have a higher self-esteem and have better social skills are more likely to establish and maintain friendships. Longitudinal studies could disentangle the causality, and one such study suggests that having friends indeed increases self-esteem (Bukowski, Newcomb, & Hoza, 1987).

Second, studies on having friends mostly not only include friends but also other members of the adolescent's network such as parents and siblings. All these people exert influence and it is therefore difficult to disentangle exactly the developmental contributions of friendships. Third, having friends usually means having good, supportive friendships, and is thus confounded with the quality of friendship, which will be described later.

2.3.2 Who the friends are

The second aspect that should be considered when describing the developmental aspects of friendships is that of who the friends are. In folk psychology, two opposing ideas exist about the identity of one's friends. One saying says 'opposites attract' whereas the other says 'birds of a feather flock together'. Empirical evidence has clearly supported the latter because adolescents are found to be more similar to their friends than to non-friends. Similarity exists on school related attitudes, aspirations and intellect (Hartup, 1996; Kandel, 1978) as well as on more normative behaviors such as drinking, smoking, and sexual activity (e.g., Dishion, Andrews, & Crosby, 1995). As the work by Stattin and Magnusson (1990) shows, the effect of friendships is related to the age of the friends. Having younger friends is associated with lower involvement in drinking alcohol compared to adolescents who have friends of their own age and for girls, having older friends, is related to early maturation.

Adolescents and their friends are also similar on aspects that are less visible such as self-esteem and perceived intelligence, while little evidence exist that friends are similar to one another on personality (Aboud & Mendelson, 1996). Similarity may sometimes indicate a developmental risk since adolescents who are aggressive and delinquent tend to affiliate with other adolescents who display similar norm-breaking behavior (Cairns, Cairns, Neckerman, Gest, & Gariepy, 1988).

Similarity can come from two sources: selection and mutual socialisation. The selection of friends is based on the human tendency to affiliate with others who are similar to themselves. The underlying assumption is that similarity is rewarding because it involves cooperation with others who have similar interests in activities and because one's views and values are validated by others who hold similar views. This is of special importance in adolescence when children are faced with the developmental task to form their identity (Erikson, 1968) and to construct a self concept (Harter, 1990). It is sometimes difficult to disentangle whether friends were similar and therefore associated with one another, or whether they became more similar as a result of their friendship, because they mutually socialize one another. It has been shown that friends do socialize one another and that this socialization can go in the direction of positive normative behaviors (Kandel & Andrews, 1987) but also in the direction of antisocial behaviors. Research of the Oregon Social Centre team (Dishion, Patterson, & Griesler, 1994) revealed that children who are at risk regarding antisocial behavior are likely to show an increase in their antisocial behaviors once they have an antisocial friend. Socialization occurs because adolescents model behavior for their friends and also are reinforced from their friends through laughter or other contingent positive reactions to rule-breaking behavior in peer groups ('deviancy training', cf. Dishion, McCord, & Poulin, 1999). Adolescents who are rewarded by peers for their deviant social behavior will probably go on displaying these behaviors or even increase it. Also, the deviancy training provides meaning and values to the aggressive adolescents, which can, therefore, serve as the cognitive basis for motivation to display deviant behavior in future.

Finally, similarity between friends may also stem from the combination of both selection and socialization. Kandel (1978) studied adolescents' marihuana use and involvement in minor delinquency over a period of one year. Results showed that friend selection and socialization equally determined similarities after one year.

2.3.3 Quality of the friendship

The third dimension that has to be distinguished when examining the developmental significance of friendships is the quality of the friendships. Whereas similarity is important in the *formation* of friendships, the quality is important in the *maintenance* of friendships. Empirical evidence has shown that the quality of adolescents' friendships is related to adjustment. For example, Burk and Laursen (2005) found that adolescents with friendship negativity was related to adjustment outcomes, such that adolescents with poorer friendship quality showed more internalizing and externalizing problems, as well as lower school grades.

Some discussion exists on how to best measure the quality of friendship. Most researchers rely

on adolescents' self-reports indicating how they perceive their relationships with their friends. Although these perceptions may be valuable in itself, they are subjective and idiosyncratic and a friendship may be more significant to one person than to his or her friendship partner (Berndt, 1996). Perceptions of the same friendship may differ and the adolescent and friend may disagree on the quality their friendship has. They may differ, for example, in the level of support they perceive (Scholte, 1998). Because relationships have characteristics that are independent of the persons involved – since they are from a different level of social complexity (Hinde, 1997) – measures should take into account the perceptions of both persons involved in the relationship (Montemayor & Gregg, 1994) and use some kind of dyadic relationship score. As research shows, it is not the perception of either relationship partner alone, but rather the discrepancy between the perceptions that correlates more strongly with adjustment difficulties (East, 1991).

2.3.4 Short- and long-term effects of friendships

As was described before, adolescents who have friends generally differ from friendless adolescents on a number of domains. The differences are related to the effects of friendships, which can be short term or immediate, as well as long term and formative. The immediate effects of friendships include positive effects on the psychological, social, and emotional adjustment of adolescents (Hartup, 1993). As Sullivan (1953) argues, this may be because friendships provide the adolescents a unique context for development, for what they learn in friendships may not be learned in other relationships. Or at least, friendships may provide developmental advantages because friends have possibilities in acquiring specific skills in their relationships (Buhrmester, 1996). Positive friendship experiences may therefore have long-term developmental formative effects on the social, emotional, and cognitive domain (Newcomb & Bagwell, 1995).

Regarding *social development*, friendships offer

the opportunities to acquire and use prosocial interpersonal skills. Adolescents learn how to establish a secure base for exchange of feelings, thoughts, and other forms of self-disclosure. In addition, adolescents learn how to maintain this affective bond with another person by sharing and cooperation. Furthermore, the resolution of conflicts in friendships has a developmental significance because conflict management is an important social skill that fosters the establishment and maintenance of close and intimate relationships later in life.

The friendship could also provide a context for *emotional development*. Within friendships adolescents have the opportunity for the affective exchange of emotions. They can learn to express and regulate their own emotions, and can learn to transfer emotions into behaviors such as helping friends or be an intimate confidant. Finally, friendships themselves are an intense emotional experience for the adolescents (Newcomb & Bagwell, 1995).

Compared to social and emotional development, much less is known about the developmental significance of adolescents' friendships for *cognitive development*. Cognitive development may be affected by friendship in several ways. First, through their more intense conversation and sharing in friendships, adolescents learn how to exchange and formulate their own ideas. Also, friendships provide the opportunity for successful problem solving through the exchange of different viewpoints and testing the ideas of others, and through taking the perspective from others (Selman, 1980).

Do friendships have positive effects only? In general, friendships are thought to be positive in nature because they have positive effects on adolescents' current adjustment as well as future functioning on a number of dimensions. Nevertheless, friendships may also have important negative effects, in part depending on who the friends are and what the quality of the friendship is. Considering who the friends are, delinquent friends can socialize one another in the direction of deviant behavior and friendship can therefore be the road that leads to more delinquency and finally to a criminal adult career (Dishion et al.,

1999). Friends also possess a crucial influence on adolescents' decisions to use tobacco, alcohol, or illicit drugs (Chassin, Presson, Montello, Sherman, & McGrew, 1986; Kandel, 1978). In addition, negative friendship experiences, indicated by low quality and negative interactions, may lead to negative behavior. Berndt and Keefe (1995), for example, found that adolescents who had trouble with their best friends, became more troublesome and disruptive in class as the school year progressed. Adolescents who have friendships that are characterized by frequent conflicts may adopt a negative interaction style that affects their interactions with others as well (Berndt, 1996). Finally, even intimate and supportive friendships may have undesirable effects (Buhrmester, 1990). Intimate friendships, especially in adolescence, are often based on self-disclosure and sharing personal feelings and thoughts. This may increase insecurity and vulnerability for betrayal (Berndt & Hanna, 1995). Also, because of the self-disclosure, friendship may lead to extreme introspection.

As described, friendships are relationships that exist between two individuals, in this case, adolescents. Friendships do not exist in isolation, however, but are usually embedded in a network of other peer relations. These relations constitute peer groups and youth cultures, which will be described next.

3. Peer groups and youth subculture

Several important transformations take place in adolescents' relationships that distinguishes them from childhood relationships (Brown, Dolcini, & Leventhal, 1997). Relationships become more stable over time and romantic relationships emerge. Maybe the most remarkable development is the formation of peer groups, which are embedded in youth subculture.

Ever since Coleman's (1961) influential study on adolescence, adolescents' peer groups are considered as having negative influences on adolescents. Coleman documented the emergence of an adolescent peer system with its own rules and values that seemed opposed to adult values. Peer groups seemed to have disconnected from adult society, and adults could not penetrate these peer groups, which made them even more suspect and prone to exhibit cross-pressure between peers and adults.

More recently, researchers acknowledge that the socialization through the peer groups should no longer be judged negatively as implied by Coleman (1961), because the relationships in these groups are characterized by symmetrical reciprocity and are organized around the principle of cooperation by equals (Youniss, McLellan, & Strouse, 1994). In this respect, they differ from relationships with adults, which are more vertical and are characterized by unilateral authority. Therefore, the relationships within the peer group offer the adolescents unique opportunities to understanding social possibilities that cannot be learned from relationships with adults such as parents (Hartup, 1983).

3.1 Peer groups

Adolescents spend time not only with their best friends, but also with their close friends and good friends. All these friends together aggregate in what in the USA are called *cliques*, which is what adolescents refer to when they talk about 'my friends'. In Europe, the term 'clique' is less prevalent, and, in this chapter, we therefore describe cliques as 'peer groups'. Peer groups are based on actual interactions that are going on between all the members of the group. An interesting question is which peers form the peer groups, or with whom peers hang out and why. In general, having mutual interests (e.g., having the same hobbies and liking the same things) is one of the driving forces for peer group formation. As Thurlow (2002) showed, boys show a strong tendency to form peer groups based on shared interests in sports and computers, but not in deviant activities such as substance use. Girls' peer orientation, contrariwise, was much more based on shared taste in clothes, music, and personal qualities such as hanging out with nice, friendly, trustworthy, open-minded people. Thurlow's study also showed that, in Great Britain, ethnicity was not important for peer affiliation.

Although peer groups are sometimes considered as mutually exclusive, adolescents can be members of more than one peer group. Youniss et al. (1994) reported that 23% of adolescents belonged to two peer groups and 10% to three or more peer groups. An informative study by Cairns, Leung, Buchanan, and Cairns (1995) showed that peer groups are rather fluid. They found that over a period of three weeks, 90% of the peer groups were found to be stable, when the criterion that at least 50% of the members of the original group remained the same was used. However, the stability substantially dropped when more stringent criteria were employed to define stability: when the criterion was that 75% of the members had to remain together, only 62% of the groups were stable, while 25% of the peer groups remained exactly the same three weeks later.

Not all adolescents who want to belong to a particular peer group are accepted and incorporated by that group. Peer groups are a strong venue for socialization, maybe even stronger than dyadic friendships. They are considered as the primary context for offering the adolescent the opportunity to develop intense friendships, to learn about society and to develop a sense of self and identity (Elkin & Handel, 1989). Peer groups, however, can also have values that are opposed to adult values such as, for example, appreciation and high value of deviant behavior (Farmer & Rodkin, 1996) and can thus have detrimental effects on adolescent behavior and development. Deviant behaviors such as drug use, vandalism and shoplifting can be encouraged in peer group members who value these behaviors (Dishion et al., 1994).

Yet, most peer groups hold views that are similar to the adult ones. As Youniss et al. (1994) show, research has recently questioned the view that cross-pressure exists between parents and peers. First, adolescents in general tend to have similar views as their parents, and not opposing views as was long believed. Second, it is now acknowledged that peers can provide opportunities for adolescents' social development because of the cooperative interactions between adolescent and peers (e.g., Youniss & Damon, 1992). Finally, it is recognized that peers and parents represent different social systems which both exert social influence on adolescents' development.

3.2 *Youth subculture*

Just as best friends are usually embedded in peer groups, are peer groups embedded in still higher order aggregates, which have been called 'crowds' in the American literature, or what can be referred to as youth culture. The youth culture differs from peer groups in that it is not necessarily formed by adolescents who are one another's friends. The youth culture contains adolescents who have similar appearances, behaviors or attitudes on various domains such as sports or antisocial behavior. In contrast to peer groups this culture is not based on interaction patterns but on a person's reputation (Brown, 1990). The youth culture has developmental significance because it can provide a context for identity development and for social skill development. Youth cultures show considerable variation in the quality of the relationships that exist inside these cultures. Sometimes, adolescents can establish friendships that will last for life (Brown et al., 1997) whereas on other occasions the relationships may be based on competition rather than cooperation and may be more superficial (Brown, Morey, & Kinney, 1994). Different social contexts, expressed in different youth cultures, provide different opportunities to master specific social skills and ways of interaction. Thus, being part of a particular youth culture, and the social skills and values that are learned in it, may not only affect the quality of the adolescent's relationships within that particular culture, but his or her future relationships as well. When friendships are superficial or genuine, later romantic relationships may be instrumental or based on commitment and altruism.

Youth cultures not only influence the opportunities for acquiring positive social skills but they also affect adolescent health behaviors, either by fostering health-enhancing or health-compromising behaviors. Marked differences between youth cultures have been observed on a number of behaviors, including substance use, delinquency, sexual intercourse, academic achievement, and emotional health (see Brown et al., 1997). These health-related differences may be a cause as well as a result of the peer relationships found in the youth culture. The perception of the display of delinquency, for example, may encourage a deviant adolescent to associate with delinquent adolescents that represent a delinquent youth culture. Aggressive adolescents indeed tend to affiliate with other adolescents who are also aggressive (Cairns et al., 1988). At the same time, group norms and sanctions for deviation of these norms can influence and direct an adolescent's behavior in a youth culture. Moreover, because youth cultures offer a social identity or status, not only peer pressure but also the adolescent's own decision to conform to the culture's values and norms, can result in continuing behaviors even if they are health compromising. Especially in adolescence when children develop an identity, the social identity offered by the youth culture may be more important to an adolescent than the adult's warnings or sanctions. Nevertheless, although youth cultures seem to be rather autonomous social systems, their influence is moderated to a certain extent by parental practices (Brown, Lamborn, Mounts, & Steinberg, 1993) or demographic factors.

Since most research on peer groups and youth cultures has been conducted in the USA, the characteristics of peer groups and youth cultures that have been described may be typically American. Some studies, however, have been conducted in Europe and can offer additional information on the developmental significance of peer groups. In Germany, Busch (1998) showed that compared to less visible peer groups, the deviant peer groups were characterized by a more hierarchical structure, clearer boundaries, and higher social pressure for conformity and solidarity. Also the work of Palmonari, Pombeni, and Kirchler on adolescent peer groups is valuable in this respect. Kirchler, Palmonari, and Pombeni (1992) found that peer groups made positive contributions to adolescent adjustment. They found that the majority of Austrian adolescents (around 80%) preferred to spend their time in informal cliques with whom they meet regularly. This finding was in line with Noack (1990), who reported that German adolescents most often formed peer groups that were informal and consisted of adolescents who met on the street and interacted freely. In the (1992) study of Kirchler et al. It was further found that Austrian adolescents who identified highly with their (nondelinquent) peer group, were likely to receive greater emotional, social and informational support when they faced problems. The associations between coping with problems and identification with the peer group were somewhat lower than the associations found in Italy. Also the number of adolescents (80%) joining informal groups was lower than the numbers of around 90% reported in Italian studies (Palmonari, Kirchler, & Pombeni, 1991; Pombeni, Kirchler, & Palmonari, 1990). This suggests that peer groups may play a greater role in Italian than in Austrian adolescents' lives. In Italy, it was found that 75% of the adolescents are members of informal peer groups, while 20% are members of a more formal peer group such as a sport group or a religious group. It is widely assumed that formal groups are better means to lead adolescents through the challenges of adolescence. As the work by Palmonari and colleagues shows, this assumption is not supported by empirical evidence. Formal and informal groups did not differ in the difficulty experienced in coping with developmental tasks. Whereas the type of group is of less importance, the identification with the peer group is significant in the development of an identity as well as in coping with adjustment problems (Pombeni et al., 1990). Palmonari et al. (1991) showed that peer groups exert negative influence on behavior particularly when adolescents identify highly with their (deviant) peer group but not with their parents.

Within peer groups, social processes like peer acceptance and peer rejection take place, resulting in adolescents having specific social positions or status inside their peer groups. Because the status is an important indicator of adjustment, several aspects will be described in the next section, including (a) the sociometric status groups, (b) stability of the status groups, and (c) the antecedents and consequences of peer rejection and aggression in adolescence.

4. Social status

The social status in the peer group is the position that an adolescent holds in his or her group, relative to the positions of all other group members. Adolescents' peer relations in general, and the social status in particular, are important indicators or precursors of adolescents' concurrent and future psychological and behavioral adjustment. Also, the current social status is related to the social status in the past, as well as to past behavior.

4.1 Social status groups

In understanding interpersonal relationship and social groups, two aspects should be considered. These aspects concern peer acceptance and rejection. Acceptance and rejection are not necessarily one another's opposites. An adolescent who is not highly accepted by his peers does not need to be rejected by those peers, but can be more or less indifferent to them. It is important to note that social status is based on a classification of acceptance and rejection that is probabilistic in nature and is relative to the peer group or class in which the status is assessed.

Although most of the empirical work on sociometric status has been conducted on children, many findings seem to be applicable to adolescents as well. For example, several studies (see Newcomb, Bukowski, & Pattee, 1993) found results on groups of adolescents that were comparable to results found in studies on children. A large body of research now shows that the social status and the way a child or adolescent interacts with peers inside a group is indicative for his or her adjustment or maladjustment. Social status has been related to positive aspects like self-esteem, well-being or prosocial behavior, as well as to negative aspects such as loneliness and isolation, drug use, aggression and delinquency.

In general, five social status groups are distinguished (Coie, Dodge, & Coppotelli, 1982; Newcomb & Bukowski, 1983). These five groups are labelled as follows:

- *Populars*: Adolescents who are liked by many and disliked by few peers. Compared to other adolescents, they show higher levels of social competence and cognitive abilities and lower levels of aggressive and disruptive behaviors, as well as loneliness and withdrawal. Popular individuals tend to have social abilities to achieve interpersonal goals yet maintain positive social relationships.

- *Rejected*: Adolescents who are more disliked than liked by their peers. Rejected adolescents are found to be more aggressive and disruptive than others, they violate social and institutional rules more easily, and have more conflicts with other peers and teachers. The display of aggression alone, however, does not account for these adolescents to be rejected. What leads to rejection is their aggression in combination with their low social competence. The rejected adolescents lack positive qualities to balance their aggressive behaviors (Newcomb et al., 1993). Rejected children and adolescents can also be more socially withdrawn and isolated, and express higher levels of depression and anxiety than their non-rejected peers. Although social withdrawal can be a consequence rather than a cause for rejection, anxiety and depression may contribute substantially to the maintenance of rejection over time. As is clear, there are two distinct factors that may lead to rejection: aggressive and disruptive behaviors on one side, and socially withdrawn and inhibited behaviors on the other.
- *Neglected*: Adolescents who are neither liked nor disliked by many peers. They receive little attention from their peers, to whom they are more or less indifferent and not well-known. These adolescents are peaceful, shy and reserved but not as socially withdrawn as some of the rejected adolescents. Although they evince less sociability than their average peers, they respect the rules and are engaged in socially accepted activities although to a lesser degree than the more accepted children and in more solitary forms. In sum, these are the adolescents who function normally, but no one notices them (Goossens, Scholte, van Aken, & Hildebrand, 2000).
- *Controversials*: Adolescents who are liked but also disliked by many peers. The controversials have higher levels of aggression,

sometimes even higher than rejected adolescents (Newcomb et al., 1993), but at the same time they show greater sociability. They are described as active, with intellectual, social, and athletic dexterity, but at the same time they easily violate established rules. Probably, they behave appropriately inside their own group of friends, but in a more aggressive and negative way toward the rest of their peers. Their social competence and friendship relations are equivalent to those of popular children and adolescents (Malik & Furman, 1993).

- *Average*: Adolescents who, compared to all other adolescents, score average on being liked and being disliked. Adolescents with an average social status never score very high on the positive features that characterize the popular or on the negative features that characterize the rejected adolescents. They are more visible or salient than the neglected adolescents.

These five social status groups have been examined in many studies in various Western countries, showing cross-cultural similarity in percentages of adolescents belonging to these groups. Cillessen and ten Brink (1991) reviewed a number of primarily American studies and found the following average percentages: 15% of the children are popular, 15% are rejected, about 5% are controversial, 7% neglected, and the rest belongs to the average group, although the percentages can vary considerably from study to study. In south European cultures that are less individualistic and more group oriented than American or northwest European cultures, more or less the same percentages are found, as was shown in a study on Greek adolescents (Hatzichristou & Hopf, 1996).

Recently, the question has risen whether the social status groups are homogeneous, or whether they are heterogeneous and include subgroups. In answering this question, most attention has focused on the status group that is most problematic, the rejected children and adolescents. On the one hand, rejected adolescents pose a risk factor for themselves, because rejection is related to internalizing problems such as depression and anxiousness. On the other hand, aggressive rejected adolescents are a threat to society because of their externalizing problem behavior such as deviancy and violent behaviors and their probability of entering criminal careers (Dishion et al., 1999).

It is now widely recognized that the status group of rejected children and adolescents, more so for boys than for girls, consists of two sub-groups that are heterogeneous with respect to the behavioral pattern typifying them. According to Rubin, LeMare and Lollis (1990), these two sub-groups, both accounting for about 50% of the rejected adolescents, can be characterized as aggressive–rejected and submissive–rejected. This distinction is crucial because it is not only linked to a different ontology of rejection, but also to different consequences in terms of concurrent and later adjustment, and to possible intervention strategies aimed at reducing the negative effects of rejection.

The subgroup of aggressive–rejected adolescents shows a clear pattern of aggressive and disruptive behavior (for more information on aggression in adolescence, see Chapter 18). The submissive–rejected adolescents are characterized by extreme social unassertiveness and low social interaction. They are actively withdrawn, avoid confrontation, and make very few requests. Consequently, they are easy targets for ridicule and bullying. This behavioral pattern does not lead to rejection in childhood, but does result in rejection in later years. This may be especially true for adolescence, when peer interactions and social competence become extremely important.

One key element in social interaction in adolescence that may lead to peer rejection seems to be the lack of expression of *prosocial* behaviors. As Parkhurst and Asher (1992) have shown, students who exhibit high levels of negative social behavior and low levels of prosocial behavior are rejected. At the same time, students who show high levels of negative social behavior as well as high levels of prosocial behavior are not rejected. These adolescents are likely to be controversial in nature, implying that they are both liked and disliked by many peers.

Although the primary reason for being rejected by peers lies in the non-social behavior of the rejected peer, especially during adolescence other factors such as physical appearance (Coie et al., 1982) athletic inability or academic achievement may also contribute to rejection. Among these characteristics, physical attractiveness has been most studied. In general, moderate correlations have been found between physical appearance and being liked by peers. Cavior and Dokecki (1973) showed that this was only true for the extremes of the continuum of being liked and disliked. Adolescents who were very attractive were liked and adolescents who were rated as unattractive were not liked: for the intermediate positions there was no relation between attractiveness and being liked. In contrast, Coie et al. (1982) argued that although physical appearance was a significant predictor of social preference among peers, adolescents' behaviors could substitute the physical appearance. In other words, it is not just the appearance or inability that leads to rejection, but more the way the adolescent deals with peer reactions and evaluations concerning his or her features (Rubin, 1990). This idea supports the assumption that social cognitions are important contributors to social or non-social behaviors.

In addition to the lack of prosocial behaviors, what both subgroups of rejected adolescents have in common is their tendency to interpret ambiguous interactions negatively (cf. social information processing, Crick & Dodge, 1994). As a consequence, they tend to react inappropriately given the real intent of the peers. Both the aggressive–rejected and submissive–rejected adolescents lack the ability to monitor and respond adequately to the peers' interpersonal cues and intents (Bierman, Smoot, & Aumiller, 1993). Moreover, these adolescents may have fewer concerns for the effects of their reactions and for others' feelings, notwithstanding the fact that, for example, withdrawn children worry much about their relationships (Parkhurst & Asher, 1992).

4.2 Stability of social status

When children grow older and enter adolescence, they not only change their behavior, but also the values they have about what behavior is appropriate and what is not. Specific qualities that were appreciated in childhood will no longer be in adolescence. Similarly, behaviors that were not perceived as very deviant before now become highly visible and possible reasons for peer rejection. Coie and Dodge (1983) found that with increasing age shyness becomes more apparent to peers. Thus, the same behavior can lead to different social status in different ages. Despite these age-related variations in peer perceptions and preferences associated with social status, data are quite consistent with respect to the correlations of high status and prosocial behaviors such as being cooperative, considerate, and helpful, and complying to the social rules across time. In general, social status is relatively stable across time, especially the status of rejection (Musitu, 1982). Even when rejected boys are placed in other groups of totally unfamiliar boys, they quickly acquire a rejected social status (Coie & Kupersmidt, 1983). In their review of all studies that reported on social status stability, Cillessen, Bukowski and Haselager (2000) found the following long-term stabilities across a period longer than three months or including school transition. Of the popular children, 35% remained popular; for the rejected children this was 45%, while it was 23% for the neglected children. Of the controversial and average children 28% and 65%, respectively, maintained their social status over this long-term period. These data concerned the median percentages of children who maintained their status over time. When the authors examined the individual status groups, while correcting for chance agreement, they found that the popular and rejected classifications were most stable across time. This indicates that children and adolescents who are popular or rejected exhibit characteristics that are relatively invariant across time and that remain positively or negatively evaluated by their peers in childhood and adolescence. When changes do occur, the direction of the change is quite patterned for each status group. It is unlikely that popular children will ever become rejected in later time, or that rejected children will ever be popular. According to Coie and Dodge (1983) the status of rejected children will shift in one of the following directions: they become neglected, they move towards average status, or they remain rejected. Children who are neglected in elementary school almost never become rejected or controversial in secondary education. Instead, it is more likely that the initially neglected children will become average or popular. Because of all children with a negative social status, the rejected boys and girls are least likely to change their status, and because rejection is associated with current and subsequent adjustment problems, adolescents with this social status have been studied most extensively.

4.3 Causes for peer rejection

As described, an adolescent's social status reflects his or her social position in the peer group, relative to the other peers. This position results from the adolescent's characteristics (e.g., aggression or withdrawal), the adolescent's social self-perceptions, and group characteristics such as group norms and values. In describing the causes for peer rejection these three perspectives need to be considered.

The social status may reflect underlying *characteristics*. In this sense, social status is a 'marker' (cf. Parker & Asher, 1987) for emotional, social cognitive or behavioral tendencies within the adolescent. For the aggressive–rejected adolescent, the status could serve as a marker of regulatory skill deficits. These skill deficits are stable across time and differentiate between aggressive–rejected and aggressive–non-rejected adolescents. These adolescents may have learned aggressive behaviors in the context of coercive interaction patterns with parents and peers (Patterson, 1982). In these interactions their negative behavior is modeled and reinforced, while the poor quality of the relationships have not provided the adolescent with opportunities to learn appropriate social skills and behaviors.

Some researchers argue that both the submissive– and the aggressive–rejected adolescents have *self-perceptions* that maintain their behavior and status. These self-perceptions may be distorted perceptions that are beyond reality. The withdrawn adolescents may underestimate their social competence (Rubin et al., 1990), while the aggressive adolescents may have rather positive but nevertheless distorted views of their social competence (Boivin & Begin, 1989) or their social position. An explanation why the self-perceptions may contribute to the stability of the social status is that children and adolescents try to maintain consistency in their conceptions (Swann, Griffin, Predmore, & Gaines, 1987), even if their perceptions are negative. In order to remain consistent they may be motivated to display behavior they have displayed before and that eventually lead to peer rejection.

Nevertheless, since the convergence of social status in different social environments is low to moderate (Coie & Kupersmidt, 1983), it is possible that some of the aggressive–rejected adolescents may actually have positive social experiences with adults and peers outside the peer group (e.g., family and neighborhood). Therefore, their perceptions may be shaped more by these positive experiences than by the negative experiences in the peer group. As was revealed by Farmer and Rodkin (1996), just like average or popular adolescents, aggressive adolescents too are members of networks of clusters or cliques inside their class. Whatever the process of social group forming may be – social exclusion or free choice – aggressive–rejected are as often reciprocally nominated by peers as being their best friend, as are average or popular children (Cairns et al., 1988). Also they may perceive the relationships and interactions they have with their friends or cluster members inside their class to be positive and supportive and may feel as accepted as the more popular adolescents. Even though they are only liked by a very small number of peers and disliked by most of them, being liked by a minority of peers who share the same values may be more important to them than being liked by the majority of the peers (Cairns et al., 1988). In Germany, Albrecht and Silbereisen (1993) also found that contact with deviant peers is of minor importance in predicting adolescent peer rejection, because the adolescents will find acceptance and recognition in the deviant peer group.

One last factor that may contribute to the rejected status concerns the *group dynamics* or processes. These group dynamics may be relatively independent of the adolescent's actual behavior, and are related both to the emergence of the rejected status and to the maintenance of the rejected status of a group member (Hymel, Wagner, & Butler, 1990). The emergence of the rejected status can result from the fact that, even before the actual interaction with a new group member takes place, group members can generate negative expectations toward the new member. These expectations can be based on peers' actual observations of the interactions of the new peer with other peers outside the class, or can be based on 'whisper' of group members. They can also result from stereotypes that the peers have about non-behavioral characteristics of the new peer which are associated with the new peer's presumed social competence.

5. Bullying and victimization

As is the case for peer rejection, bullying constitutes a negative form of peer relation. Bullying can be defined as negative actions that are repeated over time by one or more adolescents towards one or more other adolescents who are unable to defend themselves (Solberg & Olweus, 2003). These actions can be physical such as kicking, hitting, pushing or shoving, but can also be more indirect such as ignoring, isolating, gossiping and telling lies about the victim. Gender differences indicate that more boys than girls bully others and that more boys than girls are victims (e.g., Junger-Tas & van Kesteren, 1999; Solberg & Olweus, 2003), although the gender difference in being victimized is not confirmed in all studies. Recent large scale studies show that bullying is a significant problem for many adolescents. For example, in a study by Eslea et al. (2003), data from surveys among approximately 48,000 children and adolescents from seven countries revealed that up to 17% of all adolescents were bullies, 26% were victims, and 20% were bully–victims (see also Smith, Morita, Junger-Tas, Olweus, Catalano, & Slee, 1999). Substantial differences turn out to exist between European countries. Whereas in England and Ireland between 2% and 5% of children and adolescents are bullies, these rates are much higher in Italy (7–10%), Portugal (11%) and Spain (17%). Cross-cultural differences are also found for victims:

around 5% in Ireland, between 13 and 15% in England, Spain, and Portugal, and up to 26% in Italy (Eslea et al., 2003). Generally, it is believed that there is an age decline in bullying and victimization from childhood into adolescence (Smith, Madsen, & Moody, 1999). However, some studies show that this age decline may hold for self-reported victimization, but that peer reports and teacher reports do not confirm this age trend (Salmivalli, 2002).

Bullies as well as victims are characterized by specific psychosocial problems. Compared to non-involved children, bullies are found to be more aggressive, have fewer prosocial skills and are at risk for later problem behavior (Olweus, 1993). Recently, the idea that bullies are socially inadequate (i.e., the social skills deficit view of bullying) has been questioned (Sutton, Smith, & Swettenham, 1999a). It is believed that some bullies may display their behavior, because it offers them a tool to obtain socially desired goals, such as social status or dominance (Pellegrini & Long, 2002). Thus, these bullies may not lack social skills since they can accurately interpret social cues, but they use socially deviant strategies to obtain their goals. Indeed, in some research it has been found that the so-called 'ringleader' bullies – those who take the lead in bullying – are more able to understand the cognitions and emotions of peers than many other children (Sutton, Smith, & Swettenham, 1999b).

Victims are found to suffer from psychological forms of maladjustment. They tend to be more depressed and more lonely than non-victims. In addition, they are more generally and socially anxious, and tend to have negative views of themselves in the social domain and a lower self-esteem (see, for an overview, Hawker & Boulton, 2000). Victims are also found to suffer from social forms of maladjustment, in that they are more socially withdrawn, isolated, and socially rejected by peers. Although it is difficult to disentangle causes and consequences of victimization and socially maladjusted behavior, it is now widely recognized that bi-directional processes may exist. Victimization experiences may cause victims to develop specific behaviors such as withdrawal or submissive behaviors. At the same time victims

may exhibit behavioral difficulties that may contribute to victimization because their behavior may invite or reinforce bullies aggression towards them. For example, victims may reward their bullies by being insecure, compliant and submissive. Furthermore, victims may adapt their behavior to that of the bully, establishing a specific interactional pattern. This was nicely illustrated by an observational study of Menesini, Melan, and Pignatti in Italy (2000). When victims interacted with control children they were more willing to assert themselves by asking for help and explanation. However, when they interacted with bullies, they tended to express a different behavior style and were more likely to display submissive and compliant behavior.

During the last decade, bullying is increasingly viewed as a social phenomenon. Observational and survey studies have revealed that many peers are present during the bullying episodes and that 10 to 15% of the peers are willing to help the victim (Craig & Pepler, 1997; Sutton & Smith, 1999). These figures indicate that peers, more specifically friends, may intervene in some form to protect the victim. According to this 'friendship protection hypothesis' friends may protect in several ways. First, friends may threaten to retaliate or actually retaliate the bully. Second, friends may display social disapproval of the bully's behavior, resulting in possible loss of the bully's social status. Third, friends may give advice to the victim on how to react in socially threatening situations. Finally, by being in the company of friends, victims are less often alone, thus limiting opportunities to the bully to pinpoint the victim. Indeed, victims are found to have fewer reciprocal friends inside their class (Pellegrini & Long, 2002). However, the ability of friends to protect against victimization depends largely on their personal and social characteristics (e.g., Hodges, Malone, & Perry, 1997). For example, when a victim's friends are aggressive, bullies may be less inclined to target the victim (Pellegrini, Bartini, & Brooks, 1999), while having friends who are victimized themselves or who are physically less strong increases the risk for victimization (Salmivalli, Huttunen, & Lagerspetz, 1997). Given that the characteristics of friends are important for victimization, choosing friends who more or less constitute a risk factor may lead the victims to create the very social context that contributes to prolonged victimization.

As has been described, peer relations are very important during adolescence. Nevertheless, peers constitute only one part of the adolescent's social world. The other part is formed by the adolescent's family. In the next section, adolescents' relationships with their parents will be compared to their relationships with peers.

6. Parent–adolescent and peer relationships

Although peers play an increasingly important role in adolescents' lives, parents are still significant for adolescent adjustment. Even more, one cannot describe the role of peers without considering the parent–adolescent relationships. In comparing parent–adolescent relationships and friendships, we will consider both the effects of past parent–child relationships in terms of attachment and parenting practices as well as present parent–adolescent relationships and friendships. We will also describe perceived support as an important aspect of parent and peer relationships, and by which the relative importance of parents and friends can be compared.

There are two main theoretical viewpoints that focus on the parent–adolescent relationship and the adolescent friendships. On the one hand, there are theories that stress the different functions of parents and peers. On the other hand, there are theories that stress the convergence between parents and peers.

According to the first, different relationships offer different contexts for development. The most influential theory in this respect is Sullivan's (1953) interpersonal theory. As described before, Sullivan's theory suggests that different social needs emerge in different periods of life. Adolescents are embedded in myriad relationships and each of these relationships can offer fulfillment of various needs, such as the need for intimacy or companionship. Some relationships, however, are more effective in this need fulfillment. For example, during adolescence intimacy and companionship are provided more by the adolescent's friendships, whereas nurturance and attachment

are sought more in the parent–adolescent relationship. At the same time, the changes in friendship during adolescence coincide with important changes in family relationships. In adolescence, the child is concerned with the striving for autonomy (Steinberg, 1988) and the formation of identity (Erikson, 1968), which can result in a certain distancing or detachment from the parents (see also Blos, 1979). These processes are likely to change the relationships with parents, which may become less vertical in the end. Thus, adolescents seem to become less dependent on their parents and, at the same time, depend more on their friends. Friendships are thought to provide a unique context for development because, in this view, friendships differ on a number of dimensions that make them structurally different from parent–adolescent relationships. Sullivan (1953) argued that both types of relationship make unique, incremental contributions to the adolescent's development. In this sense, what is needed in friendship relationships cannot readily be learned in parent–adolescent relationships. In friendships adolescents may learn interpersonal competencies that are important in later close relationships, especially intimate and romantic relationships (Erikson, 1968). The reason for this is that friendships are more horizontal and based on equity and are therefore more similar to the future romantic relationships than the more vertical parent–adolescent relationship. Some empirical evidence for the theoretical assumption that friendships and parent–adolescent relationships may provide unique contexts for adjustment and development was partly found in the work by Furman and Buhrmester (1985) and Hunter and Youniss (1982). It was found that during early and middle adolescence there was a substantial increase in the importance of friends as intimate confidants, compared to parents. This increase, however, was relative, because although the friends' significance increased, the parents were also considered as intimate confidants, albeit at a lower level.

The second main theoretical viewpoint on relationships is found in attachment theory and related theories. Attachment theory assumes that competencies that are acquired in the early parent–child relationship experiences will manifest themselves in later relationships with friends. It is often believed that the early parent–child relationships are critical and that there is continuity in functioning across parent–child and friend relationships (see Cassidy & Shaver, 1999). This is because the early parent–child relationships serve as the basis for children's understanding of and participation in later familial and extra-familial relationships such as friendships. Early child's perceptions and understanding as well as expectations are incorporated in an internal working model (Bowlby, 1988; Bretherton, 1985). This internal working model is thought to influence the way the child enters new relationships in later life (Bretherton & Munholland, 1999). Secure attachment in early childhood will result in working models that, through peer interaction and subsequent competencies, may lead to the development of positive peer relationships in adolescence. An insecure attachment will lead to an internal working model in which interpersonal relationships are harmful or neglectful (Bretherton, 1985). In this respect, this theory assumes continuity of the developmental significance of relationships, and does not imply a unique developmental context for different types of relationship.

Some researchers take a more or less intermediate position between the assumptions that parents and peers have different functions or that they converge and are similar in function. In Germany, Krappmann (1996), for example, acknowledges that children increase their social competencies and abilities in different relationships and that new types of relationship, especially friendships in adolescence, offer unique possibilities for acquiring new skills. At the same time, early types of relationship are not fully abandoned and they exert influence on current relationships. In this developmental model earlier relationships continue to develop, thereby being influenced by the increased social competencies.

The theoretical framework used by Furman and Buhrmester (1985; Buhrmester, 1996; Furman & Buhrmester, 1992) is a modification of Sullivan's (1953) model, but incorporates other

theories as well, such as Weiss' (1974), and can therefore be seen as 'neo-Sullivanian' (Buhrmester, 1996, p. 159). Furman and Buhrmester (1985) argue that different relationships are best suited to fulfill different basic social needs but at the same time they suggest that the different relationships do not uniquely provide specific provisions. That is, although adolescents turn more to their friends for, for example, intimacy, the parents also still provide intimacy but to a lower degree (Furman & Buhrmester, 1985). Elsewhere, Buhrmester (1996) reports that friendship intimacy accounted uniquely for 16% of the variance of adolescents' interpersonal competence, while mother intimacy accounted uniquely for 9% of the variance. This finding indicates that friendships uniquely contribute to the development of social competence, independently from the parent–adolescent relationship, underlining the significant role friends play. At the same time, it shows that both parent–adolescent and friendship relationships should be considered when examining the effects of adolescents' relationships.

In Germany, Fend (1990) found that adolescents' ego strength was differentially related to parental and friend relationships. Adolescents with stable low ego strength already at age 13 perceived their friends to be more important than their parents, whereas for adolescents with a stable high ego strength parents turned out to be more important than friends until age 16. At that age, parents and friends were equally important. Also, Noack (1998) found that adolescents' relationships with parents who were high in control were related to lower school achievement, whereas high control shown by the friend was related to higher school achievement. A number of other studies (e.g., Ladd, 1989), regardless of their theoretical viewpoint, also confirm that family experiences as well as friendship experiences are important and interact in their associations with adolescent adjustment. Gauze, Bukowski, Aquan-Assee, and Sippola (1996) found that the experiences an adolescent has in the family influences the significance of having a high-quality or lower quality friendship. Adolescents who had negative friend experiences suffered less from a decrease in well-being if their parents were responsive to their demands.

These findings refer to the question whether relationships with parents can compensate for negative relationships with peers or vice versa. Especially in the parental and friend support role can compensatory or interacting effects of parent and friend relationships be examined. In general, adolescents perceive their close relationships with their friends as well as with their parents as supportive relationships (Berndt, 1988). Although during adolescence children seem to turn away from their parents in order to gain autonomy and independence, the support they perceive from their parents is still crucial. For example, parental support is related to adolescent adjustment in terms of substance use (Wills & Cleary, 1996), delinquency (Windle, 1992), emotional problems (Garnefski & Diekstra, 1996), and low self-esteem (van Aken & Asendorpf, 1997). But unlike any period in life before, the support adolescents perceive from their friends increases in importance, and equals or even surpasses the parental support.

In the scientific study of perceived support, two conceptualizations that either view support as a multidimensional or as a unidimensional construct are predominant. In the first conceptualization, the different dimensions or types of perceived support (cf. Cohen & Wills, 1985) are considered more important for the effects of support (see Scholte, van Lieshout, & van Aken, 2001). For example, Berndt (1988) distinguishes emotional support, instrumental support, information, and companionship support. Some of these dimensions overlap with the relationship dimensions that have been described by Furman and Buhrmester (1985), who identified 10 types of social provision, including affection and reliable alliance. Developmental changes indicate that on some support dimensions friends become more significant than parents. Hunter and Youniss (1982) found that perceived intimacy with friends increased systematically throughout adolescence and at age 15 surpassed the intimacy perceived from parents. Nurturance from friends also increased with increasing age, being equal to parental nurture at age 15 to age 19. In another study, Furman and Burhmester (1985) reported that, compared to friends, fathers and mothers were perceived as providing most affection, reliable alliance, enhancement of worth, and instrumental support. This indicates that parent–adolescent relationships are characterized by strong emotional bonds. From friends, by the same token, the adolescents perceived more companionship, and girls but not boys, experienced more intimacy from friends than from parents.

In these studies, then, support was considered to consist of separate dimensions and was assessed accordingly. In the second conceptualization, support is considered as a uni-dimensional construct and measured using one (aggregated) measure. Empirical evidence (Cohen, Sherrod, & Clark, 1986) indeed shows that strong correlations exist between various dimensions and that it is therefore appropriate to combine the dimensions and use this combined measure as the primary measure of support. In one study, Furman and Buhrmester (1992) examined the support that 9 to 19 year olds perceived from parents, friends, and romantic partners. In this study, because the six types of support they initially distinguished were highly correlated, support was assessed as a uni-dimensional construct. Age trends indicated that 9 year olds perceived their parents as most supportive, whereas at age 12, parents and friends were perceived equally supportive. From age 15 on, however, friends were perceived as being more supportive than parents. In our own study in the Netherlands, however (Scholte et al., 2001), we found that although during adolescence parents gradually declined and friends increased as providers of support, friends never surpassed the parents.

As regards compensatory effects, an important question is whether low support perceived from one relationship can be compensated by support from another relationship. That is, relationships may contribute uniquely to adolescent adjustment and thus compensate other relationships but relationships may also interact with each other. A number of studies has examined these compensatory patterns in terms of levels of support or in terms of differential effects of support that adolescents perceive in different relationships. Both compensatory processes can only be understood properly in a social network approach, in which different relationships are analyzed simultaneously. In several studies it has been found that low support from one relationship can be compensated by higher support from other relationships, but also that support from some relationships cannot be compensated. For example, East and Rook (1996) found that adolescents with low schoolfriend support derived relatively high sibling support. Although this sibling support was associated to lower anxiety, the effects of the compensations were minor since these adolescents remained less well-adjusted than the average adolescents. Thus, sibling support may not fully protect against the negative effects of low friend support. Similarly, Gauze et al. (1996) argued that adolescents are 'active consumers of social support', who may turn to different relationships once others do not provide satisfactory support. By doing so, the adolescents may compensate for the negative effects of the unsatisfactory support. The study of Gauze et al. (1996) revealed that friendships had enhanced significance and served as a more important source of support for adolescents who had low parental support than it did for adolescents who came from supportive families.

In a German study, van Aken and Asendorpf (1997) showed that sibling support did not compensate for low classmate support. In addition, low support from one parent could only be compensated by the support from the other parent in predicting early adolescents' general self-worth. Other studies show that support perceived from parents and from friends can have differential effects on adolescent adjustment. Reicher (1993), for example, reported that family and peer relationships had a different impact on social emotional problems. Adolescents with low parental support but high peer support showed the highest internalizing and externalizing problems, higher than all other adolescents, including those who had a low parental and low friend support. This indicates that the effects of low parental support cannot be compensated by peer relationships, and, furthermore, that some configurations of support (e.g., low parental and high peer support) can even have detrimental effects for adolescent

adjustment. In one of our own studies (Scholte et al., 2001), we used a person-centered approach to examine whether subgroups of adolescents with different configurations of parental, sibling, and friend support would exist. Results indicated that for the majority of the five groups that were found, the level of support was constant across each of these relationships. Adolescents who perceived high or average mother support also reported high or average father support, as well as high or average sibling and friend support. Surprisingly, this also held for adolescents reporting low support from all network members. This indicates that for this group no compensatory effects seemed to be present. This was also true for adolescents who reported not having a best friend: they did not turn more to their parents or siblings for support. Only a small group of adolescents, those who reported an extremely low parental support (around 9% of all adolescents under study) compensated for this low level of support by turning to their best friends for support. Compensation in terms of effects of support, however, did not occur. As was found by Reicher (1993), the adolescents who showed this configuration of perceived support were least well-adjusted. Of all adolescents, they scored highest on externalizing problems such as delinquency, substance use, and peer reported aggression and disruptiveness, as well as on some internalizing problems.

Whereas these studies focused primarily on the significance of adolescents' support perceived in the relationships with parents and peers, other studies have focused on the relation between parenting practices and adolescent adjustment. The social interaction model or coercion model, which has been widely studied by the Oregon Social Learning Centre research team (Dishion, Patterson, Stoolmiller, & Skinner, 1991), suggests that adolescent delinquency is primarily influenced by parents and peers. Nevertheless, adolescents' own deviant characteristics (e.g., personality) may also contribute to delinquency (Cairns et al., 1988). Maladaptive parenting practices consisting of harsh, inconsistent and negative parenting are believed to foster anti-social attitudes and behaviors both in the present

(Patterson, 1980) and in the future (Farrington, 1978). Aversive child behavior is reinforced within negative reciprocal parent–child exchanges (Patterson, 1982). Children learn to control and reduce their parents' limit setting by coercion, that is, by escalating aversive behavior. In the coercive interaction patterns parents reinforce their children for increasing hostile behaviors in conflict situations. The family thus constitutes the 'training ground' for deviant antisocial behavior (Bierman & Wargo, 1995). This coercive behavior may also be displayed in peer relations since children may learn to gain supremacy in peer contexts if proven successful. Evidence for the transfer of coercive behaviors from the parent–child relationship to the friendship context comes from a study by Dishion, Patterson, and Kavanagh (1992), who found that the antisocial friendships of 13- and 14-year-old adolescents provided another context in which the adolescents displayed coercive interactions. In addition, the adolescent's antisocial behaviors and attitudes may lead to peer affiliation with delinquent friends and these friendships may provide new opportunities for learning and refining antisocial and delinquent behaviors. Not only parenting practices in the past (i.e., childhood) but also in the present (i.e., adolescence) may contribute to adolescent delinquency and antisocial behavior. It is argued that parent–adolescent relationships that lack parental control and monitoring may provide the opportunity for adolescents to meet and affiliate with delinquent friends (Dishion et al., 1991). Close parental monitoring and supervision may influence the friendship choice or even encourage the dissolution of delinquent friendships. Brendgen, Vitaro, and Bukowski (2000) showed that parental monitoring distinguished adolescents who changed from delinquent to non-delinquent friends from those who maintained their delinquent friendship.

Positive parent–adolescent relationships may contribute to adolescent development and adjustment, while maladaptive parenting practices and disturbed relationships may lead to adolescent maladjustment. Disturbed relationships should be distinguished from conflicts between parents and adolescents. Although many disturbed relationships show conflicts, conflicts not necessarily lead to disturbances in the parent–adolescent relationship. As was shown in friendships, conflicts are ubiquitous in adolescent relationships and conflicts with parents, especially with the mother, may even be normative in adolescence (Laursen, 1993). Research in the USA shows that the person the adolescent has most frequent conflicts with is the mother, even more so for daughters than for sons. Whereas adolescents had one conflict with friends every six hours of interaction, the frequency of conflicts with mother was one conflict every hour of interaction (Laursen, 1995). European studies (e.g., Noack & Fingerle, 1994) also reveal that interactions with parents are more characterized by disagreement than are interactions with friends. In contrast to conflicts with friends that reflect a growing need for intimacy, equality, and reciprocity (Youniss & Smollar, 1985), conflicts with parents reflect the adolescent's striving for independence and greater control over their own lives.

Despite these frequent conflicts the parents normally remain an important source for nurturance and support (Furman & Buhrmester, 1985; Youniss & Smollar, 1985). This is because the impact of conflicts decreases with interdependence: the closest relationships usually show the most frequent but at the same time the least disruptive conflicts (Laursen, 1993). Family relationships are regulated by kinship and norms, and therefore they do not change easily and remain relatively immune for disruption. In general, parents and adolescents are able to accept conflicts as a normal part of everyday life that do not necessarily have long-term negative effects.

Thus, it shows that relationship systems, such as parent–adolescent and peer relationships are interrelated (Hinde, 1997). Continuities exist between relationship systems and these continuities probably predict developmental outcomes better than does the examination of only the parent–adolescent relationships or the peer relationships. In other words, parent–adolescent relationships and peer relationships are not separate worlds and the significance of one relationship system for adolescent development cannot be acknowledged without examining the other system.

7. Conclusion

In this chapter, various aspects of adolescents' peer relationships have been described, including adolescents' friendships, social status and the causes and consequences of rejection by peers, as well as adolescents' relationships in the larger society, that is, the youth culture. It was documented that peer relationships are of great importance for adolescent adjustment, as are adolescents' relationships with their parents.

The review in this chapter has been based not only on research conducted in the USA, but also incorporated many European studies. Nevertheless, it is difficult to infer cultural differences in peer relations between Western and non-Western countries, between Europe and the USA, or between countries within Europe. What is needed is more elaborated cross-cultural research that does not just compare different cultures, but is guided by theoretical ideas and provides a justification for cross-cultural comparison. This kind of research may be able to test hypotheses about characteristics or features of cultures that affect peer relations and lead to cultural differences in these relations. For example, one such feature is whether a culture can be characterized as collectivistic or individualistic (Schneider, 2000).

Collectivistic cultures place a higher value on group identity and collective responsibility compared to individualistic cultures that favor individual autonomy and responsibility. In a cross-cultural comparison of peer interactions between children in the collectivistic Spanish culture and the more individualistic Dutch culture, Goudena and Sanchez (1996) found that Spanish children interacted more frequently with larger groups of peers, while Dutch children interacted more frequently with dyads or small groups. In addition, in collectivistic cultures, the extended family – consisting of cousins, aunts and uncles, grandparents – plays a far more important role in people's everyday life compared to more individualistic cultures. It can be assumed that because these extended-family members provide emotional and instrumental support, children

and adolescents in collectivistic cultures may have to rely less on friends than do children in individualistic cultures (Schneider, 2000).

By the same token, cross-cultural research will not only be able to detect and examine cultural differences, but will also be able to reveal similarities in peer relations. For example, it can be expected that friendships have some functions that are present in all cultures and are therefore universal. Friendships may provide the opportunity and secure base for adolescents to talk about issues that are inappropriate to talk about with others (Krappmann, 1996).

In sum, theory-driven cross-cultural comparison may describe cultural differences as well as similarities in peer relations and will significantly broaden our understanding of these relationships. Because most studies on peer relations to date are based on children, the need for research on adolescents becomes apparent.

References

Aboud, F.E., & Mendelson, M.J. (1996). Determinants of friendship selection and quality: Developmental perspectives. In W. M. Bukowski, A. N. Newcomb, & W. W. Hartup (Eds.), *The company they keep: Friendship in childhood and adolescence* (pp. 87–112). New York: Cambridge University Press.

Albrecht, H.T., & Silbereisen, R.K. (1993). Risikofaktoren für Peerablehnung im Jugendalter: Chronische Belastungen und akute Beeinträchtigungen [Risk factors for peer rejection in adolescence: Chronic and acute stressors]. *Zeitschrift für Entwicklungspsychologie und Pädagogische Psychologie, 25*, 1–28.

Berndt, T.J. (1988). Obtaining support from friends during childhood and adolescence. In D. Belle (Ed.), *Children's social networks and social supports* (pp. 308–331). New York: John Wiley & Sons.

Berndt, T.J. (1996). Exploring the effects of friendship quality on social development. In W. M. Bukowski, A. N. Newcomb, & W. W. Hartup (Eds.), *The company they keep: Friendship in childhood and adolescence* (pp. 346–365). New York: Cambridge University Press.

Berndt, T.J. (2004). Children's friendships: Shifts over a half-century in perspectives on their development and their effects. *Merrill-Palmer Quarterly, 50*, 206–223.

Berndt, T.J., & Hanna, N.A. (1995). Intimacy and self-disclosure in friendships. In K. J. Rotenberg (Ed.),

Disclosure processes in children and adolescents (pp. 57–77). New York: Cambridge University Press.

Berndt, T.J., & Keefe, K. (1995). Friends' influence on adolescents' adjustment to school. *Child Development, 66*, 1312–1329.

Bierman, K.L., Smoot, D.L., & Aumiller, K. (1993). Characteristics of aggressive–rejected, aggressive (non-rejected), and rejected (non-aggressive) boys. *Child Development, 64*, 139–151.

Bierman, K.L., & Wargo, J.B. (1995). Predicting the longitudinal course associated with aggressive–rejected, aggressive (non-rejected), and rejected (non-aggressive) status. *Development and Psychopathology, 7*, 669–682.

Blos, P. (1979). *The adolescent passage.* New York: International Universities Press.

Boivin, M., & Begin, G. (1989). Peer status and self-perception among early elementary school children: The case of the rejected children. *Child Development, 60*, 591–596.

Bowlby, J. (1988). *A secure base: Parent–child attachment and healthy human development.* New York: Basic Books.

Brendgen, M., Vitaro, F., & Bukowksi, W.B. (2000). Stability and variability of adolescents' affiliation with delinquent friends: Predictors and consequences. *Social Development, 9*, 205–225.

Bretherton, I. (1985). Attachment theory: Retrospect and prospect. In I. Bretherton, & E. Waters (Eds.), Growing points of attachment theory and research. *Monographs of the Society for Research in Child Development, 50*, 3–35.

Bretherton, I., & Munholland, K.A. (1999). Internal working models in attachment relationships: A construct revisited. In J. Cassidy, & P. R. Shaver (Eds.), *Handbook of attachment: Theory, research, and clinical implications* (pp. 89–111). New York: Guilford.

Brown, B.B. (1990). Peer groups and peer cultures. In S. S. Feldman, & G. R. Elliott (Eds.), *At the threshold: The developing adolescent* (pp. 171–196). Cambridge, MA: Harvard University Press.

Brown, B.B., Dolcini, M.M., & Leventhal, A. (1997). Transformations in peer relationships at adolescence: Implications for health-related behavior. In J. Schulenberg, J. L. Maggs, & K. Hurrelmann (Eds.), *Health risk and developmental transitions during adolescence* (pp. 161–189). Cambridge, MA: Cambridge University Press.

Brown, B.B., Lamborn, S.D., Mounts, N.S., & Steinberg, L. (1993). Parenting practices and peer group affiliation in adolescence. *Child Development, 64*, 467–482.

Brown, B.B., Morey, M.S., & Kinney, D. (1994). Casting adolescent crowds in relational perspective: Caricature, channel and context. In R. Montemayor, G. R. Adams, & T. P. Gullotta (Eds.), *Advances in adolescent development: Vol.6. Personal relationships during adolescence* (pp. 123–167). Thousand Oaks, CA: Sage.

Buhrmester, D. (1990). Intimacy of friendship, interpersonal competence, and adjustment during preadolescence and adolescence. *Child Development, 61*, 1101–1111.

Buhrmester, D. (1996). Need fulfillment, interpersonal competence, and the developmental contexts of early adolescent friendship. In W. M. Bukowski, A. F. Newcomb, & W. W. Hartup (Eds.), *The company they keep: Friendship in childhood and adolescence* (pp. 158–185). New York: Cambridge University Press.

Bukowski, W.M., Newcomb, A.F., & Hoza, B. (1987). Friendship conceptions among early adolescents: A longitudinal study of stability and change. *Journal of Early Adolescence, 7*, 143–152.

Burk, W.J., & Laursen, B. (2005). Adolescent perceptions of friendship and their associations with individual adjustment. *International Journal of Behavioral Development, 29*, 156–164.

Busch, L. (1998). Gruppenkultur als Indikator für eine deviante Orientierung von Cliquen im Jugendalter: Entwicklung einer Skala zur Erfassung der Gruppenkultur [Group culture as an indicator of deviant clique orientation in adolescence: Development of a scale to assess group culture]. *Gruppendynamik, 29*, 421–432.

Cairns, R.B., Cairns, B.D., Neckerman, H.J., Gest, S.D., & Gariepy, J.L. (1988). Social networks and aggressive behavior: Peer support or peer rejection? *Developmental Psychology, 24*, 815–823.

Cairns, R.B., Leung, M., Buchanan, L., & Cairns, B.D. (1995). Friendships and social networks in childhood and adolescence: Fluidity, reliability, and interrelations. *Child Development, 66*, 1330–1345.

Cassidy, J., & Shaver, P.R. (1999). *Handbook of attachment: Theory, research, and clinical applications.* New York: Guilford.

Cavior, N., & Dokecki, P.R. (1973). Physical attractiveness, perceived attitude similarity, and academic achievement as contributors to interpersonal attraction among adolescents. *Developmental Psychology, 9*, 44–54.

Chassin, L., Presson, C.C., Montello, D., Sherman, S.J,. & McGrew, J. (1986). Changes in peer and parent influence during adolescence: Longitudinal versus cross-sectional perspectives on smoking initiation. *Developmental Psychology*, *22*, 327–334.

Cillessen, A.H.N., & ten Brink, P.W.M. (1991). Vaststelling van relaties met leeftijdgenoten [Assessment of relationships with peers]. *Pedagogische Studiën*, *68*, 1–14.

Cillessen, A.H.N., Bukowski, W.M., & Haselager, G.J.T. (2000). Stability of sociometric categories. In A. H. N. Cillessen, & W. M. Bukowski (Eds.), *Recent advances in the measurement of acceptance and rejection in the peer system* (pp. 75–93). San Francisco: Jossey-Bass.

Cohen, S., Sherrod, D.R., & Clark, M.S. (1986). Social skills and the stress-protective role of social support. *Journal of Personality and Social Psychology*, *50*, 963–973.

Cohen, S., & Wills, T.A. (1985). Stress, social support, and the buffering hypothesis. *Psychological Bulletin*, *98*, 310–357.

Coie, J.D., & Dodge, K.A. (1983). Continuities and changes in children's sociometric status: A five-year longitudinal study. *Merrill-Palmer Quarterly*, *29*, 261–282.

Coie, J.D., Dodge, K.A., & Coppotelli, H.A. (1982). Dimensions and types of social status: A cross-age perspective. *Developmental Psychology*, *18*, 557–569.

Coie, J.D., & Kupersmidt, J.B. (1983). A behavioral analysis of emerging social status in boys' groups. *Child Development*, *54*, 1400–1416.

Coleman, J.S. (1961). *The adolescent society*. New York: Free Press.

Craig, D., & Pepler, W. (1997). Observations of bullying and victimization in the schoolyard. *Canadian Journal of School Psychology*, *2*, 41–60.

Crick, N.R., & Dodge, K.A. (1994). A review and reformulation of social information processing mechanisms in children's social adjustment. *Psychological Bulletin*, *115*, 74–101.

Dishion, T.J., Andrews, D.W., & Crosby, L. (1995). Antisocial boys and their friendships in early adolescence: Relationship characteristics, quality, and interactional process. *Child Development*, *66*, 139–151.

Dishion, T.J., McCord, J., & Poulin, F. (1999). When interventions harm. *American Psychologist*, *54*, 755–764.

Dishion, T.J., Patterson, G.R., & Griesler, P. (1994). Peer adaptations in the development of antisocial behavior: A confluence model. In L. R. Huesmann (Ed.), *Aggressive behavior: Current perspectives* (pp. 61–95). New York: Plenum.

Dishion, T.J., Patterson, G.R., & Kavanagh, K.A. (1992). An experimental test of the coercion model: Linking theory, measurement, and intervention. In J. McCord, & R. E. Tremblay (Eds.), *Preventing antisocial behavior: Interventions from birth through adolescence* (pp. 253–282). New York: Guilford.

Dishion, T.J., Patterson, G.R., Stoolmiller, M., & Skinner, M.L. (1991). Family, school, and behavioral antecedents to early adolescent involvement with antisocial peers. *Developmental Psychology*, *27*, 172–180.

East, P.L. (1991). The parent–child relationships of withdrawn, aggressive, and sociable children: Child and parent perspectives. *Merrill-Palmer Quarterly*, *37*, 425–444.

East, P.L., & Rook, K.S. (1992). Compensatory patterns of support among children's peer relationships: A test using school friends, nonschool friends, and siblings. *Developmental Psychology*, *28*, 163–172.

Elkin, F., & Handel, G. (1989). *The child and society* (5th ed.). New York: Random House.

Epstein, J.L. (1983). Examining theories of adolescent friendship. In J. L. Epstein, & N. L. Kanweit (Eds.), *Friends in school* (pp. 39–61). New York: Academic Press.

Erikson, E.H. (1968). *Identity: Youth and crisis*. New York: Norton.

Eslea, M., Menesini, E., Morita, Y., O'Moore, M., Mora-Merchán, J.A., Pereira, B. et al. (2003). Friendship and loneliness among bullies and victims: Data from seven countries. *Aggressive Behavior*, *30*, 71–83.

Farmer, T.W., & Rodkin, P.C. (1996). Antisocial and prosocial correlates of classroom social positions: The social network centrality perspective. *Social Development*, *5*, 174–188.

Farrington, D.P. (1978). The family background of aggressive youths. In L. A. Hersov, & M. Berger (Eds.), *Aggression and antisocial behavior in childhood and adolescence* (pp. 73–93). Oxford: Pergamon.

Fend, H. (1990). Ego-strength development and pattern of social relationships. In H. A. Bosma, & A. E. Jackson (Eds.), *Coping and self-concept in adolescence* (pp. 87–109). Heidelberg, Germany: Springer-Verlag.

Furman, W., & Buhrmester, D. (1985). Children's perceptions of the personal relationships in their social networks. *Developmental Psychology*, *21*, 1016–1024.

Furman, W., & Buhrmester, D. (1992). Age and sex

differences in perceptions of networks of personal relationships. *Child Development, 63*, 103–115.

Garnefski, N., & Diekstra, R.F.W. (1996). Perceived social support from family, school, and peers: Relationship with emotional and behavioral problems among adolescents. *Journal of the American Academy of Child and Adolescent Psychiatry, 35*, 1657–1664.

Gauze, G., Bukowski, W.M., Aquan-Assee, J., & Sippola, L.K. (1996). Interactions between family environment and friendship and associations with self-perceived well-being during adolescence. *Child Development, 67*, 2201–2216.

Goossens, L., Scholte, R.H.J., van Aken, M.A.G., & Hildebrand, A. (2000, July). Loneliness, depression, and personality: Associations with sociometric status and peer reputation in early adolescence. In B. Laursen, & W. M. Bukowski (Chairs), *The self and peer relationships.* Symposium conducted at the XVIth Biennial Meetings of the International Society for the Study of Behavioral Development (ISSBD), Bejing, China.

Goudena, P., & Sanchez, J.A. (1996). Peer interaction in Andalusia and Holland: A comparative study. *Infancia y Aprentizaje, 75*, 49–58.

Harter, S. (1990). Causes, correlates, and the functional role of global self-worth: A life-span perspective. In J. Kolligian & R. Sternberg (Eds.), *Perceptions of competence and incompetence across the life-span* (pp. 67–98). New Haven, CT: Yale University Press.

Hartup, W.W. (1983). Peer relations. In P. H. Mussen, & E. M. Hetherington (Eds.), *Handbook of child psychology: Vol. 4. Socialization, personality, and social development* (4th ed., pp. 103–196). New York: John Wiley & Sons.

Hartup, W.W. (1989). Behavioral manifestations of children's friendships. In T. J. Berndt, & G. Ladd (Eds.), *Peer relations in child development* (pp. 46–70). New York: John Wiley & Sons.

Hartup, W.W. (1993). Adolescents and their friends. In B. Laursen (Ed.), *Close friendships in adolescence* (pp. 3–22), San Francisco: Jossey-Bass.

Hartup, W.W. (1996). The company they keep: Friendships and their developmental significance. *Child Development, 67*, 1–13.

Hatzichristou, C., & Hopf, D. (1996). A multiperspective comparison of peer sociometric status groups in childhood and adolescence. *Child Development, 67*, 1085–1102.

Hawker, D.S.J., & Boulton, M.J. (2000). Twenty years' research on peer victimization and psycho-social maladjustment: A meta-analytic review of cross-sectional studies. *Journal of Child Psychology and Psychiatry and Allied Disciplines, 41*, 441–455.

Hinde, R.A. (1997). *Relations: A dialectical perspective.* Hove: Psychology Press.

Hodges, E.V., Malone, M.J., & Perry, D.G. (1997). Individual risk and social risk as interacting determinants of victimization in the peer group. *Developmental Psychology, 33*, 1032–1039.

Hunter, F.T., & Youniss, J. (1982). Changes in functions of three relationships during adolescence. *Developmental Psychology, 18*, 806–811.

Hymel, S., Wagner, E., & Butler, L.J. (1990). Reputational bias: View from the peer group. In S. R. Asher, & J. D. Coie (Eds.), *Peer rejection in childhood* (pp. 156–186). New York: Cambridge University Press.

Junger-Tas, J., & van Kesteren, J. (1999). *Bullying and delinquency in a Dutch school population.* Den Haag, The Netherlands: Kugler.

Kandel, D.B. (1978). Similarity in real-life adolescent friendship pairs. *Journal of Personality and Social Psychology, 36*, 306–312.

Kandel, D.B., & Andrews, K. (1987). Processes of adolescent socialization by parents and peers. *International Journal of the Addictions, 22*, 319–342.

Kirchler, E., Palmonari, A., & Pombeni, M.L. (1992). Auf der Suche nach einem Weg ins Erwachsenenalter [Searching for a way into adulthood]. *Psychologie in Erziehung und Unterricht, 39*, 277–295.

Krappmann, L. (1991). Sozialisation in der Gruppe der Gleichaltrigen [Socialization in peer groups]. In K. Hurrelmann, & D. Ulich (Eds.), *Neues Handbuch der Sozialforschung* (pp. 82–104). Weinheim, Germany: Beltz.

Krappmann, L. (1996). The development of diverse social relationships in the social world of childhood. In A. E. Auhagen, & M. von Salisch (Eds.), *The diversity of human relationships* (pp. 36–58). New York: Cambridge University Press.

Ladd, G.W. (1989). Children's social competence and social supports: Precursors of early school adjustment? In B. H. Schneider, G. Attili, J. Nadel, & R. P. Weissberg (Eds.), *Social competence in developmental perspective* (pp. 277–291). Norwell, MA: Kluwer Academic Publishers.

Laursen, B. (1993). The perceived impact of conflict on adolescent relationships. *Merrill-Palmer Quarterly, 39*, 535–550.

Laursen, B. (1995). Conflict and social interaction in adolescent relationships. *Journal of Research on Adolescence, 5*, 55–70.

Malik, N.M., & Furman, W. (1993). Problems in children's peer relations: What can the clinician do? *Journal of Child Psychology and Psychiatry and Allied Disciplines, 34,* 1303–1326.

Mead, G.H. (1934). *Mind, self and society.* Chicago, IL: University of Chicago Press.

Menesini, E., Melan, E., & Pignatti, B. (2000). Interactional styles of bullies and victims observed in a competitive and cooperative setting. *The Journal of Genetic Psychology, 161,* 261–281.

Montemayor, R., & Gregg, V.R. (1994). Current theory and research on personal relationships during adolescence. In R. Montemayor, G. R. Adams, & T. P. Gullotta (Eds.), *Advances in adolescent development: Volume 6. Personal relationships during adolescence* (pp. 236–245). Thousand Oaks, CA: Sage.

Musitu, G. (1982). *La integración del rechazado escolar* [Integrating rejected students in school]. Actas de las II Jornadas de Orientación Escolar y Profesional (pp. 407–428). Valencia, Spain.

Newcomb, A.F., & Bagwell, C.L. (1995). Children's friendship reactions: A meta-analytic review. *Psychological Bulletin, 117,* 306–347.

Newcomb, A.F., & Bukowski, W.M. (1983). Social impact and social preference as determinants of children's peer group status. *Developmental Psychology, 19,* 856–867.

Newcomb, A.F., Bukowski, W.M., & Pattee, L. (1993). Children's peer relations: A meta analytic review of popular, rejected, neglected, controversial, and average sociometric status. *Psychological Bulletin, 113,* 99–128.

Noack, P. (1990). *Jugendentwicklung im Kontext: Zum aktiven Umgang mit sozialen Entwicklungsaufgaben in der Freizeit* [Adolescent development in context: Toward active coping with developmental tasks in leisure time]. Munich, Germany: Psychologie Verlags Union.

Noack, P. (1998). School achievement and adolescents' interactions with their fathers, mothers, and friends. *European Journal of Psychology of Education, 13,* 503–513.

Noack, P., & Fingerle, M. (1994). Gespräche Jugendlicher mit Eltern und gleichaltrigen Freunden [Adolescents' conversations with parents and same-age friends]. *Zeitschrift für Entwicklungspsychologie und Pädagogische Psychologie, 26,* 331–349.

Olweus, D. (1993). *Bullying at school: What we know and what we can do.* Oxford: Blackwell.

Palmonari, A., Kirchler, E., & Pombeni, M.L. (1991). Differential effects of identification with family and peers on coping with developmental tasks in adolescence. *European Journal of Social Psychology, 21,* 381–402.

Parker, J.G., & Asher, S.R. (1987). Peer relations and later personal adjustment: Are low-accepted children at risk? *Psychological Bulletin, 102,* 357–387.

Parkhurst, J.T., & Asher, S.R. (1992). Peer rejection in middle school: Subgroup differences in behavior, loneliness, and interpersonal concerns. *Developmental Psychology, 28,* 231–241.

Patterson, G.R. (1980). Mothers: The unacknowledged victims. *Monographs of the Society for Research in Child Development, 45* (5, Serial No. 186).

Patterson, G.R. (1982). *Coercive family process.* Eugene, OR: Castalia.

Pellegrini, A.D., Bartini, M., & Brooks, F. (1999). School bullies, victims, and aggressive victims: Factors relating to group affiliation and victimization in early adolescence. *Journal of Educational Psychology, 91,* 216–224.

Pellegrini, A.D., & Long, J.D. (2002). A longitudinal study of bullying, dominance and victimisation during the transition from primary to secondary school. *British Journal of Developmental Psychology, 20,* 259–280.

Pombeni, M.L., Kirchler, E., & Palmonari, A. (1990). Identification with peers as a strategy to muddle through the troubles of the adolescent years. *Journal of Adolescence, 13,* 351–369.

Reicher, H. (1993). Family and peer relations and social–emotional problems in adolescence. *Studia Psychologica, 35,* 403–408.

Rubin, K.H. (1990). Introduction. *Human Development, 33,* 221–224.

Rubin, K.H., LeMare, L.J., & Lollis, S. (1990). Social withdrawal in childhood: Developmental pathways to peer rejection. In S. R. Asher, & J. D. Coie (Eds.), *Peer rejection in childhood* (pp. 217–249). New York: Cambridge University Press.

Salmivalli, C. (2002). Is there an age decline in victimization by peers at school? *Educational Research, 44,* 269–277.

Salmivalli, C., Huttunen, A., Lagerspetz, K.M.J. (1997). Peer networks and bullying in schools. *Scandinavian Journal of Psychology, 38,* 305–312.

Schneider, B.H. (2000). *Friends and enemies: Peer relations in childhood.* London: Arnold.

Scholte, R.H.J. (1998). *Adolescent relationships.* Unpublished doctoral dissertation, University of Nijmegen, The Netherlands.

Scholte, R.H.J., van Lieshout, C.F.M., & van Aken, M.A.G. (2001). Perceived relational support in adolescence: Dimensions, configurations, and adolescent adjustment. *Journal of Research on Adolescence, 11*, 71–94.

Selman, R.L. (1980). *The growth of interpersonal understanding: Developmental and clinical analyses.* New York: Academic Press.

Shantz, C.U., & Hartup, W.W. (Eds.). (1992). *Conflict in child and adolescent development.* New York: Cambridge University Press.

Smith, P.K., Madsen, K., & Moody, J. (1999). What causes the age decline in reports of being bullied at school? Towards a developmental analysis of risks of being bullied. *Educational Research, 41*, 267–285.

Smith, P.K., Morita, Y., Junger-Tas, J., Olweus, D., Catalano, R., & Slee, P. (Eds). (1999). *The nature of school bullying: A cross-national perspective.* London: Routledge.

Solberg, M.E., & Olweus, D. (2003). Prevalence estimation of school bullying with the Olweus Bully/Victim Questionnaire. *Aggressive Behavior, 29*, 239–268.

Stattin, H., & Magnusson, D. (1990). *Pubertal maturation in female development.* Hillsdale, NJ: Lawrence Erlbaum Associates, Inc.

Steinberg, L. (1988). Reciprocal relation between parent–child distance and pubertal maturation. *Developmental Psychology, 24*, 122–128.

Sullivan, H.S. (1953). *The interpersonal theory of psychiatry.* New York: Norton.

Sutton, J., & Smith, P.K. (1999). Bullying as a group process: An adaptation of the participant role approach. *Aggressive Behavior, 25*, 97–111.

Sutton, J., Smith, P.K., & Swettenham, J. (1999a). Social cognition and bullying: Social inadequacy or skilled manipulation? *British Journal of Developmental Psychology, 17*, 435–450.

Sutton, J., Smith, P.K., & Swettenham, J. (1999b). Bullying and 'theory of mind': A critique of the 'Social skills deficit' view of anti-social behaviour. *Social Development, 8*, 117–127.

Swann, W.B., Jr., Griffin, J.J., Jr., Predmore, S.C., & Gaines, B. (1987). The cognitive affective crossfire: When self-consistency confronts self-enhancement. *Journal of Personality and Social Psychology, 52*, 881–889.

Thurlow, C. (2002). High-schoolers' peer orientation priorities: A snapshot. *Journal of Adolescence, 25*, 341–349.

van Aken, M.A., & Asendorpf, J.B. (1997). Support by parents, classmates, friends and siblings in pre-adolescence: Covariation and compensation across relationships. *Journal of Social and Personal Relationships, 14*, 79–93.

Weiss, R. (1974). The provisions of social relationships. In Z. Rubin (Ed.), *Doing unto others* (pp. 17–25). Englewood Cliffs, NJ: Prentice Hall.

Wills, T.A., & Cleary, S.D. (1996). How are social support effects mediated? A test with parental support and adolescent substance use. *Journal of Personality and Social Psychology, 71*, 937–952.

Windle, M. (1992). A longitudinal study of stress buffering for adolescent problem behaviors. *Developmental Psychology, 28*, 522–530.

Youniss, J., & Damon, W. (1992). Social construction in Piaget's theory. In H. Beilin, & P. B. Pufall (Eds.), *Piaget's theory: Prospects and possibilities* (pp. 267–286). Hillsdale, NJ: Lawrence Erlbaum Associates, Inc.

Youniss, J., McLellan, J.A., & Strouse, D. (1994). 'We're popular, but we're not snobs': Adolescents describe their crowds. In R. Montemayor, G. R. Adams, & T. P. Gullotta (Eds.), *Advances in adolescent development, Vol. 6: Personal relationships during adolescence* (pp. 101–122). Thousand Oaks, CA: Sage.

Youniss, J., & Smollar, J. (1985). *Adolescent relations with mothers, fathers and friends.* Chicago, IL: University of Chicago Press.

11

Sexuality and intimate relationships in adolescence

Bruna Zani and Elvira Cicognani

LEARNING OBJECTIVES

The aims of this chapter are to investigate the emergence and development of affective and sexual relationships during adolescence. Specifically, we will discuss the social and cultural context in which today's adolescents develop their affective relationships, the emergence of romantic and sexual relationships, patterns of sexual activity, preventive behaviors and risk taking in the domain of sexual relationships, and pregnancy and abortion during adolescence.

The social and cultural context in which today's adolescents develop their gender identity and begin to form affective and sexual relationships has changed considerably during the last 30–40 years. These changes have profound implications for the development of male and female gender identity during adolescence and will be mentioned in the first part of the chapter. The emergence of romantic feelings and the beginning of dating relationships will be the focus of the second part of the chapter, where we will examine how they can positively affect adolescents' development and the existing pattern of relationships with the family and the peer group. We will then move on to the issue of adolescents' patterns of sexual activity, the processes and motivations involved in the transition to coitus. An important issue concerns risk taking behaviors in the domain of sexual activity: we will examine the extent to which adolescents are taking risks from the point of view of unwanted pregnancies and HIV, and we will discuss the main theoretical explanations for such a tendency. Finally, the issue of what happens when precautionary behaviors fail (adolescent pregnancy and abortion) will be the focus of attention.

1. Introduction

1.1 Social context of adolescent romantic and sexual relationships

Over the last 40 years, in contemporary industrialized society, there have been a series of radical cultural and social changes which have had a profound effect on gender roles. In all societies, the behavior of women and men is differentiated: they are expected to hold different positions, exhibit different patterns of behavior and manifest different personality traits. All these aspects are defined by social norms and conventions that specify assigned characteristics and positions.

This change is oriented towards a diminution of the differentiation between male and female roles, by means of a reduction in stereotypic patterns of both roles and the adoption of certain characteristics of the opposite role. Since the early 1980s, the major evidence for sex role change has been reflected in labor force participation, selected aspects of family role patterns and circumstances, and sexuality.

Changes in the sphere of sexuality between male and female adolescents have occurred in the following three areas:

- a change in the *models* that regulate sexual behavior. The 'double standard' (premarital relationship is all right for the man but not for the woman), which was prevalent until the 1950s, has undergone change. Society moved away from a standard of 'sexual abstinence' for the woman to one of 'permissiveness with affection' (sexual relationships are right for both sexes under certain conditions, particularly if the relationship is stable), or even 'permissiveness with less affection'
- a change in *attitudes towards sexuality*: according to Coleman and Hendry (1990) youngsters are more open about sexual matters than previous generations, as can be seen in the franker way they speak about sex; they believe that sexual behavior is more a matter of private than public morality. Consequently, adolescents seem less

likely to make absolute judgements on what is right or wrong in individual cases. Their moral points of view are more relativistic and less evaluative. There seems to be a growing awareness of the importance of sex for stable, long-term relationships along with the belief that sex needs the context of a relationship if it is to be meaningful. As recent surveys show, most American and European adolescents believe that openness, honesty and fidelity are important elements of sexual relationships (Alan Guttmacher Institute, 1994; Steinberg, 2002)

- greater *precocity* in sexual relationships. Research studies carried out on adolescent sexual behavior over the last 30–40 years have pointed to a notable increase in sexual activity, a liberalization of the models of sexual expression (relationships with different partners, a greater frequency of relations) and a more precocious initiation in the case of young women.

During the 1990s, the spread of AIDS introduced new trends in adolescent sexual behavior: the risk of contracting sexually transmitted diseases has become a serious problem, particularly for adolescents and young people. Epidemiological data indicate that about three-quarters of individuals diagnosed with AIDS contracted the virus during their teenage years, because of the long period between infection with HIV and the onset of AIDS (Seiffge-Krenke, 1998). It is likely that the fear of getting HIV has had an impact on the increase in the age of the first intercourse.

All these issues require a special attention today, particularly in the European context, characterized by a growing number of immigrant adolescents coming from countries with different cultural norms concerning patterns of intimacy during adolescence and with different styles of sexual socialization.

1.2 Gender identity in boys and girls

Literature on the development of gender identity emphasized early adolescence as a time of heightened differentiation between masculine and feminine identity (Feiring, 1999), with boys adhering more closely to the stereotype of masculinity that emphasizes instrumental behaviors and roles and girls adhering more closely to the stereotype of femininity that emphasizes expressive behaviors and roles. Around the time of the onset of puberty, girls and boys experience an intensification of gender-related expectations. Gender intensification is seen as associated with puberty, whereas physical developments are seen as less central than the changes in social factors that influence them (Alsaker & Flammer, this volume).

By late adolescence, when some experience with romantic encounters has likely occurred, the majority of adolescents have components of their gender identity that are derived and shaped by experience in romantic relationships. For many adolescents, the self with a romantic partner will have become a more central identity and more elaborated in terms of representations of the self and of actual or potential romantic partners. As the salience of romantic relationships increases, the salience of the gender identity in romantic relationships should also increase and become more central for defining the individual's general gender identity. Furthermore, as the romantic partner becomes more central in terms of providing sexual, affiliative, caregiving, and attachment needs, the partner's positive and negative feedback about the nature of one's gender identity should become more important and more likely to change one's self-view.

The issue of *gender identity* (the gender that an individual believes he or she is psychologically) should not be confounded with *sexual orientation* (a consistent, enduring pattern of sexual desire for individuals of the same sex, the other sex, or both sexes) and *sex role behavior* (the extent to which an individual behaves in traditionally masculine or feminine ways) (Diamond & Savin-Williams, 2003). Recently, more research has focused the attention on homosexuality in adolescence, showing the difficulties encountered by sexual-minority adolescents in the process of identity construction, in the development of intimacy and in sexuality: they are forced to resolve these developmental tasks without the

same degree of social support as their heterosexual peers (D'Augelli & Patterson, 2001).

1.3 Methodological issues

Most research on adolescent sexual behavior has been conducted using self-report measures (e.g. questionnaires). The issue of reliability and validity of survey data and the likely impact of social desirability biases are particularly critical in the area of sexuality, since participants' reports cannot be substantiated by objective measures (Moore & Rosenthal, 1993). In the construction of the questionnaires, a particular attention should be given to the wording of the items, and caution is needed in generalizing the results found in samples of adolescents.

Several methods have been devised to check for the accuracy and truthfulness of self-reports, like repeated tests of the same questions separated by a period of time, comparisons between data collected with questions and face-to-face interviews, comparisons between prospective sexual behavior diaries with retrospective questionnaire responses (Siegel, Aten, & Roghmann, 1998). Results revealed that the majority of adolescents are honest in their self-reports. However, they showed a potential over-representation of sexual activity on questionnaires, particularly among male adolescents. This finding appears consistent in studies conducted in different time periods (from the late 1970s to the 1990s). It appears likely that sexually inexperienced males in our culture feel some pressure to overemphasize their actual sexual behavior in the attempt to measure up to some perceived standard of sexual prowess. This confirms the vulnerability of boys to cultural stereotypes, enforced by media images and role models. Moreover, data show also that if females are dishonest in their self-reports, this is due to their tendency to underestimate sexual behaviors. This tendency is more common among younger adolescents, and tends to disappear among older ones.

In the study of adolescent romantic and sexual relationships, other methods (besides questionnaires) can be used, like interviews and other qualitative methods (even in combination with quantitative instruments), which give the possibility to investigate more deeply adolescents' subjective experiences, beliefs and representations, subjective feelings and the meaning they attribute to their experiences and to the way in which sexuality is integrated into their identities and intimate relationships (Crockett, Raffaelli & Moilanen, 2003).

A limitation of studies conducted on romantic relationships (see next section) is the tendency to focus on the perspective of individuals and their own personal experiences, instead of considering the dyad as a unit of analysis; more attention toward the adoption of relational measures is needed.

2. Romantic relationships in adolescence

Despite the importance both theoreticians and adolescents themselves attach to romantic experiences in early and middle adolescence, research on this topic, until the end of the 1990s, has been surprisingly limited (Furman & Wehner, 1997; Montgomery & Sorell, 1998). Most of the research on adolescent partner relationships had been conducted in the USA and centered on demographic patterns of dating and sexuality (for a review, see Furman, Brown, & Feiring, 1999; Miller & Moore, 1990; Zani, 1991). Such a situation was attributable to the paucity of theoretical frameworks to guide research on romantic relationships during this developmental stage (Dowdy & Kliever, 1998; Shulman & Collins, 1997) and to the persistence of several myths that for many years hampered our progress in this area (e.g., that adolescent romantic relationships are trivial and transitory) (Collins, 2003).

Currently, research on adolescents' romantic relationships is flourishing (Bouchey & Furman, 2003; Brown, 2004). In recent years, significant contributions have been provided, and we have more information on issues like the emergence and development of early romantic attachments, their contribution to other aspects of adolescent development, and the perceptions and experiences of early and middle adolescents.

In this section we will address the emergence of romantic feelings, the beginning of dating relationships, and their consequences on adolescents' development and on the existing pattern of relationships with the family and the peer group.

2.1 *Emergence of romantic feelings*

According to Collins (2003), romantic relationships can be defined as ongoing voluntary interactions, mutually acknowledged, which have a peculiar intensity, that can be marked by expressions of affection, including physical ones, and perhaps the expectation of sexual relations eventually, if not now. In this definition, gender is not mentioned, because adolescents may have relationships of this type with partners of the same sex as well as partners of the opposite sex (Diamond & Savin-Williams, 2003).

In the literature there is some debate about when boys and girls first experience romantic feelings. During early adolescence most children become involved in romantic attachments, which appear as the first step in a sequence of events leading to a full-fledged romantic relationship in later adolescence. Among 9–11 year olds, 90% of children claimed to have a 'special' cross-gender boyfriend or girlfriend (Broderick, 1972). Montgomery and Sorell (1998) found that the age ranged from 3 to 19 years, with age 12 being the modal answer. Hatfield, Schmitz, Cornelius, and Rapson (1988) found that some children of all ages report having passionate feelings for a special boyfriend and girlfriend, and label their attachments and the feelings associated with it as 'love'. Recent studies confirm the likelihood of romantic experiences across the adolescent years (Carver, Joyner & Udry, 2003). In many cases, these early attachments are completely unreciprocated and kept secret: at least for half of the adolescents, being in love is associated with uncertain, unrequited, or fantasy relationships. Moreover, early and middle adolescents are actively reasoning about the nature and meaning of romantic feelings and experiences and take the notion of love quite seriously trying to work out its meaning for themselves and their relationship behaviors. There is evidence that young people's prototypical conceptions of 'being in love' change with age, becoming increasingly narrower and more specific (e.g., including particular notions of caring, affection, and sexual attraction). By late adolescence, 86% of young men and women report having been in love (Hendrick & Hendrick, 1986).

Brown (1999) has distinguished four phases in individuals' basic orientation toward romantic relationships:

1. *Initiation.* Pubertal development and surge in sexual drives spurs an interest in sexual expression and relationships, which inspires a new dimension to interactions with the other sex (for heterosexually oriented youth). This initial phase of adolescent romantic activity tends not to focus on the quality or features of romantic relationships, but rather on characteristics within the self. The basic objectives of the initiation phase are to broaden one's self-concept to include an 'affective romantic partner' and to gain confidence in one's capacity to relate to potential partners in romantic ways. The focus is on the self, not on relationships. Actual relationships with romantic partners can be superficial or short lived and still be quite satisfying.

2. *Status.* As adolescents gain confidence in their ability to interact effectively with romantic partners and to negotiate short-term romantic relationships, the focus turns from the self to the self's connections to others. Young people confront the pressures of having the 'right kinds' of romantic relationship with the 'right people', and of beginning and ending these relationships in socially sanctioned ways. Romantic relationships become vehicles to achieving objectives as being popular, achieving status, being accepted by a group of peers. In pursuing romantic partners, adolescents consider the consequences of a particular relationship for their image or status among peers: romantic relationships are an important means of establishing, improving, or maintaining peer group status.

3. *Affection.* At some point there is a shift away from the context in which the relationship exists toward the relationship itself. Adolescents typically gain sufficient confidence in their orientations and abilities to risk a deeper level of romantic relationships. At the same time, the power of the peer group seems to wane, as young people become more satisfied with their status and reputation in the peer group culture and sufficiently confident in themselves. The more intensive romantic relationships that characterize this phase are themselves more rewarding, both emotionally and sexually. Thus, the relationships often become a source of passion and preoccupation. In this phase, the salience of romantic relationships increases, somewhat at the expense of other social bonds. Peers serve important functions in this phase, but they cannot exercise the same level of control over romantic relationships that they did in earlier phases.

4. *Bonding.* To achieve truly mature relationships, individuals must supplement the passion of the affection stage with more pragmatic and personal concerns about the possibility of long-term commitment to one's romantic partner. There is a fourth shift that should occur in late adolescence or young adulthood, which adds an important new perspective to romantic relationships. The issue is whether or not one can and should form an extended, lifelong bond to one's partner. Prototypically, the objective of the bonding phase is 'to get married'; however, it is possible to enter into a committed or bonded relationship outside the institution of marriage.

These four phases describe what can be considered the 'normative' developmental timetable. On this point, some authors have emphasized that developmental timing of romantic experiences may show variations across cultural contexts. The planned or cultured timing of romantic experiences with biological events may exist within cultures and vary across cultures. In some cultures, initiation of romantic experiences may be timed to occur with the appearance of secondary sex characteristics, whereas in other cultures this initiation could be encouraged earlier or much later than the biological events because of a particular cultural group's desire to delay or accelerate reproduction.

Moreover, it has been pointed out that differences may occur in which type of cultural influence is most salient at a particular point in the developmental trajectory of romantic experience. Different types of cultural influence, such as family, peers, and the media, on romantic behavior may be more salient at different points along the trajectory of romantic experiences than are possible in adolescence and beyond. These influences may vary across cultural groups. For example, in more traditional societies dating and heterosexual premarital relationships are discouraged or prohibited. There is still cultural variability in the selection of romantic partners; the free choice is not a universal cultural practice: rather, adolescents need the approval from parents as well as having to accept arranged marriages (Hartfield & Rapson, 1996).

2.2 Dating relationships

The beginning of dating relationships is a natural consequence of romantic experiences. A date has been defined as a social engagement between young people with no commitment beyond the expectation that it is a pleasurable event for both (Dornbush et al., 1981). As such, dating is not synonymous with sexual intercourse or courtship. Dating is considered an end in itself, even though it may evolve in a more steady and committed relationship. It is a phenomenon of the 20th century (Roche, 1986).

In the USA, where the phenomenon of dating has been studied more extensively, the median age when adolescents begin to date declined over time, from about 16 years old in 1930 to 13 years old in 1990. In European countries, few young people in pre-adolescence date; by the time they reach adulthood, the overwhelming majority of them have dated or are dating on a regular basis.

Early dating (or 'going with') relationships are intense, salient experiences for adolescents; even though they generally turn out to be short in duration, ranging from an average of 3–4 months to 7–8 months. They are more often displays of a social form rather than a sharing of intimacy; however, various precursors of mature intimacy (the affective state identified as being in love, a reciprocity of involvement, frequent interaction, and the relationship qualities identified with close friendships) are reported by many adolescents.

Although pubertal development has a great bearing on when adolescents begin to date, dating is highly regulated and constrained by social forces (Seiffge-Krenke, 1998). It appears that peer pressures to engage in dating activities influence the onset of dating in adolescence.

Several authors have noticed that early interactions with the opposite sex often occur within the context of a crowd (Dunphy, 1963). The peer group appears as the ideal place for the development and acceptance of a close relationship. Research has shown that the presence of steady couples in peer groups of adolescents is high; in a research on Italian adolescents, over 60% of children reported that there were 'steady couples' in their group (Cagliumi, Corradini, & Zani, 1993). Montgomery and Sorell (1998) found that 88% of adolescents had gone on a 'group date'.

Dating can be described as a process involving different stages, each representing a change in the quality of the relationship (McCabe, 1984). There appears to be a progression from no involvement to group dating activities to dating activities engaged in as a couple, where more exclusive patterns of relationships such as courting and romance gradually become central areas of interest. There is a greater commitment to one another than before and this close, intimate relationship may eventually lead to engagement and marriage, or to some form of permanent relationship. This trend is consistent with the five-stage developmental model of adolescent peer group interaction elaborated by Dunphy almost half a century ago (Dunphy, 1963), which has been confirmed by recent research (Connolly, Craig, Goldberg, & Pepper, 2004): there is a transition from small unisexual cliques to associations between male and female cliques, to the formation of a larger heterosexual crowd, which provides a context for dating (first among clique leaders and then among all the members) and finally, the crowd begins to disintegrate leaving loosely associated groups of heterosexual couples. Gender differences in these social patterns are present. Boys continue to participate in group activities while beginning to date girls. Girls, contrariwise, begin to discard youth club activities and prefer smaller networks, attending heterosexual meeting places and finally going steady with one boy (Coleman & Hendry, 1990).

Several authors have found that during early stages of dating males and females differ widely in their beliefs as to what is proper sexual behavior (McCabe & Collins, 1990; Roche, 1986). There is a clear desire that sexual intimacy should increase from the first date to going steady; however, boys expect sexual intimacy sooner whereas girls tend to tie sexual intimacy to love and commitment. At later stages, this 'gender gap' virtually disappears (Zani, 1993).

Early dating is correlated with permissive sexual attitudes and early intercourse. Having a steady girlfriend or boyfriend may increase the likelihood of and pressure to engage in sexual activity (Miller, McCoy, Olson, & Wallace, 1986).

As regards adolescents' reported motivations for the search for a partner, data from a research conducted in Italy (on 15- and 18-year-old adolescents) (Zani, 1991) showed that motivations to search for a partner referred mostly to a need for affective support (to protect and facilitate the process of separation from parents), followed by maturational needs (the partner is seen as someone who helps achieve self-realisation, increase self-esteem). The needs of a sexual nature were less important. Adolescents who had already left school considered having a partner to be more important than did those at high school. Some authors (Roscoe, Diana, & Brooks, 1987) found that motivations for dating differ according to the developmental stage (immediate gratification, among younger adolescents, and intimacy, companionship and socialization, among late adolescents). Bouchey and Furman (2003) argue that the majority of work to date has focused on heterosexual experiences, neglecting the minority of youths who have sexual experiences with same-sex peers. Stigma and stereotypes still make the development of intimate relationships more complicated for sexual-minority youths than for their heterosexual peers; thus many of them (as Steinberg, 2002 has emphasized) 'end up pursu-

ing sexual activity *outside* the context of dating relationships because the prejudices and harassment of others may preclude any public display of romantic intimacy with a same-sex partner' (p. 342).

2.3 Implications of dating for adolescent social relationships

The entrance into romantic relationships represents a challenge to adolescents as individuals and to the network of relationships in which they are embedded, since it involves changes in the patterns of interdependencies with peers and the family (Laursen & Williams, 1997). Over the course of adolescence, the frequency of interaction and diversity of activity with parents, siblings, same-sex friends decrease whereas those with opposite-sex friends increase. Moreover, romantic partners are rated as more important than other figures as sources of support (the second more important in middle adolescence and the first during college years). Parallely, the salience of relationships with same-sex peers decreases as adolescents become more committed to their romantic relationships. So, romantic relationships appear to alter the dynamics of other relationships.

Important repercussions of dating relationships are found on the family. Generally, parents tend to devalue the importance of adolescent romantic relationships and focus on future relationship opportunities underestimating the current emotional significance of breakups for adolescents. In a research on adolescents' fathers and mothers (Zani, 1993), it was found that parental reactions to their own children's dating experiences varied according to the parent (father or mother) and adolescents' gender. In general, mothers feel much more involved when the daughter, as opposed to the son, begins to distance herself affectively. Contradictory and ambivalent feelings are expressed: along with the joy of seeing their daughter happy, there is sometimes a feeling of jealousy and an awareness of having lost an exclusive position in relations with the daughter; on other occasions, a sense of guilt is expressed for having failed to do something which might have pushed the daughter into finding a more satisfying affectional relationship elsewhere. Mothers of male adolescents generally claim that there has been no change in their attitudes and feelings, since what has happened is seen as 'natural', and it is considered as a positive experience. Different reactions are shown by fathers. Fathers of female adolescents show distinct profiles according to their sociocultural level. Among fathers of medium–high level the affective independence of their daughters is something expected and normal, seen as part of the developmental process. The acceptance of adolescent romantic relationships is more difficult for fathers of medium–low cultural level: they appear more concerned that the daughters might be forced into choices which are not of their own making. They appear aware that having fewer cultural opportunities brings with it a greater risk of running up against adolescent developmental problems. Fathers' attitudes toward male affective development seem more superficial. It seems that the sons are not really expected to have an emotional life at all.

2.4 Functions of dating

Some authors have claimed the important function of dating for identity formation and individuation from parents. Dating can be considered as one of the forms of peer interaction which helps adolescents clarify their identities and begin separating from their family. The consolidation of a romantic interdependent relationship may affirm an adolescent's sense of identity and his or her feeling of 'being a separate identity' (Steinberg, 2002). Dowdy and Kliever (1998) found a higher level of behavioral autonomy in adolescents who were currently dating. According to these authors, dating can be conceptualized as a social role transition, that becomes normative during middle adolescence. In dating relationship adolescents experience themselves in a different role than that of child, student or friend. As they experience this new role, behavioral patterns and existing priorities may change (e.g., regarding time spent with friends, homework etc.). Adolescents who are dating are more likely to see their relationships with others as under their jurisdiction, relative to non-daters, and are

more likely than non-daters to take control over decisions regarding with whom they spend their time. Dating will serve therefore as a catalyst for earlier autonomy development because it provides both the opportunity to practice self-governance and the motivation to do so.

Further support for the role of the involvement in dating for adolescent autonomy development has been provided by studies on the relation between dating and self-evaluation. A positive link has been found between steady dating and the perception of self-esteem and sex role identity. Adolescents who had steady dates, compared to those who did not, perceived themselves, and were perceived by their peers, as possessing higher self-esteem and higher correspondence to their gender identity (see Samet & Kelly, 1987; Zani, 1993). Moreover, heterosexual involvement offers different kinds of social satisfaction (e.g., the attention and liking of admirers, approval of parents and friends, respect of peers and achievement of a higher status), which act as an important source of self-respect and of positive self-evaluation. The early dating may have adverse effects on adolescents' mental health, but a moderate degree of dating is associated with better well-being than no dating at all. Even if it is not clear the relationships between intimacy and psychological health, they are clearly interdependent: intimacy enhances adolescents' well-being, but it is also likely that psychologically healthy adolescents are better able to make and maintain close relationships with others (Steinberg, 2002).

3. Adolescent sexual activity

In this section we turn our attention to the analysis of sexual activity in adolescence. The onset of sexual activity is a normal and important aspect of development, marking in part the transition to adulthood. Adolescents are becoming sexually active at earlier ages, and by the end of their adolescent years, more than 80% of all males and more than 70% of all females are sexually active. A great deal of research on adolescent sexual activity has been conducted in the Anglo-American context, and focused on identifying those factors related to the initiation of early sexual intercourse and the effective use of contraceptives, in part to establish profiles of pregnancy risks. Such studies were negatively biased towards sexual behavior in adolescence and treated it as a non-normative event, focusing on documenting the dangers of premarital sexual activity (e.g., unwanted pregnancies) (Seiffge-Krenke, 1998). During the 1980s, the spread of AIDS prompted new trends in sexual behavior research: it facilitated the conducting of research on sexual behavior (obtaining samples of high school students), providing a rationale to study behaviors other than sexual intercourse (oral and anal sex, and focusing more specifically on patterns of condom use), and focusing on groups previously ignored (street youth, gay males, drug users). On the whole, however, researchers tended to study adolescent sexuality outside the social and environmental contexts in which it normally occurs. Little attention was devoted to determining the role of interpersonal relationships in the development of adolescent sexuality: the typical individual approach has left a void in understanding the dynamics of sexuality.

In the following sections, we will start by discussing precursors of sexual intercourse, such as masturbation and romantic/erotic phantasizing. We will then move on considering demographic profiles of sexual activity. Subsequently discussion will focus on the meaning of sexuality for adolescents and their motivations for initiating sexual activity, as well as their reactions to the first sexual experiences. In the last section, we will consider the processes and variables involved in the explanation of adolescent transition to non-virginity.

3.1 Precursors of sexual intercourse

Much of adolescent sexual behavior is made up of substitute activities, including erotic fantasizing and masturbation (Breakwell, 1997; Seiffge-Krenke, 1998). Very little research was devoted toward understanding any of these sexual behaviors, perhaps because they were and still are regarded as very private and somewhat shameful activities. For most adolescents, masturbation is the first kind of conscious and direct sexual activity they experience. Studies on adolescent masturbation conducted in the 1980s documented

that 75% of all male adolescents and one-third of all female adolescents between 14 and 17 years old masturbated. The frequency of masturbation increases with age (Moore & Rosenthal, 1993); moreover, even though male and female continue to show different rates of masturbation, such differences narrowed over the decades. Both male and female adolescents state that they feel guilty or ashamed, and girls especially are reluctant to report or disclose details about such experiences. Data collected on Italian adolescents showed, however, that only 25% of adolescents considered masturbation something to worry about, and it was the last in a list of 12 common worries (Cagliumi et al., 1993). Whether girls' lower rates of reporting masturbation behavior reflect a real difference or simply a difference in willingness to admit a stigmatized behavior is not known. Various findings indicated that masturbation is a substitute for sexual intercourse for males, whereas for females it is a form of sexuality in its own right (Seiffge-Krenke, 1998).

Romantic/erotic fantasizing appears by far the most common sexual activity in adolescence. Adolescents mentally construct scenarios (or *scripts*; Simon & Gagnon, 1987) of romantic/sexual experiences. These are initially vague (e.g., the partner is not specified, the sexual acts are less specific) and later become more specific and detailed (e.g., the characteristics of the partner, of the acts and their sequences, e.g., the first approach, the scene of seduction, the execution of the act, etc.) (Breakwell, 1997). These fantasies, which are enacted under the pressure of growing desires, fulfill a number of different functions in the adolescent's erotic life: besides providing pleasure, they are a substitute for the satisfaction of unattainable sexual needs or help the adolescent to learn about his or her sexual needs and preferences. They allow the individual to rehearse sexual experiences, but also occur in anticipation of future sexual experiences. Fantasizing, as rehearsal and as preparation for later realization of sexual activity is extremely important for adolescents (Katchadourian, 1990).

Adolescents' worries about sexuality differ according to gender: males appear more worried about the 'mechanics' of sex, whereas females are

---

Box 11.1.   Age at first intercourse

Evidence concerning the lowering of the age at first intercourse in the last 30 years has been provided by several studies. However, the comparability of the findings is not easy, since different parameters are provided.

Considering Great Britain, in 1965 the percentages of adolescents who had sexual intercourse by age 16 was 14% among males and 5% among females (Schofield, 1965). Thirteen years later, 32% of males and 21% of females had had their first sexual intercourse by 16 (Farrell, 1978). In the 1990s, 50% of both male and female adolescents report having experienced their first intercourse by age 16, and among 19–20 year olds the percentage is 85% (Fife-Shaw & Breakwell, 1992). In Germany, the percentage of sexually experienced 18-year-old male adolescents doubled from the beginning of the 1970s to the beginning of the 1980s (increasing to 50%), whereas the percentage of sexually active females *quadrupled* (60%) (see Seiffge-Krenke, 1998). In the 1990s, almost half of all adolescents had experienced first sexual intercourse by age 16 (Meschke & Silbereisen, 1997).

The pattern found among today's British and German adolescents is analogous in other European countries. In France, a national survey found that before the age of 13, 21% of boys and 4% of girls had had sexual intercourse; at age 14–15 percentages are 27% of boys and 13% of girls; at 16–17 years of age 41% of the boys and 33% of girls; at 18 73% of the boys and 59% of the girls had had intercourse (Choquet & Ledoux, 1994). A research conducted in 2000 found that between 15 and 19 years, 45% of adolescents declare that they had sexual intercourse. This proportion increases steadily with age, from 9% of 15 year olds to 44% of 17 year olds, to 77% of 19 year olds (ORS, 2000).

In Italy, data on a nationally representative sample show that most adolescents experience their first intercourse between 15 and 18 years (Cafaro, 1998). In particular, 50% of male adolescents and 53% of females had their first intercourse at the age of 15–16.

We can compare data on European adolescents with statistics concerning US and Canadian adolescents.

A similar trend concerning the lowering of the age at first intercourse has been reported for US adolescents from 1970 to 1990 (Henshaw, 1994). In particular, in 1988, 42% of 16 year olds and 59% of 17 year olds were sexually active. Moreover, 75% of boys and 60% of girls reported having had intercourse by age 18 (Brooks-Gunn & Paikoff, 1997).

In Canada, a national survey of youth conducted at the end of the 1980s revealed that, by age 16, 50% of adolescents had engaged in sexual intercourse, and by age 18, 66% reported having had a coital experience (King, Beazley, Warren, Hankins, Robertson, & Radford, 1988).

---

more worried about relations (Breakwell, 1997). Females hold more romantic ideas, and often they construct complex systems of representations concerning romantic love, fidelity, etc. At middle adolescence, females look for a romantic and stable relation. Males are interested in sexuality for itself whereas females are interested in sexuality as a component of a couple relation. These representational systems can induce females to feel sexually inadequate if they do not succeed in finding the romantic attachment they are looking for, in the time delay they consider adequate.

3.2 *Demographic patterns of sexual activity*

As regards the patterns of adolescent sexual behaviors, changes during the last 30 years have been reported in different countries. The most striking result is a lowering of the age of the first sexual intercourse; such trend is present in most industrialized nations (Goldman & Goldman, 1988). Overall, results converge in indicating that in the 1990s, the first intercourse occurs between 15 and 17 years old for most European adolescents, and that by 19 years, 70–80% of them have experienced their first intercourse (see Box 11.1).

The trend of having intercourse at an earlier age does not seem to have persisted after 1990, however, and some authors have pointed out that it has begun to reverse its direction. Since 1990 the age of initiation for intercourse appears to have increased (Seiffge-Krenke, 1998). Data collected in Italy show an increase in the age of the first intercourse from 1993/4 to 1997/8 (Cafaro, 1998). Similar results have been reported also among Swedish adolescents from 1970 to 1996 (Magnusson, 2001). It is likely that an important influence on such phenomenon is the impact of AIDS and the fear of getting HIV as a consequence of sexual activity.

Research also revealed a narrowing of reported gender differences among younger generations. The differences between males and females have diminished with an increasing prevalence of earlier sexual activity. In some countries, there is a tendency towards establishing a pattern where young girls have more sexual experience than boys, including having their first intercourse at an earlier age (e.g., in Sweden). This is what one might expect since girls, on the average, reach physical maturation at an earlier age than boys. However, 'intergender convergence' in behavior

---

Box 11.2.   Aspects of sexual activity

Different patterns of sexual activity have been found after the first intercourse. Moore and Rosenthal (1993) found that for many adolescents, sexual intercourse is sporadic and rare. Other authors found that most adolescents regularly had sexual intercourse after the first coital experience (Seiffge-Krenke, 1998). It is likely that the frequency of intercourse is related to the nature of the relationship with one's partner: the more committed the relationship is, the more frequent the sexual activity. However, one year after the first intercourse, only every third girl and every fourth boy was still dating the partner with whom they had their first coital experience. Similar data have been reported in Italy.

Considering Great Britain, Breakwell (1997) provides percentages concerning number of sexual partners: from 16–20 years 27% of males and 34% of females declare they had one sexual partner, 16% of both male and female from two to three sexual partners, 26% of males and 19% of females four partners or more. Data collected on 17–19-year-old Italian adolescents (Cicognani & Zani, 1998a), show that among those who were sexually active, about one-third were still involved in a relationship with the first partner, another third were at the second relationship (they had not necessarily had sexual intercourse) and the remaining were alone or had had more partners.

Considering French adolescents, before 15 years of age sexual experiences are mainly one off and they become regular after 18 for 33% of boys and for 38% of girls; 2% of boys and 1% of girls had had homosexual relationships (Choquet & Ledoux, 1994).

So far, little is known about the characteristics of the partner in heterosexual relationships, except for the fact that females report that their first intercourse usually takes place with slightly older males.

Where does sexual intercourse take place? There are often few alternatives. The situation of strong external limitations means that sexual intercourse often takes place spontaneously (i.e., when the opportunity of being alone arises). Two-thirds of Australian, British, German and American adolescents engage in sexual intercourse where they are most likely to be caught in the act – at home (Gagnon et al., 1989; Moore & Rosenthal, 1993; Schmidt et al., 1994). Some Italian adolescents declare that being on holidays (e.g., at the sea) provides a good opportunity, especially for males who have the first intercourse with a partner just met (Berti Ceroni, Bonini, Cerchierini, & Zani, 1987; Cafaro, 1998).

---

regarding premarital sex need not imply a convergence in the meanings or motives held by the two sexes (Zani, 1991).

Compared to research conducted before the 1980s, we now have more information on other sexual behaviors and other aspects of adolescent sexual activity also, such as the frequency of sexual activity and the number of sexual partners, whereas limited data have been collected on issues such as the characteristics of the partner and the context in which first sexual activities occur (see Box 11.2).

There is evidence of a normative developmental pattern in the sequence of adolescent heterosexual behaviors, which starts around 13 years old, with embracing and kissing, moving through petting or fondling breasts and sexual organs, and ending with intercourse (Moore & Rosenthal, 1993).

Research shows there are differences in the ages at which the least intimate of these (kissing) and the more intimate (intercourse) are considered acceptable and are practiced (normative timetables). One study which examined directly adolescents' ideas about appropriate sexual behaviors at different ages is Rosenthal and Smith (1997), who found that (Australian) adolescents share specific norms about appropriate age-related tim-

ing for engaging in intimate behaviors with a partner. Acceptable timing is a function of three categories of intimate behaviors: kissing (12–14 years), breast and genital touching and penetrative sex (15–17 years). The modal ages for the last two sets of behaviors are mid-teens, even if a substantial minority believe that penetrative sex should be delayed until the late teens. The timetables of females matches closely the objective data about the onset of sexual behavior, but males' responses were less accurate. Adolescents' timetables appear to be influenced by autonomy timetables (age at which adolescents believe that a series of activities are appropriate for adolescents), use of common drugs, and use of sexually explicit media (the last for males).

3.3 Motivations toward initiating coital activity, and emotional reactions

Different motivations have been mentioned by adolescents for initiating sexual activity. In a study conducted with German adolescents aged 14–18 years, Neubauer (1990) found three motives for beginning heterosexual relationships: curiosity (adolescents wanted to know what sex was like), mutual affection (the adolescents were in love and wanted to belong to each other completely), and adult status (adolescents wanted to be like their friends and become an adult). These motives explain why, for a minority of young people, the initiation of sex is not voluntary.

Motivations appear to differ according to adolescent gender. In general, young females report being more motivated by love to engage in sexual intercourse, whereas young males report being more motivated by physical desire (Carroll, Volk, & Hyde, 1985). Males report less emotional attachment and commitment, whereas females are more likely to experience first coitus within what they perceive is a romantic relationship.

Such gender differences have been supported by an interview study with Italian adolescents (Zani, 1991), which sheds light also on the context of the first intercourse and adolescents' emotional reactions. The vast majority of girls first had sexual intercourse with a boy with whom they had a relationship begun some months earlier; very few girls, mainly non-student, had had their first time with someone they had not known long. Half of the girls had had a partner more grown up than themselves. Many girls had been disappointed by their first experience and had then abstained from sexual activity for a lengthy period. Others were continuing the relationship with the same person and a few had formed a new couple. In many cases, their adult partner had exerted some degree of pressure on them to 'go all the way'. Other girls declared that they had undergone a seduction. Yet others accepted or even sought a sexual experience in the vain hope that the relationship might be longer lasting.

For the boys the first time was quite different. They described their experiences as 'episodes' that had taken place without any 'real' relationship. These experiences appear to have been a kind of initiation through which a more adult partner guided them. Boys spoke of their first experience as a 'test' aiming to prove that they are normal 'men'. For this reason, they find it relatively easy to strike up a casual acquaintance, often a foreigner, on holiday, who supplies them with the desired proof. But it is precisely this absence of any genuine relationship, and hence of any sense of being in love, that constitutes one of the main causes for the disappointment that the boys said they had experienced.

Mitchell and Wellings (1998) distinguished four 'profiles' of sexual initiation, which appear to differ according to adolescent age. In some cases (generally among younger and inexperienced adolescents), the first sexual intercourse happens unexpectedly and is experienced as a shock; it is characterized by silence, confusion, embarrassment and the felt inability to discuss what happened. More typically, however, intercourse is unexpected but not a complete surprise, since they are aware of possible situational 'clues', which suggest it was a possibility. Accounts suggest that young virgin women are more likely to have certain expectations of a date but these typically do not include sex, while young men were less likely to have any expectations at all, but were open to sex as a possibility. In any case, lack of anticipation and poor communication leads to dissatisfaction with the experience. In a third group, intercourse was anticipated but not wanted. This occurred when partners had conflicting expectations, and in such cases there is a tendency for the male expectation to be fulfilled, owing to the inability of women to communicate their ambivalence to their partner before first intercourse. In such circumstances, ambivalent feelings, augmented by the frustration of feeling unable to express the ambivalence to the partner, led to subsequent feelings of regret after the event. The last group included adolescents for whom the first intercourse was planned. They were older (17 years or more) and involved in a steady relation at the time. They discussed first intercourse with the partner; this was regarded as having the potential to bring about a qualitative change in the relationships. On the whole, those who had planned and discussed first intercourse regarded it as a positive experience.

Emotional reactions to the first sexual intercourse have been explored also by other studies. Results suggest generally that males are less likely to experience guilt and more likely to experience satisfaction than are females. McCabe and Collins (1990) found that only half of the girls enjoyed the experience, whereas 40% had negative reactions such as guilt, anxiety about pregnancy, and fear of discovery. Boys, however, felt quite differently, claiming feelings of excitement and satisfaction.

3.4 Processes involved in the transition to coitus

Considerable attention has been devoted to studying the processes and the influences involved in making the transition to non-virginity, in particular in the North American context.

A strong association has been found between physical maturity and experiencing sexual intercourse (Moore & Rosenthal, 1993; Stattin & Magnusson, 1990). Although the age of first intercourse has decreased over the last 30 years, the close association of these phenomena has not changed at all. Early-maturing adolescents begin to have sexual intercourse earlier, and late-maturing adolescents begin later, each with an interval of approximately 3 years following physical maturation (Phinney, Jensen, Olsen, & Cundick, 1990).

Economic resources and the structure of the community in which adolescents live have been found to be associated with adolescents' sexual activity and age of first coital experience. As socioeconomic status descreases, rates of sexual activity increase. Living in economically disadvantaged communities where adult status behaviors, such as employment, are difficult to attain, sexual activity may be highly valued as a symbol of adult status. It is likely that economic constraints and opportunities for employment within the social context contribute to adolescents' values toward educational achievements, plans, and orientations to the future. Findings on the association between coital activity, education and aspirations for the future suggest that values toward future employment status inhibit precocious sexual intercourse. Also parents' educational attainment and expectations for their offspring are related to adolescents' school achievement and educational plans, which are inversely related to adolescent involvement in coitus (cf. Herold & Marshall, 1996).

In addition to values associated with education and future status, the values espoused by religious institutions have been found to be associated with adolescents' sexual behaviors, in particular, the delay in initiation of sexual activity (even if adolescents may engage in sexual behaviors that circumvent coitus, like oro-genital behaviors, as a way of gaining sexual experience without losing their technical virginity). A research conducted in Italy showed, however, that many adolescents who consider themselves as catholic, do not follow the directives of the church: for them virginity is no more a value, some admit the possibility of abortion (Cagliumi et al., 1993).

Family characteristics and parental attitudes are important influences on adolescents' sexual behaviors, including first coitus. Different variables can influence adolescent sexual behavior: the characteristics of the parents, relations, the structure of the family, the attitudes, the values and the norms of the members. Some authors have emphasized the role of mothers' sexual behavior when she was adolescent and the fact to have sexually active siblings. Many researches have shown the incidence of the family structure in the behavior of the sons (e.g., single-parent families). Parents' education is another meaningful variable: parents with high cultural level give more emphasis to personal realization, to school success and having a job, discouraging in their sons premature beginning of sexual activity. Among adolescents themselves, those who are more motivated in their studies and get better grades are less premature in their sexual activity.

Parental supervision (both as stated by parents and as perceived by adolescents) has been associated with the postponement of the initiation of coitus in adolescence. The degree of parental control has been found to have a curvilinear relationship with adolescent sexual behavior; adolescent participation in sexual activity was more likely with no parental control, least likely with moderate parental control, and more likely to occur under extreme parental than under moderate control. Research on communication patterns between parents and adolescents suggest that there is little discussion about sex (cf. Cicognani, 1991; Zani, 1997): when discussions occur, it is more often between mothers and daughters. Fathers have been found to report more discomfort talking with their children about sexuality, whereas their offsprings have reported that their fathers are less available for discussions. Parental values have been found to influence the timing of adolescents' first coitus: holding more traditional values has been found to be positively associated with delay of their offspring's first coitus, whereas more permissive parental values are negatively associated with offspring's age at first coitus. The degree to which adolescents identify and bond with their parents, however, mediates the effect of parental attitudes and reactions to sexual behaviors.

Another source of influence on adolescent sexual activity are peers. Research has shown that association with peers whom adolescents believe are sexually active is a much stronger predictor of transition to coitus than parental reaction to sexual behavior or adolescent attachment to parents (cf. Herold & Marshall, 1996). Furthermore, adolescents' attitudes toward sexual behavior have also been found to be significantly related to what they either knew friends thought or what they believed friends thought about premarital sexual intercourse. Adolescents themselves mention peer pressures as one of the reasons for initiation of sexual activity.

Although associations have been found between adolescent coital behavior and peer and familial influences, the mechanisms underlying these associations are ambiguous. Taris and Semin (1997, 1998) found that the relationship between parenting styles (degree of control and closeness) and adolescent sexual activity was both direct (presumably through the mediation of parental attitudes) and mediated by adolescents' perceived control and sexual self-efficacy. A lower control by parents was associated with adolescents perceiving a greater control over their behaviors, a higher self-efficacy in the sexual realm: the latter was associated with a greater involvement in sexual activities.

4. Preventive behavior and risk taking

The main risks associated with sexual activity that have been studied are the risk of pregnancy and venereal diseases, and subsequently, beginning in the 1980s, the risk of getting HIV/AIDS. The emergence of AIDS has modified the character of studies, by facilitating research on adolescent sexuality, and legitimizing questions on different types of sexual behavior, not associated with pregnancy risk but nonetheless risky from

the point of view of HIV contagion (e.g. oro-genital, anal). Moreover, while initially, from a point of view of the risk of pregnancy, the more effective contraceptive method is the pill (and studies concentrated on this), from the point of view of AIDS, the best contraceptive method is the condom (the pill is not recommended as a safe method) and studies concerned with AIDS risk focused more specifically on this precautionary method. There are therefore two different research traditions on risk and protective behaviors in adolescence, but this also means that for adolescents themselves, the problem of protection from the risks associated with sexual behavior has become cognitively more complex, since more issues have to be taken into account and possible solutions are different and even contradictory.

Research on psychosocial determinants of contraceptive behaviors has been conducted mainly in the USA, the country with the highest incidence of both adolescent pregnancies and HIV/AIDS contagion among adolescents, among western industrialized countries.

In the following, we will first consider theoretical perspectives on the process of contraceptive use. We will then present demographic data on adolescents' knowledge and use of contraceptives. We will then move on to the explanations of adolescent reluctance to use contraceptives and to take risks, by considering two principal risks: pregnancy and transmission of sexually related diseases, such as HIV/AIDS.

4.1 Theoretical perspectives on the process of contraceptive use

One of the few theoretical models explaining the processes involved in contraceptive use has been proposed by Byrne (1983). Originally it was elaborated to explain contraceptive behavior in the context of pregnancy prevention. According to Byrne (1983), the effective use of contraceptives is a complex behavior that includes various phases: (a) acquiring, elaborating and retaining in memory accurate information both on how conception can occur and on how it can be prevented; (b) being aware of the possibility to have sexual relationships; (c) obtaining adequate means of contraception; (d) talking with the partner about contraception; and (e) correctly using the chosen contraceptive. Each of these phases involves operations both at a cognitive and behavioral levels and has important implications at an affective–emotional level, since it involves problems with self-concept that the adolescent is constructing. The variety of the factors to consider is also a function of the social and cultural context.

The Byrne model can be extended to the explanation of HIV protective behavior. Generally, however, determinants of HIV/AIDS protective behaviors have mostly been studied by using different socio-psychological models of behavior change (e.g., HBM, the protection motivation theory, the theory of reasoned action and planned behavior, self-efficacy theory; cfr. Jessor, 1998; Oskamp & Thompson, 1996).

4.2 Demographic profiles of contraceptive knowledge and use

Considering knowledge about contraceptives, research conducted in several countries indicated that contraceptive methods are generally well-known, and in particular, the pill, the condom, and coil, followed by the diaphragm and coitus interruptus. Natural methods are less well-known. Knowledge increases with age and is more accurate in girls. However, adolescents' knowledge is often superficial, without a real understanding of the functioning of contraceptives. For example, the pill (the most effective method from the point of view of pregnancy prevention) is considered more harmful for health while coitus interruptus (less harmful) is considered hardly effective. Attitudes toward condoms are still negative among a certain number of adolescents, even if AIDS educational campaigns seem to have succeeded in part in modifying them.

A large percentage of adolescents hold erroneous beliefs about conception. Henshaw (1994) found that despite attendance in classes on human sexuality (American) adolescents were still misinformed about the relation between the phase of the menstrual cycle and increased likelihood for conception.

Most adolescents get information on these topics through friends, school, books and parents. As regards contraceptive behaviors, research conducted in the USA showed a significant increase in the use of contraceptive methods from the 1970s to the 1990s. Adolescent males' reports of condom use at first intercourse doubled between 1979 and 1988 from 20% to 54%. During the same time period, female contraceptive use at first intercourse also increased from 47% to 65%. However, a considerable percentage of adolescents did not use contraception. Data on German adolescents show that at the beginning of 1990 30% of the girls and 50% of the boys used inadequate contraception or did not use any at all (Schmidt, Klusmann, Zeitzschel, & Lange, 1994). In France, 25.5% of adolescents used both condoms and pill at the first intercourse, while 65.4% of them used one of them (only 9.1% of adolescents did not use any contraceptives) (ORS, 2000). In Italy, 20% of adolescents used condoms at first intercourse, 3.5% of female adolescents the pill, 25% coitus interruptus, whereas over 30% used nothing (Cafaro, 1998).

Although the condom is most often used at first intercourse, there is a trend for the pill to replace the condom as the most common method of contraception in long-term relationships. Among French adolescents, condoms are used by 71% of adolescents in casual relationships vs. 41% of those who are involved in steady relationships (who prefer the pill in 74% of the cases) (Choquet & Ledoux, 1994).

4.3 Explanations of adolescent tendency to take risks

Several explanations have been advanced for adolescents' reluctance to use contraceptives (see Box 11.3). They involve different aspects, both at the individual level (e.g., like attitudes toward contraceptives, fears about their consequences on the body, cognitive processes involved in risk perception) and at a relational level (e.g., the particular circumstances of adolescent first sexual relationships, the characteristics of the relationships themselves, difficulties at the interpersonal level). Some of them are more specific of some contraceptive methods, whereas others are more general.

Box 11.3.   Some obstacles to the use of contraceptives

1 Fear that they can interfere with the normal functioning of the body (e.g., the pill, coil).
2 Belief that sexual intercourse should be spontaneous and natural, whereas contraceptives are considered an interference to pleasure and spontaneity (birth control makes sex seem preplanned).
3 Impossibility to accept the programming of sexual intercourse.
4 Particular circumstances of adolescent first sexual experiences (often unexpected, sometimes in contrast with adolescents' beliefs and values.
5 Conviction that nothing can happen. Many female adolescents do not bother to use contraception because they are convinced that they cannot become pregnant very easily. They believe that they are too young to become pregnant or that the low frequency of sexual intercourse makes conception unlikely.
6 In the context of HIV transmission, the feeling that knowing their partner is sufficient to exclude the possibility of contagion.
7 Difficulties at an interpersonal level. Among these, the reluctance to show the partner one's availability to have sexual intercourse (for some adolescents, the use of contraceptives carries with it the possibility of being labeled as sexually expert or promiscuous). Moreover, difficulties may arise in talking about contraceptives with the partner, owing to the lack of appropriate role models (e.g., the belief that it is a boy's or a girl's responsibility to think about contraceptives).
8 Difficulties in getting hold of precautions and in overcoming feelings of embarrassment when buying them.

The emergence of AIDS made the picture of adolescent risk and precautionary behavior more complex and ambiguous in its interpretation. From the point of view of HIV, those adolescents who use the pill are seen as taking risks. In particular, the reported tendency by adolescents to shift from the use of condoms to the pill when the relationship becomes more steady (which, from the point of view of pregnancy prevention, represents safer behavior), has been interpreted as an increase in the tendency to take risks in the context of AIDS, given the reported tendency by adolescents to have short-term relationships and several partners (Breakwell, 1997).

In fact, despite the romanticism that characterizes adolescents' representation of sexuality, long-lasting relations are more the exception than the rule. Heterosexual relations appear as a series of short but intense relationships. For all their duration they are characterized by fidelity or exclusivity, strongly valued. Whichever deviation from such norms is seen like a failure of the relation and the end of it. At the beginning of these relations, the couple will adopt safe sexual practices, using condoms in order to avoid the transmission of sexual diseases. After a while, such practices will be abandoned or applied irregularly. Research studies on the profiles of sexual activities that have revealed this tendency to abandon quickly, with every new partner, safe sexual practices, have been implicitly interpreted like an evidence of risk taking.

One explanation for risk-taking tendencies makes reference to adolescents' belief to be invulnerable to risks. Such belief has been found both with reference to risk of pregnancy (Du Rant & Sanders, 1989), and to the AIDS risk (Abrams, Abrahams, Spears, & Marks, 1990; Cicognani & Zani, 1999; Perloff & Fetzer, 1986). According to some authors, the conviction of being invulnerable is a consequence of adolescent egocentrism (that is, of the inability to cognitively represent an event from a different point of view) and the 'personal fable' phenomenon. Egocentrism hinders some adolescent girls in making realistic appraisals of their chances of becoming pregnant.

There is also evidence that some individuals tend to take risks more than others. Breakwell and Fife-Shaw (1991) have identified a subgroup of adolescents (approximately 10% of the population) that tend to take risks at a sexual level (e.g., they have their first sexual intercourse earlier, more frequent and unprotected relationships, more partners, various types of sexual behaviors, declare that sex is important in their life and have greater sexual self-efficacy). Intellectual and personality variables (e.g., sensation seeking) might play a role in the explanation of such individual profiles of risk taking. It is already known that there is a common etiology for adolescents' risk behavior; for example, associations have been reported between lack of parental monitoring and multiple risk behaviors among adolescents, early initiation of sexual activity and STD risk behavior (for a review, cfr. Di Clemente & Crosby,

2003; for the Italian contexts, see Bonino, Cattelino, & Ciairano, 2003; Nizzoli & Colli, 2004).

The role of self-efficacy has been particularly emphasised in explanations of adolescents' sexual risk taking. This construct refers to the perception of having the ability to display appropriate behaviors in sexual relations. What is considered appropriate can vary but the essential point is the subject's evaluation of his or her own ability to satisfy the requirements of the sexual situation. This feeling exercises a considerable influence on behavior. Breakwell and Fife-Shaw (1991) found that it plays a role in influencing the motivated subject to adopt precautions effectively. Subjects with high self-efficacy are more likely to put into practice their intentions at the moment of the encounter. Feelings of competence imply perceptions of control over the situation (including the choice of the partner, sexual behaviors, and the moment and place in which sexual activity will happen). When adolescents expect low control on sexual relationships and the use of precautions, they are less likely to use them. There are no gender differences in global sexual self-efficacy, even if male and female adolescents differ in specific dimensions of self-efficacy; in particular female adolescents feel more capable of 'saying no' to unwanted sexual advances, whereas males have more competence in taking the initiative in sexual relationships (Cicognani & Zani, 1998a; 1998b). Adolescents' self-efficacy increases with age.

A further explanation of sexual risk taking refers to the nature of adolescent self-concept. Breakwell and Millward (1997) distinguished two dimensions of adolescents' sexual self-concept, which appear to be related to actual behavior: socio-emotional (e.g., romance, sensitivity, and eroticism) and relational (e.g., non-exploitative, non-seductive, and non-experimental). Among males, the more relationship oriented are less likely to engage in behaviors which endanger their health. The concern of these males for the relationship dimension of sexuality is associated with lower sexual activity, a tendency not to do things on impulse, a tendency to plan sexual encounters. Such males are more likely to be virgin. The socio-emotional facet of the sexual self-concept

of males is associated with a different profile of sexual activity and risk taking. Males who scored high on this dimension were likely to say that sex and being sexually attractive is important to them. They are also more likely to seek adventure and sensation-seeking experiences, yet will not necessarily do so impulsively. Although socio-emotional sexuality is associated with the likelihood of having had sex, it is not related in any way to risk-taking behavior.

For females, a high sexual assertiveness score is associated with importance of sex and of being sexually attractive. Sexual assertiveness is also related to the likelihood of being sexually active and increased likelihood of risk-taking behavior (greater number of sexual partners, frequency of alcohol consumption and cigarette smoking).

5. Adolescent pregnancy and abortion

In this section we move on to consider some consequences of adolescent sexuality, by focusing on the issues of pregnancy and abortion. After describing the main characteristics of the research on the topic, we discuss demographic profiles of pregnancy and abortion in Europe, correlates and consequences of adolescent pregnancy.

Besides being a highly risky situation from a medical perspective, adolescent pregnancy is a stressful psychological experience for the individuals involved and a serious problem for the whole society. Becoming pregnant before 18 years is associated with having had less education: in fact, adolescent mothers are more likely to abandon school, and as a consequence, their chances of getting a satisfying and well-paid job are lower. Adolescent pregnancies are more likely to end with an illegitimate birth, which is still a source of social discrimination both for the mother and the baby. An alternative solution is marriage: however, data show that the percentages of divorces among individuals who married when they were adolescents are very high (cf. Zani, 1997). Therefore, there is not a satisfying solution to this 'problem'. The adolescent girl can continue her pregnancy and give birth to a child, even if she might be unprepared to take care of him or her; she can give her child in adoption (thus facing the feelings of guilt, separation and loss);

or she can decide to have an abortion (an equally difficult choice).

5.1 Becoming a mother or a father in adolescence

Research studies describing the decision-making process of pregnant adolescents are limited, and are complicated by the fact that adolescents' responses to an unwanted pregnancy are influenced by myriad factors, including school aspirations, relationship with the father, perceptions of family support, the number of peers who have given birth to a child. Few researches have explored how adolescent girls manage these contradictory interests. What is known is that those adolescents who decide to have an abortion have more favourable perspectives as far as education is concerned, they are more likely to be of high cultural and social level, have a less religious background, have parents with more tolerant attitudes toward abortion and generally, do not have friends who became pregnant.

The issue of becoming a mother or a father during adolescence has been the topic of several research studies, often of a longitudinal nature and conducted in the Anglo-American context. Miller and Moore (1990) pointed out that in the research literature published before the 1980s, the emphasis was placed on negative aspects of adolescent motherhood, focusing on the impact of early pregnancy and motherhood on a girl's education and on concerns about the health and welfare of mother and child. Such research stressed adolescents' lack of competencies in raising children – with respect to adult mothers – their lower sensitivity to his or her needs, and their lower abilities to stimulate their child's development.

More recent research has shown, on the contrary, that the crucial issue is not the mother's age, but a series of external circumstances (including economic factors, cultural level, family support, partner support) that appear important for an optimal child development. Furstenberg, Brooks-Gunn and Chase-Lansdale (1989) in their Baltimore Study showed that long-term consequences of adolescent motherhood on children are not as negative as was expected. Different parenting styles have been found even among adolescent

mothers, associated with different consequences as regards school achievement, marriage and birth control. Dennison, Brownrigg, and Coleman (1996) reported data on British adolescent mothers which showed a more favourable picture of adolescent motherhood. Adolescent mothers interviewed enjoyed considerable emotional and practical support from their family (in particular their own mother) and were able to think of several advantages of having a baby in their teenage years: in particular, they admit having more energy and patience, more time to dedicate to their child and they believed they would be better able to relate to their children (by 'growing up' together). Disadvantages appeared to be fewer, they acknowledged that often they had less well-established material and financial environments and could not offer much stability and experience as an older mother. They were also aware that they were missing out on schooling and also had lost some of their freedom, but they also believed that they would regain this freedom and have the opportunity to carry on their education when their child went on to school. Further evidence on the importance of a high-quality relationship with the partner for adolescents' well-being have been reported by Stevenson, Maton, and Teti (1999).

We have less information on adolescent fathers; on the whole, it appears that the precocious experience of fatherhood involves fewer negative consequences. However, school career is negatively affected, and often, adolescent fathers abandon school, even if they do not marry their pregnant partner. A minority of adolescent fathers are reluctant (or refuse) to admit their responsibility in the event, in order to escape their duties as fathers. Others feel they are not capable to provide emotional support to their partner and adequate care to their child, even when they have married their partner.

In Great Britain, among illegitimate births reported during adolescence, 20% concern adolescent fathers and 60% 20- to 24-year-old fathers. The paucity of existing studies show that adolescent fathers have a lower education level and are involved in manual jobs; however, from a psychological point of view they are not different from all other adolescents. According to Break-well (1993), adolescent mothers often do not enjoy social support and show non-conventional attitudes, contrary to adolescent fathers, who can benefit from a stronger network of social relationships and stronger social support. Adolescent fathers appear conventional in their attitudes within their subculture of working-class youngsters, but nevertheless they show hostility toward authority figures.

5.2 Demographic patterns of adolescent pregnancy and abortion in Europe

Even if the data on adolescent pregnancies in Europe are less pessimistic than those concerning the USA, they are still worrying, in particular in some countries, including Great Britain (cf. Dennison et al., 1996).

The USA shows the highest rate of teenage pregnancies of any western developed nation, with 12% of women between the ages of 15 and 19 years becoming pregnant (Henshaw, 1994). About half of adolescent pregnancies result in a live birth, 36% are intentionally aborted, and 14% end in a miscarriage (Zabin & Hayward, 1993).

In Great Britain, in 1990 the teenage fertility rate was 32 births per 1000 women aged 15–19 (OPCS, 1993). The situation is less dramatic in Switzerland, the Netherlands, France and Italy (less than 10 births per 1000 women), followed by Sweden, Germany, Spain and Norway (between 10 and 20 births per 1000 women).

In France, only 5% of adolescents become pregnant. Among adolescents who become pregnant between 12 and 16 years, abortion is more frequent. Pregnancies after 17 years end with a live birth in half of cases. As regards abortion, the number of abortions among adolescents is 6000, that is 3% of all abortions undergone.

The lower pregnancy rates in European countries in comparison with the USA is attributable to a more effective contraceptive use than to lower rates of sexual intercourse.

5.3 Correlates of adolescent pregnancy

Research on the correlates of adolescent pregnancy have pointed out the role of the sociocultural context, of adolescent education, and psychological characteristics of the adolescent. A particular profile constantly emerges: adolescent mothers have a lower IQ, lower education (generally they do not finish compulsory education), lower aspirations, they are more oriented to the search for immediate gratifications than to long-term objectives. They are more likely to come from larger families, to be illegitimate daughters, and to have mothers who became pregnant during adolescence.

In a research study conducted in Great Britain, Kiernan (1980) found that adolescent mothers were more likely to have parents with lower education, holding manual jobs and who married at a younger age. They also had more siblings, scored lower on IQ tests, and had abandoned school at a younger age.

Several research studies explored the psychological profile of adolescents during pregnancy and after the birth of the child. They agree in showing that pregnant adolescents have a lower self-esteem and show devaluing tendencies. Being pregnant is associated with shame and distrust toward others, and by a feeling of incompetence in the occupational field. Other studies indicated that adolescent mothers have an external locus of control, perceive a lack of control over their lives and the events happening to them.

6. Conclusion

In this chapter, we have discussed the most significant developments that have occurred in recent research on adolescents' romantic and sexual relationships.

We reviewed some fundamental changes that have taken place in the social and cultural context in which adolescents develop their gender identity and begin to form affective and sexual relationships. Such changes appear to affect the development of male and female gender identity from early to late adolescence.

The issue of the emergence of romantic feelings has been a topic of considerable interest by researchers in recent years, and important information has been provided on the first phases of emergence of such feelings, on the developmental sequence and on the impact of early romantic relationships on the existing pattern of relationships with the family and the peer group. The need to pay greater attention to the social context in which adolescents' romantic relationships are situated has been strongly advocated (Furman, Brown, & Feiring, 1999; Smetana, Campione-Barr, & Metzger, 2006; Steinberg, 2002). More attention should be devoted to the role of the peer group, the family and the cultural expectations in adolescents' romantic experiences. Yet, researchers must also move to a higher level of analysis, considering how these various major social contexts interact, and whether they serve to reinforce each other or present young people with contradictory expectations about romantic relationships.

A further issue we considered concerns adolescents' patterns of sexual activity, by reviewing the basic trends in different sexual behaviors across different European countries, as well as the processes and motivations involved in the transition to coitus. On this issue, research data suggest that the general trend in different countries toward a greater precocity in sexual intercourse may have come to an end and that a pattern of stability or even a reversal of the tendency might be present, at least from the 1990s onward. The reasons for this change deserve greater attention. A candidate explanation might be the impact of sexually transmitted diseases like HIV/AIDS on adolescent sexual behaviors; moreover, the influence of the introduction of youth advisory centers in different European countries to help adolescents and inform them about sexually transmitted diseases and contraception should not be underestimated. The role of sex education provided to adolescents from different agencies (e.g., school, family, etc.) should also be considered.

The issue of risk-taking behaviors in the domain of sexual activity has been the focus of considerable research interest. Research has documented the ways in which adolescents are taking risks as far as unwanted pregnancies and HIV are concerned. Several explanations have been advanced for such a tendency, but research on this topic is still badly needed.

References

Abrams, D., Abraham, S.C.S., Spears, R., & Marks, D. (1990). AIDS invulnerability, relationships, sexual behavior and attitudes among 16 to 19-year-olds. In P. Aggleton, P. Davies, & G. Hart (Eds.), *AIDS: Individual, cultural and policy dimensions*. Lewes: Falmer Press.

Alan Guttmacher Institute (1994). *Sex and America's teenagers*. New York: Alan Guttmacher Institute.

Berti Ceroni, C., Bonini, C., Cerchierini, L., & Zani B. (1987). *La prima volta. Un'indagine sulla scoperta della sessualita nell'adolescenza* [The first time: A study on the discovery of sexuality during adolescence]. Milan, Italy: Angeli.

Bonino, S., Cattelino, E. & Ciarano, S. (2003). *Adolescenti e rischio* [Adolescents and risk]. Firenze, Italy: Giunti.

Bouchey, H.A., & Furman, W. (2003). Dating and romantic experiences in adolescence. In G. R. Adams, & M. D. Berzonsky (Eds.), *Blackwell handbook of adolescence* (pp. 313–329). Oxford: Blackwell.

Breakwell, G. (1993). Psychological and social characteristics of teenagers who have children. In A. Lawson, & D. Rhode (Eds.), *Politics of pregnancy: Adolescent sexuality and public policy* (pp. 159–173). Yale, CT: Yale University Press.

Breakwell, G. (1997). La sexualité à l'adolescence [Sexuality in adolescence]. In H. Rodriguez-Tome, S. Jackson, & F. Bariaud (Eds.), *Regards actuels sur l'adolescence* (pp. 179–206). Paris: Presses Universitaires de France.

Breakwell, G., & Fife-Shaw, C.R. (1991). Heterosexual anal intercourse and the risk of AIDS and HIV for 16–20 year olds. *Health Education Journal, 50*(4), 166–169.

Breakwell, G.M., & Millward, L.J. (1997). Sexual self-concept and sexual risk-taking. *Journal of Adolescence, 20*, 29–41.

Broderick, C.B. (1972). Children's romances. *Sexual Behavior, 2*, 16–21.

Brooks-Gunn, J., & Paikoff, R. (1997). Sexuality and developmental transitions during adolescence. In J. Schulenberg, J. L. Maggs, & K. Hurrelmann (Eds.), *Health risks and developmental transitions during adolescence* (pp. 190–219). Cambridge: Cambridge University Press.

Brown, B.B. (1999). 'You are going out with who?': Peer group influences on adolescent romantic relationships. In W. Furman, B. B. Brown, & C. Feiring (Eds.), *The development of romantic relationships in adolescence* (pp. 291–329). New York: Cambridge University Press.

Brown, B.B. (2004). Adolescents' relationships with peers. In R. M. Lerner, & L. Steinberg (Eds.). *Handbook of adolescent psychology* (2nd ed.) (pp. 363–394). New York: John Wiley & Sons.

Byrne, D. (1983). Sex without contraception. In D. Byrne, & W.A. Fisher (Eds.), *Adolescents, sex and contraception* (pp. 3–31). Hillsdale, NJ: Lawrence Erlbaum Associates, Inc.

Cafaro, D. (1998). *Pianeta giovani* [Planet youngsters]. Rome: ASPER.

Cagliumi, L., Corradini, A., & Zani, B. (1993). *Incontrare gli adolescenti. Modelli e strategie di intervento* [How to meet adolescents: Intervention models and strategies]. Milan, Italy: Unicopli.

Carroll, Z.L., Volk, K.D., & Hyde, J.S. (1985). Differences between males and females in motives for engaging in sexual intercourse. *Archives of Sexual Behavior, 14*, 131–139.

Carver, K, Joyner, K., & Udry, J.R. (2003). National estimates of adolescent romantic relationships. In P. Florsheim (Ed.), *Adolescent romantic relations and sexual behaviour: Theory, research and practical implications* (pp. 23–56). Mahwah, NJ: Lawrence Erlbaum Associates, Inc.

Choquet, M., & Ledoux, S. (1994). *Adolescents. Enquete nationale* [Adolescents: A national survey]. Paris: Inserm.

Cicognani, E. (1991). La comunicazione tra genitori e figli sulla sessualità: Uno sguardo alla letteratura [Parent–children communication about sexuality: A glance at the literature]. In M. C. Bonini, & B. Zani (Eds.), *Dire e non dire* (pp. 101–118). Milan, Italy: Giuffré.

Cicognani, E., & Zani, B. (1998a). *Adolescents' self-efficacy and sexual behaviors in the face of AIDS*. Paper presented at the 6th Biennial Meeting of the European Association for Research on Adolescence, Budapest, Hungary.

Cicognani, E., & Zani, B. (1998b). Chi ha paura dell'AIDS? Uno studio sulle componenti della valutazione del rischio in adolescenza [Who is afraid of AIDS? A study on the components of risk perception in adolescence]. *Bollettino di Psicologia Applicata, 226*, 47–60.

Cicognani, E., & Zani, B. (1999). La salute 'a rischio' in adolescenza: il fenomeno dell'ottimismo irrealistico [Health 'at risk' in adolescence: The phenomenon of unrealistic optimism]. *Psicologia Clinica dello Sviluppo, 3*(1), 81–100.

Coleman, J., & Hendry, L. (1990). *The nature of adolescence* (2nd ed). London: Routledge.

Collins, W.A. (2003). More than a myth: The developmental significance of romantic relationships during adolescence. *Journal of Research on Adolescence, 13*, 1–24.

Connolly, J., Craig, W., Goldberg, A. & Pepper, D. (2004). Mixed-gender groups, dating, and romantic relationships in early adolescence. *Journal of Research on Adolescence, 14*, 185–207.

Crockett, L.G., Raffaelli, M. & Moilanen, K.L. (2003). Adolescent sexuality: Behavior and meaning. In G. R. Adams & M. D. Berzonsky (Eds.), *Blackwell handbook of adolescence* (pp. 313–329). Oxford: Blackwell.

D'Augelli, A.R., & Patterson, C.J. (Eds.). (2001). *Lesbian, gay, and bisexual identities and youth: Psychological perspectives*. Oxford: Oxford University Press.

Dennison, C., Brownrigg, H., & Coleman, J. (1996, May). *Emphasising the positive. Teenage parenthood: Challenging the stereotype*. Paper presented at the 5th Biennial Meeting of the European Association for Research on Adolescence, Liege, Belgium.

Diamond, L.M. & Savin-Williams, R.C. (2003). The intimate relationships of sexual-minority youths. In G. R. Adams & M. D. Berzonsky (Eds.), *Blackwell handbook of adolescence* (pp. 393–412). Oxford: Blackwell.

Di Clemente, R.J. & Crosby, R.A. (2003). Sexually transmitted diseases among adolescents: Risk factors, antecedents, and prevention strategies. In G. R. Adams & M. D. Berzonsky (Eds.), *Blackwell handbook of adolescence* (pp. 313–329). Oxford: Blackwell.

Dornbush, S., Carlsmith, J., Gross, R., Martin, J., Jennings, D., Rosenberg, A. et al. (1981). Sexual development, age, and dating: A comparison of biological and social influences upon one set of behaviors. *Child Development, 52*, 179–185.

Dowdy, B.B., & Kliever, W. (1998). Dating, parent-adolescent conflict, and behavioral autonomy. *Journal of Youth and Adolescence, 27*, 473–491.

Dunphy, D.C. (1963). The social structure of urban adolescent peer groups. *Sociometry, 26*, 230–246.

Du Rant, R.H., & Sanders, J.M. (1989). Sexual behavior and contraceptive risk taking among sexually active adolescent females. *Journal of Adolescent Health Care, 10*, 1–9.

Farrell, W. (1978). *My mother said . . . The way young people learned about sex and birth control*. London: Routledge & Kegan Paul.

Feiring, C. (1999). Gender identity and the development of romantic relationships in adolescence. In W. Furman, B. B. Brown, & C. Feiring (Eds.), *The *development of romantic relationships in adolescence* (pp. 211–232). New York: Cambridge University Press.

Fife-Shaw, C.R., & Breakwell, G. (1992). Estimating sexual behavior parameters in the light of AIDS: A review of recent UK studies of young people. *AIDS Care, 4*(2), 187–201.

Furman, W., Brown, B.B., & Feiring, C. (1999). (Eds.). *The development of romantic relationships in adolescence.* New York: Cambridge University Press.

Furman, W., & Wehner, E.A. (1997). Adolescent romantic relationships: A developmental perspective. In S. Shulman, & W. A. Collins (Eds.), *Romantic relationships in adolescence: Developmental perspectives* (pp. 21–36). San Francisco: Jossey-Bass.

Furstenberg, F.F., Brooks-Gunn, J., & Chase-Lansdale, L. (1989). Teenaged pregnancy and childbearing. *American Psychologist, 44*, 313–320.

Gagnon, J., Lindenbaum, S., Martin, J., May, R.M., Menkey, J., Turner, C.F. et al. (1989). Sexual behavior and AIDS. In C. F. Turner, H. G. Miller, & I. E. Moses (Eds.), AIDS: *Sexual behavior and intravenous drug use* (pp. 23–48). Washington, DC: National Academy Press.

Goldman, R.G., & Goldman, J.D. (1988). *Show me yours: Understanding children's sexuality.* Ringwood: Penguin.

Hartfield, E., & Rapson, R.L. (1996). *Love and sex: Cross-cultural perspectives.* Boston, MA: Allyn & Bacon.

Hatfield, E., Schmitz, E., Cornelius, J., & Rapson, R.L. (1988). Passionate love: How early does it begin? *Journal of Psychology and Human Sexuality, 1*, 35–51.

Hendrick, C., & Hendrick, S.S. (1986). A theory and method of love. *Journal of Personality and Social Psychology, 50*, 392–402.

Henshaw, S.K. (1994). *U.S. teenage pregnancy statistics.* New York: Alan Guttmacher Institute.

Herold, E.S., & Marshall, S.K. (1996). Adolescent sexual development. In G. R. Adams, R. Montemayor, & T. P. Gullotta (Eds.), *Psychosocial development during adolescence* (pp. 62–94). Thousand Oaks, CA: Sage.

Jessor, R. (1998). *New perspectives on adolescent risk behaviors.* New York: Cambridge University Press.

Katchadourian, H. (1990). Sexuality. In S. S. Feldman, & G. R. Elliott (Eds.), *At the threshold: The developing adolescent* (pp. 330–351). Cambridge, MA: Harvard University Press.

Kiernan, K. (1980). Teenage motherhood – associated factors and consequences: The experiences of a British cohort. *Journal of Biosocial Science, 12*, 393–405.

King, A., Beazley, R., Warren, W., Hankins, C., Robertson, A., & Radford, J. (1988). *Canada youth and AIDS study.* Kingston, Ontario: Queen's University.

Laursen, B., & Williams, V. (1997). Perceptions of interdependence and closeness in family and peer relationships among adolescents with and without romantic partners. In S. Shulman, & W. A. Collins (Eds.), *Romantic relationships in adolescence: Developmental perspectives* (pp. 3–20). San Francisco: Jossey-Bass.

Magnusson, C. (2001). Adolescent girls' sexual attitudes and opposite-sex relations in 1970 and in 1996. *Journal of Adolescent Health, 28*, 242–252.

McCabe, M.P. (1984). Toward a theory of adolescent dating. *Adolescence, 19*, 159–170.

McCabe, M.P., & Collins, J.K. (1990). *Dating, relating and sex.* Sydney, Australia: Horowitz Grahame.

Meschke, L.L., & Silbereisen, R.K. (1997). The influence of puberty, family processes, and leisure activities on the timing of first sexual experience. *Journal of Adolescence, 20*, 403–418.

Miller, B.C., McCoy, J.K., Olson, T.D., & Wallace, C.M. (1986). Parental discipline and control attempts in relation to adolescent sexual attitudes and behavior. *Journal of Marriage and the Family, 48*, 503–512.

Miller, B.C., & Moore, K. (1990). Adolescent sexual behavior, pregnancy, and parenting: Research through the 1980s. *Journal of Marriage and the Family, 52*, 1025–1044.

Mitchell, K., & Wellings, K. (1998). First sexual intercourse: Anticipation and communication. Interviews with young people in England. *Journal of Adolescence, 21*, 717–726.

Montgomery, M.J., & Sorell, G.L. (1998). Love and dating experience in early and middle adolescence: Grade and gender comparisons. *Journal of Adolescence, 21*, 677–689.

Moore, S.M., & Rosenthal, D.A. (1993). *Sexuality in adolescence.* London: Routledge.

Neubauer, G. (1990). *Jugend und Sexualität* [Youth and sexuality]. Stuttgart, Germany: Enke.

Nizzoli, U. & Colli, C. (2004). *Giovani che rischiano la vita.* [Young people who risk their lives] Milan, Italy: McGraw-Hill.

OPCS (1993). *Birth statistics.* London: HMSO.

ORS (2000). *Sexualité, contraception et infections sexuellement transmissibles chez les jeunes de la région.* Nantes, France: Author.

Oskamp, S., & Thompson, S.C. (1996). *Understanding*

and preventing HIV risk behavior: Safer sex and drug use. Thousand Oaks, CA: Sage.

Perloff, L.S., & Fetzer, B. (1986). Self-other judgements and perceived vulnerability to victimisation. *Journal of Personality and Social Psychology*, *50*, 502–510.

Phinney, G.V., Jensen, L.C., Olsen, J.A., & Cundick, B. (1990). The relationship between early development and psychosexual behaviors in adolescent females. *Adolescence*, *25*, 321–332.

Roche, J.P. (1986). Premarital sex: Attitudes and behavior by dating stage. *Adolescence*, *21*, 107–121.

Roscoe, B., Diana, M.S., & Brooks, R.H. (1987). Early, middle and late adolescents' views on dating and factors influencing partner selection. *Adolescence*, *22*, 59–68.

Rosenthal, D.A., & Smith, A.M.A. (1997). Adolescent sexual timetables. *Journal of Youth and Adolescence*, *26*, 619–636.

Samet, N., & Kelly, E.W. (1987). The relationship of steady dating to self-esteem and sex role identity among adolescents. *Adolescence*, *22*, 231–245.

Schmidt, G., Klusmann, D., Zeitzschel, U., & Lange, C. (1994). Changes in adolescents' sexuality between 1970 and 1990 in West Germany. *Archives of Sexual Behavior*, *23*, 489–513.

Schofield, M. (1965). *The sexual behaviour of young people*. London: Longman.

Seiffge-Krenke, I. (1998). *Adolescents' health: A developmental perspective*. Mahwah, NJ: Lawrence Erlbaum Associates, Inc.

Shulman, S., & Collins, W.A. (Eds.). (1997). *Romantic relationships in adolescence: Developmental perspectives*. San Francisco: Jossey-Bass.

Siegel, D.M., Aten, M.J. & Roghmann, K.J. (1998). Self-report honesty among middle and high school students responding to a sexual behavior questionnaire. *Journal of Adolescent Health*, *23*, 20–28.

Simon, W., & Gagnon, J.H. (1987). A sexual scripts approach. In J. H. Greer, & W. T. O'Donohue (Eds.), *Theories of human sexuality* (pp. 363–383). New York: Plenum.

Smetana, J.G., Campione-Barr, N., & Metzger, A. (2006). Adolescent development in interpersonal and societal contexts. *Annual Review of Psychology*, *57*, (in press).

Stattin, H., & Magnusson, D. (1990). *Pubertal maturation in female development*. Hillsdale, NJ: Lawrence Erlbaum Associates, Inc.

Steinberg, L. (2002). *Adolescence* (6th ed.). New York: McGraw-Hill.

Stevenson, W., Maton, K.J., & Teti, D.M. (1999). Social support, relationship quality, and well-being among pregnant adolescents. *Journal of Adolescence*, *22*, 109–121.

Taris, T.W., & Semin, G.R. (1997). Gender as a moderator of the effects of the love motive and relational context on sexual experience. *Archives of Sexual Behavior*, *26*, 159–180.

Taris, T.W., & Semin, G.R. (1998). How mothers' parenting styles affect their children's sexual efficacy and experience. *Journal of Genetic Psychology*, *159*, 68–81.

Zabin, L., & Hayward, S. (1993). *Adolescent sexual behavior and childbearing*. Newbury Park, CA: Sage.

Zani, B. (1991). Male and female patterns in the discovery of sexuality during adolescence. *Journal of Adolescence*, *14*, 163–178.

Zani, B. (1993). Dating and interpersonal relationships in adolescence. In S. Jackson, & H. Rodriguez-Tomé (Eds.), *Adolescence and its social worlds* (pp. 95–119). Hove, UK: Lawrence Erlbaum Associates Ltd.

Zani, B. (1997). L'adolescente e la sessualità [The adolescent and sexuality]. In A. Palmonari (Ed.), *Psicologia dell'adolescenza* (pp. 177–202). Bologna, Italy: Il Mulino.

12

Adolescents in school

August Flammer and Françoise D. Alsaker

LEARNING OBJECTIVES

This chapter is about important aspects of adolescents' life in school as well as the importance of school in the life of adolescents. All adolescents in Europe go through secondary school I, very many of them also go through secondary school II. However, schools are differently organized in different countries, ranging from comprehensive to very differentiated institutions. While the first seems to be less stress inducing, they bear the risk of "underfeeding" the best students. In addition, duration of schooling, school size, class size, and diurnal organizational schemes influence perceived strain.

There is an enduring dynamic between taught subjects and students' interests. Typically, the primary interests of adolescents do not coincide readily with the school curriculum. Indeed, on average interest in school decreases during adolescence.

Special attention is paid to the procedures and the timing of transition into secondary schools, where admission is selective. The transition period is critical in terms of self-esteem and school anxiety. In addition, transition decisions (e.g., entrance exams) may coincide with stressing events in pubertal development.

School is a place both for cognitive and for social learning. While peers are very important at this stage, bullying and being bullied are serious and still frequent events.

1. Aims of schooling and historical changes

It seems natural that adolescents spend most of the daytime in school (see Figure 12.1, based on data from Alsaker & Flammer, 1999). However, some two centuries ago, most of them would not have gone to school at all. School then was a privilege for a few, mainly males from rich families. And even then it was rare that adolescents at age 14 or

15 remained in school. Today school is a public institution. It is on offer to all but also mandatory for all.

The public community has set up this institution with the intention of preparing the young generation for adult life within future society. As compared to earlier times in our culture(s), today's professional and civic life as well as private life require a greater amount of knowledge, skills, and experience in increasingly complex social and technical matters. For this reason, school has become mandatory and extended to cover some nine or more years of these young lives.

It is a general phenomenon in most countries that duration of schooling has increased over the last 100 years or so. This is not only due to societal prescriptions (laws), but also to individual students' goals. In general, students with longer

(and possibly higher) schooling will have better chances in the labor market. This is why many go far beyond the obligatory schooling stage. Going through only the minimum of schooling or even less (i.e., dropping out) drastically increases later chances of unemployment. And unemployment increases the prevalence of infringement of the law (Fergusson, Lynskey, & Horwood, 1997). By the same token, while governments are trying to reduce unemployment through more schooling opportunities as well as higher schooling requirements, for some students this leads to fatigue, stress, and greater possibility of dropping out, factors which also hamper these adolescents' chances of successful socialization. Yet early entrance into the labor market confronts many young people with a rough lifestyle that they tend to accept as a model for imitation

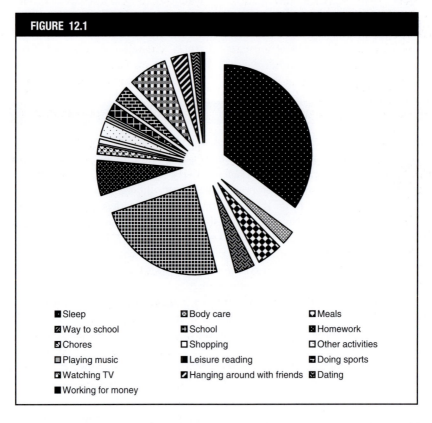

FIGURE 12.1

- ◼ Sleep
- ◪ Way to school
- ◪ Chores
- ◻ Playing music
- ◪ Watching TV
- ◼ Working for money
- ◩ Body care
- ⊞ School
- ◻ Shopping
- ◼ Leisure reading
- ◪ Hanging around with friends
- ◻ Meals
- ◪ Homework
- ◻ Other activities
- ◩ Doing sports
- ◪ Dating

NB Average calculated from 2315 participants in the Euronet study comprising adolescents from Bulgaria, CSFR [in 1992], Finland, France, Germany, Hungary, Norway, Poland, Romania, Russia, Switzerland, and USA.

Time use in 14–16-year-old adolescents on a regular school day.

(alcohol consumption, sexual attitudes, violence etc.) (Greenberger & Steinberg, 1986).

This way of looking at school triggers the question as to whether school is indeed in the best service of the students or whether it primarily serves the intentions of adult society. The answer to this question cannot be given in definitive fashion. Any answer is, furthermore, necessarily multifaceted. It has to take into account students' interests and their abilities, but also possible interests to come (adults sometimes blame their former teachers for not having sufficiently anticipated their future). However, nobody knows for sure what society will look like in the future. Furthermore, one could also ask whether everything adolescents would like to learn is actually the school's task to teach. Important socialization functions are taken over by co-educators such as parents, peers, leisure opportunities, cultural events of all sorts, sport clubs, TV, etc.

Nevertheless, schoolteachers have to make decisions and choices, taking into account all these contingencies. The sum of these more or less explicit decisions and choices make up the 'school philosophy'. As a prominent American example: a taskforce within the Carnegie Corporation divided into five categories children's and adolescents' learning goals that should be actively sustained by the school (Feagans & Bartsch, 1993, pp. 129–130). According to this categorization, schooling should lead each student:

1. to become an intellectually reflective person (writing, verbal expression, basic arts, mathematics, science)
2. to be ready to engage in work for economical reasons as well as for self-definition
3. to become a good citizen (voting, caring for the environment, respecting different cultures, understanding the nation's history)
4. to become a committed ethical person (distinguishing good and bad, and engaging for the good)
5. to become or to stay a physically and psychically healthy person.

This catalogue is clearly larger than what the formal subject matter curricula of most schools can possibly encompass.

Adolescence has been defined in many ways (Goossens, this volume). For the sake of convenience, in this chapter we restrict our discussion to those young people who attend school at so-called secondary level. In Europe, we distinguish between secondary school I or 'lower secondary education' (age 11/12 through 15/16 in most cases), and secondary school II or 'upper secondary education' (age 15/16 through 18/19 in most cases). In the majority of European countries, secondary school I is mandatory, and secondary school II is optional, compulsory education ending at the age of 16 in most countries.

Secondary school II has different names in different countries, e.g., senior high school (English-speaking countries), Gymnasium (German-speaking countries, as well as Finland, Denmark, and Sweden), lycée (French-speaking countries), lykeio (Greece), liceo (Italy), bachillerato (Spain), to mention but a few. In addition, there are several specialized schools at level II like paramedical, trade, artistic, and others. Vocational schools related to the dual vocational training system, as exists mainly in German-speaking countries, are to be found at level II, also. Professional training is treated in greater depth elsewhere in this volume.

2. Structure of schooling

Organizational aspects of schools set the boundary conditions of students' life in school. The organization of school systems and of specific single schools includes many different aspects including rules and laws of attendance, staffing, financing, decisional structures, curricula, timetables, buildings etc. We treat but a few of these aspects here.

2.1 School systems in different European countries

European school systems differ in how they organize secondary school. In some countries, secondary schools I and II are organized in different school structures, while in others they are organized in one single system. Also, in most countries lower secondary schools are conceived independently from primary schools, but in a few countries, primary school and secondary school I are one single structure. In addition, some countries distinguish between different ability levels or tracks within or among the school types in lower secondary school and offer the possibility of switching from one to the other.

In most countries, upper secondary schools provide a variety of school types and therefore offer several different curricular options. Many distinguish between general and vocational education, some also provide separate education for arts, teacher training (at the secondary level II), specific technical education, and others.

We distinguish four groups of countries according to how they organize lower secondary schooling (Table 12.1). In the first group of countries, lower secondary education represents a continuation of primary education and is organized within one single structure (mostly Scandinavian countries). All students of a given age are offered the same curriculum; there is no differentiation according to ability levels before completion of compulsory school stage. The second group, comprising Greece, France, and Italy, is very much like the first, the only differentiation being that secondary school I is organized independently from primary school. Within the third group, only common core skills are offered to all students without differentiation. The fourth group comprises those countries that offer markedly different level tracks in secondary school II, educational etc. As a consequence, admission to higher level tracks is very selective depending on results of school tests.

It is evident that these differences are not purely organizational matters but consequential for the school experience and probably also for the learning outcome in school. Hard research facts and firm generalizations are difficult to obtain, however, because school organizations are embedded in even larger societal structures and in complex cultural and historical contexts. However, as an example, a study comparing students in 6th through 9th grade in schools from group 1 and from group 4, i.e., Norway and Switzerland, has shown important differences (according as yet unreported results analyzed by the authors). For example, Norwegian students reported much less cheating in tests than Swiss students. Also, Swiss students reported that they felt more nervous before school tests than their Norwegian peers. The reason for this could be that, in Norway, school tests are informative and not decisive. Possibly as another consequence of such stressful experiences, more Norwegian than Swiss students indicated that they wanted to pursue school education beyond mandatory school.

There is possibly another side of the coin. For example, Norwegian students reported higher depression levels and more psychosomatic symptoms than their Swiss peers. Could it be that the one-track system is not challenging enough for some yet over taxing for others? Norwegian students did, in fact, report significantly higher boredom rates on school days, a poorer class climate, and less motivation to go to school than their Swiss peers. As to perceived academic competence, they were basically the same, except that the high-track Swiss students rated themselves highest of all.

2.2 Size of schools and classes

Secondary schools tend to be larger than elementary schools. This allows them to offer more and more varied learning opportunities. Large schools, however, have their disadvantages, on a variety of both performance and personality variables (Eccles & Roeser, 2003). Students often feel lost in an anonymous mass and take less responsibility for the whole school and its extracurricular activities (Garbarino, 1979). In addition, teachers in large schools feel less compelled to monitor students' development.

One matter is the size of the whole school, class size is another. European classes typically comprise 20 to 30 students. As a comparison, Japanese classes usually contain around 40 students. Evidently, given certain instructional methods, classes can be too large to be functional. But it seems that within the usual variance in Europe, class size does not systematically affect the resulting average achievements (Rutter, 1983). However, smaller classes are clearly better suited for more individualized instruction, especially for remedial instruction. But, having said that, each individual school has its own 'culture'. In a famous British study, Rutter, Maugham, Mortimer, and Ouston (1979) showed that different secondary schools

Table 12.1

Classes of secondary school organization in Western Europe (information taken from Eurydice, 1998)

| | Secondary education I ("lower") | | | | Secondary education II (= "upper") | | | | |
| | | | | | General upper secondary education | | | Vocational upper secondary education | |
	Duration and age (beginning–end) of compulsory fulltime education	Duration (years)	Age of completion	Number of ability levels (tracks)	Duration (years)	Age of completion	Number of types of schools	Duration (years)	Age of completion
Group 1	*Compulsory education organized within one single structure*								
	Identical curriculum in compulsory education								
Denmark	9 (7–16)	No distinction between primary school and lower secondary school	16	1[a]	2 or 3	19	4	2–5.5	19–20
Finland	9 (7–16)		16	1	3	19	1[b]	2–3	18–19
Sweden	9 (7–16)		16	1	3	19	1[b]	included in general upper secondary education	
Iceland	10 (6–16)		16	1	2 or 4	18–20	2	0.5–5	variable
Portugal	9 (6–15)		15	1	3	18	1	3	18
Norway	10 (6–16)		16	1	3	19	1	3	19
Group 2	*Primary and secondary education I in separate school structures*								
	Identical general curriculum in secondary education I								
Greece	9 (6–15)	3	15	1[c]	3 or 4	18–19	1	1 or 2	15 up
France	9 (6–15)	4	15	1	3	18	2	2 or 4	17–19
Italy	8 (6–14/15)	3	14/15	1	3–5	17–19	3	3–5	17–19

Group 3 — *Primary and secondary education I in separate school structures*
Common core skills in secondary education I

Belgium[d]	8–9 (6–15/16)[e]	2	1	4	18	2 or 3	4–5	18–19
Spain	10 (6–16)	4	1	2–3	18–19	2	1–3	17–19
Ireland	9 (6–15)	3	1	2–3	17–18	4	2	17
Northern Ireland	12 (4–16)	5	2	2	18	2	Pupils in post-compulsory education can take either vocational or academic courses or a combination of both	
England and Wales	11 (5–16)	5	1	2	18	2		
Scotland	11 (5–16)	4	1	2	18	1	2	18

Group 4 — *Primary and secondary education I in separate school structures*
Different school types in secondary education I

Germany	10 (6–16)[f]	6	4	3	19	1[b]	1–4[g]	19–20
Austria	9 (6–15)	4	2	4	18	1	1–5[g]	16–20
Netherlands	12 (4–16)	3–4	4	2–3	17–18	2	2–4	20
Luxembourg[d]	9 (6–15)	3	2	4	19	1	4–5	19–20
Liechtenstein	9 (6–15)	4	3	4	19	1	2–4[g]	17–19
Switzerland	9 (6/7–15/16)	3–4	2–4	2–5	17–21	3	2–4[g]	17–20

a In grades 8, 9, and 10, certain subjects are taught both in basic and in advanced courses.
b Organized in non-graded form; variable according to courses and credits.
c In some schools teaching is provided on two levels, but related to a common program.
d Secondary education is divided in three stages. In the table, we consider the first stage as lower secondary school.
e Up to age 15/16 full attendance is compulsory, then up to age 18 partial attendance is compulsory.
f Up to age 16 full attendance is compulsory, then up to age 19 partial attendance is compulsory.
g Vocational education is organized in a "dual" system, one part of the week in vocational schools and the other part on the working place.

NB The distinction between "general" and "vocational" upper secondary education is not clear in all countries. In this table, technical education is considered as a part of general education.

do indeed produce consistent differences in performance and behavior, independent of individual dispositions and extra-scholastic variables. It really depends on the school a student happens to be allocated to (for a review see Eccles & Roeser, 2003).

2.3 Entrance examinations

In many countries, entrance into the secondary schools, at least for the higher levels, requires fulfilling certain performance criteria (admission examinations). Table 12.2 offers an overview of admission criteria for secondary education I and II. The countries are grouped according to similarities of the entrance criteria to secondary school I. The first group allows free access. The second group explicitly requires successful completion of primary education. The third group demands a primary education certificate, and the fourth group sets specific additional admission criteria.

Depending on the aspirations of both the adolescents and their parents, such admission procedures can produce enormous stress, so much so that some students – the so-called test-anxious – perform worse than they would be able to under more relaxed circumstances (Sarason, 1980). In evaluative conditions, test-anxious individuals divide the allocation of their mental resources between self-preoccupied worry (rumination, self-evaluation) and on-task performance, whereas the less anxious students focus their attention more fully on task-relevant aspects.

Placing students in different levels offers the advantage of a better fit between abilities and requirements, but also bears clear risks. One risk is the possibility of misplacement. Despite the current emphasis on permeability in case of better or worse than expected performance, there is generally little new placement during the secondary school career. Another risk is the interpretation of being placed on too low a track; many of these students lose hope, motivation, and academic self-esteem (Oakes, Gamoran & Page, 1992).

2.3.1 Timing

For some adolescents admission exams collide with emotionally critical phases (e.g., conflicts with parents, pubertal maturation) so that admission decisions may be unfair to them. Petersen, Sarigiani, and Kennedy (1991) calculated adolescents' age at which they grew fastest (peak height velocity, PHV). They found 43% of girls experience this peak of maturation at about the same time as the transition from elementary to junior high school. This was the case for only 11.6% of boys. Using regression analysis they demonstrated that synchrony of pubertal and school transition was the strongest predictor of depressive mood and that it could explain the gender differences. Also, according to these researchers, students who experienced PHV more than 6 months after transition to high school had a higher self-image than those who went through PHV at least 6 months *before* transition. It might, therefore, be more likely for girls than for boys to suffer from relevant transient emotional troubles when entering higher levels of secondary schooling because of the coincidence of pubertal maturation, temporary declines in self-esteem, depressive mood, and periods of exams. Beyond this, such coincidences are risk factors for dropping out of school and for alcohol and drug consumption (Eccles, Lord, & Buchanan, 1996).

2.3.2 Transition effects

Negative effects of transition from primary to secondary school have also been found to be independent from pubertal status. In most school subjects the average self-concept of ability decreases as a consequence of this transition (Wigfield, Eccles, Mac Iver, Reuman, & Midgley, 1991), especially among the low achievers (Midgley, Feldlaufer, & Eccles, 1989). And so does the liking of school (Wigfield et al., 1991). Due to higher achievement standards and stricter grading, school anxiety has also been found to increase after transition to secondary school (Harter, Whitesell, & Kowalski, 1992).

The disruption of social networks may also contribute to the lowering of self-esteem after transition to secondary school. Having good friends (Hirsch & DuBois, 1991) and especially being able to rely on a supportive family (Eccles,

Table 12.2

Admission criteria to secondary schools I and II in Western Europe (from EDK, 1995; Eurydice, 1997; adaptations by the authors)

	Admission criteria to secondary education I	Admission criteria to secondary education II
Group 1		
Denmark	As the compulsory school is a unified structure, there is no admission selection to the secondary school I	Completion of at least the 9th year of compulsory school and recommendation for "gymnasium" and "hojere forberedelseseksamen"
Finland	As above	Graduation from secondary school I; students apply to a maximum of five institutions; selection is made on the basis of mainly average school marks
Sweden	As above	Successful completion of secondary school I; "pass" in Swedish, English and maths
Iceland	As above	Completion of the 10th year of the compulsory school
Norway	As above	Successful completion of the 9th year of compulsory school
Spain (post-reform)	Automatic access at the end of primary school	Graduation from secondary school I; students over 18 years: entrance examination to vocational education
Group 2		
Portugal	Successful completion of primary education or equivalent level of schooling	Successful completion of secondary education I or equivalent qualification
France	Completion of the consolidation stage of the primary school	Different requirements according to the chosen studies
Scotland	Completion of primary education	Admission criteria for specific courses; no conditions for "further education college" (vocational)
Group 3		
Italy	Primary education certificate	Secondary school I certificate
Greece	Primary education certificate	Secondary school I certificate
Belgium	Primary education certificate (not necessary for vocational secondary)	Secondary school I certificate
Group 4		
Ireland	Completion of the primary education; some secondary schools organize entrance examinations	No entrance criteria to secondary II

Northern Ireland	No specific conditions for "secondary schools"; "grammar schools" may include pupils' academic abilities under several admission criteria	Completion of secondary I; no formal qualifications for "further education colleges" (vocational)
England/Wales	Schools may demand ability criteria	No formal qualifications required, but some courses have specific requirements
Germany	Completion of primary school (year 4) and recommendation for "gymnasium" or for "Realschule"	Access to upper level of gymnasium requires specific qualifications
Austria	Successful completion of the primary school (year 4); (very) good marks in German, reading and maths for the "Allgemeinbildende höhere Schule" (higher level)	(Successful) completion of the year 8 or 9 of compulsory school; entrance examinations for several types of secondary II
Netherlands	Decision by an admissions board on the basis of the final primary school report	Specific certificates of secondary I
Luxembourg	Guidance procedures in the last years of primary school	Decision by the "class council" on the basis of its own guidelines
Liechtenstein	5 years of primary school; different admission procedures for "Realschule" and "Gymnasium"	9 years of compulsory education plus entrance exams, partly replaced by former and/or school results
Switzerland	(Very) good primary school marks or teacher's recommendation; opinion of the parents can be taken into consideration	9 years of compulsory education; in addition secondary I final exams or secondary II entrance exams

Lord, Roeser, Barber, & Josefowicz, 1997; Lord, Eccles, & McCarthy, 1994) seem to be important protective factors.

In a study with Parisian students aged 11 to 17 years, Rodriguez-Tomé and Bariaud (1991) found 52% of essay answers on what students were fearful of relating, among other things, to school ("worries concerning school work ..., future exams or bad test results in an extended present", p. 172); 15.6%, in part the same participants, mentioned school authorities. School-related fears, however, drastically decreasing over the researched age span, meaning that they were most frequent shortly after transition to secondary school.

Negative effects on self-image and coping have also been found for early school transition (prior to 6th grade), especially for repeated school transitions (Crockett, Petersen, Graber, Schulenberg, & Ebata, 1989). Simmons and Blyth (1987) found evidence of lower risks, especially for girls, when primary and secondary schools are within the same school setting.

Thus, while developmental psychology offers good reasons for dividing secondary from primary school at about the age of 12 years (formal operations, puberty), there are also good developmental reasons not to place this transition exactly at this age, at least if the transition is combined with decisive admission exams for higher and lower tracks and if later shifts are difficult or rare.

School organization is one important determinant of adolescents' socialization. Another is curriculum. Indeed, the hard core of what the school teaches to young people is academic disciplines such as mathematics, writing, biology etc. The next section of this chapter will therefore describe adolescents' life in the context of such academic learning. That section will be followed by considerations about more informal and social learning at school.

3. Academic learning

As its first mission, the school has to teach academic basic skills and knowledge. Secondary school continues this mission at a higher level. But in addition, secondary school prepares adolescents for professional tracks, either for imminent transition into the working world or for academic studies.

3.1 *Abstract thinking*

Some of the academic disciplines taught in the secondary school require some capacity for abstract thinking. This is especially true for mathematics and some linguistic teaching. In terms of formal operations in Piaget's sense, we know from developmental studies that many students at secondary level I do not manifest formal operations in all sorts of situations (see Lehalle, this volume). There are three ways out of this problem:

1. restrict curricula to subject matters that do not require formal operations (e.g., no algebra)
2. teach school subjects in a way that does not require formal operations (e.g., language teaching in a more intuitive way)
3. directly teaching and training formal operations (e.g., working with mathematical proportions and relating them to other operations).

The purposeful development of abstract thinking is highly desirable, not only because it is important in many everyday life contexts, but also because it allows deeper self-reflection and more efficacious critical thinking.

Generally, it is helpful to let students work on real problems in depth and over time. Formal–logical reasoning is easier, when it is embedded in understandable contents. For example, preadolescents very often are able to draw correct conclusions from a set of premises, if and only if they do not conflict with the experienced reality (Keating,

1990). Development of thinking is less a matter of stepwise climbing higher order content-free cognitive operations in Piaget's sense but more a matter of successive testing and revising subjective theories about more or less specific aspects of the real or the imagined world (Bartsch, 1993; Lehalle, this volume). Therefore, teaching to think and to think better has, in the first place, to take into account what and how the students already think about specific contents. This teaching principle implies an ongoing discourse with competent and responsive teachers (and peers) which fosters the abilities of social–cognitive exchange (Lehalle, this volume).

3.2 *Students' interests*

In most cases the curriculum is organized around scientific disciplines like mathematics, physics, language studies, biology. This is not always what corresponds to the primary interests of young students. On average, both interest in school matters *and* general well-being in school drop drastically in the first half of the second decade of life (Fend, 1997). While gifted students often show strong academic interests (Gottfried & Gottfried, 1996), average adolescent students are less inclined spontaneously towards academic learning. Teachers at this level have to undertake a formidable task:

- They have to satisfy students' interests and tie their teaching into these interests.
- They have to comply with possible later and retroactive demands or critiques in terms of what their students should have learned by then.
- They have to adequately translate societal and civic demands and necessities.

3.2.1 *Curriculum and interests*

In everyday school learning there are two types of interest–demand mismatch, one between school matters and extracurricular (often social) interests and concerns, and the other between the timing of school demands and actual interests. It is not that school learning material per se would be generally *un*interesting to the students, but the timing and the actual circumstances often clash with actual – often individual – interests and concerns. As an example, most adolescents do not hesitate to use (and to learn) mathematics when needed, for instance when it comes to decide whether it is worthwhile to take a loan in order to buy a laptop computer now instead of after earning some summer vacation income. But when the curriculum simply prescribes 'percentages and loan interests', it often comes without a motivational match on the students' side.

Contrariwise, each scientific discipline has its own logic and its own accumulated knowledge. And curricula require that students concentrate on each of these disciplines as such and eventually combine them and to apply them to practical problems. Both in order to encompass students' motivational prerequisites and to enhance the usability of learned material, modern curricula pack classical disciplines into functional complexes, be they transdisciplinary or embedded in practical problems to be solved. Especially in the second half of the second decade of life, relating school learning to real work and to later vocational activities can make learning more attractive for many adolescents (Hamilton, 1994; Toepfer, 1994).

Adolescents have many interests, and school learning is not the most prominent among them. Some studies on adolescents' interests, indirectly show a picture that is hard to reconcile with school demands, i.e., in terms of preferred leisure activities. Most adolescents really enjoy listening to music, being with friends, sports (football as well as trend sports like inline skating and snowboarding, usually boys more than girls), and parties/discos (girls more than boys) (Dybowski & Hartwig, 1996; Fitzgerald, Joseph, Hayes, & O'Regan, 1995). All these interests overlap only marginally with school activities. A Gymnasium student in 9th grade said in an interview:

> We discuss more about what to do after school. In earlier grades, the discussions in the afternoon were about what was in the morning and what to do the following day at school. (Fend, 1997, p. 12; translated by A. F.)

In the Swiss–Norway study, Alsaker and Flammer (2000) asked students to nominate those disciplines they like best. In both countries, sports were by far the most liked, although this decreased over grades. Art was liked a lot in primary school, but dropped at secondary level, more particularly in Switzerland. Religion was the most *disliked* discipline, in Norway drastically more than in Switzerland. Somewhat surprisingly, the second least liked were classes in the mother tongue (German, French, Norwegian).

The subject matter itself is one consideration, the other is the teaching style and actual learning conditions. If the success is related to interindividual rankings, students' focus is more on the outcome than on the subject matter and its potential intrinsic interest. If the student's aim is to understand, to know, to discover and to personally master what he or she wants to master, the subject matter becomes or remains intrinsically interesting (e.g., Dweck & Leggett, 1988).

3.2.2 Students' interests and timing of school learning

The partitioning of the knowledge body as is especially practiced at the secondary school levels, most often also goes along with a disruptive lesson organization. Thus, a student may start at 8 in the morning with writing, at 8:50 he or she may have to change classroom and teacher in order to go to biology, 9:40 on to geography and finally to a music class at 11. This not only demonstrates clear distinctions between learning materials, but also requires brisk interruptions of ongoing learning processes. In addition, as the different subjects put variable strain on the students, homework assignments and exam deadlines often lack coordination. Such practices produce unnecessary stress in the students.

Another aspect of possible school stress originates from school hours and their distribution over the day, the week, and the year. Most of the countries prescribe the annual minimum number of teaching hours for each subject matter. Upwards from the age of 13, only the United Kingdom and Ireland offer a totally flexible timetable (Eurydice, 1997, p. 84). The other countries vary to a great extent. As an example, the yearly number of lessons to be taught on native language (mother tongue) varies from 76 in Finland to 187 in Italy. And number yearly of lessons on foreign languages ranges from 71 lessons in Sweden to 210 in Germany.

The whole number of teaching lessons per year ranges from 800 to 1000 in most countries; Iceland prescribes about 750 lessons, and Ireland, the Netherlands, Austria, and Liechtenstein go about 1000 but all less than 1100 lessons (Eurydice, 1997).

3.2.3 Curricular choices made by students

Students' interests also influence choice of school subjects, of school tracks, and finally of professional orientations. Intrinsic motives as well as the schooling context and concrete teaching circumstances play a role (Todt, Drewes, & Heils, 1994). Some intrinsic motives are possibly gender biased and lead boys and girls to different choices (on average). Interestingly, made choices may also bias judgments of related school disciplines. For instance, Watson, McEwen, and Dawson (1994) studied 6th graders from Northern Ireland and found that the boys not only judged those subjects they typically choose as more interesting, i.e., mathematics, physics, and chemistry, but they also construed them to be more difficult, more socially beneficial, and as giving more freedom to the student in school. The same was true for girls, but related to those subjects they typically choose, i.e., English, French, history, and geography.

In choosing school types and disciplines, academically oriented students pay more attention to future professional prestige than to occupational attraction per se (Shamai, 1996). This is one of the reasons why Hamilton (1994) postulated that an optimal combination of transparency in terms of prospects and how they can be achieved and in terms of future permeability (= possibilities to move from one school or track to another) provide the key to motivate adolescents for learning in school.

Students also base their choices on their achievements, on background determinants like parents' aspirations, and on peer models and social prejudices (Fend, 1997). Thus, girls are more often channeled into language courses and

boys more into mathematics and technical courses (Hallinan, 1994; Watson et al., 1994).

Developing an adequate curriculum is a never ending task. There will always remain tensions between actual interests of students and well-founded arguments of teachers and schools whose thinking is not only theirs but also a reflection of the ongoing cultural development over history. Also, there always are minorities whose desires and aspirations must be respected and supported. Thus, some adolescent students are determined to become scientists and should not be hindered from entering the core and the logic of academic disciplines early. This is why in many countries schools offer different levels and different curricula for different types of student and different needs. However, it seems that European schools generally leave less choice to the students than US schools, for example. Contrariwise, in Europe, there seems to be more concern about whether everybody acquires a sizeable minimum of academic knowledge and skills. German schools, for example, provide more prevocational instruction than does the US system, particularly to the intellectually less gifted students, whereas the US school system seems to pay more attention to developmental and social needs of the adolescents (Petersen, Leffert, & Hurrelmann, 1993).

3.2.4 Losing interest in school

Speaking with teachers, one repeatedly learns that they most like the students in grade 3 to 6 (primary school), and for two reasons: (1) these students have learned the basic behavior discipline in school as well as the most elementary cultural techniques like writing, reading, and the elementary arithmetic operations; (2) they are very *interested in learning*. As already indicated, mean interest in school learning decreases in adolescence (Eccles, Adler, & Meece, 1984; Harter et al., 1992).

In the Swiss–Norwegian study a composite measure was calculated from several rating scales about liking and disliking school (e.g., 'I enjoy going to school', 'There are really only a few things that I like at school'). The effects were most salient in Norway, where liking school fell markedly and steadily from grade 4 to grade 9. In

Switzerland, where at the secondary school I three different level tracks are offered, this drop is less consistent. There the overall low among German Swiss was found in grade 6. In both parts of Switzerland, school liking drops from primary to secondary school I at level 2, but not at level 3 (Gymnasium; see Figure 12.2; data from Alsaker & Plammer, 1999). In addition, liking school generally decreased over primary years and secondary I years, except for the first grades of the Gymnasium.

However, interviews with secondary school II students (Gymnasium in Germany) show that later in the Gymnasium school career pleasure with school diminishes too. One of the Gymnasium students interviewed by Fend (1997, pp. 10–13; translated by A. F.) said:

Well, in 9th grade, interests are quite different from 5th grade ... Students are less interested in school. Coming from the elementary school to gymnasium, they find gymnasium great. They have new teachers and a new environment, and their first concern is to keep up ... But then school soon gets monotonous. You start to realize that it all is not so fascinating. You develop in another

direction and realize that school does not play a role in it.

Another student said:

In 5th grade they do not let you copy, because they are too afraid of their teacher. They think: 'He could get you.'

There also seems to be some group pressure to this effect:

If in 9th grade you always get good grades, then it is difficult to get rid of the label that you're a swot. ... That is why you are no longer interested in being the best. It feels 'cool' to be independent from good grades.

Adolescents, like children (and most adults), abundantly consume media offerings. In adolescence, audiovisual media are clearly preferred to the print media (VanEimeren & Maier-Lesch, 1997). Modern didactics try to fit at least partly with these preferences, but school cannot get around reading requirements. Happily, for many adolescents, reading is still one of the favorite leisure activities, especially in girls and when they

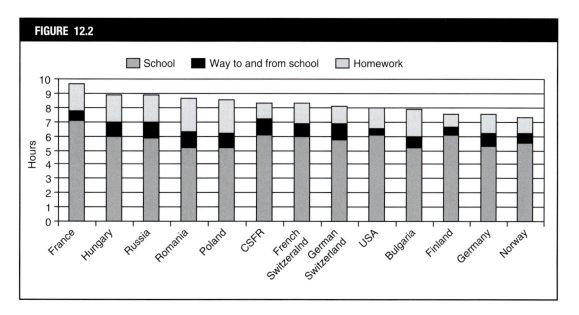

FIGURE 12.2

School-related activities in 14–16-year-old adolescents in 12 European and one US sample on a regular school day.

are in the upper levels rather than in lower school levels (Bannert & Arbinger, 1996; Flammer, Alsaker, & Noack, 1999; Gilges, 1992). As to the topics of interests in reading, romantic and social–pychological content is favored by girls. Sports, computer, and motor vehicles are favorites for boys (Fend, 1990, 1994; Palmonari, 1993; Todt, 1978). Few adolescents are interested in politics (Fischer, 1997; Palmonari & Rubini, 1993; VanEimeren & Maier-Lesch, 1997), although preparing students to become active and responsible citizens is generally taken as an important task at secondary school level. This is a special challenge for our public schools. It seems that many students at this level of development are not prepared for political education in the classical sense. But they seem to be amenable to the politics of their immediate society, e.g. the class or school. For example, in the 'just community' program by Kohlberg (1985; see also Power, 1988) students democratically develop rules for their own community life, define rewards and sanctions, and eventually apply them. Such a program is a sort of mirror of the larger political scene, adapted, however, to actual needs. Moreover, it concerns students' real everyday life and is not only a game or a mental experiment.

It seems that motivational deficits at the secondary school level are widespread, at least as far as so called intrinsic motivation is concerned. One of the Fend interviewees stated it simply like this: 'The only reason for me to stay in school is to get good finals and to become graduated in order to have a good starting position in professional life.' However, it seems to us that adolescence is too important a life phase to be spoiled by demotivation and to be filled by adverse learning experiences.

3.3 School demands and stress

School is not primarily a place for play and pleasure. Although learning is interesting and a challenge for many, the school asks for performances that necessitate huge and sustained effort. For many students, school demands are at their personal upper limit. In order not to set the demands too high, many schools in Europe offer different types of school as well as the possibility

for choosing tracks within the school career. While moving from a higher level to a lower level reduces immediate school stress, such moves also imply other, more personal stress in terms of self-esteem and societal prestige. Because all students know or believe that higher schooling offers more chances in later life, most of them prefer to stay at the highest levels possible. Some students become demotivated and perform even less well when relegated into lower levels. It is a general finding that schools and teachers who attribute (good and poor) school achievements to ability instead of effort, motivation, and actual external conditions foster anxiety and disinterest in a large proportion of students. The same is true for teachers who stress comparison *between* students instead of *individual progress* (Eccles & Roeser, 2003).

In terms of time spent in school and on activities related to school there are noticeable differences between European countries, as is shown for the selection of countries included in the Euronet study (Figure 12.3).

A Polish study serves as a good illustration of concrete school stress. Tyszkowa (1991) had 16- and 18-year-old secondary school II students write essays about 'school situations which are difficult for me'. Younger students, especially girls, reported more difficulties than older students. The most frequent of all categories was threat as reported by younger girls. One student wrote with reference to teachers' questions in mathematics: 'There are moments when everything evaporates from my mind. When I feel as though I can't count to ten' (p. 194). Interestingly, among the three main situations, impediments (e.g., 'unclear lesson, difficult formulation of questions by the teacher, impatience during pupils' answers, classmates talking during lesson') and threat (e.g., 'tests or classwork, especially where given without warning, being examined by certain teachers, expectation of bad marks') were the most frequently mentioned, more frequently than overload (e.g., 'accumulation of repetitions and tests at the end of semester, too much homework, being asked to solve very complex tasks in a short period of time') (p. 192).

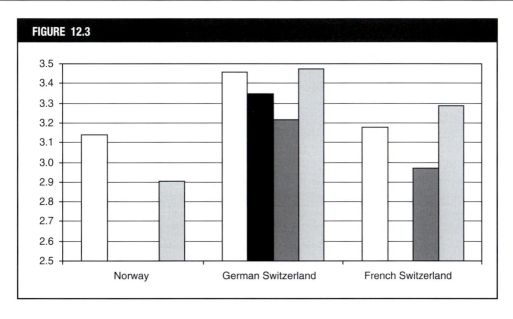

FIGURE 12.3

Liking school in primary and secondary school I (separate according to levels, where applicable)

3.3.1 School homework

School homework has many important functions in that it extends the time allocated to scholastic learning, possibly allows for leveling out certain individual differences within classes, and connects formal learning with the extra-school life such as family, home, daily routines. In a large Swiss sample, it was found that low-track and middle secondary school students spent less time on homework than high-track students (Gymnasium), and that they spent this time almost exclusively within the five school days, while Gymnasium students spent more time on homework during the weekend and most of all on Sundays (Flammer & Tschanz, 1997).

In general, the extent of homework seems to be positively related to both achievement and (positive) behavior in class (Rutter et al., 1979). Homework, however, takes up time and can also be a source of stress. In a recent study with Swiss and Norwegian adolescents, Alsaker and Flammer (1999b) found that the amount of time spent on homework was harmless for about 90% of students, but connected with psychosomatic problems for about 10%. The correlation coefficients between amount of time spent on school homework and psychosomatic symptoms such as headache, migraine, or nervousness were all positive but rather small for higher track students in the Swiss secondary schools, but highest for the lowest track students. It seems unlikely that homework per se produces psychosomatic symptoms, but it could be that such symptoms jeopardize the efficiency of the completion of homework and cause these students to work especially long hours on school homework. Given that, according to the same study, students with less school success have to spend more time on their school homework, this result allows critique on the pedagogical aim of leveling out individual differences among students.

3.3.2 Vicious circles

School is – among other things – about achievement. Not all students perform at the same level, some perform so poorly they are relegated in degrees or school level or not admitted to further/ higher schooling. School achievement also has long-term consequences for professional life, social standing, and income. Clearly, lack of success in school is frustrating and hampers further school motivation and lowers the aspiration level. And this initiates a vicious circle: poor performance lowers school motivation, and low school motivation lowers the likelihood of success in school.

Low school motivation and low educational aspirations have repeatedly been shown to be risk factors for a variety of problem behaviors (Jessor, VandenBos, Vanderryn, Costa, & Turbin, 1995), such as delinquency (McCord, 1992), drug use (Hawkins, Catalino, & Miller, 1992), and early sexual activity (Small & Luster, 1994). By the same token, high academic competence and school motivation can act as a buffer against problem behavior, e.g., substance abuse (Wills, Vaccaro, & McNamara, 1992) and internalizing problems (Dekovic, 1999). According to a study by Fergusson and Lynskey (1996, quoted in Dekovic, 1999, p. 671) enjoying school can buffer against risks emanating from the family background.

4. Social learning

Besides academic learning school also serves as a socialization agent both at the societal (= macro) level and at the group (= micro) level. Historically, public schooling was instituted in most countries with a civic purpose, i.e., to guarantee the functioning of democratic institutions. Everybody should be able to read public regulations in order to follow them, everybody should be able to read newspapers in order to form his or her opinion about public matters. Only informed people should reasonably vote and elect. Furthermore, nations have an interest in transmitting common knowledge, beliefs, and convictions in order to 'homogenize' their citizenship. Some nations even fight for linguistic homogenization of the population etc.

4.1 Civic knowledge, beliefs, and values

Citizens of a specific nation share many beliefs and values that are historically rooted but still subject to change over time. Nowadays, historians are all for revealing a shaky basis for many collective beliefs and myths. In Europe itself, there are three ready examples: (1) around the end of the 20th century, people in several European countries became aware to what extent some of their compatriots at the time took advantage from secret collaboration with the Nazis; (2) in a

comparable vein, history was being rewritten in the 1990s in several eastern European countries; (3) seemingly natural values and norms in many European countries with a Christian tradition are being challenged by the immigration of people from foreign cultures.

Among the more recent values, intentionally transmitted in European schools, are related to ecology, to justice, to worldwide famine, to refugees etc. The teaching of beliefs and values is done in formal ways through explicit curriculum contents and in informal ways, i.e., implicitly in history classes, writing classes etc.

While it is true that formal teaching of values is not experienced as attractive by some students, others are extremely interested in it. Perhaps formal value teaching comes too early for some students. They might be interested in certain principled information, but are not willing to critically study a comprehensive system of such propositions. As is shown by Lehalle (in this volume), formal operational thinking comes gradually and, for some, late. Thus, the interest might be for principles, but not for a principled system of principles (Patrick, 1991).

Political interests clearly increase during adolescence (Steiner, 1986). Fatalistic aspects in political control beliefs decrease and internal control beliefs increase (Krampen, 1991). Actual political motivation results more from concrete political events and from stimulation from parents, teachers and peers, and less from individual psychological (cognitive or emotional) development per se (Krampen, 1991). And it is exactly this kind of motivation that most fosters adolescents' social learning (Cooney & Selman, 1980; Keating, 1990). Furthermore, promoting empathy (Hatcher, Nadeau, Walsh, Reynolds, Galea, & Marz, 1994) and perspective shifts (Santilli & Hudson, 1992; Selman, 1984) are not only important social learning goals, but also important mediators of further social learning.

Despite the social interest or even enthusiasm of adolescents, there are also limits. Most adolescents and adults do not reach the highest possible stage of perspective taking and moral judgment (see, Lehalle, this volume). That is, most adolescents are capable of taking mutual perspectives (e.g., 'You know that I know that you . . .'), but not all of them are able to understand a network of perspectives that connects individuals to a social system. Similarly, most adolescents and adults attain a conventional level of moral judgment (that is recognition of both individual and social factors), but not a post-conventional level that includes a deeper analysis of the respective rights and duties of individuals and societies. In sum, adolescents are more likely than children to consider both external and internal (i.e., psychological and principled) aspects of a given problem and to integrate various features of it, but they encounter difficulties in attempting to achieve an integrated understanding of their personal and social experiences (Keating, 1990).

4.2 Integrating into the school community

To try to live in the school community is not an easy thing for adolescents. It is a major developmental task for schoolchildren to integrate into new social groups, to find his or her place in a multiplicity of necessities, desires, and tastes. In many countries, the community challenge comes gradually, starting with small Kindergarten classes, going through elementary school in a sizeable building with a dozen or so classes, and ending in complex secondary school systems with up to 1000 students. These conditions are not only learning opportunities for later adult life, but they also represent an interesting living ecology in themselves.

One challenge is to find oneself in this large community, to learn to whom one belongs (and to whom not), to learn what is regulated and what is left for free decision, and to learn what regulations come from where and how they can legally or illegally be contested. In a study about reactions of Swiss adolescents in situations where their personal freedom was sensibly limited, it was found that adolescents differentiate very much between three types of authority, i.e., authority of known persons, authority of unknown persons, and authorities of (anonymous) institutions (Flammer, Züblin, & Grob, 1988). The authority of known persons can be contacted and possibly persuaded into an alternative regulation. Institutions have neither a human face nor a human voice. Approaching them means writing to them or collecting referendum signatures, and discourse cannot generally be face to face. It seems to be easier for young people to find their way through interaction with people than with anonymous institutions and regulations. From this it can be concluded that schools and teachers can support young students' well-being and locus of control by offering them personal contacts – or hinder it by confronting them with anonymous (impersonal) authorities (King, Wold, Tudor-Smith, & Harel, 1996).

There are not only formal regulations, but also both more general and more specific norms to obey. Certain places are reserved for certain groups and forbidden for others, certain groups are attractive and others not, certain groups and people are helpful and others not. Taking part in certain activities, being accepted by certain groups can imply very different consequent obligations. We think of positive ways in the area of sports, music, religion or social commitment; and there are less positive things like legal and illegal drug taking, premature or risky sex experiences, delinquency, religious fanatism, etc.

Social factors as tied to school life co-condition the possible use of legal and illegal drugs: poor social acceptance, shyness, being at the lower end of the perfomance range in class etc. (More detailed information can be found elsewhere in this volume).

School is a promising way to train social skills at a high level. A successful method of accomplishing this is by building what is called a just community (Kohlberg, 1985; Power, 1988). Students in a school (or in a class) learn to discuss together and to democratically adopt rules of justice and desired behavior within their community. The community also controls adherence to and sanctions violations of these rules. Eventually, class members may go even further and start to discuss and decide the very rules that govern their discussions and decisions.

4.3 School and peers

As noted at the beginning of this chapter, adolescents use about one-third of their time on school-related activities. Most of this time is spent in school, which in turn means time spent with peers and teachers. Academic tasks are indeed compounded to a large extent with social situations and tasks. Adolescent students may choose certain academic topics, but they cannot choose their fellow class members. Of course, they may express their preferences towards specific students, but they can never definitely avoid the group situation. School offers a unique opportunity to meet peers and to find friends. Therefore, studies on peer relationships are almost exclusively carried out in the context of a school. (Peer relationships and friendship are addressed in Chapter 10 in this volume.) However, school not only provides opportunities to experience positive relationships, it is also a fertile soil for group-based social problems, such as bullying. In this section, we address the dark side of school as a social context, that is, specifically, bully/victim problems.

Bullying is one of many forms of aggressive behavior that can be found in a school context. It is, perhaps, easiest to define it from the perspective of the victims of bullying. It implies that a student is repeatedly harassed by schoolmates. These attacks may be overt and rough or indirect and very subtle. Direct bullying includes physical and verbal assaults, as well as intimidation, menaces, and aggressive acts against property of the victim. Indirect bullying often takes the form of isolation of a particular student. This student may be deliberately ignored, not invited at parties, never chosen for group work, etc. Other indirect forms are relational aggression (i.e., damaging others' friendship), rumors etc.

Another feature characteristic of bullying is that the victim cannot defend herself/himself, or at least not efficiently. He or she also receives only little or no support in the peer group. The victim may well have a good friend, but this friend is usually not assertive enough either to defend him or her. In other words, victims are easy targets for aggressive abuses.

Bullying is not restricted to the school context, but it prospers especially well there. Why is this? First, because bullying is most likely to occur in situations from which the victim (or potential victim) cannot escape easily. As noted earlier, this is exactly the situation of students in a school.

Should an adolescent be harassed by peers at a sport club, he could choose to quit the club and look for another one. When this happens in school, however, he *has* to remain in the same class, sometimes for many years. Let us take an example. Tom is a relatively quiet boy with more interest in music than in rough ball games. He is not very assertive and he seems to be easily scared by the rough behavior of his peers. He had no special problems in elementary school, but the transition to junior high school (secondary school) turned out to be a disaster. He ended up in a class that contained a few highly aggressive boys and girls whose school motivation is not very high. His really best friends are in another class. At the beginning of the school year, the aggressive students already start demonstrating that what they say goes in the class. They try out all kinds of nasty tricks. Most students are annoyed by this behavior but some find it really cool and join in, or at least give them positive feedback. Many students know how to set limits but Tom does not really know how to behave like this. His somewhat insecure behavior triggers the aggressiveness of the girls who use obscene gestures to make him blush in inappropriate situations. The boys laugh at him, some act jealously, finding any reason to push him against the wall, etc. Tom is scared. Some classmates feel very uneasy, but they do not know how to intervene. After some weeks things are so bad that they too are now afraid of defending Tom. Tom is stuck in this class for three years.

This example shows how vicious circles can develop over time when potential victims, potential bullies, and a passive to rewarding group of students come together in a class, all knowing that they will be there day after day. Is that all that is needed for bullying to develop? No – a major actor has been omitted: the teachers; teachers who maybe unaware of the situation, who choose to ignore it, or even may think that adolescents are old enough to solve their problems by themselves. The last group renders the situation even more difficult to bear for adolescent victims than for their younger peers, who can still expect that adults feel that they should be looking out for them.

How frequent is bullying? Studies done in over 20 countries show that bullying occurs at comparable rates in most countries. Even if bullying is more frequent among younger students, we still find between 4 and 6.5% of adolescent students (12 through 18 years) who are victims of their peers, and between 1 and 5.5% of adolescent students who can be characterized as bullies.

Adolescence is a period during which individuals are confronted with many tasks and during which peer socialization is important, and it is clear that bullying jeopardizes victims' development. Victimized students are usually unpopular (rejected sociometric status), their self-esteem suffers, they get depressive thoughts and feelings, they often have problems concentrating at school. In many cases, victims do not tell anyone about their problems. They may sometimes try to, but they may not be taken seriously and choose to try to cope with it by themselves. A few of them may even eventually take their own lives.

Programs have been developed to combat and, even better, prevent bullying in schools. The first schools-based program was developed and implemented in Norway in the early 1980s (Olweus, 1993) and consequently used in different countries around the world. The very basic prerequisites of the program are awareness of the problem and involvement on the part of the adults. The first prerequisite can be achieved through adequate information, the second requires much more from teachers and parents. Very often, adolescent peers themselves can be trained to intervene in competent ways to help solve the problem.

5. Conclusion

School functions as an extension of the young person's family in that school teaches what today's families are typically unable to teach, at least with the efficiency the school does (secondary socialization). This is true for the academic realm as well as for the social realm. In addition to the function of the extension of familial education, the school also represents something like a bridge to 'other worlds'. We distinguish two of them, i.e., the social world outside the family (synchronic dimension) and the future world or the adult world (diachronic dimension).

As shown in this chapter, most European schools at the secondary level are differentiated according to level and – some at least – according to direction in terms of content and in terms of issue. To a large degree, levels and issues are compounded in that certain issues are more difficult to attain than others. For example, to become a veterinarian requires higher school performance than to become a chimney sweep. And this compounding is consequential because issues that require higher levels of schooling are – generally speaking – more prestigious and are, certainly in professional life, better paid. Because of this, most students try to enter as high a school level as possible. Parents mostly support this and expect their children to perform well in school, often better than they actually do or can do.

This dynamic creates a high level of stress in adolescents' school life and produces frustration for many. For some students, this stress translates into a huge effort and possibly in enthusiastic pleasure in school, and for some students it translates into disappointment and divergence from school. Such divergence may phenomenally be expressed as fatigue or as intransigent critique of the school (being an ivory tower, ignorant of how colorful the world is and what 'real life' requires from adults).

Indeed, school as a public institution for life chance allocations is once more in need of justification of its activities. Psychology and especially developmental psychology is able to ask difficult questions addressed to schools. One such question has to do with the stability of individual differences in terms both of abilities (general level and profile) and of interests. It is firmly established that individual differences are less stable than that which a definite classification or selection at a given age in adolescence would justify (Flammer, 1975). This is due to individual variations in the 'growing curve' per se, but also to changing environmental conditions (dependent on specific teachers, specific schools, specific friends, specific family conditions etc.). Therefore, a school system with different tracks and levels need to introduce what is called permeability. School choices must be revisable on later occasions, possibly with the 'loss of a year'.

Many countries, especially those in Scandinavia, postpone the need of such choice of levels and directions for as long as possible. Keeping all students in the same class bears the clear advantage of postponing some of the school stress and eventual frustrations, but also includes the disadvantage of not giving the brighter students enough chance to learn and to 'get ahead'. A corresponding handicap can arise for slow learners.

Whether level decisions and orientation decisions are placed early or late in the school career, they must be made at some point. These decisions are more difficult to make today than they were in the past, but they are somehow less consequential today than they perhaps were in earlier times. They are more difficult today in that professional careers are becoming more and more differentiated. To orient oneself within the large array of professional possibilities has become an enormous task (more about these processes and the institutional help is said elsewhere in this volume). By the same token, professional choices are less consequential today, because individual life-span professional careers are less straightforward today. Today's adolescents can be pretty sure that the profession they choose and that they are going to learn will not be carried out in the way it is today for the rest of their life. They will either have to learn new procedures and rules, repeatedly, or they will simply have to shift from one profession to another, because some professional activity fields will surely become obsolete. And it is not readily predictable today which ones will become obsolete and which ones not. All this means that continued education is and will be the rule for all professional life, and that by continued education new accommodations and shifts will be possible again and again. (This too is further elaborated elsewhere in this volume.)

The last remark should be taken to mean that basically all respective problems are vanishing. Take as an example the perspective of women in professional and family life and equal opportunities among men and women. Modern schools have stopped offering different curricula for boys and girls, but actual differences in interests still exist, naturally. In addition, anticipated adult situation leads girls and boys to specific choices in school. Many girls choose a certain career because they hope it will allow them better than another might to combine professional life and family life. This could be a reasonable choice, but the question remains whether the school should not vigorously prepare their students for a radically different society to come.

Clearly, school is a meeting place of both societal interests towards the youth and the youth's legitimate expectation to become prepared for a happy life in his or her society. But society will certainly be, at least in part, different from the society that offers them their current learning opportunities and requires them to acquire specific skills, knowledge, and values.

Acknowledgments

We acknowledge the invaluable help of Irmgard Oswald in the compilation of our referencing. In addition, Irmgard Oswald and Brigitta Schaffner constructed the two tables in this chapter for us.

References

Alsaker, F.D., & Flammer, A. (Eds.). (1999a). *The adolescent experience: European and American adolescents in the 1990s*. Hillsdale, NJ: Lawrence Erlbaum Associates, Inc.

Alsaker, F.D., & Flammer, A. (1999b). Time-use by adolescents in an international perspective: II. The case of necessary activities. In F. D. Alsaker, & A. Flammer (Eds.), *The adolescent experience: European and American adolescents in the 1990s* (pp. 61–84). Hillsdale, NJ: Lawrence Erlbaum Associates, Inc.

Alsaker, F.D., & Flammer, A. (2000). *Swiss–Norwegian longitudinal study on school strain* (Technical report). University of Bern, Switzerland.

Bannert, M., & Arbinger, P.-R. (1996). Gender-related differences in exposure to and use of computers: Results of a survey of secondary school students. *European Journal of Psychology of Education, 11*, 269–282.

Bartsch, K. (1993). Adolescents' theoretical thinking. In R. M. Lerner (Ed.), *Early adolescence* (pp. 143–157). Hillsdale, NJ: Lawrence Erlbaum Associates, Inc.

Cooney, E.W., & Selman, R.L. (1980). Children's use of social conception: Toward a dynamic model of social cognition. *Personnel and Guidance Journal*, *58*, 344–352.

Crockett, L.J., Petersen, A.C., Graber, J.A., Schulenberg, J.E., & Ebata, A. (1989). School transitions and adjustment during early adolescence. *Journal of Early Adolescence*, *9*, 181–210.

Dekovic, M. (1999). Risk and protective factors in the development of problem behavior during adolescence. *Journal of Youth and Adolescence*, *28*, 667–689.

Dweck, C.S., & Leggett, E.L. (1988). A social-cognitive approach to motivation and personality. *Psychological Review*, *95*, 256–273.

Dybowski, H., & Hartwig, J. (1996). Freizeitsinteressen und -aktivitäten von Jugendlichen. Ergebnisse einer Befragung von 14–18 jährigen Braunschweiger Jugendlichen [Leisure time interests and activities of adolescents. A survey among Braunschweig adolescents aged 14 to 18]. *Soziale Arbeit*, *45*, 372–377.

Eccles, J.S., Adler, T.F., & Meece, J.L. (1984). Sex differences in achievement: A test of alternate theories. *Journal of Personality and Social Psychology*, *46*, 26–43.

Eccles, J.S., Lord, S., & Buchanan, C.M. (1996). School transitions in early adolescence: What are we doing to our young people? In J. A. Graber, J. Brooks-Gunn, & A. C. Petersen (Eds.), *Transitions through adolescence* (pp. 251–284). Hillsdale, NJ: Lawrence Erlbaum Associates, Inc.

Eccles, J.S., Lord, S.E., Roeser, R.W., Barber, B.L., & Josefowicz, D.M. (1997). The association of school transitions in early adolescence with developmental trajectories through high school. In J. Schulenberg, J. Maggs, & K. Hurrelmann (Eds.), *Health risks and developmental transitions during adolescence* (pp. 283–320). Cambridge, MA: Cambridge University Press.

Eccles, J.S., & Roeser, R.W. (2003). Schools as developmental contexts. In G. R. Adams, & M. D. Berzonsky (Eds.), *Blackwell handbook of adolescence* (pp. 129–148). Malden, MA: Blackwell.

EDK (1995). *Strukturen der allgemeinen und beruflichen Bildung in der Schweiz* [Structures of general and vocational training in Switzerland]. Bern, Switzerland: EDK.

Eurydice (1997). *Secondary education in the European Union: Structures, organisation, and administration*. Brussels, Belgium: European Unit of Eurydice.

Eurydice (1998). *http://www.eurXdice.orglEurybasel Application*.

Feagans, L.V., & Bartsch, K. (1993). A framework for examining the role of schooling during early adolescence. In R. M. Lerner (Ed.), *Early adolescence* (pp. 129–142). Hillsdale, NJ: Lawrence Erlbaum Associates, Inc.

Fend, H. (1990). *Vom Kind zum Jugendlichen* [From child to adolescent]. Bern, Switzerland: Huber.

Fend, H. (1994). *Die Entdeckung des Selbst und die Verarbeitung der Pubertät* [The discovery of the self and coping with puberty]. Bern, Switzerland: Huber.

Fend, H. (1997). *Der Umgang mit Schule in der Adoleszenz* [Adolescents' behavior in and around school]. Bern, Switzerland: Huber.

Fergusson, D.M., & Lynskey, M.T. (1996) Adolescent resiliency to family adversity. *Journal of Child Psychology*, *37*, 281–292.

Fergusson, D.M., Lynskey, M.T., & Horwood, L.J. (1997). The effects of unemployment on juvenile offending. *Criminal Behaviour and Mental Health*, *7*, 49–68.

Fischer, A. (1997). Engagement und Politik [Involvement and politics]. In Jugendwerk der Deutschen Shell (Ed.), *Jugend '97. Zukunftsperspektiven, Gesellschaftliches Engagement, Politische Orientierungen* (pp. 303–341). Opladen, Germany: Leske & Budrich.

Fitzgerald, M., Joseph, A.P., Hayes, M., & O'Regan, M. (1995). Leisure activities of adolescent schoolchildren. *Journal of Adolescence*, *18*, 349–358.

Flammer, A. (1975). *Individuelle Unterschiede im Lernen* [Individual differences in learning]. Weinheim, Germany: Beltz.

Flammer, A., Alsaker, F.D., & Noack, P. (1999). Time-use by adolescents in an international perspective: I. The case of leisure activities. In F. D. Alsaker, & A. Flammer (Eds.), *The adolescent experience in: European and American adolescents in the 1990s* (pp. 33–60). Hillsdale, NJ: Lawrence Erlbaum Associates, Inc.

Flammer, A., & Tschanz, U. (1997). Ein typischer Schulertag [A typical school day]. In A. Grob (Ed.), *Kinder und Jugendliche heute: Belastet – überlastet?* (pp. 53–68). Zurich, Switzerland: Ruegger.

Flammer, A., Züblin, C., & Grob, A. (1988). Sekundäre Kontrolle bei Jugendlichen [Secondary control in adolescents]. *Zeitschrift für Entwicklungspsychologie und Pädagogische Psychologie*, *20*, 239–262.

Garbarino, J. (1979). Entwicklung im Jugendalter: eine ökologische perspektive [Development in adolescence: An ecological perspective]. In L. Montada (Ed.), *Brennpunkte der Entwicklungspsychologie* (pp. 300–312). Stuttgart, Germany: Kohlhammer.

Gilges, M. (1992). *Lesewelten. Geschlechtsspezifische Nutzung von Büchern bei Kindern und Erwachsenen.*

[Worlds of reading: Gender-specific uses of books by children and adolescents]. Bochum, Germany: Brockmeyer.

Gottfried, A.E., & Gottfried, A.W. (1996). A longitudinal study of academic intrinsic motivation in intellectually gifted children: Childhood through early adolescence. *Gifted Child Quarterly, 40*(4), 179–183.

Greenberger, E., & Steinberg, L. (1986). *When teenagers work: The psychological and social costs of adolescent employment.* New York: Basic Books.

Hallinan, M.T. (1994): School differences in tracking effects on achievement. *Social Forces, 72*, 799–820.

Hamilton, S.F. (1994). Employment prospects as motivation for school achievement: Links and gaps between school and work in seven countries. In R. K. Silbereisen, & E. Todt (Eds.), *Adolescence in context* (pp. 267–283). New York: Springer-Verlag.

Harter, S., Whitesell, N.R., & Kowalski, P.S. (1992). Individual differences in the effects of educational transitions on young adolescents' perceptions of competence and motivational orientation. *American Educational Research Journal, 29*, 777–807.

Hatcher, S.L., Nadeau, M.S., Walsh, L.K., Reynolds, M., Galea, J., & Marz, K. (1994). The teaching of empathy for high school and college students: Testing Rogerian methods with the Interpersonal Reactivity Index. *Adolescence, 29*, 961–974.

Hawkins, J.D., Catalino, R.F., & Miller, J.Y. (1992). Risk and protective factors for alcohol and other drug problems in adolescence and early adulthood: Implications for substance abuse prevention. *Psychological Bulletin, 112*, 64–105.

Hirsch, B.J., & DuBois, D.L. (1991). Self-esteem in early adolescence: The identification and prediction of contrasting longitudinal trajectories. *Journal of Youth and Adolescence, 20*, 53–72.

Jessor, R., VandenBos, J., Vanderryn, J., Costa, F.M., & Turbin, M.S. (1995). Protective factors in adolescent problem behavior: Moderator effects and developmental change. *Developmental Psychology, 31*, 923–933.

Keating, D.P. (1990). Adolescent thinking. In S. S. Feldman, & G. R. Elliott (Eds.), *At the threshold: The developing adolescent* (pp. 54–89). Cambridge, MA: Harvard University Press.

King, A., Wold, B., Tudor-Smith, C., & Harel, Y. (1996). *The health of youth: A crossnational survey* (WHO Regional Publications, European Series No. 69). Copenhagen, Denmark: Office for Publications.

Kohlberg, L. (1985). The just community approach to moral education in theory and practice. In M. W. Berkowitz, & F. Oser (Eds.), *Moral education: Theory and application* (pp. 27–87). Hillsdale, NJ: Lawrence Erlbaum Associates, Inc.

Krampen, G. (1991). *Entwicklung politischer Handlungsorientierungen im Jugendalter. Ergebnisse einer explorativen Längsschnittsequenz-Studie* [Development of political action orientation in adolescence: Results of an explorative longitudinal sequence study]. Göttingen, Germany: Hogrefe.

Lord, S.E., Eccles, J.S., & McCarthy, K.A. (1994). Surviving the junior high school transition: Family processes and self-perceptions as protective and risk factors. *Journal of Early Adolescence, 14*, 162–199.

McCord, J. (1992). Problem behaviors. In S. S. Feldman, & G. R. Elliott (Eds.), *At the threshold. The developing adolescent* (pp. 414–430). Cambridge, MA: Harvard University Press.

Midgley, C., Feldlaufer, H., & Eccles, J.S. (1989). Student/teacher relations and attitudes toward mathematics before and after the transition to junior high school. *Child Development, 60*, 981–992.

Oakes, J., Gamoran, A., & Page, R.N. (1992). Curriculum differentiation: Opportunities, outcomes, and meanings. In P. Jackson (Ed.), *Handbook of research on curriculum* (pp. 570–608). New York: Macmillan.

Olweus, D. (1993). *Bullying at school: What we know and what we can do*. Oxford: Blackwell.

Palmonari, A. (Ed.). (1993). *Psicologia dell'adolescenza* [Psychology of adolescence]. Bologna, Italy: Il Mulino.

Palmonari, A., & Rubini, M. (1993). *School experience, orientation toward formal authorities, and political participation of young people*. Paper presented to the meetings of the European Association of Experimental Social Psychology, Lisbon, Portugal.

Patrick, J.J. (1991). Teaching the bill of rights in secondary schools: Four keys to an improved civic education. *Social Studies, 82*, 227–231.

Petersen, A.C., Leffert, N., & Hurrelmann, K. (1993). Adolescence and schooling in Germany and the United States: A comparison of peer socialization to adulthood. *Teachers College Record, 94*, 611–628.

Petersen, A.C., Sarigiani, P.A., & Kennedy, R.E. (1991). Adolescent depression: Why more girls? *Journal of Youth and Adolescence, 20*, 247–271.

Power, C. (1988). The just community approach to moral education. *Journal of Moral Education, 17*, 195–208.

Rodriguez-Tomé, H., & Bariaud, F. (1991). Anxiety in adolescence: Sources and reactions. In H. Bosma, & S. Jackson (Eds.), *Coping and self-concept in adolescence* (pp. 167–186). Berlin, Germany: Springer-Verlag.

Rutter, M. (1983). School effects on pupil progress: Research findings and policy implications. *Child Development*, *54*, 1–29.

Rutter, M., Maugham, B., Mortimer, P., & Ouston, J. (1979). *Fifteen thousand hours: Secondary schools and their effects on children.* Cambridge, MA: Harvard University Press.

Santilli, N.R., & Hudson, L.M. (1992). Enhancing moral growth: Is communication the key? *Adolescence*, *27*, 145–160.

Sarason, I.G. (Ed.). (1980). *Test anxiety: Theory, research, and applications* (pp. 349–385). Hillsdale, NJ: Lawrence Erlbaum Associates, Inc.

Selman, R.L. (1984). *The growth of interpersonal understanding: Developmental and clinical analyses.* New York: Academic Press.

Shamai, S. (1996). Elementary school students' attitudes toward science and their course of studies in high school. *Adolescence*, *31*, 677–689.

Simmons, R.G., & Blyth, D.A. (1987). *Moving into adolescence: The impact of pubertal change and school context.* New York: Aldine de Gruyter.

Small, S.A., & Luster, T. (1994). Adolescent sexual activity: An ecological, risk-factor approach. *Journal of Marriage and Family*, *56*, 181–192.

Steiner, K. (1986). *Die Entwicklung des staatspolitischen Denkens im Jugendalter* [The development of thinking about systems of government and politics in adolescence]. Mainz, Germany: University Library.

Todt, E. (1978). *Das Interesse* [Interest]. Bern, Switzerland: Huber.

Todt, E., Drewes, R., & Heils, S. (1994). The development of interests during adolescence: Social context, individual differences, and individual sig-

nificance. In R. K. Silbereisen, & E. Todt (Eds.), *Adolescence in context* (pp. 82–98). New York: Springer-Verlag.

Toepfer, C.F., Jr. (1994). Vocational/career/occupational education at the middle level: What is appropriate for young adolescents? *Middle-School Journal*, *25*(3), 59–65.

Tyszkowa, M. (1991). Coping with difficult school situations and stress resistance. In H. Bosma, & S. Jackson (Eds.), *Coping and self-concept in adolescence* (pp. 187–201). Berlin, Germany: Springer-Verlag.

VanEimeren, B., & Maier-Lesch, B. (1997). Mediennutzung und Freizeitgestaltung von Jugendlichen. Ergebnisse einer Repräsentativbefragung von rund 1000 Jugendlichen zwischen zwölf und 19 Jahren [Media use and leisure activities in young people: Results of a representative survey of about 1000 young people aged 12 to 19]. *Media Perspektiven*, *11*, 590–603.

Watson, J., McEwen, A., & Dawson, S. (1994). Sixth form A level students' perceptions of the difficulty, intellectual freedom, social benefit, and interest of science and arts subjects. *Research in Science and Technological Education*, *12*, 43–52.

Wigfield, A., Eccles, J.S., Mac Iver, D., Reuman, D.A., & Midgley, C. (1991). Transitions during early adolescence: Changes in children's domain-specific self-perceptions and general self-esteem across the transition to junior high school. *Developmental Psychology*, *27*, 552–565.

Wills, T.A., Vaccaro, D., & McNamara, G. (1992). The role of life events, family support, and competence in adolescent substance use: A test of vulnerability and protective factors. *American Journal of Community Psychology*, *20*, 249–274.

13

Youth and leisure: A European perspective

Leo B. Hendry and Marion Kloep

LEARNING OBJECTIVES

In this chapter, various kinds of leisure are described and interpreted, together with an examination of the existing literature on the topic of adolescent leisure, mainly from a European perspective. The chapter then goes on to explore some of the processes and mechanisms involved in young people's selection of leisure pursuits across adolescence. Within this chapter we consider why leisure is important to young people. What role does it play – in itself, for adolescent socialisation and towards the development of their future adult roles?:

> While being a source of enjoyment, leisure also plays a key role in development during adolescence. Leisure provides an arena for role experimentation during adolescence, assists in the learning of social norms, and provides a forum in which adolescents can experiment with the challenges that will face them as adults, including issues related to sexuality and aggression. (Raymore, Barber, Eccles & Godbey, 1999)

Furthermore, Raymore et al. (1999) have shown in a longitudinal study that leisure patterns remain fairly stable during the transition from adolescence to early adulthood. This is particularly true for 'risky' behaviours such as alcohol, drugs, and sensation seeking, and especially for males.

1. Leisure lifestyles and the economic situation in Europe

The 'affluent teenager' was initially a phenomenon of the post-war boom in Western Europe (Davis, 1990). A period of stable and relatively full employment of youth led to high earnings and a new market for consumer goods. Davis, however, has pointed out that this picture tended to gloss over differences between various groups of young people – for example, those in full-time education or those in full-time employment and the unemployed, young white men and their black counterparts, and young women. The overall spending power of adolescents may not be significant compared to other consumer groups, but the difference lies in their 'discretionary' element so that purchasing is largely concentrated in the 'non-essential' or leisure markets.

Hendry, Shucksmith and Glendinning (1997) found that in Britain social class impacts on young people's leisure interests in the sense that middle-class adolescents are more likely to be involved in organised adult-led leisure pursuits and clubs and less likely to be engaged in peer-oriented casual leisure. Even those on low incomes are under pressure to purchase designer wear, which emphasises particular leisure styles (Jones & Wallace, 1992; Tomlinson, 1990). In fashion and popular music, the once dominant influence of working-class youth declined and the middle classes became increasingly influential (Roberts & Parsell, 1994) reflecting changes in class-related income differentials stemming from the collapse of youth labour markets. While some young people have access to resources, which allow them to participate fully in the predominant patterns of youth consumption, others find themselves marginalised and excluded. Extended education and delays in entering full-time employment have provided young people with different leisure opportunities. Young people in the UK, for example, who remain in full-time education to 18 years of age (now 57% of the age group in the UK, compared to 94% in Sweden) have the highest overall levels of leisure activity, while those who are unemployed participated in fewest activities (Coleman & Schofield, 2005). In addition to financial exclusion, the unemployed may become culturally excluded because they lack the means to sustain 'appropriate' cultural identities (Hendry et al., 1997).

In Hendry's studies, in late adolescence, around the ages of 18–20 years, economic status had a particular effect on young people's leisure creating the situation where unemployed young people took less part in commercial forms of leisure and were more involved in attending youth clubs and 'hanging around on street corners'. Many of these unemployed adolescents resented the fact that they could not afford the same entertainments as their working peers. They felt trapped in a limbo between youth clubs they had outgrown and 'adult' leisure provision that was too expensive for them. Indeed, as Hendry, Shucksmith, Love and Glendinning (1993, p. 54) suggested: 'A major consequence of unemployment is to deny young people entry to the "package" of work and leisure, which is integral to "adult" lifestyle.'

The leisure patterns in other European countries reflect similar class biases. For example, Swedish youth of non-manual parents participate in all kinds of leisure-time activities (with the exception of fishing and gardening) to a higher degree than children of working-class parents (SOU, 1994). This is particularly true for organised activities, such as being members of a sports club, visiting the local library or reading a daily newspaper. Young people attending the German Hauptschule, or adolescent children of parents who have lower levels of education, are less likely to participate in organised leisure time activities than those from higher secondary school or with parents with a higher educational background.

Despite this evidence, Ziehe (1994) commented that family background, social class and regional origin have become less significant for the future lifestyle of the individual than before, and that modern society confronts youth with both the option and the pressure towards lifestyle choice. In other words, it can be argued that there is a fostering of individualism in society, which may seriously influence adolescent transitions in European societies. It is possible for people to portray a range of 'styles' since there can be a variety of overlapping groups with which they can identify and within which they can play roles associated with everyday social and leisure networks. Maffesoli (1996) makes this point when he discusses 'neo-tribes' in present-day society. Yet it is also possible to suggest that these tribal 'styles', however fluid and relatively transient, can contain within them 'embedded' social values which influence the developing adolescent's lifestyle.

2. 'Types' of leisure

In adolescence a wide variety of leisure activities are engaged in. These activities can range from relaxing home-based pursuits through organised clubs to casual peer-focused interests, some of which can be associated with sensation seeking, to leisure followed within the ambit of commercial venues of various kinds.

2.1 Home-based leisure

Jaffe (1998) tells us that about 40% of the waking hours of adolescents in the United States is spent in casual, non-directed leisure compared to 29% in 'productive' time, and 31% in 'maintenance' activities such as eating and performing chores. He stated that teenagers in other countries spend far more time than those in the United States doing schoolwork and family chores. Flammer, Alsaker and Noack (1999) confirmed this pattern when they found that European adolescents spent between four and five hours of a normal school day on leisure. However, they also found large country differences: Norwegian young people spent most time on leisure (5.59 hrs on average on the sample day), while the French spent least (2.73 hrs). American adolescents, in contrast to Jaffe's (1998) findings, did not differ hugely from their European peers: they devoted an average of 5.27 hrs. on leisure activities on the sample day. How adolescents spend their free time depends partly on their family situation. For example, young women who live in single-parent families are more likely to have a part-time job and thus less leisure time (Zick & Allen, 1996).

Many young people, like adults, are more content than younger children to spend time alone – reading, sleeping, or listening to music. Participation in many home-based leisure pursuits varies by gender – with the exception of watching television and videos and listening to the radio and popular music. Fitzgerald, Joseph, Hayes and O'Regan (1995) interviewed adolescents in Ireland about their leisure pursuits. The most popular activities of boys and girls matched those of adolescents in the United States and Britain – watching television and listening to the radio, visiting friends, listening to music, having friends visit, and reading newspapers and magazines

(see also Trew, 1997). Adolescents have become massive home consumers of media products and materials – films, television programmes, CDs, tapes, records, DVDs, computer games, comics, magazines, newspapers, and the Internet (Murray, 1997; Palladino, 1996). Arnett, Larson and Offer (1995) viewed these changes in the cultural environment as a new and important source of socialisation for adolescents since to a large extent they select their own media materials and programmes. Arnett et al. (1995) stated that adolescents use media for entertainment, identity formation, stimulation, coping, and as a way of identifying with youth culture. Roe (1995) extended this to include 'killing time', creating a desired emotional atmosphere, and 'mood control' by playing out, for example, anger or aggression with loud music: 'The media materials they choose reflect important aspects of themselves and their views of the world . . . in their pursuit of information about the possibilities of life' (Arnett et al., 1995, p. 514).

The use of computers and computer games has already pushed reading books down to the fifth place in the list of media activities, but computers still lag behind TV, CDs or tapes and radio according to a Dutch/Flemish study (Beentjes, d'Haenens, van der Voort & Koolstra, 1999).

A Canadian study (D'Amours & Robitaille, 2002) showed that girls spend as much time on the Internet as boys. However, they prefer to use the computer for personal communication, such as e-mail exchanges, while boys prefer to share activities and play more online games – a gender division that seems to mirror 'real-world' differences. Interestingly, with computers children have found a niche, where attempts at adult supervision fail (Hendry & Kloep, 2005): many parents do not feel sufficiently skilled in handling the Internet to monitor their children's activities on the net. Wolak, Mitchell and Finkelhov (2002) showed that 14% of the teenagers they interviewed reported having formed close online relationships, often leading to offline contacts such as phone calls and meetings. Yet contrary to media stories, less than half of 1% of these contacts were classified by the researchers as 'being sexual in any way'.

After the pre-adolescent years, listening to music increases in popularity, while an interest in TV viewing remains constant in European lands (Hendry, Kloep, Espnes, Ingebrigtsen, Glendinning & Wood, 1999). Larson (1995) suggested that adolescents tune into music more than television, because popular music speaks directly to adolescents' developmental issues. Thus, for many adolescents, popular music provides a means of identifying with a particular group or performer (Seelow, 1996) and a way of releasing pent-up feelings (Larson, 1995). Some adolescents idolise pop singers, and to some extent, use information about their idols in the construction of their own self-identity (Raviv, Bar-Tal, Raviv & Ben-Horin, 1996).

Flammer and colleagues' (1999) study of leisure time use of European adolescents shows that watching television and listening to music is by far the most common leisure activity: about 39% of all leisure time is used for this. Again, there are large differences between the countries, with adolescents from Eastern European countries spending most time for this activity, and the French least. It is also the activity most adolescents engage in, with no age or gender differences: in Kloep's (1998) Swedish sample, 86% reported that they watch TV, and 78% that they listen to the radio several times a week. Asked to name their favourite leisure time activity, 11% of West German, and 21% of East German 13–16 year olds named watching television, and 29 and 36%, respectively, mentioned listening to music (Fischer, 1992). Leisure reading, by the same token, is not as popular as watching TV, and in most studies, there are no differences in time spent on leisure reading across the adolescent years (Fischer, 1992; Flammer et al., 1999).

Other popular local- and family-based activities, particularly in rural areas, are connected to nature and animals. Young Swedish men, for example, seem especially enthusiastic about their hunting and fishing experiences, and young people of both genders (69% of girls, 53% of boys) spend a lot of time caring for animals both large and small (Kloep, 1998).

Zinnecker and colleagues (Behnken & Zinnecker, 1987; Zinnecker, 1990) have discussed the transition of young people's leisure from the beginning of the 1990s towards indoor, domestic leisure (i.e. 'Verhäuslichung'), because the outdoor environment is becoming less and less appropriate for young people's active leisure pursuits due to the dangers from increased traffic and strangers, and the reduction of natural play areas.

With the development of new home-based technology such as computers and PlayStations, the danger may be that the interaction with a 'rewarding' machine can encourage the young person's flight from reality into an artificial environment, with 'false' relationships and where the real self is not involved. It seems that the lower young people's level of attachment to close friends is, and the fewer pro-social attitudes they express, the higher is their involvement with the Internet (Mesch, 2001). However, that does not answer the question of whether or not Internet might be a convenient tool for shy people to try out social skills from a safe 'distance', covered by anonymity and maybe an assumed identity, or if it prevents these individuals from going out into the real world and risking the challenges of face-to-face relationships. The key questions are:

How effective would this be as a developmental 'environment' and training for the adolescent's psychosocial transitions to the world of adult society?

Will 'virtual reality' become a substitute for real-life experiences, adventures and relationships?

What effect might the increasing use of Internet chat groups have on the development of adolescents' social relationships?

Another dimension of young people's involvement with the technological society has been investigated by Griffiths (1995) in discussing adolescent gambling and playing slot machines, where elements of escapism, excitement, uncertainty and transformational flow occur. He has pointed out that this can lead on to 'technological addictions' involving human–machine interactions. He proposed a developmental model of gambling in which there can be transformations from passive viewer (television addict) to active participant (pathological gambler) over time. This may have important implications into the future with increasing access to Internet and video games. Some teenagers spend 15 or more hours a week playing video games at home or in arcades, and most video games have violence as their major theme. Thus, a large number of children and teenagers gain pleasure each day from symbolic acts of violence, often with women as victims (Strasburger, 1995). Furthermore, females portrayed in these games, even when they occupy the role of heroine, are often depicted as subordinate to male characters or are presented in terms of their sexuality. These depictions of women are detrimental to both girls *and* boys insofar as both may internalise these expectations and accept the idea that women are to be viewed as weak, as victims, and as sex objects (Dietz, 1998). It has also been proposed that violent games sometimes increase players' hostility, anxiety and aggression (Anderson & Bushman, 2001).

What has been suggested so far is that the adolescent's indoor leisure existence can be a rich and varied one, although there are some possible risks involved that should be noted. First, that this relatively passive sphere, perhaps constructed by the cultural changes in adult society, can limit the young person's involvement in more active pursuits; second, that there may be small overt and 'hidden' risks such as contact with 'virtual' strangers, becoming 'addicted' to computer games playing, developing stereotypic gender views or an exclusively home-based lifestyle; and finally, there are questions to be asked about the influence of IT and musical media on the development of adolescents' values and social skills.

2.2 Organised activities and sports

Adults can play an important role in adolescents' leisure participation. Sports clubs, hobby groups, choirs and orchestras, youth clubs and uniformed organisations all tend to be arranged for adolescents by adults, and are often closely supervised by adults. Adolescents' involvement in such adult-sponsored situations, though nominally voluntary, may not be genuinely self-chosen, and may confront young people with the dilemma of choosing to participate in a setting which if anything perpetuates adult dominance in their lives,

perhaps in exchange for the training of well-regarded skills and the advantages of acquired social status. For those adolescents who attend organised clubs and structured activities there is the opportunity to experience a wide range of social roles, and perhaps to develop a greater versatility in their social relationships by mixing with both adults and peers, while absorbing and accepting adult attitudes and values.

But as adolescents grow older they become more critical, questioning and sceptical of adult-led organisations, and wish to 'use' peers to re-affirm their emergent self-image. The need to feel independent may be a vital reason why the older adolescent moves towards commercial leisure provision. Young people begin to perceive that power and decision making in youth organisations lies with adults, though adult leaders may claim that they involve young people in decision making and that they offer truly collaborative participation with the young (Love & Hendry, 1994).

In relation to organised activities, in the 1999 study from Flammer et al., sport was the third most popular activity during adolescence, after watching TV/listening to music and meeting friends. Younger adolescents in most countries reported significantly more involvement in sport than older adolescents, and boys more than girls. Norwegian adolescents reported the highest daily time spent on sports (1hr 26), and Russians the lowest (0hrs 32). The studies of Hendry et al. (1993) and Kremer, Trew and Ogle (1997) have all indicated high involvement of school-age children in fairly regular physical activity and sport, yet differences obtain in relation to age and gender. Put simply, younger adolescents and male adolescents are most likely to be involved in physical activities and sports. There is a 'drop off' in involvement in the last few years of compulsory secondary schooling (i.e. 16 years of age in the UK), particularly when young people make the transition from school towards work, training or higher education. In rural Sweden, 63% of boys and 38% of girls (between 11 and 18 years of age) visit a sports club at least once a week. These percentages are much higher than in urban areas of Sweden, suggesting that the supply of facilities for outdoor sports (such as ski slopes, lakes, space for ball games and less traffic) play a decisive role in the choice of leisure activities. The corresponding figures for Scotland are 50% of young men and 31% of young women, while Norway shows a much higher participation with 63% of boys and 52% of girls (Hendry et al., 1999; Kloep, 1998).

Research in all European countries (Flammer et al., 1999; Hendry et al., 1999; Hurrelmann & Albert, 2002; Kloep, 1998) has consistently shown that participation in sports clubs and engagement in leisure sports decrease with increasing age, particularly into late adolescence. Asked for their reasons for dropping out, 'lack of interest' was cited as the most important reason by about 30% (Mahoney, 1997). Other reasons given by Scottish adolescents were lack of time to practise and the fact that other (social) activities had assumed more importance (Hendry et al., 1993).

Only regular exercise, which is conducted over many years into adulthood, can be expected to produce long-term effects (e.g. Rowland, 1991). Thus, a major goal of promoting physical activity in children is the establishment of habits that will persist throughout the lifecourse. However, for many adolescents long-term goals do not seem to be sufficiently motivating. For example, some years ago Hendry and Singer (1981) found that adolescent girls had positive attitudes towards physical activity for health reasons, but assigned low priority to their actual involvement in these pursuits because of 'conflicting' interests – usually of a social nature, related to visiting friends and going out, thereby sacrificing possible long-term goals for the needs of the moment. Teenagers seem to find it difficult, if not impossible, to worry about the health of a 50-year-old 'stranger' that will be themselves in their middle-aged future (Coffield, 1992).

As Wold and Hendry (1998) stated, physically active role models such as parents, siblings and peers, as well as 'star' figures and 'heroes' in the mass media, influence young people to participate – or not – in physical activity, Parents, for example, are found to promote participation through example by their own sports involvement (Hendry, Shucksmith, & Love, 1989). However, it also happens that parents can pressurise their teenage offspring to participate in sports even though the adolescent may not be particularly enthusiastic. Some adults may participate vicariously in their adolescent children's sports and in this way may experience previously unfulfilled ambitions (see, e.g., Hendry, 1971). More than one-third of males between 13 and 16 years of age in the (1993) study of Hendry et al. reported that they played competitive sport because: 'My parents like me to do it.' Further, insensitive, competitive sports coaches and physical education teachers can over-influence young people who may have unrealistic dreams about a future career in professional sport.

2.3 Socialising: Meeting and talking

Over time most teenagers come to prefer the companionship of peers to that of their family (Larson, Richards, Moneta, Holmbeck, & Duckett, 1996). Friends are less likely than parents to coerce, criticise, and lecture and are more willing to give each other personal validity, social status and shared interests. Further, peer relationships are more egalitarian than adult–child relationships; explanations and understandings are more mutually acceptable and unambiguous. Lloyd argued that:

> This allows the young person to begin the process of emotional detachment from parents. The separation process takes place over a period of years and doesn't usually mean that adolescents suddenly reject their parents or their parents' values. Instead, they gradually 'let go' in order to learn how to be emotionally self-supporting adults. (Lloyd, 1985: p. 195)

In general terms, parental and peer influences complement one another in ways that prepare adolescents for relationships in their future lives. Yet parents are sometimes concerned about their offspring's choice of friends in adolescence because young people actively select friends on the basis of similar interests, characteristics, and behaviours. In part, this may be because, in adolescence, friends and peers are encountered in settings other than the family home, and there-fore, some friends are unknown to parents. At adolescence young people move into negotiating and claiming sets of relationships on their own terms, beyond parental control.

Thus, it is not surprising that young people spend a great deal of their leisure time either with their best friend, with a group of friends, or both (Flammer et al., 1999; Hendry et al., 1993; Kloep, 1998), often 'not doing anything' but chatting, giggling and hanging around. Adolescents report spending more time simply talking to peers than in any other activity. 'Fooling around' and laugh-ter may seem rather aimless and pointless to an outsider, yet are perceived as among the most ful-filling of activities by adolescents themselves (Csikszentmihalyi & Larson, 1984). When friends cannot meet face-to-face mobile phones become important to enable the talking to continue. This is particularly true for youths in rural areas (Hendry, Glendinning, Reid & Wood, 1998).

Adolescent crowds are a common sight around many streets, parks or other public places, and represent important settings for the genders to meet. Many venues serve as meeting points. Popu-lar urban venues are shopping malls and amuse-ment arcades, though a street corner, park or other convenient assembly point may serve this function (Fisher, 1995). Older adolescents and those seeking dates may make more use of these meeting places. Conversely, those feeling threat-ened or frustrated in their hopes of romantic relationships may retreat from such places of high exposure (Silbereisen, Noack, & von Eye, 1992). However, it is important to note that the problem for rural youths is that often there is no street corner at which to meet, and friends are spread over a wide geographic area. Furthermore, climatic restrictions affect opportunities for adolescents to meet within local settings. For instance, Swedish adolescents cannot meet friends outdoors as often and as long as this is possible for Italian youths (Kirchler, Pombeni, & Palmonari, 1991; Kloep, 1998). Hence the school or youth club becomes an essential social venue and meeting point – even though it may not be an ideal context from the adolescent's perspective (Hendry et al., 1998).

2.4 'Nothing to do!'

One of the most often stated complaints young people have about their leisure time, particularly those in the age range 14 to 17 years, is that there is 'absolutely nothing to do'. In a cross-cultural study of rural youth, Hendry, Kloep, Glendin-ning, Ingebrigtsen, Espnes and Wood (2002) found that 43% of Swedish adolescents, 45% of Norwegians, and 65% of Scottish young people regarded 'nothing to do' as a serious problem in the area where they live, young women being sig-nificantly more critical than young men in all three countries. Interestingly, this complaint cor-related neither with the actual amount of time spent on leisure activities, nor with the number of different activities young people were engaged in. Kloep (1998) suggested that it might not be the quantity, but the *quality* of the activities adoles-cents can engage in that create feelings of bore-dom. What is on offer has, on the one hand, become too 'childish' and too 'adult supervised' to be of interest. On the other hand, legal and practical restrictions prevent young people in this age group from enjoying most aspects of adult leisure. Furthermore, belonging to a generation that grew up being organised and entertained by adults since early childhood, young people might lack the skills of organising and entertaining themselves (Kloep & Hendry, 2003).

In an interview study by McMeeking and Purkayasta (1995), young people indicated that regardless of location, the key issue was a shared concern about their general inability to independ-ently access leisure pursuits. Among the causes of frustration was the lack of accessible spaces as well as the social sanctions prohibiting the use of such spaces for unstructured activities. These problems were further compounded by factors such as gender, socio-economic status, race/ ethnicity and age of the young people. Shaw, Caldwell and Kleiber (1996) concluded from their study with Canadian adolescents that the fre-quent experiences of boredom and stress were not:

> [S]imply a matter of too much to do or too little to do, but were associated in a more complex way with the social construction of

adolescence and its relationship to the wider culture. Adolescents who experienced high levels of both stress and boredom may be particularly likely to resist or feel alienated from the dominant adult culture. (Shaw et al., 1996, p. 289)

Caldwell, Darling, Payne and Dowdy (1999) differentiate between psychological and social control theories in explaining 'boredom' in adolescents. While psychological theories suggest that reasons for experiencing boredom might be a lack of awareness of stimulating things to do, and/or a lack of intrinsic motivation, particularly self-determination, social control theories suggest that boredom might be a 'resistance' response to external control such as the influence of parents or other adults. As such, it might even develop into a habitual response that becomes a routine aspect of adolescent culture. In their own research, Caldwell et al. (1999) found support mainly for this latter theory.

2.5 Romance

From the onset of puberty, physical and sexual maturation and heightened sex drive increase interest in romantic relationships: 'Now the cliques of boys and girls begin self-consciously to approach one another, to pester, tease and make mock attacks instead of quietly and systematically ignoring each other' (Dunphy, 1972: p. 178).

Dating, as an important leisure pursuit, begins to complement activities with friends, and romantic partners become a crucial source of social support. Yet even if romantic relationships are formed, their intimacy and importance are unlikely to rival that of the relationship with a best friend (Lempers & Clark-Lempers, 1993). For both genders, the acquisition of romantic strategies and sexual techniques is problematic. Unlike other aspects of social learning, little useful advice and support is offered to young people by family, schools or even peers (Shucksmith & Hendry, 1998). As Kloep and Hendry (1999) have suggested, questions such as what is required to be a good lover, how to make a socially competent (sexual) approach or how to end a relationship are seldom mentioned to teenagers, or

only covered inappropriately in the pornographic material young men may access. Perhaps young women are somewhat better served in this regard by the available array of women's magazines.

The point here is that, by and large, adolescents are to a great extent left to find out information about romance, sex and relationships for themselves (e.g. Hendry, Shucksmith, & Philip, 1995). Yet romantic friendships may play a special role in the development of identity, empathy, and altruism during adolescence. Hendry, Shucksmith, Philip and Jones (1991) have shown that relational power and intimacy are two dimensions around which young people need guidance and help to understand the ways in which romantic and sexual relationships are negotiated. In particular, the dangers of learning a masculine role that separates sexual practices from emotional feelings cannot be overstated; neither can the importance of assertiveness in young women's refusal of unwanted sexual advances (Hendry et al., 1991). The creating and sustaining of an acceptable sexual reputation is clearly highly 'gendered' (Kitzinger, 1995; Wight, 1992) despite the perceived changes in attitudes to women.

If we know relatively little about young people's relationships in terms of heterosexual romantic encounters, we know even less about lesbian, gay and bisexual adolescents (e.g. Savin-Williams, 1990). Nevertheless, there has been a burgeoning literature on same-sex attractions since the early 1990s. Savin-Williams (2001) points out that young people who have same-sex desires are very similar to heterosexual teenagers in their developmental needs and concerns, and might not yet identify themselves as gay, lesbian or bisexual. With regard to leisure, Kivel and Kleiber (2000) found that sexual identity can influence the choice of leisure activities. For example, they suggest that 'closet' homosexual teenagers might abandon certain activities if continuing them would contribute to rumours that they were gay. Thus, the manner in which the need for 'invisibility' and the lack of social acceptance of the full spectrum of sexual diversity restricts young people's activities may disadvantage their health and well-being (e.g. Dempsey, Hillier, & Harrison, 2001).

2.6 Transitions, commercial activities and risks

The factors that lead adolescents towards an involvement in commercial leisure have to do with the growing adolescent's desire to be seen to be playing an independent adult-like role. Gradually, the feeling among many young people is that official clubs are too tame or over-organised to appeal to them. Pubs, discos, commercial leisure facilities such as squash or health clubs, window shopping, and even foreign travel all feature in the leisure activities of young people during this time. Clearly, participation in these sorts of pursuits is influenced by occupational status, peer-group membership, and whether or not courting relationships have been established. Additionally, available cash and employment opportunities, family commitments, associations with adult society generally, and the effects of leisure interests developed earlier in adolescence all play their part. Leisure participation is further compounded by the problematic transitions to adulthood in post-modern society.

Coleman and Warren-Adamson (1992) have pointed out that citizenship rights are inconsistent and confusing between adolescence and adulthood: some rights can be claimed at 16 years (age of sexual consent, in the UK) while others may not be assumed until 26 years of age (classed as an adult entitled to housing benefits). Parker, Aldridge and Measham (1998) have argued that the transition from childhood through adolescence and on towards adulthood and full citizenship is now a longer, more uncertain journey. While, objectively the levels of risk of 'failure' are still differentiated by race, gender, wealth, parental background, educational qualifications and neighbourhood, almost all young people subjectively experience this as a long period of uncertainty. Under the social conditions of high youth unemployment, dependency on parents, and a later average age for marriage, and where the social 'signposts' towards being considered an adult are uncertain, it is hardly surprising that young people seek pleasurable, if risky, leisure experiences from time to time as a retreat from the harsh realities of everyday life – hedonistic interludes in times of social difficulties and hard-

ships. The rave and club culture seems to epitomise this 'hedonism for hard times', where the over-riding imperative is the search for flow and escapism, and where drugs can play a central part in building up the feeling of transformation (e.g. Rietveld, 1994; Thornton, 1997).

It is clear that the process of growing up has become more complicated, and in this state of rapid societal flux adolescents take risks and weigh up enjoyment and the functional advantages of their various social and leisure habits against the dangers and pitfalls. This 'cost-benefit risk' assessment, as Parker et al. (1998) call it, is an elaborate psycho-social process in which adolescents decide how far to go to get a 'buzz' or to get 'out of it' via alcohol or drugs in their leisure lives.

In relation to all this, the concept of risk taking is ill defined. Is it part of the psychological makeup of youth – a thrill-seeking stage in the developmental transition – or a necessary step to the acquisition of adult skills and self-esteem? Or is it a consequence of a societal or cultural urge by adults to marginalise youth because in their transitions from controllable child to controlled adult they are seen as troublesome and a threat to the stability of the community? It is obvious that we need clearer definitions of what is meant by risk taking. Kloep and Hendry (1999) offered the following three categories of risk-taking behaviour:

1. *Thrill-seeking behaviours.* These are exciting or sensation-seeking behaviours that arouse and test the limits of one's capacities. Such behaviours can be observed in children as well as in adolescents and adults. What distinguishes adolescent thrill-seeking behaviour from both children, on the one hand, and adults, on the other, is frequency and a combination of increasing material resources with limited experience of their own capacities and the risks they are undertaking.

2. *Audience-controlled risk-taking behaviours.* In order to be accepted, to find place in a peer group and to establish a social position, people have to demonstrate certain

qualities and abilities. Thus, it is obvious that most risky behaviours need an audience. This may be the reason why adults do not engage so often in demonstrative risk taking: they have symbolic means of displaying their status in titles, expensive clothes or sports cars. Lacking these symbols, adolescents (but not as often as adult society claims) may turn to activities that take them to the edges of legality and thus assure them of the attention of police and media, as well as their peers.

3. *Irresponsible risk-taking behaviours*. These are not performed because of the risks they imply, but *in spite* of them, in order to achieve other desired goals. Such irresponsible behaviours demonstrate the inability of individuals to see long-term consequences, or, if these are apparent, to be unwilling to abstain from such activities because of perceived short-term advantages. It is obvious that behaviours such as getting drunk or failing to use condoms are not attractive because they are risky, but are pursued for other reasons that are temporarily more important.

As Arnett (1998) has suggested, cultures must accept a trade-off in socialisation between promoting individualism and self-expression, on the one hand, and in promoting social order, on the other. Societies such as ours pay the price for promoting individualism and achievement by having higher rates of adolescent risk taking in response to adult culture.

3. Leisure transitions

Earlier, Hendry (1983) theorised that the leisure patterns of both boys and girls move through three transitional stages: 'organised leisure', 'casual leisure' and 'commercial leisure', with boys making transitions from one phase to the next slightly later than girls. Organised leisure including sports participation and adult-led activities tends to decline from early adolescence onward. Casual leisure includes 'hanging around' with friends, and this tends to be less common after mid-adolescence. Commercial leisure becomes

the predominant form after mid-adolescence and includes cinema attendance as well as visiting discos, clubs and pubs. This study formed the background to the formulation of the focal model. A decade later, Hendry et al. (1993) still found the same general age trends in relational issues with a representative sample of over 8000 Scottish adolescents. This may seem surprising given the many societal changes that had occurred since the original theory was presented.

However, in trying to replicate these findings with rural adolescents from Norway, Sweden and Scotland, Hendry et al. (1999, 2002) discovered that cultural differences – and/or societal changes – alter the universality of the original model. For instance, involvement with friends decreases with age for young Norwegian women, while this type of leisure pursuit shows a curvilinear pattern for Scots women, reaching a peak in mid-adolescence in accordance with the model. Swedish young women's involvement decreases over adolescence, but the finding for Swedish men represents a mirror image of the results for Scottish young women. Overall, Norwegian young people seem to be more involved in casual leisure activities with friends than the other two nationalities. In contradistinction to sports, young women are more participatory in organised leisure than young men in the three countries. The Scots are more associated with organised activities than the others and younger adolescents are more involved than older youths. The 'drop-out' pattern also reveals country differences: In Scotland and Sweden the drift from adult led clubs and organised activities is apparent from early adolescence and then reaches 'steady state', whereas in Norway there is an increase in participation from early to mid-adolescence for both young men and young women, then a decline from mid- to later teens.

While the leisure focal model (Hendry, 1983) has been useful for understanding the transitions of (mainly British) urban youth it seems clear that rurality and cultural imperatives had changed these patterns of leisure transitions by the late 1990s. Involvement in casual leisure in mid-adolescence described in the original model, for instance, may have been a feature of the cultural and economic ecology of the times, where the street corner and friends' homes were peer venues for social engagement. It is possible to speculate that such settings have been replaced more and more by cafés, pizzerias and fast food restaurants as social meeting places.

Additionally, young people at the beginning of the 21st century may be more affluent and wish access to such commercial contexts of 'globalised' Western societies. In the light of media advertising, such adolescent desires do not cease at the boundaries of suburbia but continue into the rural hinterland. Hence entry to commercial leisure – in the company of peers – has accelerated down the age scale (even as far as to 4 year olds celebrating birthday parties in hamburger restaurants, wearing mini-fashions). As a feature of these earlier leisure transitions, and as a manifestation of earlier social maturity, Kloep (1999), for example, has shown in her rural Swedish study that romantic love relationships feature early as an adolescent concern, whereas 'conflicts with parents' were seen by young people as a relatively unimportant relational issue. All these findings point towards evidence of an earlier maturation – or at least social sophistication – of youth, and future research needs to consider more carefully and specifically the effects of commercialism on youth's social and leisure development.

4. Ethnic and cultural influences on leisure

However, we need to be cautious about generalising the findings of studies of white adolescents to other ethnic or racial groups or cultures. For example, partly due to racism and different cultural opportunities, the socialisation of immigrant youths – even second generation – differs to some extent from that of the host population. Because different ethnic groups often exist in relative isolation from each other in most Western societies, differences emerge in friendship patterns, preferred leisure activities and the importance of different neighbourhoods in friendship networks (Giordano, Cernkovich, & DeMaris, 1993; Urberg, Degirmenicioglu, Tolson, & Halliday-Scher, 1995). For example, involvement in sport for young black people is often cited as a means of 'getting up and out', but there is little insight into how this relates to other aspects of

their lives. Cultural and religious values affect participation in various ways. Westphal (2003) quotes the example of Muslim girls in Germany, who are even less involved in sport activities than girls in general, partly due to strict dress codes and parental opposition to mixed gender activities.

Already two decades ago, Cohen (1988) examined inter-racial attitudes and values, and what emerged from his analysis is the sheer complexity of social class, sexism and racism, which even today still creates a contradictory social milieu in which adolescents grow towards adulthood, surrounded by multicultural foods, fashions and music, but separated by racist and sexist tensions:

> Some ethnic attributes may be idealised because of their positive class and gender associations, while others are denigrated. Most typically, of course, many white working-class boys discriminate positively in favour of Afro-Caribbean subcultures as exhibiting a macho, proletarian style, and against Asian cultures as 'effeminate' and 'middle-class'. Such boys experience no sense of contradiction in wearing dreadlocks, smoking ganja and going to reggae concerts while continuing to assert that 'Pakis stink'. Split perceptions linking double standards of gender, ethnicity and class are increasingly the rule. Sexist imagery may at one moment add injury to racist insult, and in the next, unite white and black boys in displays of male chauvinism, the shared experience of sexism may in one setting bring girls together, and in another polarise them through the operation of a racial double standard. (Cohen, 1988, p. 85)

Cultural and religious values impinge especially on immigrant youth, placing them in a limbo between the traditional family culture and the values of their peers. This is illustrated in value clashes about fashion, leisure venues and activities.

Further, little is known about leisure patterns in poorer European countries. Kloep and Hendry (1997) described, for instance, the situation of young people in post-communist Albania as being similar to many working-class and minority youth in more affluent countries: At the same time as an uncensored flow of Western influences in the form of mail-order catalogues, advertisements, commercials and television shows stimulated Albanian youths' appetite for Western-style consumption, their economic opportunities were reduced and the means of participating in this new commercialism was well nigh impossible for most of them. This gap between existing, affordable goods and desired commodities creates conflict, social unrest and anomie in young people.

5. Gender and leisure

Irrespective of culture, and irrespective of the transitional routes followed by young people, there are important gender differences in sport activities, with young women in all age groups being considerably less involved than young men (Hendry et al., 1999; Mason, 1995). As a literature review by Bailey, Wellard and Dismore (2005) shows, this difference is apparent in countries as varied as Senegal, Iceland, Estonia and Singapore.

At all stages, women's leisure participation has been constrained by gender divisions (Griffin, 1993; Lees, 1993). Although there have been changes in the leisure patterns of young women in the last decades, gender has remained a strong predictor of participation in 'active' pursuits (e.g. Wold & Hendry, 1998). There are still fewer norms to restrict the activities of young males and their parents allow them to play outside unsupervised more often than girls (Inchley & Currie, 2004). In particular, leisure opportunities are restricted through conventions governing the use of 'space'. Coakley and White (1992), for instance, cited unwritten rules, which tend to prevent young women from entering snooker halls alone, while allowing women accompanying boyfriends or brothers as spectators. Hendry et al. (1993) have reported that many leisure settings are male preserves and that this lack of access to leisure 'space' for girls means that they often retreat into home-based activities. They suggested that female cultures tend to emphasise 'best friends' and close relationships in small groups,

and that this results in some psychological discomfort with collective team situations.

For example, the type of sports involvement of young men and young women is different. Young women are less likely than young men to be competitors and are more likely to play sport for fun or not at all (Bailey et al., 2005; Hendry et al., 1993). Adler, Kless and Adler (1992) showed that boys enjoyed games that were competitive, rule infused and goal directed, while girls enjoyed small intimate groups focused on enjoyment rather than winning. This reflects the play pattern of younger children: boys are more likely to play in large groups and to play outdoors, whereas girls play indoors and in pairs (Golombok & Fivush, 1994). By engaging in different types of leisure young men and young women might learn different social skills: Boys learn to negotiate conflict, to be a team member, to co-operate and to compete, while girls learn to listen, avoid conflict and to form deep relationships. The majority of the boys in Kremer and colleagues' (1997) study identified a team activity as their top sport while only a few claimed an interest in individual activities. For girls, the pattern was reversed (Scully & Clarke, 1997).

Coakley and White (1992) argued that young men regard sporting activity as congruent with the masculine role and gain kudos from engaging in competitive activities. By way of contrast, many young women are less likely to connect sports activity with the process of becoming a woman and may avoid participating in leisure activities that may be perceived as threatening to their femininity. Interestingly, the only physical activity for which participation increased with growing age among young Swedish rural women in Kloep's (1998) study was in aerobics and dance groups.

In spite of these apparent gender differences, sports clubs still tend to concentrate on competition, not on social cohesion beyond that which is necessary to produce a well-functioning team. Also in most clubs greater emphasis is placed on the male sections with better training times available for the boys. This is matched within adult society where male sports generally are given higher media coverage. Furthermore public money spent on sport is higher for traditionally male sports such as football and ice hockey, than for horse riding or dance.

The UK and Germany are two countries planning to raise the profile of sports in schools, in order to increase young people's – and particularly girls' – participation. However, a school curriculum which is dominated too heavily by competition fails to attract girls and does not transfer well to out-of-school and adult-supported participation. Inadequate physical education experiences can actually harm lifelong physical activity habits (Bailey et al., 2005; Flinton & Scraton, 2001).

Future leisure participation patterns may, however, reveal fewer gender biases, and this is already emerging in countries where social equality between the genders is more evident, such as the Scandinavian countries (Wold & Hendry, 1998). While cultural norms and values do define gender differences in physical activity, participation of girls is higher in countries with high equality between men and women than in countries low on gender equality.

Gender differences also persist beyond sports participation: young women spend more time than young men shopping with and talking to their friends, reading books and magazines (Bruno, 1996). They are more likely to go out for meals, to cinemas, theatres, concerts and churches and visit friends and relations. Young women are less active in their leisure outside the home than boys; expected to spend more of their free time helping out in the house; and are often required to return home earlier in the evening. Moreover, they receive lower wages and less pocket money and have higher 'self-maintenance costs' (Furlong, Campbell & Roberts, 1990). Young men are more likely than young women to go out, to watch sports, to play video games, and to spend time alone (Woodroffe, Glickman, Barker, & Power, 1993). Cross-culturally, boys spend more time watching TV or video than girls (Flammer et al., 1999), but they are also more likely to own their own television and their own computer than young women are (Apostolidi & Süss, 1999; Beentjes et al., 1999). Figures from the General Household Survey (Office of Population,

Censuses and Surveys, 1995) showed that young males are more likely to spend time on DIY projects and gardening, while females spent time dressmaking and knitting. Even in a country like Sweden, which is proud of its progress regarding gender equality, about 10% more young women than men report that they often help at home – but even here there are gender divisions with young women engaging in housekeeping and young men working on the farm (Kloep, 1998).

6. Processes and mechanisms

The complexity of our findings across European cultures indicates the need for a different approach towards understanding adolescence and adolescent leisure into the future. We have to move on from the idea that there is a simple and generalised story to tell about adolescence. There are many individual pathways within leisure transitions resulting from different psychologies, gender roles, social interactions and ever-changing cultural systems. We have to end our fixation with aggregated findings and single factor explanations and start to examine processes and mechanisms as Rutter (1996a, 1996b) and Hendry and Kloep (2002), among others, have proposed. It is in the disaggregation of findings culturally and across societies that facts of real importance begin to emerge. This is a somewhat similar claim to Bronfenbrenner's (1979) ecological explanation, which considers psychosocial development as the result of a series of ongoing interactions and adaptations between individuals and sets of variously overlapping social systems which range from the micro-level to the societal macro-level. These factors relate both to the developing individual and to each of these social systems within different cultures. We need to take account of these to move from rather static theoretical models to gaining a clearer understanding of the processes and mechanisms of leisure transitions within and across cultures.

If we take TV viewing as an example, we know that young women watch TV less often than young men across European countries (Alsaker & Flammer, 1999), and that they possess fewer TVs or videos of their own (e.g. Apostolidi & Süss, 1999). Is this due to their greater interest in other (more social?) pursuits, to parents favouring sons and providing them with more expensive equipment or to the male-oriented offerings of TV programmes, concentrating on sports and action films much more than on soap operas? Furthermore, why do East European young people spend more time watching TV than West Europeans? Is there little to do or is it part of a culture having the TV on all day without necessarily watching much of it? Similarly, young children today watch more TV than ever before: is it because there are more children's programmes, a whole channel available all day, or because adults use the TV as a 'babyminder'?

Culture, its traditions and restrictions, economy, gender, age, social class, opportunity and availability, personal choice, interests and motivations all interact as factors that 'produce' adolescent leisure pursuits in any society and it is important for us as researchers to try to find out how these dynamic systems function in order to understand variations in leisure patterns. This is certainly more interesting than knowing, for example, that in Norway, younger girls spend more time on playing a musical instrument than older girls and boys, while in Bulgaria, older boys play more music than younger boys and girls – when the largest difference on average is 16 minutes per day (Flammer et al., 1999)! Such future studies, looking at systems, mechanisms, processes, and functions, will demand more creative and innovative approaches utilising a vast array of research techniques – some of them as yet undiscovered.

7. Conclusion

In this chapter, we have attempted to examine the effects of rapid social and economic changes on young people's leisure transitions. Young people's leisure pursuits were looked at in relation to types of activities, to gender, to social class, to ethnicity and culture and to the leisure transitions which seem to coincide with certain relational issues as adolescents develop. It is apparent that leisure patterns follow developmental trajectories, with a typical pattern in most European societies involving a gradual evolution from home and locality-based activities to those located in the wider

social – and often commercial – setting. Leisure patterns are determined both by gender and by social background, and have been very much affected by the shift in employment patterns and career opportunities of the late 20th and early 21st century. The more limited the work prospects for an individual, the more salient leisure becomes. Where there is little satisfaction to be had from employment, a hedonistic leisure pattern may be discerned.

Hard times may lead young people to seek pleasure in the 'here and now', since there appears to be a problematic employment future. What is being suggested here is that young people's responses to the uncertainties of the 'risk society' (Beck, 1992) are in a blossoming leisure sector, which allows them to change and 'transform' and 'escape' from the hardships of everyday life to a 'play-like, leisure sphere', where risk taking appears to be more individually controllable at times via the media and Internet rather than as real-life experiences. Intentions are, in some cases, towards mood-altering experiences by the use of alcohol and other drugs. By examining some of the reasons why adolescents pursue so-called 'risky' leisure activities as responses to the ethos of modern technological societies, we proposed a set of functional categories of risk-taking behaviours: audience-controlled, irresponsible and sensation-seeking behaviours, which may be useful to future research.

We also referred to Maffesoli's (1996) ideas of the many and varied, if transient, allegiances of individuals to different social groups, which cut across gender and class boundaries. Paradoxically, such apparently personalised choices may still be influenced by traditional factors of gender, social class, education, wealth and so on.

What of the future? It has been predicted in an earlier report (Scase, 1999) that by the year 2010 40% of adults in the UK will live alone, that occupations will be less secure, and often home based, and that serious interpersonal relationships will be somewhat transient, social networks will be vital and people will be entrepreneurial and fashion conscious: in other words an economically prosperous but divided society where the more successful will be more involved in leisure, recreation, education and cultural activities. But even those who do not immediately achieve full-time employment in our increasingly competitive societies are in need of meaningful leisure skills, which can enhance their coping abilities and personal development, and can offer an alternative lifestyle in the short or longer term (e.g. Hendry, 1987; Nässtrom & Kloep, 1994). The importance of leisure for adolescents' development and transitions towards adulthood will continue to increase. Thus, it is vital that we provide an understanding of the developmental mechanisms and processes involved if we are to work with adolescents in providing structures and experiences that will enable them to use the leisure time effectively that will become available to them.

For future European societies, it will be as important for young people to learn leisure skills as it is to learn work-related, occupational ones.

References

Adler, P.A., Kless, S.J., & Adler, P. (1992). Socialization to gender roles: Popularity among elementary school boys and girls. *Sociology of Education*, *65*, 169–187.

Alsaker, F.D., & Flammer, A. (1999). European adolescents: Basically alike and excitingly different. In F. D. Alsaker, & A. Flammer (Eds.), *The adolescent experience: European and American adolescents in the 1990s* (pp. 165–175). Mahwah, NJ: Lawrence Erlbaum Associates, Inc.

Anderson, C.A., & Bushman, B.J. (2001). Effects of violent video games on aggressive behavior, aggressive cognition, aggressive affect, physiological arousal, and prosocial behavior: A meta-analytic review of the scientific literature. *Psychological Science*, *12*, 353–359.

Arnett, J. (1998). The young and the reckless. In D. Messer, & J. Dockrell (Eds.), *Developmental psychology: A reader*. London: Arnold.

Arnett, J.J., Larson, R., & Offer, D. (1995). Beyond effects: Adolescents as active media users. *Journal of Youth and Adolescence*, *25*, 511–518.

Apostolidi, C., & Süss, D. (1999, September). *Audiovisual media and computer use of young people in Greece and Switzerland: A comparative analysis of gender, age and social class interactions*. Paper presented at the IXth European Conference on Developmental Psychology, Spetses, Greece.

Bailey, R., Wellard, I. & Dismore, H. (2005). Girls and physical activities: A summary review. *Education and Health*, *23*, 3–5.

Beck, U. (1992). *Risk society: Towards a new modernity*. London: Sage.

Beentjes, H.J., d'Haenens, W.J., van der Voort, T.H.A., & Koolstra, C.M. (1999). Dutch and Flemish children and adolescents as users of interactive media. *Communications*, *24*, 145–166.

Behnken, I., & Zinnecker, J. (1987). Von Strassenkind zum verhäuslichten kind [From street child to home child]. *Sozialwissenschaftliche Informationen*, *16*, 87–96.

Bronfenbrenner, U. (1979). *The ecology of human development: Experiments by nature and design*. Cambridge, MA: Harvard University Press.

Bruno, J.E. (1996). Time perceptions and time allocation preferences among adolescent boys and girls. *Adolescence*, *31*, 109–126.

Caldwell, L.L., Darling, N., Payne, L.L., & Dowdy, B. (1999). 'Why are you bored?' An examination of psychological and social control causes of boredom among adolescents. *Journal of Leisure Research*, *31*, 103–121.

Coakley, J., & White, A. (1992). Making decisions: Gender and sport participation among British adolescents. *Sociology of Sport Journal*, *9*, 20–35.

Coffield, F. (1992). *Young people and illicit drugs. Summary Research Report*. Northern Regional Health Authority and University of Durham.

Cohen, P. (1988). The perversions of inheritance. In P. Cohen, & H. S. Bains (Eds.), *Multiracist Britain* (pp. 9–118). Basingstoke and London: Macmillan.

Coleman, J.C., & Schofield, J. (2005). *Key data on adolescence – 2005*. Brighton: Trust for the Study of Adolescence.

Coleman, J.C., & Warren-Adamson, C. (1992). *Youth policy in the 1990s*. London: Routledge.

Csikszentmihalyi, M., & Larson, R. (1984). *Being adolescent: Conflict and growth in the teenage years*. New York: Basic Books.

D'Amours, L., & Robitaille, P.A. (2002). *99% of Quebec teens use the Internet!* Cefrio. Retrieved November 29, 2004 from *http://www.cefrio.qc.ca/English/Communiques/commun_6.ofm*.

Davis, J. (1990). *Youth and the condition of Britain: Images of adolescent conflict*. London: Athlone.

Demsey, D., Hillier, L., & Harrison, L. (2001). Gendered (s)explorations among same-sex attracted young people in Australia. *Journal of Adolescence*, *24*, 67–81.

Dietz, T.L. (1998). An examination of violence and

gender role portrayals in video games: Implications for gender socialization and aggressive behavior. *Sex Roles, 38*, 425–442.

Dunphy, D.C. (1972). Peer group socialisation. In F. J. Hunt (Ed.), *Socialisation in Australia* (pp. 200–217). Sydney, Australia: Angus & Robertson.

Fischer, A. (1992). Zum Tabellenteil [About the table section]. In Jugendwerk der Deutschen Shell (Ed.), *Jugend '92. Vol. 4: Methodenberichte – Tabellen – Fragebogen* (pp. 119–220). Opladen, Germany: Leske & Budrich.

Fisher, S. (1995). The amusement arcade as a social space for adolescents. *Journal of Adolescence, 18*, 71–86.

Fitzgerald, M., Joseph, A.P., Hayes, M., & O'Regan, M. (1995). Leisure activities of adolescent schoolchildren. *Journal of Adolescence, 18*, 349–358.

Flammer, A., Alsaker, F.D., & Noack, P. (1999). Time use by adolescents in an international perspective. I: The case of leisure activities. In F. D. Alsaker, & A. Flammer (Eds.), *The adolescent experience: European and American adolescents in the 1990s* (pp. 33–60). Mahwah, NJ: Lawrence Erlbaum Associates, Inc.

Flintoff, A., & Scraton, S. (2001). Stepping into active leisure? Young women's perceptions of active lifestyles and their experiences of school physical education. *Sport, Education and Society, 6*, 5–21.

Furlong, A., Campbell, R., & Roberts, K. (1990). The effects of post-16 experiences and social class on the leisure patterns of young adults. *Leisure Studies, 9*, 213–224.

Giordano, P.C., Cernkovich, S.A., & DeMaris, A. (1993). The family and peer relations of black adolescents. *Journal of Marriage and the Family, 55*, 277–287.

Golombok, S., & Fivush, R. (1994). *Gender development*. Cambridge: Cambridge University Press.

Griffin, C. (1993). *Representations of youth*. London: Polity.

Griffiths, M. (1995). *Adolescent gambling*. London: Routledge.

Hendry, L.B. (1971). Don't put your daughter in the water, Mrs. Worthington? (A sociological examination of the sub-culture of competitive swimming). *British Journal of Physical Education, 2*, 17–29.

Hendry, L.B. (1983). *Growing up and going out*. London. Pergamon.

Hendry, L.B. (1987). Young people: From school to unemployment? In S. Fineman (Ed.), *Unemployment: Personal and social consequences* (pp. 195–218). London: Tavistock.

Hendry, L.B., Glendinning, A., Reid, M., & Wood, S. (1998). *Lifestyles, health and health concerns of rural youth: 1996–1998*. Report to the Department of Health, Scottish Office, Edinburgh.

Hendry, L.B., & Kloep, M. (2002). *Lifespan development: Resources, challenges and risks*. London: Thomson Learning.

Hendry, L.B., & Kloep, M. (2005). Talkin', doin' and bein' with friends: Leisure and communication. In A. Williams, & C. Thurlow (Eds.), *Talking adolescence: Perspectives on communication in the teenage years*. New York: Peter Lang.

Hendry, L.B., Kloep, M., Espnes, G.A., Ingebrigtsen, J.E., Glendinning, A., & Wood, S. (1999, September). *Leisure transitions – A rural perspective*. Paper presented at the IXth European Conference on Developmental Psychology, Spetses, Greece.

Hendry, L.B., Kloep, M., Glendinning, A., Ingebrigtsen, J.E., Espnes, G.A., & Wood, S. (2002). Leisure transitions: A rural perspective. *Journal of Leisure Studies, 21*, 1–14.

Hendry, L.B., Shucksmith, J., & Glendinning, A. (1997). Adolescent focal theories: Age trends in developmental transitions. *Journal of Adolescence, 19*, 307–320.

Hendry, L.B., Shucksmith, J., & Love, J.G. (1989). *Young people's leisure and lifestyles: Report of phase 1 (1985–89)*. Edinburgh: The Scottish Sports Council.

Hendry, L.B., Shucksmith, J., Love, J.G., & Glendinning, A. (1993). *Young people's leisure and lifestyles*. London: Routledge.

Hendry, L.B., Shucksmith, J., & Philip, K.L. (1995). *Educating for health: School and community approaches*. London: Routledge.

Hendry, L.B., Shucksmith, J., Philip, K., & Jones, L. (1991). *Working with young people on HIV and drugs in Grampian region*. Final Report to Grampian Health Board, Aberdeen: Department of Education, University of Aberdeen.

Hendry, L.B., & Singer, F.E. (1981). Sport and the adolescent girl: A case study of one comprehensive school. *Scottish Journal of Physical Education, 9*, 18–22.

Hurrelmann, K., & Albert, M. (2002). *Jugend 2002 – Zwischen pragmatischem Idealismus und robustem Materialismus*. 14. Shell Jugendstudie, Frankfurt, Germany: Fischer.

Inchley, J., & Currie, C. (2004). Summary of key findings from the 2003/04 pupil survey. Findings from the Physical Activity in Scottish Schoolchildren (PASS) Survey. University of Edinburgh. Retrieved

August 2005 from *http://www.education.ed.ac.uk/cahru/publications/Pass_SummaryReport0304.pdf*.

Jaffe, M.L. (1998). *Adolescence*. New York: John Wiley & Sons.

Jones, G., & Wallace, C. (1992). *Youth family and citizenship*. Buckingham: Open University Press.

Kirchler, E., Pombeni, M.L., & Palmonari, A. (1991). Sweet sixteen . . . Adolescents' problems and the peer group as source of support. *European Journal of Psychology of Education*, *6*, 393–410.

Kitzinger, J. (1995). I'm sexually attractive but I'm powerful: Young women negotiating sexual reputation. *Women's Studies International Forum*, *18*, 187–196.

Kivel, B.D., & Kleiber, D.A. (2000). Leisure in the identity formation of lesbian/gay youth: Personal but not social. *Leisure Sciences*, *22*, 215–232.

Kloep, M. (1998). *Att vara ung i Jämtland* [To be young in Jämtland]. Uddeholt, Sweden: Österåsen.

Kloep, M. (1999). Love is all you need? Focusing on adolescents' life concerns from an ecological point of view. *Journal of Adolescence*, *22*, 49–63.

Kloep, M., & Hendry, L.B. (1997). In three years we'll be just like Sweden! – Anomie, Albania and university students. *Young*, *5*, 2–19.

Kloep, M., & Hendry, L.B. (1999). Challenges, risks and coping in adolescence. In D. Messer, & S. Millar (Eds.), *Exploring developmental psychology* (pp. 400–416). London: Arnold.

Kloep, M., & Hendry, L.B. (2003). Adult control and adolescent challenge? Dilemmas and paradoxes in young people's leisure. *World Leisure*, *45*, 24–34.

Kremer, J., Trew, K., & Ogle, S. (1997). *Young people's involvement in sport*. London: Routledge.

Larson, R. (1995). Secrets in the bedroom: Adolescents' private use of media. *Journal of Youth and Adolescence*, *24*, 535–550.

Larson, R., Richards, M.H., Moneta, G., Holmbeck, G., & Duckett, E. (1996). Changes in adolescents' daily interactions with their families from ages 10 to 18: Disengagement and transformation. *Developmental Psychology*, *32*, 744–754.

Lees, S. (1993). *Sugar and spice: Sexuality and adolescent girls*. London: Penguin.

Lempers, J., & Clark-Lempers, D. (1993). A functional comparison of same-sex and opposite-sex friendships during adolescence. *Journal of Adolescent Research*, *8*, 89–103.

Lloyd, M. (1985). *Adolescence*. London: Harper & Row.

Love, J., & Hendry, L.B. (1994). Youth workers and youth participants: Two perspectives of youth work? *Youth and Policy*, *46*, 43–55.

McMeeking, D., & Purkayastha, B. (1995). I can't have my mom running me everywhere: Adolescents, leisure and accessibility. *Journal of Leisure Research*, *27*, 360–378.

Maffesoli, M. (1996). *The time of the tribes*. London: Sage.

Mahoney, A.M. (1997). Age and sport participation. In J. Kremer, K. Trew, & S. Ogle (Eds.), *Young people's involvement in sport* (pp. 98–113). London: Routledge.

Mason, V. (1995). *Young people and sport in England, 1994: A national survey*. London: Sports Council.

Mesch, G.S. (2001). Social relationships and Internet use among adolescents in Israel. *Social Science Quarterly*, *82*, 329.

Murray, B. (1997). Is the Internet feeding junk to students? *APA Monitor*, *50*, April.

Näsström, A.C., & Kloep, M. (1994). The effects of job practice on the psychological well-being of unemployed youth. *Arbete och Hälsa*, *93*, 79–88.

Office of Population Censuses and Surveys OPCS (1995). *General household survey, 1993*. London: HMSO.

Palladino, G. (1996). *Teenagers: An American history*. New York: Basic Books.

Parker, H., Aldridge, J., & Measham, F. (1998). *Illegal leisure*. London: Routledge.

Raviv, A., Bar-Tal, D., Raviv, A., & Ben-Horin, A. (1996). Adolescent idolisation of pop singers: Causes, expressions, and reliance. *Journal of Youth and Adolescence*, *25*, 631–650.

Raymore, L.A., Barber, B.L., Eccles, J.S., & Godbey, G.C. (1999). Leisure behavior pattern stability during the transition from adolescence to young adulthood. *Journal of Youth and Adolescence*, *28*, 80–103.

Rietveld, H. (1994). Living the dream. In S. Redhead (Ed.), *Rave off: Politics and deviance in contemporary youth culture* (pp. 41–78). Aldershot: Avebury.

Roberts, K., & Parsell, G. (1994). Youth cultures in Britain: The middle class take-over. *Leisure Studies*, *13*, 33–48.

Roe, K. (1995). Adolescents' use of socially disvalued media: Towards a theory of media delinquency. *Journal of Youth and Adolescence*, *24*, 617–631.

Rowland, T. (1991). Influence of physical activity and fitness on coronary risk factors in children: How *strong* an argument? *Paediatric Exercise Science*, *3*, 189–191.

Rutter, M. (1996a). Psychological adversity: Risk, resilience and recovery. In L. Verhofstadt-Deneve, I. Kienhorst, & C. Braet (Eds.), *Conflict and develop-*

ment in adolescence (pp. 21–34) Leiden, the Nether-lands: DSWO Press.

Rutter, M. (1996b). Stress research. In R. J. Haggerty, L. R. Sherrod, N. Garmezy, & M. Rutter (Eds.), *Stress, risk and resilience in children and adolescents* (pp. 354–385). Cambridge: Cambridge University Press.

Savin-Williams, R.C. (1990). *Gay and lesbian youths: Expressions of identity*. Washington, DC: Hemisphere.

Savin-Williams, R.C. (2001). A critique of research on sexual-minority youths. *Journal of Adolescence, 24,* 5–13.

Scase, J. (1999). *Britain towards 2010: The changing business environment* (ESRC Report). London: Economic and Social Research Council.

Scully, D., & Clarke, J. (1997). Gender issues in sport participation. In J. Kremer, K. Trew, & S. Ogle (Eds.), *Young people's involvement in sport* (pp. 25–56). London: Routledge.

Seelow, D. (1996). Listening to youth: Woodstock, music, America, and Kurt Cobain's suicide. *Child and Youth Care Forum, 25,* 49–60.

Shaw, S.M., Caldwell, L.L., & Kleiber, D.A. (1996). Boredom, stress and social control in the daily activities of adolescents. *Journal of Leisure Research, 28,* 274–292.

Shucksmith, J., & Hendry, L.B. (1998). *Health issues and young people: Growing up and speaking out.* London: Routledge.

Silbereisen, R.K., Noack, P., & von Eye, A. (1992). Adolescents' development of romantic friendship and change in favourite leisure contexts. *Journal of Adolescent Research, 7,* 80–93.

SOU (Statens offentliga utredningar) (1994). *Ungdomars välfärd och värderingar* [Youth welfare and values] Report No. 73. Stockholm: Civil Departement.

Strasburger, V.C. (1995). *Adolescents and the media: Medical and psychological impact.* Thousand Oaks, CA: Sage.

Thornton, S. (1997). The social logic of subcultural capital. In S. Thornton, & K. Gelder (Eds.), *The subcultures reader* (pp. 200–209). London: Routledge.

Tomlinson, A. (1990). *Consumption, identity and style.* London: Routledge.

Trew, K. (1997). Time for sport? Activity diaries of young people. In J. Kremer, K. Trew, & S. Ogle (Eds.), *Young people's involvement in sport* (pp. 126–151). London: Routledge.

Urberg, K.A., Degirmenicioglu, S.M., Tolson, J.M., & Halliday-Scher, K. (1995). The structure of adolescent peer networks. *Developmental Psychology, 31,* 540–547.

Westphal, M. (2003, September). *Geschlechtsspezifische Aspekte bei der Integration im und durch den Sport.* Paper presented at the 2nd Schnittstellenkonferenz Sportpädagogik – Jugendhilfe. Braunatal, Germany.

Wight, D. (1992). Impediments to safer heterosexual sex: A review of research with young people. *AIDSCare, 4,* 11–25.

Wolak, J., Mitchell, K.J., & Finkelhov, D. (2002). Close online relationships in a national sample of adolescents. *Adolescence, 37,* 441–456.

Wold, B., & Hendry, L.B. (1998). Social and environmental factors associated with physical activity in young people. In S. Biddle, J. Sallis, & N. Cavill (Eds.), *Young and active?* (pp. 119–132). London: Health Education Authority.

Woodroffe, C., Glickman, M., Barker, M., & Power, C. (1993). *Children, teenagers and health: Key data.* Buckingham: Open University Press.

Zick, C.D., & Allen, C.R. (1996). The impact of parents' marital status on the time adolescents spend in productive activities. *Family Relations, 45,* 65–71.

Ziehe, T. (1994). *Kulturanalyser* [Cultural analyses]. Stockholm, Sweden: Brutus.

Zinnecker, J. (1990). Vom Strassenkind zum verhäuslichten kind [From street child to home child]. In I. Behnken (Ed.), *Stadtgesellschaft und Kindheit im Prozess der Zivilisation* [Urban society and childhood in the process of socialisation] (pp. 142–162). Opladen, Germany: Leske & Budrich.

14

Adolescents' relationships to institutional order

Monica Rubini and Augusto Palmonari

LEARNING OBJECTIVES

This chapter deals with adolescents' orientation towards institutional authorities, that is, the way in which they relate to the formal system of society. Adolescents' orientations in this regard are shaped to a considerable extent, as we will illustrate, by their experiences with the school system and their interactions within the peer group. In this respect we will consider different aspects of adolescents' school experience, taking into account the pivotal role of school socialization in shaping the general orientation of individuals towards institutions. We will also look at the interplay between school experience and peer group membership in influencing attitudes and behaviours towards the formal institutions. But before we concentrate on those links, we will show how the institutional framework of society assumes special importance during adolescence. We will then look further at the components of institutional orientation, how it develops, what sort of implications it has in terms of the social identity it communicates, and starting from the communication of attitudes or from the adoption of behaviours towards the institutional system we consider what impressions are formed by others.

1. Institutions in the social world of young people

A young person does not acquire an adult identity in social isolation. The younger generations are typically accompanied in this crucial task by significant others (parents, teachers, adults with different educational roles). In the various stages of development, these socialization agents offer a variety of forms of support in coping with the multiplicity of developmental challenges entailed in working out who one is, or is becoming. During early infancy, relations with significant others are characterized by a relative informality: exchanges of communication generally begin with the direct, face-to-face encounter between the caregiver and the child.

Relational experiences accumulate, changing in structure and processes. Young people's interactions with others proceed from the relatively low levels of formality typical of family relations to the increasingly formal, institutionally regulated relations of the school and other external bodies. In these dynamic, socially organized contexts, the young begin to construct their own representation both of the roles played by the formal authorities and of how the institutional system works.

The need to understand how to relate to the institutional system on the part of someone who is not yet adult becomes particularly important during adolescence. In this period, which coincides with the acquisition – at least partial – of logical/formal thought and the refining of moral reasoning, relations with people holding formal roles are intensified. In the school environment, teachers begin systematically to expect adolescents to take direct responsibilities connected with the role of learner. Young people are now guided to adopt the appropriate behavioural repertoires, to be used both in asymmetrical relations with school authorities and in symmetrical relationships with their peers.

The growing autonomy that adolescents gain from and are given by the family enables them to purchase goods independent of family control and to experiment with other relations regulated by codified formalities and behavioural repertoires. Some adolescents, for example, experience direct relations with the staff of the health services, banks, and the local registry office. Many of them begin to interact with police authorities to reach or protect personal goals (reporting theft or loss of personal objects) or because they break the highway code or commit more serious civil offences. In addition, a number of adolescents attend religious, sports or civic institutions where, besides relations of an informal interpersonal nature, they experience the need to respect certain rules necessary for admittance to these contexts.

The scenario that we have described shows that adult public life approached at the end of adolescence is characterized by continuous relations with the institutional system and with the authorities that operate and sustain it (Emler & Reicher, 1995).

This implies that the social integration of people in the civil societies in which they live must be mediated by adequate methods of relation to the institutional system.

According to Max Weber (1922; see also Emler & Reicher, 1995) the 'bureaucratic' organization of societies, unlike other social organizations in which people live, is characterized by the impersonality and rationality of relations between the individuals and the social system to which they belong. They have rights and obligations defined by the position they hold within the system. A certain social position is achieved on the basis of technical skills and not on the basis of personal preferences or family ties. In the same vein, the authorities involved in running the institutions are obliged to act impartially and impersonally and not on the basis of affective or hostile relations towards people (Emler & Reicher, 1995).

All these characteristics of rationalization and formalization of interpersonal relations may appear distant, alienating and extremely moralistic to adolescents.

The sensation of distance and extraneousness that the institutional world produces in adolescents may, on first contact, be overcome only if these perceive the need to respect norms and rules valid for everyone with the aim of becoming a part of the greater society in a satisfactory way. In order to achieve this, the social actors, particularly the youngest and all the 'newcomers' to a certain social system, have to know and be willing to understand the rules governing the system itself so as to adapt their own behaviour to them (Berger & Berger, 1975).

Adolescents are most likely to be persuaded of the need to become part of their social communities respecting the values on which they are based and the rules guaranteeing maintenance of them if vigilance over respect for the rules is done by adults whose fundamental goal is to protect the value of people and not a rigid propensity for having the rules respected for themselves.

1.1 Notion of orientation towards formal authority

The position that adolescents adopt to relate to the formal system may be termed as orientation towards institutional authorities (Emler & Reicher, 1995; Reicher & Emler, 1985, 1987). This socio-psychological construct subsumes both the factors which are part of its development (the processes of primary socialization, school experience and peer group socialization) and the components which distinguish it (the cognitive and motivational skills necessary to understand the procedures of functioning of the institutional system, the system of attitudes towards the institutional system, the behavioural repertoires needed to relate to the system itself).

Moreover, orientation towards the institutional system has also important implications for self-presentation (with regard to the social reputation that individuals possess as a function of the attitudes and behaviours that they adopt towards the institutional system) and as a consequence of this for social relationships. The attitudes and behaviours that adolescents adopt to relate to the formal system are a communicable component of one's own identity. On the basis of them the observers build up the public reputation of other people (Emler & Reicher, 1995).

Additionally, orientation towards the institutional system may be considered as a relatively definitive solution to the developmental task regarding the need to acquire the skills to take part fully in the public life of contemporary societies, characterized by the presence of bureaucratic institutions. At the same time, as regards the individual, institutional orientation is a way to communicate one's own social identity in that it reveals the position held by each individual towards the legal system, the degree of membership of the social community in terms of citizenship, and the attitudes towards social and political issues (Emler & Reicher, 1995).

2. Components of orientation toward institutional authorities

2.1 Understanding the procedures of the institutional system

A fundamental issue linked to the position taken by individuals towards the institutional system concerns comprehension of the procedures and the aims of the system itself. During adolescence, the task of understanding how bureaucratic procedures work is facilitated by both social and individual factors. The process of exploration of the living environment (Bosma, 1994; Erikson, 1950; Marcia, 1980; Meeus, 1996), becomes more intense and is operated in greater autonomy with respect to family ties; this leads adolescents to face new experiences which often imply relations within formalized normative systems.

Some of the relations which imply formal aspects cease to be mediated by the parent figures: adolescents begin to accumulate direct experience of relations with people holding institutional and formal roles.

2.1.1 Development of formal thought

This period of life is also characterized by the achievement of formal thought (Piaget, 1972; Piaget & Inhelder, 1975) which allows people to reflect in abstract terms on their experience with the aid of refined skills of analysis and summary. Here, formal reasoning is characterized by the ability to formulate hypotheses not only of a logical mathematical type but also about one's origin, history and environment and to deduce the consequences implied in the hypotheses. This capacity for deductive hypothetical thought enables a broader comprehension of the social reality surrounding people, allows one's aspirations to be projected in time through the formulation of projects, and a dynamic balance to be found between the means considered necessary to accomplish one's projects on the basis of the resources actually available. It is clear that, in the passage from aspirations and dreams to the realistic project, the social actor must also take into account the norms and rules of social life which form 'constraints' for his/her expectations and goals. The adolescent person must therefore develop comprehension of the relatively complex system within which he/she is located and the rules which regulate and channel social behaviour.

2.1.2 Moral development

Parallel to the acquisition of formal thought, adolescents are helped to understand the advantage of respecting the institutional rules, often through assuming critical positions, by the gradual maturation of moral reasoning which during this period of life reaches Stage 4, according to Kohlberg (1981), a stage coinciding with the awareness of being members of society. From longitudinal research conducted by Kohlberg over 20 years, it emerges that adolescents who reach this stage of moral thought go beyond the consideration of others as individuals who take part in interpersonal relations but consider the equity of social systems as a basic criterion for expressing moral judgments. What regulates the relations between people and society is the sense of justice. The best way to respect this principle is for everyone to observe the law and for the laws to be applied impartially to all. As adolescents acquire such an ability to reason in moral terms, they are increasingly motivated to understand the complex functioning of the institutional system.

We have outlined here the optimal development of the adolescent situation in which expansion of the living space and of the temporal perspective, acquisition of the capacity of reasoning in hypothetical–deductive terms, maturation of moral judgment, join up to enable the individual to elaborate realistic life projects and thus become part of the social situation. In reality the process of development may take place in different ways which demand from adolescents efforts of adaptation to the context and of (expansion) autonomy of the self which are very difficult to reconcile. There are adolescents who are fascinated by the idea of creating original systems of formal rules so that they have great difficulty becoming part of the existing order and reaching the awareness that in order to change it, it has to be faced realistically as it is. Others are unable to take the step from the utopia to the project and risk remaining inert, incapable of committing themselves in the existing reality. These adolescents act in this way

because they perceive any possible result of their own action as imperfect, soon experiencing a serious decline in self-esteem. Others instead consider it of fundamental importance that their insertion in society takes place respecting ideal rules free of any compromise and adopt extreme and rigid ideological positions. Each adolescent may come up against difficulties of this type that practical experience (the fatigue of living) generally tends to smooth over in order to make a compromise with reality. Contrariwise, if these discrepancies did not exist and, above all, if adolescents did not try to go beyond what already exists, to improve reality, there would be no innovative contribution from the young generations. However there are also some adolescents who tend to conform passively to what they find in their social reality and become very sensitive to the pressure of consumerism and the logic of immediate gratification. Some authors (Canestrari, 1984) even claim that in these cases – described as 'sacrificed adolescence' – the stage of formal thought is not reached.

Finally, other individuals who live in conditions with disadvantages characterized by the lack of material resources or by the absence of significant inter-individual or social ties develop a basic cynicism towards the political and social system. These young people find it difficult to imagine a promising future in the society that they have observed and in part experimented with (Damon & Hart, 1992).

2.2 Attitudes towards the institutional system

Understanding the functioning of the procedures of the institutional system can be considered as the cognitive component of the system of attitudes towards formal authorities. However, the cognitions inherent to the institutional system, its operating procedures and the roles and responsibilities of the authorities governing it generally have a positive or negative valence. This complies with the three-dimensional specificity of attitudes. In other words, adolescents elaborate an emotive position of varying degrees of intensity towards the institutional system ('social norms limit my potential' or vice versa) which is generated when this norm or system of norms becomes important for the actor involved. In relation to these states the individual develops a drive towards action in compliance with the norm or which challenges the norm perceived as restrictive. Almost all adolescents feel the need to challenge some social norms. Others, in much more limited numbers, base their personal and group reputation on the opposition to and breaking of the social norms. And it is thus (Emler & Reicher, 1995) that enduring deviance is generated.

The study of the empirical investigation of attitudes towards the social system is not new in the field of psychology. Various authors have examined the attitudes of adolescents towards the legal system (Brown, 1974; Clark & Wenninger, 1964), towards the police (Gibson, 1967), and towards authority in general terms (Rigby & Rump, 1982). However, in none of these studies has it been contemplated that attitudes towards the different forms of institutional authority might belong to the same symbolic 'domain'. This means that, regardless of the specific institutional environment to which these attitudes refer (school, legal, judiciary etc.), it is possible to find cognitive and evaluative consistency in the semantic organization of these attitudes, to such an extent that a consistently organized network of meanings may be formed.

This theory was tested by Reicher and Emler (1985) (also see Emler & Reicher, 1987; Emler, Reicher, & Ross, 1987). These authors developed a list of statements whose contents concerned the duties of obedience of citizens towards the legal system, the latitude of transgression of norms of the formal system (the legal system and the school system for example), the impartiality of treatment of people by the legal system and the positivity of the formal system. This was done in the light of the contention of Weber (1922), according to whom complying with the legal–formal system implies obedience to the impersonal order structured legally and to its representatives who should act impartially on the basis of the power given to them by the position which they formally and legitimately fill.

The list of statements was given to a sample of high school students who expressed their opinions on the subject. On the basis of the correlation (item–whole), 24 statements were selected which constitute the scale of attitudes. This methodological tool was subsequently given to middle and high school students (12–15 years old). The results of these research studies converge to show the existence of a factor which alone explains about 30% of the variance while the other factors emerging together explain less than 10%. This indicates that the attitudes towards the institutional system constitute a consistent and distinct field of meaning, whether they refer to the school or the legal system.

These findings also show strong transcultural validity. In the first phase of our research carried out in Italy (Rubini & Palmonari, 1995), we conducted a pilot study in order to see whether attitudes towards the institutional world also imply beliefs about the social desirability and the efficiency of the acts and procedures which are part of the formal system and its representatives. On the basis of the results obtained we have developed an Italian version of the scale of institutional attitudes which was subsequently given to a sample of 444 students from different types of secondary school (lyceums, technical institutes, vocational institutes). A factor concerning the duties or the non-observance of these in relating to the institutional system explained 20% of the variance. The other three factors emerging altogether explained 26% of the variance. These concern the positivity and efficacy of the institutional system and the impartiality of the system itself.

Importantly, the factorial solutions show for each factor the co-presence of items referred both to the legal system and to the school system, offering strong empirical support to the theory that institutional attitudes form a consistent and semantically organized corpus. Similar results have been obtained in subsequent research which has made use of extensive samples of adolescents in other European countries (Portugal: Gouveia-Pereira & Pires, 1999; Gouveia-Pereira, Vala, Palmonari, & Rubini, 2003; Spain: Molpeceres, Lucas, & Pons, 2000; Greece: Rubini & Tzialla, 2001).

The factors that influence or which are correlated with institutional attitudes are many. In general terms, girls have more positive attitudes towards the social institutions than boys throughout adolescence. Age is an important factor of variation. In early adolescence at the age of 12–13 years the attitudes are basically positive, in the central stage around 14–16 years they tend to become more critical, particularly with regard to the impartiality of the institutional authorities. Towards the end of adolescence attitudes tend to acquire again a positive valence. There is also a strong connection between school experience and attitudes towards the institutional system. Those who attend more prestigious higher institutes (lyceums, for example) have more positive attitudes on the subject. What is more, both objective school achievement and the value attributed to school experience have a positive relation with the valence of institutional attitudes (Palmonari & Rubini, 1998, 1999; Rubini, 1998; Rubini & Palmonari, 1998).

Even the membership of different types of peer group bears some relation to attitudes towards the institutions. In general terms, those who belong to formal groups, in other words groups featuring the presence of explicit goals, generally of a religious or sports nature and with adult leaders responsible for the group, develop more positive attitudes towards the institutions than those who belong to informal groups, characterized simply by ties of friendship and by regular frequentation among the members of the groups. The effect due to the type of group of membership is, however, attenuated by the system of rules governing the groups in question. The attitudes of the members of groups, even informal groups, which reject strongly transgressive or deviant behaviour are more in line with the institutional system (Palmonari & Rubini, 2001).

Although there is no corpus of systematic evidence, a number of studies (Banks et al., 1991; Rubini & Palmonari, 1995) show that attitudes towards institutional authority have significant relations with the beliefs, the information and the positions held by people towards civil and political life. More positive attitudes towards the institutions are correlated with a greater knowledge of the institutional positions held by political figures, with a greater knowledge of the issues of political debate, and with less cynicism towards the efficacy of the democratic political system.

There is also a very strong relation between attitudes and behaviours towards the institutions. Emler and Reicher (1995) argue that the attitudes and behaviour taken towards the institutions are no other than two complementary ways to communicate one's own position in relation to the institutional system. These authors claim that it is very difficult to isolate the relations of cause–effect which link attitudes to behaviour, and that there is a reciprocal influence of the two components at different times. Similar conclusions have also been reached by Kohlberg and Higgins (1987) who, studying the relations between the development of moral thought (a major component of attitudes towards the institutional authorities) and social behaviour, observed that moral judgment often influences conduct, although, by the same token, becoming involved in a certain course of actions influences the moral judgment relative to the action set up. The available evidence is too limited for exhaustive conclusions to be drawn. Only research of a longitudinal nature, extended throughout adolescence, could provide more detailed responses. For the moment, in accordance with Fazio (1986) we consider it plausible that the attitudes which have been formed directly, in other words, those generated in direct contact with the object to which they refer, feature a high degree of cognitive accessibility, and are relatively predictive of the behaviours adopted by those who elaborate them. If it is true, as we will illustrate, that attitudes towards the institutional system are mainly rooted in the school experience which forms a fundamental living environment for the experimentation of the self and of one's cognitive and social skills, it is possible to argue that these attitudes derive from the direct experience of people and thus may also have a predictive function as regards how the adolescents will behave towards the formal institutions.

2.3 The institutional normative system and the behavioural repertoire

As already stated, adolescence is a period of great exploration of the surrounding reality, searching for the possible identities which could define the self (Harter, 1983). Experimentation of the new possible selves by the developing social actor also goes through the adoption of transgressive behavioural repertoires. Almost all adolescents adopt deviant behaviours but this does not imply that they will develop an enduring deviant career (Emler & Reicher, 1995; Stattin & Magnusson, 1991). Rule breaking often satisfies the need for differentiation from the adult world and the need for assimilation with the models offered by one's peers, as well as the taste for 'risk taking'. The experience of breaking social norms also allows the adolescent to appear courageous and superior to the norms, as well as seeing himself or herself as invulnerable.

As Emler and Reicher (1995) claim, the deviant action is a social action which is carried out in the presence of others or together with others. Playing truant from school is done together with one's school mates, the school register is altered in front of one's school mates, and taking illegal substances is part of a collective ritual. In other words, the deviant actions of adolescents are put into practice before an audience, usually one's peers, which observes or participates in the course of transgressive actions. In these situations adolescents share with the other social actors the same social identity of 'deviants' and communicate it through transgressive behaviour.

As already stated, not all acts of the deviant behavioural repertoire have the same gravity and not all transgressions are destined to be repeated at later times.

However, certain adolescents systematically challenge the established order and use deviant behavioural modes in different situations repeated in time. This shows that such people refuse to adapt to the norms of the formal–legal system in handling inter-individual relations. Drawing on the work of Mitchell (1969), Emler and Reicher (1995) argue that there is an implicit contract between the social actors and the formal–legal system, with the former acting in line with the rules of the system itself while the system in turn offers them protection by safeguarding their rights and promoting their social mobility.

The alternative to this implicit contract accord-

ing to Mitchell is given by a 'personal order', for which people directly protect what they think are their rights, building informal networks of reciprocal protection to defend themselves from the offences or from the attacks that they might be subjected to. Enduring deviant behaviour may develop from the common sharing of this 'personal order'.

2.3.1 Measures of transgressive behaviour

Different methods of measuring transgressive behaviour are possible (for a careful analysis of the possible methods, see Emler & Reicher, 1995). The method we have used to study the use of deviant behavioural repertoires by adolescents was that of self-reports. This method has received criticism from several sides since the compilation of self-reported measures of antisocial behaviour could be influenced variously by motivational factors linked to the norms of social desirability or to the maintenance of the self-image, and by cognitive factors regarding the distortion of information due to mnemonic recovery, which challenges its reliability. At the same time, many sources of evidence show instead that what people claim about their own delinquent activities greatly exceeds those documented by police authorities (Elmhorn, 1965; Short & Nye, 1958). This evidence has thus led us to opt for this type of measurement, considering it fairly reliable.

In order to obtain a list of transgressive behaviours relevant to those used by adolescents, we contacted a sample of about 500 secondary school students aged between 14 and 18. Participants were asked to produce a list of behaviours breaking the social and civil rules that boys and girls of their age may sometimes perform. Once this first task was concluded, the participants of the pilot study ordered the behaviours described on the basis of their perceived gravity.

The various transgressive behaviours were subsequently included in categories of broader content with respect to that implied in the specific examples. We then developed a list of transgressive behaviours adopted by adolescents taking into account the frequency with which the different behaviours where mentioned in the pilot study and the perceived gravity attributed to them. This list includes transgressive behaviours in relation to the lack of respect for road regulations (e.g., driving without a licence) or the rules of the school system (playing truant from school, tampering with the school register), consumption of illegal substances, crimes against the person (beating people up, racially insulting immigrants) and against public and private property (stealing from supermarkets, breaking the glass of telephone boxes, spraying walls with graffiti and smashing street lighting).

The instrument obtained in this way was used in several subsequent research campaigns (Rubini & Palmonari, 1998) in which we asked the participants to state whether they had ever resorted to the behaviours in question in the previous 12 months.

Every affirmative response obtained a score of one. The higher the score accumulated, the higher the degree of behavioural deviance. This measure of the behaviour towards institutional norms emerged as significantly influenced by the dimensions of the attitudes towards formal authority. This relation was in the first place highlighted by the studies of Reicher and Emler (1985, 1987) who, as we have already mentioned, argued that there is a circular influence between attitudes and behaviours and that in the final analysis, these are just two complementary ways of showing one's own convictions about institutional systems.

During the various research stages we performed on orientation towards the institutional system, we were repeatedly able to confirm the strong tie between attitudes and behaviours. The dimension of the attitudes concerning the duties of obedience and the possible transgressions of duties towards the law has repeatedly shown a strong link with the practice of relatively serious deviant behaviours (Rubini & Tzialla, 2001).

2.4 Summary
In this section we have outlined the main features of the orientation towards the institutional system. We have proposed that the development of adolescents' attitudes toward authority is facilitated by the acquisition of formal thought and moral development. We have then considered the

studies on institutional attitudes and by describing the methods through which they have been investigated. Finally, we have taken into account the behavioural facet of individuals' institutional orientation.

3. School experience and orientation towards formal institutions

3.1 Importance of school socialization
When people start attending school institutions they begin to understand that inter-individual relations are not based only on ties of a natural and affective type whose goal is the protection and satisfaction of needs or the maintenance of ties of friendship between people. Within the school environment, children and adolescents experiment relations of competition and co-operation with adults and peers for the purpose of obtaining symbolic recognition of their intellectual production. They may also discover that breaking the codes regulating the relations of competition/co-operation between the social actors in the school environment is punished. For these reasons, some investigators identify the school environment as a privileged place for analysing the socio-cognitive processes lying behind the acquisition of personal and social skills (Bandura, 1964, 1969; Harter, 1983). The repertoire of social skills which are developed and refined by taking part in the school institutions imply that people learn to respect the school authorities (the teachers) because of the position they hold and not only because of their personal characteristics.

Conceiving the roles held by the formal authorities as impersonal depends on the evaluation of the reasonableness and the advantage that this impersonal style shows. In other words, people may accept participation in relatively impersonal relations on the basis of the fact that whoever holds institutional roles acts on bases of legitimacy, applying impartially the norms and procedures that regulate social life.

Taking into account the fact that the school experience forms most individuals' first prolonged experience with a formal institution, it is likely that this provides the basis for the comprehension of the roles and functioning of other formal systems. Evidence to support this theory comes from research carried out by Emler and collaborators (Emler, Ohana, & Dickinson, 1990; Emler, Ohana, & Moscovici, 1987) who conducted transcultural research in Scotland and France, interviewing children aged between 7 and 11, on the role of teachers in the various situations of school life. The results show that children of this age are not yet able to make inferences about the legitimacy of the role of the teacher on the basis of the teachers' ability to safeguard the rights of everyone and check in an impartial manner that everyone respects one's duties. They are, however, able to describe the behaviours of their teachers in various situations, to understand if the teachers offered help to those who needed it (for example, in situations where the pupils asked the teachers for help with the homework given to them) or if they refused it to anyone, discriminating between the pupils. Thus, children of this age have not yet processed the principles on which formal authority is based but are able to describe the social behaviours from which they will subsequently deduce the foundations of how the institutional systems work. This evidence suggests that the way in which the teachers treat the pupils has very broad and long-term implications about the way in which people organize their own representation of the formal authority.

3.1.1 Role of school organization

As noted earlier, school represents the first social organization in which relations between individuals are based on relations of productivity (mainly symbolic). According to Mars (1981), there are two dimensions which explain the occupational culture of the productive organizations and thus also of the school occupational culture. One of these two dimensions concerns the categorization of the role of the individual member of the organization. If this categorization is very strict and prescriptive about the role behaviour, the individual must adapt slavishly to the ruling imposed and the breadth of variation with respect to the codified behaviour to relate to the institution will be very limited. Contrariwise, if the categorization is more flexible, there is greater space for a personal interpretation of the role

and greater tolerance for individual variations in complying with the codified expectations.

The second dimension concerns the ways in which tasks are performed within the organization. These ways are organized along a continuum which ranges from the individual to the collective. At one end, lie tasks performed on an exclusively individual basis while at the other end are the methods of collective or rather, co-operative, task execution. This dimension is highly critical for the period of adolescence. On the one hand, the collective experiences in peer groups are fundamental for restructuring the self-system, thanks to the concrete and symbolic support that peers offer in coping with the various developmental tasks. On the other hand, the school system tends in general terms to discourage collective execution of work.

The way in which these two dimensions are combined varies from school to school, and from one school order to another. However, there may be school situations in which the intersection between the two dimensions mentioned involves a rigid categorization of the way in which the student has to interpret his or her role and also a very low presence of the collective dimension in the execution of the tasks.

As Emler and Reicher (1995) have found, the metaphor which best describes this situation is that of the ass who must do nothing but carry out the task that has been assigned to it without seeking help from anyone. Faced with a proposal of this nature, from the school institution there are at least three alternatives: the first is to adapt oneself slavishly to the system, the second is to put up opposition and challenge this culture in a manner which may also be constructive, the third is to abandon the system.

The strategies that individuals adopt to relate to these extreme situations tell us much about the positions they adopt towards the school institution and have considerable implications for the long-term social reputation attributed to the individuals.

3.1.2 Teaching style and school climate

Longitudinal research by Rutter, Maughan, Mortimore, and Ouston (1982) shows that the organizational school culture reflected, in particular, in the didactic style of the teachers, is significantly linked to the school achievements of the pupils. This means that in schools where the teachers co-ordinate with each other adopting co-operative methods in achieving the educational goals, where they concentrate school time on didactic activity and spend less time on verbal invitations to observe the disciplinary norms, where there is a willingness to help the pupils whenever necessary and where there is a perception shared by all the social actors (both teachers and pupils) about the clarity and legitimacy of the school rules, the academic results of the pupils are much more satisfactory than in those situations where the teachers adopt more authoritarian styles. What is more, in schools where there is a climate of reciprocal collaboration between teachers and pupils a group identity is created which leads to the sharing of common values. This climate also contributes to the development of less oppositional and less delinquent behaviour on the part of the pupils (Carugati & Selleri, 1996).

The co-operative (centred on the group) versus the competitive (centred around the individual) school climate is also connected to different methods of evaluation of academic performance. In their longitudinal research on primary schools, Mortimore, Sammons, Stoll, Lewis, and Ecob (1987) focused on the distinction between progress (i.e., evaluation of the results obtained at different times starting from the original academic level of the individual pupils) and final result (evaluation of the academic performance of the pupils starting from a standard level set for everyone). Their findings show that in the schools where there is a collegial organizational culture of school activities (both as regards the relation between teachers and as regards the way of handling the class group), there is, generally speaking, an attention to the progress made by pupils and not only to the final results they obtain. The greatest progress may be seen in those contexts where the teachers stimulate reflection on the contents of the tasks, ask questions which encourage creative responses and activate problem-solving strategies. In a final analysis, it could be claimed that positive academic performance and school adaptation may be observed in those school contexts where there is a conception of intelligence in the plural which makes use of the contribution of the cognitive and affective energies of all the social actors involved (Mugny & Carugati, 1967), where all the pupils can make progress, and it is less important that the greatest progress is that of the more talented pupils.

The empirical evidence that we have summarized thus for all converges to show, though in different ways, that school experience has a fundamental role in structuring the skills to be used in public life. This evidence shows that the way to play the role of the teacher, the style of the teaching, the climate experienced in class and in the school institution and the social organization of school life itself, have an impact both on academic performance and on the attitudes and behaviours used to relate to the school system and, as we will illustrate, also to other institutional systems

3.1.3 School attainment

In our own research (Rubini & Palmonari, 1995), we found that objective academic performance in turn (this was operationalized as the average of the school marks obtained at the end of the four months concluded before the research study) correlates significantly with the attitudes towards the institutional authorities. This evidence confirms what has already been highlighted by Emler (1988) and Emler and St James (1990). We found also that those who have negative attitudes towards the formal institutions (school and legal system) expect to leave the school institution permanently within a short time.

As already mentioned, school experience is also directly connected to delinquent behaviour. Adolescents who perform seriously deviant acts break off relations with school before the exams of the end of the school cycle (West & Farrington, 1977) or leave school with very bad results (Hindelang, Hirschi, & Weis, 1981).

Taken together the evidence we have summarized in this paragraph reveals that school climates are linked to pupils' academic results and these in turn are related to the components of the orientation towards the institutional authorities (Rubini & Palmonari, 1995).

3.1.4 School difficulties

Tyszkova (1990) has grouped the difficulties encountered during school life into two large categories: difficulties relative to the school experience in itself (learning difficulties, for example) and difficulties relative to the relational sphere with classmates and teachers. The problems linked to school difficulties are more frequent, but those that compromise interpersonal relations and self-image are perceived as more serious and more problematic for the development of social adaptation and identity.

The importance of dealing right from the appearance of the first symptoms with school maladjustment, reflected in the inability to adapt to school rules, is highlighted by Osuna and Luna (1989). According to these authors, the difficulties of adapting to school rules may be predictive of the behaviour towards the institutional authorities and social norms. They stress the need for teachers to be made aware of how to notice the first signs of maladjustment towards the school institution and its norms since these difficulties may be solved more easily if dealt with early enough.

3.1.5 School maladjustment

Goodenow (1993) takes into consideration the relation between academic performance and school maladjustment due to low involvement and the weak sense of membership of the school group on the part of certain adolescents. This author, who has developed a psychological sense of school membership scale (PSSMS), has found that the more adolescents identify with the school groups to which they belong, the more they manage to obtain satisfactory academic results. This fairly articulated body of evidence shows therefore that what happens at school has considerable influence on the construction of personal and social identity and that school experience forms the basis for socialization concerning institutional relations and the acquisition of orientation towards the formal–bureaucratic system.

To date, however, there is not much direct evidence documenting specific links between the experience of school maladjustment and attitudes–behaviours of a deviant nature. It was our intention to see whether this link exists.

School maladjustment constitutes a multifactorial experience that may imply individual variables (such as low academic performance caused by learning difficulties, emotional vulnerability, low self-esteem or low sense of self-efficacy) or psycho-social variables such as interpersonal processes of comparison, both symmetrical (i.e., with individuals who hold the same position or social role) and asymmetrical (i.e., with people who hold social positions higher than one's own). The dynamics of social comparison characterize people's lives almost constantly and have an essential influence in the school environment characterized by co-operative and competitive relations. Thus, people in the school context confront each other during evaluation with the teachers, and the results of these asymmetrical comparisons may sometimes produce outcomes so negative that they seriously threaten important dimensions of the self-concept. Even symmetrical comparisons with classmates can often generate negative results, in the sense that on the occasions of academic assessment the student may realize that his or her classmates are better, brighter and more competent in handling social relations, so that they have a wider network of friendships, enjoy greater popularity and form more satisfactory boyfriend/girlfriend relationships.

Other sources of school maladjustment may, in addition, derive from the comparison between the structural organization of the various school cycles. In this way, the transitions from one cycle to another can create problems of school adjustment due to the growing formalization of the interpersonal relations typical of the passage to the higher school cycles.

In light of these considerations, we have developed an instrument to measure school maladjustment. We contacted a sample of about 500 students attending different types of secondary schools (lyceums, technical institutes and vocational institutes) inviting them to compile a detailed list of the experiences that make them feel good at school, plus a list of experiences and problems that make them feel bad at school. Two judges then coded the great quantity of statements generated by the adolescents on the basis of categories of content relevant to the material obtained. On the basis of the frequency of quotation of the statements included in the various categories of content, we constructed a series of 32 statements, attempting to keep as close as possible to the prototypical formulations used by the adolescents themselves. The 32 statements form the scale of measurement of school maladjustment. This scale was subsequently given to a sample of 328 adolescents whom we contacted at the meeting places of the peer groups to which they belong (church halls, sports centres, public parks or cafes). Analysis of the main components highlighted a three-factor solution, which overall explains 57.7% of the variance.

The first factor, which we have labelled 'motivation to learn', concerns the consideration of the school as a place in which it is possible to increase one's knowledge of the world as well as the desire to have teachers who are competent and qualified for the position they hold and who are able to recognize the capabilities of their students. The second factor that we have labelled 'insecurity and fear about academic assessment' groups together the negative feelings (fear and anxiety) that adolescents experience in the situations in which they are assessed. The third factor labelled 'school adjustment' concerns the capacities or difficulties that adolescents encounter in having to adapt to rules which are sometimes too strict with respect to which they have no chance of negotiation.

One of the most interesting results of this study was that the first and third factor of school maladjustment have statistically significant links both with the attitudes and with the behaviours used to relate to the institutional system. The same type of significant link was found in subsequent studies which confirm that school maladjustment may represent an important factor in relation to the development of an orientation of an oppositional nature towards the institutions. This was demonstrated both in the various studies that we carried out in Bologna (in Northern Italy) and in research carried out in Giannina (in Greece). Among the factors of school maladjustment the one that correlates most with the orientation towards the institutional system concerns adaptation to school regulations.

The importance of school maladjustment in influencing orientation towards the institutions is evident also from a study we performed on 22 minors in the Bologna juvenile prison. From interviews with these adolescents, it emerged that 50% of them abandoned their school career during primary school, and the remainder opted out during middle school. Very few managed to obtain a middle school certificate. Their accounts reveal great difficulty in communicating with the teachers, difficulty in adapting to the rules of the institution, and loss of the personal motivations necessary to complete their studies. Yet these same adolescents also expressed positive options about the importance of school, even formulating self-attributions of responsibility for the negative results obtained.

All in all, this evidence underlines the fundamental role of school experience in laying the foundations for adaptation to social public life and highlights the responsibility linked to the role of the teachers in guiding people towards an appreciation of the personal and social benefits that derive from respect of the norms regulating the various social communities (Rubini, 1998).

3.2 Summary

In this section we have outlined the multi-faceted role of school experience in shaping the orientation towards institutions. We have considered factors of different nature pertaining to the structural organization of school, teachers' features, individuals' subjective school experience, objective school performance. Taken together these factors contribute to shaping one's own attitudes and behaviour towards the social system.

4. Peer groups

So far, we have emphasized that the style of socialization of the family of origin, the organization of the school and the climate that characterizes it, and the way in which the teachers perform their roles all help to influence the quality of the orientation towards the institutional authorities in a broad sense. It is, however, equally true that during the period of adolescence a context of fundamental experience is formed by relations with peers in both school and out-of-school environments. The evidence of various studies (Palmonari, Pombeni, & Kirchler, 1992; Sherif & Sherif, 1964) shows that, during adolescence, peer groups form fundamental points of reference to cope with different developmental tasks.

If we had to name the most important developmental task that people face during adolescence, we could say that the restructuring of the self-concept forms the task which is super-ordinate to all the others. The solution (never completed, see Erikson, 1968) of this task is guided by two fundamental motivations: the need for differentiation of the self from the others (which at this stage of life coincides with the need to differentiate above all from the adults) and the need for assimilation of the self within social groups–categories with high significance for the identity that people desire to acquire (peer groups). This type of psycho-social dynamics is well articulated by Brewer (1991, 1993) in her 'optimal distinctiveness model'. According to this author, the various social identities of people are the product of contrasting needs: the necessity of reaching an optimal specificity emerges as a universal motivation satisfied by the balance between the differentiation of the self from the others through inter-group comparisons and by the inclusion of the self within the social groups or categories of membership. The ways in which people satisfy the need for optimal distinction depend on the contexts in which they live.

One of the first works to concentrate on documenting the peculiarities, the goals, and the activities of groups of adolescents was that of Sherif and Sherif (1964), who considered peer groups as social workshops in which adolescents experiment roles and identities that they would like to acquire (Harter, 1990). In these settings, young people compare their opinions and values with those of their peers (Kiesner, 2002), and support each other reciprocally in facing the various developmental tasks that characterize this period of their lives. The perception of sharing a common fate

(becoming adults) provides comfort and support in coping with the difficulties encountered.

In the Italian context it has often been verified that about 90% of adolescents belong to peer groups that meet regularly. Palmonari and colleagues (Amerio, Boggi-Cavallo, Palmonari, & Pombeni, 1990; Palmonari, Kirchler, & Pombeni, 1991; Palmonari, Pombeni, & Kirchler, 1989, 1990, 1992, 1993) show that within the adolescent group universe it is possible to distinguish between formal and informal groups.

4.1 Formal groups

Three main characteristics distinguish these groups. They are characterized by the presence of specific and explicit goals to be reached, though these may be very different from each other (e.g., goals connected with religious or sports education, or musical activities, voluntary work and politics). A second discriminating feature of formal groups concerns the fact that the public or private institutions to which they refer provide physical spaces in which the members of these groups meet with relative regularity. Finally, formal groups almost always feature the presence of leaders who are relatively adult (although often very young) with the role of guaranteeing and co-ordinating the continuity of energies produced by the members to reach the preset goals.

According to various research studies (Palmonari et al., 1989, 1990) about 25–30% of adolescents belong to formal groups of which the most popular are religious and sports groups. However, participation is not constant in time. Indeed from the age of 14 upwards, particularly when moving from middle to high school, a large percentage of adolescents abandon these groups to join informal groups. The fundamental motivation of this abandonment seems to be linked to the desire to experiment oneself within social workshops over which adults have no control.

Within the panorama of formal groups, it is worth noting that membership of political and cultural groups (such as those of environmental protection and human rights, Amnesty International, for example) is very small indeed, being about 1–2%. This figure is the same as that of other European countries (Hurrelmann & Engel, 1989).

This evidence seems to indicate limited interest in political activism on the part of the new generations. However, it should not lead us to conclude that all adolescents are characterized by political disinterest or cynicism. As we have argued in the past (Palmonari & Rubini, 1998; Rubini & Palmonari, 1995), the bases of political thought are acquired during adolescence through an interlacing of immediate and mediated communicative exchanges typical of the various contexts of development of the social actors (the family, the school, peer groups and exposure to mass media communication). So we should not draw hasty conclusions about the lack of interest in politics being a typical feature of adolescents (or even of young people) of today. It may be hypothesized instead that during adolescence a personal position is elaborated towards social institutions and rules, a process that forms for each person an important experience of introduction to politics. On this passage, however, there is still little empirical confirmation.

4.2 Informal groups

These groups are spontaneous aggregations of adolescents who meet with assiduous regularity without any superordinate goal as regards maintaining and strengthening the ties of friendship between the members of the groups. Since these spontaneous aggregations are independent of institutional contexts and not controlled by adults, the groups meet in public places such as parks, street corners, squares or coffee bars. The great majority (about 70%) of adolescents aged between 14 and 17 claims to belong to groups of this type (Palmonari et al., 1989, 1990). In addition, objective evidence shows that this type of group of adolescents is transversal to the general memberships and social classes of origin. The individual groups, however, tend to be relatively homogeneous in their composition as regards social origin, school career and achievement (this will be discussed in greater detail later), slang, appearance, method of interaction, styles of behaviour and social representations (Amerio et al., 1990; Coleman & Hendry, 1990). In other

words, adolescents choose their peer groups on the basis of the perception of sharing a common destiny with their peers (having to cope with the developmental tasks leading to adult maturity) and on the basis of perceived likenesses as regards dimensions relevant for them. Slang, appearance and tastes in music become the common denominator of the group, an element of identification and differentiation between one's own group and other groups in the same area.

While in informal groups communicational exchanges between members are relatively easy, never mediated by the presence of adults, and the structure of the roles and positions is more flexible and more variable than in formal groups, it is also true that the handling of possible intragroup conflicts may be problematic, with rifts often being created between members which are not easily healed. Amerio et al., 1990; Palmonari, Rubini, & Graziani, 2003). The same difficulties are encountered in the pursuit of the objectives of the group in that very often there is no cognitive clarity about how a certain objective may be achieved, or even defined initially. It is particularly as regards this point that informal groups pay for their isolation from adults – an isolation that is not always desired but may be imposed by events. However, Sherif and Sherif (1964) have highlighted that, even in informal groups, rules and norms are defined through interactions between members which have to be respected if the individual wants to continue to be accepted within the group. Finally, though the members of the group often do not recognize this process immediately, temporary forms of leadership appear in the different circumstances aimed at achieving the objectives to be pursued (Palmonari, Pombeni, & Kirchler, 1992).

The category of informal groups is commonly associated with the label of deviance. If it is true that about 70% of adolescents regularly participate in an informal group, the evidence available shows that only a small percentage of these groups, about 5%, is involved in serious deviant behaviour (Consiglio Nazionale dei Minori, 1990).

It is, however, equally true, as clearly documented by Emler and Reicher (1995), that adolescent delinquent conduct almost always has a collective nature. How can we then explain the relation between informal groups, to which the majority of adolescents belong, and the various forms of delinquent conduct, practised by a minority of these groups?

In one of the first stages of our empirical work on orientation towards the institutional authorities (Rubini & Palmonari, 1995), we found that with respect to the adolescents who are part of informal groups, those who belong to formal groups hold more positive attitudes towards the institutional system. This evidence would seem to confirm what is commonly believed. We formed an explanatory hypothesis of this significant difference: the fact that members of formal groups (as opposed to informal groups) have more positive attitudes towards the institutional system could be due to the earlier socialization, with respect to their peers in the informal groups, to normative systems homogeneous with the institutional systems. Early and explicit contact with formal rules could lead them to test the personal and social advantages of the institutional systems and develop more positive personal positions towards the institutional world.

To test this theory we contacted 15 different types of adolescent group (five informal groups, five sports groups, and five religious groups) directly at their meeting places. After a detailed group interview about the activities and purposes of their being together, participants were asked to compile a list of tolerated and non-tolerated behaviours within the group for the purposes of continuing being part of the group itself. The lists obtained in this way were analysed by two judges who used different categories of content for the purpose. On the basis of the statistical mode of mention of the various statements included in the various categories of content we have drawn up 22 statements that make up the scale of the group rules.

We saw that the groups differ significantly from each other in terms of acceptance/rejection of various group rules even independently of their typology. In other words: some informal groups whose members are allowed to practise transgressive and deviant behaviours while other informal groups reject deviant behaviour as a fundamental rule for continuing to belong to the group itself. We also found evidence for the fact that there is a direct relation between group rules and orientation towards institutional authorities, in the sense that the members of groups with rules of rejection towards serious transgressive behaviour have more favourable attitudes towards the institutional system and use a behavioural repertoire more in line with the norms and expectations of the system itself.

This important evidence demonstrates that it is not only the type of peer group attended that explains the differences in orientation towards institutional authorities, but, above all, the system of rules that organizes group life. The system of rules may be fairly similar to that of the institutional system or it may appear relatively in opposition to the institutional system. This implies that the system of norms shared in the group is already indicative of the position taken towards the institutional system.

This fact is in line with the findings of Emler and Reicher (1995), who also summarized previous contributions (Brake, 1985; Cloward & Ohlin, 1960; Cohen, 1955; Corrigan, 1976; Jenkins, 1983; Sherif & Sherif, 1964; Short & Strodtbeck, 1965). We were ourselves able to test this significant relation also in subsequent research carried out in other European countries (Rubini & Tzialla, 2001).

4.3 Interplay between school experience and peer groups

Among the criteria of liking that adolescents use to choose the peer groups to join, we mentioned school career and academic success. Several sources show that school careers are interwoven with experience in the peer groups; those who are good at school tend to associate with other good students. The same applies to those who have a bad academic performance. Adolescents who leave the school institution early find themselves together with adolescents who have had a similar school career. Even more interesting is the relation which links the experience of school maladjustment to the group rules. We have in fact found that significant correlations exist between the factors emerging from the factorial analyses and the dimensions emerging from the analysis of the group rules. In this specific case, it emerges that tolerance towards very serious transgressive behaviour on the part of the members of the groups of adolescents is correlated with feelings of school maladjustment linked to uncertainty about the situations of school evaluation, to low self-esteem deriving from the school experience and to the inability to adapt to school regulations. There is also a significant connection between the willingness to accept behaviours of interpersonal disloyalty between members of one's own group and the inability to adapt to school regulations. The very factor of the rules of groups of adolescents correlates negatively with the dimension of school maladjustment as regards self-esteem on the basis of the school experience (Palmonari & Rubini, 2001).

A very interesting connection thus emerges between school experience and experience with peer groups. Although definitive conclusions cannot be drawn from this evidence, it seems to us to be possible to argue that school experience really is a ground for testing and modelling social and individual skills, to such an extent that if this experience is negative and frustrating for the individual, it may be associated with the acceptance of deviant behaviour as a way of regulating social relations.

The correlations between the variables that we have examined thus show that school experience and experience with peer groups jointly influence the development of orientation towards the institutional world and place emphasis on the responsibility of the school authorities in guiding adolescents towards understanding the functioning of formal norms as a basis for an effective integration in social life.

4.4 Deviant peer groups

Having clarified this point, we shall now look further at the problem, already mentioned, of identifying the psycho-social processes explaining why a certain percentage (although small, with respect to commonly held beliefs) of groups of adolescents adopt an antagonistic position towards the social order, a position which is manifested in the adoption of behaviours that are decidedly deviant with respect to institutional rules.

One of the social explanations for adolescent deviance concerns its instrumental function of obtaining goods and resources that would otherwise be out of reach. Along the same line of thought, Short and Strodtbeck (1965) argue that deviant adolescents perceive social success as impossible to reach and try to compensate this lack through collective actions that are exciting and dangerous. In the final analysis, these explanations rest on deterministic conceptions for which, lacking sufficient access to material and symbolic resources, individuals from underprivileged social levels try to obtain them through illegal means and methods. Emler and Reicher (1995) have illustrated in detail the conceptual limits and the lack of empirical evidence for these positions.

While Emler and Reicher's (1995) own interpretation of deviance as a way of handling one's social reputation and of gaining visibility with respect to one's social fabric, on one hand, provides an innovative and more convincing contribution with respect to previous theories, it does not, on the other hand, tell us which variables lead some people to try to obtain social visibility through a negative reputation.

Rubini, Palmonari, Graziani, and Zavoli (2000) asked whether the deviant collective conducts of adolescents are associated with feelings of relative segregation and alienation from the social fabric in which they live. In addition, in the light of the arguments produced by Deaux, Read, Mizrahi, and Ethier (1999) we asked if the motivations encouraging adolescents to join peer groups are always the same or whether they are different for the different groups. We thus contacted 15 informal groups of adolescents aged between 14 and 19. On the basis of the responses of the participants to self-reported measures of deviant behaviour, we divided the groups into three subcategories: deviant groups, averagely deviant groups and non-deviant groups.

The results of this study show that there is a significant correlation between the measures of social segregation (made operative in terms of absence or scarcity of significant relations with the actors of one's own social fabric – parents, teachers, employers, neighbours – and of lack of interest in events of local, national and international import) and the adoption of deviant conducts of relative gravity ('beating up coloured immigrants' for example). Other important evidence of this research indicates that identification with the peer group is fairly high in all the members of the groups examined but is not correlated with the motivation towards intergroup (Palmonari et al., 2003). The most deviant groups are instead those characterized by motivations to compete with groups considered as rivals. From the preliminary analyses made on the data obtained it seems therefore that adolescent deviance is accompanied by strong feelings of alienation from one's own social fabric and by the desire for intergroup competition which could also imply a perception of isolation and impermeability of the group boundaries.

4.5 Summary

In this section we have considered the relationship of adolescents with their peer groups. We have distinguished between formal and informal groups arguing that they equally help adolescents to cope with the developmental task of redefining their personal and social identity after the puberal maturation. We have also highlighted a higher risk of deviance for the members of peer groups who experience feelings of relative segregation from their own social environment.

5. Conclusion

In this chapter we have seen how the orientation that adolescents take towards the institutional system of society is embodied in their attitudes towards formal authority and in their behavioural inclination to comply with or defy society's rules and regulations. Both attitudes and behaviours are influenced by adolescents' multi-faceted experience of family, school and their interactions in peer groups. Other personal factors, such as the development of formal thought and moral reasoning, have to be taken into account to explain as to why it is during adolescence that people acquire a better understanding of the functioning of formal–bureaucratic systems.

By reviewing the relevant literature and by carrying out our own research on the topic we have became aware of a crucial factor in shaping and moulding adolescents' orientation towards institutional order. This is represented by the quality of the relationships of the adolescents with their significant adults. The more adolescents perceive that adults treat them fairly the more it is likely they will develop a positive orientation towards authorities. This is an important responsibility for the people who hold authority positions within the institutional system and an issue that deserves further and deeper empirical investigation.

Adolescents' orientation to the institutional system of society is a typically European theme that has attracted considerable attention in countries such as Great Britain, Italy and various countries in southern Europe. In this particular type of research, few differences have emerged between European countries. This overall convergence of findings may derive from two facts. First, European countries largely share a common history of the development of formal structures such as the school, the judiciary system and the state. Second, informal groups of adolescents and delinquent acts conducted in these groups roughly serve the same functions (e.g., to increase social visibility as a group member or to compete with rival groups).

In conclusion the new and extensive evidence we have reviewed in this chapter highlights the multi-factorial nature of adolescent orientation towards institutional contexts.

References

Amerio, P., Boggi-Cavallo, P., Palmonari, A., & Pombeni, M.L. (1990). *Gruppi di adolescenti e processi di socializzazione* [Adolescent groups and socialisation processes]. Bologna, Italy: Il Mulino.

Bandura, A. (1964). The stormy decade: Fact or fiction? *Psychology in the Schools, 1*, 224–231.

Bandura, A. (1969). *Principles of behavior modification*. New York: Holt, Rinehart & Winston.

Banks, M., Bates, L., Breakwell, G., Bynner, J., Emler, N., Jamieson, L., & Roberts, K. (1991). *Careers and identities*. Milton Keynes: Open University Press.

Berger, P.L., & Berger, B. (1975). *Sociology: A biographical approach*. New York: Basic Books.

Bosma, H. (1994). Le développement de l'identité a l'adolescence [Development of identity in adolescence]. *Orientation Scolaire et Professionnelle, 23,* 291–311.

Brake, M. (1985). *Comparative youth culture: The sociology of youth cultures and youth subcultures in America, Britain, and Canada.* London: Routledge & Kegan Paul.

Brewer, M.B. (1991). The social self: On being the same and different at the same time. *Personality and Social Psychology Bulletin, 17,* 475–482.

Brewer, M.B. (1993). Social identity, distinctiveness, and in-group homogeneity. *Social Cognition, 11,* 150–164.

Brown, D. (1974). Cognitive development and willingness to comply with the law. *American Journal of Political Science, 18,* 583–594.

Canestrari, R. (1984). *Psicologia generale e dello sviluppo* [General and developmental psychology]. Bologna, Italy: CLUEB.

Carugati, F., & Selleri, P. (1996). *Psicologia sociale dell'educazione* [Social psychology of education]. Bologna, Italy: Il Mulino.

Clark, J.P., & Wenninger, E.P. (1964). The attitude of juveniles toward the legal institution. *Journal of Criminal Law, Criminology, and Political Science, 55,* 482–489.

Cloward, R.A., & Ohlin, L.E. (1960). *Delinquency and opportunity.* New York: Free Press.

Cohen, A.K. (1955). *Delinquent boys: The culture of the gang.* Glencoe, IL: Free Press.

Coleman, J.C., & Hendry, L. (1990). *The nature of adolescence* (2nd ed.). London: Routledge.

Consiglio Nazionale dei Minori (1990). *Secondo rapporto sulla condizione dei minori in Italia* [Second report on the juvenile condition in Italy] Milan, Italy: Franco Angeli.

Corrigan, P. (1976). Doing nothing. In S. Hall, & S. Jefferson (Eds.), *Resistance through rituals* (pp. 103–105). London: Hutchinson.

Damon, W., & Hart, D. (1992). Self-understanding and its role in social and moral development. In H. Bornstein, & M. E. Lamb (Eds.), *Developmental psychology: An advanced textbook* (3rd ed., pp. 421–464). Hillsdale, NJ: Lawrence Erlbaum Associates, Inc.

Deaux, K., Reid, A., Mizrahi, K., & Cotting, D. (1999). Connecting the person to the social: The function of social identification. In T. R. Tyler, R. M. Kramer, & O. P. John (Eds.), *The psychology of the social self* (pp. 91–113). Mahwah, NJ: Lawrence Erlbaum Associates, Inc.

Elmhorn, K. (1965). Study on self-report delinquency among school children in Stockholm. In K. O. Christiansen (Ed.), *Scandinavian studies in criminology* (pp. 117–146). London: Tavistock.

Emler, N. (1988). *Peer relations and accommodation to the institutional system.* Paper presented at ESRC16–19 First findings workshop, Harrogate, UK.

Emler, N., Ohana, J., & Dickinson, J. (1990). Children's representations of social relations. In G. Duveen, & B. Lloyd (Eds.), *Social representations and the development of knowledge* (pp. 47–69). New York: Cambridge University Press.

Emler, N., Ohana, J., & Moscovici, S. (1987). Children's belief about institutional roles: A cross-national study of representations of the teacher's role. *British Journal of Educational Psychology, 57,* 26–37.

Emler, N., & Reicher, S. (1987). Orientations to institutional authority in adolescence. *Journal of Moral Education, 16,* 108–116.

Emler, N., & Reicher, S. (1995). *Adolescence and delinquency: The collective management of reputation.* Oxford: Blackwell.

Emler, N., Reicher, S., & Ross, A. (1987). The social context of delinquent conduct. *Journal of Child Psychology and Psychiatry, 28,* 99–109.

Emler, N., & St James, A. (1990). Staying at school after sixteen: Social and psychological correlates. *British Journal of Education and Work, 3,* 60–70.

Erikson, E.H. (1950). *Childhood and society.* New York: Norton.

Erikson, E. (1968). *Identity: Youth and crisis.* London: Faber & Faber.

Fazio, R.H. (1986). How do attitudes guide behavior? In R. M. Sorrentino, & E. T. Higgins (Eds.), *Handbook of motivation and cognition: Foundations of social behavior* (pp. 204–243). New York: Guilford.

Gibson, H.B. (1967). Self-reported delinquency among schoolboys and their attitudes to the police. *British Journal of Social and Clinical Psychology, 6,* 168–173.

Goodenow, C. (1993). The psychological sense of school membership among adolescents: Scale development and educational correlates. *Psychology in the Schools, 30,* 79–90.

Gouveia-Pereira, M., & Pires, S.S. (1999). *Experiencia escolar y julgamentos acerca da autoridade* [School experience and judgements about authority]. *Analise Psicologica, 17,* 97–109.

Gouveia-Pereira, M., Vala, J., Palmonari, A., & Rubini, M. (2003). School experience, relational justice, and legitimisation of institutional authorities. *European Journal of Psychology of Education, 18,* 309–325.

Harter, S. (1983). Developmental perspectives on the self-system. In P. H. Mussen, & E. M. Hetherington (Eds.), *Handbook of child psychology: Vol. 4. Socialisation, personality and social development* (4th ed.) (pp. 275–385). New York: John Wiley & Sons.

Harter, S. (1990). Self and identity development. In S. S. Feldman, & G. R. Elliott (Eds.), *At the threshold: The developing adolescent* (pp. 352–387). Cambridge, MA: Harvard University Press.

Hindelang, M.J., Hirschi, T., & Weis, J.G. (1981). *Measuring delinquency*. Newbury Park, CA: Sage.

Hurrelmann, K., & Engel, U. (Eds.). (1989). *The social world of adolescents: International perspectives*. Berlin, Germany: de Gruyter.

Jenkins, R. (1983). *Lads, citizens, and ordinary kids: Working class youth life-style in Belfast*. London: Routledge & Kegan Paul.

Kiesner, J. (2002). Depressive symptoms in early adolescence: Their relations with classroom problem behavior and peer status. *Journal of Research on Adolescence, 12*, 463–478.

Kohlberg, L. (1981). *Essays in moral development: Vol. 1. The philosophy of moral development*. New York: Harper & Row.

Kohlberg, L., & Higgins, A. (1987). School democracy and social interaction. In W. M. Kurtines, & J. L. Gewirtz (Eds.), *Moral development through social interaction* (pp. 102–128). New York: John Wiley & Sons.

Marcia, J.E. (1980). Identity in adolescence. In J. Adelson (Ed.), *Handbook of adolescent psychology* (pp. 159–187). New York: John Wiley & Sons.

Mars, G. (1981). *Cheats at work: An anthology of work place crime*. London: Unwin.

Meeus, W. (1996). Studies on identity development in adolescence: An overview of research and some new data. *Journal of Youth and Adolescence, 25*, 569–598.

Mitchell, J.C. (1969). *Social networks in urban situations*. Manchester: Manchester University Press.

Molpeceres, M., Lucas, A., & Pons, D. (2000). Experiencia escolar y orientacion hacia la autoridad institutional en la adolescencia [School experience and orientation toward institutional authority in adolescence]. *Revista de Psicologia Social Aplicada, 15*(2), 87–105.

Mortimore, P., Sammons, P., Stoll, L., Lewis, D., & Ecob, R. (1987). *School matters: The junior years*. Tunbridge Wells: Open Books Publishing.

Mugny, G., & Carugati, F. (1967). *L'intelligence au pluriel* [Multiple intelligences]. Cousset, Switzerland: Delval.

Osuna, E., & Luna, A. (1989). Behavior at school and social maladjustment. *Journal of Forensic Sciences, 34*, 1228–1234.

Palmonari, A., Kirchler, E., & Pombeni, M.L. (1991). Differential effects of identification with family and peers on coping with developmental tasks in adolescence. *European Journal of Social Psychology, 21*, 381–402.

Palmonari, A., Pombeni, L., & Kirchler, E. (1989). Formes et fonctionnement des groupes de pairs à l'adolescence [Types and functioning of adolescent peer groups]. *L'Orientation Scolaire et Professionnelle, 18*, 299–313.

Palmonari, A., Pombeni, M.L., & Kirchler, E. (1990). Adolescents and their peer groups: A study on the significance of peers, social categorization processes and coping with developmental tasks. *Social Behaviour, 5*, 33–48.

Palmonari, A., Pombeni, M.L., & Kirchler, E. (1992). Evolution of the self-concept in adolescence and social categorisation processes. In W. Stroebe, & M. Hewstone (Eds.), *European review of social psychology* (Vol. 3, pp. 285–308). New York: John Wiley & Sons.

Palmonari, A., Pombeni, M.L., & Kirchler, E. (1993). Developmental tasks and adolescents' relationship with their peers and their family. In S. Jackson, & H. Rodriguez-Tomé (Eds.), *Adolescence and its social worlds* (pp. 145–167). Hove, UK: Lawrence Erlbaum Associates Ltd.

Palmonari, A., & Rubini, M. (1998, June). *The effect of school maladjustment and of membership of adolescent peer-groups on the orientation toward the institutional system*. Paper presented at the 6th Biennial Conference of the European Association for Research on Adolescence, Budapest, Hungary.

Palmonari, A., & Rubini, M. (1999, July). *A psychosocial approach to the study of the orientation to formal authority in adolescence*. Paper presented at the 8th General Meeting of the European Association of Experimental Social Psychology, Oxford, UK.

Palmonari, A., & Rubini, M. (2001). Adolescenti, scuola e rapporto con le autorita istituzionali [Adolescents, school, and relations with institutional authorities]. In F. P. Colucci (Ed.), Il *cambiamento imperfetto, i cittadini, la comunicazione politica, i leader* (pp. 209–217). Milan, Italy: Unicopli.

Palmonari, A., Rubini, M., & Graziani, A.R. (2003). The perceived importance of group functions in adolescent peer groups. *New Review of Social Psychology, 1*, 60–67.

Palmonari, A., Rubini, M., Graziani, A.R., & Zavoli, W. (2000, September). *I gruppi informali di adolescenti come promotori di integrazione-segregazione sociale* [Adolescent informal groups as promoters of social integration – segregation]. Paper presented at the 3rd Meeting of AIP, Parma, Italy.

Piaget, J. (1972). Intellectual evolution from adolescence to adulthood. *Human Development*, *15*, 1–12.

Piaget, J., & Inhelder, B. (1975). *The origin of the idea of chance in children*. New York: Norton.

Reicher, S., & Emler, N. (1985). Delinquent behaviour and attitudes to formal authority. *British Journal of Social Psychology*, *24*, 161–168.

Reicher, S., & Emler, N. (1987). The difference between acquiescing and not disagreeing. *British Journal of Social Psychology*, *26*, 95.

Rigby, K., & Rump, E.E. (1982). Attitudes toward authority and authoritarian personality characteristics. *Journal of Social Psychology*, *116*, 61–72.

Rubini, M. (1998). Scuola ed atteggiamenti verso le istituzioni [School and attitudes towards institutions]. In E. Morgagni (Ed.), *Adolescenti e dispersione scolastica* (pp. 173–177). Rome, Italy: Carocci.

Rubini, M., & Palmonari, A. (1995). Orientamenti verso le autorità formali e partecipazione politica degli adolescenti [Orientation towards formal authority and political participation of adolescents]. *Giornale Italiano di Psicologia*, *22*, 757–775.

Rubini, M., & Palmonari, A. (1998, June). *Peer-group membership and political cynicism in adolescence*. Paper presented at the 6th Biennial Conference of the European Association for Research on Adolescence, Budapest, Hungary.

Rubini, M., & Tzialla, P. (2001). *Percorsi scolastici e relazionali di adolescenti Greci nella costruzione dell'orientamento verso le autorità istituzionali* [School and relational experience of Greek adolescents and their orientation towards formal authority]. Manuscript under editorial consideration.

Rutter, M., Maughan, B., Mortimore, P., & Ouston, J. (1982). *Fifteen thousand hours: Secondary schools and their effects on children*. Tunbridge Wells: Open Books Publishing.

Sherif, M., & Sherif, C.W. (1964). *Reference groups: Exploration into conformity and deviation of adolescents*. New York: Harper & Row.

Short, J.F., & Nye, N.I. (1958). Extent of unrecorded delinquency: Tentative conclusion. *Journal of Criminal Law and Criminology*, *49*, 296–302.

Short, J.F., & Strodtbeck, F.L. (1965). *Group processes and gang delinquency*. Chicago, IL: University of Chicago Press.

Stattin, H., & Magnusson, D. (1991). Stability and change in criminal behaviour up to age 30. *British Journal of Criminology*, *4*, 327–346.

Tyszkova, M. (1990). Coping with difficult school situations and stress resistance. In H. Bosma, & S. Jackson (Eds.), *Coping and self-concept in adolescence* (pp. 187–201). Berlin, Germany: Springer-Verlag.

Weber, M. (1922). *Wirtschaft und Gesellschaft* [Economy and society]. Tübingen, Germany: Mohr.

West, D.J., & Farrington, D.P. (1977). *The delinquent way of life*. London: Heinemann.

Health-related behaviour: Current situation, trends, and prevention

Pierre-André Michaud, Isabelle Chossis, and Joan-Carles Suris

LEARNING OBJECTIVES

To give an insight into how adolescents see and rate their own health and their health problems. To discuss the concept of risk and experimental behaviour during adolescence; to survey several lifestyle patterns (sports and physical activity, nutrition and eating behaviours, sexuality) and their impact on health; to present some basic avenues in the field of prevention and health promotion.

1. Adolescents and their health

1.1 The health of adolescents: A developmental perspective

The way adults view adolescent health is somewhat paradoxical: on the one hand, some adults may get the impression that all adolescents are well and fit, just because the proportion who attend healthcare settings is lower than that of adults or children. On the other hand, many adults will simply depict teenagers as being drug laden, sexually promiscuous, uninhibited and deviant if not violent (Macfarlane, 1995). As with the story of the half-filled or half-empty glass: the truth lies somewhere in between: adolescence being a process, one has to remember that the mood, attitudes, behaviour and health of young people undergo rapid change during this period of life. It is indeed important, both on an individual and public health level to keep a developmental perspective of health (Juszczak & Sadler, 1999; Knight, Frazer, Goodman, Blaschke, Bravender, & Emans, 2001; Millstein, Petersen, & Nightingale, 1993; Steinberg & Morris, 2001; World Health Organization, 1996).

During early adolescence, individuals tend to focus more on their own body. Pubertal events raise a large number of issues relating to normality, body shape and individual look. Thus, health problems will be directly related to the area of growth and development. Puberty is often perceived as a disruption in one's life, even as a trauma: adolescents have less control over their body, which is developing at a fast pace, they experience sexual arousal which is beyond their control, and may get harsh comments from their family and neighbourhood about their body and appearance! This developmental stage corresponds to the phase of initiation in the individual's orientation towards romantic relationships. It is only during the later part of the adolescent process that individuals gain a real insight into the time perspective, so that during early adolescence, health attitudes and behaviour of teenagers are essentially influenced by current situation and needs, rather than the long-term consequences of their health habits and lifestyles.

During middle and late adolescence, health becomes increasingly more related to the psychosocial processes linked with this period of life: adolescents gain their independence and self-confidence through social activities with their peers. During this period, they need to experiment and socialize and health issues naturally are not always their first preoccupation, which may explain why they believe they know what is good for them, but continue to engage in behaviours and situations that place them at considerable risk.

It can easily be understood that these issues are of utmost importance when dealing with teenagers suffering from chronic diseases, which can interfere with the teenager's physical and emotional growth (Michaud, Suris, & Viner, 2004; Suris, Michaud, & Viner, 2004b): the influence of the disease and the treatment on growth, external

appearance, self-image and self-esteem should be assessed; also, in many instances, the way the patients view their illness and their future influences with both the compliance to treatment and the outcome of the disease. Finally, in some instances, heavy treatments and repeated hospitalizations may severely interfere with the process of socialization and every effort should be made to ensure adequate development (Lindstrom & Eriksson, 1993).

Not only do the adolescent's health status and behaviour need to be understood within this developmental framework, it is also important to examine lifestyles and health problems in the light of the teenager's own perceptions and representations. This, in fact, holds true both in the field of healthcare (e.g., if one wants to improve the adherence of the adolescent to any advice or treatment) and in the area of prevention and health promotion.

1.2 How do adolescents see their health?

The representations that adolescents have of their own health varies with age (Spyckerelle, Bon, Ferron, & Deschamps, 1991) as well as with their developmental stage. When questioned about the factors that can potentially affect their well-being, older adolescents are able to conceptualize health in a broad ecological & bio-psychosocial perspective. This is exemplified by a group of 17-year-old Swiss adolescents some years ago during a session devoted to health promotion (Michaud & Martin, 1982). They easily identified many of the components that influence one's state of health, stressing the fact that health is a dynamic process that mainly depends on the way individuals behave as much as on their environment (and much less on odds or constitution!). They also quite rightly complained about the fact that most adults requested them to change their habits without acknowledging the direct impact of their surroundings (Michaud, Blum, & Ferron, 1998a). For instance, why ask them to make improvements in their nutrition and eating habits if they are not provided with the nutritionally proposed food within the school setting? One interesting fact is that, as the Swiss adolescents identified, teenage habits do not include factors that may have an impact on health a fourth element that is usually cited in this kind of scheme, that is the availability and organization of healthcare. The fact that this component is missing can be readily understood, since teenagers tend to use health-care services less often than children and adults, they often do not identify health professionals as a resource in terms of health, but much more as engineers who are concerned with diseases and illnesses (Deschamps, 1987; Klein, 2000; Michaud & Martin, 1982; Spyckerelle et al., 1991).

Several surveys (Arènes, Janvrin, & Baudier, 1998; Blum & Nelson-Mmari, 2004; Choquet & Ledoux, 1994; Currie et al., 2004; Jeannin et al., 2005; Narring & Michaud, 1995) have repeatedly shown that adolescents, on one hand, consider themselves to be healthy, but on the other hand, when questioned about specific areas, display many uncovered problems and worries, which may seem a bit paradoxical. For example, in research on the proportion of young people 16 to 20 years of age reporting various health problems "for which they feel they would need help" conducted in Switzerland during 2002 among around 8000 students and apprentices (Jeannin et al., 2005), girls reported problems and needs in a far greater proportion than did boys. This difference is quasi-universal and is probably linked with the fact that boys tend to act out their problems while girls tend to focus more on their inner feelings and distress (Tiefer & Kring, 1995; van Wijk & Kolk, 1997). Another tendency which is clearly made apparent by this research is the fact that adolescents identify their main problems in such areas which cause problems, which are not just symptoms. Substance use, for instance, is often considered by adults as the main problem of young people nowadays, whereas adolescents rightly point out potential causes for such behaviour, i.e. stress or depression.

1.3 Risk versus experimental behaviour: A European perspective

For the past several years, a growing body of literature has focused on the relation between the health of adolescents and the notion of risk. Different expressions such as "psychosocial risk", "risk taking" or "problem behaviour" have been used to delineate this relationship (Jessor, 1991). Interest in risk behaviour lies in the fact that most deaths and a substantial amount of adolescent morbidity are related to behavioural and psycho-social characteristics more than to acquired illness or inherited traits. Traffic injuries, suicide and interpersonal violence are the leading causes of death among adolescents in most European countries (Kaminsky & Bouvier-Colle, 1991; Schlueter, Narring, Munch, & Michaud, 2004).

However, most behaviours considered as risk oriented are essentially developmental in nature and risk taking is, after all, part of life (Lupton, 1995). Thus, the term "risk" should be reserved for situations where the type of circumstance, the nature of the interactions with others and the particular moment in the adolescent's develop-ment create the conditions for the occurrence of a problem behaviour. Other behaviours taking place in different environmental and personal conditions should be considered as experimental and approached as such by researchers and clini-cians. Indeed, despite Jessor's efforts to promote a qualified and multicomponent definition of risk as well as a model of integrating protective fac-tors (Jessor, Turbin, & Costa, 1998), much of the research on adolescents' health behaviours per-sistently explores a single risk behaviour, often as a model, investigating objective as well as subject-ive or perceptual characteristics (Michaud et al., 1998a). While such an approach may have been useful in developing and refining discrete prevent-ive strategies for defined populations, there is a risk of generalizing from a population profile to an individual profile. Such an approach dismisses the fact that adolescents are rapidly changing and that what is true at one point in their lives is not necessarily true six months or even one week later. Very often, risk behaviours arise more because of situations which bring about new and unexpected challenges to an inexperienced youngster, than to characteristics inherent in the individual. For instance, a study conducted in a large Swiss hospital (Wyss, Rivier, Gujer, Pac-caud, Magnenat, & Yersin, 1990) shows that the percentage of individuals found with detectable levels of alcohol in their blood on arrival in the emergency ward due to a traffic injury are lower among teenagers and young adults than found among older people!

Thus, the concept of "risk" during adolescence, while proving useful, has some significant limitations. In the search for a more appropriate term than "risk-taking behaviours", some European authors have rightly proposed we use other terms such as "experimental or exploratory behaviour" (Macfarlane, 1995; Michaud et al., 1998a), for behaviours common during adolescence (e.g., having sex, drinking alcohol, trying cannabis, doing physically dangerous activities, driving too fast). Much more than a simple change in terminology, what this discussion implies is an overall shift in the conceptual framework, a change in attitude towards the behaviour of adolescents (Michaud, 1999). First, clinicians should avoid labelling behaviours as risky. Rather, they should try to understand, on an individual level, the role, the meaning, the motives and the potential consequences of these behaviours for the teenager. Second, resiliency/protective factors should also be investigated, in order to evaluate the probability of an adolescent to find his own solutions and to find support for positive health outcomes within his environment (Michaud, 1999). The resiliency framework should not only be used at an individual level. It is also important to bear in mind the positive resource-based conception of health within prevention and promotional activities (Haggerty, Sherrod, Garmezy, & Rutter, 1994), which was outlined in the Ottawa chart more than 10 years ago (Anonymous, 2004).

1.4 Psychosocial and cultural factors involved in adolescents' health status and needs

As is the case for adults, adolescents' attitudes, behaviour as well as health status and needs do vary largely depending on socioeconomic, professional and cultural background. Several surveys have clearly shown that health status and the amount and type of health problems are heavily dependent on the school environment and the level or degree attained (Jackson, Stafford, Banks, & Warr, 1983; Michaud, Ferron, Piot-Delbos, Cordonier, Narring, & Schalbetter, 1997b; Patton et al., 2000). The higher the level of school achievement, the better the health status and less prevalent the reported problems are. School dropouts, for instance, have been shown to exhibit health problems and needs at a much higher rate than their more gifted counterparts (Michaud, Delbos-Piot, & Narring, 1998b). Thus, in a Swiss study (Michaud et al., 1998b), the rate of 15- to 19-year-old girls reporting average or poor health was 35% in the dropout sample in comparison to 12% in a sample of students and apprentices of comparable age. More dropout adolescents complained about physical distress (backache, headaches and stomach-aches). Furthermore, within the dropout sample, the rate of suicide attempts was four times the rate of the general population. The problem is all the more difficult as, in many countries, it is *precisely* those dropout adolescents who have more problems who then also face more difficulties accessing proper healthcare (Hammarstrom & Janlert, 2002).

Cultural issues are also particularly important to bear in mind: several studies have focused on the health of migrant adolescents, whether they were born outside their host country or belong to the so-called "second generation" (Ferron, Haour-Knipe, Tschumper, Narring, & Michaud, 1997; Kune-Karrer & Taylor, 1995). These studies show that, given the difficulties faced in developing their own identity, migrant adolescents tend to exhibit more health problems and needs compared to their friends of the same age. However, in certain areas, due to their cultural background, they display better health-maintaining behaviour. For instance, in Switzerland, they tend to drink less alcohol and less often than Swiss teenagers (Ferron et al., 1997; Jeannin et al., 2005). The health attitudes and behaviour of these adolescents have to be appraised not only by taking into perspective the host country's culture, but also within their culture of origin, both in the healthcare setting and within research on health attitudes and behaviours (Alsaker, Flanagan, & Csapó, 1999; Michaud, Ferron, & Narring, 1996). One possible response to this challenge is to work closely with representatives from the ethnic origin of the adolescents. On an individual level, this may mean, for instance, working with cultural mediators (Kune-Karrer & Taylor, 1995). In the field of survey research, the interpretation of the results and of cross-cultural comparisons should be made with great caution, often searching for the opinions of representatives from other cultures (Michaud, Blum, & Slap, 2001a). Finally, in the field of health promotion, policymakers as well as professionals who plan and implement preventive measures should also be aware of the strong cultural and ethical aspects of any programme and thus should work – as stressed by the Ottawa chart – in close cooperation with young people from the target population.

2. Adolescent lifestyles and health-related behaviour

In this section of the chapter, we will discuss some so-called lifestyles that can be defined as "patterns of behavioural choices made from alternatives that are available to people according to their socio-economic circumstances and to the ease with which they are able to choose certain ones over the others" (Taylor, 1986). It is particularly relevant to focus on issues of lifestyles and health-related behaviours, since they are acquired during adolescence and potentially affect health in both the short and long term.

2.1 Sports activities and exercise

The next two sections focus on sports and physical activity as well as nutrition. These issues are particularly relevant, given the epidemic of obesity that many developed countries currently face (Hagarty, Schmidt, Bernaix, & Clement, 2004; Stubbs & Lee, 2004). In a recent review of the epidemiology of obesity in Europe (Lobstein & Frelut, 2003), the percentages of obese adolescents aged 14 to 17 years varied between 9% (Germany) and 23% (Cyprus). In fact, it has been clearly shown that both the level of physical activity and dieting patterns play a pivotal role in this epidemic (Stubbs & Lee, 2004). Sports can be defined as a physical activity leading to satisfaction and pleasure and which usually includes some kind of confrontation with self and/or other people. Physical activity encompasses any body movement implying energy expenditure whereas fitness is characterized by the indi-

vidual's aptitude to engage in muscular work in a satisfactory way (Rowland & Freedson, 1994). These two dimensions of health are usually well-correlated and, to a large extent, can be used interchangeably. There are sound reasons for looking at factors that impact on physical and sport activity among young people: first, we have some evidence that there is at least some tracking of physical activity from adolescence into adulthood, that is, adolescents who are physically active and practise sport before the age of 20 tend to stay more active in later years than those who do not. There is some evidence that physical and sport activity tends to decrease over one or two decades (Suris, Michaud, Chossis, & Jeannin, in press; Westerstahl, Barnekow-Bergkvist, Hedberg, & Jansson, 2003), as well as having a regular tendency to decrease throughout adolescence and into young adulthood (Aarnio, Winter, Peltonen, Kujala, & Kaprio, 2002; Michaud, Narring, Cauderay, & Cavadini, 1999; Verschuur and Kempen, 1985). The issue of physical and sports activity among children and adolescents is becoming increasingly more critical because of its impact on current and future health. There is strong evidence supporting the protective effects of physical activity against cardiovascular conditions (Baranowski et al., 1992; Bar-Or et al., 1998; Rowland, 2001). Also, given the current epidemic of obesity, increasing sports activity within this age range is one way to address this major public health issue (Caprio & Genel, 2005).

The level of physical activity as assessed by self-reports from schoolchildren varies a lot (Currie, Hurrelmann, & Settertobulte, 2000; Currie et al., 2004; Michaud et al., 1999; Raitakari et al., 1996): in 1998, according to the HBSC survey (Currie et al., 2000), about 90% of boys and 80% of Irish teenagers reported exercising at least twice a week, compared to only three-quarters of boys and less than one in two girls in countries such as France, Hungary and Greenland. In all considered surveys, boys report more physical and sports activities than girls; they also report belonging to a sports club in a higher proportion. In 1990, while about 50% of 11–15 year-old-boys from four countries attended sports club activities, the percentage was only 20–40% among girls. Another way to look at the issue of physical activity is to explore health behaviours linked with inactivity. According to the 1998 HBSC survey (Currie et al., 2000), the percentage of 11–15 year old adolescents who reported watching television for four hours a day or more was distressingly high and varied between 20 and 50% across countries, among both boys and girls.

The correlates of physical and sports activity of children and adolescents have been well-studied (Pate, Heath, Dowda, & Trost, 1996; Pate, Trost, Levin, & Dowda, 2000; Sallis, Prochaska, & Taylor, 2000). High family income and high maternal education are correlated with higher activity as well as having a better relationship with parents. Feeling well, in good health, having a good self-image are factors also linked with higher levels of physical and sports activity; depression, on the contrary, may be linked with inactivity. Regular physical and/or sports activity seems also to exert a protective effect in the field of substance use: there is a consensus that active adolescents smoke in a lower proportion to that of their inactive peers. However, the link with alcohol use and illegal drugs is more controversial: while active adolescents tend to use substances less often and in a lower proportion there is some evidence that young people engaged in team competitions tend to use alcohol as often or even more often than those who do not (Ferron, Narring, Cauderay, & Michaud, 1999). Also, specific sports disciplines such as skiing, for instance, may also be correlated to higher use of illegal drugs such as cannabis (Peretti-Watel, Guagliardo, Verger, Pruvost, Mignon, & Obadia, 2003). Another less favourable and worrying outcome of regular activity is sports injuries, as high levels of sports activity are linked with a higher prevalence of injuries, especially in certain disciplines and during the more active phase of growth characterizing mid-puberty (Michaud, Renaud, & Narring, 2001b; Suris, Jeannin, Michaud, Narring, & Diserens, 2004a).

Whatever the direction of the relationship, it seems reasonable, given the positive long-term impact of sports activity on physical and mental health, to set up programmes to increase physical activity among young people, both within and outside the school setting. For instance, health practitioners have been encouraged to assess their patient's activity and advocate regular sports activity (Glasgow, Eaken, Fisher, Bacak, & Brownson, 2001) and these strategies have proved effective. However, practitioners should be aware that it may be in some instances detrimental to force adolescents to engage in arduous exercise, as shown in a US-based longitudinal study (Taylor, Blair, Cummings, Wun, & Malina, 1999).

In summary, then, sports activity can be seen as closely linked with adolescent development. During puberty, it is one means for teenagers to adapt themselves to their new bodies and to experiment with new sensations. During middle adolescence, it often constitutes a strong means of social integration, while after 16 or 17 years of age, engaging in other activities (going out, dating) tend to increase to the detriment of sports practice.

2.2 Nutrition, eating patterns and eating disorders

2.2.1 Nutrition and eating habits
Moreover, many studies have established a possible link between food, nutrient intakes and disease prevention. Eating habits play an important role in the development of chronic diseases such as osteoporosis (Cromer and Harel, 2000; Weaver, Peacock, & Johnston, 1999), cardio-vascular disease (Hayman and Reineke, 2003) and cancer (Key, Allen, Spencer, & Travis, 2002). Recently, dietary intake and eating behaviours of young people have prompted more attention in the belief that early adoption of healthy dietary habits may help to prevent chronic diseases later in adulthood (Flodmark, Lissau, Moreno, Pietrobelli, & Widhalm, 2004; Harel, 1999; Lytle, 2002; Westenhoefer, 2002). During this period of life, as nutritional needs are high, nutriments have to ensure adequate growth and provide sufficient stores for adulthood. Moreover, several modifications occur in the adolescents' social environment: food is often consumed away from home and ready-to-eat foods and soft drinks are easily accessible (Nestle, 2000). Peer pressure, body image and changes in activity patterns all influence adolescents' choices regarding their nutrition and their eating patterns. These are all major

environmental factors, which strongly influence the food pattern and the nutritional profile of the diet.

One important difference between the teenagers' and adults' eating patterns is the fact that consumption of sweet foods and soft drinks is higher, and snacking is more frequent among the former (Decarli, Cavadini, Grin, Blondel-Lubrano, Narring, & Michaud, 2000). According to the 2002 HBSC survey (Mulvihill, Nemeth, & Vereecken, 2004), 69% of boys and 60% of girls reported to have breakfast on school days and only 30% of boys and 37% of girls reported to eat at least one item of fruit every day. Also, more boys (32%) than girls (25%) consume sugared soft drinks everyday and about one-third of adolescents eat sweets and/or chocolate every day. Between 1990 and 1998, the percentage of adolescents who eat potato crisps every day has increased in most of the European countries surveyed by the HBSC study. In Austria, for example, while 5% and 7% of 15-year-old teenagers reported such a consumption in 1990, 6 and 12% did the same in 1998. In Poland, the percentages have risen from respectively 5 and 4% to 19 and 25%! Similarly, the daily consumption of chocolate has also increased in most of the countries surveyed (Currie et al., 2000; Currie et al., 2004). Finally, the quality of the food tends to decrease from early to late adolescence, and there is also indication that its nutritional content tends to deteriorate over time, which partly explains the levelling of the prevalence of overweight and obesity in many European countries (Flodmark et al., 2004). As is the case for physical and sport activity, the nutritional content of food seems closely related to the socioeconomic status of the mother (Currie et al., 2000), that is, the more educated the mother, the more fruit and raw vegetables eaten and fewer soft drinks and crisps consumed.

The implications of these results are clear: adolescents should benefit, both on an individual and population basis, from information regarding nutrition and eating patterns (Flodmark et al., 2004; Harel, 1999; Lytle, 2002; Nestle, 2000). Dietary advice should cite the ingestion of food plants (vegetables and fruits) and should strongly encourage the choice of foods with a high micronutrient (vitamins and minerals) density, but low in fat and sugar. As it is difficult to change food habits within any population, advice and prevention programmes should not aim to drastically modify the diet, but instead target making additions to the regular diet with products rich in micronutrients. Taking into account the importance of snacking during adolescence, one way to achieve this would be to change the quality of such products, either in promoting the use of vegetables and fruits as snacks instead of "junk" food (especially within the school setting), or in adding micronutrients to the snacks that are preferred by adolescents. As nutrition patterns are heavily linked with socioeconomic and even more so to ethnic background, campaigns and preventive programmes should be culturally sensitive and not imposed in a stereotypic manner. Finally, it has to be stressed that environmental strategies focusing on the availability of healthy food and drinks, especially within the school setting (Hoelscher, Mitchell, Dwyer, Elder, Clesi, & Snyder, 2003; Parcel et al., 2003), may be more effective than mere nutritional education.

2.2.2 Eating disorders

It is difficult to separate the issue of nutritional and caloric intake during adolescence from that of body shape and body image: in almost all European countries, according to the last HBSC survey, one out of three girls and one out of five boys report some dissatisfaction with their body shape. This tendency is widespread and the rates do not differ greatly from one country to another, neither do they evolve very much between the age of 11 and 15 years (Mulvihill et al., 2004). However, there has been an increase in the prevalence of body image disturbance, eating concerns and disorders over the last two decades (Devaud, Michaud, & Narring, 1995), a trend that is most probably linked with the ideal image of the woman's body as portrayed in Western societies' media (Fombonne, 1995).

One must, however, distinguish between dieting practices – which are widespread – and eating disorders such as anorexia nervosa, bulimia and binge eating, which are clinical entities defined

TABLE 15.1
Criteria for the diagnosis of anorexia nervosa and bulimia, according to the DSM-IV
Anorexia • Refusal to maintain body weight (>15% below IBW) • Intense fear of weight gain • Distorted body perception • Preoccupation with food • Amenorrhoea, other physical signs **Bulimia** • Recurrent binge eating coupled with feelings of lack of control • Purging* (vomiting, laxatives, diuretics), fasting, over-exercise • Persistent over concern with body shape and weight • Not coupled with anorexia
* When purging behaviour are not present, the condition is named "binge eating".

according to specific criteria (Chamay-Weber, Narring, & Michaud, 2005). The most commonly used criteria (Table 15.1) are those issued by the American psychiatric association in the DSM-IV manual (American Psychiatric Association, 1994). The distinction between deviant eating behaviour and anorexia or bulimia is often not easy, and, from a clinical standpoint, it is usually recommended to follow up those adolescents who exhibit abnormal eating habits, to make sure that they do not evolve into a classical form of eating disorder, as the majority of these adolescents quit their abnormal eating pattern in the long term (Steinhausen, Seidel, & Winkler Metzke, 2000).

Classically, anorexia is more a disease of early or middle adolescence, whereas bulimia mostly appears during late adolescence and early adulthood, with some overlap and many subjects evolving from one pattern to another. While we have good data on dieting behaviour in the adolescent population (Devaud, Jeannin, Narring, Ferron, & Michaud, 1998; French, Perry, Leon, & Fulkerson, 1994; Kann, Warren, Collins, Ross, Collins, & Kolbe, 1993; Stein, Meged, Bar-Hanin, Blank, Elizur, & Weizman, 1997), it is much more difficult to assess the prevalence of anorexia and bulimia among adolescents who tend to deny their condition or refuse to participate in surveys addressing this issue (Devaud et al., 1995). Currently, it is estimated that the incidence of

anorexia in the general population is about 1/100,000 inhabitants, whereas in a defined number of "exposed population" of women aged 10 to 34, it is approximately 20 to 30/100,000 inhabitants. The rates for bulimia are at least three times higher (Devaud et al., 1995). Adolescents with anorexia or less severe forms of eating disorder also suffer from more or less severe psychiatric comorbidity, such as depression and anxiety, obsessive–compulsive tendency and impulsivity (O'Brien & Vincent, 2003). This also holds true for bulimic patients, whose eating habits often interfere with family and social life. Eating disorders have serious medical consequences (Rome & Ammerman, 2003) such as growth arrest, cardiac events, electrolytic disturbances, dental diseases and gastric complications, and, in the long term, bone disease.

The treatment of eating disorders is often complex and lengthy (Robin, Gilroy, & Dennis, 1998). Most often, it implies the intervention of multidisciplinary teams including physicians, psychiatrists or psychologists and dieticians. Fortunately, most anorectic adolescents have a fair outcome (Lewinsohn, Striegel-Moore, & Seeley, 2000; Steinhausen et al., 2000).

2.3 Sexual behaviour
Sexuality represents an essential part of adolescent development (Duncan, Dixon, & Carlson,

2003; Ponton & Judice, 2004). Indeed, it is in puberty and, in turn, the body's transformations that characterize the beginning of adolescence, which constitutes the major impetus that drives the adolescent into the process of identity constitution. The present section will essentially focus on the aspects of sexual life directly linked to health; however, one should never forget that adolescents who are not sexually active are still sexual beings, and sexual experience and intercourse is just one aspect or dimension of sexuality among those teenagers who are sexually active. Quantitative as well as qualitative research confirm the role of the emotional aspects of sexuality during adolescence, girls stressing the importance of intimacy and fidelity, while boys tend to focus more on physical pleasure (Narring, Wydler, & Michaud, 2000; Weisfeld & Woodward, 2004). Finally, it should be stressed that parental education as well as the surroundings of young people have an impact on adolescents' sexual lives, and researchers and health professionals should take into account both cultural and ethical issues when dealing with adolescent sexuality (Miller, 2002; Omar and Richard, 2004; Rose, Koo, Bhaskar, Anderson, White, & Jenkins, 2005).

2.3.1　Sexual orientation and health

The development and acknowledgement of sexual orientation plays an important role in the formation of adult identity (Savin-Williams & Cohen, 2004; Zucker, 2004). Sexual orientation is defined as the persistent pattern of physical or emotional attraction to members of the same or opposite sex (Garofalo & Harper, 2003). The assessment of sexual orientation is particularly difficult during adolescence, since some teenagers may not have yet come to terms with the process of its acknowledgement (Stronski-Huwiler & Remafedi, 1998). Sexual fantasies, emotional attraction, sexual behaviour and self-identification are considered to be dimensions of sexual orientation, and may not be congruent in each individual. It has to be stressed that homosexual behaviours during adolescence are not necessarily linked with a homosexual orientation, neither does a homosexual orientation lead to homosexual behaviour (Narring, Stronski-Huwiler, & Michaud, 2003). However, homosexual behaviour and/or orientation may constitute a threat to health. Not only can homosexual behaviour result in STIs, including HIV, but homophobia – still present in most European societies – creates serious psychosocial problems such as depression, suicide and victimization. These health problems are due, at societal levels, to the expression of negative attitudes and violence towards homosexual individuals, but also, at an individual level, they result in an internalized negative self-image (Garofalo & Harper, 2003; Narring et al., 2003; Stronski-Huwiler & Remafedi, 1998). The issue of sexual orientation should be dealt with, both within healthcare encounters (Garofalo & Harper, 2003; Stronski-Huwiler & Remafedi, 1998) as well as within sessions of sexual education, although this may prove problematic in some countries or regions (Lindley & Reininger, 2001; Rienzo, Button, & Wald, 1996).

2.3.2　First sexual experiences

Among most adolescents, the discovery of sexual activity proceeds in a step-by-step motion through experiences that go from kissing through so-called petting or "deep" petting and then sexual intercourse (Narring et al., 2000). The sequence varies from one adolescent to another, totally independent of gender. As adolescents – especially since the era of AIDS – engage in various forms of sexual communication, the emphasis placed on sexual intercourse has thus decreased (Feldmann & Middleman, 2002). Many adolescents, in fact, define sexual intercourse as any kind of physical and sexual intimacy, with or without vaginal penetration, including oral sex, petting and anal intercourse. For the past 20 years or so, the percentage of adolescents who become sexually active has not increased as much as one might think. In Switzerland, it has been steady, despite the wider availability and use of condoms linked with the preventive campaigns against AIDS (Koffi-Blanchard, Dubois-Arber, Michaud, Narring, & Paccaud, 1994). The same trend has been observed in Sweden (Haggstrom-Nordin, Hanson, & Tyden, 2002) and, to some extent, in the USA (Feldmann & Middleman, 2002; Sonenstein, Ku, Lindberg, Turner, & Pleck, 1998).

2.3.3 Use of contraception

In the 1960s, many family planning services opened in Switzerland, France, Great Britain, Germany, Sweden and the Netherlands as well as in a large number of other industrial countries. Sexual education programmes directed at adolescents – usually within the school system – were also developed. AIDS prevention campaigns have contributed to an increase in condom use and sexual preventive behaviour of adolescents in most Western European countries (Hausser & Michaud, 1994). For example, in 1996, 75.3% of Swiss girls and 76.5% of Swiss boys reported having used a condom during their first sexual intercourse (Narring et al., 2000). Surveys in France, Great Britain and the western part of Germany display similar frequency of condom use at first intercourse among 15 to 20 year olds (Lagrange & Lhomond, 1997). However, condom use tends to be lower during subsequent intercourses – especially when the partner remains steady. The use of oral contraception tends to replace condom use in the middle and long term.

In counselling young people about contraception, professionals should take into account factors that seem to have an influence on the use of adequate forms of contraception (Bearinger & Resnick, 2003). For instance, when the age at first intercourse is less than 15 years, when there is an important difference of age between the two partners (especially when the girl is much younger than the male partner), and when the first sexual intercourse takes place with a casual partner, adolescents tend to use inefficient contraceptive means (i.e. withdrawal) or take no contraceptive means at all (Narring et al., 2000). Although not subject to many publications, condom failure is nevertheless an important issue. In the already cited Swiss study (Narring et al., 2000), 7% of users declared to have experienced condom breakage and another 7% reported condom slippage. Moreover, 9.2% declared it was difficult for them to gain access to condoms, 31.7% reported having experienced difficulties in putting them on. Further, among the users of oral contraception,

22.7% of girls declare difficulties in compliance and 6.1% claim that they cannot endure it. Difficulties encountered in the use of contraception, while not typical of adolescence, are however widespread due to their relative inexperience and thus lead sexual educators, teachers and health professionals to increase the awareness and availability of emergency contraception, also known as post-coital contraception (Lindberg, 2003; Ottesen, Narring, Renteria, & Michaud, 2002). In several Western European countries, a majority of young people are aware of the existence of EC and do use it. In France, 13.6% of sexually active 15- to 19-year-old girls claim to have used EC (Arènes, Janvrin, & Baudier, 1998), whereas 20% of 16- to 20-year-old schoolgirls declare to have used it in the Swiss survey (Narring et al., 2000). Given the fact that more and more adolescents have chosen to adopt the condom, at least as a primary means of contraception, several countries have emphasized the importance of increasing knowledge about and availability of emergency contraception. Given the fact that the condom effectively protects against STIs, but contrariwise, that the pill is more effective than the condom in protecting against unplanned pregnancy, family planning centres and health professionals have come to advocate for the so-called dual contraception, that is, the simultaneous use of a condom and of oral contraception (Bearinger & Resnick, 2003).

2.3.4 Pregnancy and abortion

Despite the awareness and accessibility of contraception in Europe, adolescent pregnancy and abortion still remains a public health problem, even if most European countries do not display the alarming rates of adolescent pregnancy that the United States still have (Elfenbein & Felice, 2003). Live birth rates among women aged 15–19 years vary in Western European countries: it is low (~4.0%) in the Netherlands and Switzerland but much higher in other countries such as England and Wales (~30%) (Addor, Narring, & Michaud, 2003). The global assessment of adolescent pregnancy rates is much more difficult to establish since few countries have been able to collect reliable data on abortions. However, self-reports from adolescent health surveys provide a rough estimate of the pregnancy rates in various countries. In France 4.1% of the French 15- to 18-year-old sexually active girls and 4.8% of Swiss teenagers of the same age range do report a history of pregnancy (Arènes et al., 1998; Narring, Roulet, Addor, & Michaud, 2002). Some countries, however, record abortion rates. They are similar in Switzerland (5.2 per 1000) and in the Netherlands (4.2 per 1000, 1992), while other European countries exhibit higher rates. Sweden (17.7 per 1000, 1996), Norway (15.2 per 1000, 1995), France (8.9 per 1000, 1995) or England and Wales (23.2 per 1000 among 16 to 19 year olds, 1996) (Boonstra, 2002). Many preventive programmes have been set up to try to decrease the rate of unplanned pregnancies around the world, these programmes include sex education in school, interventions among high-risk adolescent population, media coverage, availability of family-planning facilities, exhibitions during special events or street interventions, part of which have been designed in collaboration with young people or youth leaders (Addor et al., 2003; Keller & Brown, 2002; Kirby, 2002; Kirby et al., 2004; Robin et al., 2004; Schaalma, Abraham, Gillmore, & Kok, 2004).

A recent multicentre study run in the United Kingdom suggests that peer-led education may be an effective way to achieve a reduction in unplanned pregnancies (Stephenson et al., 2004). While the United States have focused very much on abstinence-promoting programmes (Aten, Siegel, Enaharo, & Auinger, 2002), European countries have actively promoted safe-sex strategies (Chambers & Rew, 2003; Tripp & Viner, 2005). The experience shows that education has no increasing effect on the rate of adolescents becoming sexually active. Moreover, interactive strategies focusing on safe sex do have an impact on contraception and protection practices (Oakley et al., 1995).

2.3.5 Sexually transmitted infections
Although adolescence represents a period during which the potential for the spread of HIV is high (e.g., inexperience and changes of partners), in many European countries, adolescents have responded well to prevention programmes (Rotheram-Borus, O'Keefe, Kracker, & Foo, 2000). Indeed, the evaluation of the Swiss STOP-AIDS campaign (Dubois-Arber et al., 2003) has shown that adolescents are more compliant than their older counterparts in terms of condom use. As previously discussed, one of the most challenging public health issues in the field is the one of strategies that target both the issue of STIs and of unintended pregnancy, including double-contraception. More and more specialists advocate the use of "double-" contraception especially for the many adolescents who do not have a stable partner, that is the simultaneous use of the condom and the pill (Ott, Adler, Millstein, Tschann, & Ellen, 2002; Bearinger & Resnick, 2003). Two meta-analyses (Johnson, Carey, Marsh, Levin, & Scott-Sheldon, 2003; Mullen, Ramirez, Strouse, Hedges, & Sogolow, 2002) show that there are effective ways to prevent HIV contamination among adolescents, with greater success in the field of condom use: "1) in non-institutionalised populations; 2) when condoms were provided; 3) with more condom information and skills training". In other words, it may well be that both specific campaigns targeting HIV and condom use, as well as larger interventions focusing on sexual life that may be effective.

2.3.6 Forced sex and sexually abused young people
A substantial proportion of teenagers experience sexual violence or assault (Tschumper, Narring, Meier, & Michaud, 1998). Whether this event takes place during childhood or adolescence, they often disclose them during adolescence, due to the upsurge or resurgence of sexual concerns and feelings. Different surveys among adolescents, in Switzerland and in France, have recently estimated the reported rates of sexual victimization. Between 15 and 19% of the girls and 2 and 3.5% of the boys report victimization, involving physical contact (Lagrange & Lhomond, 1997; Tschumper et al., 1998). The evaluation and follow-up of such situations, once disclosed, requires careful multidisciplinary approaches, combining medical care, short- and long-term psychological support for the victims and the

family, as well as taking care of the legal issues concerning the perpetrator (Bechtel & Podrazik, 1999; Danielson & Holmes, 2004).

2.3.7 Adolescents with chronic conditions

Adolescents suffering from chronic diseases and/ or disability often face difficulties in integrating a defective body within their sexual development (Black, 2005; Finnegan, 2004; Neufeld, Klingbeil, Bryen, Silverman, & Thomas, 2002). In fact, contrary to what would be expected, adolescents with chronic health conditions tend to enter into their active sexual life earlier than their healthy counterparts (Miauton, Narring, & Michaud, 2003; Suris, Resnick, Cassuto, & Blum, 1996). Health professionals who care for these teenagers should be aware of the importance of anticipatory guidance in the field (Black, 2005; Michaud et al., 2004).

2.4 Prevention during adolescence

2.4.1 Definitions and concepts

For many years, preventive activities were essentially directed at fighting against disease or controlling behaviours potentially detrimental to health, such as smoking or eating too much fat. More recently, there has been a shift in interest to less specific interventions and activities that promote skills and healthy choices (Michaud, 2003; Millstein et al., 1993). This shift is due to several reasons. First, it has become more and more clear that specific health problems or harmful behaviour have multiple causes and that effective interventions must address as many of these potential causes as possible. Second, while many programmes used to focus mainly on changing specific "harmful" behaviours, health professionals have come to realize that such an objective was somehow autocratic, ethically highly questionable (Massé, 1995) and that it was more effective in some instance to focus on the positive "salutogenetic" aspects of health (Antonovsky, 1986). Preventive activities nowadays can be classified in the following way:

- medical intervention, such as vaccination and chemoprophylaxis
- screening for diseases (e.g., cancer) or

conditions predisposing to specific disorders (e.g., cardiovascular diseases)
- health education, aiming at attitude and behaviour modification in distinct areas (typically all interventions aiming at reducing smoking)
- broad preventive activities – specific and less specific – simultaneously directed at individuals, communities and environment (e.g., injury prevention, national aids campaign and community intervention in the field of nutrition)
- health promotion, which does not target disease but mainly well-being (e.g., life skills activities like the ones developed within the "healthy school" initiative supported by World Health Organization (World Health Organization, 1993).

2.4.2 Medical and psychosocial individual screening and counselling

It is beyond the scope of this chapter to review medical screening activities which can be applied to adolescents and which include vaccinations (such as for Hepatitis B), screening for hearing and visual defects, scoliosis, cardiovascular risk factors (e.g. obesity, hypertension and hyperlipidaemia) or HIV testing. In fact, with the shift in morbidity from pure medical conditions to psychosocial problems, much of the current activity is not confined to the medical sector but rather focuses on mental health. It has been shown that many practitioners when consulting teenagers tend to focus on the obvious reason for the consultation and so miss the opportunity to detect any underlying problems and burdens (Jacobson, Wilkinson, & Owen, 1994; Michaud & Martin, 1982). This is particularly distressing, since, in recent years, several instruments have been developed that allow for a more accurate screening of medical and psychosocial problems in an adolescent's health encounter. These tools are either self-administered questionnaires covering the whole range of the adolescent's health problems and lifestyles or they provide the health professional with a structured scheme to keep account of the medical and psychosocial history of the encounter (Dafflon & Michaud, 2000;

TABLE 15.2

The HEEADSSS concept: main fields in which screening and counseling activities should be run when caring for an adolescent (Goldenring & Rosen, 2004, p. 433)

Home (with whom does the adolescent live, socioeconomic background, etc.)
Education (school grade and degree, expectation regarding professional life, etc.)
Eating (timing and content of the meals, abnormal eating patterns)
Activities (sports and leisure time, going out with friends, etc.)
Drugs (use of legal and illegal substances, age of onset, frequency, amount, consequence)
Sexuality (orientation, activity, protection/contraception, etc.)
Safety (protective versus risk behavior: wearing helmets, driving while drunk, etc.)
Suicide (mood, depression, anxiety, suicidal thought or behavior)

Elster & Kuznets, 1994). For instance, one of the useful tools that can be used by every professional who is in charge of the guidance of adolescence is the "HEEADSSS" system, as shown in Table 15.2 (Goldenring & Rosen, 2004). Several analyses have recently shown that such screening interventions do work, as for instance in the fields of mental health (Durlak & Wells, 1998) or injury prevention (Cushman, James, & Waclawik, 1991), and one evidence-based study has recently shown that training general practitioners improves their skills in targeting such issues with their adolescent patients (Sanci et al., 2000; Sanci, Coffey, Patton, & Bowes, 2005). One issue that remains partly unsolved is whether problematic or harmful situations which are thus identified can be improved. We have, however, limited evidence that, at least in the field of substance misuse, short motivational interventions are effective (Kokotailo, Langhough, Neary, Matson, & Fleming, 1995; McCambridge & Strang, 2004; Spirito et al., 2004).

Another important issue is one of availability and relevance of healthcare structures for adolescents. Several studies have identified the factors that deter young people from taking professional advice or care (Klein, 2000; Klein, Sesselberg, Gawronski, Handwerker, Gesten, & Schettine, 2003; Oppong-Odiseng & Heycock, 1997; Veit, Sanci, Coffey, Young, & Bowes 1996). Among these factors are the perceived lack of confidentiality, too rigid time schedules, perceived lack of empathy and skills from the staff as

well as financial barriers. As an answer to this situation, the World Health Organization has developed the concept of "youth-friendly services", facilities that specifically meet adolescents' needs both in terms of organization and quality of care, as summarized in Figure 15.1 (McIntyre, 2001). The interest of this concept is that it has been validated by discussions with young people and may also be valid cross-culturally.

2.4.3 Size, targets and principles of prevention programmes

The conceptual and strategic basis of population-based prevention is quite diverse (Blum, 1998; World Health Organization, 1999). Some prevention programmes target the whole population, as is the case for media campaigns or national initiatives, like the Swiss STOP-AIDS campaign (Dubois-Arber et al., 2003). Most programmes, however, focus on specific groups of teenagers, with more or less specific profiles (pupils of specific schools, sexually active teenagers, members of a community, dropouts, etc.). The more delineated the target, the more specific and adapted the message can be. For instance, the reasons why adolescents experiment with smoking during early adolescence are different from those that make them dependent on smoking later. Futhermore, one may also choose to quit smoking during late adolescence (Bonard, Janin-Jacquat, & Michaud, 2001). It is thus essential to take into account the psychosocial development of teenagers when planning a prevention programme (Blum, 1998; Juszczak & Sadler, 1999): the issues differ from one age period to another; the issue of tobacco should be tackled before the age of 12 or 13, as many adolescents begin to smoke before the age of 15. It may be particularly appropriate to discuss the issue of nutrition around the age of 15, when adolescents begin to have more and more meals outside the family home. It is also important to adapt the wording of the message to the cognitive development of the target audience. Whatever the topic and the target audience, there are a number of issues which should be addressed when planning any intervention, which are outlined in Figure 15.2 (Michaud, Baudier, & Sandrin-Berthon, 1997a).

Interventions can focus on very specific topics such as wearing helmets while riding a bicycle or motorcycle (Cushman et al., 1991), while others tend to focus on more positive aspects of health such as resilience (Thompson, Eggert, Randell, & Pike, 2001). In the field of substance use, the shift from specific to non-specific approaches has been particularly apparent. In fact, several studies have shown the superiority of preventive activities, which aim at increasing well-being and the capacity to resist peer pressure, over those programmes focusing on the short- and long-term dangers of drug use (Foxcroft, Ireland, Lister-Sharp, Lowe, & Breen, 2002; Patton et al., 2000). In other words, many programmes currently do not tackle the issue of the behaviour itself, but, rather, issues surrounding the school, community, or even economical environment of the adolescents. A recent meta-analysis has shown the interest of those programmes using peer-led activities based on the acquisition of "life skills", skills that enable adolescents to make their own choices, to engage in sound social activities, to express their feelings and burdens and to overcome the hassles found in daily life (Tobler, Roona, Ochshorn, Marshall, Streke, & Stackpole, 2000).

2.4.4 Health promotion and community health

There are several settings that can be used for

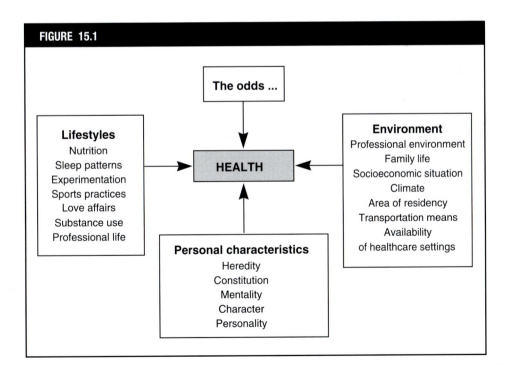

Youth-friendly services.

FIGURE 15.2

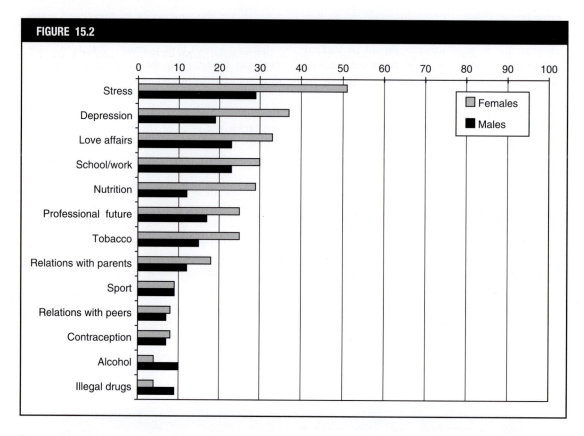

Size, targets, and principles of prevention programmes.

health promotion interventions. The school environment has obviously been much used over the years because it is one of the easiest ways of reaching adolescents where they live; also because many schools have the financial and human resources to build such programmes (World Health Organization, 1993). However, one of the major difficulties linked with school initiatives is that, if they are not taken on by the rest of the surrounding community, they expose pupils to potentially contradictory messages, which, of course, render them more vulnerable to unhealthy choices. Several studies, both in America and in Europe, have thus shown the superiority of strategies that target the whole community instead of just a target group of adolescents in any given school (Coleman et al., 2005; Ebrahim & Smith, 1997; Gilchrist, Schieber, Leadbetter, & Davidson, 2000). The philosophy behind this is much in accordance with the Ottawa chart (Anonymous, 1986), which puts emphasis on the participation of target communities in the implementation of preventive and promotional activities and which has led to the already mentioned concept of "healthy school" (World Health Organization, 1993).

As an example, the "Gatehouse" project was implemented in several schools in the region of Melbourne in Australia (Patton et al., 2000) as a randomized case control trial. It was aiming at improving the general well-being of pupils and the staff through modern paedagogic methods stressing the importance of the ethos of the school as well as a sense of coherence and connectedness (Antonovsky, 1986). Instead of focusing on pupils' behaviour itself, the programme was implemented in each school in close collaboration with the headteacher and the staff.

Various educational, interactive activities were proposed to the adolescents, who were given opportunities to take responsibility. The results of this huge effort was an impressive decrease in violent behaviour as well as a decrease in the use of substances, even though these issues had not been specifically targeted.

2.4.5 Policymaking

Beyond formal interventions in various settings, there are a number of legal and environmental dispositions that can affect the health of adolescents greatly. It is a responsibility of researchers to sensitize politicians and stake holders to the short- and long-term consequences of their decisions (Davis & Howden-Chapman, 1996; Dusenbury & Hansen, 2004; Michaud & Jeannin, 2005). Limiting access to legal psychoactive substances (i.e. an age limit for purchasing cigarettes and alcohol (Morin & Collins, 2000)), implementing new social norms (such as increasing the availability of condoms in the case of AIDS campaigns (Blake, Ledsky, Goodenow, Sawyer, Lohrmann, & Windsor, 2003) or the wearing of helmets on roads (Leblanc, Beattie, & Culligan, 2002)), implementing more stringent speed controls and limits on alcohol consumption as well as making alterations to roads (Assailly, 2004; Avery & Avery, 1982) are just some examples of measures that have proven effective. Also, one should not forget the potential effectiveness that pure economical measures bring, especially when directed at vulnerable populations such as school dropouts, newly arrived immigrants and refugees, or adolescents and families working in deprived environments.

2.4.6 Evaluation

In an era of evidence-based medicine, professionals involved in preventive activities and health promotion have been slow to embark on well-designed trials assessing the impact and effectiveness of their interventions. Moreover, European countries have been slow in evaluating prevention programmes, and most of the available literature in the field comes from North America. Indeed, the broader the focus of these interventions, the more difficult it then

becomes to bring evidence of a formal improvement of the situation. A large number of recent contributions, however, have been reflected in the field (Bury, 2003; Eriksson, 2000; Nutbeam, 2004; Pentz, 2003; Raphael, 2000). It is suggested that such evaluations concentrate less on typical randomized trials and behavioural impact and more on the processes involved in the various interventions as well as qualitative research (Raphael, 2000; Victora, Habicht, & Bryce, 2004).

3. Conclusion

In this chapter, we have shown that adolescents in Europe face several important health issues, particularly in the area of psychosocial well-being and lifestyles. To a great extent, the health problems of adolescents are similar in nature, although they clearly differ in scope and scale from one region and country to another (Blum, 1998; Blum & Nelson-Mmari, 2004; World Health Organization, 1993). A recent report issued by the European Community (Anonymous, 2000) states that: "The majority of young people enjoy good health, and the trends from the mid-1980s to the mid-1990s suggest that the situation is likely to improve in the future", but "A considerable proportion of young people suffer from poverty, family breakdown, lack of social support and of educational or professional challenges, or from low quality of food, all factors which may impede healthy growth and development." The report also adds that: "The marked differences both between and within the Member States in social and cultural determinants of health are bound to lead to increasing inequalities in young people's health between population subgroups and countries."

The EU report, as this chapter also outlines, stresses the importance of the educational and psychosocial factors that should be addressed to improve adolescent health, and the fact that attention should not be paid only to health-related lifestyles and behaviour but also to the mental health and economical environment of young people. While the United States, Canada and Australia have worked out adequate responses in creating specific facilities, in building up prevention programmes and in offering adequate training to all involved professionals, it is only recently that some European countries have developed such an approach. The time has now come to commonly reflect on the challenges that the current situations impose.

References

Aarnio, M., Winter, T., Peltonen, J., Kujala, U.M., & Kaprio, J. (2002). Stability of leisure-time physical activity during adolescence: A longitudinal study among 16-, 17- and 18-year-old Finnish youth. *Scandinavian Journal of Medicine and Science in Sports, 12*, 179–185.

Addor, V., Narring, F., & Michaud, P.A. (2003). Abortion trends 1990–1999 in a Swiss region and determinants of abortion recurrence. *Swiss Medical Weekly, 133*, 219–226.

Alsaker, F.D., Flanagan, C., & Csapó, B. (1999). Methodological challenges in cross-national research: Countries, participants, and general procedures. In F. D. Alsaker, & A. Flammer (Eds.), *The adolescent experience: European and American adolescents in the 1990s* (pp. 15–32). Mahwah, NJ: Lawrence Erlbaum Associates, Inc.

American Psychiatric Association (1994). *Diagnostic and statistical manual of mental disorders* (4th ed.). Washington, DC: American Psychiatric Association.

Anonymous (1968). *Ottawa chart for health promotion: An international conference*. Ottawa, Canada: Health and Welfare.

Anonymous (2000). *Report on the state of young people's health in the European Union*. Brussels, Belgium: European Commission, Directorate-General of Health and Consumer Protection, Unit F3: Health Promotion, Health Monitoring and Injury Prevention.

Anonymous (2004). Who is responsible for adolescent health? *Lancet, 363*, 2009.

Antonovsky, A. (1986). The salutogenic model as theory to guide health promotion. *Health Promotion International, 1*, 1–18.

Arènes, J., Janvrin, M., & Baudier, F. (1998). *Baromètre santé jeunes 97–98* [Youth health survey 97–98]. Paris: Comité Français d'Education pour la Santé.

Assailly, J.P. (2004). The prevention of young drivers' DWI (driving while intoxicated) and RWDI (riding with a driver under influence) in Europe: A social-sequential model. *Traffic Injury Prevention, 5*, 237–240.

Aten, M.J., Siegel, D.M., Enaharo, M., & Auinger, P. (2002). Keeping middle school students abstinent: Outcomes of a primary prevention intervention. *Journal of Adolescent Health, 31*, 70–78.

Avery, J.G., & Avery, P.J. (1982). Scandinavian and Dutch lessons in childhood road traffic accident prevention. *British Medical Journal, 285*, 621–626.

Baranowski, T., Bouchard, C., Bar-Or, O., Bricker, T., Heath, G., Kimm, S.Y.S. et al. (1992). Assessment, prevalence, and cardiovascular benefits of physical activity and fitness in youth. *Medicine and Science in Sports and Exercise, 24*, S237–S247.

Bar-Or, O., Foreyt, J., Bouchard, C., Brownell, K.D., Dietz, W.H., Ravussin et al. (1998). Physical activity, genetic, and nutritional considerations in childhood weight management. *Medicine and Science in Sports and Exercise, 30*, 2–10.

Bearinger, L.H., & Resnick, M.D. (2003). Dual method use in adolescents: A review and framework for research on use of STD and pregnancy protection. *Journal of Adolescent Health, 32*, 340–349.

Bechtel, K., & Podrazik, M. (1999). Evaluation of the adolescent rape victim. *Pediatric Clinics of North America, 46*, 809–823.

Black, K. (2005). Disability and sexuality: Holistic care for adolescents. *Paediatric Nursing, 17*(5), 34–37.

Blake, S.M., Ledsky, R., Goodenow, C., Sawyer, R., Lohrmann, D., & Windsor, R. (2003). Condom availability in Massachusetts high schools: Relationships with condom use and sexual behavior. *American Journal of Public Health, 93*, 955–962.

Blum, R.W.M. (1998). Healthy youth development as a model for youth health promotion: A review. *Journal of Adolescent Health, 22*, 368–375.

Blum, R.W., & Nelson-Mmari, K. (2004). The health of young people in a global context. *Journal of Adolescent Health, 35*, 402–418.

Bonard, L., Janin-Jacquat, B., & Michaud, P.A. (2001). Who are the adolescents who stop smoking? *European Journal of Pediatrics, 160*, 430–435.

Boonstra, H. (2002). Teen pregnancy: Trends and lessons learned. In *The Guttmacher report on public health* (pp. 7–19). New York: Alan Guttmacher Institute.

Bury, J.A. (2003). Evidence base in health promotion: Why bother? *Sozial- und Präventivmedizin, 48*, 277–278.

Caprio, S., & Genel, M. (2005). Confronting the epidemic of childhood obesity. *Pediatrics, 115*, 494–495.

Chamay-Weber, C., Narring, F., & Michaud, P.A. (2005). Partial eating disorders among adolescents: A review. *Journal of Adolescent Health, 37*, 417–427.

Chambers, K.B., & Rew, L. (2003). Safer sexual decision making in adolescent women: Perspectives from the conflict theory of decision-making. *Issues in Comprehensive Pediatric Nursing, 26*, 129–143.

Choquet, M., & Ledoux, S. (1994). *Adolescents: enquête nationale* [Adolescents: A national survey]. Paris: INSERM.

Coleman, K.J., Tiller, C.L., Sanchez, J., Heath, E.M., Sy, O., Milliken, G. et al. (2005). Prevention of the epidemic increase in child risk of overweight in low-income schools: The El Paso coordinated approach to child health. *Archives of Pediatrics and Adolescent Medicine, 159*, 217–224.

Cromer, B., & Harel, Z. (2000). Adolescents: At increased risk for osteoporosis? *Clinical Pediatrics, 39*, 565–574.

Currie, C., Hurrelmann, K., & Settertobulte, W.A. (2000). *Health and health behavior among young people: An HBSC WHO cross-national study.* Copenhagen, Denmark: World Health Organization.

Currie, C., Roberts, C., Morgan, A., Smith, R., Settertobulte, W., Samdal, O. et al. (2004). *Young people's health in context: Health Behaviour in School-Aged Children (HBSC) study – International report from the 2001/2002 survey.* Copenhagen, Denmark: World Health Organization.

Cushman, R., James, W., & Waclawik, H. (1991). Physicians promoting bicycle helmets for children: A randomized trial. *American Journal of Public Health, 81*, 1044–1046.

Dafflon, M., & Michaud, P.A. (2000). Un questionnaire clinique pour faciliter la consultation avec l'adolescent [A clinical questionnaire for facilitating consultation with the adolescent]. *Schweizerische Rundschau für Medizin Praxis, 89*, 24–31.

Danielson, C.K., & Holmes, M.M. (2004). Adolescent sexual assault: An update of the literature. *Current Opinion in Obstetrics and Gynecology, 16*, 383–388.

Davis, P., & Howden-Chapman, P. (1996). Translating research findings into health policy. *Social Science and Medicine, 43*, 865–872.

Decarli, B., Cavadini, C., Grin, J., Blondel-Lubrano, A., Narring, F., & Michaud, P.A. (2000). Food and nutrient intakes in a group of 11- to 16-year-old Swiss teenagers. *International Journal for Vitamin and Nutrition Research, 70*, 139–147.

Deschamps, J. (1987). Ces jeunes sont sans besoins [These young people have no needs]. *Revue Française des Affaires Sociales, 41*, 43–57.

Devaud, C., Jeannin, A., Narring, F., Ferron, C., & Michaud, P.A. (1998). Eating disorders among female adolescents in Switzerland: Prevalence and associations with mental and behavioral disorders. *International Journal of Eating Disorders, 24*, 207–216.

Devaud, C., Michaud, P.A., & Narring, F. (1995). L'anorexie et la boulimie: Des affectations en augmentation? Une revue de littérature sur l'épidémiologie des dysfonctions alimentaires [Anorexia and bulimia: Increasing disorders? A review of the literature on the epidemiology of eating disorders]. *Revue d'Epidémiologie et de Santé Publique, 43*, 347–360.

Dubois-Arber, F., Jeannin, A., Meystre-Agustoni, G., Spencer, B., Moreau-Gruet, F., Balthasar, H. et al. (2003). *Evaluation de la stratégie de prévention du sida en Suisse: Septième rapport de synthese 1999–2003* [Evaluating the AIDS prevention strategy in Switzerland: Seventh summary report 1999–2003]. Lausanne, Switzerland: Institut de Médecine Sociale et Préventive (IMSP).

Duncan, P., Dixon, R.R., & Carlson, N.J. (2003). Childhood and adolescent sexuality. *Pediatric Clinics of North America, 50*, 765–780.

Durlak, J.A., & Wells, A.M. (1998). Evaluation of indicated preventive intervention (secondary prevention) mental health programs for children and adolescents. *American Journal of Community Psychology, 26*, 775–802.

Dusenbury, L., & Hansen, W.B. (2004). Pursuing the course from research to practice. *Prevention Science, 5*, 55–59.

Ebrahim, S., & Smith, G.D. (1997). Systematic review of randomised controlled trials of multiple risk factor interventions for preventing coronary heart disease. *British Medical Journal, 314*, 1666–1674.

Elfenbein, D.S., & Felice, M.E. (2003). Adolescent pregnancy. *Pediatric Clinics of North America, 50*, 781–800.

Elster, A.B., & Kuznets, N. (1994). *AMA Guidelines for Adolescent Preventive Services (GAPS): Recommendations and rationale.* Baltimore, MA: Williams & Wilkins.

Eriksson, C. (2000). Learning and knowledge-production for public health: A review of approaches to evidence-based public health. *Scandinavian Journal of Public Health, 28*, 298–308.

Feldmann, J., & Middleman, A.B. (2002). Adolescent sexuality and sexual behavior. *Current Opinion in Obstetrics and Gynecology, 14*, 489–493.

Ferron, C., Haour-Knipe, M., Tschumper, A., Narring, F., & Michaud, P.A. (1997). Health behaviours and psychosocial adjustment of migrant adolescents in Switzerland. *Schweizerische Medizinische Wochenschrift, 127,* 1419–1429.

Ferron, C., Narring, F., Cauderay, M., & Michaud, P.A. (1999). Sport activity in adolescence: Associations with health perceptions and experimental behaviours. *Health Education Research, 14,* 225–233.

Finnegan, A. (2004). Sexual health and chronic illness in childhood. *Paediatric Nursing, 16* (7), 32–36.

Flodmark, C.E., Lissau, I., Moreno, L.A., Pietrobelli, A., & Widhalm, K. (2004). New insights into the field of children and adolescents' obesity: The European perspective. *International Journal of Obesity and Related Metabolic Disorders, 28,* 1189–1196.

Fombonne, E. (1995). Eating disorders: Time trends and possible explanatory mechanisms. In M. Rutter, & D. J. Smith (Eds.), *Psychosocial disorders in young people: Time trends and their causes* (pp. 616–685). Chichester: John Wiley & Sons.

Foxcroft, D.R., Ireland, D., Lister-Sharp, D.J., Lowe, G., & Breen, R. (2002). Primary prevention for alcohol misuse in young people. *Cochrane Database of Systematic Reviews,* CD003024.

French, S.A., Perry, C.L., Leon, G.R., & Fulkerson, J.A. (1994). Food preferences, eating patterns, and physical activity among adolescents: Correlates of eating disorders symptoms. *Journal of Adolescent Health, 15,* 286–294.

Garofalo, R., & Harper, G.W. (2003). Not all adolescents are the same: Addressing the unique needs of gay and bisexual male youth. *Adolescent Medicine, 14,* 595–611, vi.

Gilchrist, J., Schieber, R.A., Leadbetter, S., & Davidson, S.C. (2000). Police enforcement as part of a comprehensive bicycle helmet program. *Pediatrics, 106,* 6–9.

Glasgow, R.E., Eakin, E.G., Fisher, E.B., Bacak, S.J., & Brownson, R.C. (2001). Physician advice and support for physical activity: Results from a national survey. *American Journal of Preventive Medicine, 21,* 189–196.

Goldenring, J.M., & Rosen, D.S. (2004). Getting into adolescent heads: An essential update. *Contemporary Pediatrics, 21,* 64–90.

Hagarty, M.A., Schmidt, C., Bernaix, L., & Clement, J.M. (2004). Adolescent obesity: Current trends in identification and management. *Journal of the American Academy of Nurse Practitioners, 16,* 481–489.

Haggerty, R.J., Sherrod, L.R., Garmezy, N., & Rutter, M. (Eds.). (1994). *Stress, risk, and resilience in children and adolescents: Processes, mechanisms, and interventions.* Cambridge: Cambridge University Press.

Haggstrom-Nordin, E., Hanson, U., & Tyden, T. (2002). Sex behavior among high school students in Sweden: Improvement in contraceptive use over time. *Journal of Adolescent Health, 30,* 288–295.

Hammarstrom, A., & Janlert, U. (2002). Early unemployment can contribute to adult health problems: Results from a longitudinal study of school leavers. *Journal of Epidemiology and Community Health, 56,* 624–630.

Harel, Z. (1999). New developments in adolescent nutrition. *Medicine and Health – Rhode Island, 82,* 387–390.

Hausser, D., & Michaud, P.A. (1994). Does a condom-promoting strategy (the Swiss STOP-AIDS campaign) modify sexual behavior among adolescents? *Pediatrics, 93,* 580–585.

Hayman, L.L., & Reineke, P.R. (2003). Preventing coronary heart disease: The implementation of healthy lifestyle strategies for children and adolescents. *Journal of Cardiovascular Nursing, 18,* 294–301.

Hoelscher, D.M., Mitchell, P., Dwyer, J., Elder, J., Clesi, A., & Snyder, P. (2003). How the CATCH eat smart program helps implement the USDA regulations in school cafeterias. *Health Education and Behavior, 30,* 434–446.

Jackson, P.R., Stafford, E.M., Banks, M.H., & Warr, P.B. (1983). Unemployment and psychological distress in young people: The moderating role of employment commitment. *Journal of Applied Psychology, 68,* 525–535.

Jacobson, L.D., Wilkinson, C., & Owen, P.A. (1994). Is the potential of teenage consultations being missed? A study of consultation times in primary care. *Family Practice, 11,* 296–299.

Jeannin, A., Narring, F., Tschumper, A., Bonivento, L.I., Addor, V., Butikofer, A. et al. (2005). Self-reported health needs and use of primary health care services by adolescents enrolled in post-mandatory schools or vocational training programmes in Switzerland. *Swiss Medical Weekly, 135,* 11–18.

Jessor, R. (1991). Risk behavior in adolescence: A psychosocial framework for understanding and action. *Journal of Adolescent Health, 12,* 597–605.

Jessor, R., Turbin, M.S., & Costa, F.M. (1998). Protective factors in adolescent health behavior. *Journal of Personality and Social Psychology, 75,* 788–800.

Johnson, B.T., Carey, M.P., Marsh, K.L., Levin, K.D., & Scott-Heldon, L.A.J. (2003). Interventions to reduce sexual risk for the human immunodeficiency virus in adolescents, 1985–2000: A research synthesis. *Archives of Pediatrics and Adolescent Medicine, 157*, 381–388.

Juszczak, L., & Sadler, L. (1999). Adolescent development: Setting the stage for influencing health behaviors. *Adolescent Medicine: State of the Art Reviews, 10*, 1–11.

Kaminsky, M., & Bouvier-Colle, M. (1991). *La mortalité des jeunes dans les pays de la Communauté Européenne* [Youth mortality in the countries of the European Community]. Paris: Institut National de Recherche Médicale.

Kann, L., Warren, W., Collins, J.L., Ross, J., Collins, B., & Kolbe, L.J. (1993). Results from the national school-based 1991 Youth Risk Behavior Survey and progress toward achieving related health objectives for the nation. *Public Health Reports, 108* (Suppl. 1), 47–67.

Keller, S.N., & Brown, J.D. (2002). Media interventions to promote responsible sexual behavior. *Journal of Sex Research, 39*, 67–72.

Key, T.J., Allen, N.E., Spencer, E.A., & Travis, R.C. (2002). The effect of diet on risk of cancer. *Lancet, 360*, 861–868.

Kirby, D. (2002). The impact of schools and school programs upon adolescent sexual behavior. *Journal of Sex Research, 39*, 27–33.

Kirby, D.B., Baumler, E., Coyle, K.K., Basen-Engquist, K., Parcel, G.S., Harrist, R. et al. (2004). The 'Safer Choices' intervention: Its impact on the sexual behaviors of different subgroups of high school students. *Journal of Adolescent Health, 35*, 442–452.

Klein, J.D. (2000). Adolescents, health services, and access to care. *Journal of Adolescent Health, 27*, 293–294.

Klein, J.D., Sesselberg, T.S., Gawronski, B., Handwerker, L., Gesten, F., & Schettine, A. (2003). Improving adolescent preventive services through state, managed care, and community partnerships. *Journal of Adolescent Health, 32*, 91–97.

Knight, J.R., Frazer, C.H., Goodman, E., Blaschke, G.S., Bravender, T.D., & Emans, S.J. (2001). Development of a Bright Futures curriculum for pediatric residents. *Ambulatory Pediatrics, 1*, 136–140.

Koffi-Blanchard, M.C., Dubois-Arber, F., Michaud, P.A., Narring, F., & Paccaud, F. (1994). Hat sich der Beginn der Sexualität bei Jugendlichen in der Zeit von AIDS verändert? [Age of onset of sexual activity in young people: Has it changed in the era of AIDS?]. *Schweizerische Medizinische Wochenschrift, 124*, 1047–1055.

Kokotailo, P.K., Langhough, R., Neary, E.J., Matson, S.C., & Fleming, M.F. (1995). Improving pediatric residents' alcohol and other drug use clinical skills: Use of an experiential curriculum. *Pediatrics, 96*, 99–104.

Kune-Karrer, B.M., & Taylor, E.H. (1995). Toward multiculturality: Implications for the pediatrician. *Pediatric Clinics of North America, 42*, 21–30.

Lagrange, H., & Lhomond, B. (1997). *L'entrée dans la sexualité: Le comportement des jeunes dans le contexte du sida* [The onset of sexual activity: Sexual behaviour of youth in the AIDS era]. Paris: La Découverte.

Leblanc, J.C., Beattie, T.L., & Culligan, C. (2002). Effect of legislation on the use of bicycle helmets. *Canadian Medical Association Journal, 166*, 592–595.

Lewinsohn, P.M., Striegel-Moore, R.H., & Seeley, J.R. (2000). Epidemiology and natural course of eating disorders in young women from adolescence to young adulthood. *Journal of the American Academy of Child and Adolescent Psychiatry, 39*, 1284–1292.

Lindberg, C.E. (2003). Emergency contraception for prevention of adolescent pregnancy. *MCN: American Journal of Maternal Child Nursing, 28*, 199–204.

Lindley, L.L., & Reininger, B.M. (2001). Support for instruction about homosexuality in South Carolina public schools. *Journal of School Health, 71*, 17–22.

Lindstrom, B., & Eriksson, B. (1993). Quality of life for children with disabilities. *Sozial- und Präventivmedizin, 38*, 83–89.

Lobstein, T., & Frelut, M.L. (2003). Prevalence of overweight among children in Europe. *Obesity Reviews, 4*, 195–200.

Lupton, D. (1995). *The imperative of health: Public health and the regulated body*. London: Sage.

Lytle, L.A. (2002). Nutritional issues for adolescents. *Journal of the American Dietetic Association, 102*, S8–S12.

MacFarlane, A. (1995). Effectiveness in adolescent health. *Acta Paediatrica, 84*, 1089–1093.

Massé, R. (1995). *Culture et santé publique* [Culture and public health]. Montréal, Canada: Gaëtan Morin.

McCambridge, J., & Strang, J. (2004). The efficacy of single-session motivational interviewing in reducing drug consumption and perceptions of drug-related risk and harm among young people: Results from a multi-site cluster randomized trial. *Addiction, 99*, 39–52.

McIntyre, P. (2001). *Adolescent-friendly health services* [Draft report]. Geneva, Switzerland: World Health Organisation – Child and Adolescent Health.

Miauton, L., Narring, F., & Michaud, P.A. (2003). Chronic illness, life style and emotional health in adolescence: Results of a cross-sectional survey on the health of 15–20-year-olds in Switzerland. *European Journal of Pediatrics, 162,* 682–689.

Michaud, P.A. (1999). La résilience: Un regard neuf sur les soins et la prévention [Resilience: A new look at medical care and preventive pediatrics]. *Archives de Pédiatrie, 6,* 827–831.

Michaud, P.A. (2003). Prevention and health promotion in school and community settings: A commentary on the international perspective. *Journal of Adolescent Health, 33,* 219–225.

Michaud, P.A., Baudier, F., & Sandrin-Berthon, B. (1997a). L'éducation pour la santé [Health education]. In P. A. Michaud, P. Alvin, J. P. Deschamps, J. Y. Frappier, D. Marcelli, & A. Tursz (Eds.), *La santé des adolescents: Approches, soins, prévention.* Lausanne, Switzerland: Payot.

Michaud, P.A., Blum, R.W., & Ferron, C. (1998a). 'Bet you I will!': Risk or experimental behavior during adolescence? *Archives of Pediatrics and Adolescent Medicine, 152,* 224–226.

Michaud, P.A., Blum, R.W., & Slap, G.B. (2001a). Cross-cultural surveys of adolescent health and behavior: Progress and problems. *Social Science and Medicine, 53,* 1237–1246.

Michaud, P.A., Delbos-Piot, I., & Narring, F. (1998b). Silent dropouts in health surveys: Are nonrespondent absent teenagers different from those who participate in school-based health surveys? *Journal of Adolescent Health, 22,* 326–333.

Michaud, P.A., Ferron, C., & Narring, F. (1996). Immigrant status and risk behaviors. *Journal of Adolescent Health, 19,* 378–380.

Michaud, P.A., Ferron, C., Piot-Delbos, I., Cordonier, D., Narring, F., & Schalbetter, P. (1997b). La santé des jeunes en rupture d'apprentissage: Une recherche comparant la santé des apprentis et des jeunes en rupture d'apprentissage dans deux cantons romands [Health in unemployed adolescents: A study comparing the health of employed and unemployed adolescents in two French-speaking cantons]. *Revue Médicale de la Suisse Romande, 117,* 783–791.

Michaud, P.A., & Jeannin, A. (2005). Beyond the insiders' circle: Disseminating the results of adolescent health surveys. *Acta Paediatrica, 94,* 1017–1022.

Michaud, P.A., & Martin, J. (1982). La consultation de l'adolescent dans la pratique des médecins: Une étude de soins ambulatoires dans deux cantons suisses [Consultations on adolescents in medical practice: A study of ambulatory care in two Swiss cantons]. *Sozial- und Präventivmedizin, 27,* 304–309.

Michaud, P.A., Narring, F., Cauderay, M., & Cavadini, C. (1999). Sports activity, physical activity and fitness of 9- to 19-year-old teenagers in the canton of Vaud (Switzerland). *Schweizerische Medizinische Wochenschrift, 129,* 691–699.

Michaud, P.A., Renaud, A., & Narring, F. (2001b). Sports activities related to injuries? A survey among 9–19-year-olds in Switzerland. *Injury Prevention, 7,* 41–45.

Michaud, P.A., Suris, J.C., & Viner, R. (2004). The adolescent with a chronic condition. Part II: Healthcare provision. *Archives of Disease in Childhood, 89,* 943–949.

Miller, B.C. (2002). Family influences on adolescent sexual and contraceptive behavior. *Journal of Sex Research, 39,* 22–26.

Millstein, S., Petersen, A., & Nightingale, E. (1993). *Promoting the health of adolescents: New directions for the twenty-first century.* Oxford: Oxford University Press.

Morin, S.F., & Collins, C. (2000). Substance abuse prevention: Moving from science to policy. *Addictive Behaviors, 25,* 975–983.

Mullen, P.D., Ramirez, G., Strouse, D., Hedges, L.V., & Sogolow, E. (2002). Meta-analysis of the effects of behavioral HIV prevention interventions on the sexual risk behavior of sexually experienced adolescents in controlled studies in the United States. *Journal of Acquired Immune Deficiency Syndrome, 30* (Suppl. 1), S94–S105.

Mulvihill, C., Nemeth, A., & Vereecken, C. (2004). Body image, weight control and body weight. In C. Currie, C. Roberts, A. Morgan, R. Smith, W. Settertobulte, O. Samdal et al. (Eds.), *Young people's health in context: Health Behaviour in School-aged Children (HBSC) study – International report from the 2001/2002 survey.* Copenhagen, Denmark: World Health Organization.

Narring, F., & Michaud, P.A. (1995). Methodological issues in adolescent health surveys: The case of the Swiss multicenter adolescent survey on health. *Sozial- und Präventivmedizin, 40,* 172–182.

Narring, F., Roulet, N., Addor, V., & Michaud, P.A. (2002). Abortion requests among adolescents in comparison with young adults in a Swiss region (1990–1998). *Acta Paediatrica, 91,* 965–970.

Narring, F., Stronski-Huwiler, S.M., & Michaud, P.A. (2003). Prevalence and dimensions of sexual orientation in Swiss adolescents: A cross-sectional survey of 16 to 20-year-old students. *Acta Paediatrica*, *92*, 233–239.

Narring, F., Wydler, H., & Michaud, P.A. (2000). First sexual intercourse and contraception: A cross-sectional survey on the sexuality of 16–20-year-olds in Switzerland. *Schweizerische Medizinische Wochenschrift*, *130*, 1389–1398.

Nestle, M. (2000). Soft drink 'pouring rights': Marketing empty calories to children. *Public Health Reports*, *115*, 308–319.

Neufeld, J.A., Klingbeil, F., Bryen, D.N., Silverman, B., & Thomas, A. (2002). Adolescent sexuality and disability. *Physical Medicine and Rehabilitation Clinics of North America*, *13*, 857–873.

Nutbeam, D. (2004). Getting evidence into policy and practice to address health inequalities. *Health Promotion International*, *19*, 137–140.

Oakley, A., Fullerton, D., Holland, J., Arnold, S., France-Dawson, M., Kelley, P. et al. (1995). Sexual health education interventions for young people: A methodological review. *British Medical Journal*, *310*, 158–162.

O'Brien, K.M., & Vincent, N.K. (2003). Psychiatric comorbidity in anorexia and bulimia nervosa: Nature, prevalence, and causal relationships. *Clinical Psychology Review*, *23*, 57–74.

Omar, H., & Richard, J. (2004). Cultural sensitivity in providing reproductive care to adolescents. *Current Opinion in Obstetrics and Gynecology*, *16*, 367–370.

Oppong-Odiseng, A.C., & Heycock, E.G. (1997). Adolescent health services: Through their eyes. *Archives of Disease in Childhood*, *77*, 115–119.

Ott, M.A., Adler, N.E., Millstein, S.G., Tschann, J.M., & Ellen, J.M. (2002). The trade-off between hormonal contraceptives and condoms among adolescents. *Perspectives on Sexual and Reproductive Health*, *34*, 6–14.

Ottesen, S., Narring, F., Renteria, S.C., & Michaud, P.A. (2002). Comment améliorer l'utilisation de la contraception d'urgence par les adolescents? [How to improve use of emergency contraception by adolescents?]. *Journal de Gynécologie, Obstétrique et Biologie de la Reproduction*, *31*, 144–151.

Parcel, G.S., Perry, C.L., Kelder, S.H., Elder, J.P., Mitchell, P.D., Lytle, L.A. et al. (2003). School climate and the institutionalization of the CATCH program. *Health Education and Behavior*, *30*, 489–502.

Pate, R.R., Heath, G.W., Dowda, M., & Trost, S.G. (1996). Associations between physical activity and other health behaviors in a representative sample of US adolescents. *American Journal of Public Health*, *86*, 1577–1581.

Pate, R.R., Trost, S.G., Levin, S., & Dowda, M. (2000). Sports participation and health-related behaviors among US youth. *Archives of Pediatrics and Adolescent Medicine*, *154*, 904–911.

Patton, G.C., Glover, S., Bond, L., Butler, H., Godfrey, C., Di Pietro, G. et al. (2000). The Gatehouse Project: A systematic approach to mental health promotion in secondary schools. *Australian and New Zealand Journal of Psychiatry*, *34*, 586–593.

Pentz, M.A. (2003). Evidence-based prevention: Characteristics, impact, and future direction. *Journal of Psychoactive Drugs*, *35*, 143–152.

Peretti-Watel, P., Guagliardo, V., Verger, P., Pruvost, J., Mignon, P., & Obadia, Y. (2003). Sporting activity and drug use: Alcohol, cigarette and cannabis use among elite student athletes. *Addiction*, *98*, 1249–1256.

Ponton, L.E., & Judice, S. (2004). Typical adolescent sexual development. *Child and Adolescent Psychiatric Clinics of North America*, *13*, 497–511, vi.

Raitakari, O.T., Taimela, S., Porkka, K.V.K., Leino, M., Telama, R., Dahl, M. et al. (1996). Patterns of intense physical activity among 15- to 30-year-old Finns: The Cardiovascular Risk in Young Finns Study. *Scandinavian Journal of Medicine and Science in Sports*, *6*, 36–39.

Raphael, D. (2000). The question of evidence in health promotion. *Health Promotion International*, *15*, 355–367.

Rienzo, B.A., Button, J., & Wald, K.D. (1996). The politics of school-based programs which address sexual orientation. *Journal of School Health*, *66*, 33–40.

Robin, A.L., Gilroy, M., & Dennis, A.B. (1998). Treatment of eating disorders in children and adolescents. *Clinical Psychology Review*, *18*, 421–446.

Robin, L., Dittus, P., Whitaker, D., Crosby, R., Ethier, K., Mezoff, J. et al. (2004). Behavioral interventions to reduce incidence of HIV, STD, and pregnancy among adolescents: A decade in review. *Journal of Adolescent Health*, *34*, 3–26.

Rome, E.S., & Ammerman, S. (2003). Medical complications of eating disorders: An update. *Journal of Adolescent Health*, *33*, 418–426.

Rose, A., Koo, H.P., Bhaskar, B., Anderson, K., White, G., & Jenkins, R.R. (2005). The influence of primary caregivers on the sexual behavior of early adolescents. *Journal of Adolescent Health*, *37*, 135–144.

Rotheram-Borus, M.J., O'Keefe, Z., Kracker, R., & Foo, H.H. (2000). Prevention of HIV among adolescents. *Prevention Science, 1*, 15–30.

Rowland, T.W. (2001). The role of physical activity and fitness in children in the prevention of adult cardiovascular disease. *Progress in Pediatric Cardiology, 12*, 199–203.

Rowland, T.W., & Freedson, P.S. (1994). Physical activity, fitness, and health in children: A close look. *Pediatrics, 93*, 669–672.

Sallis, J.F., Prochaska, J.J., & Taylor, W.C. (2000). A review of correlates of physical activity of children and adolescents. *Medicine and Science in Sports and Exercise, 32*, 963–975.

Sanci, L., Coffey, C., Patton, G., & Bowes, G. (2005). Sustainability of change with quality general practitioner education in adolescent health: A 5-year follow-up. *Medical Education, 39*, 557–560.

Sanci, L.A., Coffey, C.M.M., Veit, F.C.M., Carr-Gregg, M., Patton, G.C., Day, E. et al. (2000). Evaluation of the effectiveness of an educational intervention for general practitioners in adolescent health care: Randomised controlled trial. *British Medical Journal, 320*, 224–230.

Savin-Williams, R.C., & Cohen, K.M. (2004). Homoerotic development during childhood and adolescence. *Child and Adolescent Psychiatric Clinics of North America, 13*, 529–549, vii.

Schaalma, H.P., Abraham, C., Gillmore, M.R., & Kok, G. (2004). Sex education as health promotion: What does it take? *Archives of Sexual Behavior, 33*, 259–269.

Schlueter, V., Narring, F., Munch, U., & Michaud, P.A. (2004). Trends in violent deaths among young people 10–24 years old in Switzerland, 1969–1997. *European Journal of Epidemiology, 19*, 291–297.

Sonenstein, F.L., Ku, L., Lindberg, L.D., Turner, C.F., & Pleck, J.H. (1998). Changes in sexual behavior and condom use among teenaged males: 1988 to 1995. *American Journal of Public Health, 88*, 956–959.

Spirito, A., Monti, P.M., Barnett, N.P., Colby, S.M., Sindelar, H., Rohsenow, D.J. et al. (2004). A randomized clinical trial of a brief motivational intervention for alcohol-positive adolescents treated in an emergency department. *Journal of Pediatrics, 145*, 396–402.

Spyckerelle, Y., Bon, N., Ferron, C., & Deschamps, J. (1991). Perceived health and health requests in a French adolescent population. *International Journal of Adolescent Medicine and Health, 5*, 161–175.

Stein, D., Meged, S., Bar-Hanin, T., Blank, S., Elizur, A., & Weizman, A. (1997). Partial eating disorders in a community sample of female adolescents. *Journal of the American Academy of Child and Adolescent Psychiatry, 36*, 1116–1123.

Steinberg, L., & Morris, A.S. (2001). Adolescent development. *Annual Review of Psychology, 52*, 83–110.

Steinhausen, H.C., Seidel, R., & Winkler Metzke, C. (2000). Evaluation of treatment and intermediate and long-term outcome of adolescent eating disorders. *Psychological Medicine, 30*, 1089–1098.

Stephenson, J.M., Strange, V., Forrest, S., Oakley, A., Copas, A., Allen, E. et al. (2004). Pupil-led sex education in England (RIPPLE study): Cluster-randomised intervention trial. *Lancet, 364*, 338–346.

Stronski-Huwiler, S.M., & Remafedi, G. (1998). Adolescent homosexuality. *Advances in Pediatrics, 45*, 107–144.

Stubbs, C.O., & Lee, A.J. (2004). The obesity epidemic: Both energy intake and physical activity contribute. *Medical Journal of Australia, 181*, 489–491.

Suris, J.C., Jeannin, A., Michaud, P.A., Narring, F., & Diserens, C. (2004a). Unintentional injuries among 16- to 20-year-old students in Switzerland. *International Journal of Adolescent Medicine and Health, 16*, 265–273.

Suris, J.C., Michaud, P., Chossis, I., & Jeannin, A. (in press). Towards a sedentary society: Trends in adolescent sport practice in Switzerland 1993–2002. *Journal of Adolescent Health*.

Suris, J.C., Michaud, P.A., & Viner, R. (2004b). The adolescent with a chronic condition. Part I: Developmental issues. *Archives of Disease in Childhood, 89*, 938–942.

Suris, J.C., Resnick, M.D., Cassuto, N., & Blum, R.W. (1996). Sexual behavior of adolescents with chronic disease and disability. *Journal of Adolescent Health, 19*, 124–131.

Taylor, S. (1986). *Health psychology*. New York: Random House.

Taylor, W.C., Blair, S.N., Cummings, S.S., Wun, C.C., & Malina, R.M. (1999). Childhood and adolescent physical activity patterns and adult physical activity. *Medicine and Science in Sports and Exercise, 31*, 118–123.

Thompson, E.A., Eggert, L.L., Randell, B.P., & Pike, K.C. (2001). Evaluation of indicated suicide risk prevention approaches for potential high school dropouts. *American Journal of Public Health, 91*, 742–752.

Tiefer, L., & Kring, B. (1995). Gender and the organization of sexual behavior. *Psychiatric Clinics of North America, 18*, 25–37.

Tobler, N.S., Roona, M.R., Ochshorn, P., Marshall, D.G., Streke, A.V., & Stackpole, K.M. (2000). School-based adolescent drug prevention programs: 1998 meta-analysis. *Journal of Primary Prevention, 20*, 275–336.

Tripp, J., & Viner, R. (2005). ABC of adolescence: Sexual health, contraception, and teenage pregnancy. *British Medical Journal, 330*, 590–593.

Tschumper, A., Narring, F., Meier, C., & Michaud, P.A. (1998). Sexual victimization in adolescent girls (age 15–20 years) enrolled in post-mandatory schools or professional training programmes in Switzerland. *Acta Paediatrica, 87*, 212–217.

Van Wijk, C.M.T.G., & Kolk, A.M. (1997). Sex differences in physical symptoms: The contribution of symptom perception theory. *Social Science and Medicine, 45*, 231–246.

Veit, F.C., Sanci, L.A., Coffey, C.M., Young, D.Y., & Bowes, G. (1996). Barriers to effective primary health care for adolescents. *Medical Journal of Australia, 165*, 131–133.

Verschuur, R., & Kemper, H.C.G. (1985). The pattern of daily physical activity. In H. C. G. Kemper (Ed.), *Growth, health, and fitness of teenagers: Longitudinal research in international perspective* (pp. 169–185). Basel, Switzerland: Karger.

Victora, C.G., Habicht, J.P., & Bryce, J. (2004). Evidence-based public health: Moving beyond randomized trials. *American Journal of Public Health, 94*, 400–405.

Weaver, C.M., Peacock, M., & Johnston, C.C. Jr. (1999). Adolescent nutrition in the prevention of postmenopausal osteoporosis. *Journal of Clinical Endocrinology and Metabolism, 84*, 1839–1843.

Weisfeld, G.E., & Woodward, L. (2004). Current evolutionary perspectives on adolescent romantic relations and sexuality. *Journal of the American Academy of Child and Adolescent Psychiatry, 43*, 11–19; discussion 20–23.

Westenhoefer, J. (2002). Establishing dietary habits during childhood for long-term weight control. *Annals of Nutrition and Metabolism, 46* (Suppl. 1), 18–23.

Westerstahl, M., Barnekow-Bergkvist, M., Hedberg, G., & Jansson, E. (2003). Secular trends in body dimensions and physical fitness among adolescents in Sweden from 1974 to 1995. *Scandinavian Journal of Medicine and Science in Sports, 13*, 128–137.

World Health Organization (1993). *The European Network of Health Promoting Schools.* Copenhagen, Denmark: World Health Organization.

World Health Organization (1993). *The health of young people.* Geneva, Switzerland: World Health Organization.

World Health Organization (1996). *A picture of health: A review of health and annotated bibliography of the health of young people in developing countries.* Geneva, Switzerland: World Health Organization.

World Health Organization (1999). *Programming for adolescent health and development.* Geneva, Switzerland: World Health Organization.

Wyss, D., Rivier, L., Gujer, H.R., Paccaud, F., Magnenat, P., & Yersin, B. (1990). Characteristics of 167 consecutive traffic accident victims with special reference to alcohol intoxication: A prospective emergency room study. *Sozial- und Präventivmedizin, 35*, 108–116.

Zucker, K.J. (2004). Gender identity development and issues. *Child and Adolescent Psychiatric Clinics of North America, 13*, 551–568, vii.

16

Depression and suicide

Françoise D. Alsaker and Andreas Dick-Niederhauser

LEARNING OBJECTIVES

The aim of this chapter is to contribute to an understanding of the developmental processes that may lead to depression and suicide or suicidal attempts during adolescence. Specifically, we intend to promote readers' knowledge on (1) what adolescent depression is, (2) who is at risk in becoming depressed or in attempting suicide during adolescence, (3) what kind of developmental models of adolescent depression and suicide may be inferred from empirical research, (4) and what conclusions can be drawn for treatment and prevention.

This chapter is divided into three main sections. In the first section we deal with adolescent depression, covering definition, diagnostic classification, epidemiology, and comorbidity, as well as important processes in the etiology of adolescent depression. The second section deals with suicide during adolescence, presenting specific epidemiological data for adolescents, analyzing risk factors and looking at possible pathogenetic processes. In the third section we address the question of how depression and suicide attempts might possibly be prevented and what needs to be taken into account for working efficiently with adolescents with depressive disorders and adolescents who have attempted suicide.

1. Depression in adolescence

In the past, professionals and public opinion held that moodiness was a normal characteristic of adolescence young people would eventually grow out of as they entered adulthood. Adolescent depression began to be considered as being of major clinical importance some decades ago after research evidence pointed to the fact that many adolescents traverse this period of life *without* significant psychological difficulties (Douvan & Adelson, 1966; Offer, 1969), while, contrariwise, depressed adolescents are at an increased risk of developing depressive disorders and other serious psychiatric disorders in adulthood (Harrington, 1993; Merikangas & Angst, 1995; Rutter, 1986; Rutter, Graham, Chadwick, & Yule, 1976; Weiner & DelGaudio, 1976). There is evidence indicating that the prevalence of depression increases dramatically during adolescence (Fleming & Offord, 1990; Rutter, 1986), and that this rise may in certain cases even be associated with biological and social factors specific to puberty or pubertal timing (Brooks-Gunn & Warren, 1989; Stattin & Magnusson, 1990; see also Alsaker & Flammer, this volume).

1.1 Description and diagnostic classification

Depression, especially when occurring in adolescents and children, is viewed as belonging to the group of "internalizing" disorders together with anxiety, eating disorders, social isolation, and problems of low self-esteem. In comparison to "externalizing" disorders such as delinquency, substance abuse, and antisocial behavior internalizing disorders are usually given less attention by laypeople and educators, because they are less obvious and commonly produce less problems for the social environment. Even though depression in childhood and adolescence was not considered as a nosological entity prior to 1960, there exist descriptions of melancholia in children as far back as the middle of the 18th century (Merikangas & Angst, 1995). During the last decades depression in childhood and adolescence has received much research interest, which led to considerable differences between authors in the use of the term. What exactly is juvenile or adolescent depression?

There is general agreement on the fact that, phenomenologically speaking, adolescent depression is similar to adult depression. Depression has been characterized by "emotional emptyness" and a "feeling of flatness" (Harrington, 1993, p. 2), obscuring all perception of oneself and the exterior like a black cloud (Hamilton, 1982). Another central element of depression can be described by the term *anhedonia*, an inability to feel joy and to delight in activities that have previously been a source of pleasure. These phenomenological descriptions make it clear that depression is not identical to sadness or unhappiness, even though depressed individuals may use these terms to describe their state of mind. In the last decades, researchers and practitioners have much emphasized the cognitive features of depression; Beck (1976) postulates a typical cognitive set in depressed patients, consisting of a negative evaluation of oneself, of the world, and of the future. Furthermore, individuals with depression tend to attribute negative events to themselves, viewing their failures as being stable over time and global in validity (Seligman, Peterson, Kaslow, Tannenbaum, Alloy, & Abramson, 1984).

It is important to note that the term *depression* can be used to characterize a multitude of heterogeneous symptoms. Hautzinger (1998) groups these different symptoms into the following five categories:

1. *observable behavior*, such as a limp and drooped posture, a sad and worried facial expression, slow and monotonous speech, restricted movements
2. *emotional symptoms*, such as feeling low, lost, helpless, lonely, empty, guilty, hostile, worried, distanced
3. *physiological symptoms*, such as agitation, tension, irritability, exhaustion, seasonal fluctuations, loss of appetite, weight loss, decrease in sexual drive, general physical complaints
4. *cognitive symptoms*, such as self-depreciation, pessimism, self-consciousness, insecurity, hypochondria, slow thinking, inability to concentrate, constant rumination, delusions, suicidal ideas
5. *motivational symptoms*, such as social isolation and retreat, avoidance of responsibility, expectation of failure, subjective loss of control, lack of reinforcement, dependency on others, suicide.

Depression can be regarded as a construct representing a continuum from normal reactions to negative life events on one pole and extreme emotional states of deep melancholia, total apathy, or suicidal danger on the other pole. Whether or not adolescent depression is of clinical significance is thus dependent on the severity of the symptoms. The problem that many researchers are trying to figure out is where to draw the line between normal depressive reactions and a clinical depression (Angold, 1988).

Harrington (1993) distinguishes between depression as an isolated symptom, which he regards as part of the normal range of human emotional reactions experienced by many people at some time during their lives, and depression as a syndrome, which is usually defined as a combination of depressed mood with certain associated symptoms. Petersen, Compas, Brooks-Gunn, Stemmler, Ey, and Grant (1993) differentiate between three categories of adolescent depression: (1) depressed mood, (2) depressive syndromes, and (3) clinical depression. Depressed mood is identical to Harrington's definition of depression as a symptom. It often occurs together with other negative emotions, such as fear, guilt, anger, contempt, or disgust, but never with happiness (Watson & Kendall, 1989). Petersen et al. (1993) view the depressive syndrome as a constellation of behaviors and emotions consistently occurring together. In contrast to Harrington (1993), Petersen et al. (1993) refer to a depressive syndrome only when criteria for a clinical depression according to the categorization of mental disorders by the American Psychiatric Association (1994; DSM-IV) or by the World Health Organization (1990; ICD-10) are not met. A clinical depression according to DSM-IV and ICD-10 requires not only the presence of an identifiable syndrome but also a significant level of current distress or disability with an increased risk for impairment in the individual's functioning.

According to the DSM-IV, adolescents may be diagnosed as experiencing a major depressive disorder, a dysthymic disorder, or both. *Major depressive disorder* requires the presence of at least one major depressive episode, which is characterized by the presence of at least five of the following symptoms during the same two-week period:

1. depressed or irritable mood most of the day

2. markedly diminished interest or pleasure in almost all activities
3. loss of appetite or increased appetite and corresponding weight changes
4. insomnia or hypersomnia
5. psychomotor agitation or retardation
6. fatigue or loss of energy
7. feelings of worthlessness or excessive or inappropriate guilt
8. diminished ability to think or concentrate
9. recurrent thoughts of death, recurrent suicidal ideation, a suicide attempt, or a specific plan for committing suicide.

Either the first or the second symptom has to be present, and the symptoms have to represent a change from previous functioning.

A *dysthymic disorder* is diagnosed when the adolescent has experienced depressed mood for most of the day for at least one year plus at least two of the following symptoms:

1. poor appetite or overeating
2. insomnia or hypersomnia
3. low energy or fatigue
4. low self-esteem
5. poor concentration or difficulty making decisions
6. feelings of hopelessness.

If adolescents fulfill criteria for dysthymic disorder as well as for major depressive disorder, both may be coded.

The occurrence of depressive symptoms when a loved one dies is considered normal and does not constitute a clinical disorder. If however, the symptoms are not characteristic of a "normal" grief reaction (for example in case of a morbid preoccupation with feelings of worthlessness) the diagnosis of *bereavement* may be given.

Depressive symptoms that do not meet criteria for major depression or dysthymia and develop within three months after the onset of an identifiable psychosocial stressor are diagnosed as *adjustment disorder with depressed mood* or *adjustment disorder with anxiety and depressed mood*.

In spite of these methodological developments the diagnostic classification of depressive disorders in adolescents remains challenging. Depression is now considered a very heterogeneous disorder, combining many different symptoms (Cicchetti & Toth, 1998), and it is increasingly described as a dimension rather than a clear diagnostic category (Groen & Petermann, 2002).

On the basis of a review of the literature on symptoms presented by depressive children and adolescents, Groen and Petermann (2002) came to the conclusion that there were changes in the kind of symptom and the rate to which they were presented before and after puberty. Whereas irritability, somatic complaints, a depressive look, psychomotoric restlessness, separation anxiety could be considered typical in children, symptoms such as anhedonia, feelings of hopelessness, hypersomnia, weight changes, suicidal thoughts and behavior appeared or increased significantly in adolescents.

1.2 Epidemiology and comorbidity

Concerning depressed mood in nonclinical samples Petersen et al. (1993) report figures of 10–20% of nonreferred boys and 15–20% of non-referred girls, who experienced depression in the previous six months based on parents' reports. On the basis of adolescents' self-reports, 20–35% of boys and 25–40% of girls experienced depressed mood. Merikangas and Angst (1995) report percentages varying between 23% and 50% according to eight different community surveys. In a recent representative study conducted among 7428 Swiss adolescents aged 16 through 20 years (Swiss Multicenter Adolescent Survey on Health – SMASH 2002, Narring et al., 2004) 5.6% of boys and 10% of girls were found to be depressive according to an instrument tapping depressive mood, hopelessness, depressive cognitions and thoughts about death (see Alsaker, 1992; Holsen, Kraft & Vitterso, 2000).

Concerning clinical depression Petersen et al. (1993) found an average of 7% clinically depressed adolescents in 14 studies of nonclinical samples. Merikangas and Angst (1995) reported point prevalence rates of major depression to vary between 0.4% and 5.7% in several nonclinical samples. The average six-month prevalence rate (three studies) was 5.1%. Lifetime rates of major depression in adolescents ranged from 1.9% to 18.4%.

Even though these data are rather fragmentary, several preliminary conclusions can be drawn. First, depressed mood is quite common in adolescents, with about every fourth adolescent boy and about every third adolescent girl reporting having experienced depressed mood in the previous six months. Second, parents seem to underestimate depressed mood in their children (or their children tend to overestimate it). Third, in nonclinical samples prevalence rates and lifetime risk of depression for adolescents is comparable to data across all ages, where point prevalence is estimated at about 5% and lifetime risk at about 10% (Hautzinger, 1998). Fourth, in clinical samples of adolescents, depression constitutes a common disorder (Petersen et al., 1993).

As already mentioned, the diagnosis of depressive disorders as well as depressed mood seem to increase dramatically from childhood to adolescence (Fleming & Offord, 1990; Rutter, 1986; Rutter et al. 1976) and this increase seems to be most pronounced during early adolescence (Sund & Wichstrøm, 2002).

In studies using DSM-III criteria, the point prevalence of major depression among children has generally been found to fall in the range of 0.5–2.5% (Harrington, 1993), which is considerably lower than the percentages reported for adolescents (see earlier). The incidence of depression increases continually throughout early adulthood, peaking at the age of 45 to 55 (Lewinsohn, Duncan, Stanton, & Hautzinger, 1986). Harrington (1993) points to the explanation that depression in adolescence might be due to a decrease in protective factors rather than to an increase in risk factors; the reduction of family support during adolescence might make young people more susceptible to stress, or maybe young children are protected from depression by their limited cognitive abilities which protect them from specific negative cognitions that some theorists consider to be crucial in the etiology of depression (see earlier). In the same vein, Galambos, Leadbeater, and Barker (2004) found decreases in social support over a four-year period to be significantly associated with increases in depressive symptoms in adolescents aged 12 to 17 at the first time of measurement. Several authors have shown that increases in depressive disorders and mood seem to be greater for girls than boys during adolescence (Kandel & Davies, 1982; Kashani et al., 1987). Whereas boys show greater rates of depression than girls prior to age 12, a reversal in the sex ratio takes place thereafter (McGee, Feehan, Williams, & Anderson, 1992), which seems to be associated with poorer self-esteem and a more negative body image in girls (Allgood-Merton, Lewinsohn, & Hops, 1990). Girls who mature early are especially at an increased risk of developing depression and other internalizing problems. The latter might be due to the fact that they are less satisfied with their looks (Alsaker, 1992, 1995; Stattin & Magnusson, 1990; see also Alsaker & Flammer, this volume). Furthermore, girls might experience more challenges during puberty, e.g., girls are more likely than boys to go through puberty just before or during the transition to secondary school (Petersen, Sarigiani, & Kennedy, 1991). Studies examining whether the gender difference in adolescent depression might be due to artifacts such as differences in the answering style or in disclosure have concluded that the gender difference indeed appears to be a true effect (e.g. Nolen-Hoeksema, Girgus, & Seligman, 1991; Weissman & Klerman, 1977). Nolen-Hoeksema (1987) found that men and women may have different patterns of reaction or coping styles. Whereas women ruminate on their depressed mood and thus amplify it, men tend to distract themselves. However, the reasons for gender differences in adolescent depression still remain hypothetical, and further research on this topic is certainly needed. It is rather clear, however, that girls are at a higher risk than boys to develop depression in adolescence, and that early-maturing girls are at an especially high risk.

Several epidemiological studies have found that a considerable number of adolescents who experience a depressive disorder also have a comorbid disorder at a rate significantly higher than expected from the base rate and higher than the rate for depressed adults (Essau, Karpinski, Petermann, & Conradt, 1998, report 57.6%;

Lewinsohn, Hops, Roberts, Seeley, & Andrews, 1993, report 42.8%; Rohde, Lewinsohn, & Seeley, 1991, report 42%). Cicchetti and Toth (1998) estimated that 40% to 70% of depressed children and adolescents develop at least one comorbid disorder. The comorbidity in adolescents is highest for anxiety disorders, conduct disorders, eating disorders and substance abuse (Kovacs, 1990; Kovacs, Akiskal, Gatsonis, & Parrone, 1994; Petersen et al., 1993; Rohde et al., 1991). A high incidence of borderline personality disorders has been reported among depressed adolescents and suicide attempters (Clarkin, Friedman, Hurt, Corn, & Aronoff, 1984), and deficits in interpersonal functioning also seem to be associated with depression in adolescence (Hammen, 1991). Since most data referring to comorbidity in depressed adolescents were obtained by cross-sectional and retrospective studies we know only little about the course of development of depressive and other disorders in childhood and adolescence. It was found, however, that anxiety and conduct disorders often precede depressive disorders (Kovacs, Gatsonis, Paulauskas, & Richards, 1989; Last, Hansen, & Franco, 1997; Reinherz, Stewart-Berhauer, Pakiz, Frost, Moeykens, & Holmes, 1989; Rohde et al., 1991), while substance abuse often develops following a depressive disorder (Anderson & McGee, 1994; Deykin, Buka, & Zeena, 1992; Hammen, Burge, Burney, & Adrian, 1990).

1.3 Risk factors and developmental processes

For didactical purposes, it seems reasonable to distinguish between risk factors of adolescent depression and developmental models, even though this distinction is not based on clear-cut theoretical arguments or empirical findings. In order to better understand the developmental processes leading to depression and possibly maintaining it, it is nevertheless necessary to first report the most important associations between depression and biological, psychological and social variables that may be considered risk factors. In the discussion of risk factors, two things should be kept in mind: First, co-occurrence does not mean causality, even if it may suggest it; co-occurrent variables may be causes, mere by-products or consequences of depression; second, co-occurrent variables may help to understand the causes as well as the maintenance of depressive disorders.

1.3.1 Risk factors

1.3.1.1 Biological and genetic factors

These seem to play a certain role in adolescent depression. It has been shown that affective disorders tend to run in families (Andreasen, Endicott, Spitzer, & Winikur, 1977; Weissman, Leaf, Holzer, Myers & Tischler, 1984), and identical twins were found to be four to five times more likely than fraternal twins to show concordance for major depression (Kendler, Heath, Martin, & Eaves, 1986; Wender, Kety, Rosenthal, Schulsinger, Ortmann, & Lunde, 1986). There is, however, no clear evidence so far that biological dysregulation in hormones occurs with depressive episodes (Shelton, Hollon, Purdon, & Loosen, 1991; Dahl et al., 1991). The genetic factor has generally proved to be far less important in unipolar than in bipolar depression (Merikangas & Angst, 1995); neither the onset nor the maintenance of depressive symptoms can be explained by heritability to any large extent, suggesting that psychological and social factors probably play a more important role.

1.3.1.2 Family

Children of depressed parents are at a considerably higher risk of developing a depressive disorder themselves than children of non-depressed parents (Downey & Coyne, 1990). This risk increases when both parents are afflicted by an affective disorder (Merikangas, Prussoff, & Weissman, 1988), when the parent's depression manifested early (Neumann, Geller, Rice, & Todd, 1997; Weissman, Gammon, John, Merikangas, Prusoff, & Sholomskas, 1987), when it showed a high level of severity and was comorbid with other disorders, and finally when it showed a relapsing development (Mufson, Weissman, & Warner, 1992; Warner, Mufson, & Weissman, 1995). There is greater covariance between parents' and their offspring's depressive

symptoms in girls than in boys (Boyle & Pickles, 1997; Davies & Windle, 1997). However, depression in parents is more strongly associated with anxiety disorders than with depression in their offspring (Merikangas & Angst, 1995). Several factors have been made responsible for this transmission of depressive disorders from parents to their children:

1. *genetic predisposition* and *biological vulnerability*
2. *emotional unavailability* of depressed parents (e.g., Cicchetti & Toth, 1998) and low satisfaction of their children's needs, thereby affecting the child's attachment to his or her parents. For example, Sund and Wichstrøm (2002) found that adolescents' insecure attachment to their parents (using the scale described in Armsden & Greenberg, 1987) seems to be a risk factor for future depressive symptoms in early adolescence
3. *low parenting competencies* and dysfunctional parent–child interactions (depressed mothers being more likely to severely punish their children and to show inconsistent patterns of interaction with their children (Cohen, Brook, Cohen, Velez, & Garcia, 1990; Holmes & Robins, 1988; Parker, 1979))
4. *family discord*, marital conflicts, and other stressful events and experiences within the family system such as divorce, rejection and abuse (Angold, 1988; Angst, Vollrath, Merikangas, & Ernst, 1990; Downey & Coyne, 1990).

1.3.1.3 Peers

To be treated unlovingly by parents is considered a major risk factor in adolescent depression; to be unpopular with peers, however, has hardly been a topic in depression research. In a nonclinical sample, Jacobsen, Lahey, and Strauss (1983) found low peer popularity to be related to depressed mood. Poor peer relations in adolescence are one of the strongest predictors of adult disorder (Sroufe & Rutter, 1984). Rejection by peers and victimization have also been shown to correlate with self-derogation and depression (Alsaker, 2003; Alsaker & Olweus, 2002). Alsaker

(2000) also found that depressed adolescents more often reported being rejected and isolated by peers, making more negative experiences with peers, believing less in their ability to control the outcome of peer conflicts, and feeling uncomfortable in peer groups. However, the same depressed adolescents also reported having a best friend just as often as non-depressed adolescents did, and they rated the quality of their relationships with friends just as favorable, which suggests that the reported negative experiences of depressed adolescents with their peers are not only the result of a depressive cognitive distortion, because then the quality of friendships would also have been rated to be poor. Depressive adolescents thus seem to distinguish strongly between dyadic relations with friends, which they find to be agreeable, and being in peer groups, which seems problematic for them.

1.3.1.4 Activities

In accordance with these findings, depressed adolescents have also been found to be significantly less active socially, e.g. going out less often, more often reporting just "hanging out", spending more time watching television on weekends, and spending more time daydreaming (Alsaker, 2000). This finding is compatible with Lewinsohn's (1974) theory of depression, assuming that depressed individuals experience little social reinforcement to a large extent because they do not engage in behavior that leads to pleasant consequences, which may result from a lack of social skills necessary to obtain rewards.

1.3.1.5 Cognitive factors

These can play an important role in the development and maintenance of depressive symptoms. As postulated by different cognitive theories of depression in adults (Beck, 1967; Nezu & Ronan, 1985; Seligman, Abramson, Semmel, & von Baeyer, 1979), many studies with normal and clinical samples of children and adolescents confirmed specific dysfunctional cognitive patterns including internal, global and stable negative attributions, negative self-evaluations, poor self-control beliefs, helplessness, a lack of problem-solving competencies, and negative cog-

nitions in regard to social relationships (Groen & Petermann, 1998). A few longitudinal studies were able to show that negative cognitions can indeed predict depressive symptoms or a depressive episode in adolescence (Cole, Martin, & Powers, 1997; Hammen, Burge, Daley, Davila, Paley, & Rudolph, 1995; Lewinsohn, Gotlib, & Seeley, 1995; Nolen-Hoeksema, Girgus, & Seligman, 1992; Robinson, Garber, & Hilsman, 1995).

1.3.1.6 Temperament

Longitudinal studies from normal and risk samples show that temperamental features predict the subsequent development of psychopathology (Graham, Rutter, & George, 1973; Prior, 1992; Thomas & Chess, 1982). Children of mentally ill parents with high-risk temperamental attributes have been found to be twice as likely to develop a psychiatric disturbance as temperamentally easy children (Rutter & Quinton, 1984). However, to date there is very little research on temperamental characteristics of children and adolescents with depressive disorders. An examination of six cases of depression in the 133 subjects of the New York Longitudinal Study (Chess, Thomas, & Hassibi, 1983) revealed no significant influence of the child's temperament on the development of major depression (two cases), but all three cases of dysthymic disorder and the one case of adjustment disorder with depressive mood showed extreme scores on temperamental traits (persistence, distractibility and short attention span, or difficult temperament). Subsequent analyses suggested that there might be indirect mechanisms linking difficult temperament to a predisposition of depression, for example, through behavior that increases the likelihood of adverse reactions of others. Given the very small number of cases these results should be interpreted with great caution.

1.3.1.7 Pubertal changes

It has already been noted that the rise of depression in early adolescence might be associated with the numerous biological, psychological and social changes occurring during puberty, and that early-developing girls are at a higher risk of developing a negative body image, negative self-esteem or a depressive disorder.

1.3.1.8 Early adverse experiences and life events

According to attachment theory (Bowlby, 1980), insecure attachment to the mother in infancy is likely to predispose individuals to become depressed when experiencing stressful life events later in their life. Especially early separation from and loss of the mother are thought to be linked to depressive disorders in adolescence and adulthood. Despite a large number of studies examining the association between early loss and later depression, the findings are ambiguous (Crook & Elliot, 1980; Granville-Grossman, 1968; Paykel, 1982). Parker (1992) assumes that the decisive variable is *lack of care* instead of separation or loss. Several studies confirmed that the effect of loss of mother on later depression seems to be dependent on family disruption, parental attitudes and continued vs. interrupted support (Bifulco, Brown, & Harris, 1987; Brown, Harris, & Bifulco, 1986; Quinton, Rutter, & Liddle, 1984; Rodgers, 1990), thus suggesting that depression is probably mediated largely through psychosocial adversities that follow the loss. Many other specific adverse experiences in childhood have been studied with regard to the etiology of later depression, e.g. bereavement, parental divorce, natural disasters, academic problems, physical and sexual abuse. There are obviously marked individual variations in children's responses to these experiences, and the majority of children who experience an adverse event will not develop a depressive disorder. However, this does not mean that adverse experiences may not play an important role in the development of depressive disorders in adolescents, but there is probably little specificity in the association of adverse experiences and adolescent depression (Harrington, 1993; Wilde, Kienhorst, Diekstra, & Wolters, 1992). Daily stressors such as conflicts with peers, parental restrictions, etc. seem to reinforce the association between stressful life events and depression and possibly weaken coping resources (Compas, Howell, Phares, Williams, & Ledoux, 1989; Wagner, Compas, & Howell, 1988).

1.3.2 Pathways to adolescent depression

Even though there is a large body of findings on associations between risk factors and depression, there is no consensus on any integrative model of the development of depression during adolescence. It was found that depression tends to be most stable over time for individuals who received a diagnosis of depression early in their life, whose depression co-occurs with some other mental disorder, or who show recurrent episodes of depression (Merikangas & Angst, 1995). However, answers to the question of why certain adolescents develop a depressive disorder and why others remain healthy even though they may be exposed to serious risk factors still remain very hypothetical.

Many risk factors of adolescent depression are unspecific in their nature, representing risks for different psychological occurrences in childhood and adolescence. Up to now, no specific causes of depression have been identified, and, as stated by Cicchetti and Toth (1998), single factors can rarely be conceived as resulting in depression. Petersen et al. (1993) distinguish three kinds of pathways leading to depression in adolescents: (1) environmental events trigger biological dysregulation that leads to depression; (2) a series of stressful environmental and biological events and processes closely related to each other lead to depression; (3) chronic or extreme stress becomes overwhelming for the individual, thus leading to depression. Apart from these *causal* pathways, there are also processes *maintaining* a once established depressive disorder. Another conceptual distinction has been made by distinguishing *predisposing* factors and processes of depression making an individual vulnerable to mental disorders and *precipitating* events and processes leading to a manifest depressive disorder.

The last distinction is based on the concept of *vulnerability*, which has been an important issue in research on the effects of life stress in children and adolescents, and which is closely related to the concept of *resilience*. Seligman and Peterson (1986) proposed that neither individual characteristics (in their model: attributional style) nor external events alone can lead to helplessness and depression, but that only their *co-occurrence* may result in a manifest depressive disorder. According to this view, predisposing vulnerability factors increase the risk of a disorder in the presence of factors such as adverse life events; however, they are negligible when the precipitating events are absent.

The concepts of vulnerability and resilience have been criticized for their implication of a linear cause–effect model of psychopathology and the neglect of reciprocal interactions between individual and environment (Cicchetti & Schneider-Rosen, 1984, 1986). Apart from these more general and abstract models of vulnerability and resilience, there are two major models of depression in young people that have gained considerable empirical support and that make assumptions about specific mental and environmental processes and their relationship to the development of juvenile depression: cognitive–behavioral models and family systems models.

The *cognitive–behavioral models* include Seligman's attribution theory of depression (Abramson, Seligman, & Teasdale, 1978; Seligman, 1975), Beck's cognitive theory (Beck, 1976), and Lewinsohn's lack of positive reinforcement theory of depression (Lewinsohn, 1974).

According to Seligman (Abramson et al., 1978), the belief that the cause of a bad event is stable leads to the chronic feeling of helplessness as well as to hopelessness in regard to the future; the global and internal attribution leads to feelings of self-devaluation and in consequence to a low self-esteem. Attribution style could possibly provide an explanation for the increased rates of depression during early adolescence and the sex differences appearing at the same time; only older children seem to display situation-specific learned helplessness, whereas younger children under the age of 7 have not been found to attribute their failures to global and stable personality traits (Dweck & Elliot, 1983; Rholes, Blackwell, Jordan, & Walters, 1980). However, it has also been found that among children aged 9 to 13 years, girls reported significantly more depressive symptoms, but only slightly more internal attributions for bad events than boys (Seligman & Peterson, 1986), suggesting that the sex differences in juven-

ile depression may not be explained by differences in attributional style. Most studies examining the relationship between depressive symptoms and attributional styles in children and adolescents point to the conclusion that a negative attributional style may be a state-dependent symptom of depression rather than a trait-like predisposition (Harrington, 1993). At the same time and in seeming contradiction to these findings, there is considerable evidence that the attributional style is of familial origin, children's self-critical remarks being strongly related to maternal criticism (Jaenicke et al., 1987; Seligman & Peterson, 1986). Other studies have also confirmed Beck's view of an association between negative cognitive biases and depression in young people (self-punitive bias; lower self-esteem, less recall of positive experiences, more negative self-evaluations; Kaslow, Rehm, & Siegel, 1984; Kazdin, French, Unis, Esveldt-Dawson, & Sherick, 1983; Kendall, Stark, & Adam, 1990; McCauley, Mitchell, Burke, & Moss, 1988).

Attributional style and other cognitive biases of depressive adolescents are possibly being transmitted early on within the family setting and increase children's and young people's risk of getting depressed when encountering adverse situations such as peer rejection and harassment or parental rejection. Dysfunctional schemata and the cognitive bias associated with them become activated when adolescents experience negative social events and acute stress. At the same time, when being activated by external events, dysfunctional schemata act as a trigger of a depressive episode, representing an internal stressor. Once activated, a depressive explanatory style and the cognitive bias can play an important role in the maintenance of symptoms, independent of what came first, depression or the cognitive bias.

According to this view, the young child is assumed to construct mental representations of the self and of others – so-called "inner working models" (Bowlby, 1969) or "representations of interactions generalized" (Stern, 1977) – through the interaction with parents, peers and other people. Two sets of representations are assumed to develop in close complementarity, representations of the self and representations of the "others". When, for example, children experience rejection from their caregivers, they will be likely to construct a working model of a worthless self (Bretherton, 1990; Bretherton & Munholland, 1999). If through later experiences, the self-devaluating set of this working model is being activated, the individual is likely to respond with feelings of depression.

Especially adolescents with low social competencies seem to be at an elevated risk of activating such depressive cognitive–emotional schemata, since they often receive negative feedback from others and are more likely to lose social support (Adams & Adams, 1991; Cole, 1991; Patterson & Capaldi, 1990; Wilson & Cairns, 1988). According to Lewinsohn's theory of depression (Lewinsohn, 1974), individuals with low social competencies are likely to experience a lower rate of positive reinforcements, which may result in depression. As a consequence of the depressive symptoms that are being transmitted to others through the nonverbal and verbal behavior of depressed individuals, other people tend to withdraw and thus consolidate this vicious circle. Depressed adolescents are already more likely than others to feel rejected, independent of the cause of their depressive state, and they explain the experienced rejection in internal, stable and global terms. On such a basis, these adolescents have no reason to believe that a relationship could be rewarding at any point and thus they show little motivation to engage in peer relationships (Alsaker, 2000).

From the viewpoint of *family systems theory* depression is regarded as a result of dysfunctional maintenance of the family equilibrium. The depressed individual merely represents the weakest element of a family system, which works according to rules that, due to their rigidity, no longer permit an efficient and well-adaptive development of all family members. For example, in families with "enmeshed" boundaries with little differentiation between family members, the adolescent may not be allowed to freely develop his or her autonomy and may thus become depressed in order to maintain the myth of family unity (e.g. Oster & Caro, 1990). Empirical studies investigat-

ing family environments of children and adolescents found that depressive symptoms and other psychiatric disorders were associated with the number of conflicts with the parents (Forehand, Neighbors, & Wierson, 1991), a lack of parents' supportiveness, and "enmeshed" family boundaries (Stark, Humphrey, Crook, & Lewis, 1990).

Systems theory has been criticized for not providing a complete model of depression, because it neglects the emotional or intrapsychic aspect of depression (Harrington, 1993). The construct of "inner working models" could provide the missing link between intrapsychic experiences of the individual and a systemic perspective of the family: an "enmeshed" family system at the point of manifestation of a depressive disorder might correspond to certain types of emotional experiences in early childhood, which are partly responsible for the development of cognitive and emotional representations in the child and that become activated in adolescence when the developmental task of autonomy collides with the rules of the family system (for research evidence linking attachment to depression, see Cole-Detke & Kobak, 1996; Fonagy et al., 1996; Rosenstein & Horowitz, 1996).

When examining possible pathways to adolescent depression, the processes that maintain a depressive disorder are just as important as those that cause it. For aggressive and antisocial behavior it was found that bullies very often show delinquent behavior from childhood up to young adulthood (Olweus, 1991), suggesting that the behavior of bullies can be seen as part of an aggressive or antisocial personality orientation. For depression, too, it seems likely that a depressive personality orientation develops if the recurrent feedback loops between negative self-perceptions, social withdrawal, adverse and rejecting behavior by others and subsequent confirmation of negative self-evaluations are not interrupted through protective factors such as social support, close friendships, or through professional help. The social withdrawal of depressed adolescents can be seen primarily as a consequence of their biased perceptions, suggesting that depressed individuals regulate their behavior in terms of minimization of pain rather than maximization of pleasure (Alsaker, 2000).

1.3.3 An integrative model of the development of depression in adolescence

In our view, a general model of adolescent depression should take into account five distinct types of process that are more or less closely related to each other:

1. *inherited temperament* and *predisposing factors of depression*, which are partly responsible for interactions between the child and her/his primary caregivers and significant others (thus affecting his or her self-representations)
2. *environmental factors*, especially relationships to family members and peers (including experiences of victimization) as well as important life events, early adverse experiences and chronic stress that determine what kind of representations of self and others the child develops
3. the *continuous influence* of these representations on behavior, thus establishing a vicious circle of dysfunctional schemata, problematic behavior (e.g., social withdrawal, subordination), negative reactions of others (e.g., rejection and exclusion), and confirmation of the negative self-schemata
4. *later life events* and *acute stress* acting as triggers of depression or depressive mood, leading to the activation of the cognitive–emotional–motivational schemata responsible for the display of the well-known symptoms of depression (simultaneously activating neurobiological processes in the brain)
5. the *maintenance of depressive symptoms* through further social withdrawal and self-fulfilling prophecies, thus (possibly) leading to a depressive personality orientation (see Alsaker, 2000) and a chronic development of recurrent depressive episodes (see Figure 16.1).

This model explains why some adolescents who are exposed to serious risk factors never become depressed, because they either did not develop negative self-representations through childhood (process 2), or they had enough social skills or social support to compensate for their vulnerability (process 3), or they have learned to counter the activation of negative schemata by helpful coping strategies (process 5) (see also Garmezy, 1985). The model might eventually also be able to explain why many risk factors associated with adolescent depression are not specific for depression: life events and acute stress are not depression specific, but simply activate the underlying depressive schemata. Accordingly, we would assume that these self-schemata and the appraisal processes associated with them are indeed specific to depression and that they are responsible for what kind of disorder an individual eventually manifests (Epstein, 1987; Greenberg, Rice, & Elliott, 1993; Lazarus, 1991).

This general model can serve as a framework for many different individual paths to depression in adolescence and might explain why some adolescents become deeply depressed and commit suicide (see later), while others experience only a passing tinge of depressive mood. We would assume clinical forms of depression to be associated with stable negative "working models" about oneself and the world, while depressive mood due to external events in its milder forms does not involve a long history of negative self-perception with the development of dysfunctional self-schemata. A recent epidemiological study in Switzerland would seem to support this view (Steinhausen & Metzke, 2000).

2. Suicide in adolescence

Suicide and suicidal behavior can be defined as a preoccupation or an act that aims to inflict death to oneself. However, many suicides or suicide attempts in adolescence are not motivated by a wish to die, but rather to express feelings of despair, hopelessness or anger. Suicidal behavior is usually divided into three categories:

1. *suicidal ideation*, referring to cognitions ranging from the thought that life is not worth living through concrete plans for killing oneself to an intense delusional preoccupation with self-destruction

FIGURE 16.1

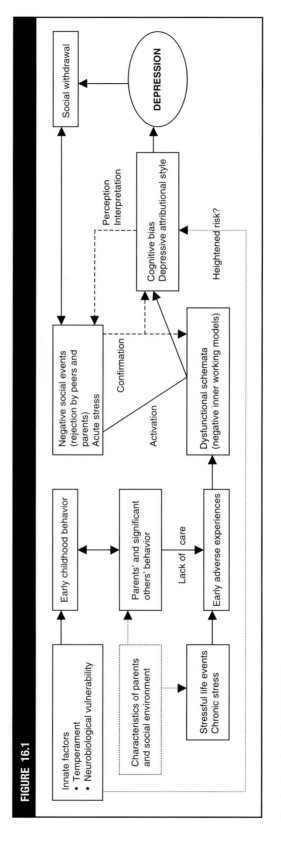

Developmental model of depression.

2. *parasuicide* (attempted suicide), referring to any deliberate, nonhabitual act with nonfatal outcome that (without the intervention from others) might cause or actually causes self-harm

3. *suicide*, referring to any death that is the direct or indirect result of an act accomplished by an individual, knowing or believing that the act will lead to one's death (Diekstra, 1995).

Indirect suicide such as high risk taking in road traffic is thought by some authors to be particularly common in adolescence and young adulthood (Farberow, 1980). Research tends to support the notion of a continuity between youth suicidal ideation, parasuicide, and suicide (Brent et al., 1988).

2.1 Epidemiology

Suicide rates in adolescence vary considerably between countries. In Europe, Finland has the highest suicide rates for adolescents between the age of 15 and 24, followed by New Zealand, Switzerland and Austria. The Netherlands, the United Kingdom, Italy, and Spain have relatively low suicide rates (Cantor, Neulinger, & De Leo, 1999; Platt, Bille-Brahe, & Kerkhof, 1992). The WHO/Euro Multicentre Study on Parasuicide established average European prevalence rates of 165.5 per 100,000 for males and 284.4 per 100,000 for females in young people aged between 15 and 24 for the years 1989–1992 (Bille-Brahe & Schmidtke, 1995).

It is a well-established fact that suicide rates increase during adolescence (e.g., Seroczynski, Jacquez, & Cole, 2003) and that suicide in childhood under the age of 10 is very rare. The rate of parasuicide compared to suicide varies greatly according to different studies with a broad range in the estimates of the ratio of suicide attempts to completed suicides in youths from 10:1 to 220:1 (Cairns & Cairns, 1994). In Switzerland, Narring, et al. (2004) found that 1.6% of adolescent males (16–20 years) and 3.44% of same-age females reported a suicide attempt in the previous 12 months. Also, 3.2% of males and 8.2% of females reported at least one suicide attempt in their life.

Part of the discrepancy in reported rates of suicide and suicide attempts between studies may be due to differences in males and females in the ratio of attempted to completed suicide. Kosky (1982) found a sharp differential age-related increase in suicide rates among boys and girls under the age of 15 admitted to all Western Australian government hospitals with a diagnosis of attempted suicide between 1969 and 1978. The rates for girls showed a dramatic rise after the age of 12 years. The male to female ratio in rate of suicide attempts was 1:3.6, but the male to female ratio in rate of completed suicides was 3:1. This sex difference between attempted and completed suicide is generally explained by the use of more violent or lethal suicidal actions among boys than among girls.

There has been a real increase in suicide risk among the white urban adolescents and young adults of Europe and North America over the past two decades. Furthermore, there is a significant difference in trends between the sexes over the period 1970 to 1986. In most countries suicide rates for males increased in all age groups. The increase was most pronounced in adolescents and young adults (with a mean change of +70%). In the majority of countries the increase was less pronounced among females than males (with a mean change of +40%; Diekstra, 1995). Similar findings are reported in Australia for the period between 1964 and 1997 (Cantor et al., 1999).

Bille-Brahe and Schmidtke (1995) identified a subgroup of adolescent with parasuicidal repetitions within a short period of time (at least two suicide attempts within 12 months) of about 19 percent for both boys and girls between the age of 15 to 24. This subgroup (repeated suicide attempts) also seems to have become larger during the last 15 years, at least for Germany.

How can the increase of parasuicide and suicide in adolescence compared to childhood be explained? And what might be the reasons for an increase in suicides in young adults over the past 20 years? Some of the answers to these questions will become clearer when we take a closer look at the risk factors for suicide and suicide attempts in adolescence.

2.2 Risk factors

Depression is considered one of the major risk factors for suicide in adolescence with recent studies showing a significant higher rate of depression in suicide attempters when compared to nonsuicidal adolescents (Brent, 1993; Brent, Perper, Moritz, Baugher, Schweers, & Roth, 1994; Laederach, Fischer, Bowen, & Ladame, 1999; Seroczynski et al., 2003). A high proportion of suicide attempters are actually found to be depressed (Rotheram-Borus & Trautman, 1988; Spirito, Overholser, Ashworth, Morgan, & Benedict-Drew, 1988). However, affective disorders alone are not sufficient, *comorbidity* seems to be an important factor in adolescent suicide. Pawlak, Pascual-Sanchez, Raë, Fischer, and Ladame (1999) found adolescents with anxiety disorders who developed a major depression to be at a high risk for suicide attempts. Of 24 patients aged 15 to 20 years with anxiety disorders who attempted suicide, 21 (95%) fulfilled criteria for associated major depression, compared to five out of 21 (24%) patients with anxiety disorders who had not attempted suicide. In a study by Lewinsohn, Rohde, and Seeley (1995), the diagnoses with the strongest association with suicide attempts were combinations of depressive disorder with substance use, disruptive behavior, or anxiety. Another strong correlation exists between affective disorders, attempted suicide, and borderline personality disorder (Clarkin et al., 1984; Crumley, 1979).

Nock and Kazdin (2002) have argued that cognitive factors associated with depression are of greater importance than the affective dimension of depression in predicting suicide-related outcomes in children and young adolescents (psychiatric inpatients aged 6 through 13 years). Controlling for depressed mood, they could show that negative automatic thoughts, hopelessness about the future and anhedonia were closely related to suicidal thoughts, intentions, and behaviors.

Even though suicide in adolescence can often be linked to depression, as shown earlier, the stereotype of the withdrawn and inward turning suicidal adolescent fails to capture a large proportion of suicidal adolescents. Shaffer (1974, 1985), who analyzed all suicides that occurred among children aged 16 years and younger in England and Wales between 1958 and 1970, found that two-thirds of the suicides were characterized by acting-out problems. This points to an important cluster of risk factors of adolescent suicide: *behavior problems, especially aggressive and assaultive behavior, low tolerance for stress and frustration*, and *impulsivity*.

Kashden, Fremouw, Callahan, and Franzen (1993), who compared nonsuicidal and suicidal adolescent psychiatric inpatients to community high school students, found suicidal inpatients to be characterized by greater impulsivity, hopelessness, and depression than both nonsuicidal inpatients and high school students. Cairns and Cairns (1994) found a history of prior acting-out, impulsive, and aggressive behaviors in many adolescents with suicidal ideation. The pathway for these adolescents often lead from acting-out behavior via substance abuse to suicidal actions. In a study with 800 extremely aggressive adolescents up to 18 years of age, Cairns, Peterson, and Neckerman (1988) found 13.2% of the subjects to report suicide attempts. Certain subgroups were considerably more vulnerable to suicide attempts than others: Among white females in the 14–15 age group, 39% had attempted to kill themselves!

The changes in alcohol consumption (measured in liters of pure alcohol) have been found to have the highest single correlation (0.70) with change in suicide rates in selected European countries over the period from 1960 to 1985 (Diekstra, 1995). This points to the increasing emergence of a pattern of behavior in adolescents involving the *use or abuse of psychoactive substances* to cope with life problems and depressive reactions. The incidence of suicide and parasuicide has been shown to be particularly high among psychoactive substance abusers (Kirkpatrick-Smith, Rich, Bonner, & Jans, 1992; Miles, 1978; Rich, Sherman, & Fowler, 1990). The role of substance abuse in the increase of suicidal behaviors may, however, be restricted to young men. Gould, Shaffer, and Davies (1991), in a case control study of teenage suicides, found that 37% of the male suicides were associated with a substance abuse disorder (as compared to 7% of the normal group), whereas only 5% of the female suicides had such a disorder (as compared to 7% of the normal group).

Cairns and Cairns (1994) suggest three different reasons for an association between externalizing problem behavior and suicide:

1. Suicide and aggression are both manifestations of poor impulse control. Poor impulse control and low tolerance for stress and frustration can lead to self-directed harm (suicide) and aggressive behavior towards others depending in part on social issues.
2. Aggressive juveniles or those with conduct disorders are more likely to act out their impulses when they are depressed, frustrated or fearful. They have a lower threshold than their less aggressive peers to react with self-destructive actions.
3. Aggressive behavior may be a reflection of irritability accompanying an agitated depression. The symptoms of depression might not be properly recognized by clinicians in assaultive juveniles, because their aggressive features are more salient.

Several studies showed that adolescents attempting suicide have extremely *strained relationships with their parents* and exhibit a *difficult family history* with emotional neglect and physical or sexual abuse. Pfeffer (1981a) found the following characteristics in many families of suicidal adolescents: an absence of generational boundaries between the parents of these adolescents and their own parents; dependency conflicts in spousal relationships with parental anger inappropriately displaced onto the children; the parents of these children discourage the autonomy process, thus maintaining the same symbiotic ties to their children as their parents maintain to them. Even though this family environment might seem very close at first sight, parents and children are often emotionally detached from each other, resulting in most young people feeling unloved and unwanted (see also Dundas, 1999: "dysfunctional closeness").

Many studies have confirmed that lack of par-

ental love and support puts adolescents at risk for suicide (Allen, 1987; Asarnow, Carlson, & Guthrie, 1987; Cohen-Sandler, Berman, & King, 1982; Paluszny, Davenport, & Kim, 1991; Paykel, 1989; Pfeffer, 1989; Tishler, McKenry, & Morgan, 1981). Some researchers have even suggested that in certain cases parental rejection goes so far as to encourage the child to commit suicide (Molin, 1986; Pfeffer, 1981b; Rosenkrantz, 1978). Another kind of perceived parental neglect may occur as a result of the death of a parent. Stanley and Barter (1970) reported that a group of 38 hospitalized suicidal adolescents were more likely to have lost a parent before the age of 12 than patients in the nonsuicidal control group. Adolescents who have a parent with an affective disorder, alcohol abuse or suicidal tendencies show a four to five times increased suicide risk compared to other adolescents (Pfeffer, 1989). "Psychological autopsy" studies of juvenile suicide victims, which look for risk factors retrospectively after completed suicide, identified stressors such as disciplinary crises and mental illness in the family (Shaffer, 1974, 1988; Shafii, Carrigan, Whittinghill, & Derrick, 1985). Adolescents who had a history of physical abuse were four times more likely to attempt suicide than adolescents who did not have a history of abuse (Deykin, Alpert, & McNamarra, 1985). In a longitudinal study examining the long-term consequences of sexual abuse during childhood or adolescence, Silverman, Reinherz, and Giaconia (1996) found a particularly elevated level of suicidality among the girls; one-fourth of sexually abused girls had attempted to commit suicide before the age of 21.

In 1989, the United States Department of Health and Human Services issued a report on youth suicide, which found that *gay youths* are two to three times more likely to attempt suicide than heterosexual youths. Homosexual adolescents may comprise up to 30% of completed youth suicides annually (Alcohol, Drug Abuse, and Mental Health Administration, 1989). The increased risk of suicide facing these adolescents may be linked to growing up in a society that teaches them to hide and to hate themselves. Studies comparing homosexually oriented suicide attemptors with nonattemptors highlight social risk factors such as gender nonconformity, early awareness of homosexuality, gay-related stress, victimization by violence, lack of social support, school dropout, family problems, suicide attempts by friends or relatives, and homelessness (see Remafedi, 1999, for a review).

Teenagers with a sad family history with lack of parental support and emotional deprivation may look for another very close companionship with a boyfriend or girlfriend. In some cases the relationship becomes so close that they withdraw from other friends. Doing this, they become very vulnerable if this new love relationship breaks up, and, confronted with their isolation and loneliness as well as the sadness of their relationship history, they may decide in desperation to commit suicide (Davidson, Rosenberg, Mercy, Franklin, & Simmons, 1989; Teicher & Jacobs, 1966). Among adolescents who spontaneously described suicide attempts and suicidal ideas in Cairns' and Cairns' longitudinal study (1994), the rupture of a close relationship was often depicted as a pivotal trigger. According to a study by Diekstra and Kerkhof (1989), adolescents are more vulnerable to *social and interpersonal adversities* than are adults. Adults and adolescents showed a significant difference in estimated probability of suicide under adverse social conditions such as loss of job, break-up of a (love) relationship, unwanted pregnancy and the like. The adolescents and young adults rated the probability that they or others would commit suicide under such circumstances much higher than the older age groups.

A number of reports indicate that adverse social conditions such as unemployment and economic hardship, interpersonal difficulties and losses, parental mental disorders, and physical and sexual abuse have increased over the last three to four decades (Coleman & Husen, 1985; Preston, 1984). It has been suggested that the *breakdown of traditional family group structures and of religious attitudes and social norms* is to be held responsible for the increased availability and acceptability of drugs in industrialized countries and other negative social changes, especially increasing social isolation, resulting in a higher rate of suicide attempts (Diekstra, 1995).

For most people social isolation is in itself an unpleasant situation. In periods when contact with peers and friends is crucial for the development of social competence and self-worth, or at times when a person needs social support to surmount aversive events, social isolation may have detrimental consequences. Also, social isolation may be used as a powerful victimization strategy (Alsaker, 2003; Alsaker & Brunner, 1999). It was mentioned earlier that victimization has been found to correlate with negative self-evaluations and depression (Alsaker & Olweus, 2002). Sometimes the victimization situation is associated with such an experience of hopelessness that the victim commits suicide. An accumulation of suicides following sustained victimization among young adolescents was indeed the reason why the Norwegian government decided to launch a nationwide campaign against bullying in schools in the early 1980s (Olweus, 1993).

In addition, over the past 150 years the average onset of puberty has occurred at an increasingly lower age (see Alsaker & Flammer, this volume), causing a *disjunction of biological and psychosocial development* until the end of the teenage years (Hamburg, 1989). This might pose stresses on some adolescents that exceed their coping abilities and those of their families. Even if this secular acceleration is probably due to a general health increase in the population, we might agree with Diekstra that: "Despite a general rise in standard of living and physical health, it remains doubtful whether the quality of mental life and of social well-being for many adolescents has improved. It also remains doubtful whether adolescents at the lower end of the social continuum today are better off than their peers fifty or a hundred years ago" (1995, p. 238).

It remains controversial whether *suicidal behavior among family members and acquaintances* can be regarded as a risk factor for suicide in adolescence. Brent, Moritz, Bridge, Perper, and Canobbio (1996) and Pfeffer et al. (1997) have concluded that even though there is an impact in terms of increased risk for depression, anxiety, and posttraumatic stress disorder, exposure to suicide among friends and relatives does not result in an increased risk of suicidal behavior. By the same token, Laederach et al. (1999) in their study of 148 adolescents admitted to a hospital after attempting suicide (no control group) have found that more than one-third of their subjects knew a person among family or friends who had attempted suicide. One adolescent in seven had been confronted by a completed suicide of a family member or a friend. An imitation effect has also been observed with models not belonging to family or other immediate social networks, such as celebrities or fictional and non-fictional young people, whose suicide has been highlighted by the media (Diekstra, 1995).

Cairns and Cairns (1994) found *gun availability and ownership* to be startlingly high among teenage males. This gender difference in ownership and availability of firearms accounts for a higher incidence of injury and death in adolescent males.

Also, a *past history of suicidal behavior* has been shown to be a strong predictor of future suicidal behavior in adolescents (Corbitt, Malone, Haas, & Mann, 1996; Lewinsohn, Rohde, & Seeley, 1994; Nock & Kazdin, 2002). Granboulan, Rabain, and Pasquin (1995) examined the outcome of teenage suicide attempts at an average of 11.5 years after the first hospital admission. More than half of the 127 subjects that could be traced, were either unchanged (i.e., the symptoms were the same as in adolescence), or worse (the symptoms were more severe than in adolescence with a lower level of adjustment). Fifteen subjects (12%) had died, only one of them from natural causes, and 39 subjects (31%) had made at least one further suicide attempt. An important finding from the recent Swiss study on adolescent health (Narring et al., 2004) was that around 40% of the adolescents who reported a suicide attempt in their life had already made several suicide attempts. These figures show the importance of juvenile suicide attempt for the development of these young individuals and the need for effective prevention and intervention. The fact that most of the Swiss adolescents who reported a suicide attempt during the last 12 months (70%) had not had any opportunity to talk with someone about their suicidal behavior, demonstrates clearly how important it would be to develop structures that are easily accessible to adolescents in need of help.

With regard to developmental pathways to adolescent suicide and suicidal attempts, we ought to distinguish between *triggers* of suicidal acts, such as the break-up of a friendship, and underlying *causes*, which usually are much more complex and multivariate, even though these two theoretical concepts cannot always be clearly separated empirically. With regard to the underlying causes, we should differentiate more clearly between a *psychopathological perspective* that looks for associations between suicidal behavior and psychological disorders and a *psychosocial perspective* that tries to link important childhood experiences, the family environment, interpersonal relations and other adverse events to suicidality in adolescence. Especially in regards to the latter perspective, much research work remains to be done, since too many suicide studies simply focus on psychopathology. There should be more prospective studies of individual pathways to suicide in adolescence that attempt to identify typical pathways leading to juvenile suicide, parasuicide or suicidal ideation.

3. Considerations for prevention and treatment

What are the implications of the current knowledge on the nature of juvenile depression and suicide for prevention and treatment?

In order to alleviate depressive symptoms many psychiatrists and other physicians use antidepressants in the adolescent population, most commonly selective serotonin re-uptake inhibitors (SSRI). However, a recent analysis by the United States Food and Drug Administration of the published and unpublished data available for SSRI use in children and adolescents indicates that there is evidence of an increased risk of suicidality, including suicidal ideation, suicide attempts, and self-harm events, associated with each of the SSRIs that were evaluated (Mosholder, 2004). The recently published Treatment for Adolescents with Depression Study (TADS, 2004) found that at the completion of therapy fluoxetine was beneficial for the treatment of depression in adolescents with mild to severe symptoms of major depressive disorder. Treatment with fluoxetine plus cognitive–behavioral therapy was more beneficial and decreased suicidal ideation compared with placebo by the end of the treatment period. During therapy with fluoxetine there was, however, an increase in some adverse events such as acts and ideation of suicide, self-harm, and violence. It is generally recognized that medication for the treatment of adolescent depression should be used only in conjunction with psychotherapeutic interventions with inclusion of parents into treatment and careful monitoring for the emergence of suicide ideation and behavior (Kutcher, 2004).

A variety of psychological therapies have shown efficacy in depression in youths, particulary cognitive–behavioral therapy and interpersonal therapy. In cognitive–behavioral therapy, therapists primarily aim at reducing symptoms of sadness and irritability by focusing on how adolescents think and by improving their social skills. One of the best-known cognitive–behavioral approaches for adolescents is the Coping with Depression Course for Adolescents that consists of 16 sessions with a group of teens and a separate group of parents (Clarke, DeBar, & Lewinsohn, 2003; see also Hautzinger, 1998). This approach teaches depressed adolescents to monitor their own mood, to improve social skills, to identify, and engage in pleasant activities, to identify negative thoughts and their cause, to use relaxation effectively during periods of stress, and to improve problem-solving skills.

Although cognitive–behavioral therapy for depression has the most extensive evidence base with children and adolescents, recent evidence suggests that interpersonal psychotherapy for adolescents may also be beneficial (Mufson, Pollack Dorta, Moreau, & Weissman, 2004). This treatment approach focuses on common adolescent developmental issues such as separation from parents, development of peer relationships, and dealing with peer pressure. The program usually lasts between 12 and 15 sessions and consists of three phases. In the first phase, the therapist works with adolescents and their parents to assess relationships and to decide which interpersonal problem areas to focus on. In the second phase, therapist and adolescent work directly on the designated problem areas to induce behavior change.

In the third phase, the adolescent works toward ending the relationships with the therapist and establishing future competence to deal with problems.

In terms of our developmental model of depression (see Figure 16.1), cognitive–behavioral therapy focuses on the cognitive bias of depressed adolescents in interpreting (social) events, on dysfunctional schemata and negative attribution styles as well as on social withdrawal and subsequent peer rejection. Interpersonal therapy, by way of contrast, focuses mainly on the developmental and relational experiences and adverse events that lead up to negative working models and dysfunctional schemata and that help sustain them. According to our model, there is thus reason to believe that it might be beneficial to combine a cognitive–behavioral approach with an interpersonal approach in the treatment of adolescent depression.

Most prevention and early intervention programs for adolescent depression have concentrated on highly selected at-risk samples with the aim of modifying a single risk factor, usually a stressful live event (e.g., parental divorce, death of a parent), or subclinical symptoms of depression (see Dick-Niederhauser & Silverman, 2004, for review). Only relatively few studies have attempted to prevent the incidence of adolescent depression by targeting an entire population that has not been identified on the basis of any risk factor. Australian researchers have dominated this universal prevention approach to depression in youths, most of them using the Penn Prevention Project by Jaycox, Reivich, Gillham, and Seligman (1994), which is based on changing negative explanatory styles, cognitive deficits, dysfunctional attitudes, poor interpersonal problem solving, and low expectations for self-performance. About half of these studies found significant improvements in coping skills, attributional style, and perceived control at the end of the program. Most of these studies, however, did not lead to any significant reduction in depressive symptoms.

According to our developmental model of adolescent depression (Figure 16.1), the young person's social environment (family, peers, school) should be taken into consideration for prevention and early intervention. Cole and Siegel (1990) proposed three levels of service delivery in schools:

1. *primary prevention services* provided to all staff and students by sharing information about issues and resources
2. *secondary prevention services* developed for staff and students at risk
3. *tertiary prevention* and/or *crisis intervention services* designed for staff and students who are experiencing acute difficulties in school.

In the United States and Canada, mutidiscipli-nary "in-school teams" have been in operation for about three decades, designed to support educators in providing appropriate interventions for students in need (e.g., Miezitis, 1992).

Any adolescent who has attempted suicide should be offered treatment. According to Ret-terstøl (1990), the primary health service and the social services should identify suspected or mani-fest mental diseases for treatment in a hospital or by a psychiatrist or psychologist. Ideally, the patient will be referred with his own consent to a crisis intervention center, where a specialist can examine the patient and evaluate what kind of treatment is necessary. It is often necessary to motivate the patient and his family for a psychi-atric or psychological examination and treatment. The period following a suicide attempt is a very good time for reviewing the patient's life situ-ation. Retterstøl (1990) points to the fact that, unfortunately, there often is a massive disparity between the technical apparatus employed to save the patient's life and the apparatus employed to understand his mental background, help him with his problems, and prevent a recurrence.

Even though suicide is among the leading causes of death in adolescents and depression is the most common diagnosis in adolescents who have attempted suicide, little is known about what treatment is best for depressed adolescent suicide attempters since they are usually excluded from participation in research studies. Randomized clinical trials with suicidal patients are difficult to conduct due to clinical and ethical concerns about control groups. Therefore, "treatment as

usual" comparison groups have been proposed as ethically defensible alternatives to control groups. However, treatment as usual for suicidal patients is rarely characterized in clinical trials. Spirito, Stanton, Donaldson, and Boergers (2002) studied treatment as usual in 63 adolescent suicide attempters aged 12 to 19 years. Following a suicide attempt, adolescents reported attending zero to 22 outpatient psychotherapy sessions, with an average of seven sessions, with 52% of the ado-lescents reported attending six or fewer sessions. Supportive psychotherapy techniques were reported by three-fourths of the sample, psycho-dynamic and cognitive techniques by one-half of the sample, and behavioral techniques by one-third of the sample. Results suggest that treat-ment as usual with adolescent suicide attempters is highly variable, both in terms of the number of sessions attended and type of treatment received.

The search for efficacious treatments for ado-lescent suicide attempters is receiving increased scrutiny from public health authorities. The National Institute of Mental Health in the United States is currently recruiting patients for a clinical trial comparing the effects of three types of treatment (antidepressant medication; cogni-tive–behavioral therapy; combination of anti-depressants and cognitive–behavioral therapy) for depressed teenagers who have attempted sui-cide. Katz, Cox, Gunasekara, and Miller (2004) have recently demonstrated preliminary effective-ness for dialectical behavior therapy in a general child and adolescent psychiatric inpatient unit. Sixty-two adolescents with suicide attempts or suicidal ideation were admitted to one of two psychiatric inpatient units. Dialectical behavior therapy significantly reduced behavioral incidents during admission when compared with treatment as usual. Both groups demonstrated highly sig-nificant reductions in parasuicidal behavior, depressive symptoms, and suicidal ideation at one year.

According to Freeman and Reinecke (1993), a major focus of therapy with suicidal adolescents lies in the acceptance of the current restrictions associated with their age, such as, for example, lack of mobility or some legal constraints. This should be especially important for those juvenile suicide attempters who mainly show behavioral problems, aggressive and assaultive behavior, and low tolerance for stress and frustration. As our review has shown, depression is not the only risk factor in adolescent suicide. Behavior problems, impulsivity, low stress tolerance, substance abuse, difficult family relationships, and interpersonal adversities can all contribute to the development of suicidality in teenagers. Gay teenagers are at a particularly high risk of experiencing social rejection from family and peers. All these factors should be taken into consideration when treating adolescent suicide attempters or teenagers with suicidal ideation.

Regarding the prevention of suicide in adolescents, Shaffer and Piacentini (1994) suggest four general approaches: (1) case finding, (2) crisis management, (3) educational programs, and (4) limiting access to potential methods for committing suicide. We will briefly discuss each of these four approaches.

In order to identify high-risk cases, indirect case finding is used in some suicide education programs to train students, teachers, and parents to spot the warning signs of suicide among their classmates, friends, or children. However, teenagers who have received systematic training in case finding are no more likely to recommend treatment to their distressed friends than those who did not (Vieland, Whittle, Garland, Hicks, & Shaffer, 1991). Direct case finding tries to elicit risk status from suicidal teenagers themselves. A number of self-report forms have been developed to identify presuicidal states in teenagers (e.g., adolescent suicide questionnaire; Pearce & Martin, 1994), but their value in predicting suicide-prone teenagers has not yet been sufficiently demonstrated.

Crisis services aim at the psychological ambivalence that arises in the context of mental disturbance prior to a suicide attempt. They are usually provided by so-called telephone hotlines. Empirical evidence suggests that crisis services have no or only very limited effects on suicide rate (Barraclough et al., 1977; Bridge, Potkin, Zung, & Soldo, 1977; Jennings, Barraclough, & Moss, 1978; Miller, Coombs, Leeper, & Barton, 1984), probably because the callers are mostly females, who are at a lower risk for suicide, the quality of the advice given is usually somewhat mediocre, and significant proportions of suicides occur when the victim is in an agitated state in which he or she may not be able to make an appropriate call (Shaffer & Piacentini, 1994).

Educational programs of suicide prevention try to heighten awareness of the problem by giving information about suicide and parasuicide. They promote indirect case finding (see earlier) and disclosure of suicidal ideation, and they provide staff and students with information about the accessibility of mental health resources. However, the overwhelming number of adolescents who are exposed to these programs carry no risk for suicide. In addition, all these educational efforts to reduce suicide rates may make the situation even worse for adolescents at risk and may produce imitation effects. Siegel, Mesago, and Christ (1990) suggest that "high risk" groups such as the children of depressed parents, or children who have just experienced an adverse event, or children who are just about to experience an adverse event such as a bereavement should be targeted specifically. Speaker and Petersen (2000) delineated an integrative model for preventing adolescent suicide and school violence based on a nationwide survey in 15 school districts in the United States. The model addresses each of the five factors that have been found to contribute to school violence and suicide in youths:

1. to counteract the decline in family structure, the family should be included in prevention programs
2. to overcome a lack of school resources and skills in dealing with violence and suicide attempts, changes in teacher and administrator roles are necessary
3. to counteract the breakdown in ethical education of youth, education and teaching should focus on helping student develop a success identity
4. to deal with family violence and adolescent drug use conflict mediation may be helpful
5. to raise students' awareness of violence in the media, the authors suggest improving students visual literacy.

4. Conclusion

Limiting access to suicide methods can prevent suicide in some instances, but often only leads to a transient effect until other methods are more frequently chosen.

"It could be said in a simple way that preventing suicide and attempted suicide involves removing the causes", Retterstøl (1990) concludes. It seems that there has not been enough done to address the actual causes of suicidal actions. This is probably due to the still unsatisfactory knowledge on the developmental pathways leading to suicide. Suicide prevention often aims at reducing depression and hopelessness. However, especially in adolescents, increased attention should be given to young people's social situation and interpersonal problem-solving skills and to how both of these crucial factors in teenagers' lives may be improved.

References

Abramson, L.Y., Seligman, M.E.P., & Teasdale, J.D. (1978). Learned helplessness in humans: Critique and reformulation. *Journal of Abnormal Psychology*, *87*, 49–74.

Adams, M., & Adams, J. (1991). Life events, depression, and perceived problem solving alternatives in adolescence. *Journal of Child Psychology and Psychiatry*, *32*, 811–820.

Alcohol, Drug Abuse, and Mental Health Administration (1989). *Report of the secretary's task force on youth suicide: Risk factors for youth suicide (vol. 2)*. Unpublished manuscript, United States Department of Health and Human Services.

Allen, B.P. (1987). Youth suicide. *Adolescence*, *22*, 271–290.

Allgood-Merton, B., Lewinsohn, P.M., & Hops, H. (1990). Sex differences and adolescent depression. *Journal of Abnormal Psychology*, *99*, 55–63.

Alsaker, F.D. (1992). Pubertal timing, overweight, and psychosocial adjustment. *Journal of Early Adolescence*, *12*, 396–419.

Alsaker, F.D. (1995). Timing of puberty and reactions to pubertal changes. In M. Rutter (Ed.), *Psychosocial disturbances in young people: Challenges for prevention* (pp. 37–82). New York: Cambridge University Press.

Alsaker, F.D. (2000). The development of a depressive personality orientation: The role of the individual. In W. J. Perrig, & A. Grob (Eds.), *Control of human behaviour, mental processes and awareness* (pp. 345–359). Hillsdale, NJ: Lawrence Erlbaum Associates, Inc.

Alsaker, F.D. (2003). *Quälgeister und ihre Opfer. Mobbing unter Kindern – und wie man damit umgeht* [Bullies and their victims. Victimization among children – and how to handle it]. Bern: Huber.

Alsaker, F.D., & Brunner, A. (1999). Switzerland. In P. K. Smith, Y. Morita, J. Junger-Tas, D. Olweus, R. Catalino, & P. T. Slee (Eds.), *The nature of school bullying: A cross-national perspective* (pp. 250–263). London: Routledge.

Alsaker, F.D., & Olweus, D. (2002). Stability and change in global self-esteem and self-related affect. In T. M. Brinthaupt, & R. P. Lipka (Eds.), *Understanding the self of the early adolescent* (pp. 193–223). New York: State University of New York Press.

American Psychiatric Association (1994). *Diagnostic and statistical manual of mental disorders* (4th ed.). Washington, DC: APA.

Anderson, J.C., & McGee, R. (1994). Comorbidity of depression in children and adolescents. In W. M. Reynolds, & H. F. Johnston (Eds.), *Handbook of depression in children and adolescents* (pp. 581–601). New York: Plenum.

Andreasen, N.C., Endicott, J., Spitzer, R.L., & Winikur, G. (1977). Family history method using diagnostic criteria. *Archives of General Psychiatry*, *34*, 1223–1229.

Angold, A. (1988). Childhood and adolescent depression: 1. Epidemiological and aetiological aspects. *British Journal of Psychiatry*, *152*, 601–617.

Angst, J., Vollrath, M., Merikangas, K.R., & Ernst, C. (1990). Comorbidity of anxiety and depression in the Zurich cohort study of young adults. In J. D. Maser, & C. R. Cloninger (Eds.), *Comorbidity of mood and anxiety disorders* (pp. 123–138). Washington, DC: American Psychiatric Press.

Armsden, G.C., & Greenberg, M.T. (1987). The inventory of parent and peer attachment: Individual differences and their relationship to psychological well-being in adolescence. *Journal of Youth and Adolescence*, *16*, 427–454.

Asarnow, J.R., Carlson, G., & Guthrie, D. (1987). Coping strategies, self-perceptions, hopelessness, and perceived family environments in depressed and suicidal children. *Journal of Consulting and Clinical Psychology*, *55*, 361–366.

Barraclough, B.M., Jennings, C., Moss, J.R., Hawton, K., Cole, D., O'Grady, J., & Osborne, M. (1977). Suicide prevention by the Samaritans. *Lancet*, *2*, 237–238.

Beck, A.T. (1967). *Depression: Clinical, experimental and theoretical aspects*. New York: Harper & Row.

Beck, A.T. (1976). *Cognitive therapy and the emotional disorders*. New York: International Universities Press.

Bifulco, A., Brown, G.W., & Harris, T.O. (1987). Childhood loss of parent, lack of adequate parental care and adult depression: A replication. *Journal of Affective Disorders, 12*, 115–118.

Bille-Brahe, U., & Schmidtke, A. (1995). Conduites suicidaires des adolescents: La situation en Europe [Suicidal behaviors in adolescence: The situation in Europe]. In F. Ladame (Ed.), *Adolescents et suicide* (pp. 18–38). Paris: Masson.

Bowlby, J. (1969). *Attachment and loss: Vol. I. Attachment*. London: Hogarth Press.

Bowlby, J. (1980). *Attachment and Loss: Vol. III. Sadness and depression*. New York: Basic Books.

Boyle, M.H., & Pickles, A. (1997). Maternal depressive symptoms and ratings of emotional disorder symptoms in children and adolescents. *Journal of Child Psychology and Psychiatry, 38*, 981–992.

Brendt, D.A., Moritz, G., Bridge, J., Perper, J., & Canobbio, R. (1996). Long-term impact of exposure to suicide: A three-year controlled follow-up. *Journal of the American Academy of Child and Adolescent Psychiatry, 35*, 646–653.

Brent, D.A., Johnson, B., Bartle, S., Bridge, J., Rather, C., Matta, J., et al. (1993). Personality disorder, tendency to impulsive violence, and suicidal behavior in adolescents. *Journal of the American Academy of Child and Adolescent Psychiatry, 32*, 69–75.

Brent, D.A., Perper, J.A., Goldstein, C.E., Kollco, D.J., Allan, M.J., Allman, et al. (1988). Risk factors for adolescent suicide: A comparison of adolescent suicide victims with suicidal inpatients. *Archives of General Psychiatry, 45*, 581–588.

Brent, D.A., Perper, J.A., Moritz, G., Baugher, M., Schweers, J., & Roth, C. (1994). Suicide in affectively ill adolescents: A case-control study. *Journal of Affective Disorders, 31*, 193–202.

Bretherton, I. (1990). Open communication and internal working models: Their role in the development of attachment relationships. In R. A. Thompson (Ed.), *Nebraska symposium on motivation: Vol. 36. Socioemotional development* (pp. 57–113). Lincoln, NE: University of Nebraska Press.

Bretherton, L., & Munholland, K.A. (1999). Internal working models in attachment relationships: A construct revisited. In J. Cassidy, & P. R. Shaver (Eds.), *Handbook of attachment: Theory, research, and clinical applications* (pp. 89–111). New York: Guilford.

Bridge, T.P., Potkin, S.G., Zung, W.W., & Soldo, B.J. (1977). Suicide prevention centers: Ecological study of effectiveness. *Journal of Nervous and Mental Disease, 164*, 18–24.

Brooks-Gunn, J., & Warren, M.P. (1989). Biological and social contributions to negative affect in young adolescent girls. *Child Development, 60*, 40–55.

Brown, G.W., Harris, T.O., & Bifulco, A. (1986). Long-term effects of early loss of parent. In M. Rutter, C. E. Izard, & P. B. Read (Eds.), *Depression in young people: Clinical and developmental perspectives* (pp. 251–296). New York: Guilford.

Cairns, R.B., & Cairns, B.D. (1994). *Lifelines and risks: Pathways of youth in our time*. Cambridge: Cambridge University Press.

Cairns, R.B., Peterson, G., & Neckerman, J.J. (1988). Suicidal behavior in aggressive adolescents. *Journal of Clinical Child Psychology, 17*, 298–309.

Cantor, C.H., Neulinger, K., & De Leo, D. (1999). Australian suicide trends 1964–1997: Youth and beyond? *Medical Journal of Australia, 171*, 137–141.

Chess, S., Thomas, A., & Hassibi, M. (1983). Depression in childhood and adolescence: Prospective study of six cases. *Journal of Nervous and Mental Disease, 171*, 411–420.

Cicchetti, D., & Schneider-Rosen, K. (1984). Toward a transactional model of childhood depression. In D. Chicchetti, & K. Schneider-Rosen (Eds.), *Childhood depression* (New directions for child development, No. 26; pp. 5–27). San Francisco: Jossey-Bass.

Cicchetti, D., & Schneider-Rosen, K. (1986). An organizational approach to childhood depression. In M. Rutter, C. E. Izard, & P. B. Read (Eds.), *Depression in young people: Developmental and clinical perspectives* (pp. 71–134). New York: Guilford.

Cicchetti, D., & Toth, S.L. (1998). The development of depression in children and adolescents. *American Psychologist, 53*, 221–241.

Clarke, G.N., DeBar, L.L., & Lewinsohn, P.M. (2003). Cognitive–behavioral therapy for adolescent depression: Comparative efficacy, mediation, moderation, and effectiveness. In A. E. Kazdin, & J. R. Weisz (Eds.), *Evidence-based psychotherapies for children and adolescents* (pp. 120–134). New York: Guilford.

Clarkin, J.F., Friedman, R.C., Hurt, S.W., Corn, R., & Aronoff, M. (1984). Affective and character pathology of suicidal adolescent and young adult inpatients. *Journal of Clinical Psychiatry, 45*, 19–22.

Cohen, P., Brook, J.S., Cohen, J., Velez, N., & Garcia, M. (1990). Common and uncommon pathways to adolescent psychopathology and problem behavior.

In L. Robins, & M. Rutter (Eds.), *Straight and devious pathways from childhood to adulthood* (pp. 242–258). London: Cambridge University Press.

Cohen-Sandler, R., Berman, A.L., & King, R.A. (1982). A follow-up study of hospitalized suicidal children. *Journal of the American Academy of Child Psychiatry*, *21*, 398–403.

Cole, D.A. (1991). Preliminary support for a competency-based model of depression in children. *Journal of Abnormal Psychology*, *100*, 181–190.

Cole, D.A., Martin, J.M., & Powers, B. (1997). A competency-based model of child depression: A longitudinal study of peer, parent, teacher, and self-evaluations. *Journal of Child Psychology and Psychiatry*, *38*, 505–514.

Cole, E., & Siegel, J. (1990). *Effective consultation in school psychology*. Toronto, Canada: Hogrefe & Huber.

Cole-Detke, H., & Kobak, R. (1996). Attachment processes in eating disorder and depression. *Journal of Consulting and Clinical Psychology*, *64*, 282–290.

Coleman, E.A., & Husen, T. (1985). *Becoming an adult in a changing society*. Paris: OECD.

Compas, B.E., Howell, D.C., Phares, V., Williams, R., & Ledoux, N. (1989). Parent and child stress and symptoms: An integrative analysis. *Developmental Psychology*, *25*, 550–559.

Corbitt, E.M., Malone, K.M., Haas, G.L., & Mann, J.J. (1996). Suicidal behavior in patients with major depression and comorbid personality disorders. *Journal of Affective Disorders*, *39*, 61–72.

Crook, T., & Elliot, J. (1980). Parental death during childhood and adult depression: A critical review of the literature. *Psychology Bulletin*, *87*, 252–259.

Crumley, F.E. (1979). Adolescent suicide attempts. *Journal of the American Medical Association*, *241*, 2404–2407.

Dahl, R.E., Ryan, N.D., Puig-Antich, J., Nguyen, N.A., Al-Shabbout, M., Meyer, V.A. et al. (1991). 24-hour cortisol measures in adolescents with major depression: A controlled study. *Biological Psychiatry*, *30*, 25–36.

Davidson, L.E., Rosenberg, M.L., Mercy, J.A., Franklin, J., & Simmons, J.T. (1989). An epidemiologic study of risk factors in two teenage suicide clusters. *Journal of the American Medical Association*, *262*, 2687–2692.

Davies, P.T., & Windle, M. (1997). Gender-specific pathways between maternal depressive symptoms, family discord, and adolescent adjustment. *Developmental Psychology*, *33*, 657–668.

Deykin, E.Y., Alpert, J.J., & McNamarra, J.J. (1985). A pilot study of the effect of exposure to child abuse or neglect on adolescent suicidal behavior. *American Journal of Psychiatry*, *142*, 1299–1303.

Deykin, E.Y., Buka, S.L., & Zeena, T.H. (1992). Depressive illness among chemically dependent adolescents. *American Journal of Psychiatry*, *149*, 1341–1347.

Dick-Niederhauser, A., & Silverman, W.K. (2004). Prevention and early detection of emotional disorders. In H. Remschmidt, M. L. Belfer, & I. Goodyer (Eds.), *Facilitating pathways: Care, treatment, and prevention in child and adolescent mental health* (pp. 272–286). Berlin: Springer-Verlag.

Diekstra, R.F.W. (1995). Depression and suicidal behaviors in adolescence: Sociocultural and time trends. In M. Rutter (Ed.), *Psychosocial disturbances in young people: Challenges for prevention* (pp. 212–243). New York: Cambridge University Press.

Diekstra, R.F.W., & Kerkhof, A.J.F.M. (1989). Attitudes toward suicide: The development of a suicide attitude questionnaire (SUIATT). In R. F. W. Diekstra, R. Maris, S. Platt, A. Schmidtke, & G. Sonneck (Eds.), *Suicide and its prevention: The role of attitude and imitation* (WHO copublication; pp. 91–107). Canberra, Australia: Leinde.

Douvan, E.A., & Adelson, J. (1966). *The adolescent experience*. New York: John Wiley & Sons.

Downey, G., & Coyne, J.C. (1990). Children of depressed parents: An integrative review. *Psychological Bulletin*, *108*, 50–76.

Dundas, I. (1999). *Functional and dysfunctional closeness: Family interactions and children's adjustment*. Unpublished dissertation, Department of Psychosocial Science, Faculty of Psychology, University of Bergen, Norway.

Dweck, C.S., & Elliot, E.S. (1983). Achievement motivation. In P. H. Mussen, & E. M. Hetherington (Eds.), *Handbook of child psychology: Vol. 4. Socialization, personality, and social development* (4th ed., pp. 643–691). New York: John Wiley & Sons.

Epstein, S. (1987). Implications of cognitive self-theory for psychopathology and psychotherapy. In N. Cheshire & H. Thomae (Eds.), *Self, symptoms, and psychotherapy*. New York: John Wiley & Sons.

Essau, C.A., Karpinski, N.A., Petermann, F., & Conradt, J., (1998). Häufigkeit und Komorbidität psychischer Störungen bei Jugendlichen: Ergebnisse der Bremer Jugendstudie [Frequency and comorbidity of psychological disorders in young people: Results from the Bremen Youth Study]. *Zeitschrift für Klinische Psychologie, Psychiatrie und Psychotherapie*, *46*, 105–124.

Farberow, N.L. (Ed.). (1980). *The many faces of suicide: Indirect self-destructive behaviour.* New York: McGraw-Hill.

Fleming, J.E., & Offord, D.R. (1990). Epidemiology of childhood depressive disorders: A critical review. *Journal of the American Academy of Child and Adolescent Psychiatry, 29,* 571–580.

Fonagy, P., Leigh, T., Steele, M., Steele, H., Kennedy, R., Mattoon, G. et al. (1996). The relations of attachment status, psychiatric classification, and response to psychotherapy. *Journal of Consulting and Clinical Psychology, 64,* 22–31.

Forehand, R., Neighbors, B., & Wierson, M. (1991). The transition to adolescence: The role of gender and stress in problem behavior and competence. *Journal of Child Psychology and Psychiatry, 32,* 929–937.

Freeman, A., & Reinecke, M.A. (1993). *Cognitive therapy of suicidal behavior: A manual for treatment.* New York: Springer-Verlag.

Galambos, N.L., Leadbeater, B.J., & Barker, E.T. (2004). Gender differences in and risk factors for depression in adolescence: A 4-year longitudinal study. *International Journal of Behavioral Development, 28*(1), 16–25.

Garmezy, N. (1985). Stress-resistant children: The search for protective factors. In J. Stevenson (Ed.), *Recent advances in developmental psychopathology.* Oxford: Pergamon.

Gould, M.S., Shaffer, D., & Davies, M. (1991). Truncated pathways from childhood into adulthood: Attrition in follow-up studies due to death. In L. Robins, & M. Rutter (Eds.), *Straight and devious pathways from childhood into adulthood* (pp. 3–9). New York: Cambridge University Press.

Graham, P., Rutter, M., & George, S. (1973). Temperamental characteristics as predictors of behavior disorders in children. *American Journal of Orthopsychiatry, 43,* 328–339.

Granboulan, V., Rabain, D., & Pasquin, M. (1995). The outcome of adolescent suicide attempts. *Acta Psychiatrica Scandinavica, 91,* 265–270.

Granville-Grossman, K.L. (1968). The early environment in affective disorder. In A. Coppen, & A. Walk (Eds.), *Recent developments in affective disorders.* London: Royal Medico-Psychological Association.

Greenberg, L.S., Rice, L., & Elliott, R. (1993). *Facilitating emotional change: The moment to moment processes.* New York: Guilford.

Groen, G., & Petermann, F. (1998). Depression [Depression]. In F. Petermann, M. Kusch, & K. Niebank (Eds.), *Entwicklungspsychopathologie* (pp. 327–361). Weinheim, Germany: Beltz.

Groen, G., & Petermann, F. (2002). *Depressive Kinder und Jugendliche* [Depressive Children and Adolescents]. Göttingen, Germany: Hogrefe.

Hamburg, D. (1989). Preparing for life: The critical transition of adolescence. In R. W. F. Diekstra (Ed.), *Preventive interventions in adolescence* (pp. 4–15). Toronto, Canada: Hogrefe & Huber.

Hamilton, M. (1982). Symptoms and assessment of depression. In E. Paykel (Ed.), *Handbook of affective disorders* (pp. 3–11). Edinburgh: Churchill Livingstone.

Hammen, C. (1991). *Depression runs in families.* New York: Springer-Verlag.

Hammen, C., Burge, D., Burney, E., & Adrian, C. (1990). Longitudinal study of diagnoses in children of women with unipolar and bipolar affective disorders. *Archives of General Psychiatry, 47,* 465–474.

Hammen, C.L., Burge, D., Daley, S.E., Davila, J., Paley, B., & Rudolph, K.D. (1995). Interpersonal attachment cognitions and prediction of symptomatic responses to interpersonal stress. *Journal of Abnormal Psychology, 104,* 436–443.

Harrington, R. (1993). *Depressive disorder in childhood and adolescence.* Chichester: John Wiley & Sons.

Hautzinger, M. (1998). *Depression* [Depression] (Fortschritte der Psychotherapie. Manuale für die Praxis, Vol. 4). Göttingen, Germany: Hogrefe.

Holmes, S.J., & Robins, L.N. (1988). The role of parental disciplinary practices in the development of depression and alcoholism. *Psychiatry, 51,* 24–36.

Holsen, I., Kraft, P., & Vitterø, J. (2000). Stability in depressed mood in adolescence: Results from a 6-year longitudinal panel study. *Journal of Youth and Adolescence, 29,* 61–78.

Jacobsen, R.H., Lahey, B.B., & Strauss, C.C. (1983). Correlates of depressed mood in normal children. *Journal of Abnormal Child Psychology, 11,* 29–39.

Jaenicke, C., Hammen, C., Zupan, B., Hiroto, D., Gordon, D., Adrian, C. et al. (1987). Cognitive vulnerability in children at risk for depression. *Journal of Abnormal Child Psychology, 15,* 559–572.

Jaycox, L.H., Reivich, K.J., Gillham, J., & Seligman, M.E.P. (1994). Prevention of depressive symptoms in school children. *Behaviour Research and Therapy, 32,* 801–816.

Jennings, C., Barraclough, B.M., & Moss, J.R. (1978). Have the Samaritans lowered the suicide rate? A controlled study. *Psychological Medicine, 8,* 413–422.

Kandel, D.B., & Davies, M. (1982). Epidemiology of

depressive mood in adolescents. *Archives of General Psychiatry*, *39*, 1205–1212.

Kashani, J.H., Carlson, G.A., Beck, N.C., Hoeper, E.W., Corcoran, C.M., McAllister, J.A. et al. (1987). Depression, depressive symptoms, and depressed mood among a community sample of adolescents. *American Journal of Psychiatry*, *147*, 313–318.

Kashden, J., Fremouw, W.J., Callahan, T.S., & Franzen, M.D. (1993). Impulsivity in suicidal and nonsuicidal adolescents. *Journal of Abnormal Child Psychology*, *21*, 339–553.

Kaslow, N.J., Rehm, L.P., & Siegel, A.W. (1984). Social–cognitive and cognitive correlates of depression in children. *Journal of Abnormal Child Psychology*, *12*, 605–620.

Katz, L.Y., Cox, B.J., Gunasekara, S., & Miller, A.L. (2004). Feasibility of dialectical behavior therapy for suicidal adolescent inpatients. *Journal of the American Academy of Child and Adolescent Psychiatry*, *43*, 276–282.

Kazdin, A.E., French, N.H., Unis, A.S., Esveldt-Dawson, K., & Sherick, R.B. (1983). Hopelessness, depression and suicidal intent among psychiatrically disturbed children. *Journal of Consulting and Clinical Psychology*, *53*, 201–210.

Kendall, P.C., Stark, K.D., & Adam, T. (1990). Cognitive deficit or cognitive distortion in childhood depression. *Journal of Abnormal Child Psychology*, *18*, 255–270.

Kendler, K.S., Heath, A., Martin, N.G., & Eaves, L.J. (1986). Symptoms of anxiety and depression in a volunteer twin population. *Archives of General Psychiatry*, *43*, 213–221.

Kirkpatrick-Smith, J., Rich, A., Bonner, R., & Jans, F. (1992). Psychological vulnerability and substance abuse as predictors of suicide ideation among adolescents. *Omega: Journal of Death and Dying*, *24*, 21–33.

Kosky, R. (1982). Suicide and attempted suicide among Australian children. *Medical Journal of Australia*, *1*, 124–126.

Kovacs, M. (1990). Comorbid anxiety disorders in childhood-onset depressions. In J. D. Maser, & C. R. Cloniger (Eds.), *Comorbidity of mood and anxiety disorders* (pp. 272–281). Washington, DC: American Psychiatric Press.

Kovacs, M., Akiskal, H.S., Gatsonis, C., & Parrone, P. (1994). Childhood-onset dysthymic disorder: Clinical features and prospective naturalistic outcome. *Archives of General Psychiatry*, *51*, 365–374.

Kovacs, M., Gatsonis, C., Paulauskas, S.L., & Richards, C. (1989). Depressive disorders in childhood: IV. A longitudinal study of comorbidity with and risk for anxiety disorders. *Archives of General Psychiatry*, *46*, 776–782.

Kutcher, S. (2004). Medications. In H. Remschmidt, M. L. Belfer, & I. Goodyer (Eds.), *Facilitating pathways: Care, treatment, and prevention in child and adolescent mental health* (pp. 208–221). Berlin: Springer-Verlag.

Laederach, J., Fischer, W., Bowen, P., & Ladame, F. (1999). Common risk factors in adolescent suicide attempters revisited. *Crisis*, *20*, 15–22.

Last, C.G., Hansen, C., & Franco, N. (1997). Anxious children in adulthood: A prospective study of adjustment. *Journal of the American Academy of Child and Adolescent Psychiatry*, *36*, 645–652.

Lazarus, R.S. (1991). *Emotion and adaptation*. New York: Oxford University Press.

Lewinsohn, P.H. (1974). A behavioral approach to depression. In R. J. Friedman, & M. M. Katz (Eds.), *The psychology of depression: Contemporary theory and research*. Washington, DC: John Wiley & Sons.

Lewinsohn, P.M., Duncan, E.M., Stanton, A.K., & Hautzinger, M. (1986). Age at first onset for nonbipolar depression. *Journal of Abnormal Psychology*, *95*, 378–383.

Lewinsohn, P.M., Gotlib, I.H., & Seeley, J.R. (1995). Adolescent psychopathology: IV. Specificity of psychosocial risk factors for depression and substance abuse in older adolescents. *Journal of the American Academy of Child and Adolescent Psychiatry*, *34*, 1221–1229.

Lewinsohn, P.M., Hops, H., Roberts, R.E., Seeley, J.R., & Andrews, J.A. (1993). Adolescent psychopathology: I. Prevalence and incidence of depression and other DSM-III-R disorders in high school students. *Journal of Abnormal Psychology*, *102*, 133–144.

Lewinsohn, P.M., Rohde, P., & Seeley, J.R. (1994). Psychosocial risk factors for future adolescent suicide attempts. *Journal of Consulting and Clinical Psychology*, *62*, 297–305.

Lewinsohn, P.M., Rohde, P., & Seeley, J.R. (1995). Adolescent psychopathology: III. The clinical consequences of comorbidity. *Journal of the American Academy of Child and Adolescent Psychiatry*, *34*, 510–519.

McCauley, E., Mitchell, J.R., Burke, P., & Moss. S. (1988). Cognitive attributes of depression in children and adolescents. *Journal of Consulting and Clinical Psychology*, *56*, 903–908.

McGee, R., Feehan, M., Williams, S., & Anderson, J. (1992). DSM-III disorders from age 11 to age 15 years. *Journal of the American Academy of Child and Adolescent Psychiatry*, *31*, 50–59.

Merikangas, K.R., & Angst, J. (1995). The challenge of depressive disorders in adolescence. In M. Rutter (Ed.), *Psychosocial disturbances in young people: Challenges for prevention* (pp. 131–165). New York: Cambridge University Press.

Merikangas, K.R., Prusoff, B.A., & Weissman, M.M. (1988). Parental concordance for affective disorders: Psychopathology in offspring. *Journal of Affective Disorders*, *15*, 279–290.

Miezitis, S. (1992). *Creating alternatives to depression in our schools: Assessment, intervention, prevention.* Seattle, WA: Hogrefe & Huber.

Miles, C.P. (1978). Conditions predisposing to suicide: A review. *Journal of Nervous and Mental Disease*, *164*, 231–246.

Miller, H.L., Coombs, D.W., Leeper, J.D., & Barton, S. (1984). An analysis of the effects of suicide prevention facilities on suicide rates in the United States. *American Journal of Public Health*, *74*, 340–343.

Molin, R.S. (1986). Covert suicide and families of adolescents. *Adolescence*, *21*, 177–184.

Mosholder, A.D. (2004). *Suicidality in pediatric clinical trials of antidepressant drugs: Comparisons between previous analyses and Columbia University Classification.* Center for Drug Evaluation and Research, Food and Drug Administration, 16 August 2004.

Mufson, L., Pollack Dorta, K., Moreau, D., & Weissman, M.M. (2004). *Interpersonal psychotherapy for depressed adolescents* (2nd ed.). New York: Guilford.

Mufson, L., Weissman, M.M., & Warner, V. (1992). Depression and anxiety in parents and children: A direct interview study. *Journal of Anxious Disorders*, *6*, 1–13.

Narring, F., Tschumper, A., Inderwildi, L., Jeannin, A., Addor, V., Bütikofer, A., et al. (2004). *Gesundheit der Jugendlichen in der Schweiz (2002)* [SMASH 2002 Swiss multicenter adolescent study on health 2002]. Schlussbericht. Bern, Switzerland: Institut für Psychologie.

Neumann, R.J., Geller, B., Rice, J.P., & Todd, R.D. (1997). Increased prevalence and earlier onset of mood disorders among relatives of prepubertal versus adult probands. *Journal of the American Academy of Child and Adolescent Psychiatry*, *36*, 466–473.

Nezu, A.M., & Ronan, G.F. (1985). Life stress, current problems, problem solving, and depressive symptoms: An integrative model. *Journal of Consulting and Clinical Psychology*, *53*, 693–697.

Nock, M.K., & Kazdin, A.E. (2002). Examination of affective, cognitive, and behavioral factors in suicide-related outcomes in children and young adolescents. *Journal of Clinical Child and Adolescent Psychology*, *31*, 48–58.

Nolen-Hoeksema, S. (1987). Sex differences in unipolar depression: Evidence and theory. *Psychological Bulletin*, *101*, 259–282.

Nolen-Hoeksema, S., Girgus, J.S., & Seligman, M.E.P. (1991). Sex differences in depression and explanatory style in children. *Journal of Youth and Adolescence*, *20*, 233–246.

Nolen-Hoeksema, S., Girgus, J.S., & Seligman, M.E.P. (1992). Predictors and consequences of childhood depressive symptoms: A 5-year longitudinal study. *Journal of Abnormal Psychology*, *101*, 405–422.

Offer, D. (1969). *The psychological world of the teenager: A study of normal adolescent boys.* New York: Basic Books.

Olweus, D. (1991). Bully/victim problems among school children: Basic facts and effects of a school based intervention program. In D. Pepler, & K. Rubin (Eds.), *The development and treatment of childhood aggression* (pp. 441–448). Hillsdale, NJ: Lawrence Erlbaum Associates, Inc.

Olweus, D. (1993). *Bullying at school: What we know and what we can do.* Oxford: Blackwell.

Oster, G.D., & Caro, J.E. (1990). *Understanding and treating depressed adolescents and their families.* New York: John Wiley & Sons.

Paluzny, M., Davenport, C., & Kim, W.J. (1991). Suicide attempts and ideation: Adolescents evaluated on a pediatric ward. *Adolescence*, *26*, 208–215.

Parker, G. (1979). Parental characteristics in relation to depressive disorders. *British Journal of Psychiatry*, *134*, 138–147.

Parker, G. (1992). Early environment. In E. S. Paykel (Ed.), *Handbook of affective disorders* (2nd ed., pp. 171–183). Edinburgh: Churchill Livingstone.

Patterson, G.R., & Capaldi, D.M. (1990). A mediational model for boys' depressed mood. In J. Rolf, A. S. Masten, D. Chicchetti, K. H. Nuechterlein, & S. Weintraub (Eds.), *Risk and protective factors in the development of psychopathology* (pp. 141–163). Cambridge: Cambridge University Press.

Pawlak, C., Pascual-Sanchez, T., Raë, P., Fischer, W., & Ladame, F. (1999). Anxiety disorders, comorbidity, and suicide attempts in adolescence: A preliminary investigation. *European Psychiatry*, *14*, 132–136.

Paykel, E.S. (1982). Life events and early environment. In E. S. Paykel (Ed.), *Handbook of affective disorders* (pp. 146–161). Edinburgh: Churchill Livingstone.

Paykel, E.S. (1989). Stress and life events. In ADAMHA, *Report of the secretary's task force on youth suicide: Vol. 2. Risk factors for youth suicide* (US Department of Health and Human Services publication No. ADM 89–1622.) Washington, DC: Government Printing Office.

Pearce, C.M., & Martin, G. (1994). Predicting suicide attempts among adolescents. *Acta Psychiatrica Scandinavica, 90*, 324–328.

Petersen, A.C., Compas, B.E., Brooks-Gunn, J., Stemmler, M., Ey, S., & Grant, K.E. (1993). Depression in adolescence. *American Psychologist, 48*, 155–168.

Petersen, A.C., Sarigiani, P.A., & Kennedy, R.E. (1991). Adolescent depression: Why more girls? *Journal of Youth and Adolescence, 20*, 247–271.

Pfeffer, C.R. (1981a). The family system of suicidal children. *American Journal of Psychotherapy, 35*, 330–341.

Pfeffer, C.R. (1981b). Suicidal behavior of children: A review in the implications for research and practice. *American Journal of Psychiatry, 138*, 154–159.

Pfeffer, C.R. (1989). Family characteristics and support systems as risk factors for youth suicidal behavior. In ADAMHA, *Report of the secretary's task force on youth suicide: Vol. 2. Risk factors for youth suicide* (US Department of Health and Human Services publication No. ADM 89–1622.) Washington, DC: Government Printing Office.

Pfeffer, C.R., Martins, P., Mann, J., Sunkenberg, M., Ice, A., Damore, J.P. et al. (1997). Child survivors of suicide: Psychosocial characteristics. *Journal of the American Academy of Child and Adolescent Psychiatry, 36*, 65–174.

Platt, S., Bille-Brahe, U., & Kerkhof, A.J.F.M. (1992). Parasuicide in Europe: The WHO/Euro multicentre study on parasuicide: I. Introduction and preliminary analysis for 1989. *Acta Psychiatrica Scandinavica, 85*, 97–104.

Preston, S.H. (1984). Children and elderly in the U.S. *Scientific American, 251*(6), 36–41.

Prior, M. (1992). Childhood temperament. *Journal of Child Psychology and Psychiatry, 33*, 249–279.

Quinton, D., Rutter, M., & Liddle, C. (1984). Institutional rearing, parenting difficulties and marital support. *Psychological Medicine, 14*, 107–124.

Reinherz, H.Z., Stewart-Berhauer, G., Pakiz, B., Frost, A.K., Moeykens, B.A., & Holmes, W.M. (1989). The relationship of early risk and current mediators to depressive symptomatology in adolescence. *Journal of the American Academy of Child and Adolescent Psychiatry, 28*, 942–947.

Remafedi, G. (1999). Suicide and sexual orientation: Nearing the end of controversy? *Archives of General Psychiatry, 56*, 885.

Remschmidt, H. (2000). Affektive Störungen [Affective disorders]. In H. Remschmidt (Ed.), *Kinder- und Jugendpsychiatrie. Eine praktische Einfuhrung* (3th ed., pp. 196–206). Stuttgart, Germany: Thieme.

Retterstøl, N. (1990). *Suicide: A European perspective.* Cambridge: University Press.

Rholes, W.S., Blackwell, J., Jordan, C., & Walters, C. (1980). A developmental study of learned helplessness. *Developmental Psychology, 16*, 616–624.

Rich, C.L., Sherman, M., & Fowler, R.C. (1990). San Diego suicide study: The adolescents. *Adolescence, 25*, 855–865.

Robinson, N.S., Garber, J., & Hilsman, R. (1995). Cognitions and stress: Direct and moderating effects on depressive versus externalising symptoms during the junior high school transition. *Journal of Abnormal Psychology, 104*, 453–463.

Rodgers, B. (1990). Influences of early-life and recent factors on affective disorder in women: An exploration of vulnerability models. In L. N. Robins, & M. Rutter (Eds.), *Straight and devious pathways from childhood to adulthood* (pp. 314–327). Cambridge: Cambridge University Press.

Rohde, P., Lewinsohn, P.M., & Seeley, J.R. (1991). Comorbidity of unipolar depression: II. Comorbidity with other mental disorders in adolescents and adults. *Journal of Abnormal Psychology, 100*, 214–222.

Rosenkrantz, A.L. (1978). A note on adolescent suicide: Incidence, dynamics, and some suggestions for treatment. *Adolescence, 13*, 209–213.

Rosenstein, D.S., & Horowitz, H.A. (1996). Adolescent attachment and psychopathology. *Journal of Consulting and Clinical Psychology, 64*, 244–253.

Rotheram-Borus, M.J., & Trautman, P.D. (1988). Hopelessness, depression, and suicidal intent among adolescent suicide attempters. *Journal of the American Academy of Child and Adolescent Psychiatry, 27*, 700–704.

Rutter, M. (1986). The developmental psychopathology of depression: Issues and perspectives. In M. Rutter, C. E. Izard, & P. B. Read (Eds.), *Depression in young people: Developmental and clinical perspectives* (pp. 3–32). New York: Guilford.

Rutter, M., Graham, P., Chadwick, O.F.D., & Yule, W. (1976). Adolescent turmoil: Fact or fiction? *Journal of Child Psychology and Psychiatry, 17*, 35–56.

Rutter, M., & Quinton, D. (1984). Parental psychiatric

disorder: Effects on children. *Psychological Medicine, 14*, 853–880.

Seligman, M.E.P. (1975). *Helplessness: On depression, development and death*. San Francisco: Freeman.

Seligman, M.E.P, Abramson, L., Semmel, A., & Von Baeyer, C. (1979). Depressive attributional style. *Journal of Abnormal Psychology, 88*, 222–247.

Seligman, M.E.P., & Peterson, C. (1986). A learned helplessness perspective on childhood depression: Theory and research. In M. Rutter, C. E. Izard, & P. B. Read (Eds.), *Depression in young people: Developmental and clinical perspectives* (pp. 223–250). New York: Guilford.

Seligman, M.E.P., Peterson, C., Kaslow, N., Tannenbaum, R., Alloy, L., & Abramson, L. (1984). Attributional style and depressive symptoms among children. *Journal of Abnormal Psychology, 93*, 235–238.

Seroczynski, A.D., Jacquez, F.M., & Cole, D.A. (2003). Depression and suicide during adolescence. In M. D. Berzonsky, & G. R. Adams (Eds.), *Blackwell handbook of adolescence* (pp. 550–572). Malden, MA: Blackwell.

Shaffer, D. (1974). Suicide in childhood and early adolescence. *Journal of Child Psychology and Psychiatry, 15*, 275–291.

Shaffer, D. (1985). Depression, mania and suicidal acts. In M. Rutter, & L. Hersov (Eds.), *Child and adolescent psychiatry* (2nd ed., pp. 698–719). London: Blackwell.

Shaffer, D. (1988). The epidemiology of teen suicide: An examination of risk factors. *Journal of Clinical Psychiatry, 49*, 36–41.

Shaffer, D., & Piacentini, J. (1994). Suicide and attempted suicide. In M. Rutter, E. Taylor, & L. Hersov (Eds.), *Child and adolescent psychiatry: Modern approaches* (pp. 407–424). London: Blackwell.

Shafii, M., Carrigan, S., Whittinghill, J.R., & Derrick, R.N. (1985). Psychological autopsy of completed suicide in children and adolescents. *American Journal of Psychiatry, 142*, 1061–1064.

Shelton, R.C., Hollon, S.D., Purdon, S.E., & Loosen, P.T. (1991). Biological and psychological aspects of depression. *Behavior Therapy, 22*, 201–228.

Siegel, K., Mesago, F.P., & Christ, G. (1990). A prevention program for bereaved children. *American Journal of Orthopsychiatry, 60*, 168–175.

Silverman, A.B., Reinherz, H.Z., & Giaconia, R.M. (1996). The long-term sequelae of child and adolescent abuse: A longitudinal community study. *Child Abuse and Neglect, 20*, 709–723.

Speaker, K.M., & Petersen, G.J. (2000). School violence and adolescent suicide: Strategies for effective intervention. *Educational Review, 52*, 65–73.

Spirito, A., Overholser, J., Ashworth, S., Morgan, J., & Benedict-Drew, C. (1988). Evaluation of a suicide awareness curriculum for high school students. *Journal of the American Academy of Child and Adolescent Psychiatry, 27*, 705–711.

Spirito, A., Stanton, C., Donaldson, D., & Boergers, J. (2002). Treatment-as-usual for adolescent suicide attempters: Implications for the choice of comparison groups in psychotherapy research. *Journal of Clinical Child and Adolescent Psychology, 31*, 41–47.

Sroufe, A., & Rutter, M. (1984). The domain of developmental psychopathology. *Journal of Child Development, 55*, 17–29.

Stanley, E.J., & Barter, J.T. (1970). Adolescent suicidal behavior. *American Journal of Orthopsychiatry, 40*, 87–96.

Stark, K.D., Humphrey, L.L., Crook, K., & Lewis, K. (1990). Perceived family environments of depressed and anxious children: Child's and maternal figure's perspectives. *Journal of Abnormal Child Psychology, 18*, 527–547.

Stattin, H., & Magnusson, D. (1990). *Pubertal maturation in female development*. Hillsdale, NJ: Lawrence Erlbaum Associates, Inc.

Steinhausen, H.C., & Metzke, C.W. (2000). Adolescent self-rated depressive symptoms in a Swiss epidemiological study. *Journal of Youth and Adolescence, 29*, 427–440.

Stern, D. (1977). *The first relationship: Infant and mother*. Cambridge, MA: Harvard University Press.

Sund, A.M., & Wichstrøm, L. (2002). Insecure attachment as a risk factor for future depressive symptoms in early adolescence. *Journal of the American Academy of Child & Adolescent Psychiatry, 41*, 1478–1485.

Teicher, J.D., & Jacobs, J. (1966). Adolescents who attempt suicide: Preliminary findings. *American Journal of Psychiatry, 122*, 1248–1257.

Thomas, A., & Chess, S. (1982). Temperament and follow-up to adulthood. In R. Porter, & G. M. Collins (Eds.), *Temperamental differences in infants and young children* (pp. 168–175). New York: New York University Press.

Tishler, C.L., McKenry, P.C., & Morgan, K.C. (1981). Adolescent suicide attempt: Some significant factors. *Suicide and Life-Threatening Behavior, 11*, 86–92.

Treatment for Adolescents with Depression Study

(TADS) Team (2004). Fluoxetine, cognitive–behavioral therapy and their combination for adolescents with depression. *Journal of the American Medical Association, 292,* 807–820.

Vieland, V., Whittle, B., Garland, A., Hicks. R., & Shaffer, D. (1991). The impact of curriculum-based suicide prevention programs for teenagers: An 18-month follow-up. *Journal of the American Academy of Child and Adolescent Psychiatry, 30,* 811–815.

Wagner, B.M., Compas, B.E., & Howell, D.C. (1988). Daily and major life events: A test of an integrative model of psychosocial stress. *American Journal of Community Psychology, 16,* 189–205.

Warner, V., Mufson, L., & Weissman, M.M. (1995). Offspring at high and low risk for depression and anxiety: Mechanisms of psychiatric disorders. *Journal of the American Academy of Child and Adolescent Psychiatry, 34,* 786–797.

Watson, D., & Kendall, P.C. (1989). Common and differentiating features of anxiety and depression: Current findings and future directions. In P. C. Kendall, & D. Watson (Eds.), *Anxiety and depression: Distinctive and overlapping features* (pp. 493–508). San Diego, CA: Academic Press.

Weiner, I.B., & DelGaudio, A. (1976). Psychopathology in adolescence. *Archives of General Psychiatry, 34,* 98–111.

Weissman, M.M., & Klerman, G.L. (1977). Sex differences and the epidemiology of depression. *Archives of General Psychiatry, 35,* 1304–1311.

Weissman, M.M., Gammon, G.D., John, K., Merikangas, K.R., Prusoff, B.A., & Sholomskas, D. (1987). Children of depressed parents: Increased psychopathology and early onset of major depression. *Archives of General Psychiatry, 44,* 847–853.

Weissman, M.M., Leaf, P.J., Holzer, C.E., III, Myers, J.K., & Tischler, G.L. (1984). The epidemiology of depression: An update on sex differences in rates. *Journal of Affective Disorders, 7,* 179–188.

Wender, P.H., Kety, S.S., Rosenthal, D., Schulsinger, F., Ortmann, J., & Lunde, I. (1986). Psychiatric disorders in the biological and adoptive families of adopted individuals with affective disorders. *Archives of General Psychiatry, 43,* 923–929.

Wilde, E.J., Kienhorst, I.C.W.M., Diekstra, R.F.W., & Wolters, W.H.G. (1992). The relationship between adolescent suicidal behaviour and life events in childhood and adolescence. *American Journal of Psychiatry, 149,* 45–51.

Wilson, R., & Cairns, E. (1988). Sex-role attributes, perceived competence and the development of depression in adolescence. *Journal of Child Psychology and Psychiatry, 29,* 635–650.

World Health Organization (1990). *International classification of diseases and related health* (10th revision). Geneva: WHO.

17

Epidemiology and psychosocial risk factors associated with adolescent drug consumption

Sofia Buelga, Marcella Ravenna, Gonzalo Musitu, and Marisol Lila

LEARNING OBJECTIVES

Adolescence is a critical period in a person's lifetime in relation to the initiation and regular practice of risk behaviours. This chapter deals with drug consumption during this stage of life. First, we carried out an epidemiological analysis of this behaviour, where we studied factors such as the age of initiation, regular use, and prevalence or consumption patterns of legal and illegal drug use. Second, after reviewing the various explanatory models and current theories on drug consumption, we explored this behaviour from a psychosocial perspective. Finally, we carefully examined the factors that account for the use of drugs during adolescence within different interrelated contexts (individual, microsocial and macrosocial).

1. Introduction

The widespread use of illicit drugs in Europe is a recent phenomenon that has developed from the post-war period until the present day. Over time, it has taken on different characteristics and forms of expression: in the mid-1960s, the age and typology of the drug user changed; drug use became a specifically teenage youth reality; the number of drug users increased, different types of drug were introduced and various forms of excessive and destructive consumption greatly increased (Ravenna, 1997). In social life, drug use appears as a dynamic phenomenon that is in constant evolution. This dynamism can also be found in the relationship that individuals establish with the different substances.

Studies carried out since the late 1970s, in both epidemiological and psychosocial spheres, have shown that adolescence is the crucial time for experimenting with both licit and illicit drugs. It is specifically between the ages of 11 and 18 that premises are established for types of drug use that do not involve any great risk and for those that can turn into abuse and addiction (Elliot, Orr, Watson, & Jackson, 2005). The specific characteristics that the phenomenon has acquired do not allow that it be explained through pathological or deviant processes of the person, but through a more complex framework of psychological processes related to adolescence (Hansen & O'Malley, 1996; Hawkins, Catalino, & Arthur, 2002; Musitu, Buelga, Lila, & Cava, 2000).

Drug consumption is defined by the World Health Organization (WHO, 1998) as the use of a substance, which, once introduced in a live organism, can modify one or several of its functions. It is, therefore, a kind of risk behaviour such as unsafe sexual practices, inadequate nourishment and criminal behaviour (Buelga & Musitu, 2004). From this perspective, drug consumption is considered to be closely related to the various developmental tasks that adolescents must cope with at this specific stage of their lives; and especially those tasks are related to the reorganization of self-concept (Pinquart, Silbereisen, & Wiesner, 2005).

The importance of this risk behaviour involves considerable effort on the part of researchers and scholars to explain the mechanisms underlying drug consumption. The complexity of this topic has resulted in the appearance of different theories and models in which the concept of drug itself is, from the start, difficult to define. The conceptualization of what is considered to be a drug is more influenced by sociocultural circumstances of a given historical period than by the quality of a given substance and its effects on living organisms (Ravenna, 2005).

Among the many taxonomies proposed to classify the different psychoactive substances, one of the simplest and most widespread in the scientific literature classifies drugs in accordance with their different pharmacological effects on the central nervous system (WHO, 1998). From this perspective, drugs are classified into three large groups of substances: depressant, stimulant and psychodysleptic or psychotometic. Alcohol, opiates, hypnotics and sedatives are some of the various depressant substances that affect neural and motor activities, while amphetamine and other synthetic drugs (such as ecstasy), cocaine, xanthine (tea and coffee) and tobacco activate or stimulate the functions of the central nervous system. Finally, hallucinogens (LSD, mescaline), derivatives from cannabis, inhalants, and other chemicals, such as antidepressants, corticosteroids, and beta blocking are regarded as psychodysleptic substances, which can modify or disturb the activity of the central nervous system by producing more or less intense perceptive distortions, illusions, and hallucinations in the individual.

There is currently already well-sustained evidence of the existing relationship between the different substances in the progression of drug consumption. Thus, authors point out the influence of legal drug consumption (alcohol, tobacco) on the initiation of illicit drug consumption. A classic study by Kandel (1980) outlines the existence of a sequence of four stages in the consumption of various substances: wine and beer; tobacco, or alcoholic drinks with higher alcohol content; marijuana; and other dangerous drugs, such as cocaine. Following this model, which is known as the *gateway theory*, the author emphasizes the facilitating effect of legal drugs on the use of illicit drugs. This model is based on the idea that the use of alcohol, tobacco, and marijuana at early stages acts as a "gateway" to experimenting with other drugs such as amphetamines, cocaine, hallucinogens, or heroin. However, consuming a specific substance in one phase of the sequence does not necessarily imply the subsequent consumption of other substances. In fact, the gateway effect is complex and cannot be reduced to a simple model (Buelga & Musitu, 2004; Kandel & Jessor, 2002).

The consumption of any kind of drug generally follows a course with an initial phase, a development phase (a combination of change, fluctuation, and stabilization) and an end phase. A complex weave of factors that have a diversified role in the different stages of the development of this course comes into play (Ravenna, 1997). In the approach stage, the adolescent decides whether or not to try consumption. If the adolescent continues (the stabilization phase), different styles of consumption may be adopted (occasional or regular), alternating between the two or breaking off completely. The willingness to try substances is, in fact, the result of a process of social construction which may imply different strategies of elaboration. In some cases this process is influenced by the stimuli present at a particular time in the surrounding environment (Ravenna & Cavazza, 2003; Rohrbach, Sussman, Dent, & Sun, 2005).

2. Epidemiological studies on licit and illicit drug consumption in childhood and adolescence in Europe

Most European countries have made significant efforts in the past few years to determine the current trends in licit and illicit drug consumption among teenagers. However, when interpreting the results of these studies, the different methodologies applied in each country and the cultural diversity among the European countries should be taken into acount. In spite of these limitations, epidemiological studies are a valuable source of information about drug consumption patterns among young people.

2.1 Licit drugs

Smoking is currently one of the most serious health problems of the 21st century. It is the most important avoidable cause of disease and premature death (WHO, 2004a). Tobacco use often starts before adulthood. About 80% of adult smokers start before the age of 18 (WHO, 2005).

Adolescence is, consequently, a decisive period for determining the use of tobacco in adulthood.

The last report of the European School Survey Project on Alcohol and Other Drug Use among students in 35 European countries (ESPAD, 2003) shows that the habit of smoking has decreased in the last five years. Although this habit is still widespread and varies considerably across countries, there seems to be an encouraging decline in cigarette smoking among young people in many European countries. The prevalence of cigarette smoking during the last 30 days among 15 and 16 year olds decreased between 1999 and 2003, from 37% to 35% (Hibell et al., 2004).

Despite this promising finding, tobacco is, together with alcohol, the drug most commonly used by young people. The mean age for the onset of smoking is about 12.5 years old; for regular consumption, it is about 15 years old (WHO, 2004a). Both experimental and regular consumption increase significantly with age (ESPAD, 2003). In France, for example, the proportion of daily smokers (at least one cigarette per day) increases from 9% to 25% between the ages of 14 and 18 in boys, and from 10% to 28% in girls (Choquet, 2004).

The starting age seems to be related to the regular consumption of tobacco. Godeau, Rahav, and Hubbet (2004) found that among 15 years old, 49% of daily smokers started smoking (for the first time) *before the age of 11*. This early age suggests that regular smoking seems to be associated with lower ages of experimental smoking. Obviously, a majority of adolescents who experiment at an early age with tobacco do not repeat this experience and do not acquire the habit of smoking.

Another interesting result is related to gender differences in tobacco use. The Health Behaviour in School-Aged Children Survey (HBSC 2001/2002), which was carried out in 35 countries in the WHO European region and North America, and the ESPAD survey (2003) found a gender gap depending on geographical areas and regions of Europe (see Figure 17.1). In eastern European countries, more boys smoke than girls. In northern and western Europe, the pattern reverses: more girls smoke than do boys. In the southern

FIGURE 17.1

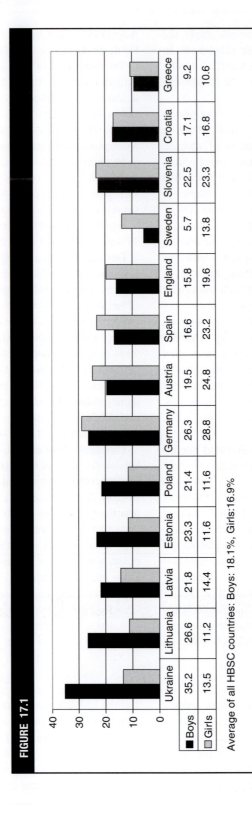

	Ukraine	Lithuania	Latvia	Estonia	Poland	Germany	Austria	Spain	England	Sweden	Slovenia	Croatia	Greece
■ Boys	35.2	26.6	21.8	23.3	21.4	26.3	19.5	16.6	15.8	5.7	22.5	17.1	9.2
☐ Girls	13.5	11.2	14.4	11.6	11.6	28.8	24.8	23.2	19.6	13.8	23.3	16.8	10.6

Average of all HBSC countries: Boys: 18.1%, Girls:16.9%

Daily smoking among 15-year-old adolescents in several European countries (%).

Average of all HBSC countries: Boys: 18.1%, Girls:16.9%.

Adapted from HBSC 2001/2002 survey

and central countries of Europe, the rates are similar for both genders.

These data indicate that in Ukraine, Lithuania, Estonia and Poland, boys smoke twice as much as girls. In Ukraine for example, there are almost three times more boy smokers than girl smokers (35.2% vs. 13.5% respectively). Moreover, in these countries, instead of decreasing, the habit of smoking has significantly increased in recent years among young people. For example, in Lithuania and Estonia, daily smoking rates for 15-year-old adolescents have increased 12% with respect to 1998 (Godeau et al., 2004).

The data for northern and western Europe indicate the reverse in gender pattern. Although differences between boys and girls are not as marked as in eastern Europe, in Germany, Austria, Spain and England, the results show that there are more girl smokers (24.1%) than boy smokers (19.5%). These gender differences are much more evident in Sweden, where the rate of young smokers is one of the lowest. In this Nordic country, twice as many girls smoke as boys (13.8% girls vs. 5.7% boys).

Tobacco is highly addictive (Atrens, 2001), which explains the dependence and maintenance of its use after adolescence. Moreover, it seems to facilitate the use of other drugs (Kandel, 1980; Kandel & Jessor, 2002). In this sense, Lloyd and Lucas (1998) point out that the experimentation and use of alcohol is more frequent among smokers than among non-smokers. These authors also found that whereas 90% of non-smokers had not experimented with cannabis, 84% of smokers had done so. Indeed, some of these smokers continue smoking cannabis occasionally (28%) and some frequently (34%).

Nowadays, if tobacco and caffeine are excluded, alcohol is the drug that is most experimented with and consumed by young people (EMCDA, 2003). Young people start experimenting with alcohol at very early ages of adolescence (see Table 17.1.). The mean age of the onset of alcohol drinking is 12.6 years old (as is the case for tobacco). The first experience of drunkenness occurs at about 13.7 years old (HBSC, 2001/ 2002). Boys are more precocious in these experiences of initiation and in the use and regular abuse of this drug (ESPAD, 2003; Schmid & Gabhainn, 2004; WHO, 2005).

This gender gap is more obvious for specific patterns of alcohol consumption. Differences between sexes are smaller for the age of onset of drinking and drunkenness and are larger for weekly drinking and frequency of drunkenness (Schmid & Gabhainn, 2004). One-third more boys than girls drink weekly and a higher proportion of boys repeat situations of drunkenness (HBSC, 2001/2002).

The frequency and quantity of alcohol consumed from the ages of 15 and 16 until early adulthood are becoming significantly higher. In Spain, a study by Pons, Buelga, and Lehalle (1999) reveals that 18.4% of 15- to 19-year-old adolescents are abusive consumers. In fact, at 15 years old, 30% of European students show a pattern of regular alcohol consumption (HBSC, 2001/2002). Countries like England, the Netherlands and

TABLE 17.1

Alcohol consumption variables among 15 year olds (from HBSC 2001/2002 survey)

	Age at onset of drinking	Age at onset of drunkenness	Drinking weekly (%)	Drinking beer weekly (%)	Drinking spirits weekly (%)	Drinking wine weekly (%)	Drunkenness 2 or more times (%)
Boys	12.3	13.6	34.3	26.0	12.4	8.3	39.8
Girls	12.9	13.9	23.9	11.2	9.7	6.2	31.4
All	12.6	13.7	29.1	18.6	11.0	7.25	35.6

FIGURE 17.2

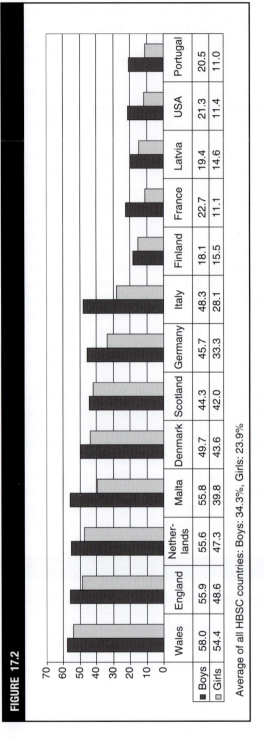

	Wales	England	Nether-lands	Malta	Denmark	Scotland	Germany	Italy	Finland	France	Latvia	USA	Portugal
■ Boys	58.0	55.9	55.6	55.8	49.7	44.3	45.7	48.3	18.1	22.7	19.4	21.3	20.5
□ Girls	54.4	48.6	47.3	39.8	43.6	42.0	33.3	28.1	15.5	11.1	14.6	11.4	11.0

Average of all HBSC countries: Boys: 34.3%, Girls: 23.9%

Percentage of 15-year-old adolescents who drink alcohol weekly in several European countries and the United States.

Average of all HBSC countries: Boys: 34.3%, Girls: 23.9%.

Adapted from HBSC 2001/2002 survey

Wales are significantly above the average rate of consumption. More than 50% of students report drinking weekly (WHO, 2005; see Figure 17.2). The opposite case has been observed in Portugal (15%) and the USA, Latvia, France and Finland (16–17%).

In these countries of low alcohol consumption, there is an interesting gender gap. Boys drink alcohol regularly twice as much as girls. This is the case in France, the USA, and Portugal. These gender differences are much lower in countries with high alcohol consumption. In Wales and Scotland, for example, the proportion of girls (48%) who drink regularly is almost equal to the proportion of boys (51%) who drink regularly. In contrast, in Malta and Italy, which are countries that show high alcohol consumption, gender differences are large. In these two Mediterranean countries, there may be cultural factors that can explain why girls drink much less alcohol in comparison with boys.

Although there are important differences in drinking cultures among countries, beer and spirits are the beverages more consumed by young people. In fact, beer is the most popular drink for European youth. It is more consumed by boys than girls. This gender preference is true for the western parts of Europe.

Data from the HBSC 2001/2002 survey show that almost half of 15-year-old Danish boys (47.7%) drink beer weekly; and more than one-third of boys also consume this drink in Wales, the Netherlands, Germany, England and Belgium (Flemish) (33.2%–43.1%). Moreover, boys prefer beer over spirits and wine in other parts of Europe like Malta, Ukraine, the Czech Republic and Italy (35.1%–40.1%). Girls also show this same preference in some of these countries. The highest consumption of beer is found in Denmark (31.5%). Other high prevalence countries for girls include the Czech Republic, Italy, Germany, the Netherlands and Belgium (16.7%–23.1%).

In the Baltic countries and the Balkans, although the consumption of beer in boys is not as high, they drink four times more than girls. In this sense, in Croatia, Slovenia and Estonia, 26.6% of boys drink beer, but the proportion decreases to 6.3% for girls. The lowest consump-

tion of beer among young people (boys and girls), with a percentage of 9% or less, is found in Finland, Spain, Portugal and Ireland (7.5%–9%).

With regard to the consumption of wine, Finland, Portugal, Ireland and Norway, present the lowest rate of consumption among young people (2.5% or less). Actually, the regular consumption of this drink among 15-year-old adolescents is very low (under 0%). However, it is significantly higher in countries where wine is part of the traditional culture, with the exception of Spain. In comparison with the average consumption (7.25%), about one-quarter of students (23.9.%) in Malta drink wine weekly and about one-fifth (18.4%) in Italy. In Hungary, which is a wine-producing country, the proportion of regular drinkers (16.9%) is twice the average consumption. And, also, in all these countries, more than twice the number of boys drink wine in comparison with girls.

These gender differences are reversed in some countries of western Europe. In England, Austria and Wales, the percentage of girls who drink wine (13.5%–15.5%) is twice the European average (7.25%). It is also double the consumption of boys (6.1%–9.6%). In Germany, which has low consumption rates, girls also drink more wine than boys (8.2% vs. 5.7% respectively). In the rest of Europe and North America, with the exception of the the Czech Republic, boys consume more wine than girls (Schmid & Gabhainn, 2004).

With regard to the consumption of spirits, boys consume more than girls (12.4% for boys vs. 9.7% for girls). Countries with higher rates of spirits consumption are Malta, England, Scotland and Denmark (28.8%–34.8%). In these countries, almost one-third of 15-year-old adolescents regularly drink these strong beverages.

In England, Scotland and Wales, girls show a clear preference for the newly designed premixed drinks (alcopops). Since their recent appearance on the market in the mid-1990s, these alcoholic drinks, which are often characterized by sweet tastes and fruity flavours, have increased in popularity among young people, mainly girls. This is the case of the United Kingdom, Ireland, Norway, Denmark, and Switzerland. In Ireland, for example, alcopops consumption has increased among girls from 3% in 1998 to 8% in 2002 (National Health and Life Style Survey, 2003). The Swiss Institute of Prevention of the Alcoholism and Other Drug Addictions reveals that, in that country, the sale of alcopops between 2000 and 2002 multiplied by 40 (ISPA, 2003). In Norway, 50% of 15- to 17-year-old adolescents drank three or more bottles the last time they consumed alcopops (Norwegian Gallup on behalf of Alkokutt, 2003).

With regard to the regular consumption of alcoholic drinks, a major concern is related to the increase in levels of drunkenness and bingeing for recreational purposes among young people. The practice of binge drinking, that is to say, having five or more drinks in a row, seems to have increased among adolescents in northern and western Europe (Hibell et al., 2004). In fact, in Denmark, Ireland, the Isle of Man, the Netherlands, Norway, Poland, and the United Kingdom, approximately 24%–32% of 15-year-old students have practised this behaviour in the last month. This excessive consumption of alcohol is logically associated with episodes of intoxication. In Denmark and Ireland, about one-quarter of students have been drunk three times or more during the last month (ESPAD, 2003). Also, in the United Kingdom, the Isle of Man, and Austria, between 22% and 27% of young people have had repeated experiences of intoxication.

It becomes obvious that an excessive or abusive use of alcohol at any stage of a person's lifetime represents a problem that affects the different vital contexts of individuals in significant ways: friendship, health, family life, profession, studies and economy (Babor, Del Boca, & Griffith, 2002; Jernigan & Mosher, 2005). The fact is that about 55,000 young people die of alcohol-related causes in the European region every year (WHO, 2005).

2.2 Illicit drugs

Different research lines suggest that the pattern of illicit drug consumption is different from that of legal drugs. Thus, the existence of a curvilinear relationship between age and illicit drug use has been outlined. The frequency and quantity of consumption remain low until the age of 14 (Ravenna, 1993, 2005). As age increases, so does illicit drug consumption, until the maximum level is reached in the first stage of adulthood. This can be set, depending on the different authors, between the ages of 18 and 25 (Nyberg, 1979; Sloboda & Bukoski, 2003). After this age, consumption decreases significantly, when the acquisition of an adult social role takes place. An exception to this might be cannabis consumption. In fact, the regular use of cannabis is very usual until the age of 25; and this drug consumption is extremely high among young adults between 25 and 34 years old (EMCDDA, 2004).

Currently, cannabis is the illicit drug that is most frequently consumed by both adolescents and adults. During the 1990s, its consumption significantly increased among adolescents (EMCDDA, 2004). For instance, between 1995 and 1999, the experimental use of cannabis by 15- and 16-year-olds students doubled in several countries, including Finland and Norway. Nowadays this consumption is beginning to stabilize and even to decrease in countries like Ireland, which 10 years ago had one of the highest rates of experimental consumption in Europe.

Today, the highest rates of experimental consumption in 15-year-old adolescents are in other countries like Switzerland and Canada (HBSC, 2001/2002). The lifetime prevalence of cannabis use is over 40% in Canada and 37% in Switzerland (see Table 17.2). Additionally, more than one-third of 15-year-old students have tried this drug in very different and geographically distant countries such as Greenland, the United States, Spain, England and Scotland. With the exception of Greenland, the data also suggest that a significant proportion of these adolescents repeat the consumption of this substance between three and 39 times a year. These adolescents perceive the regular use of cannabis as normal behaviour in the culture of the peer group (Ter Bogt, Fotiou, & Gabhainn, 2004; WHO, 2005).

In Canada, almost 20% of adolescents aged 15 are regular users. Switzerland (17.4%) and Spain (15%) also stand out because of their high prevalence rates. These numbers contrast with those found in eastern European countries, where the experimental and recreational consumption are particularly low. In countries like the former

TABLE 17.2

Cannabis use by 15 year olds (%) (from HBSC 2001/2002 survey)

	Canada	Switzerland	Greenland	USA	England & Scotland	Spain	France	Belgium (French)	Italy
Lifetime	40.4	37.8	33.6	31.3	32.6	30.4	27.5	24.1	20.5
Regular	19.2	17.4	10.8	13.3	13.6	15	13.3	10.7	8.5
Heavy	8.1	9.4	2.8	7.9	6.3	5.1	4.5	4.8	3.3

	Germany	Netherlands	Denmark	Russia	Latvia	Lithuania	TFYR Macedonia	HBSC average
Lifetime	18.5	21.6	21.3	8.7	8	5.9	3.05	18.8
Regular	8	10.5	9.7	2.3	2.1	1.3	0.6	7.9
Heavy	2.3	2.8	1.4	0.4	0.4	0.3	0.1	2.8

Yugoslav Republic of Macedonia, Lithuania, Latvia and the Russian Federation, less than 3% of young people are regular consumers of cannabis.

Most of the other western European countries, such as Germany, the Netherlands or Denmark have a moderate prevalence rate and fall between these two extremes. It is interesting to note that, in the Netherlands, where the sale and the use of cannabis are allowed in about 1200 coffee shops (Barendregt, 1996), the consumption of this drug is relatively moderate. In fact, this consumption is lower than in many other European countries and North America, although it is higher than in some other countries.

In all countries and for all patterns of cannabis consumption, boys consume more than girls. Gender differences are much more significant in the eastern and southern countries of Europe (EMCDDA, 2004). In France, for example, this gender pattern becomes more noticeable with age (Choquet, 2004). At 17 years old, twice the number of boys than girls consume cannabis (14% vs. 6% respectively). And at 18 years old, this figure increases to three times (21% boys vs. 7% girls).

The heavy consumption of cannabis (more than 40 times within a year) is also much more frequent in boys than in girls. Actually, an important minority of young people are heavy users (EMCDDA, 2004; WHO, 2005). This kind of consumption may be associated with problems at school, depression, risk taking and deviance (Ter Bogt et al., 2004).

The 2001/2002 HBSC survey found that the country with the heaviest consumption is Switzerland. Almost 10% of adolescents aged 15 years old are heavy users. Other countries with high prevalence rates are Canada, the USA, England, Scotland and Spain (5–8%). However, in the vast majority of European countries, the group of heavy users is less than 3%. Many authors emphasize that cannabis consumption in adolescence commonly takes place within a group of friends. Thus, the consumption of this drug with other users may provide a platform of acceptability for trying other drugs (Pudney, 2002; Shillington & Clapp, 2002). Moreover, this concomitant exposure to other consumers increases the probability of access to illegal markets, which also might influence the gateway effect for other illicit drugs (EMCDDA, 2004).

After cannabis, inhalants are currently the illicit drugs that are most consumed by adolescents (EMCDDA, 2003). These drugs, which contain many different chemical components (glue, petrol, paint thinners, domestic polish, aerosol sprays, poppers) are normally used between late childhood and early adolescence. According to the National Survey on Drug Use and Health (NSDUH, 2003), the first use of inhalants occurs on average about age 12. According to data from ESPAD (2003), the highest prevalence of inhalants is reported in Greenland, where 22% of adolescents have used them at some time. There are also high rates of consumption in the Isle of Man, Ireland, Cyprus, Malta and Slovenia (15%–19%). By contrast, in Romania, only 1% have used it; and in Bulgaria, Hungary and Turkey, consumption is reported to be 5% or under.

In general, the use of inhalants decreases dramatically with age, so that its consumption in the school-aged population is mainly experimental and occasional (NSDUH, 2003). In fact, the abuse of inhalants in both developing and developed countries is a problem that most affects the poorest sectors of society, in particular, street children and indigenous young people (Mallett, Rosenthal, & Keys, 2005; WHO, 2005). In Brazil, for example, 88% of street youths use inhalants and solvents daily or several times a week (Inciardi & Surratt, 1998).

A very different reality exists with regard to other illicit drugs that are preferentially consumed in recreational settings related to rave culture. Indeed, the consumption of some synthetic drugs, mainly ecstasy (MDMA) and its derivates (MMDA, MDA, MDEA, MDBM) is most frequent by rave party visitors in dance music settings (techno, house.) (Calafat et al., 1998; Engels & Ter Bogt, 2004).

Different researchers confirm that the small but significant group of adolescents who frequent recreational environments of this kind commonly consume this drug (Panagopoulus & Ricciardelli, 2005). A research study with a sample of 1121 Dutch ravers showed that the lifetime prevalence of the use of ecstasy was 81% (Van de Wijngaart, Braam, De Bruin, Fris, Maalsté, & Verbraeck, 1999). In techno dance settings, lifetime prevalence in the United Kingdom was 85% (EMCDDA, 2003), and in the Netherlands, 22% of young people who attend rave parties consume this synthetic drug weekly (EMCDDA, 2004). Ecstasy consumption among young people

significantly increased during the 1990s. This increase has been very noticeable in some countries like the United Kingdom, the Netherlands, Germany, and Spain (Calafat et al., 1998). Actually, the use of this designer drug, which is more frequently consumed by boys than girls, has exceeded the consumption of amphetamines in these and other countries. This synthetic substance is one of the illicit drugs that is most commonly used by adolescents (EMCDDA, 2004). In the Czech Republic, the data indicate that not only has the use of ecstasy increased, but also the use of methamphetamines (mainly pervitin), principally among girls.

Since coming on the scene, evidence suggests that, even though the prevalence in the use of ecstasy is very high in many countries, the use of this drug among young people has stabilized and decreased. In Spain, for example, the consumption of ecstasy doubled between 1998 and 2000 and has recently decreased to almost half. In fact, the National Drug Plan of Spain indicates that the use of this drug in the past 12 months among adolescents aged 15 to 18 diminished between the years 2000–2004, from 6.7% to 3.7% (DGPNSD, 2005). However, in this country, the use of ecstasy begins at an earlier age (around 15.5 years old) in comparison with other countries. In Switzerland, the age of maximum prevalence in the consumption of this drug according to Graf (1997) is between 18 and 26. In the United Kingdom, the age of maximum prevalence seems to range between 19 and 24 years (Chivite-Matthews et al. 2005).

Polyconsumption is a widely extended practice among ecstasy consumers (Degenhardt, Barker, & Topp, 2004; NSDUH, 2003). According to Graf (1997), 94% of ecstasy consumers have also tried other illicit drugs during the past 12 months. Likewise, in Italy, 86% of ecstasy users have consumed this substance along with other drugs (Schifano, Di Furi, Miconi, & Bricolo, 1996). Schifano's study reveals that more than half of these consumers have used ecstasy jointly with cannabis or alcohol, and one-third with poppers or cocaine (see Figure 17.3).

Cocaine is another illicit drug whose consumption has also increased in the last decade in

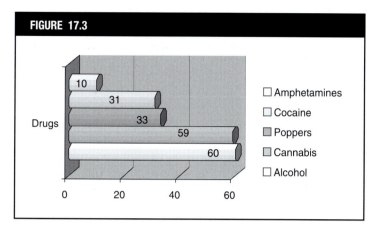

Percentage of ecstasy consumers who combine this drug with other substances.

Adapted from Schifano, Di Furi, Miconi, & Bricol, 1996

many European countries. This increasing trend contrasts with the generalized decrease in the use of hallucinogens (LSD and hallucinogenic mushrooms).

The increase in cocaine use seems to have occurred in the same countries where ecstasy consumption has also risen: the United Kingdom, Denmark, Germany, the Netherlands, and Spain. Recent surveys in these countries have found a lifetime prevalence in the use of cocaine between 5 and 13% among 15- to 24-year-old males (EMCDDA, 2004).

Although cocaine consumption is limited in the European school-aged population, in countries like Spain, the use of cocaine has consistently increased in recent years. In 2004 the consumption of this drug was three and even four times higher among 15- to 18-year-old adolescents, in comparison with 1994. In 1994 practically no adolescent had tried cocaine in the last 12 months (0.9%), while in 2004 3.2% had tried it. This number was four times higher at the age of 17 (from 2.7% in 1994 to 14.0% in 2004).

It is clear that the growing tendency in the use of certain drugs has become a worrisome challenge in Europe in the 21st century. In recent years there has been an important increase in the number of cases seeking help and assistance for psychological dependency on these drugs within a context of clubbing and party going (Green, O'Shea, & Colado, 2004; Maxwell, 2003). In add-

ition, some studies are already reporting deaths and psychiatric illnesses related to these new drugs (Gill, Hayes, DeSouza, Marker, & Stajic, 2002; Green et al., 2004). In the United Kingdom, for instance, ecstasy-related deaths increased from 16 in 1998 to 55 in 2001 (EMCDDA, 2004).

For all these reasons, it has become a major priority to implement preventive strategies to fight the growing consumption of drugs in adolescence. Therefore, a psychosocial perspective of the various factors associated with drug use is essential. These factors span a continuum from individual to macro-environmental factors and are probably different for recreational and serious use.

3. Factors associated with drug consumption: A biopsychosocial approach

3.1 Initial approach

Even though each substance has its own specific domain, and the consequences of tobacco consumption, abuse of alcohol or, abuse of other drugs are essentially different, there are clear similarities in their models of development. Thus, the abuse of tobacco, alcohol, and illicit drugs show similar epidemiological and aetiological models and reveal numerous coincidences in the approaches to the treatment and prevention of these problems (Hansen & O'Malley, 1996). Furthermore, on many occasions, it has been demonstrated that social influence is an important factor that promotes the experimentation, increased use, and continued consumption of all these substances regardless of the differences in the pharmacological effects of each one.

From this perspective, researchers point out two general factors that influence substance consumption. First, it is clear that previous consumption of a substance is a determinant factor of subsequent consumption, as stated earlier. Some substances produce addiction by generating symptoms of abstinence and psycho-pharmacological tolerance (Hodgkins, Cahill, Seraphine, Frost-Pineda, & Gold, 2004). Second, previous studies have also shown that psychosocial factors, such as the influence of peers, play an important role in the initiation and progressive development of substance consumption (Musher-Eizenman, Holub, & Arnett, 2003).

In this sense, Becker (1974) emphasizes the importance of the interaction with others in the approximation and initiation stages of drug consumption. This author regards the progression in drug consumption to be the result of a complex succession of psychological and social experiences, in which the context of interaction with other consumers reinforces or modifies the pre-existing attitudes towards drug consumption (a predisposition towards consumption or towards rejection). The moment and conditions in which that interaction takes place become particularly important, because they represent a change from a simple predisposition to direct experimentation with a substance.

The underlying complexity of drug consumption in both the initiation and continued drug consumption stages has led to important efforts by researchers to develop theoretical models that are powerful enough to explain at least some of the main processes and factors that are related to this social problem.

3.2 Development of interpretative models: From an intrapersonal approach to an ecological perspective

The initial approaches developed in the 1960s were focused on explanations of drug consumption through unidimensional factors. Thus, individual or situational factors were considered to

be predictive factors of the use of substances. Some of the variables outlined in these approaches concerned specific personality features, deficits in identity development, influence of behaviour models or disorders in the relationship between the subject and the social context.

Subsequent studies disregard explanations of this kind and support the fact that the personality variables, as well as any other unidimensional factor cannot be predictive of drug behaviour. Furthermore, the epidemiological data obtained in the 1970s show that drug consumption is not a specific reality of a few individuals, but rather a behaviour pattern that is widespread in the adolescent population (Ravenna, 1993). Widespread drug consumption allows researchers to definitely rule out interpretations that consider drug consumption to be something specific to a restricted number of disturbed or deviant subjects. Other factors related to adolescent life styles should be introduced into the analysis (Coslin, 2002; Moffitt, 1993).

Even though a unitary model has not been achieved as yet, a great number of theories have attempted to explain drug consumption in adolescence. Nowadays, some of the most widely accepted approaches are those that are based on the patterns obtained from a psychosocial framework that moves from the subject to the community (FearnowKenney, Hansen, & McNeal, 2002; Musitu et al., 2000).

One of the most relevant proposals of the interdisciplinary approach to risk behaviours is the problem behaviour theory proposed by Jessor and Jessor (1980). This theory considers adolescent risk behaviours to be an interrelation between risk factors and protective factors. This approach distributes the factors that contribute to adolescent risk behaviours in five areas: (1) biological or genetic factors; (2) social environment, which includes factors such as poverty and marginality; (3) perceived environment, which refers to how adolescents perceive their own environment; (4) personality factors, which include variables such as self-esteem, expectations about their own future, their tendency to assume risks, and values related to achievement and health; and (5) behavioural factors, such as school attendance and alcohol consumption. This theory also emphasizes the importance of the protective factors that mitigate the adolescents' participation in risk behaviours.

The problem behaviour theory also suggests that the behaviour of drug consumption is related to an underlying trend towards deviation (Jessor, 1991, 1993). The initiation into the use of substances is considered to be the milestone from which the trend to be implicated in a deviated behavioural style increases. Furthermore, the initiation into the use of substances, on the one hand, conveys an increasingly important and negative influence of the deviated peers, and, on the other hand, becomes the gateway to more problematic behaviours, such as alcoholism or the abuse of other drugs (Gossman, 1992; Shillington & Clapp, 2002). Field studies in Italy have fully confirmed that a specific risk behaviour is generally associated with other problematic behaviours. This association is more evident in those adolescents who are more involved with drug consumption (Ravenna & Cavazza, 2000; Ravenna & Kirchler, 2000).

Longitudinal studies on the influence of problematic behaviours at an early age (before the age of 15) in adolescent psychosocial development show that the consequences arising from these behaviours increase the probability of initiating drug consumption (Rohrbach, et al., 2005). According to Robins and McEvoy (1990) there exists a significant relationship between the number or extent of problematic behaviours at early ages, and the age in which the initiation in drug consumption takes place. Thus, the initiation in drug use at more precocious ages increases with the number of problematic behaviours (Buelga & Lila, 1999; Wills, Walker, & Resko, 2005).

The biopsychosocial model proposed by Igra and Irwin (1996) also emphasizes the importance of using a psychosocial perspective in order to explain the adolescent risk behaviours. With reference to the consumption of different drugs, these authors identify several risk factors associated to the subjects and the social system. They emphasise the interrelationship of these factors within a biopsychosocial model, which also includes an evaluation of cultural factors. The authors

propose some biological and psychological factors as individual risk variables. Specifically, the biological ones are genetic predisposition, direct hormonal influences, hormonal interactions and the age of puberty development. The adolescents' cognitive ability and the predisposing personality features are judged as decisive elements in relation to the psychological area. With regard to the social or environmental system, authors suggest that the role of peers and parents, the family structure, and the social institutions are important factors that contribute to risk behaviours.

Finally, another interesting proposal is the model by Hawkins, Catalino and Miller (1992). This model is based on the assumption that the different risk factors that configure the biopsychosocial matrix do not occur independently or in isolation but frequently take place in combination, thus affecting different areas of the adolescent's performance. Adolescents susceptible to high-risk behaviours show problems in multiple areas and tend to belong to social networks that foster the development of these risk behaviours and reinforce their continued performance (Hawkins et al., 2002). These authors consider it necessary to study the different risk factors that are present in substance consumption from an ecological perspective, which takes into account five basic contexts: individuals, school, family, peers, and community. In this respect, they consider laws and normative behaviours, availability of substances, economic deprivation, neighbourhood disorganization and mobility to be important risk factors for substance consumption in the society–community context. In the family context, organization, practices of family control, conflicts, and parental styles are also considered to be relevant risk factors. In the academic area, some significant factors are recurrent absenteeism, low academic performance, little connection with the school environment and the existence of persistent and early antisocial behaviours. In relation to the peer group, Hawkins et al. (1992, 2002) regard peer rejection (or indifference at elementary school), favourable attitudes to substance consumption as well as behaviours of substance use by peers to be facilitator factors of drug consumption. Finally, in an individual context, biological and cognitive factors, rebellion against normative attitudes and values of society, lack of coping abilities, and a precocious initiation in deviant behaviours are considered by these authors to be important predictors of substance consumption.

4. Applying constructs from the biopsychosocial model to initiation and continued drug use

In accordance with the main contexts (individual, family, peer group and community) proposed in the biopsychological theories just mentioned, we will now try to integrate the different concepts and constructs on which these approaches are based in an explicative model that is focused on the risk factors associated to the different phases of drug consumption.

As is shown in more detail in the following, while a considerable number of these risk factors concern the individual at different levels (biological, psychological, and socio-demographical), some refer to the influences of significant others (family and peers), and some refer to elements of a macro social order.

4.1 The individual: Biological, psychological, and structural variables

4.1.1 Biological variables

The studies carried out in this field have shown that various drugs that produce an increase in a positive mood or euphoria, such as nicotine and alcohol, directly or indirectly affect the inhibiting neurotransmitter GABA, dopamine in the accubems nucleus or in the prefrontal cortex (Hodgkins et al., 2004; Tomkins & Sellers, 2001). The stimulation of these dopaminergic mechanisms represents the most important factor in explaining the strengthening effects and the potential addiction of various abusive substances. In addition to dopamine, it has been confirmed that certain proteins and other neurotransmitters contribute to the pathophysiology of the individual risk of drug dependency (Smith & Capps, 2005).

4.1.2 Psychological variables

Several studies have underscored the importance of certain psychological variables as vulnerability factors in drug consumption: cognitive and motivational factors, sensation and excitement seeking, and social facilitation. These and other psychological variables will be explained in detail.

4.1.2.1 Cognitive factors

The literature on this topic suggests that the first experimentation of any substance can be predicted from positive attitudes, expectations, and attributions on consumption. In this respect, Jessor (1991) argues that attitudes and expectations about the consequences of consumption predict the initial use. Also, Cook, Lounsbury, and Fontenell (1980) with reference to Fishbein and Ajzen's (1975) model have pointed out that a favourable attitude to drug behaviour is correlated to drug consumption.

Underestimating the risks associated with the drug use, overrating one's own abilities of self-control and the spread in drug use in one's own living environment or among friends are all elements that can facilitate and support drug use behaviour (Ravenna & Nicoli, 1991a, 1991b). In this sense, the "false consensus effect" is due to the fact that real or potential drug users, who tend to form relationships with others that share the same beliefs and behaviour, are in general led to believe that the number of drug users is higher than it actually is. This increases the attributes of normality and attractiveness of drug use, rendering it more acceptable in certain aspects (Pudney, 2002; Ravenna, 2005).

Likewise, the values system seems to be another important variable. Thus, according to Schwartz's model (1992), the dimension of "openness to changes", which comprises individual needs such as hedonism and stimulation, as opposed to the more pro-socially biased dimension of "self-transcendence", becomes predictive both in the initial stage of drug use and in the continued consumption patterns. The literature has found some differences in the values system of drug consumers and non-consumers (Buelga & Pons, 2004). Whereas consumers attribute more importance to the values related to individual needs, such as the seeking of pleasure and activation, non-consumers assign more importance to values directed to common welfare (Pons et al., 2000).

Hawkins et al. (1992) suggest that the rejection of the normative attitudes and values of society and the rejection of the commitment to social aims constitute important risk factors for substance consumption. From this point of view, for some adolescents, illicit drug use represents an expression of rebellion or transgression against the establishment in a reactive attempt to build up a specific identity, which is different from the one offered by society. Moreover, the transgression incentive to carry out a forbidden action diminishes with age. This incentive is more important for adolescents aged 15 to 18 than for youths aged 19 to 24; for this second age group, it is more relevant than for those aged 25 to 29.

4.1.2.2 Motivational factors

Personal expectations and beliefs about the effects of various drugs play an important role both in favouring initial contact and in strengthening drug habits over time. In the first case, these expectations are founded on the adolescents' own elaboration about their relationship with the environment; in the second case, they are mainly based on direct experience (Allen, 2003). Much of the evidence from different conceptual and effective approaches shows that teenagers and young adults use licit and illicit drugs to look for states of excitement that make their relationships with others more intense and satisfying and that make their spare time activities more stimulating (Bonino, 1999; Palmonari & Ravenna,1988). They also look for states that stimulate the different processes of identification with their peers and that reduce the degree of embarrassment that is associated with growing up (Ravenna & Nicoli, 1991a; Schlaadt & Shannon, 1994).

4.1.2.3 Self-enhancement and regulation of emotions

Adolescents also adopt certain types of behaviour to enhance important aspects and dimensions of the self and identity. Since the definition of the self is a particularly crucial question in adolescence, certain behaviours may be undertaken to maintain or increase certain personal attributes (Buelga & Musitu, 2004). As the need to try different experiences increases, there is a greater

probability for adolescents to identify smoking, drinking alcohol or taking illegal drugs either as a way of experimenting with their own physical and psychological possibilities, or of trying out different social behaviours (possible selves) (Bonino, 1999; Palmonari, 1997). Being a smoker, a drinker, or a drug taker is of immediate value in the subject's relationship with significant others (Emler & Reicher, 1995). This behaviour provides information about the self that allows adolescents to be treated by the peer group as someone who is more adult, more emancipated, more capable of controlling their own life autonomously.

In certain circumstances, young people who feel insecure about their own abilities may resort to alcohol or other drugs in order to preserve a positive self-image. They can avoid being blamed for possible failures and lay the blame on their state of intoxication. Therefore, as Jones and Berglas (1978) point out, they basically adopt a criterion according to which it is better to be seen as drunk or high rather than as incompetent. Although, many teenagers can recognize the emotions they feel, know how to express them, and understand how these emotions influence their behaviour, they are not able to control their emotional states. In other words, they are unable to produce positive emotional reactions or to play down negative ones in situations that require it (Labouvie, 1986). Difficulty or failure in facing states of anger, extreme excitement, or depression may help them to identify drugs as an effective strategy to obtain immediate gratification effects and increase feelings of self-control (Boys & Marsden, 2003; Panagopoulus & Ricciardelli, 2005).

4.1.2.4 Stress reduction

The more adolescents become aware of the difficulties in constructively facing the tasks of growing up, the more attractive drugs will be as a mean to reduce feelings of inadequacy and negative psychological states such as anxiety, anger, insecurity, depression (Palmonari, 1997; Wagner, 2001).

Drugs can allow adolescents to distance themselves from a present that is perceived to be highly unsatisfying (Bonino, 1999; Sher, Bartholow, &

Wood, 2003). Adolescents who feel particularly overwhelmed by rules, norms, expectations and constraints in their daily lives may live intentionally sought experiences through drugs, in which they abandon the experience of the self in ordinary life for a limited period of time (Ricci Bitti, 1997). The results of Labouvie's research (1986) on 677 young drug users show that an environment that is unable to stimulate satisfying social relationships may contribute to increasing feelings of helplessness, behaviour directed towards the search for sensations and a greater involvement in drug use.

Drugs are also taken to find some way of adapting to social pressures related to competition and success. In these cases, drugs are identified as a means for reducing the conflict between certain personal needs and the strict demands made by the environment (Palmonari, 1993; Wagner, 2001).

4.1.2.5 Sensation and excitement seeking, modification of states of conscience

The need to modify states of conscience by taking the most disparate substances is nothing new. It has existed throughout human history and in every kind of society, and it has always pushed people to discover and invent new substances to achieve their goals (Gossop, 1987). Weil (1986) believes that the need to alter states of conscience is felt not only by young people and adults, but also by small children. This author hypothesizes that this need evolves during the different stages of life and different solutions are found at each stage. The experiences that alter normal psychological states satisfy an innate inner need (like the sexual need). The experience of pleasure that is obtained can be reached in different ways: through games (spinning round until one feels dizzy, breathing deeply and quickly until a state of hyperventilation is reached, having one's chest or neck compressed until one feels faint), or by taking drugs to find those specific sensations that characterize the intermediate stage between waking and sleeping.

Adolescence is the time to expand the boundaries of one's own living space, to experiment with new and different styles of behaviour and to search for adventurous and unusual experiences (Ames, Sussman, Dent, & Stacy, 2005; Palmonari, 1997). From this perspective, Zuckerman (1979) explains young people's attraction for reckless behaviour as the manifestation of a personality trait that is characterized by the desire to have new and different experiences. These experiences imply a certain degree of risk that they are prepared to run for the fun of it. The need for strong sensations is greater among males and is negatively correlated with age (Wagner 2001). It is closely tied to the use of psychoactive substances (Acton, 2003; Carrol, Zuckerman, & Vogel, 1982) and is included with other numerous personality traits and characteristics such as hypomania, impulsive, antisocial or psychopathic tendencies, extroversion, non-conformity, creativity, independence from the field and the need for change, self-esteem and display (Sher et al., 2003).

Other explanations include the role of cultural influences in the search and display (in a variety of fields: sport, sex, travel) of extreme experiences that are considered to be unique and unrepeatable. These influences also affect the experiences that adolescents have with drugs; for example, when they do not know the real composition of the substance, or when they take massive doses to get the best high. Somehow, this type of behaviour promotes the idea "that there is a desire to be put to an extreme test, like pulling the rope to see how far you get. The desire is to succeed, to be the only ones capable of making it" (Le Breton, 1991).

4.1.2.6 Personality factors

Some authors consider that certain personality features are related to different levels of drug abuse (Kashdan, Vetter, & Collins, 2005). One of the most important formulations is the contribution of Eysenck (1988), who suggests that certain personality traits, such as psychopathy, neuroticism and antisocial personality are related to substance consumption. In this sense, extroversion and psychopathy are the dimensions that are most closely related to tobacco consumption. As explained earlier, impulsiveness and sensation seeking, and/or pessimistic states, depression and low self-esteem are all factors associated with alcohol and illicit substance consumption (Acton, 2003; Sher et al. 2003).

Shedler and Block's longitudinal research study (1990) analysed the relationship between the use of/abstention from drugs and the presence/absence of specific personal traits and characteristics in a sample of 101 subjects from 5 to 18 years old. Results show that, long before contact with drugs and before adolescence, regular users already had different symptoms of emotional suffering. These symptoms could be framed in a coherent syndrome characterized by alienation, impulsiveness, and social stress. It was precisely because they were unable to invest energy in relationships with others, at school, and at work, that they felt unhappy and inadequate to the point of progressively isolating themselves from others. According to the authors, this lack of interest and involvement in the different environments of daily life triggered emotional instability and a lack of direction and planning, which increased the importance of acting based on short-lived subjective aspects. These adolescents were attracted to drugs because they eased feelings of isolation, inadequacy, and the inability to achieve more lasting and significant gratification. In a longitudinal study on a group of 100 children from age 7 to age 20, van Aken and Heutinck (1998) found that adolescents who take drugs at 20 years old are characterized by higher levels of impulsiveness and extroversion and by lower satisfaction and responsibility. This study also found that the use of drugs by 20 year olds can be predicted by levels of impulsiveness between the ages of 7 and 12.

In contrast, other authors support the idea that there are no specific personality characteristics associated with drug consumption (Hawkins et al. 2002; Musitu et al. 2000; Ravenna, 1993). In this perspective, it is believed that initiation is influenced, in most cases, by a series of features in the non-conventionality area or by temporary negative emotional states, rather than being associated to psychopathological–structured disorders. In relation to this, Moffitt (1993) underlines that risk behaviour is not associated with any type of psychological alteration, but rather

with a basic human characteristic (curiosity) which is especially relevant during adolescence. Some authors consider, from a basically statistical point of view, that the previous, more frequent type of personality among drug abusers is the normal personality. Most forms of drug consumption and other risk behaviours among young people involve neither abuse nor social deviation; neither can they be attributed to abnormal personalities or pathological socialization processes. These kinds of behaviour even present characteristics of normativeness.

4.1.2.7 Social competence, coping, self-esteem, problem behaviour

Social competence, or the capacity to behave appropriately in interpersonal relationships and situations, also plays an important role in drug use. The authors who base their works on Shiffman and Wills' coping theory (1985) claim the following: children and young people that have not had the opportunity to learn the appropriate social abilities, or have been poorly supported and valued in their experience of coping, or exposed to particularly negative events, have less probability of acquiring these adapting abilities and more risk for developing non-conventional behaviours.

From this perspective, coping strategies are essential to explain both initiation and continued drug use (Folkman, Lazarus, Gruen, & De Longis, 1986). Resorting to drugs allows the subject to escape from the adverse situations of daily life (see also "stress reduction"). The way problems are faced are different for users and non-users. Tackling problems by facing the situation that generates them is less frequent in the groups that consume alcohol and illicit drugs. Furthermore, those that only consume illicit drugs use the strategy of lack of responsibility for the events that affect them more frequently (Minehan, Newcomb, & Galaif, 2000).

According to different studies, active coping strategies, such as cognitive redefinition or problem resolution are related to higher self-esteem. Thus, self-esteem is also a resource that people possess to face the different situations that occur in their lives (Lila, Musitu, & Buelga, 2001).

A low self-esteem represents an important risk factor for continued drug use (Bonino & Cattelino, 1998; Bonino & Ciairano, 1998; Bonino & Gangarossa, 1998).

Other research has studied the relationship between early problematic behaviour and the use or abuse of drugs. Robins and McEvoy's retrospective study (1990) on a sample of 5188 drug users shows that the early manifestation (before the age of 15) of problematic behaviour (unruliness, truancy, being expelled from school, running away from home, vandalism, thieving and so on) increases the likelihood of drug consumption. This study also shows that the more frequently this type of behaviour occurs, the earlier the first contact with drugs. The amount of abuse also increases. In a longitudinal study on 545 young people between the ages of 13 and 25, Anderson, Bergman, and Magnusson (1989) found that what increases the risk of abuse of alcohol in adolescence and adulthood is not one single kind of problematic behaviour (psychomotor unrest, aggressiveness, lack of concentration, low aspirations and educational motivation, poor peer relationships) but rather a "serious cluster of behaviours" before the age of 13. This finding is positively correlated to problems of deviancy and mental health.

4.1.2.8 Social facilitation

Expectations and beliefs connected with sociability carry great weight in teenage drug behaviour. The basic idea is that resorting to drugs strengthens comradeship, helps to create an atmosphere of cooperation, facilitates communication and the sharing of feelings and experiences, and permits the different processes of peer identification (Allen, Donohue, Griffin, Ryan, & Turner, 2003). This may take on different forms. Resorting to a type of drug may permit experiences of similarity with one's own group of drug-using friends (intragroup similarity). It may constitute a rite of bonding that is achieved by sharing the actions connected to the drug consumption while at the same time confirming and strengthening membership of a group (Atkinson, Richard, & Carlson, 2002; Bonino, 1999). It also allows teenagers to show their own diversity from those who do not

engage in this kind of behaviour (intergroup differentiation). This may help to make the adolescents feel braver, stronger, and freer and at the same time, allows them to build up their own reputation and status within the group (Emler & Reicher, 1995).

For younger adolescents, an experience with drugs may represent a challenge to the rules and norms put forward by parents; it is a way of distancing themselves from their world (Buelga & Musitu, 2004). Such an experience can also accelerate their identification with an older age bracket, thus allowing them to feel like they have taken a shortcut to adulthood (Coslin, 2002). This is particularly true for those teenagers who want to enjoy the advantages of adult life without waiting, and for those who are more sensitive to peer pressure to appear more grown-up, independent and cocky (Ravenna, 1997).

Resorting to drugs may also favour experiences of union between the individual and a larger group as in the processes of de-individuation described by Zimbardo (1969). A specific example of this is drug use that is linked to the discotheque, where the combination created by music, drug use and the rites associated with these environments favour a collective experience defined as *"participation mystique"*. This experience responds to the need to feel part of a large group and to be absorbed into a transforming and welcoming whole (Bricolo, 1996). Feeling anonymous in a group, focusing on the immediate present, is subjecting oneself to an overload of sensorial stimuli or the effects of the drugs are all conditions in which people's actions are guided more by momentary psychological states than by careful, far-reaching thought processes (Zimbardo, 1988).

4.1.3 Structural variables

4.1.3.1 Gender and age

Gender is considered to be one of the most relevant risk factors associated with continued drug use as well as with the consumption patterns of the various substances. Many studies have found that the consumption of alcohol and illicit drugs is more frequent among male adolescents (Kashdan et al., 2005; Wagner, 2001). This trend is more evident when regular or frequent consumption is taken into account, with a male/female proportion of approximately 2:1 (EMCDDA, 2003, 2004, 2005).

The prevalence of males in the use of the various substances is explained in a similar way to that of other illicit or reprehensible behaviours. This prevalence is accounted for by the different styles of socialisation and control. Boys are given more freedom to adopt non-conventional behaviours, whereas there is stronger pressure on girls to comply with social norms (Estevez, Musitu, & Herrero, 2005). It is also explained in accordance with the different kinds of attachments that both sexes have. Girls have a closer involvement in family and school life, while boys are more closely involved with their peers (Svensson, 2003)

It has been consistently demonstrated that age is a variable closely related to substance consumption. As mentioned earlier, it has become evident that there is a curvilinear relationship between illicit drug consumption patterns and age; as adolescents grow older, consumption increases, with a peak between the ages of 18 and 25 followed by a general decrease in the use of substances (Hansen & Malley, 1996; Sloboda & Bukoski, 2003).

4.1.3.2 Academic achievement and level

The educational context is the relational environment and space where intellectual development takes place. It is one of the most important systems for the prevention of behaviour problems. Poor academic performance, lack of commitment, and integration with the education received, are all factors that are frequently considered to explain risk behaviours, specifically, drug consumption (Lillehoj, Trudeau, & Spoth, 2005; Sutherland & Shepherd, 2001).

In this respect, various studies confirm the existence of a relationship between negative school performance and substance consumption (Bryant, Schulenberg, O'Malley, Bachman, & Johnston, 2003; Lillehoj et al., 2005). Students who repeat courses and those with a negative school or academic self-image show the highest levels of consumption of tobacco, alcohol, and

illicit drugs. Academic level also appears to be related to consumption patterns (Jeynes, 2002).

4.1.3.3 Habitat and social class

Different studies have focused on habitat and social class. The contradictory results emerging probably depend on the influence of other modulating variables. Several studies show that young people who work (particularly those who work long hours) are more prone to drug use (EMCDDA, 2003). The unemployed also appear to be a group that is at risk of substance consumption (Zanis, 2004).

4.1.3.4 Affordability and leisure time

There are some connections between disposable income (pocket money) and regular drug consumption. Thus, significant relationships between becoming a regular consumer and having more money for weekly expenses have been found. These relationships are found in the consumption of all the substances: tobacco, alcohol and illicit drugs.

Another interesting question is the amount of leisure time available to young people and the kind of activities they participate in in that period. Undoubtedly, there are more hours of leisure time at weekends and holidays. An important part of their leisure time is spent in interaction with their groups of reference; some of the most common activities are talking with friends, dancing and drinking. To a large extent, these activities are associated with the consumption of various substances (Ravenna, & Cavazza, 2000; Ravenna & Kirchler, 2000). In relation to alcohol consumption, a number of studies have found that participation in religious activities is significantly associated in an inverse proportion with alcohol consumption. Likewise, participation in sports activities (Escarti, 2003), although not directly related to low alcohol consumption, does reduce the frequency of drunkenness. Therefore, a connection between participation in sports activities and a lower frequency of drunkenness is found. This relationship has already been highlighted in a study carried out among young athletes in Italy (Donato & Assanellieu, 1994).

4.2 Microsocial factors: Family and peers

4.2.1 The family

The family, which is regarded as one of the most important support systems for the welfare and adjustment of its members, has also been analysed in studies investigating certain risk factors associated with substance consumption. Some of the most important factors are educational parenting style, the relationship between parents and children, and the parents' role as behaviour models for their children (Barker & Hunt, 2004; Buelga & Pons, 2004; Kumpfer, Alvarado, & Whiteside, 2003; Lila & Gracia, 2005).

4.2.1.1 Parenting style

Educational style is one of the principal ways for parents to alter their children's involvement in drug consumption. The scientific literature suggests that both the authoritarian parenting style (where parenting control prevails over affective warmth), and the permissive parenting style (where affection prevails over the control of the children's behaviour) are related to adolescent drug use (Martínez, Fuertes, Ramos, & Hernández, 2003).

Another style is the authoritative parenting style. In contrast with the other, this authoritative style is an important factor in the prevention of substance consumption among adolescents (Baumrind, 1991). The main characteristics of this educational style are affective warmth/acceptance and monitorization/discipline. These characteristics seem to be particularly important in promoting a form of autonomy in children that is based on the ability to form deep relationships and prevent risk behaviours (Lila & Gracia, 2005).

Moreover, the studies suggest that the harmony/discrepancy level in the values system concerning the children's education is related to risk behaviours (McIntosh, MacDonald, & McKeganey, 2005). Thus, family cohesion and the consistency of the points of view on the children's education seem to influence drug consumption indirectly in two ways: (1) it diminishes the appearance of negative self-images, while promoting self-esteem, and (2) it reduces the excessive dependency of adolescents on their peer groups (Martínez et al., 2003).

4.2.1.2 Family relationships

The nature of the relationships between parents and children constitutes a family factor that also seems to be connected with drug consumption. One of the most widely accepted theories suggests that a positive parent–child relationship, in which the emotional link prevails, may act as a prevention mechanism in drug use (Buelga & Pons, 2004; Kumpfer et al., 2003). Consumers of legal and illicit drugs perceive greater conflict in their family environment than non-consumers. Important factors that are associated with drug use are: lack of parent–child communication or negative communication patterns, such as double messages or criticism; and a family atmosphere with frequent conflicts and arguments between parents and children, and/or between parents (Musitu et al., 2000; Williams, McDermitt, Bertrand, & Davis, 2003).

4.2.1.3 Parental consumption model

The parents' level of drug use has been consistently related to the children's future level of consumption. A number of studies have also revealed a consistent correlation between adolescent drug abuse and parental use of alcohol and tobacco (Bonino & Cattelino, 1998; Bonino & Ciairano, 1998). Thus, there is a higher frequency of tobacco and alcohol consumption by adolescents when one or both parents smoke or drink alcohol. It is generally assumed that parents' drug consumption influences their children's drug behaviour, even though parents express negative verbal messages against these conducts. Parental drug use and a verbal message against consumption may lead to ambiguous behaviour in children regarding the identification of consumption with the status of adulthood (Barker & Hunt, 2004).

Parental modelling influences are an important learning factor in the development of drug consumption behaviour. Nevertheless, the imitation of a parental model is not produced in a direct way. It is biased by other modulating variables, such as the model's credibility, the interpretation of the model's behaviour and the perception of the model's attitudes and behaviour (Bandura, 1999).

4.2.2 The peer group

4.2.2.1 Group influence

As stated earlier (see social facilitation), peer group influence is undoubtedly one of the most frequently recognized factors in the scientific literature (Allen et al., 2003; Musher-Eizenman et al., 2003). Therefore, even though the parental behaviour of legal substance consumption appears to be important for initiation into tobacco and alcohol consumption, the role of the peer group is fundamental for both the continued consumption of these substances and for the initiation into illicit drugs (Atkinson et al., 2002).

According to Rosenbaum (1979), there are also differences depending on the person who induces the adolescent to experiment with these drugs. In the case of boys, the person that commonly offers an illicit substance is a friend of the same sex. In the case of girls, it is generally a male friend or boyfriend.

In the peer group, the suggestion to experiment is frequently made by people with a higher status (from the adolescence's perspective). Consumption may have different meanings for different people. While for some, drug consumption may represent a ritual to reach maturity, for others, it is a ritual that allows them to take part in leisure activities and become integrated in the group. Illicit substance consumption is certainly a key criterion in defining membership to a group (Atkinson et al., 2002; Bonino, 1999). Those groups that commonly consume illicit substances can use drugs as a social identifier and/or a part of the established social rituals. A number of research data confirm that the initiation and the continued use of different drugs is, in most cases, produced through the influence of the group of friends (Allen et al., 2003).

4.2.2.2 The selection and projection model

In another work concerning group influence, Bauman and Ennet's proposal (1996) questions whether or not friends determine drug consump-

tion. These authors emphasize that peer group influence has been overestimated with reference to the use of substances. It overlooks the fact that friendships are largely determined by drug consumption (selection), and that adolescents frequently attribute their own behaviour to their friends (projection). Thus, both the selection model (which places drug consumption at the base of friendship) and the projection model (which sees the behaviour attributed to friends as the consequence of one's own drug consumption) are employed by Bauman and Ennet (1996) to question the importance of the group influence model. Note that, in most cases, the results obtained in different studies on adolescent drug consumption have not accounted for these processes of selection and projection. This probably depends on the fact that the researchers have generally employed cross-sectional research models, which are inadequate for studying the influence of selection.

4.3 Macrosocial Factors

4.3.1 Social marginality

It is difficult to establish the relationship between marginality and drug consumption when the term marginality itself has different connotations. This term is, in fact, associated with the following characteristics: poverty and the consequent lack of resources; the lack of stable or healthy housing; malnutrition; low cultural level; lack of any type of power and absence of social participation channels (Compas, Hinden, & Gerhardt, 1995; Freisthler, Lascala, Gruenewald, & Treno, 2005).

Although drug consumption also occurs in all social groups, research shows that the use and abuse of drugs, delinquency, and other risk behaviours are relatively more frequent among the marginal groups in a situation of serious poverty, homeless people, or those living in very dilapidated neighbourhoods (Edmonds, Sumnall, McVeigh, & Bellis, 2005; Freisthler et al., 2005). Studies related to this topic also point out that, in marginal populations, particularly among young people, the age of initiation with the various drugs is lower, and that multi-consumption and multi-toxicomania prevail (Jotcham, 2001; Mallett et al., 2005).

4.3.2 Substance availability

It is widely recognized that experimenting with or consuming different substances depends, to a large extent, on the availability of the product. Undoubtedly, the nearer and more easily available the substance is, the greater the probability of consumption (Knibbe et al., 2005). Easy access to a product, in terms of availability and price, significantly influences its use, especially among new consumers, who want to try a substance to test its effects (Komro, Flay, Hu, Zelli, Rashid, & Amuwo, 1998). This access in terms of availability and price also accounts for the continued consumption of many substances.

Easy access to tobacco and alcohol on the part of minors in the family environment, and also in public premises and shops, becomes an important facilitating factor for initiation as well as for continued consumption. In some countries, problems can arise from the fact that alcohol and tobacco are legal drugs, but their purchase, possession, and use by children under 16 is illegal. Thus, even though there are regulations preventing sales to minors, adolescents can easily access these drugs. These substances are frequently available in supermarkets, where they are cheaper and less controlled. Access to illicit substances such as synthetic drugs or hallucinogens is also relatively easy at discos and nightclubs.

4.3.3 Mass media

The influence of the media is nowadays so great, that it is difficult to analyse the problems of society without relating them to radio, television, and the written press. For adolescents, watching television is one of their favourite leisure activities. Those aged 13 to 15 spend approximately 1500 hours per year in front of the television and witness approximately 670 murders, 858 fights, and 18 cases of drug consumption (sniffing, intravenous consumption) a *week* (De Noray & Parvex, 1994).

Adolescents increasingly have to cope with contradictory messages. They receive information from campaigns against drugs, which clearly reject drug consumption. They also observe advertising messages for legal drugs, which enhance the value of the product through its connection with fam-

ous people. This is done by relating their consumption to supposedly positive effects: escape, unity and integration with the peer group and entertainment (Priester, 2001).

5. Conclusion

The use of legal and illicit drugs is currently a phenomenon that is particularly common among the adolescent population, principally in male adolescents (Kashdan et al., 2005; Wagner, 2001). This situation is constantly changing with regard to the type of substances taken, the circumstances, and the activities connected with drug use. As we have discussed here, it is no easy task to obtain a homogeneous view of the trends of this phenomenon, since the epidemiological studies performed in the various countries use different data collection methodologies. With respect to subjective experience, drug consumption responds to the diversified needs that are linked with overcoming the specific development tasks of this stage of life, especially those relating to the definition of the self and identity. Drug consumption has been classified as a risk behaviour that does not occur in isolation. It is mainly associated with other risky or problematic behaviours. There are a number of factors that tend to favour initial contact and also consolidate consumption habits over time. Among these are individual, microsocial and macrosocial factors, which play a crucial role. Although adolescents are often subject to the restrictions and influences of their social environment and to fortuitous circumstances, they actively construct their own relationship with drugs and are not limited to simply reacting to the circumstances and to the models of behaviour they are faced with.

Valuable examples of the possible relationships that exist among the various risk factors (biological, psychological, and those relative to social influences) are given in relevant interactionist theories such as Jessor and Jessor's theory of problematic behaviour (1980, 1990), Igra and Irvin's biopsychosocial theory (1996) and the 1992 model of Hawkins et al., which have all proved to be instrumental in perceiving the multidimensional nature of drug use phenomenon.

References

Acton, G.S. (2003). Measurement of impulsivity in a hierarchical model of personality traits: Implications for substance use. *Journal of Substance Use and Misuse, 38*, 67–83.

Allen, D. (2003). Treating the cause not the problem: Vulnerable young people and substance misuse. *Journal of Substance Use, 8*, 42–46.

Allen, M., Donohue, W.A., Griffin, A., Ryan, D., & Turner, M.M. (2003). Comparing the influence of parents and peers on the choice to use drugs: A meta-analytic summary of the literature. *Criminal Justice and Behavior, 30*, 163–186.

Ames, S.L., Sussman, S., Dent, C.W., & Stacy, A.W. (2005). Implicit cognition and dissociative experiences as predictors of adolescent substance use. *American Journal of Drug and Alcohol Abuse, 31*(1), 129–162.

Anderson, T., Bergman, L.R., & Magnusson, D. (1989). Patterns of adjustment problems and alcohol abuse in early adulthood: A prospective longitudinal study. *Development and Psychopathology, 1*, 119–131.

Atkinson, J.S., Richard, A.J., & Carlson, J.W. (2002). The influence of peer, family, and school relationships in substance use among participants in a youth jobs program. *Journal of Child and Adolescent Substance Abuse, 11*, 45–54.

Atrens, D.M. (2001). Nicotine as an addictive substance: A critical examination of the basic concepts and empirical evidence. *Journal of Drug Issues, 31*, 325–394.

Babor, T.F., Del Boca, F.K., & Griffith, E. (Eds.). (2002). *Treatment matching in alcoholism.* Cambridge: University Press.

Bandura, A. (1999). A sociocognitive analysis of substance abuse: An agentic perspective. *Psychological Science, 10*, 214–217.

Barendregt, C. (1996). El problema de las drogas y la respuesta de Holanda [The drug question and Holland's answers]. *Interdependencias, 16*, 9–11.

Barker, J.C., & Hunt, G. (2004). Representations of family: A review of the alcohol and drug literature. *International Journal of Drug Policy, 15*, 347–356.

Bauman, K.E., & Ennet, S.T. (1996). On the importance of peer influence for adolescent drug use: Commonly neglected considerations. *Addiction, 91*, 185–198.

Baumrind, D. (1991). The influence of parenting style on adolescent competence and substance use. *Journal of Early Adolescence, 11*, 56–95.

Becker, M.H. (1974). The health belief model and personal health behavior. *Health Education Monographs, 2*, 324–473.

Bonino, S. (1999). Il rischio nell'adolescenza: L'erba "leggera" [Risk in adolescence: "Light" grass]. *Psicologia Contemporanea, 151*, 40–48.

Bonino, S., & Cattelino, E. (1998). *Assunzione di sigarette* [Cigarette smoking]. Regione Piemonte, Assessorato sanità.

Bonino, S., & Ciairano, S. (1998). *Il fumo di sigarette* [Cigarette smoke]. Torino, Regione Piemonte, Assessorato sanità.

Bonino, S., & Gangarossa, G. (1998). *L'uso di marijuana* [The use of marijuana]. Regione Piemonte, Assessorato sanità.

Boys, A., & Marsden, J. (2003). Perceived functions predict intensity of use and problems in young polysubstance users. *Addiction, 98*, 951–963.

Bricolo, R. (1996). Intervista citata. In F. Bagozzi, *Generazione in ecstasy* [Generation in ecstasy]. Torino: Edizioni Gruppo Abele.

Bryant, A.L., Schulenberg, J.E., O'Malley, P.M., Bachman, J.G., & Johnston, L.D. (2003). How academic achievement, attitudes, and behaviors relate to the course of substance use during adolescence: A 6-year, multiwave national longitudinal study. *Journal of Research on Adolescence, 13*, 361–397.

Buelga, S., & Lila, M.S. (1999). *Adolescencia y conducta antisocial* [Adolescence and antisocial behaviour]. Valencia: CSV.

Buelga, S., & Musitu, G. (2004). *Famille et adolescence: Prévention de conduite à risque.* [Family and adolescence: Prevention of risk behaviours]. Plenary conference presented at the XIX symposium Scientific Psychology of French Language. Current adolescence. Caen, France.

Buelga, S., & Pons, J. (2004). Alcohol y adolescencia: ¿Cuál es el papel de la familia? [Alcohol and adolescence: What is the role of the family?]. *Encuentros en Psicología Social, 1*(1), 34–43.

Calafat, A., Stocco, P., Mendes, F., Simon, J., Van de Wijngaart, G., Sureda, M.P., et al. (1998). *Characteristics and social representation of ecstasy in Europe.* Palma of Mallorca: IREFREA.

Carrol, E.N., Zuckerman, M., & Vogel, W.H. (1982). A test of the optimal level of arousal theory of sensation seeking. *Journal of Personality and Social Psychology, 42*, 572–575.

Chivite-Matthews, N., Richardson, A., O'Shea, J., Becker, J., Owen, N., Roe, S., et al. (2005). *Drug misuse declared: Findings from the 2003/04 British Crime Survey.* London: Home Office. Research, Development and Statistics Directorate.

Choquet, M. (2004). *Evolution des adolescents durant les 10 dernières années, constats et significations* [Evolution of the teenagers during the last 10 years, reports and meanings]. Plenary conference presented at the XIX symposium Scientific Psychology of French Language. Current adolescence. Caen, France.

Compas, B.E., Hinden, B.R., & Gerhardt, C.A. (1995). Adolescent development: Pathways and processes of health risk and resilience. *Annual Review of Psychology, 46,* 265–293.

Cook, M.P., Lounsbury, J.W., & Fontenell, G.A. (1980). An application on Fishbein and Ajzen's attitude subjective norms model to the study of drug use. *Journal of Social Psychology, 110,* 193–201.

Coslin, P. (2002). *Psychologie de l'adolescent* [Psychology of adolescence]. Paris: Armand Colin.

De Noray, M.L., & Parvex, R. (1994). *Los medios de comunicación frente a la drogas* [Mass media and drugs] Bilbao, Spain: Servicio Central de Publicaciones del País Vasco.

Degenhardt, L., Barker, B., & Topp, L. (2004). Patterns of ecstasy use. *Addiction, 99,* 187–195.

Donato, F., & Assanelliu, D. (1994). Alcohol consumption among high school students and young athletes in north Italy. *Revue Epidémiologique de Santé Publique, 42,* 198–206.

Edmonds, K., Sumnall, H., McVeigh, J., & Bellis, M.A. (2005). *Drug prevention among homeless young people.* Liverpool: John Moores University.

Elliott, L., Orr, L., Watson, L., & Jackson, A. (2005). Secondary prevention interventions for young drug users: A systematic review of the evidence. *Adolescence, 40*(157), 1–22.

Emler, N., & Reicher, S. (1995). *Adolescence and delinquency.* Oxford: Blackwell.

Engels, R.C., & Ter Bogt, T. (2004). Outcome expectancies and ecstasy use in visitors of rave parties in the Netherlands. *European Addiction Research, 10,* 156–162.

Escartí, A. (2003). Socializacion deportiva [Sport socialization]. In A. Hernandez-Mendo (Ed.), *Psicología del deporte* [Sport psychology] (pp. 88–103). Buenos Aires, Brazil: Tulio Guterman.

Estevez, E., Musitu, G., & Herrero, J. (2005). The influence of violent behavior and victimization at school on psychological distress: The role of parents and teachers. *Adolescence, 40*(157), 183–196.

European Monitoring Centre for Drugs and Drug Addiction [EMCDDA] (2003). *Annual report on the state of the drugs problem in the European Union and Norway.* Lisbon, Portugal: European Monitoring Centre for Drugs and Drug Addiction.

European Monitoring Centre for Drugs and Drug Addiction [EMCDDA] (2004). *Annual report on the state of the drugs problem in the European Union and Norway.* Lisbon, Portugal: European Monitoring Centre for Drugs and Drug Addiction.

European Monitoring Centre for Drugs and Drug Addiction [EMCDDA] (2005). *Differences in patterns of drug use between women and men.* Lisbon, Portugal: European Monitoring Centre for Drugs and Drug Addiction.

European School Survey Project on Alcohol and Other Drug Use Among Students in 35 European Countries [ESPAD] (2003). The Swedish Council for Information on Alcohol and Other Drugs and the Pompidou Group at the Council of Europe.

Eysenck, H.J. (1988). The respective importance of personality cigarrette smoking and interaction effects for the genesis of cancer and coronary heart disease. *Personality and Individual Differences, 9,* 453–464.

FearnowKenney, M., Hansen, W.B., & McNeal, R.B. (2002). Comparison of psychosocial influences on substance use in adolescents: Implications for prevention programming. *Journal of Child and Adolescent Substance Abuse, 11,* 1–24.

Fishbein, M., & Ajzen, I. (1975). *Belief, attitude, intention and behavior: An introduction to theory and research.* Reading, MA: Addison-Wesley.

Folkman, S., Lazarus, R.S., Gruen, R.J., & De Longis, A. (1986). Appraisal, coping, health status, and psychological symptoms. *Journal of Personality and Social Psychology, 50,* 571–579.

Freisthler, B., Lascala, E.A., Gruenewald, P.J., & Treno, A.J. (2005). An examination of drug activity: Effects of neighborhood social organization on the development of drug distribution systems. *Substance Use and Misuse, 40,* 671–686.

Gill, J.R., Hayes, J.A., DeSouza, I.S., Marker, E., & Stajic, M. (2002). Ecstasy (MDMA) deaths in New York City: A case series and review of the literature. *Journal of Forensic Sciences, 47,* 121–126.

Godeau, E., Rahav, G., & Hubbet, A. (2004). Tobacco smoking. In C. Currie, C. Robert, A. Morgan, R. Smith, W. Settertobulte, O. Samdal et al. (Eds.), *International report from the 2001/2002 survey. Young people's health in context. Health behaviour in school-aged children (HBSC) study* (pp. 63–71). Copenhagen, Denmark: WHO Regional Office for Europe.

Gossman, F.K. (1992). Risk and resilience in young

adolescents. *Journal of Youth and Adolescence, 21*, 529–550.

Gossop, M. (1987). *Living with drugs*. London: Willwood House.

Government Delegation of the Drug National Plan (DGPNSD) (2005). *State survey on use of drugs among students*. Madrid, Spain: Government Delegation of the Drug National Plan.

Graf, M. (1997). Ecstasy in Switzerland: Data and interpretation. *Addictions, 9*, 293–300.

Green, A.R., O'Shea, E., & Colado, M.I. (2004). A review of the mechanisms involved in the acute MDMA (ecstasy)-induced hyperthermic response. *European Journal of Pharmacology, 500*, 3–13.

Hansen, W.B., & O'Malley, P.M. (1996). Drug use. In R. J. DiClemente, W. B. Hansen, & L. E. Ponton (Eds.), *Handbook of adolescent health risk behavior*. New York: Plenum.

Hawkins, J.D., Catalino, R.F., & Arthur, M.W. (2002). Promoting science-based prevention in communities. *Addictive Behaviors, 27*(6), 951–976.

Hawkins, J.D., Catalano, R.F., & Miller, J.Y. (1992). Health risk and protective factors for alcohol and others drug problems in adolescence and early adulthood: Implications for substance use prevention. *Psychological Bulletin, 112*, 64–105.

Health Behaviour in School-aged Children [HBSC] (2001/2002). *Survey of young people's health in context*. Copenhagen, Denmark: WHO Regional Office for Europe.

Hibell, B., Andersson, B., Bjarnason, T., Ahlström, S., Balakireva, O., Kokkevi, A., & Morgan, M. (2004). *The ESPAD Report 2003. Alcohol and other drug use among students in 35 European countries*. Stockholm, Sweden: The Swedish Council for Information on Alcohol and Other Drugs (CAN) and the Pompidou Group at the Council of Europe.

Hodgkins, C.C., Cahill, K.S., Seraphine, A.E., Frost-Pineda, K., & Gold, M.S. (2004). Adolescent drug addiction treatment and weight gain. *Journal of Addictive Diseases, 23*, 55–65.

Igra, V., & Irwin, C.E. (1996). Theories of adolescent risk-taking behavior. In R. J. DiClemente, W. B. Hansen, & L. E. Ponton (Eds.), *Handbook of adolescent health risk behavior* (pp. 35–51). New York: Plenum.

Inciardi, J., & Surratt, H. (1998). Children in the streets of Brazil: Drug use, crime, violence, and HIV risks. *Journal of Substance Use and Misuse, 33*, 1461–1480.

Jernigan, D.H., & Mosher, J.F. (2005). Alcohol and youth. Public health perspectives. *Journal of Public Health Policy, 26*, 286–291.

Jessor, R. (1991). Risk behaviour in adolescence: A psychosocial framework for understanding and action. *Journal of Adolescent Health, 12*, 597–605.

Jessor, R. (1993). Successful adolescent development among youth in high-risk settings. *American Psychology, 48*, 117–126.

Jessor, R., & Jessor, S. (1980). A social-psychological framework for studying drug use. In D. J. Lettieri, M. Sayers, & H. Wallestein Pearson (Eds.), *Theories on drug abuse* (pp.102–109). Washington, DC: US Government Printing Office.

Jeynes, W.H. (2002). The relationship between the consumption of various drugs by adolescents and their academic achievement. *American Journal of Drug and Alcohol Abuse, 28*, 15–35.

Jones, E.E., & Berglas, S. (1978). Control of attribution about the self through self-handicapping strategies: The appeal of alcohol and the role of underachievement. *Personality and Social Psychology Bulletin, 4*, 200–206.

Jotcham, J. (2001). Homeless, young and on drugs. *Addiction Today, 12*, 20–21.

Kandel, D.B. (1980). Drug and drinking behavior among youth. *Annual Review of Sociology, 6*, 235–285.

Kandel, D.B., & Jessor, R. (2002). The gateway hypothesis revisited. In D. Kandel (Ed.), *Stages and pathways of drug involvement: Examining the gateway hypothesis* (pp. 365–372). Cambridge: Cambridge University Press.

Kashdan, T.B., Vetter, C.J., & Collins, R.L. (2005). Substance use in young adults: Associations with personality and gender. *Addictive Behaviors, 30*, 259–269.

Knibbe, R.A., Joosten, J., Derickx, M., Choquet, M., Morin, D., Monshouwer, K. et al. (2005). Perceived availability of substances, substance use and substance-related problems: A cross-national study among French and Dutch adolescents. *Journal of Substance Use, 10*, 151–163.

Komro, K.A., Flay, B.R., Hu, F.B., Zelli, A., Rashid J., & Amuwo, S. (1998). Urban pre-adolescents report perceptions of easy access to drugs and weapons. *Journal of Child and Adolescent Substance Abuse, 8*, 77–90.

Kumpfer, K.L., Alvarado, R., & Whiteside, H.O. (2003). Family-based interventions for substance use and misuse prevention. *Substance Use and Misuse, 38*(11), 1759–1787.

Labouvie, E.W. (1986). Alcohol and marijuana use in relation to adolescent stress. *The International Journal of Addiction, XX*, 333–345.

Le Breton, D. (1991). *Passions du risque* [A lust for risk]. Paris: Editions Métailliè.

Lila, M.S., & Gracia, E. (2005). Determinantes de la aceptación–rechazo parental [Determinants of parental aceptance–rejection]. *Psicothema, 15*(2), 161–166.

Lila, M.S., Musitu, G., & Buelga, S. (2001). Adolescentes colombianos y españoles: Diferencias, similitudes y relaciones entre la socialización familiar, la autoestima y los valores [Colombian and Spanish teenagers: Differences, similarities and relations among family socialization, self-esteem and values]. *Revista Latinoamericana de Psicología, 32*, 301–319.

Lillehoj, C.J., Trudeau, L., & Spoth, R. (2005). Longitudinal modeling of adolescent normative beliefs and substance initiation. *Journal of Alcohol and Drug Education, 49*, 7–41.

Lloyd, B., & Lucas, K. (1998). *Smoking in adolescence.* London: Routledge.

Mallett, S., Rosenthal, D., & Keys, D. (2005). Young people, drug use and family conflict: Pathways into homelessness. *Journal of Adolescence, 28*(2), 185–199.

Martínez, J.L., Fuertes, A., Ramos, M., & Hernández, A. (2003). Consumo de drogas en la adolescencia: Importancia del afecto y de la supervisión parental [Substance use in adolescence: Importance of parental warmth and supervision]. *Psicothema, 15*(2), 161–166.

Maxwell, J.C. (2003). The response to club drug use. *Current Opinion in Psychiatry, 16*, 279–289.

McIntosh, J., MacDonald, F., & McKeganey, N. (2005). The reasons why children in their pre and early teenage years do or do not use illegal drugs. *International Journal of Drug Policy, 16*, 254–326.

Minehan, J.A., Newcomb, M.D., & Galaif, E.R. (2000). Predictors of adolescent drug use: cognitive abilities, coping strategies and purpose in life. *Journal of Child and Adolescent Substance Abuse, 10*, 33–52.

Moffitt, T.E. (1993). Adolescence-limited and life-course-persistent antisocial behavior: A developmental taxonomy. *Psychological Review, 100*, 674–701.

Musher-Eizenman, D.R., Holub, S.C., & Arnett, M. (2003). Attitude and peer influences on adolescent substance use: The moderating effect of age, sex, and substance. *Journal of Drug Education, 33*, 1–23.

Musitu, G., Buelga, S., Lila, M.S., & Cava, M.J. (2000). *Familia y adolescencia.* [Family and adolescence]. Madrid, Spain: Síntesis.

National Health and Life Style [NHLS] (2003). *Survey 2003.* Dublin: Health Promotion Unit, Department of Health and Children.

National Survey on Drug Use and Health [NSDUH] (2003). *Results from the 2003 national survey on drug use and health: National findings.* Rockville, MD: Office of Applied Studies.

Norwegian Gallup on behalf of Alkokutt (2003). *Report 2003.* Oslo, Norway: Norwegian Gallup.

Nyberg, K.L. (1979). Drug abuse and drug programs in rural America. In R. I. Dupont, A. Goldstein, & J. O'Donnel (Eds.), *Handbook on drug abuse.* Rockville, MD: NIDA.

Palmonari, A. (1993). Droga aspetti socio-psicologici [Drug socialpsychological aspects]. *Enciclopedia delle Scienze Sociali* (Vol.3, pp.261–270). Roma: Istituto dell'Enciclopedia Italiana.

Palmonari, A. (1997). *Psicologia dell'adolescenza* [Psychology of adolescence] (2nd ed.). Bologna, Italy: Il Mulino.

Palmonari, A., & Ravenna, M. (1988). I processi socio-psicologici del consumo controllato o dipendente di eroina [The socio-psychological processes of controlled or addicted heroin consumption]. *Appuntamenti, 2*, 13–40.

Panagopoulus, I., & Ricciardelli, L.A. (2005). Harm reduction and decision making among recreational ecstasy users. *International Journal of Drug Policy, 16*, 54–64.

Pinquart, M., Silbereisen, R.K., & Wiesner, M. (2005). Changes in discrepancies between desired and present states of developmental tasks in adolescence: A 4-process model. *Journal of Youth and Adolescence, 33*(6), 467–477.

Pons, J., Buelga, S., & Lehalle, H. (1999). Consommation d'alcool et système de valeurs chez les adolescents [Adolescent alcohol consumption and value system]. *International Review of Social Psychology, 12*(2), 67–77.

Priester, J.R. (2001). Sex, drugs, and attitudinal ambivalence: How feelings of evaluative tension influence alcohol use and safe sex behaviours. In W. D. Crano, & M. Burgoon (Eds.), *Mass media and drug prevention: Classic and contemporary theories and research* (pp.145–162). Mahwah, NJ: Lawrence Erlbaum Associates, Inc.

Pudney, S. (2002) *The road to ruin? Sequences of initiation into drug use and offending by young people in Britain.* Home Office Research Study 253. London: Home Office.

Ravenna, M. (1993). *Adolescenti e droga. Percorsi e processi socio-psicologici del consumo* [Adolescents and drugs. Socio-psychological processes and routes of consumption]. Bologna, Italy: Il Mulino.

Ravenna, M. (1997). *Psicologia delle tossicodipendenze* [Psychology of drug addiction]. Bologna, Italy: Il Mulino.

Ravenna, M. (2005). Il fascino delle droghe [The charm of drugs]. In G. Speltini (Ed.), *Minori, disagio e aiuto psicologico* (pp.121–153). Bologna, Italy: Il Mulino.

Ravenna, M., & Cavazza, N. (2000). Rappresentazioni dello "sballo" ed atteggiamenti nei confronti della discoteca in un campione di giovani consumatori di sostanze psico-attive [Representations of "getting high" and attitudes to the disco in a sample of young consumers of psycho-active substances]. *Psicologia Clinica dello Sviluppo, 3*, 415–440.

Ravenna, M., & Cavazza, N. (2003). Rappresentazioni del fenomeno droga e percezione dell'insicurezza in adolescenza [Drugs representations and insecurity perception in adolescence]. In B. Zani (Ed.), *Sentirsi insicuri in città* (pp. 195–219). Bologna, Italy: Il Mulino.

Ravenna, M., & Kirchler, E. (2000). Giovani e tempo del *loisir*. Ricerca di eccitazione, percezione del rischio e rappresentazioni del giorno e della notte [Youth and leisure time. Excitement research, risk perception and day and night representations]. *Giornale Italiano di Psicologia, XXVII*(3), 573–604.

Ravenna, M. & Nicoli, M.A. (1991a). Iniziazione all'uso di droghe leggere e pesanti: Analisi di sequenze discorsive [Initiation towards the use of light and hard drugs: Analysis of discursive sequences]. *Giornale Italiano di Psicologia, XVIII*(3), 473–489.

Ravenna, M., & Nicoli, M.A. (1991b). Il consolidarsi dell'uso di droghe leggere e pesanti attraverso l'analisi di sequenze discorsive [Consolidation of the use of light and hard drugs through the analysis of discursive sequences]. *Età Evolutiva, 10*, 44–55.

Ricci Bitti, P.E. (1997). Organizzare la vita quotidiana e progettare il futuro: L'esperienza temporale degli adolescenti [Organizing daily life and planning the future: The temporal experience of adolescents]. In A. Palmonari (Ed.), *Psicologia dell'adolescenza* (pp.169–199). Bologna, Italy: Il Mulino.

Robins, L.N., & McEvoy, L. (1990). Conduct problems as predictors of substance abuse. In L. N. Robins, & M. Rutter (Eds.), *Straight and deviant pathways from childhood to adulthood* (pp.182–204). Cambridge: Cambridge University Press.

Rohrbach, L.A., Sussman, S., Dent, C.W., & Sun, P. (2005). Tobacco, alcohol, and other drug use among high-risk young people: A five-year longitudinal study from adolescence to emerging adulthood. *Journal of Drug Issues, 35*, 333–356.

Rosenbaum, M. (1979). Becoming addicted: The woman addict. *Contemporary Drug Problems, 8*, 141–167.

Schifano, F., Di Furi, L., Miconi, L., & Bricolo, R. (1996). MDMA y amfetamino-simili, aspetti epidemiologici e clinici [MDMA and amphetamine-types, epidemiological and clinical aspects]. *2nd Congresso Nazionale di Medicina Nelle Dipendenze* (pp 97–108). Verona, Italy: GICS.

Schlaadt, R.G., & Shannon, P.T. (1994). *Drugs, use, misuse, and abuse*. Englewood Cliffs, NJ: Prentice Hall.

Schmid, H., & Gabhainn, S.N. (2004). Alcohol use. In C. Currie, C. Robert, A. Morgan, R. Smith, W. Settertobulte, O. Samdal, et al. (Eds.), *International report from the 2001/2002 survey. Young people's health in context. Health behaviour in School-aged Children (HBSC) study* (pp. 73–83). Copenhagen, Denmark: WHO Regional Office for Europe.

Schwartz, S. (1992). Universals in the content and structure of values: Theoretical advances and empirical tests in 20 countries. *Advances in Experimental Social Psychology, 25*, 1–65.

Sher, K.J., Bartholow, B.D., & Wood, M.D. (2003). Personality and substance use disorders: A prospective study. In R. N. Rosenthal (Ed.), *Dual diagnosis* (pp.149–172). New York: Brunner Routledge.

Shiffman, S., & Wills, T.A. (1985). *Coping and substance use*. New York: Academic Press.

Shillington, A.M. & Clapp, J.D. (2002) Beer and bongs: Differential problems experienced by older adolescents using alcohol only compared to combined alcohol and marijuana use. *American Journal Drug Alcohol Abuse, 28*, 379–397.

Sloboda, Z., & Bukoski, W.J. (Eds.) (2003). *Handbook of drug abuse prevention: Theory, science, and practice*. New York: Kluwer.

Smith, R.L., & Capps, F. (2005). The major substances of abuse and the body. In P. Stevens, & R. L. Smith (Eds), *Substance abuse counseling: Theory and practice* (pp.36–82). Auckland, NZ: Prentice Hall.

Sutherland, I., & Shepherd, J.P. (2001). Social dimensions of adolescent substance use. *Addiction, 96*, 445–458.

Svensson, R. (2003). Gender differences in adolescent drug use: The impact of parental monitoring and peer deviance. *Journal of Youth and Society, 34*, 300–329.

Swiss Institute for Prevention of Alcoholism and Other Drug Addictions [ISPA] (2003). *Alcopops*.

Lausanne, Switzerland: Swiss Institute for Prevention of Alcoholism and Other Drug Addictions.

Ter Bogt, T., Fotiou, A., & Gabhainn, S. (2004). Cannabis use. In C. Currie, C. Robert, A. Morgan, R. Smith, W. Settertobulte, O. Samdal, et al. (Eds.), *International report from the 2001/2002 survey. Young people's health in context. Health behaviour in School-aged Children (HBSC) study* (pp. 84–89). Copenhagen, Denmark: WHO Regional Office for Europe.

Tomkins, D.M., & Sellers, E.M. (2001). Addiction and the brain: The role of neurotransmitters in the cause and treatment of drug dependence. *Canadian Medical Association Journal, 164*, 817–821.

Van Aken, M.A., & Heutinck, C. (1998). *Personality in elementary school as a precursor of anti-social behavior in late adolescence.* Paper presented at ISSBD, Berne.

Van de Wijngaart, R.B., de Bruin, D., Fris, M., Maalsté, N.J.M., & Verbraeck, H.T. (1999). Ecstasy use at large-scale dance events in the Netherlands. *Journal of Drug Issues, 29*, 679–702.

Wagner, M.K. (2001). Behavioral characteristics related to substance abuse and risk-taking, sensation-seeking, anxiety sensitivity, and self-reinforcement. *Addictive Behaviors, 26*, 115–120.

Weil, A. (1986). *The natural mind.* Boston, MA: Houghton-Mifflin.

Williams, R.J., McDermitt, D.R., Bertrand, L.D., & Davis, R.M. (2003). Parental awareness of adolescent substance use. *Addictive Behaviors, 28*, 803–809.

Wills, T.A, Walker, C., & Resko, J.A. (2005). Longitudinal studies of drug use and abuse. In Z. Sloboda (Ed.), *Epidemiology of drug abuse* (p.177–192). Rockville, MD: National Institute of Drug Abuse Research Monograph.

World Health Organization [WHO] (1998). Concept. *Press releases, fact and feature.* Geneva, Switzerland: WHO.

World Health Organization [WHO] (2004a). *Building blocks for tobacco control: A handbook.* Geneva, Switzerland: WHO.

World Health Organization [WHO] (2004b). *Young people's health in context. Health behaviour in school-aged children (HBSC) study. International report from the 2001/2002 survey.* Copenhagen, Denmark: WHO Regional Office for Europe.

World Health Organization [WHO] (2005). *The European health report. Public health action for healthier children and populations.* Copenhagen, Denmark: Who Regional Office for Europe.

Zanis, D.A. (2004). The most critical unresolved issue associated with contemporary vocational rehabilitation for substance users. *Journal of Substance Use and Misuse, 39*, 2619–2620.

Zimbardo, P. (1969). The human choice: Individuation, reason and order versus deindividuation, impulse and chaos. In W. J. Arnold, and D. Levine (Eds), *Nebraska symposium on motivation* (Vol. XVII, pp. 237–307). Lincoln, NE: University of Nebraska Press.

Zimbardo, P. (1988). *Psychology and life.* Glenview, NJ: Foresman and Co.

Zuckerman, M. (1979). *Sensation seeking: Beyond the optimal level of arousal.* New York: John Wiley & Sons.

18

Development of aggression and its linkages with violence and juvenile delinquency

Willem Koops and Bram Orobio de Castro

1. Introduction

There are good reasons to consider adolescence as a recent historical discovery, or cultural invention (Koops & Zuckerman, 2003). Jean Jacques Rousseau (1763) was the first author after the Middle Ages who wrote about adolescence and Stanley Hall (1904) extended the basic ideas of Rousseau into a multidisciplinary classical (hand)book that more or less shaped current modern ideas about adolescence. In the Rousseau–Stanley Hall tradition adolescence has been considered as a period of "normative turmoil", "storm and stress", and "oscillations and oppositions". In the last decades, however, it has become clear that empirical data offer very little, if any, support for the traditional core idea of normative

turmoil. Petersen (1988) for the first time reviewed the relevant research, refuting many of the "classical" hypotheses on adolescence. There is even some reason to call into question the special developmental status of the period of adolescence, as Arnett (1999) did, in a recent review of the available empirical data on "storm and stress". Arnett concluded that there is, at best, some support for a "modified storm and stress view", but only if we recognize that hormones and genes play hardly any role in it. Arnett rejected all assumptions about a universal phenomenon of adolescence and emphasized instead the large differences in the experience of adolescence between cultures and even among individuals within a culture.

Scott and Grisso (1997) wrote an interesting paper on these changing ideas on adolescence and its effects on the juvenile justice reform in the USA. They explain that originally (based on the traditional idea of adolescence) the juvenile court was shaped in important ways by a conception of errant youth as "childlike, psychologically troubled, and malleable" (p. 137). But in the last decennia this picture totally changed (and the juvenile justice system became much harsher), as is nicely expressed by the following quote: "Juvenile offenders are criminals who happen to be young, not children who happen to be criminal" (p. 141).

Realizing these recently "revolutionized" conceptions of adolescence we write this chapter from the perspective that adolescence is to be considered as continuous with long-term – earlier and later – developmental processes. We therefore start this chapter with a general discussion of the *developmental approach*. We then turn to the most important area of behavior that is involved in youth delinquency, that is *aggression*. We then concentrate on the *development of aggression* and its linkages with *delinquent violence* in adolescence. Then we discuss *developmental trajectories in aggression and violence* and concentrate very much on the problem of *causality*. The chapter will conclude with a plea for research into causal mechanisms, including intervention research.

2. A developmental approach

Drawing on Jack Wohlwill's (1973) classic, we distinguish three fundamental approaches within psychology: the *experimental*, the *differential*, and the *developmental* approach. The first approach searches for causes of momentary behavior with the aid of experimental manipulations; the second systematically details and attempts to explain natural individual differences, and the third approach focuses on the development of behavior, on the systematics of psychological changes in childhood and adolescence. The history of psychology and the nature of current research clearly demonstrate that these three approaches cannot be reduced to a single common denominator. Instead they complement one another in essential

ways and together form the *trinity of human behavioral science*.

The ultimate goal in developmental psychology is to find and understand causes of development. Philosophically the concept of causality is extremely complex and multifarious (Hopkins & Butterworth, 1990). But within the frame of developmental psychology one could without many problems agree about the empirical approach of causality. We will follow here the helpful analysis of Bryant (1990). Fortunately, the developmental psychologist who simply wants to get on with his research can turn to Peter Bryant's down-to-earth analysis in the chapter following that of Hopkins and Butterworth (Bryant, 1990). He begins with the proposal that developmental psychologists face two issues. The first concerns mapping the developmental course. How, for example, does the aggressive behavior of a 4 year old differ from that of a 10 year old? Are there qualitative differences between physical aggression among preschoolers, children at elementary school, and adolescents? The second issue concerns causes. Once developmental changes have been outlined they need to be explained; the researcher needs to establish why they take place. Bryant shows that developmental psychology has sadly expended infinitely more energy on mapping the course of development than on investigating its causes. In his opinion, this discrepancy can be traced to two stumbling blocks encountered when looking for explanations. The first is related to the nature of classical developmental theories, the second has to do with a methodological problem.

Practically all developmental psychologists accept the assumption that one thing leads to another: excessive physical aggression at an early age can lead to antisocial behavior in adolescence and to violent criminal offences in adulthood (Farrington, 1994; Frick et al., 1993; Kokko & Pulkkinen, 2005; Loeber, 1998; Loeber & Hay, 1994; Loeber & Schmaling, 1985; Loeber, et al. 1993; Stattin & Magnusson, 1989; Tremblay, 1998). But what causes such a connection? Many influential developmental theories offer an *external factor* as explanation. These are what Bryant refers to as "*deus ex machina theories*".

He starts by illustrating that Piaget's theory on the development of thought, which dominated much if not *all* research in developmental psychology throughout the world for around three-quarters of a century, falls into this category. Piagetian tradition can be seen as prototypical for the whole of developmental thinking and therefore we shortly discuss the essence of his theoretical position. Piaget saw development as driven by the causal factors assimilation, accommodation, and equilibration, referred to by Flavell (1963) as "*functional invariants*". A good term, which immediately conveys the essence: these causal factors keep working in the same way and will always do so, whether they are applied to the responses of 7 year olds to simple logical problems or to the way in which university students conduct scientific experiments. Despite the fact that Piaget and his adherents carried out and published an unprecedented number of studies into the cognitive functioning of children at various ages, they devoted *hardly any* [sic] empirical studies to the working of the functional invariants.

Why then, asks Bryant, has such a deus ex machina theory been so widely embraced? Because in Piaget's case there is no alternative; no explanation can be derived from the developmental course of cognitive actions itself, since the early phases are always *negatively* formulated. Piaget's theory is a *deficit theory* (see also Koops, 1992, 2000); he indicates what children *cannot yet do* compared to adults. Bryant points out that Piaget and his associates always claimed that "*il y a trois stades*", namely a stage in which the particular cognitive competence was absent, followed by its tentative partial presence and the eventual, stable accomplishment. The principal objection is that the roots of a later development can hardly be discovered in an earlier one, if this earlier one in fact consists of a deficiency. To quote Bryant (1990, p. 38) once again: "Deficits cannot cause abilities any more than holes can cause hills." Piaget's theory may be regarded as a prototype of the classic deficit theories. His theory harks back to Rousseau and thereby to a long tradition of deficit–theoretical thought (Koops, 1992, 2000), as we will see in connection with developmental research into aggression.

The conclusion of Bryant's analysis must be that classical developmental theories generally cannot infer the causes of development from the developmental course and are thus *compelled* to develop a deus ex machina theory on causes. These external causes are usually so general in nature that no connection can be made empirically with developing behavior and the causes of the development are usually *presumed*, but not empirically validated, causes. This brings us to the second stumbling block of research into causes of development, still according to Bryant.

Bryant emphasizes that a unique, or best, method to test a causal developmental hypothesis does not exist. All methods have inherent strengths and weaknesses and our job is to combine the methods in such a way that the weaknesses of the one are compensated for by the strengths of the other and vice versa. The longitudinal method allows us to establish all sorts of relations between earlier and later behaviors. But the relationships we thus find, and sometimes even succeed in making theoretically plausible, offer no decisive answers with regard to causality as any number of unnamed third factors may be at work, unbeknown to the researcher. To establish causality we will therefore have to experiment. In the words of Dearborn, tutor of the renowned developmental psychologist Urie Bronfenbrenner: "If you want to understand something, Urie, try to change it" (quoted in Bronfenbrenner, 1979, p. 107).

If we want to trace the causes of development, we shall have to conduct an experimental manipulation in such a way that the course of development of the particular behavior is influenced (e.g., Development & Psychopathology, 2002). It is for this reason that the developmental approach cannot be reduced to the experimental or differential approach: within the developmental approach the other approaches always have to be linked to the *developmental course of behavior*. An experimental manipulation within the developmental approach implies an *intervention*, not a brief manipulation within a laboratory setting but the influencing of children and adolescents in everyday situations on a relatively large scale for a relatively long period. Such a manipulation is laborious and complicated on all counts, even regarding ethical issues much has to be arranged and explained. This is counterbalanced by the fact that a successful experimental intervention has high yields: not only a demonstration of causality, but also a parenting strategy, a child psychiatric or clinical psychological treatment program, an educational intervention, etc.

Given that there is an adequate control group, that measurements are reliable, and so on, an intervention study can provide conclusive evidence as to how change can be brought about. A disadvantage is that we do not know whether our manipulation is artificial or whether it resembles what happens in real life. Thus, a longitudinal study can reveal relationships between earlier and later behaviors but offers no preclusion with regard to causality, while an intervention study reveals a causal relationship between behaviors, but cannot prove that this relationship exists beyond the artificially created situation. But, in combination, these two methods produce a powerful test for a causal hypothesis! The reason: a study designed to test that factor A determines later development B, and that shows that A predicts B and that increased experience with A accelerates the development of B, or changes B quantitatively or qualitatively, may be regarded as convincing evidence that A influences B (see Bryant, 1990, p. 41). Unfortunately, to date, few such causal studies have been carried out, although the area of research we will be discussing shortly, the development of aggression, offers promising possibilities.

In sum, causes of development are hard to find in the research literature, since early developmental stages are often defined in negative terms. What remain are deus ex machina explanations, often based more on assumption than on research. The field of developmental psychology will have to collect better longitudinal data and, to identify causes, will have to conduct experimental research in which the course of development is manipulated by interventions. Now let us see whether these basic insights are or can be applied to the development of aggression.

3. What is aggression? Notes on terminology

The authoritative, four-volume standard work in which research in developmental psychology during the last century is summarized (Damon, 1998) includes a chapter by Coie and Dodge entitled "Aggression and antisocial behavior" (Coie & Dodge, 1998). The first comment we wish to make on this subject has been borrowed from Tremblay (2000), who remarked that an analogous title in the field of botany would be "Apples and fruit". Indeed, Coie and Dodge do portray aggression as antisocial behavior (Coie & Dodge, 1998, p.781, denote aggression literally as "that form of antisocial behavior") and, in this sense, Tremblay is right, but at the same time it is not necessary to view aggression as antisocial behavior *by definition*, so on that score Tremblay has got it wrong. Indeed, he himself is keen to stress that aggression can also be seen as *pro*social behavior: Most parents would not mind hearing that their son is an aggressive tennis player; many sales managers aim to employ aggressive salespersons (Tremblay, 2000, p. 130). And we can add to this list the example of many older academics who would still like to be an "angry young man". We are not particularly convinced by Coie and Dodge's argument (1998, p. 781) that the so-called comorbidity (read: correlation) of aggression and other social behaviors such as disobedience to parents, alcohol and drug abuse, delinquency, lying and cheating, high-risk sexual behavior, and vandalism suggests that we can better understand the developmental course of aggression by including it in the broader category of antisocial behaviors. When one considers that one of the most widely used rating scales, the child behavior checklist (CBCL; Achenbach & Edelbrock, 1983), contains very few questions regarding direct aggression and many on antisocial behaviors – and is used in clinical practice alternately to identify "aggressive", "externalizing", and "antisocial" children, or children with "conduct disorders", it becomes clear that a good deal of tautology is involved. The same can be said of the so-called aggression scale discussed by Tremblay (Tremblay, 2000, p. 130). This scale was used in one of the few large-scale longitudinal studies into the development of aggressive behavior (Huesman, Eron, Lefkowitz, & Walder, 1984) and includes the following items: "disobeys teacher, gives dirty looks, makes up stories and lies, does things that bother others, gets in trouble". All antisocial actions without doubt, but we cannot see how they can add up to "aggression". In short, Coie and Dodge's suggestion seems to us to be scientifically highly disputable: if aggression is so poorly defined that it can include all sorts of antisocial behaviors in research studies, then to suggest studying aggression in the context of antisocial behavior is by no means the solution to the problem, but merely a tautological argument for an existing, debatable research practice.

It should by now be clear that in the practice of research, the boundaries between aggression and multitude forms of antisocial behavior are, unfortunately, ill defined and poorly guarded. In theory, however, a number of attempts have been made to come to distinct definitions, predominantly based on, respectively, the *intention* of the aggressor, and the *harm* caused by the aggressor.

These two aspects are expressed in Parke and Slaby's (1983, p.50) definition of aggression. They define aggression ("in a minimal way", by their own admission) as "behavior that is aimed at harming or injuring other persons". The phrase "aimed at" signifies that the aggressor *intends* to inflict harm on another person. The problem with intentions, however, is that they are invisible, presenting researchers with a difficult task; another problem is that young children are considered unable to distinguish intentions (see, for example, Kagan, 1974, p. 109; Tremblay, 2000), neither their own nor those of others, and this would mean that young children, *by definition*, cannot be aggressive. A point of view that may enjoy widespread popularity, but that is unfortunately not empirically falsifiable: if we decide a priori that aggressive behavior cannot exist before a certain age, then we preclude falsification of what should have been a hypothesis (see Tremblay, 2000, p. 131). Another implication of this viewpoint that is difficult to accept is that animals cannot be aggressive, a position that immediately brings us into conflict with ethologists (see Lorenz,

1968)[1] and besides that with our own everyday use of language.

The second element, causation of harm, is also a widely used referent of aggression. Loeber and Hay (1997) for example write: "Aggression is defined as those acts that inflict bodily or mental harm on others." However, the idea of harm, the idea that another individual is made to *suffer* is problematic: if an ungainly movement of mine causes someone else to fall from an escalator and that person breaks a leg, was I being aggressive? If, in a fit of rage, I try to shoot someone, but my gun is jammed, am I not showing aggression?

This brief account hopefully illustrates that the concept of aggression is decidedly less clearly defined than one would wish for the starting point of empirical studies of behavior and behavioral development; and all this despite an enormous body of research and a huge, multidisciplinary effort. We cannot solve this problem here without causing huge analytical conceptual problems in reviewing the existing literature. What we will do here is sticking close to the usual (although disputable) definitions just discussed. Predominantly we will consider explicit ("intentional") harmdoing to others as aggression. At the same time we concentrate our discussion mainly on one form of aggression, that is easy to observe: *physical aggression*. Furthermore our interest particularly concerns aggression with relatively grave consequences for the victim: serious injury or other serious (psychological) damage. This severe aggression is usually indicated as *violence*. Loeber and Stouthamer-Loeber for instance define violence as follows: "Violence is defined as those aggressive acts causing serious harm, such as aggravated assault, rape, robbery, and homicide" (Loeber & Stouthamer-Loeber, 1998, p. 242). It will be clear that these forms of aggression are usually considered as antisocial, and as criminal.

So, in the following we will use the term aggres-

---

[1] Incidentally, it is remarkable that in his classic and influential book Lorenz invests virtually no effort in defining aggression. To Lorenz, as illustrated by the foreword, aggression is "the fighting spirit aimed at members of the same species, among both animals and humans" (Lorenz, 1968, p. 7). He proceeds to refer to aggression as an instinct throughout the book, and with that the reader simply has to make do. (See also Parke & Slaby, 1983, p. 550.)

sion in accordance with the usual definitions within developmental psychology by stressing here the negative, harm-oriented side of it. We will use the term violence for high levels of this aggression and connect violence with criminality. In doing so, youth delinquency in this chapter will be reduced to violent aggression in adolescence. We will demonstrate that the limitation of our discussion of youth delinquency to violence is quite defendable in terms of actual empirical data on crime rates. Since our orientation is developmental and seeks to understand adolescent development from a wider developmental perspective, we will first devote some attention to the general developmental study of aggression.

4. Development of aggression

Let us begin by stating that the classic view of the development of aggression suffers to an even greater extent from the same shortcoming as the classic developmental theory of Piaget: in the case of aggression development there is also a deficit theory which is, if possible, even more radical. Since Rousseau's *Émile* (1763) we regard the child as innocent and virtually angelic, brought into the world without sin or vice by the Creator, and only tainted by people, in particular the parent figures, thereby possibly developing aggression. The renowned opening sentence of *Émile* is: "Tout est bien sortant des mains de l'Auteur des choses, tout dégénère entre les mains de l'homme." By "tout" Rousseau means, in the first place, the child.

Tremblay (2000; Tremblay et al., 1999) rightly pointed out that Bandura's (1973) influential social learning approach is compatible with this line of thinking: for decades his view that childhood aggression is based on social learning, and that children follow the bad example set by adults, was the basic premise of international research into aggression. Among other things this led to research into the influence of violent television programs on aggressive behavior in children (Huesmann & Eron, 1986; Huesmann & Miller, 1994). And although on the basis of an immense body of research literature it can no longer be denied that violent TV programs can stimulate antisocial aggression somewhat among children

under certain conditions, the overriding influence assigned by researchers like Huesmann (1998) to mass media is almost implausible. As Tremblay remarked ironically, one can hardly imagine how people can ever have been aggressive before the invention of film and television. It is clear that on the basis of the Rousseau–Bandura tradition young children *of themselves* are considered incapable of aggression. Research on aggression among babies and toddlers is therefore not commonplace, as a result of which we have long remained in the dark when it comes to possible early precursors of later antisocial aggression.

Recent data, however, shed some light on this issue. The age curves for aggression comprised from several large longitudinal studies (e.g. Tremblay, 1998; Termblay et al., 2004) show very clearly that physical aggression *decreases* continually from the age of 4. At the same time, so-called *indirect aggression* – mainly verbal in nature and including bad mouthing a peer with whom one is angry – increases at the same rate. Research by Tremblay, Phil, Vitaro, and Dobkin (1994) shows that mothers are of the opinion that their 2 year olds "hit, kick, and bite" more often than at any other age. Between the ages of 2 and 12 this aggression continues to decrease. Tremblay remarks, and records elsewhere (Tremblay, 1998, p. 44), that independent research has revealed a similar developmental course for temper tantrums: these also hit a peak at around the second year and subsequently subside. It is with good reason that we speak of "the terrible twos". If we add these data to the previously mentioned age curves, it becomes apparent that physical aggression peaks at the age of 2 and subsequently decreases, while indirect aggression gradually increases from the same tender age. It is important to realize when considering the literature on these kinds of age curves that they usually concern the *perception* of aggression by adults (mainly parents, crèche workers, teachers) and only seldom refer to behavior *observed and registered* by the researchers themselves. Fortunately, in this case a fair amount of direct observational data is available and they show, among other things, that the frequency of threats and the struggle for toys peak at the age of 2 in crèches and play schools and gradually reduce from this age onwards (Tremblay, 1998, p. 44). Thus it would appear that on this issue, ratings and direct observations show a high degree of concurrence.

In the literature it pretty much goes without saying that severe forms of aggression have their roots in childhood (Loeber & Stouthamer-Loeber, 1998, p. 244 ff.). Since Olweus (1979) published his data on the stability of aggression over the years, it is generally accepted that in terms of correlations, the stabilities of aggression and intelligence are equally high. One must bear in mind that in both cases the correlation coefficients, in the order of .70, do not divulge a wealth of information with regard to developmental processes. In the first place, they reveal nothing about individual development, but only concern the relative aggression of an individual, compared to that of peers in earlier and later moments in the course of development. In the second place, they provide no clues as to the developmental course of aggressive behavior in terms of increase and attenuation. And, in the third place, even correlation coefficients that high still leave approximately half of the existing behavioral variance *un*explained. In developmental psychological terms, and incidentally also in terms of possibilities for intervention and professional help, it is precisely that *un*explained part that interests us. The interesting questions do not concern stability, but rather *in*stability. Since we now know that all children function at a top level of aggression around their second year, it strikes us as particularly interesting to establish why the majority of children subsequently discontinue this behavior, and a substantial proportion do not. In the research literature this discontinuance of aggression or antisocial behavior is referred to as *desistance*. The opposites of desistance are, on the one hand, the term *persistence* and, on the other hand, the term *onset*, the beginning of aggression. Since persistence has just been discussed in the context of stability, we will now turn our attention to *desistance* and *onset*.

Remarkably little research has been done on the desistance of aggression. Generally, research on desistance concerns delinquency, that is several forms of delinquent behavior, not aggression

specifically. A well-known example of such research is research by Moffitt (Moffitt, Caspi, Dickson, Silva, & Stanton, 1996; Moffitt, Caspi, Harrington, & Milne, 2002), who distinguished two types of delinquent on the basis of her longitudinal data: lifecourse persistent delinquents and adolescent-limited delinquents. Her distinction, however, is based on general data on general delinquency and not on specific data regarding aggression and violence (see Loeber & Stouthamer-Loeber, 1998). The relevant data and conclusions on desistance of aggression can be summarized as follows.

In the first place, it is clear that, as discussed previously with regard to research by Tremblay, aggression decreases dramatically between the ages of 2 and 12. Research from Australia underscores this finding: of the children identified by researchers as aggressive and studied between the ages of 2 and 8, approximately one-third desisted between their second and eighth year. (For more detailed documentation, see Loeber & Stouthamer-Loeber, 1998.)

Loeber and Stouthamer-Loeber (1998) show that desistance can also occur in adolescence. Countless studies reveal that particularly male physical aggression can cease in adolescence. According to some studies substantial desistance takes place from the age of 13, other studies pinpoint desistance mainly between 15 and 17 years of age. It is important to note that – contrary to the expected statistical regression effect – desistance is seen more often in the case of less serious forms of aggression than with more serious forms of aggression. This leads to the conclusion that serious aggression and violence can more often already be seen at young ages. In effect two groups can be identified: where fighting decreases in one group, in the other group it continues to increase. Unfortunately, and this is a serious shortcoming of the research until now, *little or nothing is known about the causes of desistance*, according to Loeber and Stouthamer-Loeber.

Another interesting insight to be gleaned from the literature is that much, but not all, aggression and violent behavior at a later age necessarily has its roots in early childhood. Loeber and Stouthamer-Loeber (1998) identify three types on the basis of their data on *age of onset*: a *lifecourse type*, a *limited-duration type*, and a *late-onset type* (Loeber and Stouthamer-Loeber's categorization builds on the model of Moffitt, referred to earlier (Moffitt, 1993; Moffitt et al., 1996, 2002). The first type is seen most frequently and justifies the view that the causes and potential for prevention are to be found in early childhood. It appears though that a portion of the persistently aggressive group is characterized by onset in the preschool years and a – smaller – portion by onset during adolescence. The second type refers to children who desist either in the preschool period or in adolescence. Finally, there is the third type, a small group (6% of the population; see Loeber & Stouthamer-Loeber, 1998, p. 246), for whom onset only occurs in adulthood. Two longitudinal studies (Farrington, 1978, 1994; Magnusson, Stattin, & Duner, 1983) have shown that a minority of individuals committing acts of violence as adults had no history of aggression during childhood.

Nevertheless, it is by no means certain that aggression later in life suddenly materializes out of thin air. Loeber and Stouthamer-Loeber also point out that there are various explanations for late onset. They derive one of these from a number of authors who propose that late-onset violence may well be preceded by earlier problems, presumably mainly the problem of overcontrol. The idea is that some children are highly inhibited and that they are only able to transpose their anger into violence once high inhibitory thresholds have been exceeded. Loeber and Stouthamer-Loeber take the view that it is very doubtful whether the childhood years of the late-onset group were indeed problem free. The available data (including Pulkkinen, 1982; Windle & Windle, 1995) reveal that the late-onset type shows evidence of *more emotional problems* during childhood than was the case in comparison groups.

We may conclude from these data that the terms early and late onset may be misleading: the terms may refer to our lack of knowledge of the relationship between different aspects of behavior, or, to put it differently, to our lack of knowledge of latent variables. We are in need

of the theoretical understanding of age-related expressions of aggression. The designation "late onset" may be the result of new deficiency theories that we create, in which onset and desistance pop up as natural phenomena that simply come and go. This is linked to the despairing cry of Loeber and Stouthamer-Loeber concerning the lack of knowledge about the stability and the *causes* of desistance and onset (Loeber & Stouthamer-Loeber, 1998, p. 244). They take the view, and we are in total agreement with them in this regard, that we need to understand the *causes* of onset and desistance. In the next section, we will concentrate on aggression and delinquency in adolescence, and we will evaluate developmental theories that can support the search for developmental causes.

5. Delinquency in adolescence

It is well known, by scientists as well as laypeople, that adolescence is a period with increased danger of deviant behavior. The rapid increase in deviant behavior during adolescence, which is followed by an equivalently rapid decrease, has been labeled the age–crime curve (Farrington, 1986; Tremblay, 2000). Tremblay (2000) reminds us that this age–crime curve was described for the first time by the Belgian mathematician–astronomer–biosocial scientist Adolphe Quetelet in his 1833 book. Figure 18.1 is a reproduction of Quetelet's curve. It is in our eyes a misunderstanding to interpret this curve as proof for the "normative turmoil" hypothesis, for two reasons. The first is that the "normative turmoil" interpretation may be an expression of what Felson (1998, pp. 11–14) called the "innocent youth fallacy". This fallacy leads to the conception that young criminals must be innocents corrupted by older ("real") criminals. However, the data show a very strong presence of young people in various aspects of crime (Felson, 1998; Gottfredson & Hirschi, 1990) and no evidence for the usual "innocence" hypothesis. The second reason that the "normative turmoil" hypothesis may be misleading is that it prevents fruitful developmental thinking. It may be the case that aggression and violence in particular have earlier developmental roots. Quetelet sensed this possibility: his explanation for the increase in

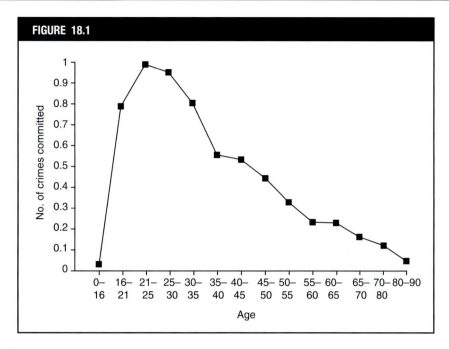

FIGURE 18.1

Male age–crime curve.

Adapted from Quetelet, 1833.

crime was that it developed "in proportion to the intensity of physical strength and passions in man" (Quetelet, 1833, p. 65). Such an interpretation permits the assumption that the roots may exist earlier in development than the expression by delinquent violence during adolescence.

Before we discuss theoretical developmental interpretations of aggression and delinquent violence in adolescence, we briefly take a look at data on juvenile crime in Europe in our time. General data on juvenile crime in Europe are far from complete and the data that do exist hardly permit comparisons between countries. There are two sources that offer relevant data on most of the western European countries: Estrada (1999), and Pfeiffer (1998). To offer an impression of general trends we will summarize the findings of these two authors.

Table 18.1 summarizes the findings of Estrada. Generally, it turns out that the number of juvenile offenders is leveling off: this means that the post-war period is *not* characterized by an ever expanding population of young criminals. Exceptions are England, Germany and Finland. Since violence among young people has recently become a focus for the interest of the general public, the media and criminologists, Estrada offers separate findings on this small part of the total juvenile offences. Interestingly trends in juvenile violence deviate from the underlying general crime trends: *in all countries the crime statistics display a rise in juvenile violence.* In England and Finland this rise has been continuous through the period 1980–1995. The increase in Denmark, Germany, the Netherlands, Norway, Sweden and Switzerland reflects a trend shift at the end of the 1980s.

Pfeiffer describes general juvenile crime trends as falling in Denmark, England, Switzerland and Sweden. In Germany and Austria, Pfeiffer sees a rise from the end of the 1980s. Juvenile crime in the Netherlands is presented as stable since 1985. Finland, Norway and Scotland are not included in Pfeiffer's analyses. Differences between the data from Estrada and Pfeiffer are due to Pfeiffer's exclusive reliance on official crime statistics while Estrada uses other alternative data, such as self-reports. However, in particular, the data of both criminologists on violent juvenile

TABLE 18.1

Summary of juvenile crime trends in postwar Europe (based on Estrada, 1999)

Country	Validity	Underlying trend 1950–1995	Trends in juvenile violence
Austria	–	Model 2: Stable since 1970	?
Switzerland	–	Model 2: sharp upward trend to beginning of 1970s, followed by "leveling off"	No increase during 1980s. Possible break in this trend and increase during 1990s
Finland	±	Model 1: unbroken increase to 1990, followed by reduction	Contradictory indicators. Increase according to assault statistics. Decrease during 1990s according to victim surveys
Scotland	±	Model 2: upward trend to beginning of 1980s followed by "leveling off"	No increase according to victim surveys and assault statistics
Denmark	+	Model 2: sharp upward to first half of 1970s, followed by "leveling off"	Contradictory indicators. Increasing during 1990s according to assault statistics. Stable according to hospital data
England	+	Model 1: unbroken increase throughout the period	Rising throughout the period according to both assault statistics and victim surveys
Germany	+	Model 1: unbroken increase during the entire period	Stable between 1984–1989. Thereafter, sharp increase during 1990s according to official crime statistics
Netherlands	+	Model 2: sharp upward trend to beginning of 1980s, followed by "leveling off"	Stable to end of 1980s. Thereafter, rising during 1990s according to both assault and alternative statistics
Norway	+	Model 2: sharp upward trend to first half 1970s followed by "leveling off"	Contradictory indicators during 1980s. Increase during 1990s according to both assault statistics and victim surveys
Sweden	+	Model 2: sharp upward trend to first half of 1970s, followed by "leveling off"	Contradictory indicators. Increase during 1990s according to assault statistics. Stable according to self-report data and victim surveys

NB The symbols for "validity" are based on Estrada's critical comments: – refers to his notion that his materials collected for Austria and Switzerland are "doubtful", ± for Scotland and Finland intermediate ("acceptable") and + for the rest "good". Model 1 means "the linear upward trend model"; model 2 means: "an initial increase followed by a leveling off". Data sets and sources on which this table has been based are to be found in Estrada, 1999.

crime are, on the whole, very similar. Both authors find indications of increasing violence among juveniles in the 1990s according to the crime statistics in several countries.

We may simply conclude from these statistics that there is no general increase in juvenile crime, but that there is a serious and substantial increase in delinquent juvenile violence. This justifies our focus on aggression and violence in this chapter.

In the following three paragraphs, we offer an overview of the developmental data, that is of the *developmental trajectories* of aggression and delinquent violence. Thereafter we will discuss the literature on risk and protective factors from which investigators try to *predict development*. However, the analysis of changes is not the same as knowledge of *causal mechanisms*. We will therefore finally discuss theories that offer some clues for the understanding of causal mechanisms.

6. Developmental trajectories of aggression and violence

For a long time, the only information regarding the development of aggressive and violently delinquent behavior consisted of retrospective reports made by violent delinquents concerning their histories. This was highly problematic, as retrospective information from such a select group tells us nothing about the development of adolescents who did *not* turn into violent delinquents, making it impossible to assess which factors in the violent delinquents' histories were actually associated with their problematic development. Fortunately, in the past decades several large, prospective longitudinal studies have been conducted, following samples of children from birth or early childhood, well into young adulthood. These large-scale studies of the general population make it possible to assess how aggressive and delinquently violent behavior develops over time, and which factors are associated with delinquent "outcomes" in adolescence. On the flip side, these studies were only conducted in New Zealand (Moffitt et al., 1996, 2002), the USA (Loeber, & Stouthamer-Loeber, 1998; Tolan, Gorman-Smith, & Loeber, 2000), Canada (Tremblay et al., 1994, 2004), and England (Farrington, 1995; Rutter, 1989), leaving the generalizability of findings to other (European) countries an open question.

Recent advances in methodology (Koops & Orobio de Castro, 2004; Nagin, 1999; Nagin & Tremblay, 2001) make it possible to derive from these studies models describing individual developmental trajectories of aggressive behavior.

Groups of children with similar developmental trajectories can then be identified and the predictive value of being in a particular trajectory for later violent delinquency can be assessed, making it possible to infer prognoses and select children "at risk" based on their previous development.

Generalizing over studies (such as those by Moffitt, Loeber & Stouthamer-Loeber, Farrington and others, as discussed earlier in this chapter) four developmental trajectories can be identified. A small percentage of children (5% in Moffitt, in press) is usually found in a chronically high (also erroneously called "early-onset") trajectory. These children were irritable and aggressive as infants, remained so throughout childhood and are the most seriously violent in adolescence. This group also shows the most continuity in young adulthood, with the highest rates of (marital) violence and severe associated problems, such as depression and unemployment. A second group consists of "desisters" (±15%). They start off irritable and quite aggressive in infancy, although somewhat less so than the chronic group. They then become less aggressive in mid-childhood and remain so. A third group is known as "adolescent limited" or – again misleadingly – "late onset". Children in this group (±20%) were not irritable or difficult in early and middle childhood, but do commit violent acts in adolescence. In young adulthood most children in this group desist from such behavior, although not all do so. Finally, the majority of children rarely acted excessively aggressively at any point in their development and chances are that they will rarely do so as adults (but, as discussed earlier, a limited number of cases seemingly show "late onset" in adulthood). Recent studies that made use of the statistical trajectory technique of Nagin more or less fit in with this general scheme. Trajectories as distinguished by Nagin and Tremblay (2001) – increasers, decreasers and no-changers – or as distinguished by Côté, Zoccolollo, Tremblay, Nagin, and Vitaro (2001) – low, medium, medium–high, and high trajectories – are covered reasonably well by the general scheme that we have just described.

The identification of these trajectories is clearly

very important for understanding violent delinquency in adolescence. Only by identifying these trajectories does it become clear that the same violently delinquent behavior in adolescents may have very different roots and causes in different children: for the chronic group it can be seen as the continuation of a behavior pattern that was already there, while for the adolescence limited group it appears that there must be different causes that promote violent behavior during only this time period.

Thus, developmental studies show that we may need different theories to explain delinquent violence in adolescence, depending on its developmental course. This has important implications: if delinquent violence results from different developmental trajectories in different adolescents, prevention and intervention need to be tailored to these differential trajectories.

The trajectory studies still have important limitations. Most importantly, the findings described earlier do not explain *why* the different developmental trajectories exist. Causality is not yet satisfactorily addressed in these studies. Distinction of trajectories tends to be purely explorative, leaving it to statistical procedures to do the job (see Koops & Orobio de Castro, 2004; Merk, 2005). To find explanations for the development of aggression, causal theories concerning the development of aggression need to be developed and tested. This is a complicated task, that necessarily will include intervention studies such as that by Wohlwill. Before discussing theoretical possibilities, we will now first turn to the analyses of risk and protective factors.

7. Predicting development in adolescence from "risk" and "protective" factors

Delinquency in adolescence cannot only be predicted from the development of aggression itself, but also from organismic and environmental factors correlated with children's development. Numerous studies have been conducted to identify such factors, which are generally called risk factors (that increase the chance of violent delinquency later in life) and protective factors (suppressing the increased chances associated with risk factors). Handbooks and review studies offer nearly inexhaustible lists of potential risk and protective factors. The OJJD (Office of Juvenile Justice and Delinquency Prevention) study group (co-chaired by Loeber & Farrington) for instance distinguished 26 categories of predictors. Each category exists out of several partly interlinked factors, to be divided in risk and protective ones. Furthermore the study group describes many complex relationships between factors across categories. It may be clear that there is no beginning in listing the complete findings on risk and protective factors, so we will only summarize some main findings very briefly (for reviews see Hawkins, Herrenkohl, Farrington, Brewer, Catalona, & Harachi, 1998; Lipsey & Derzon, 1998).

Predictions of adolescent violence from any single factor are highly inaccurate (Farrington, 1995). There is no single gene, biological or environmental factor that predicts violence in adolescence by itself. The best single predictor is earlier problematic behavior for a prolonged period of time, which follows directly from the above identified patterns and trajectories. Even this factor is not a very good predictor, given its inclusion of both chronics and desisters. However, prediction becomes highly accurate when multiple factors are combined, particularly if factors from different contexts are combined. In the UK and the USA, over 80% of accurate predictions from childhood to late adolescence are reported for combinations of multiple factors (e.g., Farrington, 1995; Loeber, 1998; Tolan et al., 2002). Factors in such predictions include child factors (difficult temperament, low intelligence, among others), family factors (inconsequent parenting, marital conflict, poverty, parental problems, etc.), school factors (learning problems, drop out, and others), peer factors (rejection by peers, aggressive friends, and so on), and neighborhood factors (bad housing, unsafety, etc.).

Evidently, risk factors are often interdependent: families with violently delinquent fathers frequently also become single-parent families and if a child is highly aggressive, chances are that there will be more psychosocial problems for the parents too. Likewise, the outcomes predicted by risk factors tend not to be limited to violent delinquency, but to encompass a broad variety of other negative outcomes as well, such as social problems and internalizing problems (McMahon, Grant, Compas, Thurm, & Ey, 2003). It appears that the *accumulation* of factors from different contexts is the best predictor. Interactions between different factors dramatically improve prediction (Farrington, 1995; Loeber et al., 1993). For example, there is a modest relation between child maltreatment and later aggression. For children who where not maltreated, there is no association between genes and adolescent aggression. However, within the group of children who were maltreated, the chance that they will later behave severely violent is reduced if a specific gene encodes low monoamine oxidase A (MAO A) activity (Caspi et al., 2002). Thus, this particular gene by itself is not related to aggression, but the interaction with maltreatment is. Similarly, children from single-parent families are in general at no greater risk for later aggressive behavior than other children. But if the father is violently delinquent, *absence* of the father is a protective factor (Moffitt, 2002).

So far, we discussed prediction of the very broad descriptor "delinquent violence". One would expect different kinds of violent behavior to have different predictors. Currently, evidence accumulates distinguishing between so called "reactive aggression" and "proactive aggression" (Dodge, 1991). The former being aggressive reactions to (presumed) threats involving strong physical arousal and the latter being unprovoked, planful use of aggression, not involving high physical arousal. It appears that, though related, these two different patterns of aggressive behavior follow different developmental courses (Lansford, Dodge, Bates, & Pettit, 2002), have different predictors and correlates (Dodge, Lochman, Harnish, Bates, & Pettit, 1997; Merk, 2005), and different prognoses (Vitaro, Gendreau, Tremblay, & Oligny, 1998). Reactive aggression appears to be more stable over time and is uniquely associated with early attention problems, difficult temperament, peer rejection, and harsh parenting, whereas proactive aggression is uniquely associated with aggressive models, positive attitude towards aggression, and bully-

ing. More comprehensive longitudinal studies are currently underway to test the differential development of these two kinds of aggression.

Intriguing and strong as the findings on risk factors are, they remain unsatisfactory, as they do not explain *why* certain combinations of factors predict later violent behavior. They are mere descriptions of relations over time, but do not provide any explanation of causal mechanisms. As we explained in an earlier section (the developmental approach) we need theories specifying such mechanisms and we need to do intervention research to test these. We now turn to several leading theories on the development of aggression and violence.

8. Causal mechanisms in theories on juvenile (delinquent) violence

Numerous theories have been forwarded to explain the development of violent delinquency in adolescence, the simplest, perhaps, being proposed by former US politician Dole, who once said: "There are three causes for criminality: criminals, criminals, and criminals." Here, we limit ourselves to the most prominent and best supported theories to date (not Dole's). We first discuss learning theories, then biologically oriented theories, information processing approaches, and finally integration of these perspectives in transactional models.

Learning theorists proposed that aggressive behavior may be learned through conditioning and vicarious learning. There is considerable evidence that both mechanisms operate in concert. Patterson and colleagues (e.g., Patterson, 1982) conducted milestone studies on operant conditioning at the Oregon Social Learning Center in the USA. They carefully coded time series of family interactions and experimentally manipulated these interactions in a large number of families in Oregon. This permitted them to demonstrate that a process of mutual operant conditioning between aggressive children and their parents and peers called "coercive interactions" causes persistence and escalation of aggressive and oppositional behaviors. A series of coercive interactions consists of (1) a demand made by one interaction partner, (2) an aggressive refusal to meet this demand by the other interaction partner, (3) the first partner giving in, in response to the aggression, and (4) the aggressive interaction partner stopping the aggression and getting his or her way. In terms of learning theory, the third and fourth steps in this sequence are crucial, as the aggressive person is rewarded for being aggressive, and the non-aggressive interaction partner is rewarded for rewarding the aggression. Over time this pattern makes the aggressor more likely to aggress and the other more likely to reward this, thereby further conditioning the aggressor's aggression.

Patterson's colleagues later demonstrated the same interaction pattern in peer groups, where positive attention and rejection were found to serve reinforcing functions for aggressive behavior in aggressive peer groups (Dishion, Spracklen, Andrews, & Patterson, 1996). Patterson and colleagues' studies not only demonstrate the predictive value of these exchanges in both families and peer groups, they also demonstrate that experimental interventions to change these interaction patterns lead to decreases in aggressive behavior, thereby demonstrating causality (Eddy & Chamberlain, 2001). Studies of vicarious learning were initiated by Bandura's social learning theory (1973). Although we do not accept the idea that *all* aggression and violence has been learned (see our earlier discussion on deficiency theories in the Rousseau–Bandura tradition) it cannot be denied that Bandura's theory offered insight into an effective principle of learning: *vicarious conditioning*. If other people are seen (or believed) to be rewarded for particular behaviors, these behaviors are also reinforced in the observer. Ample evidence exists for the importance of this phenomenon (see Anderson & Bushman, 2002), although no rigorous experimental tests for long-term causal effects have been conducted.

Both operant conditioning and vicarious learning may explain links between constellations of risk factors and later aggressive behavior. Increased risk for children who experience inconsequential parenting or neighborhood violence may, for example, be explained by these mechanisms. They are, however, less useful to explain why certain children are more susceptible to these environmental risks than others. Not all children become more aggressive under inconsequential parenting or after witnessing neighborhood violence, and learning theory does not explain why this is so. Several theories attempt to fill in this caveat by focusing on individual differences in children's susceptibilities to environmental influences.

Even though the field of behavior genetics is a minefield of methodological problems and unwarranted generalizations (see Rutter, 2002), the approach has justly spurred renewed interest in biological explanations of the development of aggression. Current biological theories concerning aggression do not maintain they provide completely biological explanations for the development of aggression, but rather propose interactions between children's physiological (not necessarily inherited) characteristics and their environment. Current theories in this field generally propose that a certain physiological characteristic makes children either more prone to engage in aggressive behavior (e.g., "sensation seeking"), less sensitive to environmental influences that discourage engagement in such behavior ("fearlessness", "callousness", "dominance of the behavior activation system over the behavior inhibition system") or that evokes environmental responses that promote the development of aggressive behavior ("hyperactivity", "irritability"). Some theorists argue that such characteristics are stable, inherited traits, whereas others suggest that these characteristics may have been shaped by early environmental influences or interactions between the two.

Unfortunately, research on physiological theories of aggression in adolescence is still scarce. Most studies in this field have been conducted with children or adults and do apply more to the life-persistent trajectory than to the adolescence-limited trajectory. Moreover, findings in children are often contradictory (see Snoek, 2002, for an overview of conflicting findings on androgens, norepinephrine, dopamine, serotonine, and 5-ht) and all human studies in this field are correlational, making it impossible to draw conclusions concerning causality. Nonetheless, research in this field does show certain stable findings in children that may be relevant to the development of aggression in adolescence. Highly aggressive children show a remarkably lower resting heart rate than their peers (Raine et al., 1997 in Snoek, 2002), and two studies with children with diagnoses of disruptive behavior disorders have found that these children's cortisol responses to stress are lower than in comparison children (Snoek, 2002; van Goozen, Matthys, Cohen-Kettenis, Gispen-Wied, de Wiegant, & van Engeland, 1998).

It is unclear what mechanisms cause these differences and whether they play any causal role in the development of aggression in adolescence. Possibly, severe stress and/or physical harm alter the serotenergic system, thereby making children more susceptible to the development or continuation of aggressive behavior later in life. As yet, this is clearly pure speculation. On a more optimistic note, Raine, Venables, Dalais, Mellingen, Reynolds, and Mednick recently (2001) demonstrated with Mauritian children that environmental enrichment in nursery school resulted in enhanced performance on psychophysiological measures six to eight years later. Although no data on aggressive behavior were obtained, this finding clearly demonstrates the malleability of psychophysiology and thereby the feasibility of longitudinal–experimental studies into the causal role of psychophysiology in the development of aggression.

A host of theories propose that transactions between organismic and environmental characteristics cause aggressive behavior in adolescence. Examples are attachment theory, Gottfredson and Hirschi's general theory of crime (Gottfredson & Hirschi, 1990) and a number of "biopsychosocial" models. Even though their general "transactional" claim (i.e., the claim that there are complicated mutual effects) seems likely – and indeed somewhat too obvious – these theories are particularly vague about the exact mechanisms that *cause* the aggressive behavior resulting from these so-called transactions. We therefore do not further discuss here such theories.

A detailed model of the exact manner in which individual differences in aggressive behavior develop is given by the social information processing approach (Crick & Dodge, 1994). According to this approach, whether people respond aggressively to violent stimuli or not depends on their processing of the social information at hand. Combinations of cognitive information processing capabilities, on the one hand, and a "database" with schemata and skills derived from experiences, on the other hand, cause people to process information differently, with different behavior as a result.

For reactively aggressive behavior, the theory proposes that a combination of attention problems and/or low intelligence with frequent experiences of hostility, rejection, and/or aggression causes children to miss important social cues and to attribute hostile intentions to others, leading to a tendency to respond angrily and aggressively in many social situations. In contrast, for proactively aggressive behavior, the theory posits that frequent experiences or witnessing of benefits of aggressive behavior (and absence of such experiences with non-aggressive behavior) causes positive outcome expectancies for aggressive behaviors, and thereby leads to frequent aggressive behaviors in many social situations (Dodge, 1991; Dodge et al., 1997).

Extensive research has shown that aggression is indeed related to the expected social information processing patterns (Dodge, 1993; Orobio de Castro, Veerman, Koops, Bosch, & Monshouwer, 2002). Longitudinal studies have shown that the specific social information processing patterns for reactive and proactive aggression are preceded by the expected differences in developmental histories, and that the relations between histories and aggressive behaviors are partially mediated by social information processing (Dodge et al., 1997; Weiss, Dodge, Bates, & Pettit, 1992). Experimental manipulations have shown that changes in social information processing cause modest changes in aggressive behavior (Hudley & Graham, 1993; Lochman & Lenhart, 1993; Lochman & Wells, 2002; Van Manen, Prins, & Emmelkamp, 2004) and evidence is emerging that these may be specific to reactive or proactive aggression, depending on the aspects of social information processing that are subjected to intervention (e.g., Barker & Orobio de Castro, submitted).

In all, there is robust support for the approach. However, effects and explained variance are mostly modest, which may be due to measurement problems in this area (Orobio de Castro et al., 2002), but may also indicate that the theory only explains part of the puzzle.

Although the model itself has been widely studied, less is known about the "information processing capacities" and the "database" that are supposed to drive the whole process. An approach that fits the database idea particularly well is the idea of "inflated self-esteem" posited by Baumeister, Smart, and Boden (1996). High levels of aggression have long been assumed to be related to low self-esteem. Based on this assumption, countless prevention and intervention programs aim to bolster children's self-esteem, expecting this will reduce or prevent aggressive behavior problems. Numerous empirical studies with children and adults have, however, never demonstrated any relation between low self-esteem and aggressive behavior. Moreover, there is no clear theoretical rationale as to *why* one would expect low self-esteem and aggressive behavior to be related. Recently Baumeister and colleagues (1996) gave a different view on this topic, proposing that aggressive behavior does not result from low, but rather from unrealistically *high* self-esteem. They specifically expect aggressive behavior to occur when an unrealistically positive evaluation of oneself is disputed or threatened by others. In popular media, Baumeister simplified this hypothesis to the expectation of a general relation between high self-esteem and aggressive behavior. In recent studies (e.g., Brendgen, Vitaro, Turgeon, Poulin, & Wanner, 2004; van Boxtel, Orobio de Castro, & Goossens, 2004), support was found for Baumeister and colleagues' original hypothesis in children: discrepancies between positive self-evaluation and evaluations by peers were strongly related to physical aggression. The simplified hypothesis was not supported. It should, however, be noted that research on this theory has only just begun and does not yet involve adolescent participants.

In reviewing current theories, it is clear that some theories explain part of the picture and even some possible causal mechanisms. However, it may be evident these potential causes are probably interrelated, and that some causes are in fact likely consequences of other causes, mentioned in other theories. In many cases, a vicious cycle may develop over time, where multiple factors strengthen each other's effects. For example, a baby who cries a lot is by itself no major problem, but in the case of parents who work at irregular hours and have no friends or family to help out, may impose a significant stress on them. This may, in turn, result in frequent marital conflict and inconsequent parenting practices. These inconsequent parenting practices may reinforce the child's temper tantrums. When the child enters kindergarten and still has these temper tantrums, other children are likely to resent that and frequent conflicts with peers may arise, etc. Over time problems may accumulate to an extent where the aforementioned mechanisms of coercive interactions, vicarious learning of aggression, inadequate emotion regulation and social information processing all operate simultaneously, causing the established stability or even aggravation in the chronic trajectory. Thus, transactions between factors may cause this development, even though no single factor could have caused it by itself.

We would expect that in the coming years more complex transactional models will be specified and tested. It will be necessary to devise theories that take into account multi-causality over time. And it will be necessary to execute more intervention research to test the precise claims of these multi-causal models.

9. Conclusion

Inspired by Wohlwill (1973), we take the view that the apotheosis of all developmental investigations should consist of experimental research to identify the causes of development, a view that was further clarified by Bryant (1990). Fortunately, numerous creative developmental psychologists were not prepared to put aside the development of intervention programs until the ideal set of developmental psychological data became available. It was mainly developmental psychologists of the American learning theory tradition, who carried out the most prominent and successful pioneering work in this area. Once again we refer to the work of Patterson and his colleagues at the renowned Oregon Social Learning Center (Patterson, 1982; Patterson, Capaldi, & Bank, 1991; Patterson, Dishion, & Bank, 1984). In the entire social learning theory tradition the solution, that is prevention and intervention, is primarily sought by the use of *parent management training*, on the one hand (Kazdin, 2001), and *training children in social problem solving*, on the other.

Most of these programs are quite massive and consist of many components. The therapists, parents and trainers involved are many and varied. One does not need an extensive training in methodology to see that while the effects of such programs can be measured, it is generally quite difficult to determine which specific components have been effective. The therapeutic work referred to here is clearly of major importance in terms of clinical practice. However, if *parent management training* is seen as an experimental manipulation for influencing the development of aggression, then its scientific usefulness will be extremely limited. To date, no evaluations of training programs have involved sufficient numbers of repeated measurements over a sufficiently protracted period of time to justify statements about development. Furthermore, it is true to say that even if parent management training is reasonably effective, it does not necessarily follow that the development of aggression can be attributed to the child-rearing behavior of parents. While Bandura showed that violent aggression can be learned by following the behavioral models provided by adults, the parent management training programs revealed that excessive social aggression can indeed be mitigated by parents. However, it does not follow that *all* aggression, or even the larger part of the variance, is based on social learning.

As regards *training the children* instead of the adults, this is also carried out in accordance with the principles of learning theory and its derivative, behavioral therapy. One example of a thoroughly investigated and reasonably effective program is the *anger coping program* developed by Lochman (Lochman, Lampron, Gemner, & Harris, 1987;

Lochman, & Wells, 2002; Matthys, 1998). The essence of this program is that aggressive and antisocial boys are taught to recognize and control their anger by means of instructions, self-talk and exercises. They have since combined their program with a related parent training course in parenting skills and called it the *coping power program* (Lochman & Wells, 1996; 2002).

Sadly, we cannot justifiably claim that developmental psychology has sufficient longitudinal data on aggression to attempt the obvious experimental manipulation that would enable us to track down the causes of the development of aggression. What is missing is the relation of existing intervention and prevention programs to developmental theory and data on developmental causes. The main progress made thus far, is that delinquent violent behavior in adolescence has been brought into a developmental scientific frame. A simple phase-specific interpretation like "normative turmoil" cannot suffice any more. The future of research into adolescent (delinquent) violence will be in the hands of developmental theoreticians, who creatively detect developmental causal mechanisms by testing them with clear-cut theory-driven interventions.

References

Achenbach, T.M., & Edelbrock, C. (1983). *Manual for the child behavior checklist and revised child behavior profile*. Burlington, VT: University of Vermont, Department of Psychiatry.

Anderson, C.A., & Bushman, B.J. (2002). Human aggression. *Annual Review of Psychology, 53*, 27–51.

Arnett, J.J. (1999). Adolescent storm and stress reconsidered. *American Psychologist, 54*, 317–326.

Bandura, A. (1973). *Aggression: A social learning analysis*. New York: Holt.

Barker, E.D., & Orobio de Castro, B. (2006). *Testing etiological models of proactive and reactive aggression through interventions*. Symposium to be presented at the biennial meeting of the International Society for the Study of Behavioral Development. Melbourne, Australia.

Baumeister, R.F., Smart, L., & Boden, J.M. (1996). Relation of threatened egotism to violence and aggression: The dark side of high self-esteem. *Psychological Review, 103*, 5–33.

Brendgen, M., Vitaro, F., Turgeon, L., Poulin, F., & Wanner, B. (2004). Is there a dark side of positive illusions? Overestimation of social competence and subsequent adjustment in aggressive and nonaggressive children. *Journal of Abnormal Child Psychology*, *32*(3), 305–320.

Bronfenbrenner, U. (1979). Een experimentele ecologie van de menselijke ontwikkeling. In W. Koops, & J. J. van der Werff (Eds.), *Overzicht van de ontwikkelingspsychologie* (pp 407–423). Groningen The Netherlands: Wolters-Noordhoff.

Bryant, P. (1990). Empirical evidence for causes in development. In G. Butterworth, & P. Bryant (Eds.), *Causes of development. Interdisciplinary perspectives* (pp. 33–45). London: Harvester Wheatsheaf.

Butterworth, G., & Bryant, P. (1990). *Causes of development: Interdisciplinary perspectives*. London: Harvester Wheatsheaf.

Caspi, A., McClay, J., Moffitt, T.E., Mill, J., Martin, J., Craig, I.W. et al. (2002). Role of genotype in the cycle of violence in maltreated children. *Science*, *2*, 851–854.

Coie, J.D., & Dodge, K.A. (1998). Aggression and antisocial behavior. In W. Damon, & N. Eisenberg (Eds.), *Handbook of child psychology: Social, emotional, and personality development* (Vol.3, pp. 779–862). Toronto, Canada: John Wiley & Sons.

Côté, S., Zoccololo, M., Tremblay, R.E., Nagin, D., & Vitaro, F. (2001). Predicting girls' conduct disorder in adolescence from childhood trajectories of disruptive behavior. *Journal of the American Academy of Child Adolescent Psychiatry*, *40*, 678–684.

Crick, N.C., & Dodge, K.A. (1994). A review and reformulation of social information-processing mechanisms in children's social adjustment. *Psychological Bulletin*, *115*, 74–101.

Damon, W. (1999). *Handbook of child psychology*. (Volumes I, II, III, and IV). New York: John Wiley & Sons.

Development & Psychopathology (2002). Special issue: Prevention and intervention science: Contributions to developmental theory. *Development & Psychopathology*, *14*, 4.

Dishion, T.J., Spracklen, K.M., Andrews, D.W., & Patterson, G.R. (1996). Deviancy training in male adolescents' friendships. *Behavior Therapy*, *27*, 373–390.

Dodge, K.A. (1991). The structure and function of reactive and proactive aggression. In D. Pepler, & K. H. Rubin (Eds), *The development and treatment of childhood aggression* (pp. 201–218). Hillsdale, NJ: Lawrence Erlbaum Associates, Inc.

Dodge, K.A. (1993). Social–cognitive mechanisms in the development of conduct disorder and depression. *Annual Review of Psychology*, *44*, 559–584.

Dodge, K.A., Lochman, J.E., Harnish, J.D., Bates, J.E., & Pettit, S. (1997). Reactive and proactive aggression in school children and psychiatrically impaired chronically assaultive youth. *Journal of Abnormal Psychology*, *106*, 37–51.

Eddy, J.M., & Chamberlain, P. (2001). Family management and deviant peer association as mediators of the impact of treatment condition on youth antisocial behavior. *Journal of Consulting and Clinical Psychology*, *68*, 857–863.

Estrada, F. (1999). Juvenile crime trends in post-war Europe. *European Journal on Criminal Policy and Research*, *7*, 23–42.

Farrington, D.P. (1978). The family background of aggressive youths. In L. A. Hersov, M. Berger, & D. Schaffer (Eds.), *Aggression and antisocial behavior in childhood and adolescence* (pp. 73–93). Oxford: Pergamon.

Farrington, D.P. (1986). Age and crime. In M. Tonry, & N. Morris (Eds.), *Crime and justice: An annual review of research* (Vol. 7, pp. 189–250). Chicago, IL: University of Chicago Press.

Farrington, D.P. (1994). Childhood, adolescent, and adult features of violent males. In L. R. Huesmann (Ed.), *Aggressive behavior: Current perspectives* (pp. 215–240). New York: Plenum.

Farrington, D.P. (1995). The development of offending and antisocial behaviour from childhood: Key findings from the Cambridge study in delinquent development. The Twelfth Jack Tizard Memorial Lecture. *Journal of Child Psychology and Psychiatry and Allied Disiplines*, *360*, 929–964.

Felson, M. (1998). *Crime and everyday life*. Thousand Oaks, CA: Pine Forge.

Flavell, J. (1963). *The developmental psychology of Jean Piaget*. New York: Van Nostrand.

Frick, P.J., Lahey, B.B., Loeber, R., Tannenbaum, L., Van Horn, Y., Christ, M.A.G. et al. (1993). Oppositional defiant disorder and conduct disorder: A meta-analytic review of factor analyses and cross-validation in a clinic sample. *Clinical Psychology Review*, *13*, 319–340.

Gottfredson, M., & Hirschi, T. (1990). *A general theory of crime*. Stanford, CA: Stanford University Press.

Hall, G.S. (1904). *Adolescence: Its psychology and its relation to physiology, anthropology, sociology, sex, crime, religion and education* (2 volumes). New York: Appleton.

Hawkins, J.D., Herrenkohl, T., Farrington, D.P., Brewer, D., Catalino, R.F., & Harachi, T.W. (1998). A review of predictors of youth violence. In R. Loeber, & D. P. Farrington (Eds.), *Serious & violent juvenile offenders: Risk factors and successful interventions.* Thousand Oaks, CA: Sage.

Hopkins, B., & Butterworth, G. (1990). Concepts of causality in explanations of development. In G. Butterworth, & P. Bryant (Eds.), *Causes of development: Interdisciplinary perspectives* (pp. 3–32). London: Harvester Wheatsheaf.

Hudley, C., & Graham, S. (1993). An attributional intervention to reduce peer-directed aggression among African-American boys. *Child Development, 64,* 124–138.

Huesmann, L.R. (1998). *An information processing theory for understanding the interaction of emotions and cognitions in the development and instigation of aggressive behavior.* Presidential address. Ramapo College, NJ: International Society for Research on Aggression.

Huesmann, L.R., & Eron, L.D. (1986). *Television and the aggressive child: A cross-national comparison.* Hillsdale, NJ: Lawrence Erlbaum Associates, Inc.

Huesmann, L.R., Eron, L.D., Lefkkowitz, M.M., & Walder, L.O. (1984). Stability of aggression over time and generations. *Developmental Psychology, 20,* 1120–1134.

Huesmann, R.L., & Miller, L.S. (1994). Long-term effects of repeated exposure to media violence in childhood. In L. R. Huesmann (Ed.), *Aggressive behavior: Current perspectives* (pp. 153–186). New York: Plenum.

Kagan, J. (1974). Development and methodological considerations in the study of aggression. In J. De Wit & W. W. Hartup (Eds.), *Determinants and origins of aggressive behavior* (pp. 107–114). Den Haag, The Netherlands: Mouton.

Kazdin, A.E. (2001). Treatment of conduct disorders. In J. Hill, & B. Maugham (Eds), *Conduct disorders in childhood and adolescence* (pp. 408–448). Cambridge: Cambridge University Press.

Kokko, K., & Pulkkinen, L. (2005). Stability of aggressive behavior from childhood to middle age in women and men. *Aggressive Behavior, 31*(5), 485–497.

Koops, W. (1992). Is de eeuw van het kind eindelijk voorbij? *Nederlands Tijdschrift voor de Psychologie, 47,* 264–277.

Koops, W. (2000). *Gemankeerde volwassenheid. Over eindpunten van de ontwikkeling en doelen van de pedagogiek.* Houten/Diegem, The Netherlands: Bohn Stafleu Van Loghum.

Koops, W., & Orobio de Castro, B. (2004). Development of aggression: Causes and trajectories. In G. Bruinsma, H. Elffers, & J. de Keijser (Eds.), *Developments in criminology and criminal justice research: Punishment, places, and perpetrators* (pp. 232–246). Devon: Willan Publishing.

Koops, W., & Zuckerman, M. (2003). *Beyond the century of the child.* Philadelphia, PA: University of Pennsylvania Press.

Lansford, J.E., Dodge, K.A., Bates, J.E., & Pettit, G.S. (2002). *Developmental trajectories of reactive and proactive aggression: Similarities and differences over time.* Paper presented at the XVth world meeting of the International Society for Research on Aggression. Montreal, Canada.

Lipsey, M.W., & Derzon, J.H. (1998). Predictors of violent or serious delinquency in adolescence and early adulthood: A synthesis of longitudinal research. In R. Loeber, & D. P. Farrington (Eds.), *Serious and violent juvenile offenders: Risk factors and successful interventions* (pp. 86–105). Thousand Oaks, CA: Sage.

Lochman, J., Lampron, L., Gemner, T., & Harris, S. (1987). Anger coping intervention with aggressive children: A guide to implementation in school settings. In P. Keller, & S. Heyman (Eds), *Innovations in clinical practice: A source book* (Vol. 6) (pp. 339–356). Sarasota, FL: Professional Resource Exchange.

Lochman, J.E., & Lenhart, L.A. (1993). Anger coping intervention for aggressive children: Conceptual models and outcome effects. *Clinical Psychology Review, 13,* 785–805.

Lochman, J., & Wells, K., (1996). A social–cognitive intervention with aggressive children: Prevention effects and contextual implementation issues. In R. Peters, & R. McMahon (Eds.), *Preventing childhood disorders, substance abuse, and delinquency* (pp. 111–143). Thousand Oaks, CA: Sage.

Lochman, J.E., & Wells, K.C. (2002). Contextual social–cognitive mediators and child outcome: A test of the theoretical model in the coping power program. *Development and Psychopathology, 14*(4), 945–967.

Loeber, R., (1998). Ontwikkelingspaden en risicopatronen. In W. Koops, & N.W. Slot, (Eds.), *Van lastig tot misdadig* (pp. 15–32). Houten/Diegem, The Netherlands: Bohn Stafleu Van Loghum.

Loeber, R., & Hay, D.F. (1994). Developmental approaches to aggression and conduct problems. In

M. Rutter, & D. F. Hay (Eds.), *Development through life: A handbook for clinicians* (pp. 488–516). Malden, MA: Blackwell.

Loeber, R., & Hay, D.F. (1997). Key issues in the development of aggression and violence from childhood to early adulthood. *Annual Review of Psychology*, *48*, 371–410.

Loeber, R., & Schmaling, K.B. (1985). Empirical evidence for overt and covert patterns of antisocial conduct problems: A meta-analysis. *Journal of Abnormal Child Psychology*, *13*, 337–352.

Loeber, R., & Stouthamer-Loeber, M. (1998). Development of juvenile aggression and violence. *American Psychologist*, *53*, 242–259.

Loeber, R., Wung, P., Keenan, K., Giroux, B., Stouthamer-Loeber, M. van Kammen, W.B. et al. (1993). Developmental pathways in disruptive child behavior. *Development and Psychopathology*, *5*, 101–132.

Lorenz, K. (1968). *Over agressie bij dier en mens.* Amsterdam: Ploegsma.

Magnusson, D., Stattin, H., & Duner, A. (1983). Aggression and criminality in a longitudinal perspective. In K. T. Van Dusen, & S. A. Mednick (Eds.), *Antecedents of aggression and antisocial behavior* (pp. 277–301). Boston, MA: Kluwer-Nijhoff.

Matthys, W. (1998). Groepstraining in sociale probleemoplossing voor kinderen met oppositioneel-opstandige en antisociale gedragsstoornissen. In W. Koops, & N. W. Slot (Eds.), *Van lastig tot misdadig* (pp.145–156). Houten/Diegem, The Netherlands: Bohn Stafleu Van Loghum.

McMahon, S.D., Grant, K.E., Compas, B.E., Thurm, A.E., & Ey, S. (2003). Stress and psychopathology in children and adolescents: Is there evidence of specificity? *Journal of Child Psychology and Psychiatry and Allied Disciplines*, *44*(1), 107–133.

Merk, W. (2005). *Development of reactive and proactive aggression in boys.* Unpublished doctoral dissertation. Utrecht University, The Netherlands.

Moffitt, T.E. (1993). Adolescence-limited and life-course-persistent antisocial behavior: A developmental taxonomy. *Psychological Review*, *100*, 674–701.

Moffitt, T.E. (2002). *Behavioral genomics of antisocial behavior: How genetic research pushes environmental theories forward.* Paper presented at the biennial meeting of the International Society for the Study of Behavioral Development, Ottawa, Canada.

Moffitt, T.E., Caspi, A., Dickson, N., Silva, P., & Stanton, W. (1996). Childhood-onset versus adolescent-onset antisocial conduct problems in males:

Natural history from ages 3 to 18 years. *Development and Psychopathology*, *8*, 399–424.

Moffitt, T.E., Caspi, A., Harrington, H., & Milne, B.J. (2002). Males on the life-course-persistent and adolescence-limited antisocial pathways: Follow-up at age 26 years. *Development and Psychopathology*, *14*(1), 179–207.

Nagin, D.S. (1999). Analyzing developmental trajectories: Semi-parametric, group-based approach. *Psychological Methods*, *4*, 139–177.

Nagin, D.S., & Tremblay, R.E. (2001). Analyzing developmental trajectories of distinct but related behaviors: A group-based method. *Psychological Methods*, *6*, 18–34.

Olweus, D. (1979). Stability and aggressive reaction patterns in males: A review. *Psychological Bulletin*, *86*, 852–875.

Orobio de Castro, B., Veerman, J.W., Koops, W., Bosch, J.D., & Monshouwer, H.J. (2002). Hostile attribution of intent and aggressive behavior: A meta-analysis. *Child Development*, *73*, 916–934.

Parke, R.D., & Slaby, R.G. (1983). The development of aggression. In P. H. Mussen (Ed.), *Handbook of Child Psychology* (Volume IV) (pp. 547–640). New York: John Wiley & Sons.

Patterson, G.R. (1982). *A social learning approach to family intervention: III. Coercive family process.* Eugene, OR: Castalia.

Patterson, G.R., Capaldi, D., & Bank, L. (1991). An early starter model for predicting delinquency. In D. J. Pepler, & K. H. Rubin (Eds.), *The development and treatment of childhood aggression* (pp. 139–168). Hillsdale: NJ: Lawrence Erlbaum Associates, Inc.

Patterson, G.R., Dishion, T.J., & Bank, L. (1984). Family interaction: A process model of deviancy training. *Aggressive Behavior*, *10*, 253–267.

Petersen, A.C. (1988). Adolescent development. *Annual Review of Psychology*, *39*, 583–607.

Pfeiffer, C. (1998). Juvenile crime and violence. Crime and justice. *A Review of Research*, *23*, 255–328.

Pulkkinen, L. (1982). Self-control and continuity from childhood to adolescence. In P. B. Baltes, & O. G. Brim (Eds.), *Life-span development and behavior* (Vol. 4) (pp. 63–105). Hillsdale, NJ: Lawrence Erlbaum Associates, Inc.

Quetelet, A. (1833). *Research on the propensity for crime at different ages.* Brussels: M. Hayez, Printer to the Royal Academy.

Raine, A., Venables, P.H., Dalais, C., Mellingen, K., Reynolds, C., & Mednick, S.A. (2001). Early educational and health enrichment at age 3–5 years is associated with increased autonomic and central nervous system arousal and orienting at age 11 years: Evidence from the Mauritius Child Health Project. *Psychophysiology*, *38*, 254–266.

Rousseau, J.J. (1763). *Emile on education*. London: Nourse and Vaillant. (Original work published 1762)

Rutter, M. (1989). Pathways from childhood to adult life. *Journal of Child Psychology and Psychiatry and Allied Disciplines*, *30*, 23–51.

Rutter, M. (2002). Nature, nurture, and development: From evangelism through science toward policy and practice. *Child Development*, *73*, 1–21.

Scott, E., & Grisso, T. (1997). The evolution of adolescence: A developmental perspective on juvenile justice reform. *Journal of Criminal Law & Criminology*, *88*, 137–190.

Snoek, H. (2002). *Psychoneuroendocrinological aspects of aggressive behavior in children*. Dissertation, Utrecht University, The Netherlands.

Stattin, H., & Magnusson, D. (1989). The role of early aggressive behavior in the frequency, seriousness, and types of later crime. *Journal of Consulting and Clinical Psychology*, *57*, 710–718.

Tolan, P., Gorman-Smith, D., & Loeber, R. (2000). Developmental timing of onsets of disruptive behaviors and later delinquency of inner-city youth. *Journal of Child and Family Studies*, *9*, 203–220.

Tremblay, R.E. (1998). De ontwikkeling en preventie van fysieke agressie. In W. Koops, & N. W. Slot (Eds.), *Van lastig tot misdadig. Een ontwikkelingsbenadering van lastige en misdadige kinderen en adolescenten: diagnostiek, behandeling en beleid* (pp. 33–51). Houten/Diegem, The Netherlands: Bohn Stafleu Van Loghum.

Tremblay, R.E. (2000). The development of aggressive behaviour during childhood: What have we learned in the past? *International Journal of Behavioral Development*, *24*, 129–141.

Tremblay, R.E., Japel, C., Pérusse, D., Boivin, M., Zoccolillo, M., Montplaisir, J. et al. (1999). The search for the age of "onset" of physical aggression:

Rousseau and Bandura revisited. *Criminal Behavior and Mental Health*, *9*, 8–23.

Tremblay, R.E., Nagin, D.S., Seguin, J.R., Zoccolillo, M., Zelazo, P.D., Boivin, M. et al. (2004). Physical aggression during early childhood: Trajectories and predictors. *Pediatrics*, *114*(1), 343–350.

Tremblay, R.E., Phil, R.O., Vitaro, F., & Dobkin, P.L. (1994). Predicting early onset of male antisocial behavior from preschool behavior. *Archives of General Psychiatry*, *51*, 732–738.

Van Boxtel, H., Orobio de Castro, B., & Goossens, F.A. (2004). Frequent fighting is related to high self-esteem in rejected children. *European Journal of Developmental Psychology*, *1*, 205–214.

van Goozen, S.H.M., Matthys, W., Cohen-Kettenis, P.T., de Gispen-Wied, C., Wiegant, V. M., & van Engeland, H. (1998). Salivary cortisol and cardiovascular activity during stress in oppositional defiant disorder boys and normal controls. *Biological Psychiatry*, *43*, 156–158.

Van Manen, T.G., Prins, P.J.M., & Emmelkamp, P.M.G. (2004). Reducing aggressive behavior in boys with a social cognitive group treatment: Results of a randomized, controlled trial. *Journal of the American Academy of Child and Adolescent Psychiatry*, *43*(12), 1478–1487.

Vitaro, F., Gendreau, P.L., Tremblay, R.E., & Oligny, P. (1998). Reactive and proactive aggression differentially predict later conduct problems. *Journal of Child Psychology and Psychiatry and Allied Disciplines*, *39*, 377–385.

Weiss, B., Dodge, K.A., Bates, J.E. & Pettit, G.S. (1992). Some consequences of early harsh discipline: Child aggression and a maladaptive information processing style. *Child Development*, *63*, 1321–1335.

Windle, R.C., & Windle, M. (1995). Longitudinal patterns of physical aggression: Associations with adult social, psychiatric, and personality functioning and testosterone levels. *Development and Psychopathology*, *5*, 563–585.

Wohlwill, J.F. (1973). *The study of behavioral development*. New York: Academic Press.

Author index

Subject index